ONE TO

Bilingual Dictionary

English-Cantonese
Cantonese-English
Dictionary

Compiled by
Nisa Yang

STAR Foreign Language BOOKS

This Edition : 2023

Published by

STAR Foreign Language BOOKS

a unit of
Star Books

56, Langland Crescent
Stanmore HA7 1NG, U.K.
info@starbooksuk.com
www.bilingualbooks.co.uk

Printed in India at
Star Print-O-Bind, New Delhi-110 020

About this Dictionary

Developments in science and technology today have narrowed down distances between countries, and have made the world a small place. A person living thousands of miles away can learn and understand the culture and lifestyle of another country with ease and without travelling to that country. Languages play an important role as facilitators of communication in this respect.

To promote such an understanding, **STAR Foreign Language BOOKS** has planned to bring out a series of bilingual dictionaries in which important English words have been translated into other languages, with Roman transliteration in case of languages that have different scripts. This is a humble attempt to bring people of the word closer through the medium of language, thus making communication easy and convenient.

Under this series of *one-to-one dictionaries*, we have published almost 57 languages, the list of which has been given in the opening pages. These have all been compiled and edited by teachers and scholars of the relative languages.

Publishers

Bilingual Dictionaries in this Series

English-Afrikaans / Afrikaans-English	Abraham Venter
English-Albanian / Albanian-English	Theodhora Blushi
English-Amharic / Amharic-English	Girun Asanke
English-Arabic / Arabic-English	Rania-al-Qass
English-Bengali / Bengali-English	Amit Majumdar
English-Bosnian / Bosnian-English	Boris Kazanegra
English-Bulgarian / Bulgarian-English	Vladka Kocheshkova
English-Burmese (Myanmar) / Burmese (Myanmar)-English	Kyaw Swar Aung
English-Cambodian / Cambodian-English	Engly Sok
English-Cantonese / Cantonese-English	Nisa Yang
English-Chinese (Mandarin) / Chinese (Mandarin)-Eng	Y. Shang & R. Yao
English-Croatian / Croatain-English	Vesna Kazanegra
English-Czech / Czech-English	Jindriska Poulova
English-Danish / Danish-English	Rikke Wend Hartung
English-Dari / Dari-English	Amir Khan
English-Dutch / Dutch-English	Lisanne Vogel
English-Estonian / Estonian-English	Lana Haleta
English-Farsi / Farsi-English	Maryam Zaman Khani
English-French / French-English	Aurélie Colin
English-Georgian / Georgina-English	Eka Goderdzishvili
English-Gujarati / Gujarati-English	Sujata Basaria
English-German / German-English	Bicskei Hedwig
English-Greek / Greek-English	Lina Stergiou
English-Hindi / Hindi-English	Sudhakar Chaturvedi
English-Hungarian / Hungarian-English	Lucy Mallows
English-Italian / Italian-English	Eni Lamllari
English-Japanese / Japanese-English	Miruka Arai & Hiroko Nishimura
English-Korean / Korean-English	Mihee Song
English-Latvian / Latvian-English	Julija Baranovska
English-Levantine Arabic / Levantine Arabic-English	Ayman Khalaf
English-Lithuanian / Lithuanian-English	Regina Kazakeviciute
English-Malay / Malay-English	Azimah Husna
English-Nepali / Nepali-English	Anil Mandal
English-Norwegian / Norwegian-English	Samuele Narcisi
English-Pashto / Pashto-English	Amir Khan
English-Polish / Polish-English	Magdalena Herok
English-Portuguese / Portuguese-English	Dina Teresa
English-Punjabi / Punjabi-English	Teja Singh Chatwal
English-Romanian / Romanian-English	Georgeta Laura Dutulescu
English-Russian / Russian-English	Katerina Volobuyeva
English-Serbian / Serbian-English	Vesna Kazanegra
English-Sinhalese / Sinhalese-English	Naseer Salahudeen
English-Slovak / Slovak-English	Zuzana Horvathova
English-Slovenian / Slovenian-English	Tanja Turk
English-Somali / Somali-English	Ali Mohamud Omer
English-Spanish / Spanish-English	Cristina Rodriguez
English-Swahili / Swahili-English	Abdul Rauf Hassan Kinga
English-Swedish / Swedish-English	Madelene Axelsson
English-Tagalog / Tagalog-English	Jefferson Bantayan
English-Tamil / Tamil-English	Sandhya Mahadevan
English-Thai / Thai-English	Suwan Kaewkongpan
English-Tigrigna / Tigrigna-English	Tsegazeab Hailegebriel
English-Turkish / Turkish-English	Nagme Yazgin
English-Ukrainian / Ukrainian-English	Katerina Volobuyeva
English-Urdu / Urdu-English	S. A. Rahman
English-Vietnamese / Vietnamese-English	Hoa Hoang
English-Yoruba / Yoruba-English	O. A. Temitope

STAR Foreign Language BOOKS

ENGLISH-CANTONESE

A

a *a.* 一 yat
aback *adv.* 向後 heurng ho
abaction *n* 強搶 keurng cheurng
abactor *n* 強搶者 keurng cheurng jeh
abandon *v.t.* 遺棄 way hey
abase *v.t.* 踩低 tai day
abasement *n* 踩低 tai day
abash *v.t.* 慚愧 tarm kwai
abate *v.t.* 減低 garm day
abatement *n.* 減低 garm day
abbey *n.* 寺院 ji yoon
abbreviate *v.t.* 簡稱 gan ting
abbreviation *n* 簡稱 gan ting
abdicate *v.t,* 放棄 forng hay
abdication *n* 放棄 forng hay
abdomen *n* 腹部 fuk bo
abdominal *a.* 腹部嘅 fuk bo geh
abduct *v.t.* 拐走 gwai jow
abduction *n* 綁架 borng ga
abed *adv.* 喺床度 hay chorng dow
aberrance *n.* 唔正常 hm jing seurng
abet *v.t.* 唆擺 sor bai
abetment *n.* 唆擺 sor bai
abeyance *n.* 擱置 gok ji
abhor *v.t.* 憎 jang
abhorrence *n.* 痛恨 tung han
abide *v.i* 容忍 yung yan
abiding *a* 永恆嘅 wing han geh
ability *n* 能力 lang lik
abject *a.* 賤格 jeen gak
ablactate *v.t* 戒奶 gai lai
ablactation *n* 戒奶 gai lai
ablaze *adv.* 着火 jeurk for
able *a* 可以 hor yi
ablepsy *n* 盲 mang
ablush *adv* 面紅 meen hung
ablution *n* 沐浴 muk yuk

abnegate *v. t* 否認 fow ying
abnegation *n* 否認 fow ying
abnormal *a* 唔正常 hm jing seurng
aboard *adv* 上咗 seurng jor
abode *n* 住所 ju sor
abolish *v.t* 廢除 fay chuy
abolition *v* 廢除 fay chuy
abominable *a* 討厭 tow yeem
aboriginal *a* 本地 bwun day
aborigines *n. pl* 原住民 yoon ju man
abort *v.i* 終止 jung jee
abortion *n* 墮胎 dor toy
abortive *adv* 失敗 sat bai
abound *v.i.* 有好多 yow ho dor
about *adv* 大概 dai koy
about *prep* 關於 gwan yu
above *adv* 以上 yee seurng
above *prep.* 上面 seurng meen
abreast *adv* 並肩 bing geen
abridge *v.t* 縮短 suk doon
abridgement *n* 摘要 jak yiew
abroad *adv* 出國 chut gwok
abrogate *v. t.* 廢除 fay chuy
abrupt *a* 突然間 dak yeen gan
abruption *n* 中斷 jung toon
abscess *n* 膿腫 lung jung
absonant *adj* 唔一致 hm yat jee
abscond *v.i* 逃走 tow jow
absence *n* 缺席 koot tik
absent *a* 缺席 koot tik
absent *v.t* 缺席 koot tik
absolute *a* 絕對 joot duy
absolutely *adv* 絕對 joot duy
absolve *v.t* 解除 gai chuy
absorb *v.t* 吸收 kap sow
abstain *v.i.* 戒 gai
abstract *a* 抽象 tow jeurng
abstract *n* 摘要 jak yiew
abstract *v.t* 抽出 tow chut
abstraction *n.* 抽象嘅概念 tow

jeurng geh koy leem

absurd *a* 荒謬 forng mow

absurdity *n* 荒謬 forng mow

abundance *n* 充足 chung juk

abundant *a* 充足嘅 chung juk geh

abuse *v.t.* 虐待 yeurk doy

abuse *n* 濫用 larm yung

abusive *a* 侮辱嘅 mow yuk geh

abutted *v* 連接住 leen jeep ju

abyss *n* 深處 sam chu

academic *a* 學術嘅 hok sut geh

academy *n* 學院 hok yoon

acarpous *adj.* 無果嘅植物 mow gwor geh jik mat

accede *v.t.* 同意 tung yee

accelerate *v.t* 加速 ga chuk

acceleration *n* 加速 ga chuk

accent *n* 口音 ho yam

accent *v.t* 強調 keurng diew

accept & 接受 jeep sow

acceptable *a* 可以接受 hor yi jeep sow

acceptance *n* 接受 jeep sow

access *n* 用 yung

accession *n* 就任 jow yam

accessory *n* 飾物 sik mat

accident *n* 意外 yee ngoy

accidental *a* 唔小心 hm siew sam

acclaim *v.t* 讚 jan

acclaim *n* 讚 jan

acclamation *n* 歡呼 fwun fu

acclimatise *v.t* 適應 sik ying

accommodate *v.t* 容納 yung lap

accommodation *n.* 住宿 ju suk

accompaniment *n* 伴奏 bwun jow

accompany *v.t.* 伴 bwun

accomplice *n* 伴 bwun

accomplish *v.t.* 搞掂 gao deem

accomplished *a* 搞掂咗 gao deem jor

accomplishment *n.* 成就 sing

jow

accord *v.t.* 符合 fu hap

accord *n.* 一致 yat jee

accordingly *adv.* 按照 on jiew

account *n.* 戶口 wu ho

account *v.t.* 講明 gorng ming

accountable *a* 有責任 yow jak yam

accountancy *n.* 會計 wuy gey

accountant *n.* 會計師 wuy gey see

accredit *v.t.* 委任 way yam

accrementition *n* 增長 jang jeurng

accrete *v.t.* 增加 jang ga

accrue *v.i.* 增值 jang jik

accumulate *v.t.* 積累 jik luy

accumulation *n* 積累緊 jik luy gan

accuracy *n.* 準確性 jun kok sing

accurate *a.* 準確 jun kok

accursed *a.* 被詛咒嘅 bay juy jow geh

accusation *n* 控告 hung gow

accuse *v.t.* 控告 hung gow

accused *n.* 被人告 bay yan gow

accustom *v.t.* 習慣 jap gwan

accustomed *a.* 慣咗 gwan jor

ace *n* 高手 gow sow

acentric *adj* 唔正常 hm jing seurng

acephalous *adj.* 無首領嘅 mo sow ling geh

acephalus *n.* 無頭 mo tow

acetify *v.* 醋化 cho far

ache *n.* 痛 tung

ache *v.i.* 痛 tung

achieve *v.t.* 實現 yeen sat

achievement *n.* 成就 sing jow

achromatic *adj* 無色嘅 mo sik geh

acid *a* 酸味 shoon may

acid *n* 酸 shoon
acidity *n.* 酸性 shoon sing
acknowledge *v.* 承認 sing ying
acknowledgement *n.* 承認 sing ying
acne *n* 粉刺 fan tee
acorn *n.* 橡果 jeurng gwor
acoustic *a* 原聲 yoon seng
acoustics *n.* 音效 yam hao
acquaint *v.t.* 瞭解 liew gai
acquaintance *n.* 識嘅人 sik geh yan
acquest *n* 攞到 lor dow
acquiesce *v.i.* 順從 sun chuung
acquiescence *n.* 默然接受 mak yeen jeep sow
acquire *v.t.* 要 yiew
acquirement *n.* 需要嘅嘢 suy yiew geh yeh
acquisition *n.* 得到 dak dow
acquit *v.t.* 判無罪 pwun mow juy
acquittal *n.* 被判無罪 bay pwun mow juy
acre *n.* 英畝 ying mow
acreage *n.* 大幅田地 dai fuk teen day
acrimony *n* 尖刻嘅說話 jeem hak geh shoot wah
acrobat *n.* 雜技師 jap gey see
across *adv.* 橫過 wang gwor
across *prep.* 對面 duy meen
act *n.* 行爲 hang way
act *v.i.* 演 yeen
acting *n.* 演技 yeen gey
action *n.* 動作 dung jok
activate *v.t.* 開動 hoy dung
active *a.* 活躍 wut yeurk
activity *n.* 活動 wut dung
actor *n.* 演員 yeen yoon
actress *n.* 女演員 luy yeen yoon
actual *a.* 真正嘅 tan ting geh
actually *adv.* 其實 key sat

acumen *n.* 敏銳 man yuy
acute *a.* 嚴重 yeem jung
adage *n.* 格言 gak yeen
adamant *a.* 堅決 geen koot
adamant *n.* 堅決 geen koot
adapt *v.t.* 適應 sik ying
adaptation *n.* 改編嘅 goy peen geh
adays *adv* 日頭 yat tow
add *v.t.* 加 ga
addict *v.t.* 上癮 seurng yan
addict *n.* 上癮者 seurng yan jeh
addiction *n.* 癮 yan
addition *n.* 加上 ga seurng
additional *a.* 加上 ga seurng
addle *adj* 糊涂 wu tow
address *v.t.* 稱呼 ting fu
address *n.* 地址 day jee
addressee *n.* 收件人 sow geen yan
adduce *v.t.* 舉出 kuy chut
adept *n.* 擅長 seen cheurng
adept *a.* 熟練 suk leen
adequacy *n.* 恰當 hap dong
adequate *a.* 適合 sik hap
adhere *v.i.* 遵守 jun sow
adherence *n.* 遵守 jun sow
adhesion *n.* 黐住 tee ju
adhesive *n.* 膠水 gao suy
adhesive *a.* 黐 tee
adhibit *v.t.* 引入 yan yap
adieu *n.* 再見 joy geen
adieu *interj.* 再見 joy geen
adjacent *a.* 隔籬 gak lay
adjective *n.* 形容詞 ying yung tee
adjoin *v.t.* 連埋 leen mai
adjourn *v.t.* 押後 at ho
adjournment *n.* 延期 yeen kay
adjudge *v.t.* 裁定 choy ding
adjunct *n.* 附屬 fu suk
adjure *v.t.* 命令 ming ling
adjuration *n* 懇求 han ko

adjust *v.t.* 調整 tiew jing
adjustment *n.* 調整 tiew jing
administer *v.t.* 掌管 jeung gwun
administration *n.* 行政 hang jing
administrative *a.* 行政嘅 hang jing geh
administrator *n.* 行政人員 hang jing yan yoon
admirable *a.* 令人欣賞 ling yan yan seurng
admiral *n.* 司令 see ling
admiration *n.* 欣賞 yan seurng
admire *v.t.* 欣賞 yan seurng
admissible *a.* 可以接受 hor yi jeep sow
admission *n.* 收 sow
admit *v.t.* 承認 sing yan
admittance *n.* 入去 yap huy
admonish *v.t.* 責怪 jak gwai
admonition *n.* 警告 ging gow
adnascent *adj.* 寄生 gey sang
ado *n.* 事 see
adobe *n.* 黏土 leem tow
adolescence *n.* 青春期 ting chun kay
adolescent *a.* 青少年 ting siew leen
adopt *v.t.* 收養 sow yeurng
adoption *n* 收養 sow yeurng
adorable *a.* 可愛 hor ngoy
adoration *n.* 愛慕 ngoy mo
adore *v.t.* 愛 ngoy
adorn *v.t.* 裝扮 jorng ban
adscititious *adj* 後天性 ho teen sing
adscript *adj.* 後寫 ho seh
adulation *n* 奉承 fung sing
adult *a* 成熟 sing suk
adult *n.* 成年人 sing leen yan
adulterate *v.t.* 溝咗嘢 kow jor yeh
adulteration *n.* 溝嘢 kow yeh
adultery *n.* 通姦 tung garn

advance *v.t.* 進攻 jun gung
advance *n.* 預先 yu seen
advancement *n.* 晉升 jun sing
advantage *n.* 好處 ho chu
advantage *v.t.* 有利 yow lay
advantageous *a.* 着數 jerk sow
advent *n.* 出現 chut yeen
adventure *n* 冒險 mo heem
adventurous *a.* 大膽 dai dam
adverb *n.* 副詞 fu tee
adverbial *a.* 副詞嘅 fu tee geh
adversary *n.* 對手 duy sow
adverse *a* 不利 bat lay
adversity *n.* 困境 kwun ging
advert *v.* 廣告 gworng gow
advertise *v.t.* 推廣 tuy gworng
advertisement *n* 廣告 gworng gow
advice *n* 意見 yee geen
advisable *a.* 適宜 sik yee
advisability *n* 適當性 sik dong sing
advise *v.t.* 畀意見 bay yee geen
advocacy *n.* 支持 jee tee
advocate *n* 辯方律師 been forng lut see
advocate *v.t.* 支持 jee tee
aerial *a.* 空中嘅 hung jung geh
aerial *n.* 天線 teen seen
aeriform *adj.* 無形嘅 mo ying geh
aerify *v.t.* 氣體化 hey tay far
aerodrome *n* 機場 gey cheurng
aeronautics *n.pl.* 航空學 horn hung hok
aeroplane *n.* 飛機 fay gey
aesthetic *a.* 美學嘅 may hok geh
aesthetics *n.pl.* 美感 may gam
aestival *adj* 夏天嘅 har teen geh
afar *adv.* 遠 yoon
affable *a.* 好好人士 ho ho yan see
affair *n.* 婚外情 fan ngoy ting
affect *v.t.* 影響 ying heurng

affectation *n* 扮晒嘢 ban sai yeh

affection *n.* 感情 gam ting

affectionate *a.* 深情嘅 sam ting geh

affidavit *n* 誓章 say jeurng

affiliation *n.* 關係 gwan hay

affinity *n* 密切嘅關係 mat teet geh gwan hay

affirm *v.t.* 肯定 hang ding

affirmation *n* 證實 ting sat

affirmative *a* 肯定嘅 hang ding geh

affix *v.t.* 貼住 teep ju

afflict *v.t.* 折磨 jeet mor

affliction *n.* 痛苦 tung fu

affluence *n.* 富裕 fu yu

affluent *a.* 有錢 yow cheen

afford *v.t.* 負擔 fu dam

afforest *v.t.* 綠化 luk far

affray *n* 爭執 jang jap

affront *v.t.* 侮辱 mo yuk

affront *n* 侮辱 mo yuk

afield *adv.* 遠處 yoon chu

aflame *adv.* 燒緊 siew gan

afloat *adv.* 浮住 fow ju

afoot *adv.* 進行緊 jun hang gan

afore *prep.* 之前 jee teen

afraid *a.* 驚 geng

afresh *adv.* 重新 chung san

after *prep.* 之後 jee ho

after *adv* 後來 ho lay

after *conj.* 以後 yee ho

after *a* 後 ho

afterwards *adv.* 之後 ji ho

again *adv.* 再 joy

against *prep.* 反對 fan duy

agamist *n* 未婚人世 may fan yan see

agape *adv.,* 擘大個口 mak dai gor ho

agaze *adv* 望住 mong ju

age *n.* 年齡 leen ling

aged *a.* 老咗 lo jor

agency *n.* 代理處 doy lay chu

agenda *n.* 議程表 yee ting biew

agent *n* 經紀人 ging gey yan

aggravate *v.t.* 激嬲 gik lo

aggravation *n.* 激嬲 gik lo

aggregate *v.t.* 總數 jung so

aggression *n* 攻擊性 gung gik sing

aggressive *a.* 霸道 ba dow

aggressor *n.* 侵略者 tam leurk jeh

aggrieve *v.t.* 受委屈 sow way wat

aghast *a.* 嚇到傻咗 hak dow sor jor

agile *a.* 敏捷 man jeet

agility *n.* 敏捷度 man jeet dow

agitate *v.t.* 激動 gik dung

agitation *n* 憂慮 yow luy

agist *v.t.* 照顧馬匹 jiew gu ma pat

aglow *adv.* 發光 fat gwong

ago *adv.* 之前 jee teen

agog *adj.* 渴望 hot mong

agonist *n* 興奮劑 hing fan jay

agonize *v.t.* 苦悶 fu mun

agony *n.* 痛苦 tung fu

agronomy *n.* 農學 lung hok

agoraphobia *n.* 懼曠症 guy kwong jing

agrarian *a.* 農業嘅 lung yeep geh

agree *v.i.* 同意 tung yee

agreeable *a.* 可以接受 hor yi jeep sow

agreement *n.* 協議書 heep yee shu

agricultural *a* 農業嘅 lung yeep geh

agriculture *n* 農業 lung yeep

agriculturist *n.* 農業家 lung yeep ga

ague *n* 發冷 fat lang

ahead *adv.* 前面 teen meen

aheap *adv* 堆積嘅 duy jik geh

aid *n* 援助 woon jor
aid *v.t* 幫助 bong jor
aigrette *n* 白鷺 bak lo
ail *v.t.* 困擾 kwun yiew
ailment *n.* 小病 siew beng
aim *n.* 目標 muk biew
aim *v.i.* 瞄準 miew jun
air *n* 空氣 hung hey
aircraft *n.* 飛機 fay gey
airy *a.* 空氣流通 hung hey low tung
ajar *adv.* 半開 bun hoy
akin *a.* 類似 luy tee
alacrious *adj* 興奮 hing fan
alacrity *n.* 爽快 song fai
alamort *adj.* 去死 huy sey
alarm *n* 警報 ging bo
alarm *v.t* 驚動 ging dung
alas *interj.* 唉 ay
albeit *conj.* 就算 jow shoon
albion *n* 英國 ying gwok
album *n.* 專輯 joon tap
albumen *n* 蛋白 dan bak
alchemy *n.* 煉金術 leen gam sut
alcohol *n* 酒精 jow jing
ale *n* 麥芽啤酒 mak ngar beh jow
alegar *n* 麥芽醋 mak ngar cho
alert *a.* 警覺 ging gok
alertness *n.* 警覺性 ging gok sing
algebra *n.* 代數 doy sing
alias *n.* 化名 far meng
alias *adv.* 化名 far meng
alibi *n.* 不在場證據 bat joy cheurng jing guy
alien *a.* 外國人 ngoy gwok yan
alienate *v.t.* 疏遠 sor yoon
aliferous *adj.* 有翼嘅 yow yik geh
alight *v.i.* 燒緊 siew gan
align *v.t.* 對齊 duy chay
alignment *n.* 形成直線 ying sing jik seen
alike *a.* 相同 seurng tung

alike *adv* 差唔多 cha hm dor
aliment *n.* 營養 ying yeurng
alimony *n.* 贍養費 seen yeurng fey
aliquot *n.* 徐得盡 chuy dak jun
alive *a* 在生 joy sang
alkali *n* 鹼 gan
all *a.* 全部 choon bo
all *n* 一切 yat chai
all *adv* 完全 yoon choon
all *pron* 所有 sor yow
allay *v.t.* 減輕 garm heng
allegation *n.* 指控 jee hung
allege *v.t.* 聲稱 sing ting
allegiance *n.* 忠誠 jung sing
allegorical *a.* 有意義嘅 yow yee yee geh
allegory *n.* 寓意 yu yee
allergy *n.* 敏感 man gam
alleviate *v.t.* 減輕 gam heng
alleviation *n.* 減輕 gam heng
alley *n.* 小巷 siew hong
alliance *n.* 聯盟 loon mang
alligator *n* 鈍吻鱷 dun man ok
alliterate *v.* 押頭韻 at tow wan
alliteration *n.* 押頭韻 at tow wan
allocate *v.t.* 分配 fan puy
allocation *n.* 分配到嘅嘢 fan puy dow geh yeh
allot *v.t.* 分配 fan puy
allotment *n.* 份 fan
allow *v.t.* 準 jun
allowance *n.* 津貼 jun teep
alloy *n.* 合金 hap gam
allude *v.i.* 暗示 am see
allure *v.t.* 誘惑 yow wak
allurement *n* 誘惑 yow wak
allusion *n* 暗示 am see
allusive *a.* 暗指 am jee
ally *v.t.* 結盟 geet mang
ally *n.* 盟國 mang gwok
almanac *n.* 通勝 tung sing
almighty *a.* 全能嘅 choon lang

geh

almond *n.* 杏仁 hang yan

almost *adv.* 差唔多 cha hm dor

alms *n.* 救濟品 gao jay ban

aloft *adv.* 喺上面 hay seurng meen

alone *a.* 自己 jee gey

along *adv.* 一齊 yat chai

along *prep.* 順住 sun ju

aloof *adv.* 冷淡 lang dam

aloud *adv.* 大聲 dai seng

alp *n.* 高山 go san

alpha *n* 阿爾法 ah yee fat

alphabet *n.* 字母 jee mo

alphabetical *a.* 字母順序 jee mo sun juy

alpinist *n* 爬山家 pa san ga

already *adv.* 已經 yee ging

also *adv.* 而且 yee cher

altar *n.* 祭壇 jay tan

alter *v.t.* 改 goy

alteration *n* 修改 sow goy

altercation *n.* 爭論 jang lun

alternate *a.* 輪流 lun low

alternate *v.t.* 輪流 lun low

alternative *n.* 代替品 doy tay ban

alternative *a.* 代替 doy tay

although *conj.* 雖然 suy yeen

altimeter *n* 高度計 go dow gey

altitude *n.* 海拔 hoy bat

alto *n* 女低音 luy day yam

altogether *adv.* 一齊 yat chai

aluminate *n.* 鋁酸鹽 luy shoon yeem

aluminium *n.* 鋁 luy

alumna *n* 女畢業生 luy bat yeep sang

always *adv* 成日 sing yat

alveary *n* 蜂竇 fung dow

alvine *adj.* 腸嘅 cheurng geh

am 係 hay

amalgam *n* 混合體 wan hap tay

amalgamate *v.t.* 合併 hap ping

amalgamation *n* 合併 hap ping

amass *v.t.* 累積 luy jik

amateur *n.* 業餘愛好者 yeep yu ngoy ho jeh

amatory *adj* 戀愛嘅 loon ngoy geh

amaurosis *n* 黑內障 hak loy jeurng

amaze *v.t.* 驚奇 ging kay

amazement *n.* 驚奇 ging kay

ambassador *n.* 大使 dai see

amberite *n.* 琥珀炸藥 fu pak ja yeurk

ambient *adj.* 周圍嘅 jow way geh

ambiguity *n.* 模糊 mow wu

ambiguous *a.* 模糊 mow wu

ambition *n.* 理想 lay seurng

ambitious *a.* 恆心 hang sam

ambry *n.* 櫃 gway

ambulance *n.* 救護車 gao wu cher

ambulant *adj* 可以嘟 hor yee yuk

ambulate *v.t* 行 hang

ambush *n.* 埋伏 mai fuk

ameliorate *v.t.* 改良 goy leurng

amelioration *n.* 改良 goy leurng

amen *interj.* 阿門 ah mun

amenable *a* 順從 sun chung

amend *v.t.* 修改 sow goy

amendment *n.* 修改 sow goy

amends *n.pl.* 修改 sow goy

amenorrhoea *n* 月經不調 yoot ging bat tiew

amiability *n.* 親切性 tan teet sing

amiable *a.* 平易近人 ping yee gan yan

amicable *adj.* 心平氣和 sam ping hay wor

amid *prep.* 中 jung

amiss *adv.* 唔正常 hm jing seurng

amity *n.* 和睦 wor muk

ammunition *n.* 彈藥 dan yeurk

amnesia *n* 失憶 sat yik

amnesty *n.* 大赦 dai she

among *prep.* 之中 jee jung
amongst *prep.* 之中 jee jung
amoral *a.* 唔遵守道德 hm jun sow dow dak
amount *n* 數額 sow ak
amount *v.i* 總計 jung gey
amount *v.* 等於 dang yu
amorous *a.* 性慾 sing yuk
amour *n* 私情 see ting
ampere *n* 安(培) on (puy)
amphibious *adj* 水陸兩棲 suy luk leurng chay
amphitheatre *n* 古羅馬劇場 gu lor ma kek cheurng
ample *a.* 足夠 juk gow
amplification *n* 擴大 kwong dai
amplifier *n* 擴音器 kwong yam hey
amplify *v.t.* 放大 fong dai
amuck *adv.* 癲狂 deem kwong
amulet *n.* 護身符 wu san fu
amuse *v.t.* 氹人 tam yan
amusement *n* 娛樂 yu lok
an *art* 一 yat
anabaptism *n* 再洗禮 joy say lay
anachronism *n* 過晒時 gwor sai see
anaclisis *n* 依賴 yee lai
anadem *n* 花冠 far gwun
anaemia *n* 貧血 pan hoot
anaesthesia *n* 麻醉 ma juy
anaesthetic *n.* 麻醉藥 ma juy yeurk
anal *adj* 注重小事 ju jung siew see
analogous *a.* 相似 seurng tee
analogy *n.* 比喻 bei yu
analyse *v.t.* 分析 fan sik
analysis *n.* 分析結果 fan sik geet gwor
analyst *n* 分析員 fan sik yoon
analytical *a* 分析嘅 fan sik geh

anamnesis *n* 病歷 beng lik
anamorphous *adj* 再次形成 joy tee ying sing
anarchism *n.* 無政府主義 mo ting fu ju yee
anarchist *n* 無政府主義者 mo jing fu juu yee jeh
anarchy *n* 無政府 mo jing fu
anatomy *n.* 解剖學 gai fo hook
ancestor *n.* 祖先 jo seen
ancestral *a.* 祖先嘅 jo seen geh
ancestry *n.* 祖先 jo seen
anchor *n.* 錨 mao
anchorage *n* 停泊處 ting pak chu
ancient *a.* 古老 gu low
ancon *n* 肱木 gung muk
and *conj.* 同埋 tung mai
androphagi *n.* 食人族 sik yan juk
anecdote *n.* 短故事 doon gu see
anemometer *n* 風速計 fung chuk gey
anew *adv.* 重新 chung san
anfractuous *adj* 九曲十三彎 gow kuk sap sam wan
angel *n* 天使 teen see
anger *n.* 怒火 low for
angina *n* 心絞痛 sam gao tung
angle *n.* 角度 gok dow
angle *n* 觀點 gwoon deem
angry *a.* 嬲 low
anguish *n.* 苦惱 fu lo
angular *a.* 有角嘅 yow gok geh
anigh *adv.* 近 kan
animal *n.* 動物 dung mat
animate *v.t.* 製作成動畫片 jai jok sing dung wah peen
animate *a.* 變活躍 been wut yeurk
animation *n* 動畫 dung wah
animosity *n* 仇恨 sow han
animus *n* 敵意 dik yee
aniseed *n* 洋茴香 yeurng wuy heurng

ankle n. 腳踝 geurt ngan
anklet n 腳鍊 geurt leen
annalist n. 史官 see gwun
annals n.pl. 歷史記載 lik see gey joy
annectant adj. 連接緊 leen jeep gen
annex v.t. 吞併 tun ping
annexation n 吞併 tun ping
annihilate v.t. 毀滅 way meet
annihilation n 毀滅 way meet
anniversary n. 紀念日 gey leem yat
announce v.t. 宣佈 shoon bo
announcement n. 宣佈 shoon bo
annoy v.t. 煩 fan
annoyance n. 煩惱 fan lo
annual a. 一年一次嘅 yat leen yat tee geh
annuitant n 領養老金人 ling yeurng low gam yam
annuity n. 養老金 yeurng low gam
annul v.t. 廢除 fay chuy
annulet n 小環 siew wan
anoint v.t. 搽油 cha yow
anomalous a 異常嘅 yee seurng geh
anomaly n 異常 yee seurng
anon adv. 好快 ho fai
anonymity n. 匿名 lik ming
anonymous a. 匿名 lik ming
another a 另外 ling ngoy
answer n 答案 dap on
answer v.t 回答 wuy dap
answerable a. 負責 fu jak
ant n 蟻 ay
antacid adj. 抗酸劑 kong shoon jay
antagonism n 敵意 dik yee
antagonist n. 敵人 dik yan
antagonize v.t. 對抗 duy kong
antarctic a. 南極 larm gik

antecede v.t. 存在先過 choon jor seen gwor
antecedent n. 前因 teen yan
antecedent a. 之前嘅 jee teen geh
antedate n 預期 yu kay
antelope n. 羚羊 ling yeurng
antenatal adj. 產前嘅 chan teen geh
antennae n. 觸鬚 juk so
antenuptial adj. 結婚前嘅 geet fan teen geh
anthem n 國歌 gwok gor
anthology n. 選集 shoon jap
anthropoid adj. 似人嘅猿 chee yan geh yoon
anti pref. 反 fan
anti-aircraft a. 防空 forng hung
antic n 蠱惑 gu wak
anticardium n 腹上部 fuk seurng bo
anticipate v.t. 預料 yu liew
anticipation n. 預計 yu gey
antidote n. 解藥 gai yeurk
antinomy n. 矛盾 mao tun
antipathy n. 反感 fan gam
antiphony n. 輪住唱 lun ju cheurng
antipodes n. 剛剛相反 gong gong seurng fan
antiquarian a. 古文物嘅 gu man mat geh
antiquarian n 古物收藏家 gu mat sow chong gar
antiquary n. 古物收藏家 gu mat sow chong gar
antiquated a. 過晒時 gwor sai see
antique a. 古董 gu dung
antiquity n. 古代 gu doy
antiseptic n. 防腐劑 forng fu jay
antiseptic a. 消過毒嘅 siew gwor duk geh
antithesis n. 對立 duy lap

antitheist *n* 無神論者 mow san lun jeh

antler *n.* 鹿角 luk gok

antonym *n.* 反義詞 fan yee tee

anus *n.* 肛門 gong mun

anvil *n.* 鐵砧 teet tam

anxiety *a* 憂慮 yow luy

anxious *a.* 憂慮 yow luy

any *a.* 任何 yam hor

any *adv.* 任何 yam hor

anyhow *adv.* 點都好 deem dow ho

apace *adv.* 快 fai

apart *adv.* 分開 fan hoy

apartment *n.* 單位 dan way

apathy *n.* 冷漠 lang mok

ape *n* 猿 yoon

ape *v.t.* 模仿 mo fong

aperture *n.* 孔徑 hung ging

apex *n.* 窿 lung

aphorism *n* 格言 gak yeen

apiary *n.* 養蜂場 yeurng fung cheurng

apiculture *n.* 養蜂業 yeurng fung yeep

apish *a.* 好似猿咁 ho chee yoon gam

apnoea *n* 窒息 jat sik

apologize *v.i.* 道歉 dow heep

apologue *n* 寓言 yu yeen

apology *n.* 道歉 dow heep

apostle *n.* 信徒 sun tow

apostrophe *n.* 撇號 peet ho

apotheosis *n.* 高峰 go fung

apparatus *n.* 儀器 yee hey

apparel *n.* 服裝 fuk jorng

apparel *v.t.* 裝飾 jorng sik

apparent *a.* 明顯 ming heen

appeal *n.* 上訴 seurng so

appeal *v.t.* 吸引 kap yan

appear *v.i.* 出現 chut yeen

appearance *n* 外表 ngoy biew

appease *v.t.* 安撫 on fu

appellant *n.* 上訴人 seurng so yan

append *v.t.* 附加 fu ga

appendage *n.* 附件 fu geen

appendicitis *n.* 盲腸炎 mang cheurng yeem

appendix *n.* 闌尾 !an may

appendix *n.* 附錄 fu luk

appetence *n.* 慾望 yuk mong

appetent *adj.* 渴望 hot mong

appetite *n.* 胃口 way ho

appetite *n.* 慾望 yuk mong

appetizer *n* 頭盤 tow poon

applaud *v.t.* 鼓掌 gu jeurng

applause *n.* 掌聲 jeurng sing

apple *n.* 蘋果 ping gwor

appliance *n.* 器具 hay guy

applicable *a.* 適合 sik hap

applicant *n.* 申請人 san ting yan

application *n.* 申請表 san ting biew

apply *v.t.* 申請 san ting

appoint *v.t.* 委任 way yam

appointment *n.* 預約 yu yeurk

apportion *v.t.* 分配 fan puy

apposite *adj* 適合 sik hap

apposite *a.* 恰當 hap dong

appositely *adv* 貼切 teep teet

approbate *v.t* 批准 pay jun

appraise *v.t.* 評價 ping ga

appreciable *a.* 感覺到 gam gok dow

appreciate *v.t.* 欣賞 yan seurng

appreciation *n.* 感激 gam gik

apprehend *v.t.* 拉 lai

apprehension *n.* 擔心 dam sam

apprehensive *a.* 擔心嘅 dam sam geh

apprentice *n.* 徒弟 tow day

apprise *v.t.* 通知 tung jee

approach *v.t.* 接近 jeep gan

approach *n.* 方式 fong sik

approbation *n.* 認可 ying hor

appropriate v.t. 盜用 dow yung
appropriate a. 適當 sik dong
appropriation n. 經費 ging fay
approval n. 批准 pay jun
approve v.t. 批准 pay jun
approximate a. 大概 dai koy
apricot n. 杏子 hang jee
appurtenance n 附屬物 fu suk mat
apron n. 圍裙 way kwun
apt a. 適當嘅 sik dong geh
aptitude n. 天賦 teen fu
aquarium n. 水族館 suy juk gwun
aquarius n. 水瓶座 suy ping jor
aqueduct n 輸水管 shuy suy gwun
arable adj 適合耕種嘅 sik hap gang jung geh
arbiter n. 裁判 choy pwun
arbitrary a. 武斷 mo doon
arbitrate v.t. 裁判 choy poon
arbitration n. 仲裁 jung choy
arbitrator n. 仲裁人 jung choy yan
arc n. 弧 wu
arcade n 拱廊 gung long
arch n. 拱 gung
arch v.t. 弯曲 wan kuk
arch a 調皮 tiew pay
archaic a. 古代嘅 gu doy geh
archangel n 天使長 teen see jeurng
archbishop n. 大主教 dai ju gao
archer n 弓箭手 gung jeen sow
architect n. 建築師 geen juk see
architecture n. 建築學 geen juk hok
archives n.pl. 存檔 choon dong
Arctic n 北極 bat gik
ardent a. 熱情 yeet ting
ardour n. 熱情 yeet ting
arduous a. 艱難 garn lan
area n 地方 day forng

areca n 檳榔樹 ban long shu
arefaction n 乾 gon
arena n 舞台 mo toy
argil n 陶土 tow tow
argue v.t. 嗌交 ay gao
argument n. 鬧交 lao gao
argute adj 尖叫 jeem giew
arid adj. 乾燥 gorn cho
aries n 牡羊座 muk yeurng jor
aright adv 正確 jing kok
aright adv. 啱 ngam
arise v.i. 出現 chut yeen
aristocracy n. 貴族 gway juk
aristocrat n. 一個貴族 yat gor gway juk
aristophanic adj 諷刺喜劇風 fung chee hey kek fung
arithmetic n. 算術 shoon sut
arithmetical a. 算術嘅 shoon sut geh
ark n 方舟 forng jow
arm n. 手臂 sow bay
arm v.t. 裝備 jorng bay
armada n. 艦隊 lam duy
armament n. 軍備 gwan bay
armature n. 轉子 joon jee
armistice n. 休戰 yow jeen
armlet a 臂釧 bay choon
armour n. 盔甲 kway gap
armoury n. 軍械庫 gwan hai fu
army n. 軍隊 gwan duy
around prep. 周圍 jow wey
around adv 到處 dow chu
arouse v.t. 激起 gik hey
arraign v. 提審 tay sam
arrange v.t. 安排 on pai
arrangement n. 安排 on pai
arrant n. 衰到徹尾 suy dow cheet mey
array v.t. 大堆 dai duy
array n. 佈置 bo jee
arrears n.pl. 債 jai

arrest *v.t.* 拉 lai
arrest *n.* 拘留 kuy low
arrival *n.* 到達 dow dat
arrive *v.i.* 到 dow
arrogance *n.* 自大 jee day
arrogant *a.* 囂張 hiew cheurng
arrow *n* 箭 jeen
arrowroot *n.* 竹芋 juk yu
arsenal *n.* 武器 mow hay
arsenic *n* 砒霜 pay seurng
arson *n* 縱火罪 jung for juy
art *n.* 藝術 ngay sut
artery *n.* 動脈 dung mak
artful *a.* 巧妙 hao miew
arthritis *n* 關節炎 gwan jeet yeem
artichoke *n.* 朝鮮薊 tiew seen ging
article *n* 文章 man jeurng
articulate *a.* 清楚表達 ting chor biew dat
artifice *n.* 手段 sow doon
artificial *a.* 人造嘅 yan jo geh
artillery *n.* 大炮 dai pao
artisan *n.* 工匠 gung jeurng
artist *n.* 藝術家 ngay sut ga
artistic *a.* 藝術嘅 ngay sut geh
artless *a.* 天真 teen jan
as *adv.* 同...一樣 tung...yat yeurng
as *conj.* 因為 yan way
as *prep..* 做 jow
asafoetida *n.* 阿魏樹脂 ah ay shu jee
asbestos *n.* 石棉 sek meen
ascend *v.t.* 升 sing
ascent *n.* 爬高 pa go
ascertain *v.t.* 查明 cha ming
ascetic *n.* 禁慾 gam yuk
ascetic *a.* 禁慾 gam yuk
ascribe *v.t.* 歸因於 gway yan yu
ash *n.* 灰 fuy
ashamed *a.* 慚愧 tarm kway
ashore *adv.* 上岸 seurng ngon

aside *adv.* 一邊 yat been
aside *n.* 旁邊 pong been
asinine *adj.* 蠢 chun
ask *v.t.* 問 man
asleep *adv.* 瞓咗覺 fan jor gao
aspect *n.* 方面 fong meen
asperse *v.* 誹謗 fey bong
aspirant *n.* 有上進心嘅人 yow seurng jun sam geh yan
aspiration *n.* 志向 jee heurng
aspire *v.t.* 立志做 lap jee jo
ass *n.* 驢 lo
assail *v.* 攻擊 gung gik
assassin *n.* 刺客 tee hak
assassinate *v.t.* 行刺 hang tee
assassination *n.* 刺殺 tee sat
assault *n.* 襲擊 jap gik
assault *v.t.* 毆打 ow da
assemble *v.t.* 招集 jiew jap
assembly *n.* 晨會 san wuy
assent *v.i.* 贊成 jan sing
assent *n.* 同意 tung yee
assert *v.t.* 肯定 hang ding
assess *v.t.* 評估 ping gu
assessment *n.* 評價 ping ga
asset *n.* 資產 jee chan
assibilate *v.* 齒音化 tee yam far
assign *v.t.* 指派 jee pay
assignee *n.* 受託人 sow tok yan
assimilate *v.* 吸收 kap sow
assimilation *n* 吸收 kap sow
assist *v.t.* 幫助 bong jor
assistance *n.* 幫助 bong jor
assistant *n.* 助手 jor sow
associate *v.t.* 聯想 loon seurng
associate *a.* 有關係嘅 yow gwan hay geh
associate *n.* 同事 tung see
association *n.* 協會 heep wuy
assoil *v.t.* 赦免 seh meen
assort *v.t.* 分類 fan luy
assuage *v.t.* 減輕 garm heng

assume *v.t.* 假設 ga cheet
assumption *n.* 假設 ga cheet
assurance *n.* 保證 bo jing
assure *v.t.* 保證 bo jing
astatic *adj.* 唔穩定 hm wan ding
asterisk *n.* 星號 sing ho
asterism *n.* 星群 sing kwun
asteroid *adj.* 小行星 siu hang sing
asthma *n.* 哮喘 hao choon
astir *adv.* 轟動 gwun dung
astonish *v.t.* 驚訝 ging ngar
astonishment *n.* 驚訝 ging ngar
astound *v.t* 令到...驚訝 ling dow...
ging ngar
astray *adv.,* 當失路 dong sat lo
astrologer *n.* 占星師 jeem sing
see
astrology *n.* 占星學 jeem sing hok
astronaut *n.* 太空人 tai hung yan
astronomer *n.* 天文學家 teen man
hok ga
astronomy *n.* 天文學 teem man
hok
asunder *adv.* 碎 suy
asylum *n* 精神病院 jing san beng
yoon
at *prep.* 喺 hay
atheism *n* 無神論 mo san lun
atheist *n* 無神論者 mo san lun jeh
athirst *adj.* 渴望 hot mong
athlete *n.* 運動員 wan dung yoon
athletic *a.* 運動型 wan dung ying
athletics *n.* 田徑運動 teen ging
wan dung
athwart *prep.* 橫過 wang gwor
atlas *n.* 地圖 day tow
atmosphere *n.* 氣氛 hey fan
atoll *n.* 環狀珊瑚島 wan jorng san
wu dow
atom *n.* 原子 yoom jee
atomic *a.* 原子嘅 yoom jee geh
atone *v.i.* 彌補 lay bo

atonement *n.* 補償 bo seurng
atrocious *a.* 殘忍 tarn yan
atrocity *n* 殘暴行爲 tarn bo hang
way
attach *v.t.* 附加 fu gar
attache *n.* 使館館員 see gwun
gwun yoon
attachment *n.* 附件 fu geen
attack *n.* 襲擊 jap gik
attack *v.t.* 襲擊 jap gik
attain *v.t.* 獲得 wok dak
attainment *n.* 成就 sing jow
attaint *v.t.* 恥辱 tee yuk
attempt *v.t.* 嘗試 seurng see
attempt *n.* 嘗試 seurng see
attend *v.t.* 出席 chut jik
attendance *n.* 出席率 chut jik lut
attendant *n.* 服務員 fuk mo yoon
attention *n.* 注意 ju yee
attentive *a.* 留心 low sam
attest *v.t.* 證實 jing sat
attire *n.* 衫 sam
attire *v.t.* 打扮 da ban
attitude *n.* 態度 tai dow
attorney *n.* 受權人 sow koon yan
attract *v.t.* 吸引 kap yan
attraction *n.* 吸引 kap yan
attractive *a.* 好靚 ho leng
attribute *v.t.* 歸因於 gway yan yu
attribute *n.* 屬性 suk sing
auction *n* 拍賣 pak mai
auction *v.t.* 拍賣 pak mai
audible *a* 聽到嘅 teng dow geh
audience *n.* 觀衆 gwoon jung
audit *n.* 審查 sam ta
audit *v.t.* 審計 sam gey
auditive *adj.* 聽覺嘅 ting gok geh
auditor *n.* 審計員 sam gey yoon
auditorium *n.* 觀衆席 gwun jung
jik
auger *n.* 螺絲鑽 luy see joon
aught *n.* 任何嘢 yam hor yeh

augment *v.t.* 增加 jang ga

augmentation *n.* 增加 jang ga

August *n.* 八月 bat yoot

august *n* 威嚴 way yeem

aunt *n.* 姨 yee

auriform *adj.* 耳狀 yee jorng

aurilave *n.* 洗耳器 say yee hay

aurora *n* 極光 gik gwong

auspicate *v.t.* 做好意頭嘅嘢 jo ho yee tow geh yeh

auspice *n.* 預兆 yu siew

auspicious *a.* 吉利嘅 gat lay geh

austere *a.* 樸素 pok so

authentic *a.* 真正嘅 tan jing geh

author *n.* 作者 jok jeh

authoritative *a.* 有權威 yow koon way

authority *n.* 權力 koon lik

authorize *v.t.* 批准 pay jun

autobiography *n.* 自傳 jee joon

autocracy *n* 獨裁政治 duk choy jing ji

autocrat *n* 獨裁者 duk choy jeh

autocratic *a* 專橫 joon wang

autograph *n.* 簽名 teem meng

automatic *a.* 自動 ji dung

automobile *n.* 車 cher

autonomous *a* 自治 jee ji

autumn *n.* 秋天 chow teen

auxiliary *a.* 輔助嘅 fu jor geh

auxiliary *n.* 輔助人員 fu jor yan yoon

avale *v.t.* 下降 har gong

avail *v.t.* 有用 yow yung

available *a* 得閒 dak harn

avarice *n.* 貪錢 tarm teen

avenge *v.t.* 報仇 bo sow

avenue *n.* 大街 dai gai

average *n.* 平均數 ping gwun so

average *a.* 平均 ping gwun

average *v.t.* 平均爲 ping gwun way

averse *a.* 反對做 fan duy jo

aversion *n.* 反感 fan gam

avert *v.t.* 避免 bay meen

aviary *n.* 大雀籠 dai jeurk lung

aviation *n.* 航空 hong hung

aviator *n.* 飛機師 fey gey see

avid *adj.* 熱愛 yeet ngoi

avidity *adv.* 熱情 yeet ting

avidly *adv* 渴望咁 hot morn gam

avoid *v.t.* 避開 bay hoy

avoidance *n.* 避開 bay hoy

avow *v.t.* 聲明 sing ming

avulsion *n.* 撕裂 see leet

await *v.t.* 等緊 dang gan

awake *v.t.* 醒 seng

awake *a* 醒 seng

award *v.t.* 頒獎 barn jeurng

award *n.* 獎 jeurng

aware *a.* 知道 jee dow

away *adv.* 走 jow

awe *n.* 敬畏 ging way

awful *a.* 好衰 ho suy

awhile *adv.* 一陣 yat jan

awkward *a.* 尷尬 gam gai

axe *n.* 斧頭 fu tow

axis *n.* 軸 kuk

axle *n.* 車軸 cher kuk

B

babble *n.* 胡言亂語 wu yeen lun yu

babble *v.i.* 胡言亂語 wu yeen lun yu

babe *n.* 寶貝 bo bwuy

babel *n* 嘈雜聲 cho jap seng

baboon *n.* 狒狒 fut fut

baby *n.* B B B B

bachelor *n.* 單身男人 dan san larm yan

back *n.* 背脊 bwuy jek
back *adv.* 後面 how meen
backbite *v.t.* 中傷 jung seurng
backbone *n.* 脊骨 jek gwut
background *n.* 背景 bwuy ging
backhand *n.* 反手 fan sow
backslide *v.i.* 退步 tuy bo
backward *a.* 退後 tuy ho
backward *adv.* 向後 heurng ho
bacon *n.* 煙肉 yeen yuk
bacteria *n.* 細菌 sey kwun
bad *a.* 差 ta
badge *n.* 徽章 fay jeurng
badger *n.* 獾 gwun
badly *adv.* 差 ta
badminton *n.* 羽毛球 yu mo kow
baffle *v.t.* 困擾 kwan yiew
bag *n.* 袋 doy
bag *v.i.* 入袋 yap doy
baggage *n.* 行李 hang lay
bagpipe *n.* 風笛 fung dek
bail *n.* 保釋 bo sik
bail *v.t.* 保釋 bo sik
bailable *a.* 畀保釋嘅 bay bo sik geh
bailiff *n.* 執達員 jap dat yoon
bait *n* 餌 leay
bait *v.t.* 放餌 forng lay
bake *v.t.* 焗 guk
baker *n.* 麵包師 meen bao see
bakery *n* 餅店 beng deem
balance *n.* 餘額 yu ak
balance *v.t.* 平衡 ping hang
balcony *n.* 陽台 yeurng toy
bald *a.* 光頭 gwong tow
bale *n.* 大包 dai bao
bale *v.t.* 打成大包 da sing dai bao
baleful *a.* 有惡意 yow ok yee
baleen *n.* 鯨鬚 king so
ball *n.* 波 bor
ballad *n.* 情歌 ting gor

ballet *sn.* 芭蕾舞 ba luy mo
balloon *n.* 氣球 hey kow
ballot *n* 選票 shoon piew
ballot *v.i.* 無記名投票 mo gey meng tow piew
balm *n.* 香油 heurng yow
balsam *n.* 香脂 heurng jee
bam *n.* 嘭 pang
bamboo *n.* 竹 juk
ban *n.* 禁止 gam jee
ban *n* 禁令 gam ling
banal *a.* 平凡 ping fan
banana *n.* 香蕉 heurng jiew
band *n.* 樂團 ngok toon
bandage *~n.* 繃帶 bang dai
bandage *v.t* 包紮 bao jat
bandit *n.* 強盜 keurng dow
bang *v.t.* 撞 jong
bang *n.* 巨響 guy heurng
bangle *n.* 手鈪 sow ak
banish *v.t.* 驅逐 kuy juk
banishment *n.* 驅逐 kuy juk
banjo *n.* 班卓琴 ban jeurk kam
bank *n.* 銀行 an hong
bank *v.t.* 存錢 choon teen
banker *n.* 銀行家 an hong ga
bankrupt *n.* 破產 por tan
bankruptcy *n.* 破產 por tan
banner *n.* 橫額 wang ak
banquet *n.* 宴會 yeen wuy
banquet *v.t.* 筵席 yeen jik
bantam *n.* 矮腳雞 doon geurt gey
banter *v.t.* 講笑 gong siew
banter *n.* 玩笑 wun siew
bantling *n.* 細路 say lo
banyan *n.* 榕樹 yung shu
baptism *n.* 洗禮 say lay
baptize *+v.t.* 受洗 sow say
bar *n.* 酒吧 jow ba
bar *v.t* 封住 fung ju
barb *n.* 倒鈎 dow oh
barbarian *a.* 野蠻 yeh man

barbarian *n.* 野蠻人 yeh man yan
barbarism *n.* 野蠻 yeh man
barbarity *n* 殘忍 tan yan
barbarous *a.* 殘酷 tan huk
barbed *a.* 有刺 yow tee
barber *n.* 理髮師 lay fat see
bard *n.* 時人 see yan
bare *a.* 空 hung
bare *v.t.* 除 chuy
barely *adv.* 僅僅 gan gan
bargain *n.* 平貨 peng for
bargain *v.t.* 講價 gong ga
barge *n.* 駁船 bok shoon
bark *n.* 樹皮 shu pay
bark *v.t.* 吠叫聲 hoon giew seng
barley *n.* 大麥 dai mak
barn *n.* 穀倉 guk chorng
barnacles *n* 藤壺 tang wu
barometer *n* 氣壓計 hay ngat gey
barouche *n.* 馬車 ma cher
barrack *n.* 兵營 bing ying
barrage *n.* 彈幕射擊 dan mok she gik
barrator *ns.* 教唆犯 gao sor fan
barrel *n.* 桶 tung
barren *n* 不育 bat yuk
barricade *n.* 路障 lo jeurng
barrier *n.* 障礙 jeurng ngoy
barrister *n.* 大律師 dai lut see
barter1 *v.t.* 以物換物 yee mat wun mat
barter2 *n.* 交換 gao wun
barton *n.* 農場 lung cheurng
basal *adj.* 基礎 gey chor
base *n.* 根基 gan gey
base *a.* 卑鄙 bay pay
base *v.t.* 設喉 teet hay
baseless *a.* 無低 mo day
basement *n.* 地下室 day har sat
bashful *a.* 怕醜 pa cho
basic *a.* 基本 gey bwun
basil *n.* 羅勒 lor lak

basin *n.* 盆 pwun
basis *n.* 基礎 gey chor
bask *v.i.* 曬太陽 sai tai yeurng
basket *n.* 籃 larm
baslard *n.* 刀 dow
bass *n.* 男低音 larm day yam
bastard *n.* 私生子 see sang jee
bastard *a* 衰人 suy yan
bat *n* 蝙蝠 peen fuk
bat *n* 球拍 kow pak
bat *v.i* 拍 pak
batch *n* 批 pay
bath *n* 浴缸 yuk gong
bathe *v.t* 沖涼 chung leurng
baton *n* 接力棒 jeep lik pang
batsman *n.* 擊球手 gik kow so
battalion *n* 軍隊 gwan duy
battery *n* 電池 deem tee
battle *n* 戰鬥 jeen dow
battle *v.i.* 搏鬥 bok dow
bawd *n.* 妓女 gey luy
bawl *n.i.* 大喊 dai harm
bawn *n.* 圍牆 way cheurng
bay *n* 海灣 hoy wan
bayard *n.* 貝爾德 bwuy yee dak
bayonet *n* 刺刀 tee dow
be *v.t.* 存在 choon joy
be *pref.* 喉 hay
beach *n* 沙灘 sa tan
beacon *n* 燈塔 dang tap
bead *n* 珠 ju
beadle *n.* 儀仗官 yee jeurng gwun
beak *n* 鳥喙 niew hok
beaker *n* 燒杯 siew bwuy
beam *n* 光線 gwong seen
beam *v.i* 容光煥發 yung gwong wun fat
bean *n.* 豆 dow
bear *n* 熊 hung
bear *v.t* 承受 sing sow
beard *n* 鬍鬚 wu so
bearing *n* 方位 forng way

beast *n* 野獸 yeh so

beastly *a* 野獸咁嘅 yeh so gam geh

beat *v. t.* 打 da

beat *n* 拍子 pak jee

beautiful *a* 靚 leng

beautify *v. t* 美化 may far

beauty *n* 美麗 mey lay

beaver *n* 海狸 hoy lay

because *conj.* 因為 yan way

beck *n.* 小溪 siew kay

beckon *v.t.* 吸引 kap yan

beckon *v. t* 招手 chiew so

become *v. i* 變成 been sing

becoming *a* 合適 hap sik

bed *n* 床 chorng

bedevil *v. t* 長期困擾 cheurng key kwan yiew

bedding *n.* 寢具 tam guy

bedight *v.t.* 裝飾 jorng sik

bed-time *n.* 瞓覺時間 fan gao see gan

bee *n.* 蜜蜂 mat fung

beech *n.* 山毛櫸 san mo guy

beef *n* 牛肉 ngow yuk

beehive *n.* 蜂竇 fung dow

beer *n* 啤酒 beh jow

beet *n* 甜菜 teem choy

beetle *n* 甲蟲 gap chung

befall *v. t* 降臨到 gong lam dow

before *prep* 之前 jee teen

before *adv.* 以前 yee teen

before *conj* 之前 jee teen

beforehand *adv.* 事先 see seen

befriend *v. t.* 做朋友 jo pang yow

beg *v. t.* 求 kow

beget *v. t* 引發 yan fat

beggar *n* 乞兒 hat yee

begin *n* 開始 hoy tee

beginning *n.* 開始 hoy tee

begird *v.t.* 圍繞 way yiew

beguile *v. t* 呃 ak

behalf *n* 代表 doy biew

behave *v. i.* 表現 biew yeem

behaviour *n* 行為 hang way

behead *v. t.* 斬頭 jam tow

behind *adv* 後面 ho meen

behind *prep* 後面 ho meen

behold *v. t* 睇到 tay dow

being *n* 生物 sang mat

belabour *v. t* 強調 keurng diew

belated *adj.* 遲咗嘅 tee jor geh

belch *v. t* 打嗝 da ert

belch *n* 打嗝聲 da ert seng

belief *n* 信仰 sun yeurng

believe *v. t* 信 sun

bell *n* 鈴 ling

belle *n* 靚女 leng luy

bellicose *a* 想鬥 seurng dow

belligerency *n* 交戰 gao jeen

belligerent *a* 好鬥 ho dow

belligerent *n* 交戰國 gao jeen gwok

bellow *v. i* 呼喝 fu hot

bellows *n.* 叫聲 giew seng

belly *n* 肚 tow

belong *v. i* 屬於 suk yu

belongings *n.* 財物 choy mat

beloved *a* 深愛嘅 sam ngoy geh

beloved *n* 心愛嘅人 sam ngoy geh yan

below *adv* 下面 ha meen

below *prep* 少於 siew yu

belt *n* 皮帶 pay dai

belvedere *n* 望景樓 morng ging low

bemask *v. t* 隱藏 yan chorng

bemire *v. t* 整到成身泥 jing dow sing san lay

bemuse *v. t* 困擾 kwan yiew

bench *n* 長凳 cheurng dang

bend *n* 彎 wan

bend *v. t* 彎 wan

beneath *adv* 下面 ha meen

beneath *prep* 下面 ha meen
benefaction *n.* 捐款 goon fwun
benefice *n* 聖俸 sing fung
beneficial *a* 有利嘅 yow lay geh
benefit *n* 津貼 jun teep
benefit *v. t.* 有利於 yow lay yu
benevolence *n* 善心 seen sam
benevolent *a* 有愛心 yow ngoy sam
benight *v. t* 落後 lok ho
benign *adj* 善良 seen leurng
benignly *adv* 善良咁 seen leurng gam
benison *n* 祝福 juk fuk
bent *n* 彎咗 wan jor
bequeath *v. t.* 遺留 way low
bereave *v. t.* 喪失 song sat
bereavement *n* 喪失親友 song sat tan yow
berth *n* 鋪位 po way
beside *prep.* 側邊 jak been
besides *prep* 徐咗 chuy jor
besides *adv* 而且 yee cher
beslaver *v. t* 噴口水 pan ho suy
besiege *v. t* 圍攻 way gung
bestow *v. t* 賜贈 tee jang
bestrew *v. t* 散佈 san bo
bet *v.i* 賭 dow
bet *n* 預計 yu gey
betel *n* 檳榔葉 ban long yeep
betray *v.t.* 背叛 bwuy bun
betrayal *n* 背叛 bwuy bun
betroth *v. t* 許配 huy pwuy
betrothal *n.* 訂婚 ding fan
better *a* 較好 gao ho
better *adv.* 更好 gang ho
better *v. t* 叻過 lek gwor
betterment *n* 改善 goy seen
between *prep* 之間 jee gan
beverage *n* 飲品 yam ban
bewail *v. t* 歎息 tan sik
beware *v.i.* 提防 tay forng

bewilder *v. t* 混亂 wan loon
bewitch *v.t* 迷惑 may wak
beyond *prep.* 超出 tiew chut
beyond *adv.* 更遠 gang yoon
bi *pref* 雙 seurng
biangular *adj.* 雙角嘅 seurng gok
bias *n* 偏心 peen sam
bias *v. t* 有偏見 yow peen geen
biaxial *adj* 雙軸嘅 seurng kuk geh
bibber *n* 酒鬼 jow gway
bible *n* 聖經 sing ging
bibliography *+n* 參考書目 tarm hao shu muk
bibliographer *n* 書目編著者 shu muk peen ju jeh
bicentenary *adj* 二百週年 yee bak jow leen
biceps *n* 二頭肌 yee tow gey
bicker *v. t* 拗 ai
bicycle *n.* 單車 dan cher
bid *v.t* 出價 chut ga
bid *n* 投標 tow biew
bidder *n* 投家 tow ga
bide *v. t* 等 dang
biennial *adj* 兩年一次嘅 leurng leen yat chi geh
bier *n* 棺材架 gwoon choy ga
big *a* 大 dai
bigamy *n* 重婚罪 chung fan juy
bight *n* 海灣 hoy wan
bigot *n* 頑固 wan gu
bigotry *n* 頑固 wan gu
bile *n* 膽汁 dam jap
bilingual *a* 雙語 seurng yu
bill *n* 單 dan
billion *n* 十億 sap yik
billow *n* 巨浪 guy lorng
billow *v.i* 大量冒出 dai leurng mo chut
biliteral *adj* 兩個字母嘅 leurng gor jee mo geh
bilk *v. t.* 呃 ak

bimensal *adj* 每兩個月 mwuy leurng gor yoot

bimonthly *adj.* 隔個月嘅 gak gor yoot geh

binary *adj* 二進制 yee jun jay

bind *v.t* 綁 bong

binding *a* 必需遵守嘅 beet suy jun so geh

binocular *n.* 望遠鏡 mong yoon geng

biographer *n* 傳記作家 joon gey jok ga

biography *n* 傳記 joon gey

biologist *n* 生物學家 sang mat hok ga

biology *n* 生物學 sang mat hok

bioscope *n* 放映機 forng ying gey

biped *n* 兩足動物 leurng juk dung mat

birch *n.* 樺樹 wah shu

bird *n* 雀 jeurk

birdlime *n* 鳥膠 liew gao

birth *n.* 出生 chut sang

biscuit *n* 餅乾 beng gon

bisect *v. t* 平分 ping fan

bisexual *adj.* 雙性戀 seurng sing loon

bishop *n* 主教 ju gao

bison *n* 野牛 yeh ngow

bisque *n* 濃湯 lung tong

bit *n* 一啲 yat dee

bitch *n* 賤女人 jeen luy yan

bite *v. t.* 咬 ao

bite *n* 一啖 yat dam

bitter *a* 苦 fu

bi-weekly *adj* 兩星期一次 leurng sing kay yat tee

bizarre *adj* 奇怪 kay gwai

blab *v. t. & i* 亂噏 loon ap

black *a* 黑色 hak sik

blacken *v. t.* 整黑 jing hak

blackmail *n* 勒索 lak sok

blackmail *v.t* 勒索 lak sok

blacksmith *n* 鐵匠 teet jeurng

bladder *n* 膀胱 pong gwong

blade *n.* 刀片 dow peen

blain *n* 水泡 suy pao

blame *v. t* 責怪 jak gwai

blame *n* 責任 jak yam

blanch *v. t. & i* 變白 been bak

bland *adj.* 無味 mo may

blank *a* 空白 hung bak

blank *n* 空格 hung gak

blanket *n* 毛氈 mo jeen

blare *v. t* 刺耳嘅聲 tee yee geh seng

blast *n* 爆炸 bao ja

blast *v.i* 炸爛 ja lan

blaze *n* 火焰 for yeem

blaze *v.i* 燃燒 yeen siew

bleach *v. t* 漂白水 piew bak suy

blear *v. t* 模糊 mo wu

bleat *n* 羊叫聲 yeurng giew seng

bleat *v. i* 咩咩叫 meh meh giew

bleb *n* 水泡 suy pao

bleed *v. i* 流血 low hoot

blemish *n* 瑕疵 har tee

blend *v. t* 溝勻 kow wan

blend *n* 混合品 wan hap ban

bless *v. t* 祝福 juk fuk

blether *v. i* 囉唆 lor sor

blight *n* 損害 shoon hoy

blind *a* 盲 mang

blindage *n* 掩體 yeem tay

blindfold *v. t* 蒙住眼 mung ju ngan

blindness *n* 失明 sat ming

blink *v. t. & i* 眨眼 jam ngan

bliss *n* 喜悅 hay yoot

blister *n* 水泡 suy pao

blizzard *n* 暴風雪 bo fung shoot

bloc *n* 國家集團 gwok ga jap toon

block *n* 一嚿 yat gow

block *v.t* 阻塞 jor sat

blockade *n* 封鎖 fung sor

blockhead *n* 蠢材 chun choy

blood *n* 血 hoot

bloodshed *n* 傷亡 seurng mong

bloody *a* 血淋淋 hoot lum lum

bloom *n* 花 fa

bloom *v.i.* 開花 hoy fa

blossom *n* 花朵 far dor

blossom *v.i* 開花 hoy fa

blot *n.* 污漬 wu jik

blot *v. t* 吸乾 kap gorn

blouse *n* 襯衫 tan sam

blow *v.i.* 吹 chuy

blow *n* 打擊 da gik

blue *n* 藍色 larm sik

blue *a* 憂鬱 yow wat

bluff *v. t* 虛張聲勢 huy jeurng sing say

bluff *n* 嚇人 hak yan

blunder *n* 錯 chor

blunder *v.i* 做錯 jow chor

blunt *a* 鈍 dun

blur *n* 模糊 mo wu

blurt *v. t* 衝口而出 chung ho yee chut

blush *n* 面紅 meen hung

blush *v.i* 面紅 meen hung

boar *n* 野豬 yeh ju

board *n* 板 ban

board *v. t.* 上 seurng

boast *v.i* 曬命 sai meng

boast *n* 曬命 sai meng

boat *n* 船 shoon

boat *v.i* 撐船 tang shoon

bodice *n* 上身 seurng san

bodily *a* 身體嘅 san tay geh

bodily *adv.* 全身嘅 choon san geh

body *n* 身 san

bodyguard *n.* 保鏢 bo biew

bog *n* 沼澤 jiew jak

bog *v.i* 阻止 jor jee

bogle *n* 廁所 tee sor

bogus *a* 假嘅 gar geh

boil *n* 黃水瘡 wong suy chorng

boil *v.i.* 滾 gwun

boiler *n* 鍋爐 wok lo

bold *a.* 大膽 dai dam

boldness *n* 膽量 dam leurng

bolt *n* 門閂 mun san

bolt *v. t* 鎖門 sor mun

bomb *n* 炸彈 ja dan

bomb *v. t* 炸 ja

bombard *v. t* 轟炸 gwun ja

bombardment *n* 轟炸 gwun ja

bomber *n* 放炸彈嘅人 forng ja dan geh yan

bonafide *adv* 誠實嘅 sing sat geh

bonafide *a* 真正嘅 jan jing geh

bond *n* 關係 gwan hay

bondage *n* 束縛 chuk bok

bone *n.* 骨 gwat

bonfire *n* 大火堆 dai for duy

bonnet *n* 引擎蓋 yan king goy

bontebok *n* 南非羚羊 larm fay ling yeurng

bonus *n* 意外收穫 yee ngoy so wok

book *n* 書 shu

book *v. t.* 訂 deng

book-keeper *n* 記帳人 gey jeurng yan

book-mark *n.* 書籤 shu teem

book-seller *n* 書商 shu seurng

book-worm *n* 書蟲 shu chung

bookish *n.* 蛀書蟲 ju shu chung

booklet *n* 小冊子 siew tak jee

boon *n* 有利於 yow lay yu

boor *n* 粗人 cho yan

boost *n* 幫 borng

boost *v. t* 提升 tay sing

boot *n* 靴 hur

booth *n* 卡位 ka way

booty *n* 贓物 jorng mat

booze *v. i* 狂飲酒 kwong yam jow

border *n* 邊界 been gai	**boyhood** *n* 童年 tung leen
border *v.t* 鑲邊 seurng been	**brace** *n* 牙箍 ngar ku
bore *v. t* 悶 mun	**bracelet** *n* 手鏈 sow leen
bore *n* 煩人 fan yan	**brag** *v. i* 吹水 chuy suy
born *v.* 出生 chut sang	**brag** *n* 曬 sai
born rich *adj.* 出生富裕 chut sang fu yu	**braille** *n* 盲文 mang man
borne *adj.* 攜帶 kway dai	**brain** *n* 腦 lo
borrow *v. t* 借 jeh	**brake** *n* 刹車 sat ter
bosom *n* 胸部 hung bo	**brake** *v. t* 刹車 sat ter
boss *n* 老細 lo say	**branch** *n* 樹枝 shu jee
botany *n* 植物學 jik mat hok	**brand** *n* 牌子 pai jee
botch *v. t* 輪盡 lun jun	**brandy** *n* 白蘭地 bak lan day
both *a* 雙方 seurng forng	**brangle** *v. t* 嗌交 ai gao
both *pron* 兩個 leurng gor	**brass** *n.* 黃銅 wong tung
both *conj* 而且 yee ter	**brave** *a* 大膽 dai dam
bother *v. t* 麻煩 ma fan	**bravery** *n* 膽量 dam leurng
botheration *n* 煩惱 fan lo	**brawl** *v. i. & n* 打鬥 da dow
bottle *n* 樽 jun	**bray** *n* 驢叫聲 lo giew seng
bottler *n* 裝樽機 jorng jun gey	**bray** *v. i* 刺耳 tee yee
bottom *n* 低 day	**breach** *n* 違法 way fat
bough *n* 大樹枝 dai shu jee	**bread** *n* 麵包 meen bao
boulder *n* 大石 dai sek	**breaden** *v. t. & i* 麵包整嘅 meen bao jing geh
bouncer *n* 保鏢 bo biew	**breadth** *n* 闊度 fwut dow
bound *n.* 跳 tiew	**break** *v. t* 整爛 ting lan
boundary *n* 邊界 been gai	**break** *n* 休息 yow sik
bountiful *a* 大方 dai forng	**breakage** *n* 破損 por shoon
bounty *n* 慷慨 hon koy	**breakdown** *n* 故障 gu jeurng
bouquet *n* 一紮花 yat jak fa	**breakfast** *n* 早餐 jo tan
bout *n* 一陣 yat jan	**breakneck** *n* 飛速 fay chuk
bow *v. t* 鞠躬 guk gung	**breast** *n* 胸 hung
bow *n* 鞠躬 guk gung	**breath** *n* 氣 hey
bow *n* 蝴蝶結 wu deep geet	**breathe** *v. i.* 唞氣 tow hey
bowel *n.* 腸 cheurng	**breeches** *n.* 半長褲 bwun cheurng fu
bower *n* 涼亭 leurng ting	**breed** *v.t* 交配繁殖 gao pwuy fan jik
bowl *n* 碗 wun	**breed** *n* 品種 ban jung
bowl *v.i* 投球 tow kow	**breeze** *n* 微風 may fung
box *n* 箱 seurng	**breviary** *n.* 摘要 jak yiew
boxing *n* 拳擊 koon gik	**brevity** *n* 簡潔 gan geet
boy *n* 男仔 larm jai	**brew** *v. t.* 沖茶 chung cha
boycott *v. t.* 抵制 day jay	
boycott *n* 抵制 day jay	

brewery *n* 啤酒廠 beh jow chorng
bribe *n* 賄賂 kwuy lo
bribe *v. t.* 賄賂 kwuy lo
brick *n* 磚 joon
bride *n* 新娘 san leurng
bridegroom *n.* 新郎 san long
bridge *n* 橋 kiew
bridle *n* 馬勒 mah lak
brief *a.* 簡單 gan dan
brigade *n.* 陸軍 luk gwan
brigadier *n* 陸軍準將 luk gwan jun jeurng
bright *a* 光 gwong
brighten *v. t* 變光啲 been gwong dee
brilliance *n* 光彩 gwong choy
brilliant *a* 精彩 jing choy
brim *n* 邊沿 been yoon
brine *n* 鹽水 yeem suy
bring *v. t* 帶 dai
brinjal *n* 茄子 keh jee
brink *n.* 邊緣 been yoon
brisk *adj* 快 fai
bristle *n* 短而硬嘅毛 doon yee ngan geh mo
british *adj* 英國嘅 ying gwok geh
brittle *a.* 脆 chuy
broad *a* 闊 fwut
broadcast *n* 廣播 gwong bor
broadcast *v. t* 廣播 gwong bor
brocade *n* 錦緞 gam doon
broccoli *n.* 西蘭花 say lan far
brochure *n* 手冊 sow tak
brochure *n* 假日指南 ga yat jee larm
broker *n* 經紀人 ging gey yan
brood *n* 一竇 yat dow
brook *n.* 小溪 siew kay
broom *n* 掃把 so bar
bronze *n. & adj* 青銅 teng tung
broth *n* 肉湯 yuk tong
brothel *n* 妓院 gey yoon

brother *n* 兄弟 hing day
brotherhood *n* 手足之情 sow juk jee ting
brow *n* 額頭 ak tow
brown *a* 棕色 jung sik
brown *n* 棕色 jung sik
browse *n* 搜索 sow sok
bruise *n* 瘀 yu
bruit *n* 散播 san bor
brush *n* 掃 so
brustle *v. t* 摩擦 mor tat
brutal *a* 殘忍 tan yan
brute *n* 禽獸 kam so
bubble *n* 泡泡 pao pao
bucket *n* 水桶 suy tung
buckle *n* 扣住 kowju
bud *n* 花蕾 fa luy
budge *v. i. & n* 嘟 yuk
budget *n* 預算 yu shoon
buff *n* 愛好者 ngoy ho jeh
buffalo *n.* 水牛 suy ngow
buffoon *n* 小丑 siew cho
bug *n.* 昆蟲 kwun chung
bugle *n* 號角 ho gok
build *v. t* 起 hey
build *n* 體格 tay gak
building *n* 建築 geen juk
bulb *n.* 燈泡 dang pao
bulk *n* 大部分 dai bo fan
bulky *a* 龐大 pong dai
bull *n* 牛 ngow
bulldog *n* 牛頭犬 ngow tow hoon
bull's eye *n* 靶心 ba sam
bullet *n* 子彈 jee dan
bulletin *n* 公告 gung go
bullock *n* 閹牛 yeem ngow
bully *n* 惡霸 ok ba
bully *v. t.* 蝦人 har yan
bulwark *n* 堡壘 bo luy
bumper *n.* 保險槓 bo heem gong
bumpy *adj* 崎嶇 kay kuy
bunch *n* 紮 jat

bundle *n* 包 bao
bungalow *n* 平房 ping forng
bungle *v. t* 失敗 sat bai
bungle *n* 失誤 sat hm
bunk *n* 臥鋪 ngor po
bunker *n* 地堡 day bo
buoy *n* 浮標 fow biew
buoyancy *n* 浮力 fow lik
burden *n* 包袱 bao fuk
burden *v. t* 負擔 fu dam
burdensome *a* 難以承擔 larn yee sing dam
bureau *n.* 事務處 see mo chu
Bureacuracy *n.* 官僚主義 gwun liew ju yee
bureaucrat *n* 官僚 gwun liew
burglar *n* 賊 tak
burglary *n* 盜竊 tow seet
burial *n* 葬禮 jorng lay
burk *v. t* 蠢材 chun choy
burn *v. t* 燒 siew
burn *n* 燒 siew
burrow *n* 地道 day dow
burst *v. i.* 爆 bao
burst *n* 爆破 bao por
bury *v. t* 埋 mai
bus *n* 巴士 ba see
bush *n* 矮樹 ngai shu
business *n* 生意 sang yee
businessman *n* 生意人 sang yee yan
bustle *v. t* 催 chuy
busy *a* 忙 mong
but *prep* 但係 dan hay
but *conj.* 不過 bat gwor
butcher *n* 屠夫 tow fu
butcher *v. t* 屠殺 tow sat
butter *n* 牛油 ngow yow
butter *v. t* 搽牛油 ta ngow yow
butterfly *n* 蝴蝶 wu deep
buttermilk *n* 脫脂奶 toot jee lai
buttock *n* 屁股 pay gu

button *n* 鈕 low
button *v. t.* 扣鈕 kow low
buy *v. t.* 買 mai
buyer *n.* 買家 mai ga
buzz *v. i* 嗡嗡聲 wung wung seng
buzz *n.* 嗡嗡聲 wung wung seng
by *prep* 靠近 kao gan
by *adv* 經過 ging gwor
bye-bye *interj.* 拜拜 bai bai
by-election *n* 補選 bo shoon
bylaw, bye-law *n* 地方法 day forng fat
bypass *n* 旁路 pong lo
by-product *n* 副產品 fu tan ban
byre *n* 牛棚 ngow pang
byword *n* 俗語 juk yu

C

cab *n.* 的士 dik see
cabaret *n.* 歌舞表演 gor mo biew yeen
cabbage *n.* 生菜 sang choy
cabin *n.* 船艙 shoon chorng
cabinet *n.* 櫥櫃 chu gway
cable *n.* 電纜 deen larm
cable *v. t.* 打電報 da deen bo
cache *n* 隱藏物 chorng mat chu
cachet *n* 威信 way sun
cackle *v. i* 嘎嘎聲笑 ga ga seng siew
cactus *n.* 仙人掌 seen yan jeurng
cad *n* 無賴 mo lai
cadet *n.* 軍校生 gwan hao sang
cadge *v. i* 乞 hat
cadmium *n* 鎘 gak
cafe *n.* 咖啡店 ga feh deem
cage *n.* 籠 lung
cain *n* 殺兄弟者 sat hing day jeh
cake *n.* 蛋糕 dan go

calamity *n.* 災難 jor larn
calcium *n* 鈣 koy
calculate *v. t.* 計 gey
calculator *n* 計數機 gey so gey
calculation *n.* 計算 gey shoon
calendar *n.* 日曆 yat lik
calf *n.* 小腿 siew tuy
call *v. t.* 叫 giew
call *n.* 電話 deen wah
caller *n* 來電者 loy deen jeh
calligraphy *n* 書法 shu fat
calling *n.* 使命感 see ming gam
callow *adj* 幼稚 yow jee
callous *a.* 冷酷無情 lang huk mo ting
calm *n.* 冷靜 lang jing
calm *n.* 平靜 ping jing
calm *v. t.* 鎮靜 jan jing
calmative *adj* 鎮靜嘅 jan jing geh
calorie *n.* 卡路里 ka lo lay
calumniate *v. t.* 誹謗 fay borng
camel *n.* 駱駝 lok tor
camera *n.* 相機 seurng gey
camlet *n* 駝毛布 tor mo bo
camp *n.* 度假營 dow ga ying
camp *v. i.* 露營 lo ying
campaign *n.* 活動 wut dung
camphor *n.* 樟腦 jeurng lo
can *n.* 罐 gwun
can *v. t.* 可以 hor yi
can *v.* 裝罐 jorng gwun
canal *n.* 運河 wan hor
canard *n* 假新聞 ga san man
cancel *v. t.* 取消 chuy siew
cancellation *n* 取消 chuy siew
cancer *n.* 癌症 ngam jing
candid *a.* 公正 gung jing
candidate *n.* 申請人 san ting yan
candle *n.* 蠟燭 lap juk
candour *n.* 誠懇 sing han
candy *n.* 糖 tong
candy *v. t.* 用糖煮 yung tong ju

cane *n.* 藤條 tang tiew
cane *v. t.* 用藤條打 yung tang tiew da
canister *n.* 小罐 siew gwun
cannon *n.* 大炮 dai pao
cannonade *n. v. & t* 連續炮轟 leen juk pao gwun
canon *n* 原則 yoon jak
canopy *n.* 罩篷 jao fung
canteen *n.* 食堂 sik tong
canter *n* 騎馬慢跑 keh mah man pao
canton *n* 行政區 hang jing kuy
cantonment *n.* 兵營 bing ying
canvas *n.* 帆布 fan bo
canvass *v. t.* 拉票 lai piew
cap *n.* 帽 mo
cap *v. t.* 盒蓋 hap goy
capability *n.* 能力 lang lik
capable *a.* 有能力 yow lang lik
capacious *a.* 寬敞 fwun torng
capacity *n.* 容量 yung leurng
cape *n.* 披肩 pay geen
capital *n.* 首都 sow dow
capital *a.* 死刑嘅 say ying geh
capitalist *n.* 資本主義者 jee bun ju yee jeh
capitulate *v. t* 屈服 wat fuk
caprice *n.* 任性 yam sing
capricious *a.* 善變 seen been
Capricorn *n* 魔羯座 mor keet jor
capsicum *n* 辣椒 lat jiew
capsize *v. i.* 翻 fan
capsular *adj* 膠囊狀 gao lorng jorng
captain *n.* 隊長 duy jeurng
captaincy *n.* 隊長職位 duy jeurng jik way
caption *n.* 插圖說明 tap tow shoot ming
captivate *v. t.* 迷住 may ju
captive *n.* 俘虜 fu lo

captive *a.* 被監禁 bay garm gum

captivity *n.* 監禁 garm gum

capture *v. t.* 捉 juk

capture *n.* 捉 juk

car *n.* 車 cher

carat *n.* 卡 ka

caravan *n.* 旅行拖車 luy hang tor cher

carbide *n.* 碳化物 tan far mat

carbon *n.* 碳 tam

card *n.* 卡 ka

cardamom *n.* 豆蔻 dow kow

cardboard *n.* 紙皮 jee pay

cardiacal *adjs* 心臟嘅 sam jorng geh

cardinal *a.* 最重要 juy jung yiew

cardinal *n.* 樞機主教 shu gey ju gao

care *n.* 照顧 jiew gu

care *v. i.* 關心 gwan sam

career *n.* 職業生涯 jik yeep sang ngai

careful *a* 小心 siew sam

careless *a.* 大意 dai yee

caress *v. t.* 撫摩 fu mor

cargo *n.* 貨 for

caricature *n.* 諷刺畫 fung tee wah

carious *adj* 腐爛 fu lan

carl *n* 粗人 cho yan

carnage *n* 大屠殺 dai tow sat

carnival *n* 嘉年華 ka leen wah

carol *n* 頌歌 jung gor

carpal *n.* 腕骨 wun gwat

carpenter *n.* 木匠 muk jeurng

carpentry *n.* 木工 muk gung

carpet *n.* 地氈 dey jeen

carriage *n.* 車廂 cher seurng

carrier *n.* 運輸公司 wan shu gung see

carrot *n.* 紅蘿蔔 hung lor bak

carry *v. t.* 攞 lor

cart *n.* 馬車 ma cher

cartage *n.* 運輸費 wan shu fay

carton *n* 盒 hap

cartoon *n.* 動畫 dung wah

cartridge *n.* 盒 hap

carve *v. t.* 刻 hak

cascade *n.* 小瀑布 siew buk bo

case *n.* 箱 seurng

cash *n.* 現金 yeen gam

cash *v. t.* 兌現支票 duy yeen jee piew

cashier *n.* 收銀員 sow an yoon

casing *n.* 箱 seurng

cask *n* 木桶 muk tung

casket *n* 細盒 say hap

cassette *n.* 錄音帶 luk yam dai

cast *v. t.* 投射 tow she

cast *n.* 全體演員 choon tey yeen yoon

caste *n* 社會地位 seh wuy day way

castigate *v. t.* 嚴厲批評 yeem lay pay ping

casting *n* 角色分配 gok sik fan pwuy

cast-iron *n* 鑄鐵 ju teet

castle *n.* 城堡 sing bo

castor oil *n.* 蓖麻油 bay ma yow

castral *adj* 營嘅 ying geh

casual *a.* 平常 ping seurng

casualty *n.* 遇難者 yu lan jeh

cat *n.* 貓 mao

catalogue *n.* 目錄 muk luk

cataract *n.* 大瀑布 dai buk bo

catch *v. t.* 捉 chuk

catch *n.* 接 jeep

categorical *a.* 絕對 joot duy

category *n.* 種類 jung luy

cater *v. i* 提供飲食 tay gung yam sik

caterpillar *n* 毛蟲 mo chung

cathedral *n.* 大教堂 dai gao tong

catholic *a.* 天主教嘅 teen ju gao

geh
cattle *n.* 牛 ngow
cauliflower *n.* 椰菜花 yeh choy fa
causal *adj.* 因果關係 yan gwor gwan hay
causality *n* 因果關係 yan gwor gwan hay
cause *n.* 起因 hey yan
cause *v.t* 令到 ling dow
causeway *n* 堤道 tay dow
caustic *a.* 腐蝕性 fu sik sing
caution *n.* 警告 ging go
caution *v. t.* 提醒 tay sing
cautious *a.* 謹慎 gan san
cavalry *n.* 騎兵 keh bing
cave *n.* 山洞 san dung
cavern *n.* 大山洞 dai san dung
cavil *v. t* 抱怨 po yoon
cavity *n.* 窿 lung
caw *n.* 鴉叫聲 ngar giew seng
caw *v. i.* 鴉叫 ngar giew
cease *v. i.* 終止 jung jee
ceaseless *~a.* 不停嘅 bat ting geh
cedar *n.* 雪松 shu chung
ceiling *n.* 天花板 teen far ban
celebrate *v. t. & i.* 慶祝 hing juk
celebration *n.* 慶祝活動 hing juk wut dung
celebrity *n* 名人 ming yan
celestial *adj* 天上嘅 teen seurng geh
celibacy *n.* 獨身生活 duk san sang wut
celibacy *n.* 獨身 duk san
cell *n.* 細胞 say bao
cellar *n* 地窖 day gao
cellular *adj* 細胞嘅 say bao geh
cement *n.* 水泥 suy lay
cement *v. t.* 加強 ga keurng
cemetery *n.* 墓園 mo yoon
cense *v. t* 焚香致敬 fan heurng jee ging

censer *n* 香爐 heurng lo
censor *n.* 審查官 sam cha gwun
censor *v. t.* 刪剪 san jeen
censorious *adj* 奄尖 yeem jeem
censorship *n.* 審查 sam cha
censure *n.* 批評 pay ping
censure *v. t.* 譴責 heen jak
census *n.* 人口調查 yan ho tiew ta
cent *n* 仙 seen
centenarian *n* 人瑞 yan suy
centenary *n.* 一百週年 yat bak jow leen
centennial *adj.* 一百週年 yat bak jow leen
center *n* 中心 jung sam
centigrade *a.* 攝氏 seep see
centipede *n.* 蜈蚣 hm gung
central *a.* 中心 jung sam
centre *n* 中心 jung sam
centrifugal *adj.* 離心 lay sam
centuple *n. & adj* 百倍 bak pwuy
century *n.* 世紀 say gey
ceramics *n* 陶瓷 tow chee
cerated *adj.* 塗咗蠟嘅 tow jor lap geh
cereal *n.* 穀物 guk mat
cereal *a* 穀類 guk luy
cerebral *adj* 大腦嘅 dai lo geh
ceremonial *a.* 禮儀 lay yee
ceremonious *a.* 講究禮儀 gong go lay yee
ceremony *n.* 儀式 yee sik
certain *a* 特定 dak ding
certainly *adv.* 當然 dong yeen
certainty *n.* 確定性 kok ding sing
certificate *n.* 獎狀 jeurng jorng
certify *v. t.* 證實 jing sat
cerumen *n* 耳垢 yee go
cesspool *n.* 垃圾坑 lap sap hang
chain *n* 鍊 leen
chair *n.* 凳 dang
chairman *n* 主席 ju jik

chaise *n* 馬車 ma cher
chaise *n* 躺椅 tong yee
challenge *n.* 挑戰 tiew jeen
challenge *v. t.* 挑戰 tiew jeen
chamber *n.* 會議廳 wuy yee teng
chamberlain *n* 管家 gwun ga
champion *n.* 冠軍 gwun gwan
champion *v. t.* 聲援 sing wun
chance *n.* 機會 gey wuy
chancellor *n.* 總理 jung lay
chancery *n* 檔案室 dong on sat
change *v. t.* 改變 goy been
change *n.* 改變 goy been
channel *n* 台 toy
chant *n* 反覆呼叫 fan fuk fu giew
chaos *n.* 混亂 wan loon
chaotic *adv.* 混亂 wan loon
chapel *n.* 細教堂 say gao tong
chapter *n.* 章 jeurng
character *n.* 角色 gok sik
charge *v. t.* 收費 so fay
charge *n.* 告 go
chariot *n* 戰車 jeen cher
charitable *a.* 慈善嘅 tee seen geh
charity *n.* 慈善 tee seen
charm1 *n.* 魅力 may lik
charm2 *v. t.* 吸引 kap yan
chart *n.* 圖表 tow biew
charter *n* 憲章 heen jeurng
chase1 *v. t.* 追 juy
chase2 *n.* 追捕 juy bo
chaste *a.* 純潔 sun geet
chastity *n.* 忠貞 jung jing
chat1 *n.* 傾偈 king gey
chat2 *v. i.* 傾偈 king gey
chatter *v. t.* 亂噏 look ap
chauffeur *n.* 司機 see gey
cheap *a* 平 peng
cheapen *v. t.* 降價 gorng ga
cheat *v. t.* 出貓 chut mao
cheat *n.* 騙子 peen jee
check *v. t.* 檢查 geem cha

check *n* 檢查 geem cha
checkmate *n* 將軍 jeurng gwan
cheek *n* 面珠 meen ju
cheep *v. i* 吱吱叫 jee jee giew
cheer *n.* 歡呼聲 fwun fu seng
cheer *v. t.* 喝彩 hot choy
cheerful *a.* 高興 go hing
cheerless *a* 陰暗 yam am
cheese *n.* 芝士 jee see
chemical *a.* 化學嘅 far hok geh
chemical *n.* 化學物品 far hok mat ban
chemise *n* 無袖連衣裙 mo jow leen yee kwan
chemist *n.* 化學家 far hok ga
chemistry *n.* 化學 far hok
cheque *n.* 支票 jee piew
cherish *v. t.* 珍惜 jan sik
cheroot *n* 雪茄煙 shoot ka yeen
chess *n.* 國際象棋 gwok jay jeurng kay
chest *n* 心口 sam ho
chestnut *n.* 栗子 lut jee
chew *v. t* chiew
chevalier *n* 騎士 keh see
chicken *n.* 雞 gey
chide *v. t.* 指責 jee jak
chief *a.* 首要嘅 sow yiew geh
chieftain *n.* 首領 sow ling
child *n* 細路仔 say lo jai
childhood *n.* 童年 tung leen
childish *a.* 幼稚 yow jee
chill *n.* 寒冷 hon lang
chilli *n.* 辣椒 lat jiew
chilly *a* 凍 dung
chiliad *n.* 一千 yat teen
chimney *n.* 煙囪 yeen tung
chimpanzee *n.* 黑猩猩 hak sing sing
chin *n.* 下巴 ha pa
china *n.* 瓷器 tee hay
chirp *v.i.* 吱喳叫 jee ja giew

chirp *n* 吱喳叫聲 jee ja giew seng
chisel *n* 鑿 jok
chisel *v. t.* 雕 diew
chit *n.* 欠單 heem dan
chivalrous *a.* 體貼 tay teep
chivalry *n.* 體貼 tay teep
chlorine *n* 氯氣 luk hay
chloroform *n* 氯仿 luk forng
choice *n.* 選擇 shoon jak
choir *n* 合唱團 hap cheurng toon
choke *v. t.* 哽 kang
cholera *n.* 霍亂 fok loon
chocolate *n* 朱古力 ju gu lik
choose *v. t.* 揀 gan
chop *v. t* 斬 jam
chord *n.* 和弦 wor yoon
choroid *n* 脈絡膜 mak lok mok
chorus *n.* 副歌 fu gor
Christ *n.* 耶穌 yeh so
Christendom *n.* 基督教徒 gey duk gao tow
Christian *n* 基督徒 gey duk tow
Christian *a.* 基督徒 gey duk tow
Christianity *n.* 基督教 gey duk gao
Christmas *n* 聖誕節 sing dan jeet
chrome *n* 鉻 gok
chronic *a.* 慢性 man sing
chronicle *n.* 編年史 peen leen see
chronology *n.* 年表 leen biew
chronograph *n* 記時器 gey see hay
chuckle *v. i* 笑 siew
chum *n* 好朋友 ho pang yow
church *n.* 教堂 gao tong
churchyard *n.* 教堂墓地 gao tong mo day
churl *n* 下賤嘅人 ha jeen geh yan
churn *v. t. & i.* 攪 gao
churn *n.* 攪乳機 gao yu gey
cigar *n.* 雪茄 shoot ka
cigarette *n.* 煙 yeen

cinema *n.* 戲院 hey yoon
cinnabar *n* 朱砂 ju sar
cinnamon *n* 肉桂粉 yuk gway fan
cipher, cipher *n.* 暗號 am ho
circle *n.* 圓圈 yoon hoon
circuit *n.* 線路 seen lo
circumfluence *n.* 環流 wan low
circumspect *adj.* 慎重 san jung
circular *a* 圓形 yoon ying
circular *n.* 傳單 choon dan
circulate *v. i.* 環繞 wan yiew
circulation *n* 循環 chun wan
circumference *n.* 圓周 yoon jow
circumstance *n* 情況 ting forng
circus *n.* 馬戲團 ma hay toon
cist *n* 石棺 sek gwun
citadel *n.* 堡壘 bo luy
cite *v. t* 舉出 guy chut
citizen *n* 市民 see man
citizenship *n* 公民權利 gung man koon lay
citric *adj.* 檸檬 ling mung
city *n* 城市 sing see
civic *a* 城市嘅 sing see geh
civics *n* 公民學 gung man hok
civil *a* 平民嘅 ping man geh
civilian *n* 平民 ping man
civilization *n.* 文明社會 man ming seh wuy
civilize *v. t* 開化 hoy far
clack *n. & v. i* 噼拍 pik pak
claim *n* 宣稱 shoon ting
claim *v. t* 聲稱 sing ting
claimant *n* 要求者 yiew kow jeh
clamber *v. i* 攀登 pan dang
clamour *n* 吵鬧聲 tao lao seng
clamour *v. i.* 大聲要求 dai seng yiew kow
clamp *n* 夾鉗 geep keem
clandestine *adj.* 秘密嘅 bay mat geh
clap *v. i.* 拍手 pak sow

clap *n* 鼓掌 gu jeurng

clarify *v. t* 澄清 ting ting

clarification *n* 澄清 ting ting

clarion *n.* 喇叭 la ba

clarity *n* 清晰 ting sik

clash *n.* 分歧 fan kay

clash *v. t.* 撞 jorng

clasp *n* 捉緊 juk gan

class *n* 班 ban

classic *a* 典型 deen ying

classic *n* 經典 ging deen

classical *a* 古典 gu deen

classification *n* 種類 jung luy

classify *v. t* 分類 fan luy

clause *n* 條款 tiew fwun

claw *n* 爪 jao

clay *n* 泥土 lay tow

clean *n.* 乾淨 gon jeng

clean *v. t* 清潔 ting geet

cleanliness *n* 乾淨 gon jeng

cleanse *v. t* 清洗 ting say

clear *a* 清楚 ting chor

clear *v. t* 搬走 bwun jow

clearance *n* 清除 ting chuy

clearly *adv* 明顯 ming heen

cleft *n* 裂口 leet ho

clergy *n* 牧師 muk see

clerical *a* 辦公室嘅 ban gung sat geh

clerk *n* 文員 man yoon

clever *a.* 叻 lek

clew *n.* 線毯 seen kow

click *n.* 點擊 deem gik

client *n..* 客 hak

cliff *n.* 懸崖 yoon ai

climate *n.* 氣候 hay ho

climax *n.* 高潮 go tiew

climb *n.* 攀登 pan dang

climb *v.i* 爬 pa

cling *v. i.* 捉緊 juk gan

clinic *n.* 診所 tan sor

clink *n.* 丁噹聲 ding dong seng

cloak *n.* 斗篷 dow fung

clock *n.* 鐘 jung

clod *n.* 泥塊 lay fai

cloister *n.* 修院 sow yoon

close *n.* 掘頭巷 gwat tow horng

close *a.* 近 kan

close *v. t* 閂 san

closet *n.* 壁櫃 bik gway

closure *n.* 停業 ting yeep

clot *n.* 蠢人 chun yan

clot *v. t* 凝結 ying geet

cloth *n* 布 bo

clothe *v. t* 着 jeurk

clothes *n.* 衫 sam

clothing *n* 衫 sam

cloud *n.* 雲 wan

cloudy *a* 多雲 dor wan

clove *n* 丁香 ding heurng

clown *n* 小丑 siew cho

club *n* 會 wuy

clue *n* 提示 tay see

clumsy *a* 輪盡 lun jun

cluster *n* 群 kwun

cluster *v. i.* 聚集 juy jap

clutch *n* 離合 lay hap

clutter *v. t* 亂 loon

coach *n* 大巴 dai ba

coachman *n* 馬車夫 ma cher fu

coal *n* 炭 tan

coalition *n* 聯合政府 loon hap jing fu

coarse *a* 粗 cho

coast *n* 海岸 hoy ngon

coat *n* 褸 lo

coating *n* 覆蓋層 fuk koy tang

coax *v. t* 氹 tam

cobalt *n* 鈷 gu

cobbler *n* 鞋匠 hai jeurng

cobra *n* 眼睛蛇 ngan geng seh

cobweb *n* 蜘蛛網 jee ju morng

cocaine *n* 可卡因 hor ka yan

cock *n* 公雞 gung gey

cocker v. t 嬌養 giew yeurng
cockle v. i 鳥蛤 liew ha
cock-pit n. 駕駛艙 ga say chorng
cockroach n 甲由 gat jat
coconut n 椰子 yeh jee
code n 密碼 mat ma
co-education n. 男女同校 larm luy tung hao
coefficient n. 係數 hay so
co-exist v. i 共存 gung choon
co-existence n 共存 gung choon
coffee n 咖啡 ga feh
coffin n 棺材 gwun choy
cog n 輪齒 lun tee
cogent adj 有說服力 yow suy fuk lik
cognate adj 同族 tung juk
cognizance n 同族 ling hm
cohabit v. t 同居 tung guy
coherent a 合乎邏輯 hap fu lor tap
cohesive adj 有凝聚力 yow ying juy lik
coif n 頭巾 tow gan
coin n 銀仔 an jai
coinage n 硬幣 ang bay
coincide v. i 同時發生 tung see fat sang
coir n 椰殼纖維 yeh hok teem way
coke v. t 變焦炭 been jiew tan
cold a 凍 dung
cold n 感冒 gam mo
collaborate v. i 合作 hap jok
collaboration n 合作 hap jok
collapse v. i 暈低 wan day
collar n 領 leng
colleague n 同事 tung see
collect v. t 收集 so jap
collection n 系列 hay leet
collective a 集體 jap tay
collector n 收集家 so jap ga
college n 學院 hok yoon

collide v. i. 碰撞 pung jorng
collision n 碰撞 pung jorng
collusion n 串通 choon tung
colon n 冒號 mo ho
colon n 結腸 geet cheurng
colonel n. 上校 seurng gao
colonial a 殖民嘅 jik man geh
colony n 殖民地 jik man day
colour n 顏色 ngan sik
colour v. t 染色 yeem sik
colter n 犁刀 lay dow
column n 欄 lan
coma n. 昏迷 fan may
comb n 梳 sor
combat1 n 搏鬥 bok dow
combat v. t. 防止 forng jee
combatant1 n 戰士 jeen see
combatant a. 戰鬥 jeen dow
combination n 組合 jo hap
combine v. t 結合 geet hap
come v. i. 嚟 lay
comedian n. 喜劇家 hay kek ga
comedy n. 喜劇 hay kek
comet n 彗星 way sing
comfit n. 糖 tong
comfort1 n. 舒服 shu fuk
comfort v. t 安慰 on way
comfortable a 舒服 shu fuk
comic a 戲劇嘅 hay kek geh
comic n 漫畫 man wah
comical a 好笑嘅 ho siew geh
comma n 逗號 dow ho
command n 命令 ming ling
command v. t 命令 ming ling
commandant n 司令 see ling
commander n 指揮官 jee fay gwun
commemorate v. t. 紀念 gey leem
commemoration n. 紀念 gey leem
commence v. t 開始 hoy tee

commencement *n* 開始 hoy tee
commend *v. t* 表揚 biew yeurng
commendable *a.* 值得讚嘅 jik dak jan geh
commendation *n* 嘉許 ga huy
comment *v. i* 表達意見 biew dat yee geen
comment *n* 評論 ping lun
commentary *n* 評論 ping lun
commentator *n* 評論員 ping lun yoon
commerce *n* 貿易 mo yik
commercial *a* 商業嘅 seurng yeep geh
commiserate *v. t* 同情 tung ting
commission *n.* 佣金 yung gam
commissioner *n.* 委員 way yoon
commissure *n.* 接合處 jeep hap chu
commit *v. t.* 做 jow
committee *n* 委員會 way yoon wuy
commodity *n.* 貨 for
common *a.* 常見 seurng geen
commoner *n.* 平民 ping man
commonplace *a.* 普遍嘅 po peen geh
commonwealth *n.* 英聯邦 ying loon bong
commotion *n* 騷亂 so loon
commove *v. t* 激動 gik dung
communal *a* 共享嘅 gung heurng geh
commune *v. t* 群體 kwan tay
communicate *v. t* 溝通 kow tung
communication *n.* 通訊 tung sun
communiqué *n.* 公報 gung bo
communism *n* 共產主義 gung tan ju yee
community *n.* 社會 seh wuy
commute *v. t* 減刑 garm ying
compact *a.* 壓縮嘅 at suk geh

compact *n.* 合同 hap tung
companion *n.* 伴 bwun
company *n.* 公司 gung see
comparative *a* 相比 seurng bay
compare *v. t* 比較 bay gao
comparison *n* 比較 bay gao
compartment *n.* 間隔 gan gak
compass *n* 指南針 jee larm jam
compassion *n* 同情 tung ting
compel *v. t* 強迫 keurng bik
compensate *v.t* 賠償 pwuy seurng
compensation *n* 賠償 pwuy seurng
compete *v. i* 競爭 ging jang
competence *n* 能力 lang lik
competent *a.* 有能力 yow lang lik
competition *n.* 比賽 bay choy
competitive *a* 競爭力 ging jang lik
compile *v. t* 編寫 peen she
complacent *adj.* 得戚 dak tik
complain *v. i* 投訴 tow so
complaint *n* 投訴 tow so
complaisance *n.* 殷勤 yan kan
complaisant *adj.* 順從 sun chung
complement *n* 補充物 bo chung mat
complementary *a* 互補 wu bo
complete *a* 完整 yoon jing
complete *v. t* 完成 yoon sing
completion *n.* 完成 yoon sing
complex *a* 複雜 fuk jap
complex *n* 建築群 geen juk kwan
complexion *n* 膚色 fu sik
compliance *n.* 順從 sun chung
compliant *adj.* 順從 sun chung
complicate *v. t* 複雜化 fuk jap fa
complication *n.* 複雜化 fuk jap fa
compliment *n.* 讚揚 jan yeurng

compliment *v. t* 讚 jan
comply *v. i* 服從 fuk chung
component *n.* 組件 jo geen
compose *v. t* 作 jok
composition *n* 作品 jok ban
compositor *n.* 排版師 pai ban see
compost *n* 肥料 fay liew
composure *n.* 鎮定 jan ding
compound *n* 化合物 fa hap mat
compound *a* 混合 wan hap
compound *n* 復合詞 fuk hap tee
compound *v. i* 惡化 ok fa
compounder *n.* 製藥公司 jay yeurk gung see
comprehend *v. t* 理解 lay gai
comprehension *n* 領悟力 ling hm lik
comprehensive *a* 全部嘅 choon bo geh
compress *v. t.* 壓縮 at suk
compromise *n* 和解 wor gai
compromise *v. t* 妥協 tor heep
compulsion *n* 強迫 keurng bik
compulsory *a* 一定要 yat ding yiew
compunction *n.* 內疚 loy gow
computation *n.* 計算 gey shoon
compute *v.t.* 計算 gey shoon
comrade *n.* 戰友 jeen yow
conation *n.* 意圖 yee tow
concave *adj.* 凹 lup
conceal *v. t.* 隱瞞 yan mun
concede *v.t.* 承認 sing ying
conceit *n* 驕傲 giew oh
conceive *v. t* 想像 seurng jeurng
concentrate *v. t* 專心 joon sam
concentration *n.* 專心 joon sam
concept *n* 概念 koy leem
conception *n* 構思 kow see
concern *v. t* 涉及 seep kap
concern *n* 關心 gwan sum

concert *n.* 演唱會 yeen cheurng wuy
concert2 *v. t* 達成 dat sing
concession *n* 妥協 tor heep
conch *n.* 海螺殼 hoy lor hok
conciliate *v.t.* 安撫 on fu
concise *a* 簡潔 gan geet
conclude *v. t* 結束 geet chuk
conclusion *n.* 結論 geet lun
conclusive *a* 確鑿嘅 kok jok geh
concoct *v. t* 調製 tiew jay
concoction *n.* 調製品 tiew jay ban
concord *n.* 和諧 wor hai
concrescence *n.* 愈合 yu hap
concrete *n* 混凝土 wan ying tow
concrete *a* 確實嘅 kok sat geh
concrete *v. t* 用混凝土 yung wan ying tow
concubinage *n.* 同居 tung guy
concubine *n* 妾 teep
conculcate *v.t.* 踩 tai
condemn *v. t.* 指責 jee jak
condemnation *n* 譴責 heen jak
condense *v. t* 壓縮 at suk
condite *v.t.* 醃 yeep
condition *n* 條件 tiew geen
conditional *a* 附帶條件 fu dai tiew geen
condole *v. i.* 哀悼 oi dow
condolence *n* 慰問 way man
condonation *n.* 寬恕 fwun shu
conduct *n* 行為舉止 hang way guy jee
conduct *v. t* 安排 on pai
conductor *n* 指揮家 jee fey ga
cone *n.* 圓錐形 yoon juy ying
confectioner *n* 甜食商 teem sik seurng
confectionery *n* 甜食 teem sik
confer *v. i* 商討 seurng tow
conference *n* 會議 wuy yee

confess *v. t.* 承認 sing yan
confession *n* 表白 biew bak
confidant *n* 知己 jee gey
confide *v. i* 透露 tow lo
confidence *n* 信心 sun sam
confident *a.* 有信心 yow sun sam
confidential *a.* 機密 gey mat
confine *v. t* 限制 han jay
confinement *n.* 監禁 garm gam
confirm *v. t* 確認 kok ying
confirmation *n* 確定 kok ding
confiscate *v. t* 充公 chung gung
confiscation *n* 沒收 mut so
conflict *n.* 爭論 jang lun
conflict *v. i* 衝突 chung dat
confluence *n* 匯流處 wuy low chu
confluent *adj.* 匯合 wuy hap
conformity *n.* 遵守 jun sow
conformity *n.* 同其他人一樣 tung kay ta yan yat yeurng
confraternity *n.* 團體 toon tay
confrontation *n.* 對質 duy jat
confuse *v. t* 混亂 wan loon
confusion *n* 混亂 wan loon
confute *v.t.* 駁 bok
conge *n.* 辭職 tee jik
congenial *a* 適合 sik hap
conglutinate *v.t.* 愈合 yu hao
congratulate *v. t* 恭喜 gung hey
congratulation *n* 祝賀 juk hor
congress *n* 國會 gwok wuy
conjecture *n* 猜測 tai tak
conjecture *v. t* 推測 tuy tak
conjugal *a* 夫妻間嘅 fu tay gan geh
conjugate *v.t. & i.* 動詞變化 dung tee been fa
conjunct *adj.* 結合 geet hap
conjunctiva *n.* 結膜 geet mok
conjuncture *n.* 緊急關頭 gan gao gwan tow

conjure *v.t.* 呼喚 fu wun
conjure *v.i.* 變魔術 been mor sut
connect *v. t.* 連接 leen jeep
connection *n* 關連 gwan leen
connivance *n.* 縱容 jung yung
conquer *v. t* 征服 jing fuk
conquest *n* 征服 jing fuk
conscience *n* 良心 leurng sam
conscious *a* 清醒 ting sing
consecrate *v.t.* 聖化 sing fa
consecutive *adj.* 連續 leen juk
consecutively *adv* 連續咁 leen juk gam
consensus *n.* 共識 gung sik
consent *n.* 允許 wan huy
consent *v. i* 同意 tung yee
consent3 *v.t.* 允許 wan huy
consequence *n* 後果 ho gwor
consequent *a* 後果 ho gwor
conservative *a* 保守 bo so
conservative *n* 保守黨支持者 bo so dong jee tee jeh
conserve *v. t* 保存 bo choon
consider *v. t* 考慮 hao luy
considerable *a* 相當大嘅 seurng dong dai geh
considerate *a.* 體貼 tay teep
consideration *n* 仔細考慮 jee say hao luy
considering *prep.* 考慮到 hao luy dow
consign *v.t.* 交畀 gao bay
consign *v. t.* 打發 da fat
consignment *n.* 運送貨 wan sung for
consist *v. i* 包含 bao ham
consistence,-cy *n.* 連貫性 leen gwan sing
consistent *a* 一直 yat jik
consolation *n* 安慰 on way
console *v. t* 安慰 on way
consolidate *v. t.* 加強 ga keurng

consolidation *n* 強化 keurng fa
consonance *n.* 和音 wor yam
consonant *n.* 輔音 fu yam
consort *n.* 配偶 pwuy oh
conspectus *n.* 大網 dai morng
conspicuous *a.* 明顯 ming heen
conspiracy *n.* 陰謀 yam mow
conspirator *n.* 共謀者 gung mo jeh
conspire *v. i.* 密謀 mat mo
constable *n* 警察 ging tat
constant *a* 一直 yat jik
constellation *n.* 星群 sing kwan
constipation *n.* 便秘 been bay
constituency *n* 選區 shoon kuy
constituent *n.* 選民 shoon man
constituent *adj.* 組成 jow sing
constitute *v. t* 被認爲 bay ying way
constitution *n* 憲法 heen fat
constrict *v.t.* 縮窄 suk jak
construct *v. t.* 起 hay
construction *n* 結構 geet kow
consult *v. t* 詢問 sun man
consultation *n* 商討會 seurng tow wuy
consume *v. t* 消耗 siew ho
consumption *n* 消耗量 siew ho leurng
consumption *n* 消費 siew fay
contact *n.* 接觸 jeep juk
contact *v. t* 聯絡 loon lok
contagious *a* 傳染 choon yeem
contain *v.t.* 有 yow
contaminate *v.t.* 污染 wu yeem
contemplate *v. t* 考慮 hao luy
contemplation *n* 考慮緊 hao luy gan
contemporary *a* 現代 yeen doy
contempt *n* 鄙視 pay see
contemptuous *a* 輕視 hing see
contend *v. i* 聲稱 sing ting

content *a.* 滿足 mun juk
content *v. t* 知足 jee juk
content *n* 內容 loy yung
content *n.* 目錄 muk luk
contention *n* 觀點 gwun deem
contentment *n* 滿意 mun yee
contest *v. t* 爭辯 jang been
contest *n.* 比賽 bay choy
context *n* 上下文 seurng har man
continent *n* 洲 jow
continental *a* 歐洲大陸嘅 oh jow dai luk geh
contingency *n.* 可能發生嘅事 hor lang fat sang geh see
continual *adj.* 連續 leen juk
continuation *n.* 持續 tee juk
continue *v. i.* 繼續 gey juk
continuity *n* 連續性 leen juk sing
continuous *a* 不斷嘅 bat doon geh
contour *n* 輪廓 lun kok
contra *pref.* 正相反 jing seurng fan
contraception *n.* 避孕 bay yan
contract *n* 合約 hap yeurk
contract *v. t* 伸縮 san suk
contrapose *v.t.* 對照 duy jiew
contractor *n* 承辦商 sing ban seurng
contradict *v. t* 反駁 fan bok
contradiction *n* 矛盾 mao tun
contrary *a* 相反 seurng fan
contrast *v. t* 對比 duy bay
contrast *n* 對照 duy jiew
contribute *v. t* 捐 goon
contribution *n* 貢獻 gung heen
control *n* 控制權 hung jay koon
control *v. t* 控制 hung jay
controller *n.* 遙控 yiew hung
controversy *n* 爭論 jang lun
contuse *v.t.* 挫傷 chor seurng
conundrum *n.* 難題 lan tay

convene *v. t* 召集 jiew jap
convener *n* 召集人 jiew jap yan
convenience *n.* 方便 forng been
convenient *a* 方便 forng been
convent *n* 女修道院 luy sow dow yoon
convention *n.* 集會 jap wuy
conversant *a* 熟悉 suk sik
conversant *adj.* 熟 suk
conversation *n* 傾偈 king gey
converse *v.t.* 傾 king
conversion *n* 轉換 joon wun
convert *v. t* 換 wun
convert *n* 轉宗教嘅人 joon jung gao geh yan
convey *v. t.* 表達 biew dat
conveyance *n* 傳送 choon sung
convict *v. t.* 宣判有罪 shoon pwun yow juy
convict *n* 罪犯 juy fan
conviction *n* 判罪 pwun juy
convince *v. t* 說服 suy fuk
convivial *adj.* 容易相處 yung yee seurng chu
convocation *n.* 集會 jap wuy
convoke *v.t.* 召集 jiew jap
convolve *v.t.* 捲 goon
coo *n* 細聲 say seng
coo *v. i* 咕咕叫 gu gu giew
cook *v. t* 煮 joo
cook *n* 廚師 choo see
cooker *n* 爐 lo
cool *a* 涼 leurng
cool *v. i.* 變涼 been leurng
cooler *n* 冷卻器 lang keurk hay
coolie *n* 苦力 fu lik
co-operate *v. i* 合作 hap jok
co-operation *n* 合作 hap jok
co-operative *a* 配合 pwuy hap
co-ordinate *a.* 協調 heep tiew
co-ordinate *v. t* 協調 heep tiew
co-ordination *n* 協調 heep tiew

coot *n.* 白骨頂 bak gwat ding
co-partner *n* 拍檔 pak dong
cope *v. i* 應付 ying fu
coper *n.* 馬販 ma fan
copper *n* 銅 tung
coppice *n.* 矮林 ay lam
coprology *n.* 糞石學 fan sek hok
copulate *v.i.* 交配 gao pwuy
copy *n* 複製品 fuk jay ban
copy *v. t* 複製 fuk jay
coral *n* 珊瑚 san wu
cord *n* 細繩 say sing
cordial *a* 好好人 ho ho yan
corbel *n.* 梁托 leurng tok
cordate *adj.* 心形 sam ying
core *n.* 果心 gwor sam
coriander *n.* 芫荽 yoon say
Corinth *n.* 科林斯 for see lam
cork *n.* 酒塞 jow sat
cormorant *n.* 鸕鷀 lo tee
corn *n* 粟米 suk may
cornea *n* 角膜 gok mok
corner *n* 角落 gok lok
cornet *n.* 短號 doon ho
cornicle *n.* 腹管 fuk gwun
coronation *n* 加冕典禮 ga meen deen lay
coronet *n.* 冠冕 gwun meen
corporal *a* 身體嘅 san tay geh
corporate *adj.* 公司嘅 gung see geh
corporation *n* 大公司 dai gung see
corps *n* 兵團 bing toon
corpse *n* 屍體 see tay
correct *a* 正確 jing kok
correct *v. t* 更改 gang goy
correction *n* 改正 goy jing
correlate *v.t.* 互相依賴 wu seurng yee lai
correlation *n.* 相關 seurng gwan
correspond *v. i* 符合 fu hap

correspondence *n.* 通信 tung sun

correspondent *n.* 記者 gey jeh

corridor *n.* 走廊 jow long

corroborate *v.t.* 證實 jing sat

corrosive *adj.* 腐蝕性嘅 fu sik sing geh

corrupt *v. t.* 破壞 por wai

corrupt *a.* 唔誠實 hm sing sat

corruption *n.* 貪污 tam wu

cosier *n.* 更舒適 gang shu sik

cosmetic *a.* 表面 biew meen

cosmetic *n.* 化妝品 fa jorng ban

cosmic *adj.* 宇宙嘅 yu jow geh

cost *v.t.* 損失 shoon sat

cost *n.* 價格 gar gak

costal *adj.* 肋骨嘅 lak gwat geh

cote *n.* 小屋 siew uk

costly *a.* 貴 gway

costume *n.* 服裝 fuk jorng

cosy *a.* 舒適 shu sik

cot *n.* 幼兒床 yow yee chorng

cottage *n* 小屋 siew uk

cotton *n.* 棉 meen

couch *n.* 梳化 sor fa

cough *n.* 咳 kat

cough *v. i.* 咳 kat

council *n.* 政務委員會 jing mo way yoon wuy

councillor *n.* 市議員 see yee yoon

counsel *n.* 建議 geen yee

counsel *v. t.* 勸 hoon

counsellor *n.* 顧問 gu man

count *n.* 點數 deem so

count *v. t.* 數 so

countenance *n.* 面色 meen sik

counter *n.* 櫃台 gway toy

counter *v. t* 反駁 fan bok

counteract *v.t.* 抵消 day siew

countercharge *n.* 反控 fan hung

counterfeit *a.* 偽造 ay jow

counterfeiter *n.* 偽造者 ay jow jeh

countermand *v.t.* 撤銷 teet siew

counterpart *n.* 對應事物 duy ying see mat

countersign *v. t.* 副署 fu ju

countess *n.* 伯爵夫人 bak jeurk fu yan

countless *a.* 無數 mo so

country *n.* 國家 gwok ga

county *n.* 縣 yoon

coup *n.* 政變 jing been

couple *n* 一對 yat duy

couple *v. t* 連接 leen jeep

couplet *n.* 對聯 duy loon

coupon *n.* 優惠券 yow way goon

courage *n.* 勇氣 yung hey

courageous *a.* 勇敢 yung gam

courier *n.* 專遞公司 joon day gung see

course *n.* 課程 for ting

court *n.* 法庭 fat ting

court *v. t.* 討好 tow ho

courteous *a.* 有禮貌 yow lay mao

courtesan *n.* 情婦 ting fu

courtesy *n.* 禮貌 lay mao

courtier *n.* 朝臣 tiew san

courtship *n.* 求愛期 kow ngoy kay

courtyard *n.* 庭院 ting yoon

cousin *n.* 表親 biew tan

covenant *n.* 合同 hap tung

cover *v. t.* 遮住 jeh ju

cover *n.* 封面 fung meen

coverlet *n.* 床罩 chorng jao

covet *v.t.* 渴望 hot morng

cow *n.* 牛 ngow

cow *v. t.* 恐嚇 hung hak

coward *n.* 膽小鬼 dam siew gway

cowardice *n.* 懦弱 loy yeurk

cower *v.i.* 退縮 tuy suk

cozy *a.* 舒適 shu sik
crab *n* 蟹 hai
crack *n* 裂痕 leet han
crack *v. i* 裂開 leet hoy
cracker *n* 薄脆餅乾 bok chuy beng gon
crackle *v.t.* 劈里啪啦 pi lee pa la
cradle *n* 搖籃 yiew larm
craft *n* 手藝 sow ngay
craftsman *n* 工匠 gung jeurng
crafty *a* 狡猾 gao wat
cram *v. t* 塞 sat
crambo *n.* 對韻遊戲 duy wan yow hay
crane *n* 吊車 diew cher
crankle *v.t.* 彎曲 wan kuk
crash *v. i* 撞 jorng
crash *n* 碰撞 pung jorng
crass *adj.* 粗魯 cho lo
crate *n.* 板條箱 ban tiew seurng
crave *v.t.* 渴望 hot morng
craw *n.* 嗉囊 so long
crawl *v. t* 爬 pa
crawl *n* 慢速 man chuk
craze *n* 熱潮 yeet tiew
crazy *a* 黐線 tee seen
creak *v. i* 嘎吱聲 ga jee seng
creak *n* 嘎吱聲 ga jee seng
cream *n* 奶油 lai yow
crease *n* 摺痕 jeep han
create *v.t* 整 jing
creation *n* 作品 jok ban
creative *adj.* 創意 chorng yee
creator *n* 創作者 chorng jok jeh
creature *n* 生物 sang mat
credible *a* 可靠嘅 hor kao geh
credit *n* 信譽 sun yu
creditable *a* 值得讚嘅 jik dak jan geh
creditor *n* 債主 jai ju
credulity *adj.* 輕易相信 hing yee seurng sun

creed *n.* 原則 yoon jak
creed *n* 信念 sun leem
creek *n.* 小溪 siew kay
creep *v. i* 爬 pa
creeper *n* 攀緣植物 pan yoon jik mat
cremate *v. t* 火化 for far
cremation *n* 火化 for far
crest *n* 徽章 fay jeurng
crevet *n.* 熔爐 yung lo
crew *n.* 工作人員 gung jok yan yoon
crib *n.* 幼兒床 yow yee chorng
cricket *n* 板球 ban kow
crime *n* 罪 juy
crimp *n* 起皺 hay jow
crimple *v.t.* 蜷曲 goon kuk
criminal *n* 罪犯 juy fan
criminal *a* 犯法嘅 fan fat geh
crimson *n* 深紅色 sam hung sik
cringe *v. i.* 畏縮 way suk
cripple *n* 跛 bay
crisis *n* 危機 ngay gey
crisp *a* 脆 chuy
criterion *n* 標準 biew jun
critic *n* 批評家 pay ping ga
critical *a* 唔穩定 hm wan ding
criticism *n* 批評 pay ping
criticize *v. t* 批評 pay ping
croak *n.* 青蛙聲 ting wa seng
crockery *n.* 陶器 tow hay
crocodile *n* 鱷魚 ok yu
croesus *n.* 大富豪 dai fu yung
crook *a* 唔舒服 hm shu fuk
crop *n* 農作物 lung jok mat
cross *v. t* 過 gwor
cross *n* 十字架 sap jee ga
cross *a* 嬲 low
crossing *n.* 人行橫道 yan hang wang dow
crotchet *n.* 四分音符 say fan yam fu

crouch *v. i.* 跍低 mo day
crow *n* 烏鴉 wu ngar
crow *v. i* 得戚 dak tik
crowd *n* 一班人 yat ban yan
crown *n* 皇冠 wong gwun
crown *v. t* 加冕 ga meen
crucial *adj.* 決定性 koot ding sing
crude *a* 簡略 gan leurk
cruel *a* 殘忍 tan yan
cruelty *n* 殘暴行為 tan bo hang way
cruise *v.i.* 搭船遊覽 dap shoon yow larm
cruiser *n* 巡洋艦 chun yeurng larm
crumb *n* 碎 suy
crumble *v. t* 碎 suy
crump *adj.* 脆 chuy
crusade *n* 鬥爭 dow jang
crush *v. t* 壓 at
crust *n.* 麵包皮 meen bao pay
crutch *n* 腋杖 yik jeurng
cry *n* 叫聲 giew seng
cry *v. i* 喊 harm
cryptography *n.* 密碼學 mat ma hok
crystal *n* 水晶 suy jing
cub *n* 幼獸 yow sow
cube *n* 立方形 lap forng ying
cubical *a* 立方體 lap forng tay
cubiform *adj.* 立方形 lap forng ying
cuckold *n.* 戴綠帽嘅人 dai luk mo geh yan
cuckoo *n* 杜鵑鳥 dow goon liew
cucumber *n* 青瓜 teng gwa
cudgel *n* 棍棒 gwun pang
cue *n* 提示 tay see
cuff *n* 袖口 jow ho
cuff *v. t* 拍 pak
cuisine *n.* 風味 fung may
cullet *n.* 碎玻璃 suy bo lay

culminate *v.i.* 告終 go jung
culpable *a* 難辭其咎 lan tee kay gow
culprit *n* 罪犯 juy fan
cult *n* 時尚 see sseurng
cultivate *v. t* 耕 gang
cultrate *adj.* 尖銳 jeem yu
cultural *a* 文化嘅 man far geh
culture *n* 文化 man far
culvert *n.* 排水管 pai suy gwun
cunning *a* 狡猾嘅 gao wat geh
cunning *n* 狡猾 gao wat
cup *n.* 杯 bwuy
cupboard *n* 櫃 gway
Cupid *n* 邱比特 yow bay dak
cupidity *n* 貪心 tam sam
curable *a* 可以醫嘅 hor yi yee geh
curative *a* 有療效嘅 yow liew hao geh
curb *n* 控制 hung jay
curb *v. t* 控制 hung jay
curcuma *n.* 鬱金香 wat gam heurng
curd *n* 凝乳 ying yu
cure *n* 藥 yeurk
cure *v. t.* 醫好 yee ho
curfew *n* 宵禁令 siew gam ling
curiosity *n* 好奇心 ho kay sam
curious *a* 好奇 ho kay
curl *n.* 捲 goon
currant *n.* 提子乾 tay jee gon
currency *n* 貨幣 for bay
current *n* 水流 suy low
current *a* 流行嘅 low hang geh
curriculum *n* 課程 for ting
curse *n* 咒 jow
curse *v. t* 詛咒 juy jow
cursory *a* 倉促 chorng choot
curt *a* 簡短而無禮 gan doon yee mo lay
curtail *v. t* 限制 han jay

curtain *n* 窗簾 cheurng leem
curve *n* 曲線 kuk seen
curve *v. t* 彎 wan
cushion *n* 墊 jeen
cushion *v. t* 緩和撞擊 wun wor jorng gik
custard *n* 奶油凍 lai yow dung
custodian *n* 監護人 garm wu yan
custody *v* 監護權 garm wu koon
custom *n.* 習俗 jap juk
customary *a* 習俗 jap juk
customer *n* 客 hak
cut *v. t* 剪 jeen
cut *n* 傷口 seurng ho
cutis *n.* 皮膚 pay fu
cuvette *n.* 細玻璃管 say bo lay gwun
cycle *n* 循環 chun wan
cyclic *a* 循環嘅 chun wan geh
cyclist *n* 單車手 dan cher sow
cyclone *n.* 旋風 shoon fung
cyclostyle *n* 復印機 fuk yan gey
cyclostyle *v. t* 複印 fuk yan
cylinder *n* 圓柱型 yoon chu ying
cynic *n* 憤世嫉俗者 fan say jat juk jeh
cypress *n* 柏樹 pak shu

dabble *v. i.* 玩 wan
dacoit *n.* 賊 tak
dacoity *n.* 搶劫 cheurng geep
dad, daddy *n* 爹地 deh dee
daffodil *n.* 黃水仙 wong suy seen
daft *adj.* 蠢 chun
dagger *n.* 匕首 bay sow
daily *a* 每日嘅 mwuy yat geh
daily *adv.* 每日 mwuy yat
daily *n.* 日報 yat bo

dainty *a.* 嬌小 giew siew
dainty *n.* 美食 may sik
dairy *n* 奶類 lai luy
dais *n.* 台 toy
daisy *n* 雛菊 chor guk
dale *n* 山谷 san guk
dam *n* 水壩 suy ba
damage *n.* 損壞 shoon wai
damage *v. t.* 破壞 por wai
dame *n.* 女爵士 luy jeurk see
damn *v. t.* 抵死 day say
damnation *n.* 天譴 teen heen
damp *a* 濕 sap
damp *n* 潮濕 tiew sap
damp *v. t.* 整濕 jing sap
damsel *n.* 少女 siew luy
dance *n* 舞 mo
dance *v. t.* 跳舞 tiew mo
dandelion *n.* 蒲公英 po gung ying
dandle *v.t.* 搖BB yiew bee bee
dandruff *n* 頭皮 tow pay
dandy *n* 花花公子 fa fa gung jee
danger *n.* 危險 ngay heem
dangerous *a* 危險 ngay heem
dangle *v. t* 吊 diew
dank *adj.* 陰濕 yam sap
dap *v.i.* 跳 tiew
dare *v. i.* 夠膽 gow dam
daring *n.* 大膽 dai dam
daring *a* 勇敢嘅 yung gam geh
dark *a* 黑 hak
dark *n* 黑暗 hak am
darkle *v.i.* 漸暗 jeem am
darling *n* 寶貝 bo bwuy
darling *a* 可愛嘅 hor ngoy geh
dart *n.* 飛鏢 fay biew
dash *v. i.* 閃 seem
dash *n* 快閃 fai seem
date *n* 日期 yat kay
date *v. t* 拍拖 pak tor
daub *n.* 塗料 tow liew
daub *v. t.* 搽 ta

daughter *n* 女 luy
daunt *v. t* 嚇 hak
dauntless *a* 勇敢嘅 yung gam geh
dawdle *v.i.* 慢吞吞 man tun tun
dawn *n* 黎明 lay ming
dawn *v. i.* 變清楚 been ting chor
day *n* 日頭 yat tow
daze *n* 迷茫 may morng
daze *v. t* 凝視 ying see
dazzle *n* 迷惑 may wak
dazzle *v. t.* 迷惑 may wak
deacon *n.* 執事 jap see
dead *a* 死 say
deadlock *n* 僵局 geurng guk
deadly *a* 致命 jee ming
deaf *a* 聾 lung
deal *n* 交易 gao yik
deal *v. i* 發牌 fat pai
dealer *n* 貿易商 mo yik seurng
dealing *n.* 處理 chu lay
dean *n.* 主任 ju yam
dear *a* 親愛 tan ngoi
dearth *n* 缺乏 koot fat
death *n* 死亡 say morng
debar *v. t.* 禁止 gam jee
debase *v. t.* 降價 gorng ga
debate *n.* 爭論 jang lun
debate *v. t.* 討論 tow lun
debauch *v. t.* 令人墮落 ling yan dor lok
debauch *n* 放蕩 forng dong
debauchee *n* 浪蕩者 lorng dong jeh
debauchery *n* 放蕩 forng dong
debility *n* 虛弱 huy yeurk
debit *n* 借記 jeh gey
debit *v. t* 記入賬戶 gey yap jeurng wu
debris *n* 殘骸 tan hai
debt *n* 債 jai
debtor *n* 債務人 jai mo yan

decade *n* 十年 sap leen
decadent *a* 墮落 dorlok
decamp *v. i* 逃走 tow jow
decay *n.* 腐爛 fu lan
decay *v. i* 腐爛 fu lan
decease *n* 死亡 say morng
decease *v. i* 死 say
deceit *n* 呃人 ak yan
deceive *v. t* 呃 ak
december *n* 十二月 sap yee yoot
decency *n* 禮儀 lay yee
decennary *n.* 十年 sap leep
decent *a* 似樣 tee yeurng
deception *n* 騙局 peen guk
decide *v. t* 決定 koot ding
decillion *n.* 千嘅十一乘方 teen geh sap yat sing forng
decimal *a* 十進位 sap jun way
decimate *v.t.* 毀滅 way meet
decision *n* 決定 koot ding
decisive *a* 關鍵嘅 gwan geen geh
deck *n* 甲板 gap ban
deck *v. t* 佈置 bo jee
declaration *n* 聲明 sing ming
declare *v. t.* 宣佈 shoon bo
decline *n* 下降 ha gong
decline *v. t.* 拒絕 kuy joot
declivous *adj.* 傾斜嘅 king ter geh
decompose *v. t.* 分解 fan gai
decomposition *n.* 分解 fan gai
decontrol *v.t.* 撤銷 teet siew
decorate *v. t* 裝修 jorng sow
decoration *n* 裝飾 jorng sik
decorum *n* 得體 dak tay
decrease *v. t* 減少 garm siew
decrease *n* 降低 gorng day
decree *n* 裁決 choy koot
decree *v. i* 裁定 choy ding
decrement *n.* 降低 gorng day
dedicate *v. t.* 奉獻 fung heen
dedication *n* 奉獻 fung heen

deduct v.t. 扣除 kow chuy
deed n 行爲 hang way
deem v.i. 認爲 ying way
deep a. 深 sam
deer n 鹿 luk
defamation n 誹謗 fay borng
defame v. t. 中傷 jung seurng
default n. 違約 way yeurk
defeat n 失敗 sat bai
defeat v. t. 擊敗 gik bai
defect n 缺點 koot deem
defence n 防禦 fong yu
defend v. t 防守 fong so
defendant n 被告 bay go
defensive adv. 自衛嘅 jee way geh
deference n 尊重 joon jung
defiance n 違抗 way korng
deficit n 赤字 tek jee
deficient adj. 有缺陷嘅 yow koot ham geh
defile n. 山路 san lo
define v. t 解釋 gai sik
definite a 肯定嘅 hang ding geh
definition n 解釋 gai sik
deflation n. 通貨緊縮 tung for gan suk
deflect v.t. & i. 轉移 joon yee
deft adj. 靈巧 ling hao
degrade v. t 降低身分 gorng day san fan
degree n 學位 hok way
dehort v.i. 勸阻 hoon jor
deist n. 自然神論者 jee yeen san lun jeh
deity n. 神 san
deject v. t 灰心 fwuy sam
dejection n 沮喪 juy sorng
delay v.t. & i. 延遲 yeen tee
delibate v.t. 試 see
deligate1 n 代表 doy biew
delegate v. t 委託 way tok

delegation n 代表團 doy biew toon
delete v. t 刪除 san chuy
deliberate v. i 仔細考慮 jee say hao luy
deliberate a 特登 dak dang
deliberation n 深思熟慮 sam see suk luy
delicate a 脆弱 chuy yeurk
delicious a 美味 mey mey
delight n 高興 go hing
delight v. t. 高興 go hing
deliver v. t 送 sung
delivery n 速遞 chuk day
delta n 三角洲 sam gok jow
delude n.t. 呃 at
delusion n. 錯覺 chor gok
demand n 需求 suy kow
demand v. t 強烈要求 keurng leet yiew kow
demarcation n. 界線 gai seen
dement v.t 發顛 fat deen
demerit n 過失 gwor sat
democracy n 民主 man ju
democratic a 民主 man ju
demolish v. t. 拆除 tak chuy
demon n. 魔鬼 mor gway
demonetize v.t. 停止通用 ting jee tung yung
demonstrate v. t 示範 see fan
demonstration n. 示範 see fan
demoralize v. t. 意志消沉 yee jee siew tam
demur n 猶豫 yow yee
demur v. t 反對 farn duy
demurrage n. 滯留費 jay low fay
den n 竇 dow
dengue n. 登革熱 dang gak yeet
denial n 否認 fow ying
denote v. i 象徵 jeurng jing
denounce v. t 指責 jee jak
dense a 濃密 lung mat

density *n* 密度 mat dow
dentist *n* 牙醫 ngar yee
denude *v.t.* 剝光 mok gwong
denunciation *n.* 指責 jee jak
deny *v. t.* 否認 fow ying
depart *v. i.* 離開 lay hoy
department *n* 部門 bo mun
departure *n* 離開 lay hoy
depauperate *v.t.* 變窮 been kung
depend *v. i.* 依賴 yee lai
dependant *n* 受養人 sow yeurng yan
dependence *n* 依賴 yee lai
dependent *a* 依靠嘅 yee kao geh
depict *v. t.* 描繪 miew kwuy
deplorable *a* 可悲 hor bay
deploy *v.t.* 部署 bo chu
deponent *n.* 證人 jing yan
deport *v.t.* 離境 lay ging
depose *v. t* 罷免 ba meen
deposit *n.* 按金 on gam
deposit *v. t* 放低 forng day
depot *n* 貨倉 for chorng
depreciate *v.t.i.* 跌價 deet ga
depredate *v.t.* 貶價 been ga
depress *v. t* 憂鬱 yow wat
depression *n* 抑鬱症 yik wat jing
deprive *v. t* 剝奪 mok doot
depth *n* 深度 sam dow
deputation *n* 代表團 doy biew toon
depute *v. t* 授權 sow koon
deputy *n* 副手 fu sow
derail *v. t.* 出軌 chut gway
derive *v. t.* 得到 dak dow
descend *v. i.* 降落 gorng lok
descendant *n* 後代 how doy
descent *n.* 降落 gorng lok
describe *v. t* 形容 ying yung
description *n* 描述 miew sut
descriptive *a* 描述 miew sut
desert *v. t.* 拋棄 pao hay

desert *n* 沙漠 sa mok
deserve *v. t.* 應得 ying dak
design *v. t.* 設計 teet gey
design *n.* 設計 teet gey
desirable *a* 值得做嘅 jik dak jow geh
desire *n* 渴望 hot morng
desire *v.t* 渴望 hot morng
desirous *a* 希望 hay morng
desk *n* 書枱 shu toy
despair *n* 絕望 joot morng
despair *v. i* 絕望 joot morng
desperate *a* 急 gap
despicable *a* 卑鄙 bay pay
despise *v. t* 憎 jang
despot *n* 暴君 bo gwan
destination *n* 目的地 muk di dey
destiny *n* 命運 ming wan
destroy *v. t* 破壞 por wai
destruction *n* 毀滅 way meet
detach *v. t* 分開 fan hoy
detachment *n* 分遣隊 fan heen duy
detail *n* 細節 say jeet
detail *v. t* 詳述 cheurng sut
detain *v. t* 扣留 kow low
detect *v. t* 探測 □□tak
detective *a* 偵探嘅 jing tam geh
detective *n.* 偵探 jing tam
determination *n.* 決心 koot sam
determine *v. t* 決定 koot ding
dethrone *v. t* 罷免 ba meen
develop *v. t.* 研發 yeen fat
development *n.* 成長 sing jeurng
deviate *v. i* 偏離 peen lay
deviation *n* 偏離 peen lay
device *n* 儀器 yee hay
devil *n* 魔鬼 mor gway
devise *v. t* 發明 fat ming
devoid *a* 完全無 yoon choon mo
devote *v. t* 專心 joon sam
devotee *n* 愛好者 ngoy ho jeh

devotion *n* 熱心 yeet sam
devour *v. t* 狼哽 lorng kang
dew *n.* 露水 lo suy
diabetes *n* 糖尿病 tong liew beng
diagnose *v. t* 診斷 tan doon
diagnosis *n* 診斷 tan doon
diagram *n* 圖表 tow biew
dial *n.* 打 da
dialect *n* 方言 fong yeen
dialogue *n* 錶盤 biew pwun
diameter *n* 直徑 jik ging
diamond *n* 鑽石 joon sek
diarrhoea *n* 肚屙 tow or
diary *n* 日記 yat gey
dice *n.* 骰 sik
dice *v. i.* 切粒 teet lap
dictate *v. t* 口述 ho sut
dictation *n* 口述 ho sut
dictator *n* 獨裁者 duk choy jeh
diction *n* 用詞 yung tee
dictionary *n* 字典 jee deen
dictum *n* 格言 gak yeen
didactic *a* 教誨 gao fwuy
die *v. i* 死 sey
die *n* 壓模 at mo
diet *n* 日常飲食 yat seurng yam sik
differ *v. i* 有差異 yow tar yee
difference *n* 差異 tar yee
different *a* 唔同 hm tung
difficult *a* 難 larn
difficulty *n* 難度 larn dow
dig *n* 輕撞 hing jorng
dig *v.t.* 掘 gwat
digest *v. t.* 消化 siew far
digest *n.* 摘要 jak yiew
digestion *n* 消化 siew far
digit *n* 數位 so way
dignify *v.t* 有尊嚴 yow joon yem
dignity *n* 尊嚴 joon yeem
dilemma *n* 困境 kwan ging
diligence *n* 努力 low lik

diligent *a* 勤力 kan lik
dilute *v. t* 稀釋 hey sik
dilute *a* 稀釋 hey sik
dim *a* 暗 am
dim *v. t* 變暗 been am
dimension *n* 尺寸 tek choon
diminish *v. t* 減少 garn siew
din *n* 嘈雜聲 cho jap seng
dine *v. t.* 食飯 sik fan
dinner *n* 飯 fan
dip *n.* 調味醬 tiew may jeurng
dip *v. t* 點 deem
diploma *n* 文憑課程 man pang for ting
diplomacy *n* 外交 ngoy gao
diplomat *n* 外交官 ngoy gao gwun
diplomatic *a* 外交嘅 ngoy gao geh
dire *a* 嚴重 yeem jung
direct *a* 直接 jik jeep
direct *v. t* 指導 jee dow
direction *n* 方向 forng heurng
director *n.* 導演 dow yeen
directory *n* 電話簿 deen wah bo
dirt *n* 泥 lay
dirty *a* 污糟 wu jow
disability *n* 缺陷 koot ham
disable *v. t* 令到無效 ling dow mow hao
disabled *a* 殘廢 tan fay
disadvantage *n* 不利因素 bat lay yan so
disagree *v. i* 唔同意 hm tung yee
disagreeable *a.* 乞人憎 hat yan jang
disagreement *n.* 分歧 fan kay
disappear *v. i* 消失 siew sat
disappearance *n* 失蹤 sat jung
disappoint *v. t.* 失望 sat morng
disapproval *n* 反對 fan duy
disapprove *v. t* 反對 fan duy

disarm *v. t* 繳械 giew hai
disarmament *n.* 裁減軍備 choy garm gwan bay
disaster *n* 災難 jor lan
disastrous *a* 極差 gik ta
disc *n.* 磁碟 tee deep
discard *v. t* 掟 deng
discharge *v. t* 釋放 sik forng
discharge *n.* 獲准離開 wok jun lay hoy
disciple *n* 信徒 sun tow
discipline *n* 紀律 gey lut
disclose *v. t* 透露 tow low
discomfort *n* 唔舒服 hm shu fuk
disconnect *v. t* 切斷 teet toon
discontent *n* 不滿 bat mun
discontinue *v. t* 停止 ting jee
discord *n* 紛爭 fan jang
discount *n* 折頭 jeet tow
discourage *v. t.* 阻止 jor jee
discourse *n* 論文 lun man
discourteous *a* 失禮 sat lay
discover *v. t* 發現 fat yeen
discovery *n.* 發現 fat yeen
discretion *n* 謹慎 gan san
discriminate *v. t.* 歧視 kay see
discrimination *n* 歧視 kay see
discuss *v. t.* 討論 tow lun
disdain *n* 鄙視 pay see
disdain *v. t.* 藐視 miew see
disease *n* 病 beng
disguise *n* 偽裝 ngay jorng
disguise *v. t* 假扮 gar ban
dish *n* 碟 deep
dishearten *v. t* 沮喪 juy sorng
dishonest *a* 唔誠實 hm sing sat
dishonesty *n.* 唔誠實 hm sing sat
dishonour *v. t* 違背 way bwuy
dishonour *n* 恥辱 tee yuk
dislike *v. t* 唔鐘意 hm jung yee
dislike *n* 反感 fan gam
disloyal *a* 唔忠心 hm jung sam

dismiss *v. t.* 解散 gai san
dismissal *n* 解雇 gai gu
disobey *v. t* 違抗 way korng
disorder *n* 失調 sat tiew
disparity *n* 差異 ta yee
dispensary *n* 藥房 yeurk forng
disperse *v. t* 分散 fan san
displace *v. t* 取代 chuy doy
display *v. t* 展示 jeen see
display *n* 展覽 jeen lan
displease *v. t* 得罪 dak juy
displeasure *n* 不滿 bat mun
disposal *n* 處理 chu lay
dispose *v. t* 揼 dum
disprove *v. t* 反駁 fan bok
dispute *n* 爭論 jang lun
dispute *v. i* 質疑 jat yee
disqualification *n* 取消資格 chut siew jee gak
disqualify *v. t.* 取消資格 chut siew jee gak
disquiet *n* 不安 bat on
disregard *n* 忽視 fat see
disregard *v. t* 唔理 hm lay
disrepute *n* 喪失名譽 sorng sat ming yu
disrespect *n* 唔尊敬 hm joon ging
disrupt *v. t* 打斷 da toon
dissatisfaction *n* 不滿 bat mun
dissatisfy *v. t.* 唔滿意 hm mun yee
dissect *v. t* 解剖 gai fow
dissection *n* 解剖 gai fow
dissimilar *a* 不同嘅 bat tung geh
dissolve *v.t* 溶解 yung gai
dissuade *v. t* 勸 hoon
distance *n* 距離 kuy lay
distant *a* 遠嘅 yoon geh
distil *v. t* 蒸餾 jing low
distillery *n* 釀酒廠 yeurng jow chorng

distinct *a* 明顯 ming heen
distinction *n* 差別 ta beet
distinguish *v. i* 分別 fan beet
distort *v. t* 扭曲 low kuk
distress *n* 憂慮 yow luy
distress *v. t* 憂慮 yow luy
distribute *v. t* 分配 fan pwuy
distribution *n* 分佈 fan bo
district *n* 地區 day kuy
distrust *n* 唔信 hm sun
distrust *v. t.* 唔信 hm sun
disturb *v. t* 騷擾 so yiew
ditch *n* 渠 kuy
ditto *n.* 同上 tung seurng
dive *v. i* 潛水 teem suy
dive *n* 潛水 teem suy
diverse *a* 唔同嘅 hm tung geh
divert *v. t* 轉移 joon yee
divide *v. t* 分 fan
divine *a* 神聖嘅 san sing geh
divinity *n* 神學 san hok
division *n* 除法 chuy fat
divorce *n* 離婚 lay fan
divorce *v. t* 離婚 lay fan
divulge *v. t* 爆料 bao liew
do *v. t* 做 jo
docile *a* 溫順 wan sun
dock *n.* 碼頭 ma tow
doctor *n* 醫生 yee sang
doctorate *n* 博士學位 bok see hok way
doctrine *n* 政策 jing tak
document *n* 文件 man geen
dodge *n* 詭計 gway gey
dodge *v. t* 避 bay
doe *n* 雌鹿 tee luk
dog *n* 狗 gow
dog *v. t* 折磨 jeet mor
dogma *n* 教條 gao tiew
dogmatic *a* 自以爲是 jee yee way see
doll *n* 公仔 gung jay

dollar *n* 蚊 man
domain *n* 領域 ling wik
dome *n* 圓頂屋 yoon deng uk
domestic *a* 家庭嘅 gar ting geh
domestic *n* 工人 gung yan
domicile *n* 住所 ju sor
dominant *a* 顯著嘅 heen ju geh
dominate *v. t* 控制 hung jay
domination *n* 控制 hung jay
dominion *n* 統治權 tung jee koon
donate *v. t* 捐 goon
donation *n.* 捐款 goon fwun
donkey *n* 驢 low
donor *n* 捐贈者 goon jang jeh
doom *n* 厄運 ak wan
doom *v. t.* 注定失敗 ju ding sat bai
door *n* 門 mun
dose *n* 一劑 yat jay
dot *n* 點 deem
dot *v. t* 加點 gar deem
double *a* 雙倍嘅 seurng pwuy geh
double *v. t.* 加倍 ga pwuy
double *n* 兩倍 leurng pwuy
doubt *v. i* 猶疑 yow yee
doubt *n* 疑問 yee man
dough *n* 麵團 meen toon
dove *n* 鴿 gap
down *adv* 向下 heurng har
down *prep* 下面 har meen
down *v. t* 飲 yam
downfall *n* 下滑 har wat
downpour *n* 大雨 dai yu
downright *adv* 徹底咁 teet day gam
downright *a* 完全 yoon choon
downward *a* 下降 har gorng
downward *adv* 向下 heurng har
downwards *adv* 向下 heurng har
dowry *n* 嫁妝 gar jorng
doze *n.* 瞓陣 fan jan

doze *v. i* 瞌眼瞓 hap ngan gan
dozen *n* 一打 yat da
draft *v. t* 草擬 cho yee
draft *n* 草稿 cho go
draftsman *n* 起草者 hay cho jeh
drag *n* 絆腳石 bwun geurt sek
drag *v. t* 拉 lai
dragon *n* 龍 lung
drain *n* 排水管 pai suy gwun
drain *v. t* 流 low
drainage *n* 排水 pai suy
dram *n* 少量嘅酒 siew leurng geh jow
drama *n* 戲劇 hay kek
dramatic *a* 戲劇化 hay kek fa
dramatist *n* 編劇 peen kek
draper *n* 布商 bo seurng
drastic *a* 極端 gik doon
draught *n* 通風 tung fung
draw *v.t* 畫 wak
draw *n* 打和 da wor
drawback *n* 缺點 koot deem
drawer *n* 櫃桶 gway tung
drawing *n* 畫 wah
drawing-room *n* 客廳 hak teng
dread *n* 恐懼 hung guy
dread *v.t* 擔心 dam sam
dread *a* 驚 geng
dream *n* 夢 mung
dream *v. i.* 夢 mung
drench *v. t* 濕晒 sap sai
dress *n* 裙 kwan
dress *v. t* 着 jeurk
dressing *n* 調料 tiew liew
drill *n* 鑽 joon
drill *v. t.* 鑽 joon
drink *n* 飲品 yam ban
drink *v. t* 飲 yam
drip *n* 滴 dik
drip *v. i* 滴 dik
drive *v. t* 楂車 ja cher
drive *n* 路程 lo ting

driver *n* 司機 see gey
drizzle *n* 細雨 sai yu
drizzle *v. i* 落細雨 lok sai yu
drop *n* 滴 dik
drop *v. i* 跌 deet
drought *n* 乾旱 gorn hon
drown *v.i* 沈 tam
drug *n* 毒品 duk ban
druggist *n* 藥劑師 yeurk jay see
drum *n* 鼓 gu
drum *v.i.* 打鼓 da gu
drunkard *n* 醉酒佬 juy jow low
dry *a* 乾 gon
dry *v. i.* 整乾 jing gon
dual *a* 雙 seurng
duck *n.* 鴨 ap
duck *v.i.* 踎低 mo day
due *a* 因爲 yan way
due *n* 應得嘅嘢 ying dak geh yeh
due *adv* 正向 jing heurng
duel *n* 決鬥 koot dow
duel *v. i* 決鬥 joot dow
duke *n* 公爵 gung jeurk
dull *a* 無聊 mo liew
dull *v. t.* 變麻木 been mar muk
duly *adv* 適當嘅 sik dorng geh
dumb *a* 蠢 chun
dunce *n* 遲鈍嘅人 tee dun gen yan
dung *n* 動物糞 dung mat fan
duplicate *a* 複製嘅 fuk jay ghe
duplicate *n* 副本 fu bwun
duplicate *v. t* 複製 fuk jay
duplicity *n* 奸詐行爲 gan ja hang way
durable *a* 耐用 loy yung
duration *n* 期間 kay gan
during *prep* 喺 hay
dusk *n* 黃昏 wong fan
dust *n* 塵 tan
dust *v.t.* 抹 mat
duster *n* 撢 tan
dutiful *a* 盡職嘅 jun jik geh

duty *n* 責任 jak yam
dwarf *n* 矮人 ai yan
dwell *v. i* 住 ju
dwelling *n* 住所 ju sor
dwindle *v. t* 減少 garm siew
dye *v. t* 染 yeem
dye *n* 染料 yeem liew
dynamic *a* 有活力嘅 yow wut lik geh
dynamics *n.* 動態 dung tai
dynamite *n* 炸藥 ja yeurk
dynamo *n* 發電機 fat deen gey
dynasty *n* 朝代 tiew doy
dysentery *n* 痢疾 lay jat

E

each *a* 每個 mwuy gor
each *pron.* 各自 gok jee
eager *a* 心急 sam gap
eagle *n* 鷹 ying
ear *n* 耳 yee
early *adv* 早 jow
early *a* 早 jow
earn *v. t* 賺 jan
earnest *a* 認真 ying tan
earth *n* 地球 dey kow
earthen *a* 土製嘅 tow jay geh
earthly *a* 人間嘅 yan gan geh
earthquake *n* 地震 dey jan
ease *n* 輕易 hing yee
ease *v. t* 舒緩 shu wun
east *n* 東 dung
east *adv* 向東 heurng dung
east *a* 東方嘅 dung forng geh
easter *n* 復活節 fuk wut jeet
eastern *a* 東方 dung fong
easy *a* 容易 yung yee
eat *v. t* 食 sik
eatable *n.* 食用 sik yung

eatable *a* 可以食嘅 hor yi sik geh
ebb *n* 退潮 tuy tiew
ebb *v. i* 衰弱 suy yeurk
ebony *n* 烏木 wu muk
echo *n* 回音 wuy yam
echo *v. t* 回音 wuy yam
eclipse *n* 日蝕 yat sik
economic *a* 經濟嘅 ging jay geh
economical *a* 經濟嘅 ging jay geh
economics *n.* 經濟學 ging jay hok
economy *n* 經濟 ging jay
edge *n* 邊 been
edible *a* 可以食嘅 hor yi sik geh
edifice *n* 大廈 dai har
edit *v. t* 修葺 so top
edition *n* 版 ban
editor *n* 編輯 peen top
editorial *a* 編輯嘅 peen top geh
editorial *n* 評論 ping lun
educate *v. t* 教 gao
education *n* 教育 gao yuk
efface *v. t* 消除 siew chuy
effect *n* 效果 hao gwor
effect *v. t* 引起 yan hey
effective *a* 有效 yow hao
effeminate *a* 好乸 ho la
efficacy *n* 功效 gung hao
efficiency *n* 效率 hao lut
efficient *a* 效率高 hao lut go
effigy *n* 雕像 diew jeurng
effort *n* 努力 lo lik
egg *n* 雞蛋 gey dan
ego *n* 自我 jee ngor
egotism *n* 自負 jee fu
eight *n* 八 bat
eighteen *a* 十八 sap bat
eighty *n* 八十 bat sap
either *a.,* 其中一個 kay jung yat gor
either *adv* 或者 wak jeh

eject *v. t.* 噴出 pan chut

elaborate *v. t* 詳細描述 cheurng say miew sut

elaborate *a* 詳細嘅 cheurng say geh

elapse *v. t* 消逝 siew say

elastic *a* 有彈性 yow dan xing

elbow *n* 手踭 so jang

elder *a* 年長 leen jeurng

elder *n* 長者 jeurng jeh

elderly *a* 老人 lo yan

elect *v. t* 選 shoon

election *n* 選舉 shoon kuy

electorate *n* 全體選民 choon tay shoon man

electric *a* 電 deen

electricity *n* 電 deen

electrify *v. t* 興奮 hing fan

elegance *n* 優雅 yow ngar

elegant *adj* 優雅 yow ngar

elegy *n* 輓詩 wan see

element *n* 要素 yiew so

elementary *a* 基本嘅… gey bun geh

elephant *n* 大笨象 dai ban jeurng

elevate *v. t* 提高 tay go

elevation *n* 海拔 hoy bat

eleven *n* 十一 sap yat

elf *n* 精靈 jing ling

eligible *a* 有資格 yow jee gak

eliminate *v. t* 除去 chuy huy

elimination *n* 除去 chuy huy

elope *v. i* 私奔 see ban

eloquence *n* 口才 ho choy

eloquent *a* 流利 low lay

else *a* 唔同嘅 hm tung geh

else *adv* 其他 kay ta

elucidate *v. t* 講清楚 gorng ting chor

elude *v. t* 避開 bay hoy

elusion *n* 逃避 tow bay

elusive *a* 難以捉摸 larn yee juk

mor

emancipation *n.* 解放 gai forng

embalm *v. t* 防腐 forng fu

embankment *n* 堤 tay

embark *v. t* 開始 hoy tee

embarrass *v. t.* 尷尬 gam gai

embassy *n* 使館 see gwun

embitter *v. t* 沮喪 juy sorng

emblem *n* 象徵 jeurng jing

embodiment *n* 典型 deen ying

embody *v. t.* 代表 doy biew

embolden *v. t.* 變大膽 been dai darm

embrace *v. t.* 抱 po

embrace *n* 接受 jeep sow

embroidery *n* 刺繡 tee sow

embryo *n* 胚胎 bwuy toy

emerald *n* 綠寶石 luk bo sek

emerge *v. i* 出現 chut yeen

emergency *n* 緊急 gan gap

eminance *n* 顯赫 heen hak

eminent *a* 著名嘅 ju ming geh

emissary *n* 密使 mat see

emit *v. t* 散發出 san fat chut

emolument *n* 糧 leurng

emotion *n* 感情 gam ting

emotional *a* 感情豐富 gam ting fung fu

emperor *n* 皇帝 wong day

emphasis *n* 強調 keurng diew

emphasize *v. t* 強調 keurng diew

emphatic *a* 強調嘅 keurng diew geh

empire *n* 帝國 day gwok

employ *v. t* 請 teng

employee *n* 僱員 gu yoon

employer *n* 僱主 gu joo

employment *n* 工作 gung jok

empower *v. t* 授權 sow koon

empress *n* 皇后 wong ho

empty *a* 空 hung

empty *v* 倒 dow

emulate *v. t* 模仿 mo forng

enable *v. t* 激活 gik wut

enact *v. t* 通過 tung gwor

enamel *n* 琺瑯質 fat lonrg jat

enamour *v. t* 傾心 king sam

encase *v. t* 圍住 way ju

enchant *v. t* 着迷 jeurk may

encircle *v. t.* 圍繞 way yiew

enclose *v. t* 附 fu

enclosure *n.* 附件 fu geen

encompass *v. t* 包含 bao ham

encounter *n.* 遭遇 jo yu

encounter *v. t* 相遇 seurng yu

encourage *v. t* 鼓勵 gu lay

encroach *v. i* 侵佔 tam jeem

encumber *v. t.* 阻礙 jor ngoy

encyclopaedia *n.* 百科全書 bak for choon shu

end *v. t* 結束 geet chuk

end *n.* 完 yoon

endanger *v. t.* 危及 ngay kap

endear *v.t* 受歡迎 sow fwun ying

endearment *n.* 愛 ngoy

endeavour *n* 嘗試 seurng see

endeavour *v.i* 盡力 jun lik

endorse *v. t.* 宣傳 shoon choon

endow *v. t* 資助 jee jor

endurable *a* 耐用嘅 loy yung geh

endurance *n.* 耐力 loy lik

endure *v.t.* 忍 yan

enemy *n* 敵人 dik yan

energetic *a* 有活力嘅 yow wut lik geh

energy *n.* 力量 lik leurng

enfeeble *v. t.* 變虛弱 been huy yeurk

enforce *v. t.* 執行 jap hang

enfranchise *v.t.* 授權投票 sow koon tow piew

engage *v. t* 吸引 kap yan

engagement *n.* 訂婚 ding fan

engine *n* 引擎 yan king

engineer *n* 工程師 gung ting see

English *n* 英文 ying man

engrave *v. t* 刻 hak

engross *v.t* 全神貫注 choon san gwun ju

engulf *v.t* 吞沒 tun mwut

enigma *n* 謎 may

enjoy *v. t* 享受 heurng so

enjoyment *n* 愉快 yu fai

enlarge *v. t* 放大 forng dai

enlighten *v. t.* 啓發 kay fat

enlist *v. t* 入伍 yap hm

enliven *v. t.* 搞生 gao sang

enmity *n* 仇恨 sow han

ennoble *v. t.* 封爲貴族 fung way gway juk

enormous *a* 好大嘅 ho dai geh

enough *a* 夠 gow

enough *adv* 足夠 juk gow

enrage *v. t* 激 gik

enrapture *v. t* 着迷 jeurk may

enrich *v. t* 變豐富 been fung fu

enrol *v. t* 入學 yap hok

enshrine *v. t* 放入神龕 forng yap san am

enslave *v.t.* 奴役 lo yik

ensue *v.i* 因而產生 yan yee tan sang

ensure *v. t* 保證 bo jing

entangle *v. t* 捲入 goon yap

enter *v. t* 入 yap

enterprise *n* 企業 kay yeep

entertain *v. t* 娛樂 yu lok

entertainment *n.* 娛樂 yu lok

enthrone *v. t* 登位 dang way

enthusiasm *n* 熱心 yeet sam

enthusiastic *a* 熱情 yeet ting

entice *v. t.* 引誘 yan yow

entire *a* 全部 choon bo

entirely *adv* 完全 yoon choon

entitle *v. t.* 有權 yow koon

entity *n* 實體 sat tay

entomology *n.* 昆蟲學 kwan chung hok

entrails *n.* 內臟 loy jorng

entrance *n* 入口 yap ho

entrap *v. t.* 設陷阱 teet ham jing

entreat *v. t.* 求 kow

entreaty *n.* 懇求 han kow

entrust *v. t* 委託 way tok

entry *n* 入 yap

enumerate *v. t.* 列舉 leet guy

envelop *v. t* 包 bao

envelope *n* 信封 sun fung

enviable *a* 令人羨慕 ling yan seen mo

envious *a* 妒忌 dow gey

environment *n.* 環境 wan ging

envy *v* 羨慕 seen mo

envy *v. t* 妒忌 dow gey

epic *n* 史詩 si see

epidemic *n* 流行病 low hang beng

epigram *n* 詼諧短詩 fwuy hai doon see

epilepsy *n* 羊癇症 yeurng gan jing

epilogue *n* 後記 ho gey

episode *n* 集 jap

epitaph *n* 碑文 bay man

epoch *n* 時代 see doy

equal *a* 相同嘅 seurng tung geh

equal *v. t* 等於 dang yu

equal *n* 同等 tung dang

equality *n* 平等 ping dang

equalize *v. t.* 變平等 been ping dang

equate *v. t* 相等於 seurng dang yu

equation *n* 方程式 fong ting sik

equator *n* 赤道 tek dow

equilateral *a* 等邊嘅 dang been geh

equip *v. t* 裝備 jorng bay

equipment *n* 器材 hey choy

equitable *a* 公平嘅 gung ping geh

equivalent *a* 相等於 seurng dang yu

equivocal *a* 說話模糊 shoot wah mo wu

era *n* 時代 see doy

eradicate *v. t* 鏟除 tan chuy

erase *v. t* 刪除 san chuy

erect *v. t* 創立 chorng lap

erect *a* 直立嘅 jik lap geh

erection *n* 建立 geen lap

erode *v. t* 侵蝕 tam sik

erosion *n* 侵蝕 tam sik

erotic *a* 性愛嘅 sing ngoy geh

err *v. i* 犯錯 fan chor

errand *n* 差事 tai see

erroneous *a* 錯嘅 chor geh

error *n* 錯誤 chor ng

erupt *v. i* 爆發 bao fat

eruption *n* 爆發 bao fat

escape *n* 逃避 tow bay

escape *v. i* 逃走 tow jow

escort *n* 護送者 wu sung jeh

escort *v. t* 護送 wu sung

especial *a* 特別嘅 dak beet geh

essay *n.* 論文 lun man

essay *v. t.* 企圖 kay tow

essayist *n* 散文家 san man ga

essence *n* 精髓 jing suy

essential *a* 必需嘅 beet suy geh

establish *v. t.* 成立 sing lap

establishment *n* 成立 sing lap

estate *n* 住宅區 ju jak kuy

esteem *n* 尊敬 joon ging

esteem *v. t* 尊敬 joon ging

estimate *n.* 估計 gu gey

estimate *v. t* 估 gu

estimation *n* 判斷 pwun doon

etcetera *adv.* 等等 dang dang

eternal *a.* 永遠 wing yoon

eternity *n* 永恒 wing hang

ether *n* 醚 may

ethical *a* 道德 dow dak

ethics n. 道德標準 dow dak biew jun

etiquette n 禮節 lay jeet

etymology n. 詞源學 tee yoon hok

eunuch n 太監 tai garm

evacuate v. t 疏散 sor san

evacuation n 疏散 sor san

evade v. t 避開 bay hoy

evaluate v. t 評估 ping gu

evaporate v. i 蒸發 jing fat

evasion n 逃避 tow bay

even a 平嘅 ping geh

even v. t 擺平 bai ping

even adv 甚至連 sam jee leen

evening n 挨晚 ai man

event n 活動 wut dung

eventually adv. 最終 juy jung

ever adv 曾 tang

evergreen a 常綠嘅 seurng luk geh

evergreen n 常綠樹 seurng luk shu

everlasting a. 永恆嘅 wing hang geh

every a 每個 mwuy gor

evict v. t 逐出 juk chut

eviction n 逐出 juk chut

evidence n 證據 jing guy

evident a. 清楚 ting chor

evil n 邪惡 ter ok

evil a 惡毒嘅 ok duk geh

evoke v. t 引起 yan hay

evolution n 進化 jun far

evolve v.t 進化 jun far

ewe n 母羊 mo yeurng

exact a 準確嘅 jun kok geh

exaggerate v. t. 誇大 kwa dai

exaggeration n. 誇張 kwa jeurng

exalt v. t 高度讚揚 go dow jan yeurng

examination n. 考試 hao see

examine v. t 檢查 geem cha

examinee n 考生 hao sang

examiner n 考官 hao gwun

example n 例子 lay jee

excavate v. t. 挖掘 wat gwut

excavation n. 挖掘 wat gwut

exceed v.t 超越 tiew yoot

excel v.i 超過 tiew gwor

excellence n. 優秀 yow sow

excellency n 優點 yow deem

excellent a. 優秀嘅 yow sow geh

except v. t 唔包括 hm bao kwut

except prep 徐咗 chuy jor

exception n 例外 lay ngoy

excess n 多餘 doryu

excess a 多餘嘅 dor yu geh

exchange n 交換 gao wun

exchange v. t 交換 gao wun

excise n 消費稅 siew fay suy

excite v. t 興奮 hing fan

exclaim v.i 叫 giew

exclamation n 感歎詞 gam tan tee

exclude v. t 撇除 peet chuy

exclusive a 獨有嘅 duk yow geh

excommunicate v. t. 逐出教會 juk chut gao wuy

excursion n. 遠足 yoon juk

excuse v.t 原諒 yoon leurng

excuse n 藉口 jik ho

execute v. t 執行 jap hang

execution n 處決 choo koot

executioner n. 行刑者 hang ying jeh

exempt v. t. 免除 meen chuy

exempt a. 免除 meen chuy

exercise n. 運動 wan dung

exercise v. t 鍛鍊 doon leen

exhaust v. t. 筋疲力盡 gan pay lik jun

exhibit n. 展覽品 jeen lam ban

exhibit v. t 展出 jeen chut

exhibition *n.* 展覽 jeen lam

exile *n.* 流放 low forng

exile *v. t* 放逐 forng juk

exist *v.i* 存在 choon joy

existence *n* 存在 choon joy

exit *n.* 出口 chut ho

expand *v.t.* 擴大 kwong dai

expansion *n.* 擴張 kwong jeurng

ex-parte *a* 單方面嘅 dan forng meen geh

ex-parte *adv* 單方 dan forng

expect *v. t* 預計 yu gey

expectation *n.* 期望 key morng

expedient *a* 權宜之計 koon yee jee gey

expedite *v. t.* 加速 gar chuk

expedition *n* 遠征 yoon jing

expel *v. t.* 趕出 gorn chut

expend *v. t* 花費 fa fay

expenditure *n* 消費 siew fay

expense *n.* 開支 hoy jee

expensive *a* 貴 gwey

experience *n* 經驗 ging yeem

experience *v. t.* 經歷 ging lik

experiment *n* 實驗 sat yeem

expert *a* 經驗豐富 ging yeem fung fu

expert *n* 專家 joon ga

expire *v.i.* 過期 gwor kay

expiry *n* 到期 dow kay

explain *v. t.* 解釋 gai sik

explanation *n* 解釋 gai sik

explicit *a.* 清楚 ting chor

explode *v. t.* 爆炸 bao ja

exploit *n* 英勇行爲 ying yung hang way

exploit *v. t* 利用 lay yung

exploration *n* 勘察 ham tat

explore *v.t* 探索 tam sok

explosion *n.* 爆炸 bao ja

explosive *n.* 炸藥 ja yeurk

explosive *a* 爆炸性 bao ja sing

exponent *n* 擁護者 yung wu jeh

export *n* 出口 chut ho

export *v. t.* 出口 chut ho

expose *v. t* 暴露 bo lo

express *v. t.* 表達 biew dat

express *a* 快 fai

express *n* 特快列車 dak fai leet cher

expression *n.* 表情 biew ting

expressive *a.* 表示 biew see

expulsion *n.* 逐出 juk chut gao wuy

extend *v. t* 延長 yeen cheurng

extent *n.* 限度 han dow

external *a* 外面嘅 ngoy meen geh

extinct *a* 絕種嘅 joot jung geh

extinguish *v.t* 撲熄 pok sik

extol *v. t.* 讚 jan

extra *a* 額外嘅 ak ngoy geh

extra *adv* 額外 ak ngoy

extract *n* 提取物 tay chuy mat

extract *v. t* 提煉 tey leen

extraordinary *a.* 異常嘅 yee seurng geh

extravagance *n* 大使 dai say

extravagant *a* 大使嘅 dai say geh

extreme *a* 偏激 peen gik

extreme *n* 極端 gik doon

extremist *n* 極端分子 gik doon fan jee

exult *v. i* 興奮 hing fan

eye *n* 眼 ngan

eyeball *n* 眼球 ngan kow

eyelash *n* 眼睫毛 ngan jeet mo

eyelet *n* 眼孔 ngan hung

eyewash *n* 洗眼液 say ngan yik

F

fable n. 寓言 yu yeen
fabric n 布料 bo liew
fabricate v.t 虛構 huy kow
fabrication n 製作 jay jok
fabulous a 太好啦 tai ho la
facade n 正面 jing meen
face n 面 meen
face v.t 面對 meen duy
facet n 方面 forng meen
facial a 面部嘅 meen bo geh
facile a 輕率 hing sut
facilitate v.t 幫 borng
facility n 設施 teet see
facsimile n 傳真 choon jan
fact n 事實 see sat
faction n 派 pai
factious a 派別嘅 pai beet geh
factor n 因素 yan so
factory n 工廠 gung chorng
faculty n 科系 for hay
fad n 短暫嘅狂熱 doon jam geh kwong yeet
fade v.i 甩色 lut sik
faggot n 柴把 tai ba
fail v.i 失敗 sat bai
failure n 失敗 sat bai
faint a 微弱 may yeurk
faint v.i 暈 wan
fair a 公平 gung ping
fair n. 露天遊樂場 lo teen yow lok cheurng
fairly adv. 公平 gung ping
fairy n 小仙女 siew seen luy
faith n 信念 sun leem
faithful a 忠誠嘅 jung sing geh
falcon n 獵鷹 leep ying
fall v.i. 跌 deet
fall n 跌 deet
fallacy n 謬論 mo lun

fallow a 休閒 yow han
false a 假 gar
falter v.i 衰退 suy tuy
fame n 名氣 ming hay
familiar a 熟 suk
family n 屋企人 uk kay yan
famine n 飢荒 gey forng
famous a 出名 chut meng
fan n 風扇 fung seen
fanatic a 入迷 yap may
fanatic n 狂迷 kwong may
fancy n 幻想 wan seurng
fancy v.t 鐘意 jung yee
fantastic a 太好啦 tai ho la
far adv. 遠 yoon
far a 遠 yoon
far n 小麥 siew mak
farce n 鬧劇 lao kek
fare n 票價 piew ga
farewell n 告別 go beet
farewell interj. 送別 sung beet
farm n 農場 lung cheurng
farmer n 農夫 lung fu
fascinate v.t 吸引 kap yap
fascination n. 吸引力 kap yan lik
fashion n 時裝 see jorng
fashionable a 流行嘅 low hang geh
fast a 快 fai
fast adv 快 fai
fast n 齋戒期 jai gai kay
fast v.i 齋戒 jai gai
fasten v.t 扣 kow
fat a 肥 fei
fat n 脂肪 jee forng
fatal a 致命嘅 jee ming geh
fate n 緣份 yoon fan
father n 爹地 deh dee
fathom v.t 理解 lay gai
fathom n 英尋 ying tam
fatigue n 疲勞 pay lo

fatigue *v.t* 厭 yeem
fault *n* 過錯 gwor chor
faulty *a* 壞嘅 wai geh
fauna *n* 動物群 dung mat kwan
favour1 *n* 事 see
favour *v.t* 比較鐘意 bay gao jung yee
favourable *a* 有利 yow lay
favourite *a* 最鐘意嘅 juy jung yee geh
favourite *n* 最鐘意嘅人 juy jung yee geh yan
fear *n* 恐懼 hung guy
fear *v.i* 驚 geng
fearful *a.* 驚 geng
feasible *a* 行得通嘅 hang dak tung geh
feast *n* 宴會 yeen wuy
feast *v.i* 盡情享用 jung ting heurng yung
feat *n* 功績 gung jik
feather *n* 羽毛 yu mo
feature *n* 特點 dak deem
February *n* 二月 yee yoot
federal *a* 聯邦嘅 loon borng geh
federation *n* 聯邦 loon borng
fee *n* 票價 piew ga
feeble *a* 虛弱 huy yeurk
feed *v.t* 餵 way
feed *n* 一餐 yat tan
feel *v.t* 摸 mor
feeling *n* 感覺 gam gok
feign *v.t* 扮 ban
felicitate *v.t* 祝賀 juk hor
felicity *n* 幸福 hang fuk
fell *v.t* 跌 deet
fellow *n* 同事 tung see
female *a* 女性嘅 luy sing geh
female *n* 女性 luy xing
feminine *a* 女性嘅 luy sing geh
fence *n* 圍欄 way lan
fence *v.t* 圍住 way ju

fend *v.t* 抵擋 day dorng
ferment *n* 政治騷動 jing jee so dung
ferment *v.t* 發酵 fat hao
fermentation *n* 發酵 fat hao
ferocious *a* 惡 ok
ferry *n* 郵輪 yow lun
ferry *v.t* 用船運送 yung shoon wan sung
fertile *a* 肥沃 fay yuk
fertility *n* 生育力 sang yuk lik
fertilize *v.t* 受精 sow jing
fertilizer *n* 肥料 fay liew
fervent *a* 熱烈 yeet leet
fervour *n* 熱情 yeet ting
festival *n* 節日 jeet yat
festive *a* 喜慶嘅 hay hing geh
festivity *n* 慶祝活動 hing juk wut dung
festoon *n* 花彩 fa choy
fetch *v.t* 攞 lor
fetter *n* 束縛 chuk bok
fetter *v.t* 限制 han jay
feud *n.* 世仇 say sow
feudal *a* 封建 fung geen
fever *n* 發燒 fat siew
few *a* 幾個 gey gor
fiasco *n* 慘敗 tarm bai
fibre *n* 纖維 teem way
fickle *a* 易變 yee been
fiction *n* 小說 siew shoot
fictitious *a* 虛構嘅 huy kow geh
fiddle *n* 騙局 peen guk
fiddle *v.i* 亂搞 loon gao
fidelity *n* 忠實 jung sat
fie *interj* 唓 ter
field *n* 田 teen
fiend *n* 惡魔 ok mor
fierce *a* 惡 ok
fiery *a* 暴躁 bo cho
fifteen *n* 十五 sap ng
fifty *n.* 五十 ng sap

fig *n* 無花果 mo fa gwor
fight *n* 打交 da gao
fight *v.t* 打 da
figment *n* 虛構 huy gou
figurative *a* 比如嘅 bay yu geh
figure *n* 身形 san ying
figure *v.t* 認爲 ying way
file *n* 文件 man gene
file *v.t* 提交 tay gao
file *n* 指甲銼 jee gap chor
file *v.t* 銼 chor
file *n* 一行人 yat horng yan
file *v.i.* 排成一行 pai sing yat horng
fill *v.t* 裝滿 jorng mun
film *n* 電影 deen ying
film *v.t* 錄影 luk ying
filter *n* 過濾器 gwor luy hay
filter *v.t* 過濾 gwor luy
filth *n* 污物 wu mat
filthy *a* 污糟 wu jo
fin *n* 鰭 kay
final *a* 最後 juy ho
finance *n* 財政 choy jing
finance *v.t* 提供資金 tay gung jee gam
financial *a* 財政嘅 choy jing geh
financier *n* 金融家 gam yung ga
find *v.t* 搵 wan
fine *n* 罰款 fat fwun
fine *v.t* 罰款 fat fwun
fine *a* 高質量 go jat leurng
finger *n* 手指 so jee
finger *v.t* 用手指摸 yung so jee mor
finish *v.t* 完成 yoon sing
finish *n* 結局 geet guk
finite *a* 有限嘅 yow han geh
fir *n* 冷杉 lang tam
fire *n* 火 for
fire *v.t* 發射 fat seh
firm *a* 結實 geet sat
firm *n.* 公司 gung see

first *a* 第一個 day yat gor
first *n* 第一個 day yat gor
first *adv* 首先 sow seen
fiscal *a* 財政嘅 choy jing geh
fish *n* 魚 yu
fish *v.i* 釣魚 diew yu
fisherman *n* 漁人 yu yan
fissure *n* 裂痕 leet han
fist *n* 拳頭 koon tow
fistula *n* 瘻管 low gwun
fit *v.t* 啱身 am san
fit *a* 健康 geen horng
fit *n* 發作 fat jok
fitful *a* 斷斷續續 toon toon juk juk
fitter *n* 安裝師傅 on jorng see fu
five *n* 五 ng
fix *v.t* 整好 jing ho
fix *n* 困境 kwun ging
flabby *a* 鬆弛 sung tee
flag *n* 旗 kay
flagrant *a* 明目張膽 ming muk jeurng darm
flame *n* 火焰 for yeem
flame *v.i* 燃燒 yeen siew
flannel *n* 法蘭絨 fat lan yung
flare *v.i* 燒 siew
flare *n* 火光 for gwong
flash *n* 閃光 seem gwong
flash *v.t* 閃 seem
flask *n* 燒瓶 siew ping
flat *a* 平嘅 ping geh
flat *n* 平嘅 ping geh
flatter *v.t* 討好 tow ho
flattery *n* 奉承 fung sing
flavour *n* 味道 mey dow
flaw *n* 瑕疵 har chee
flea *n.* 蚤 sat
flee *v.i* 閃人 seem yam
fleece *n* 羊毛 yeurng mo
fleece *v.t* 敲詐 hao ja
fleet *n* 艦隊 larm duy
flesh *n* 肉 yuk

flexible *a* 柔軟 yow yoon
flicker *n* 閃 seem
flicker *v.t* 閃閃下 seem ha
flight *n* 班機 ban gey
flimsy *a* 質地差 jat day ta
fling *v.t* 掟 deng
flippancy *n* 輕率 hing sut
flirt *n* 調情 tiew ting
flirt *v.i* 放電 forng deen
float *v.i* 漂 piew
flock *n* 群 kwan
flock *v.i* 擁埋 yung mai
flog *v.t* 賣 mai
flood *n* 水浸 suy jam
flood *v.t* 浸 jam
floor *n* 地下 dey ha
floor *v.t* 鋪地板 po day ban
flora *n* 植物群 jik mat kwan
florist *n* 花商 far seurng
flour *n* 麵粉 meen fan
flourish *v.i* 興旺 hing worng
flow *n* 流動 low dung
flow *v.i* 流 low
flower *n* 花 far
flowery *a* 花嘅 far geh
fluent *a* 流利 low lay
fluid *a* 流暢 low cheurng
fluid *n* 液體 yik tay
flush *v.i* 沖洗 chung say
flush *n* 面紅 meen hung
flute *n* 長笛 cheurng dek
flute *v.i* 吹笛 chuy dek
flutter *n* 飄動 piew dung
flutter *v.t* 飛 fay
fly *n* 烏蠅 wu ying
fly *v.i* 飛 fay
foam *n* 泡沫 po mut
foam *v.t* 起泡 hay po
focal *a* 重要嘅 jung yew geh
focus *n* 焦點 jiew deem
focus *v.t* 專注 joon ju
fodder *n* 飼料 jee liew

foe *n* 敵人 dik yan
fog *n* 霧 mo
foil *v.t* 制止 jay jee
fold *n* 摺 jeep
fold *v.t* 摺 jeep
foliage *n* 葉 yeep
follow *v.t* 跟住 gan ju
follower *n* 追隨者 juy chuy jeh
folly *n* 蠢 chun
foment *v.t* 挑起 tiew hay
fond *a* 鐘意 jung yee
fondle *v.t* 撫摸 fu mor
food *n* 食物 sik mat
fool *n* 蠢材 chun choy
foolish *a* 蠢嘅 chun geh
foolscap *n* 大頁紙 dai yeep jee
foot *n* 腳 geurt
for *prep* 畀 bay
for *conj.* 因為 yan way
forbid *v.t* 禁止 gam jee
force *n* 暴力 bo lik
force *v.t* 強迫 keurng bik
forceful *a* 堅強嘅 geen keurng geh
forcible *a* 強行嘅 keurng hang geh
forearm *n* 前臂 teen bay
forearm *v.t* 有備無患 yow bay mo wan
forecast *n* 預告 yu go
forecast *v.t* 預測 yu tak
forefather *n* 祖先 jo seen
forefinger *n* 食指 sik jee
forehead *n* 額頭 ak tow
foreign *a* 外國嘅 ngoy gwok geh
foreigner *n* 外國人 ngoy gwok yan
foreknowledge *n.* 預知 yu jee
foreleg *n* 前腳 teen geurt
forelock *n* 額髮 ak fat
foreman *n* 工頭 gung tow
foremost *a* 最重要嘅 juy jung yiew geh

forenoon *n* 上午 seurng hm

forerunner *n* 預兆 yu siew

foresee *v.t* 預見 yu geen

foresight *n* 先見之明 seen geen jee ming

forest *n* 森林 sam lam

forestall *v.t* 先發制人 seen fat jay yan

forester *n* 林務官 lam mo gwun

forestry *n* 林業 lam yeep

foretell *v.t* 預言 yu yeen

forethought *n* 預謀 yu mow

forever *adv* 永遠 wing yoon

forewarn *v.t* 預先警告 yu seen ging go

foreword *n* 序 juy

forfeit *v.t* 沒收 mwut sow

forfeit *n* 罰金 fat gam

forfeiture *n* 喪失 sorng sat

forge *n* 煉爐 leen lo

forge *v.t* 偽造 ngay jo

forgery *n* 偽造品 ngay jo ban

forget *v.t* 唔記得 hm gey dak

forgetful *a* 無記性 mo gey sing

forgive *v.t* 原諒 yoon leurng

forgo *v.t* 放棄 forng hay

forlorn *a* 孤苦伶仃 gu fu ling ding

form *n* 表格 biew gak

form *v.t.* 形成 ying sing

formal *a* 正式 jing sik

format *n* 格式 gak sik

formation *n* 隊形 duy ying

former *a* 昔日嘅 sik yat geh

former *pron* 前者 teen jeh

formerly *adv* 以前 yee teen

formidable *a* 可怕 hor pa

formula *n* 公式 gung sik

formulate *v.t* 規劃 kway wak

forsake *v.t.* 離棄 lay hay

forswear *v.t.* 放棄 forng hay

fort *n.* 堡壘 bo luy

forte *n.* 專長 joon cheurng

forth *adv.* 向前 heurng teen

forthcoming *a.* 即將發生嘅 jik jeurng fat sang geh

forthwith *adv.* 立刻 lap hak

fortify *v.t.* 增強 jang keurng

fortitude *n.* 耐力 loy lik

fort-night *n.* 兩個禮拜 leurng gor lay bai

fortress *n.* 城堡 sing bo

fortunate *a.* 好彩 ho choy

fortune *n.* 財產 choy tan

forty *n.* 四十 sey sap

forum *n.* 論壇 lun tan

forward *a.* 前 teen

forward *adv* 向前 heurng teen

forward *v.t* 轉寄 joon gey

fossil *n.* 化石 fa sek

foster *v.t.* 領養 ling yeurng

foul *a.* 臭 chow

found *v.t.* 搵到 wan dow

foundation *n.* 基礎 gey chor

founder *n.* 創立人 chorng lap yan

foundry *n.* 鑄造廠 ju jow chorng

fountain *n.* 噴水池 pan suy tee

four *n.* 四 sey

fourteen *n.* 十四 sap sey

fowl *n.* 家禽 ga kam

fowler *n.* 獵人 leep yan

fox *n.* 狐狸 wu lay

fraction *n.* 小部份 siew bo fan

fracture *n.* 骨折 gwat jeet

fracture *v.t* 折斷 jeet toon

fragile *a.* 脆弱 chuy yeurk

fragment *n.* 碎片 suy peen

fragrance *n.* 香味 heurng mey

fragrant *a.* 香嘅 heurng geh

frail *a.* 弱 yeurk

frame *v.t.* 鑲 seurng

frame *n* 框 kwang

franchise *n.* 特許經營權 dak huy ging ying koon

frank *a.* 坦白 tan bak

frantic *a.* 瘋狂 fung kwong
fraternal *a.* 兄弟嘅 hing day geh
fraternity *n.* 群體 kwan tay
fratricide *n.* 殺兄弟姊妹罪 sat hing day jee mwuy juy
fraud *n.* 騙子 peen jee
fraudulent *a.* 欺詐嘅 hay ja geh
fraught *a.* 充滿 chung mun
fray *n* 磨損 mor shoon
free *a.* 自由 jee yow
free *v.t* 放 forng
freedom *n.* 自由 jee yow
freeze *v.i.* 凍結 dung geet
freight *n.* 貨 for
French *a.* 法國嘅 fat gwok geh
French *n* 法國人 fat gwok yan
frenzy *n.* 狂熱 kwong yeet
frequency *n.* 頻率 pan lut
frequent *a.* 密 mat
fresh *a.* 新鮮 san seen
fret *n.* 煩惱 fan lo
fret *v.t.* 煩 fan
friction *n.* 摩擦力 mor chat lik
Friday *n.* 星期五 sing kay ng
fridge *n.* 雪櫃 shoot gway
friend *n.* 朋友 pang yow
fright *n.* 驚嚇 ging hak
frighten *v.t.* 嚇 hak tan
frigid *a.* 冷淡 lang dam
frill *n.* 褶邊 jeep been
fringe *n.* 陰 yam
fringe *v.t* 加緣飾 ga yoon sik
frivolous *a.* 輕佻 hing tiew
frock *n.* 裙 kwun
frog *n.* 青蛙 ting wa
frolic *n.* 歡樂 fwun lok
frolic *v.i.* 玩 wan
from *prep.* 從 chung
front *n.* 前 teen
front *a* 前面 teen meen
front *v.t* 面向 meen heurng
frontier *n.* 邊界 been gai

frost *n.* 霜 seurng
frown *n.* 皺眉 jow mey
frown *v.i* 皺眉 jow mey
frugal *a.* 慳家 han ga
fruit *n.* 生果 sang gwor
fruitful *a.* 有效 yow hao
frustrate *v.t.* 煩 fan
frustration *n.* 煩惱 fan lo
fry *v.t.* 炸 jar
fry *n* 魚苗 yu miew
fuel *n.* 燃料 yeen liew
fugitive *a.* 走佬嘅 jow lo geh
fugitive *n.* 通緝犯 tung tap fan
fulfil *v.t.* 達成 dat sing
fulfilment *n.* 成就感 sing jow gam
full *a.* 滿 mun
full *adv.* 滿嘅 mun geh
fullness *n.* 豐滿度 fung mun dow
fully *adv.* 完全 yoon choon
fumble *v.i.* 亂摸 loon mor
fun *n.* 好玩 ho wan
function *n.* 功能 gung lang
function *v.i* 運作 wan jok
functionary *n.* 官員 gwun yoon
fund *n.* 資金 jee gam
fundamental *a.* 基本嘅 gey bwun geh
funeral *n.* 喪禮 song lay
fungus *n.* 真菌 jan kwan
funny *n.* 搞笑 gao siew
fur *n.* 毛 mo
furious *a.* 超嬲 tiew low
furl *v.t.* 捲埋 goon mai
furlong *n.* 弗隆 fut lung
furnace *n.* 火爐 for low
furnish *v.t.* 佈置 bo jee
furniture *n.* 家私 ga see
furrow *n.* 皺紋 jow man
further *adv.* 更遠嘅 gang yoon geh

further *a* 更進一步 gang jun yat bo

further *v.t* 增進 jang jun

fury *n.* 怒火 low for

fuse *v.t.* 結合 geet hap

fuse *n* 保險絲 bo heem see

fusion *n.* 結合 geet hap

fuss *n.* 麻煩 ma fan

fuss *v.i* 大驚小怪 dai geng siew gwai

futile *a.* 無用 mo yung

futility *n.* 無益 mo yik

future *a.* 未來嘅 may loy geh

future *n* 將來 jeurng loy

G

gabble *v.i.* 含糊不清 ham wu bat ting

gadfly *n.* 麻煩人 ma fan yan

gag *v.t.* 作嘔 jok oh

gag *n.* 笑話 siew wah

gaiety *n.* 高興 go hing

gain *v.t.* 增 jang

gain *n* 好處 ho chu

gainsay *v.t.* 唔認同 hm ying tung

gait *n.* 行法 hang fat

galaxy *n.* 星系 sing hay

gale *n.* 颱風 toy fung

gallant *a.* 勇敢 yung gam

gallant *n* 型男 ying larm

gallantry *n.* 勇敢 yung gam

gallery *n.* 畫廊 wah lorng

gallon *n.* 加侖 ga lun

gallop *n.* 飛奔 fay ban

gallop *v.t.* 奔跑 ban pao

gallows *n. .* 絞刑架 gao ying ga

galore *adv.* 好多 ho dor

galvanize *v.t.* 激勵 giklay

gamble *v.i.* 賭 dow

gamble *n* 賭博 dow bok

gambler *n.* 賭仔 dow jay

game *n.* 遊戲 yow hai

game *v.i* 賭 dow

gander *n.* 雄鵝 hung or

gang *n.* 一班 yat ban

gangster *n.* 蠱惑仔 gu wak jay

gap *n* 罅 la

gape *v.i.* 目定口呆 muk ding ho ngoy

garage *n.* 車房 cher forng

garb *n.* 打扮 da ban

garb *v.t* 着 jeurk

garbage *n.* 垃圾 lap sap

garden *n.* 花園 far yoon

gardener *n.* 園藝家 yoon ngay ga

gargle *v.i.* 口 lorng ho

garland *n.* 花環 far wan

garland *v.t.* 戴花冠 dai far gwun

garlic *n.* 蒜蓉 shoon yung

garment *n.* 衫 sam

garter *n.* 吊襪帶 diew mat dai

gas *n.* 煤氣 mwuy hay

gasket *n.* 墊圈 deen hoon

gasp *n.* 深呼吸 sam fu kap

gasp *v.i* 喘氣 choon hay

gassy *a.* 多氣體 dor hay tay

gastric *a.* 胃嘅 way geh

gate *n.* 閘 jap

gather *v.t.* 收集 sow jap

gaudy *a.* 俗 juk

gauge *n.* 計議器 gey yee hay

gauntlet *n.* 鐵手套 teet sow tow

gay *a.* 同性戀 tung sing loon

gaze *v.t.* 望住 morng ju

gaze *n* 凝視 ying see

gazette *n.* 公報 gung bo

gear *n.* 檔 dorng

geld *v.t.* 閹 yeem

gem *n* 寶石 bo sek

gender *n.* 性別 sing beet

general *a.* 普遍嘅 po peen geh

generally adv. 通常 tung seurng
generate v.t. 產生 tan sang
generation n. 一代人 yat doy yan
generator n. 發電器 fat deen hay
generosity n. 寬宏大量 fwun wang dai leurng
generous a. 大方 dai forng
genius n. 天才 teen choy
gentle a. 溫柔 wan yow
gentleman n. 紳士 san see
gentry n. 上等人 seurng dang yan
genuine a. 真嘅 tan geh
geographer n. 地理學家 day lay hok ga
geographical a. 地理嘅 day lay geh
geography n. 地理學 day lay hok
geological a. 地質嘅 day jat geh
geologist n. 地質學家 day jat hok ga
geology n. 地質學 day jat hok
geometrical a. 幾何學嘅 gey hor hok geh
geometry n. 幾何學 gey hor hok
germ n. 病菌 beng kwan
germicide n. 殺菌劑 sat kwan jay
germinate v.i. 發芽 fat ngar
germination n. 成長 sing jeurng
gerund n. 動名詞 dung ming tee
gesture n. 手勢 sow say
get v.t. 攞 lor
ghastly a. 恐怖 hung bo
ghost n. 鬼 gway
giant n. 巨人 guy yan
gibbon n. 長臂猿 cheurng bay yoon
gibe v.i. 串人 choon yan
gibe n 侮辱 mo yuk
giddy a. 激動 gik dung
gift n. 禮物 lay mat
gifted a. 有才華嘅 yow choy wah geh

gigantic a. 巨大嘅 guy dai geh
giggle v.i. 格格笑 gak gak siew
gild v.t. 鍍金 dow gam
gilt a. 鍍金 dow gam
ginger n. 姜 geurng
giraffe n. 長頸鹿 cheurng geng luk
gird v.t. 準備 jun bay
girder n. 大梁 dai leurng
girdle n. 腰帶 yiew dai
girdle v.t 圍繞 way yiew
girl n. 女仔 luy jay
girlish a. 女性化 luy sing fa
gist n. 要點 yiew deem
give v.t. 畀 bay
glacier n. 冰河 bing hor
glad a. 高興 go hing
gladden v.t. 高興 go hing
glamour n. 吸引力 kap yan ik
glance n. 一眼 yat ngan
glance v.i. 望 morng
gland n. 腺 seen
glare n. 眼倔倔 ngan gwat gwat
glare v.i 眼倔倔咁望 ngan gwat gwat gam morng
glass n. 草 cho
glaucoma n. 青光眼 teng gwong ngan
glaze v.t. 發呆 fat ngoy
glaze n 釉 yow
glazier n. 玻璃工人 bor lay gung yan
glee n. 高興 go hing
glide v.t. 滑 wat
glider n. 滑翔機 wat cheurng gey
glimpse n. 一眼 yat ngan
glitter v.i. 閃 seem
glitter n 閃粒 seem lap
global a. 全球嘅 choon kow geh
globe n. 地球 day kow
gloom n. 幽暗 yow am

gloomy *a.* 陰暗 yam am

glorification *n.* 讚揚 jan yeurng

glorify *v.t.* 吹捧 chuy pung

glorious *a.* 光榮嘅 gwong wing geh

glory *n.* 榮譽 wing yu

gloss *n.* 光澤 gwong jak

glossary *n.* 詞彙表 tee wuy biew

glossy *a.* 光滑嘅 gwong wat geh

glove *n.* 手套 sow tow

glow *v.i.* 發光 fat gwong

glow *n* 暗光 am gwong

glucose *n.* 葡萄糖 po tow tong

glue *n.* 膠水 gao suy

glut *v.t.* 超量供應 tiew leurng gung ying

glut *n* 供過於求 gung gwor yu kow

glutton *n.* 為食嘅人 way sik geh yan

gluttony *n.* 暴飲暴食 bo yam bo sik

glycerine *n.* 甘油 gam yow

go *v.i.* 去 huy

goad *n.* 激勵 gik lay

goad *v.t* 招惹 tiew yeh

goal *n.* 目標 muk biew

goat *n.* 山羊 san yeurng

gobble *n.* 狼吞虎嚥 lorng tun fu yeen

goblet *n.* 酒杯 jow bwuy

god *n.* 上帝 seurng day

goddess *n.* 女神 luy san

godhead *n.* 上帝 seurng day

godly *a.* 虔誠嘅 keen sing geh

godown *n.* 倉庫 chorng fu

godsend *n.* 天賜之物 tteen tee jee mat

goggles *n.* 護眼鏡 wu ngan geng

gold *n.* 金 gam

golden *a.* 金色嘅 gam sik geh

goldsmith *n.* 金匠 gam jeurng

golf *n.* 高爾夫球 go yee fu kow

gong *n.* 鑼 lor

good *a.* 好嘅 ho geh

good *n* 好處 ho chu

good-bye *interj.* 再見 joy geen

goodness *n.* 美德 may dak

goodwill *n.* 善意 seen yee

goose *n.* 鵝 or

gooseberry *n.* 醋栗 cho lut

gorgeous *a.* 好靚 ho leng

gorilla *n.* 猩猩 sing sing

gospel *n.* 福音 fuk yam

gossip *n.* 閒話 han wah

gourd *n.* 葫蘆 wu low

gout *n.* 通風病 tung fung beng

govern *v.t.* 統治 tung jee

governance *n.* 統治方式 tung jee forng sik

governess *n.* 家庭女教師 ga ting luy gao see

government *n.* 政府 jing fu

governor *n.* 州長 jow jeurng

gown *n.* 女禮服 luy lay fuk

grab *v.t.* 捉住 juk ju

grace *n.* 優美 yow may

grace *v.t.* 裝飾 jorng sik

gracious *a.* 仁慈 yan tee

gradation *n.* 階段 gai doon

grade *n.* 級 kap

grade *v.t* 分級 gan kap

gradual *a.* 逐漸 juk jeem

graduate *v.i.* 畢業 bat yeep

graduate *n* 畢業生 bat yeep sang

graft *n.* 移植物 yee jik mat

graft *v.t* 移植 yee jik

grain *n.* 一粒 yat lap

grammar *n.* 文法 man fat

grammarian *n.* 文法家 man fat ga

gramme *n.* 克 hak

gramophone *n.* 留聲機 low seng gey

granary n. 糧倉 leurng chorng
grand a. 壯麗嘅 jorng lay geh
grandeur n. 宏偉 wang way
grant v.t. 畀 bay
grant n 撥款 pwut fwun
grape n. 提子 tay jee
graph n. 圖表 tow biew
graphic a. 繪畫嘅 kwuy wah geh
grapple n. 格鬥 gak dow
grapple v.i. 扭打 low da
grasp v.t. 捉住 juk ju
grasp n 掌握 jeurng ak
grass n 草 cho
grate n. 爐條 lo tiew
grate v.t 磨碎 mor suy
grateful a. 感激 gam gik
gratification n. 滿足感 mun juk gam
gratis adv. 免費嘅 meen fay geh
gratitude n. 感激 gam gik
gratuity n. 貼士 teep see
grave n. 墳頭 fan tow
grave a. 嚴肅 yeem suk
gravitate v.i. 被吸引到 bay kap yan dow
gravitation n. 引力 yan lik
gravity n. 地心吸引力 day sam kap yan lik
graze v.i. 食草 sik cho
graze n 擦傷 tat seurng
grease n 油脂 yow jee
grease v.t 擦油 tat yow
greasy a. 多油 dor yow
great a 好好 ho ho
greed n. 貪慾 tam yuk
greedy a. 貪心 tam sam
Greek n. 希臘人 hay lap yan
Greek a 希臘文 hay lap man
green a. 綠色嘅 luk sik geh
green n 綠色 luk sik
greenery n. 綠色植物 luk sik jik mat

greet v.t. 打招呼 da jiew fu
grenade n. 手榴彈 sow low dan
grey a. 灰色嘅 fwuy sik geh
greyhound n. 灰狗 gwuy gow
grief n. 悲痛 bay tung
grievance n. 委屈 way wat
grieve v.t. 傷心 seurng sam
grievous a. 令人痛苦 ling yan tung fu
grind v.i. 磨碎 mor suy
grinder n. 磨碎機 mor suy gey
grip v.t. 捉實 juk sat
grip n 控制 hung jay
groan v.i. 嘆息 tan sik
groan n 呻吟聲 san yam seng
grocer n. 雜貨店 jap for deem
grocery n. 雜貨店 jap for deem
groom n. 新郎 san lorng
groom v.t 梳毛 sormo
groove n. 紋 man
groove v.t 鎅 gai
grope v.t. 猥瑣 wuy sor
gross n. 總收入 jung sao yap
gross a 核突 wat dat
grotesque a. 荒謬嘅 forng mo geh
ground n. 地 day
group n. 一組 yat jow
group v.t. 組成 jow sing
grow v.t. 生 sang
grower n. 種植者 jung jik jeh
growl v.i. 吼叫 hung giew
growl n 吼叫聲 hung giew seng
growth n. 發育 fat yuk
grudge v.t. 勉強做 meen keurng jo
grudge n 怨恨 yoon han
grumble v.i. 發牢騷 fat low sow
grunt n. 呼嚕 fu low
grunt v.i. 呼嚕聲 fu low seng
guarantee n. 保養 bo yeurng
guarantee v.t 擔保 dan bo

guard *v.i.* 守衛 sow way

guard *n.* 護衛 wu way

guardian *n.* 守護者 sow wu jeh

guava *n.* 番石榴 fan sek low

guerilla *n.* 游擊戰 yow gik jeen

guess *n.* 猜測 tai tak

guess *v.i* 估 gu

guest *n.* 嘉賓 gar ban

guidance *n.* 指導 jee dow

guide *v.t.* 指引 jee yan

guide *n.* 指南 jee lam

guild *n.* 協會 heep wuy

guile *n.* 蠱惑 gu wak

guilt *n.* 內疚 loy gow

guilty *a.* 內疚 loy gow

guise *n.* 外表 ngoy biew

guitar *n.* 結他 geet ta

gulf *n.* 海灣 hoy wan

gull *n.* 海鷗 hoy ow

gull *n* 受騙者 sow peen jeh

gull *v.t* 呃 ak

gulp *n.* 一大啖 yat dai dam

gum *n.* 牙肉 ngar yuk

gun *n.* 槍 cheurng

gust *n.* 一陣風 yat jan fung

gutter *n.* 水槽 suy cho

guttural *a.* 喉嚨嘅 ho lung geh

gymnasium *n.* 體育館 tay yuk gwun

gymnast *n.* 體操員 tay cho yoon

gymnastic *a.* 體操嘅 tay cho geh

gymnastics *n.* 體操 tay cho

habeas corpus *n.* 人身保護令 yan san bo wu ling

habit *n.* 習慣 jap gwan

habitable *a.* 適合住嘅 sik hap ju geh

habitat *n.* 棲息地 tay sik day

habitation *n.* 居住 guy ju

habituate *v. t.* 習慣咗 jap gwan jor

hack *v.t.* 侵入 tam yap

hag *n.* 醜女 tow luy

haggard *a.* 憔悴 tiew suy

haggle *v.i.* 講價 gorng ga

hail *n.* 冰雹 bing pao

hail *v.i* 讚 jan

hail *v.t* 招手 jiew sow

hair *n* 頭髮 tow fat

hale *a.* 硬朗 ang lorn

half *n.* 一半 yat bwun

half *a* 半 bwun

hall *n.* 禮堂 lay tong

hallmark *n.* 特徵 dak jing

hallow *v.t.* 崇敬 sung ging

halt *v. t.* 停止 ting jee

halt *n* 停止 ting jee

halve *v.t.* 分半 fan bwun

hamlet *n.* 細村莊 sai choon jorng

hammer *n.* 槌仔 chuy jay

hammer *v.t* 揼 dap

hand *n* 手 sow

hand *v.t* 畀 bay

handbill *n.* 傳單 choon dan

handbook *n.* 手冊 sow tak

handcuff *n.* 手扣 sow kow

handcuff *v.t* 鎖 sor

handful *n.* 少數 siew sow

handicap *v.t.* 阻礙 jor ngoy

handicap *n* 殘疾 tan jat

handicraft *n.* 手工藝 sow gung ngay

handiwork *n.* 手工 sow gung

handkerchief *n.* 手巾 sow gan

handle *n.* 手柄 sow beng

handle *v.t* 處理 chu lay

handsome *a.* 靚仔 leng jay

handy *a.* 方便 forng been

hang *v.t.* 掛 gwa

hanker *v.i.* 渴望 hot morng

haphazard *a.* 無秩序 mo deet juy

happen *v.t.* 發生 fat sang

happening *n.* 事 see

happiness *n.* 快樂 fai lok

happy *a.* 開心 hoy sam

harass *v.t.* 騷擾 sow yiew

harassment *n.* 騷擾 sow yiew

harbour *n.* 港 gorng

harbour *v.t* 窩藏 wor chorng

hard *a.* 難 lan

harden *v.t.* 硬化 ang far

hardihood *n.* 大膽 dai dam

hardly *adv.* 幾乎無 gey fu mow

hardship *n.* 艱難 gan lan

hardy *adj.* 適應力強 sik ying lik keurng

hare *n.* 野兔 yeh tow

harm *n.* 損害 shoon hoy

harm *v.t* 傷害 seurng hoy

harmonious *a.* 和諧嘅 wor hai geh

harmonium *n.* 風琴 fung kam

harmony *n.* 和睦 wor muk

harness *n.* 馬具 ma guy

harness *v.t* 控制 hung jay

harp *n.* 豎琴 shu kam

harsh *a.* 刻薄 hak bok

harvest *n.* 收成 sow sing

havester *n.* 收割機 sow got gey

haste *n.* 匆忙 chung morng

hasten *v.i.* 促進 chuk jun

hasty *a.* 草率 cho sut

hat *n.* 帽 mo

hatchet *n.* 斧頭 fu tow

hate *n.* 仇恨 sow han

hate *v.t.* 憎 jang

haughty *a.* 高傲自大嘅 gow oh jee dai geh

haunt *v.t.* 鬼魂出沒 gway wan chut mwut

haunt *n* 成日去嘅地方 sing yat huy geh day forng

have *v.t.* 有 yow

haven *n.* 避難所 bay lan sor

havoc *n.* 浩劫 ho geep

hawk *n* 鷹 ying

hawker *n* 小販 siew fan

hawthorn *n.* 山楂樹 san ja shu

hay *n.* 乾草 gon cho

hazard *n.* 危險 ngay heem

hazard *v.t* 冒險 mo heem

haze *n.* 薄霧 bok mo

hazy *a.* 模糊 mo wu

he *pron.* 佢 kuy

head *n.* 頭 tow

head *v.t* 去 huy

headache *n.* 頭痛 tow tung

heading *n.* 標題 biew tay

headlong *adv.* 輕率 hing sut

headstrong *a.* 硬頸 ang geng

heal *v.i.* 醫好 yee ho

health *n.* 健康 geen horng

healthy *a.* 健康 geen horng

heap *n.* 一堆 yat duy

heap *v.t* 堆積 duy jik

hear *v.t.* 聽 teng

hearsay *n.* 傳聞 choon man

heart *n.* 心 sam

hearth *n.* 爐低 lo day

heartily *adv.* 盡情咁 jun ting gam

heat *n.* 熱 yeet

heat *v.t* 加熱 ga yeet

heave *v.i.* 搬 bwun

heaven *n.* 天堂 teen tong

heavenly *a.* 天堂嘅 teen tong geh

hedge *n.* 樹籬 shu lay

hedge *v.t* 轉彎抹角 joon wan mwut got

heed *v.t.* 注意 ju yee

heed *n* 留心 low sam

heel *n.* 腳睜 geurt jang

hefty *a.* 重 chung

height *n.* 高度 go dow

heighten *v.t.* 增高 jang gow

heinous *a.* 非常惡毒嘅 fay seurng ok duk geh

heir *n.* 繼承人 gey sing yan

hell *a.* 地獄 dey yuk

helm *n.* 舵輪 tor lun

helmet *n.* 頭盔 tow kway

help *v.t.* 幫 borng

help *n* 幫助 borng jor

helpful *a.* 樂於助人 lok yu jor yan

helpless *a.* 無用嘅 mo yung geh

helpmate *n.* 伴侶 bwun luy

hemisphere *n.* 半球 bwun kow

hemp *n.* 大麻 dai ma

hen *n.* 母雞 mo gey

hence *adv.* 因此 yan tee

henceforth *adv.* 從此以後 chung tee yee ho

henceforward *adv.* 從今以後 chung gam yee ho

henchman *n.* 親信 tan sun

henpecked *a.* 怕老婆 pa lo por

her *pron.* 佢 kuy

her *a* 佢嘅 kuy geh

herald *n.* 宣佈 shoon bo

herald *v.t* 預兆 yu siew

herb *n.* 藥草 yeurk cho

herculean *a.* 力大無比嘅 lik dai mo bay geh

herd *n.* 一群 yat kwan

herdsman *n.* 牧人 muk yan

here *adv.* 呢度 lee dow

hereabouts *adv.* 呢頭附近 lee tow fu gan

hereafter *adv.* 從此以後 chung tee yee ho

hereditary *n.* 遺傳嘅 way choon geh

heredity *n.* 遺傳 way choon

heritable *a.* 可以遺傳嘅 hor yee way choon geh

heritage *n.* 遺產 way tan

hermit *n.* 隱士 yan see

hermitage *n.* 隱居處 yan guy chu

hernia *n.* 突出 dat chut

hero *n.* 英雄 ying hung

heroic *a.* 英勇嘅 ying yung geh

heroine *n.* 女主角 luy ju gok

heroism *n.* 英雄精神 ying hung jing san

herring *n.* 鯡魚 fay yu

hesitant *a.* 猶豫嘅 yow yee geh

hesitate *v.i.* 猶豫 yow yee

hesitation *n.* 猶豫 yow yee

hew *v.t.* 劈 pek

heyday *n.* 高峰時期 go fung see kay

hibernation *n.* 冬眠 dung meen

hiccup *n.* 打嗝 da gut

hide *n.* 藏身處 chorng san chu

hide *v.t* 收埋 sow mai

hideous *a.* 核突 wat dat

hierarchy *n.* 等級制度 dang kap jay dow

high *a.* 高 go

highly *adv.* 非常 fay seurng

Highness *n.* 殿下 deen ha

highway *n.* 大路 dai low

hilarious *a.* 好搞笑 ho gao siew

hilarity *n.* 高興 go hing

hill *n.* 山 san

hillock *n.* 小丘 siew yow

him *pron.* 佢 kuy

hinder *v.t.* 阻礙 jor ngoy

hindrance *n.* 防礙 forng ngoy

hint *n.* 提示 tay see

hint *v.i* 暗示 am see

hip *n* 臀部 toon bo

hire *n.* 租用 jow yung

hire *v.t* 租 jow

hireling *n.* 工人 gung yan

his *pron.* 佢嘅 kuy geh

hiss *n* 嘶嘶聲 see see seng

hiss *v.i* 發嘶嘶聲 fat see see seng

historian *n.* 歷史學家 lik see hok ga

historic *a.* 歷史性嘅 lik see sing geh

historical *a.* 歷史嘅 lik see geh

history *n.* 歷史 lik see

hit *v.t.* 打 da

hit *n* 打擊 da gik

hitch *n.* 故障 gu jeurng

hither *adv.* 到呢度 dow lee dow

hitherto *adv.* 直到而家 jik dow yee ga

hive *n.* 蜂房 fung forng

hoarse *a.* 沙啞 sar ngar

hoax *n.* 惡作劇 ok jok kek

hoax *v.t* 整蠱 jing gu

hobby *n.* 嗜好 see ho

hobby-horse *n.* 木馬 muk mah

hockey *n.* 曲棍球 kun gwan kow

hoist *v.t.* 吊起 diew hay

hold *n.* 控制 hung jay

hold *v.t* 揸住 ja ju

hole *n* 窿 lung

hole *v.t* 打窿 da lung

holiday *n.* 旅行 luy hang

hollow *a.* 空心嘅 hung sam geh

hollow *n.* 洞 dung

hollow *v.t* 整凹 jing lap

holocaust *n.* 大屠殺 dai tow sat

holy *a.* 神聖嘅 san sing geh

homage *n.* 敬意 ging yee

home *n.* 屋企 uk kay

homicide *n.* 殺人罪 sat yan juy

homoeopath *n.* 同種療法師 tung jung liew fat see

homeopathy *n.* 同種療法 tung jung liew fat

homogeneous *a.* 同類嘅 tung luy geh

honest *a.* 誠實 sing sat

honesty *n.* 誠實 sing sat

honey *n.* 蜜糖 mat torng

honeycomb *n.* 蜂巢 fung tao

honeymoon *n.* 度蜜月 dow may yoot

honorarium *n.* 酬金 chow gam

honorary *a.* 義務嘅 yee mo geh

honour *n.* 榮譽 wing yu

honour *v. t* 尊敬 joon ging

honourable *a.* 品加高尚 ban gak go seurng

hood *n.* 帽 mow

hoodwink *v.t.* 呃 ak

hoof *n.* 蹄 tay

hook *n.* 鉤 oh

hooligan *n.* 飛仔 fay jay

hoot *n.* 喇叭聲 la ba seng

hoot *v.i* 響 heurng

hop *v. i* 單腳跳 dan geurt tiew

hop *n* 單腳跳 dan geurt tiew

hope *v.t.* 希望 hay morng

hope *n* 希望 hay morng

hopeful *a.* 滿懷希望 mun wai hay morng

hopeless *a.* 無望 mo morng

horde *n.* 一大班人 yat dai ban yan

horizon *n.* 地平線 day ping seen

horn *n.* 角 gok

hornet *n.* 大黃峰 dai wong fung

horrible *a.* 恐怖嘅 hung bo geh

horrify *v.t.* 嚇 hak

horror *n.* 恐怖 hung bo

horse *n.* 馬 ma

horticulture *n.* 園藝 yoon ngay

hose *n.* 水管 suy gwun

hosiery *n.* 襪類 mat luy

hospitable *a.* 好客嘅 ho hak geh

hospital *n.* 醫院 yee yoon

hospitality *n.* 好客 ho hak

host *n.* 主持 ju tee

hostage *n.* 人質 yan jee

hostel *n.* 旅舍 luy she

hostile *a.* 強烈反對 keurng leet fan duy

hostility *n.* 對抗 duy korng
hot *a.* 熱 yeet
hotchpotch *n.* 一大堆嘢 yat dai duy yeh
hotel *n.* 酒店 jow deem
hound *n.* 獵犬 leep hoon
hour *n.* 鐘頭 jung tow
house *n* 屋 uk
house *v.t* 收容 sow yung
how *adv.* 點樣 deem yeurng
however *adv.* 不過 bat gwor
however *conj* 但係 dan hay
howl *v.t.* 大聲叫 dai seng giew
howl *n* 喊叫聲 ham giew seng
hub *n.* 輪轂
hubbub *n.* 嘈雜聲 cho jap seng
huge *a.* 好大嘅 ho dai geh
hum *v.i* 哼 hang
hum *n* 嗡嗡聲 wung wung seng
human *a.* 人類 yan luy
humane *a.* 有人性嘅 yow yan sing geh
humanitarian *a* 人道主義嘅 yan dow ju yee geh
humanity *n.* 人類 yan luy
humanize *v.t.* 變得適合人 been dak sik hap yan
humble *a.* 謙虛 heem huy
humdrum *a.* 單調 dan diew
humid *a.* 焗 guk
humidity *n.* 濕度 sap dow
humiliate *v.t.* 落面 lok meen
humiliation *n.* 恥辱 tee yuk
humility *n.* 謙虛 heem huy
humorist *n.* 幽默作家 yow mak jok ga
humorous *a.* 幽默 yow mak
humour *n.* 幽默感 yow mak gam
hunch *n.* 直覺 jik gok
hundred *n.* 一百 yat bak
hunger *n* 渴望 hot morng
hungry *a.* 肚餓 tow or

hunt *v.t.* 打獵 da leep
hunt *n* 搵 wan
hunter *n.* 獵人 leep yan
huntsman *n.* 獵人 leep yan
hurdle1 *n.* 跨欄 kwa lan
hurdle2 *v.t* 跳過 tiew gwor
hurl *v.t.* 大力咁掉 dai lik gam deng
hurrah *interj.* 好啊 ho ah
hurricane *n.* 颱風 toy fung
hurry *v.t.* 趕 gon
hurry *n* 急住 gap ju
hurt *v.t.* 受傷 sow seurng
hurt *n* 委屈 way wat
husband *n* 老公 lo gung
husbandry *n.* 農牧業 lung muk yeep
hush *n* 變安靜 been on jing
hush *v.i* 唔好講嘢 hm ho gorng yeh
husk *n.* 外殼 ngoy hok
husky *a.* 沙啞 sa ngar
hut *n.* 茅屋 mao uk
hyaena, hyena *n.* 鬣狗 leep gow
hybrid *a.* 雜種嘅 jap jung geh
hybrid *n* 雜種 jap jung
hydrogen *n.* 氫氣 hing hay
hygiene *n.* 衛生 way sang
hygienic *a.* 衛生嘅 way sang geh
hymn *n.* 聖歌 sing gor
hyperbole *n.* 誇張 kwa jeurng
hypnotism *n.* 催眠術 chuy meen suy
hypnotize *v.t.* 催眠 chuy meen
hypocrisy *n.* 虛偽 huy ngay
hypocrite *n.* 偽君子 ngay gwan jee
hypocritical *a.* 虛偽嘅 huy ngay geh
hypothesis *n.* 假設 ga teet
hypothetical *a.* 假設 ga teet

hysteria *n.* 大驚小怪 dai geng siew gwai

hysterical *a.* 情緒激動 ting suy gik dung

```
I
```

I *pron.* 我 ngor

ice *n.* 冰 bing

iceberg *n.* 冰山 bing san

icicle *n.* 冰柱 bing ju

icy *a.* 冰 bing

idea *n.* 想法 seurng fat

ideal *a.* 理想嘅 lay seurng geh

ideal *n* 理想 lay seurng

idealism *n.* 理想主義 lay seurng ju yee

idealist *n.* 理想主義者 lay seurng ju yee jeh

idealistic *a.* 理想主義 lay seurng ju yee

idealize *v.t.* 理想化 lay seurng far

identical *a.* 一樣嘅 yat yeurng geh

indentification *n.* 身分證明 san fan jing ming

identify *v.t.* 辨認 been ying

identity *n.* 身分 san fan

idiocy *n.* 愚蠢行為 yu chun hang way

idiom *n.* 成語 sing yu

idiomatic *a.* 地道嘅 day dow geh

idiot *n.* 白癡 bak tee

idiotic *a.* 蠢嘅 chun geh

idle *a.* 無嘢做 mo yeh jow

idleness *n.* 閒散 han san

idler *n.* 遊手好閒嘅人 yow sow ho han geh yan

idol *n.* 偶像 oh jeurng

idolater *n.* 崇拜者 sung bai jeh

if *conj.* 如果 yu gwor

ignoble *a.* 唔光彩嘅 hm gwong choy geh

ignorance *n.* 無知 mo jee

ignorant *a.* 無知 mo jee

ignore *v.t.* 忽視 fat see

ill *a.* 病 beng

ill *adv.* 差 ta

ill *n* 病 beng

illegal *a.* 犯法 fan fat

illegibility *n.* 模糊不清 mow wu bat ting

illegible *a.* 難讀 lan duk

illegitimate *a.* 私生嘅 see sang geh

illicit *a.* 非法嘅 fay fat geh

illiteracy *n.* 文盲 man mang

illiterate *a.* 文盲 man mang

illness *n.* 病 beng

illogical *a.* 唔合邏輯嘅 hm hap lor tap geh

illuminate *v.t.* 照 jiew

illumination *n.* 光源 gwong yoon

illusion *n.* 錯覺 chor gok

illustrate *v.t.* 加圖 ga tow

illustration *n.* 插圖 tap tow

image *n.* 圖片 tow peen

imagery *n.* 意象 yee jeurng

imaginary *a.* 幻想 wan seurng

imagination *n.* 想像力 seurng jeurng lik

imaginative *a.* 有想像力 yow seurng jeurng lik

imagine *v.t.* 想像下 seurng jeurng ha

imitate *v.t.* 模仿 mo forng

imitation *n.* 模仿 mo forng

imitator *n.* 模仿者 mo forng jeh

immaterial *a.* 唔緊要 hm gan yiew

immature *a.* 幼稚 yow jee

immaturity *n.* 未成年 may sing

leen

immeasurable *a.* 無限嘅 mo han geh

immediate *a* 即刻 jik hak

immemorial *a.* 古老嘅 gu low geh

immense *a.* 巨大嘅 guy dai geh

immensity *n.* 巨大 guy dai

immerse *v.t.* 浸 jam

immersion *n.* 浸 jam

immigrant *n.* 移民 yee man

immigrate *v.i.* 移民 yee man

immigration *n.* 移民 yee man

imminent *a.* 即將發生 jik jeurng fat sang

immodest *a.* 唔謙虛 hm heem huy

immodesty *n.* 唔謙虛 hm heem huy

immoral *a* 不道德 bat dow dak

immorality *n.* 邪惡 ter ok

immortal *a.* 不死嘅 bat say geh

immortality *n.* 永生 wing sang

immortalize *v.t.* 名垂千古 ming suy teen gu

immovable *a.* 固定嘅 gu ding geh

immune *a.* 有免疫力嘅 yow meen yik lik geh

immunity *n.* 免疫力 meen yik lik

immunize *v.t.* 免疫 meen yik

impact *n.* 影響力 ying heurng lik

impart *v.t.* 通知 tung jee

impartial *a.* 中立嘅 jung lap geh

impartiality *n.* 公平 gung ping

impassable *a.* 過唔到 gwor hm dow

impasse *n.* 死路 say low

impatience *n.* 無耐性 mo loy sing

impatient *a.* 無耐性 mo loy sing

impeach *v.t.* 告 gow

impeachment *n.* 告 gow

impede *v.t.* 阻止 jor jee

impediment *n.* 障礙 jeurng ngoy

impenetrable *a.* 穿唔過嘅 choon hm gwor geh

imperative *a.* 急嘅 gap geh

imperfect *a.* 唔完美 hm yoon may

imperfection *n.* 瑕疵 har tee

imperial *a.* 皇帝嘅 worng day geh

imperialism *n.* 帝國統治 day gwok tung jee

imperil *v.t.* 陷入險境 ham yap heem ging

imperishable *a.* 不死嘅 bat say geh

impersonal *a.* 冷淡 lang dam

impersonate *v.t.* 模仿 mo forng

impersonation *n.* 模仿 mo forng

impertinence *n.* 無禮嘅 mow lay geh

impertinent *a.* 不敬 bat ging

impetuosity *n.* 衝動 chung dung

impetuous *a.* 輕率 hing sut

implement *n.* 工具 gung guy

implement *v.t.* 執行 jap hang

implicate *v.t.* 牽涉 heen seep

implication *n.* 牽連 heen leen

implicit *a.* 唔懷疑 hm wai yee

implore *v.t.* 求 kow

imply *v.t.* 暗示 am see

impolite *a.* 無禮貌 mow lay mao

import *v.t.* 進入 jun yap

import *n.* 引進 yan jun

importance *n.* 重要性 jung yiew sing

important *a.* 重要 jung yiew

impose *v.t.* 推行 tuy hang

imposing *a.* 令人印象深刻 ling yan yan jeurng sam hak

imposition *n.* 實施 sat see

impossibility *n.* 無可能性 mow

hor lang sing

impossible *a.* 無可能 mow hor lang

impostor *n.* 騙子 peen jee

imposture *n.* 假冒行騙 ga mow hang peen

impotence *n.* 無能 mo lang

impotent *a.* 性無能嘅 sing mo lang geh

impoverish *v.t.* 變窮 been kung

impracticability *n.* 無法事實 mo fat sat see

impracticable *a.* 不切實際嘅 bat teet sat jay geh

impress *v.t.* 驚喜 ging hay

impression *n.* 印象 yan jeurng

impressive *a.* 印象深刻 yan jeurng sam hak

imprint *v.t.* 印 yan

imprint *n.* 壓印 ngat yan

imprison *v.t.* 軟禁 yoon gam

improper *a.* 唔正當嘅 hm jing dong geh

impropriety *n.* 唔合合適嘅行爲 hm hap sik geh hang way

improve *v.t.* 進步 jun bo

improvement *n.* 進步 jun bo

imprudence *n.* 輕率 hing sut

imprudent *a.* 唔明智嘅 hm ming jee geh

impulse *n.* 衝動 chung dung

impulsive *a.* 衝動 chung dung

impunity *n.* 免責 meen jak

impure *a.* 唔純潔嘅 hm sun geet geh

impurity *n.* 雜質 jap jat

impute *v.t.* 歸咎於 gway gow yu

in *prep.* 喺 hay

inability *n.* 無能力 mo lang lik

inaccurate *a.* 唔準確 hm jun kok

inaction *n.* 唔做嘢 hm jow yeh

inactive *a.* 唔活躍 hm wut yeurk

inadmissible *a.* 唔允許 hm wan huy

inanimate *a.* 無生命嘅 mow sang ming geh

inapplicable *a.* 唔適合 hm sik hap geh

inattentive *a.* 無心裝載 mo sam jorng joy

inaudible *a.* 聽唔到 teng hm dow

inaugural *a.* 開創嘅 hoy chorng geh

inauguration *n.* 就職 jow jik

inauspicious *a.* 不祥嘅 bat cheurng geh

inborn *a.* 天生嘅 teen sang geh

incalculable *a.* 計唔到嘅 gey hm dow geh

incapable *a.* 無能力 mo lang lik

incapacity *n.* 無能力 mo lang lik

incarnate *a.* 人體化嘅 yan tay far geh

incarnate *v.t.* 具體化 guy tay far

incarnation *n.* 化身 far san

incense *v.t.* 激人 gikyan

incense *n.* 香 heurng

incentive *n.* 鼓勵 gu lay

inception *n.* 開始 hoy tee

inch *n.* 寸 choon

incident *n.* 事 see

incidental *a.* 唔重要嘅 hm jung yiew geh

incite *v.t.* 激發 gik fat

inclination *n.* 意願 yee yoon

incline *v.i.* 傾向 king heurng

include *v.t.* 包括 bao kwut

inclusion *n.* 包括 bao kwut

inclusive *a.* 包括 bao kwut

incoherent *a.* 唔清唔楚 hm ting hm chor

income *n.* 收入 sow yap

incomparable *a.* 無得比 mo dak bay

incompetent a. 無能力 mo lang lik

incomplete a. 未完成 may yoon sing

inconsiderate a. 唔體諒 hm tay leurng

inconvenient a. 唔方便 hm forng been

incorporate v.t. 加入 ga yap

incorporate a. 合併 hap ping

incorporation n. 納入 lap yap

incorrect a. 錯 chor

incorrigible a. 無藥可救 mo yeurk hor gow

incorruptible a. 清廉 ting leem

increase v.t. 增加 jang ga

increase n 增加 jang ga

incredible a. 難以置信 lan yee jee sun

increment n. 增值 jang jik

incriminate v.t. 牽連 heen leen

incubate v.i. 孵 fu

inculcate v.t. 灌輸 gwun shu

incumbent n. 現任者 yeen yam jeh

incumbent a 有責任 yow jak yam

incur v.t. 惹 yeh

incurable a. 無得醫 mo dak yee

indebted a. 感激 gam gik

indecency n. 不雅行為 bat ngar hang way

indecent a. 唔恰當 hm hap dong

indecision n. 優柔寡斷 yow yow gwa doon

indeed adv. 的確 dik kok

indefensible a. 無法防守 mo fat forng sow

indefinite a. 無限期 mo han kay

indemnity n. 保障 bo jeurng

independence n. 獨立 duk lap

independent a. 獨立 duk lap

indescribable a. 難以形容 lan yee ying yung

index n. 索引 sok yan

Indian a. 印度嘅 yan dow geh

indicate v.t. 指出 jee chut

indication n. 顯示 heen see

indicative a. 表示 biew see

indicator n. 跡象 jik jeurng

indict v.t. 起訴 hay sow

indictment n. 控告 hung gow

indifference n. 漠不關心 mok bat gwan sam

indifferent a. 唔好 hm how

indigenous a. 當地嘅 dorng day geh

indigestible a. 難消化 lan siew far

indigestion n. 消化不良 siew far bat leurng

indignant a. 憤慨 fan koy

indignation n. 憤慨 fan koy

indigo n. 靛藍 deen larm

indirect a. 間接 gan jeep

indiscipline n. 無紀律 mow gey lut

indiscreet a. 唔謹慎 hm gan san

indiscretion n. 唔檢點行為 hm geem deem hang way

indiscriminate a. 不加選擇 bat ga shoon jak

indispensable a. 不可缺乏嘅 bat hor koot fat geh

indisposed a. 唔舒服 hm shu fuk

indisputable a. 無得拗 mo dak ao

indistinct a. 模糊 mow wu

individual a. 個別嘅 gor beet geh

individualism n. 個性 gor sing

individuality n. 個性 gor sing

indivisible a. 分唔到 fan hm dow

indolent a. 懶 lan

indomitable a. 堅毅不屈 geen

ngay bat wat

indoor *a.* 室內嘅 sat loy geh

indoors *adv.* 室內 sat loy

induce *v.t.* 引起 yan hay

inducement *n.* 引誘 yan yow

induct *v.t.* 正式就職 jing sik jow jik

induction *n.* 就任 jow yam

indulge *v.t.* 沈迷 tam may

indulgence *n.* 縱容 jung yung

indulgent *a.* 縱容 jung yung

industrial *a.* 工業嘅 gung yeep geh

industrious *a.* 勤力 kan lik

industry *n.* 行業 horng yeep

ineffective *a.* 無效 mow hao

inert *a.* 惰性 dor sing

inertia *n.* 慣性 gwan sing

inevitable *a.* 無可避免 mow hor bay meen

inexact *a.* 唔準確 hm jun kok

inexorable *a.* 耳仔軟 yee jay yoon

inexpensive *a.* 唔貴 hm gway

inexperience *n.* 無經驗 mo ging yeem

inexplicable *a.* 無法解釋 mow fat gai sik

infallible *a.* 萬無一失 man mow yat sat

infamous *a.* 聲名狼藉 sing ming lorng jik

infamy *n.* 惡行 ok hang

infancy *n.* 初期 chor kay

infant *n.* 細路仔 say low jay

infanticide *n.* 殺嬰罪 sat ying juy

infantile *a.* 細佬仔 say low jay

infantry *n.* 步兵 bo ping

infatuate *v.t.* 迷戀 may loon

infatuation *n.* 著迷 jeurk may

infect *v.t.* 傳染 choon yeem

infection *n.* 感染 gam yeem

infectious *a.* 傳染性 choon yeem sing

infer *v.t.* 推斷 tuy doon

inference *n.* 結論 geet lun

inferior *a.* 較差 gao ta

inferiority *n.* 自卑感 jee bay gam

infernal *a.* 好討厭嘅 ho tow yeem geh

infinite *a.* 無限嘅 mow han geh

infinity *n.* 無限 mow han

infirm *a.* 體弱 tay yeurk

infirmity *n.* 體弱 tay yeurk

inflame *v.t.* 激起 gik hay

inflammable *a.* 易燃 yee yeen

inflammation *n.* 發炎 fat yeem

inflammatory *a.* 發炎 fat yeem

inflation *n.* 價格通脹 ga gak tung jeurng

inflexible *a.* 無彈性 mo dan sing

inflict *v.t.* 加害 ga hoy

influence *n.* 影響 ying heurng

influence *v.t.* 影響 ying heurng

influential *a.* 有影響力 yow ying heurng lik

influenza *n.* 流感 low gam

influx *n.* 湧入 yung yao

inform *v.t.* 通知 tung jee

informal *a.* 日常嘅 yat seurng geh

information *n.* 資料 jee liew

informative *a.* 提供資訊嘅 tay gung jee sun geh

informer *n.* 告密者 gow mat jeh

infringe *v.t.* 侵犯 tam fan

infringement *n.* 違反 way fan

infuriate *v.t.* 激 gik

infuse *v.t.* 注入 ju yap

infusion *n.* 灌輸 gwun shu

ingrained *a.* 日常 yat seurng

ingratitude *n.* 忘恩負義 morng yan fu yee

ingredient *n.* 材料 choy liew

inhabit *v.t.* 居住於 guy ju yu

inhabitable *a.* 適合住嘅 sik hap
ju geh

inhabitant *n.* 居民 guy man

inhale *v.i.* 吸入 kap yap

inherent *a.* 固有嘅 gu yow geh

inherit *v.t.* 繼承 gey sing

inheritance *n.* 遺產 way tan

inhibit *v.t.* 阻止 jor jee

inhibition *n.* 拘謹 kuy gan

inhospitable *a.* 唔適合住嘅 hm
sik hap ju geh

inhuman *a.* 冷酷無情 lang huk
mo ting

inimical *a.* 不利 bat lay

inimitable *a.* 獨特嘅 duk dak geh

initial *a.* 最初 juy chor

initial *n.* 第一個字母 dai yat gor
jee mow

initial *v.t* 草簽 cho teem

initiate *v.t.* 發起 fat hay

initiative *n.* 主動性 ju dung sing

inject *v.t.* 注射 ju she

injection *n.* 打針 da jam

injudicious *a.* 不當 bat dorng

injunction *n.* 禁制令 gam jay ling

injure *v.t.* 傷害 seurng hoy

injurious *a.* 有害 yow hoy

injury *n.* 傷 seurng

injustice *n.* 唔公正 hm gung jing

ink *n.* 墨 mak

inkling *n.* 略知 leurk jee

inland *a.* 陸地 luk day

inland *adv.* 陸地 luk day

in-laws *n.* 姻親 yan tan

inmate *n.* 同住者 tung ju jeh

inmost *a.* 內心深處 loy sam sam
chu

inn *n.* 細旅館 say luy gwun

innate *a.* 天生嘅 teen sang geh

inner *a.* 裡面嘅 luy meen geh

innermost *a.* 內心深處 loy sam
sam chu

innings *n.* 局 guk

innocence *n.* 天真 teen jan

innocent *a.* 無辜 mow gu

innovate *v.t.* 引入 yan yap

innovation *n.* 新思想 san see
seurng

innovator *n.* 創新者 chorng san
jeh

innumerable *a.* 無數嘅 mow sow
geh

inoculate *v.t.* 打預防針 da yu
forng jam

inoculation *n.* 預防接種 yu forng
jeem jung

inoperative *a.* 無效 mow hao

inopportune *a.* 唔合時 hm hap
see

input *n.* 投入 tow yap

inquest *n.* 審訊 sam sun

inquire *v.t.* 打聽 da ting

inquiry *n.* 詢問 sun man

inquisition *n.* 盤問 pwun man

inquisitive *a.* 八卦 bat gwa

insane *a.* 癡線 tee seen

insanity *n.* 精神病 jing san beng

insatiable *a.* 唔知足嘅 hm jee
juk geh

inscribe *v.t.* 提 tay

inscription *n.* 題字 tan jee

insect *n.* 昆蟲 kwan chung

insecticide *n.* 殺蟲劑 sat chung
jay

insecure *a.* 唔安全 hm on choon

insecurity *n.* 危險 ngay heem

insensibility *n.* 不省人事 bat
sing yan see

insensible *a.* 無反應 mow fan
ying

inseparable *a.* 分唔開 fan hm
hoy

insert *v.t.* 插 tap

insertion *n.* 插入 tap yap

inside *n.* 內側 loy jak
inside *prep.* 入邊 yap been
inside *a* 入邊 yap been
inside *adv.* 入邊 yap been
insight *n.* 瞭解 liew gai
insignificance *n.* 唔重要 hm jung yiew
insignificant *a.* 唔重要 hm jung yiew
insincere *a.* 唔誠實 hm sing sat
insincerity *n.* 虛偽 huy ngay
insinuate *v.t.* 暗示 am see
insinuation *n.* 影射 ying she
insipid *a.* 無味 mow may
insipidity *n.* 無味 mow may
insist *v.t.* 堅持 geen tee
insistence *n.* 堅持 geen tee
insistent *a.* 堅決 geen koot
insolence *n.* 無禮 mow lay
insolent *a.* 無禮 mow lay
insoluble *n.* 唔溶 hm yung
insolvency *n.* 破產 por tan
insolvent *a.* 無力還 mow lik wan
inspect *v.t.* 視察 see tat
inspection *n.* 檢查 geem ta
inspector *n.* 檢察官 geem tat gwun
inspiration *n.* 靈感 ling gam
inspire *v.t.* 啓發 kay fat
instability *n.* 唔穩定性 hm wan ding sing
install *v.t.* 安裝 on jorng
installation *n.* 安裝 on jorng
instalment *n.* 一期付款 yat kay fu fwun
instance *n.* 例子 lay jee
instant *n.* 一刻 yat hak
instant *a.* 即刻 jik hak
instantaneous *a.* 立即 lap jik
instantly *adv.* 即刻 jik hak
instigate *v.t.* 煽動 seen dung
instigation *n.* 煽動 seen dung

instil *v.t.* 慢慢灌輸 man man gwun shu
instinct *n.* 直覺 jik gok
instinctive *a.* 直覺嘅 jik gok geh
institute *n.* 機構 gey gow
institution *n.* 機構 gey gow
instruct *v.t.* 指示 jee see
instruction *n.* 指示 jee see
instructor *n.* 教練 gao leen
instrument *n.* 樂器 ok hay
instrumental *a.* 樂器演奏 ok hay yeen jow
instrumentalist *n.* 樂器家 ok hay ga
insubordinate *a.* 唔順從嘅 hm sun chung geh
insubordination *n.* 犯上 dan seurng
insufficient *a.* 唔夠 hm gow
insular *a.* 保守 bo sow
insularity *n.* 孤立 gu lap
insulate *v.t.* 隔熱 gak yeet
insulation *n.* 隔離 gak lay
insulator *n.* 緣絕物 yoon joot mat
insult *n.* 侮辱 mow yuk
insult *v.t.* 侮辱 mow yuk
insupportable *a.* 難以接收 lan yee jeep sow
insurance *n.* 保險 bo heem
insure *v.t.* 投保 tow bo
insurgent *a.* 叛亂嘅 pwun loon geh
insurgent *n.* 作反者 jok fan jeh
insurmountable *a.* 克服唔到嘅 hak fuk hm dow geh
insurrection *n.* 叛亂 pwun loon
intact *a.* 完整 yoon jing
intangible *a.* 難以形容 lan yee ying yung
integral *a.* 必需嘅 beet suy geh
integrity *n.* 完整 yoon jing
intellect *n.* 智力 jee lik

intellectual *a.* 理智 lay jee
intellectual *n.* 知識分子 jee sik fan jee
intelligence *n.* 聰明才智 chung ming choy jee
intelligent *a.* 聰明 chung ming
intelligentsia *n.* 知識分子 jee sik fan jee
intelligible *a.* 易明嘅 yee ming geh
intend *v.t.* 打算 da shoon
intense *a.* 緊張 gan jeurng
intensify *v.t.* 加強 ga keurng
intensity *n.* 強度 keurng dow
intensive *a.* 密集嘅 mat jap geh
intent *n.* 目的 muk dik
intent *a.* 熱切 yeet teet
intention *n.* 目的 muk dik
intentional *a.* 故意 gu yee
intercept *v.t.* 截住 jeet ju
interception *n.* 攔截 lan jeet
interchange *n.* 交換 gao wun
interchange *v.* 交換 gao wun
intercourse *n.* 交流 gao low
interdependence *n.* 互相依賴 wu seurng yee lai
interdependent *a.* 互相依賴 wu seurng yee lai
interest *n.* 興趣 hing chuy
interested *a.* 有興趣 yow hing chuy
interesting *a.* 有興趣 yow hing chuy
interfere *v.i.* 干預 gorn yu
interference *n.* 干預 gorn yu
interim *n.* 間歇 gan keet
interior *a.* 室內嘅 sat loy geh
interior *n.* 室內 sat loy
interjection *n.* 感歎詞 gam tan tee
interlock *v.t.* 相連 seurng leen
interlude *n.* 間歇 gan keet

intermediary *n.* 中間人 jung gan yan
intermediate *a.* 中間嘅 jung gan geh
interminable *a.* 太長 tai cheurng
intermingle *v.t.* 混合 wan hap
intern *v.t.* 扣留 kow low
internal *a.* 內部嘅 loy bo geh
international *a.* 國際 gwok jay
interplay *n.* 互相影響 wu seurng ying heurng
interpret *v.t.* 翻譯 fan yik
interpreter *n.* 翻譯 fan yik
interrogate *v.t.* 審問 sam man
interrogation *n.* 審問 sam man
interrogative *a.* 提問 tay man
interrogative *n* 疑問詞 yee man tee
interrupt *v.t.* 插嘴 tap juy
interruption *n.* 打擾 da yiew
intersect *v.t.* 交叉 gao ta
intersection *n.* 交點 gao deem
interval *n.* 間隔 gan gak
intervene *v.i.* 介入 gai yap
intervention *n.* 介入 gai yap
interview *n.* 面試 meen see
interview *v.t.* 訪問 forng man
intestinal *a.* 腸嘅 cheurng geh
intestine *n.* 腸 cheurng
intimacy *n.* 親密 tan mat
intimate *a.* 密切 mat teet
intimate *v.t.* 暗示 am see
intimation *n.* 暗示 am see
intimidate *v.t.* 威脅 way heep
intimidation *n.* 恐嚇 hung hak
into *prep.* 入 yap
intolerable *a.* 頂唔順嘅 ding hm sun geh
intolerance *n.* 無法忍受 mo fat yan sow
intolerant *a.* 唔容忍 hm yung yan
intoxicant *n.* 酒類飲品 jow luy

yam ban
intoxicate *v.t.* 令人飲醉 ling yan
yam juy
intoxication *n.* 醉 juy
intransitive *a. (verb)* 不及物 bat
kap mat
interpid *a.* 勇敢 yung gam
intrepidity *n.* 大膽 dai dam
intricate *a.* 複雜 fuk jap
intrigue *v.t.* 激起興趣 gik hay
hing chuy
intrigue *n* 陰謀 yam mow
intrinsic *a.* 內在嘅 loy joy geh
introduce *v.t.* 介紹 gai siew
introduction *n.* 介紹 gai siew
introductory *a.* 初步嘅 chor bo
geh
introspect *v.i.* 反省 fan sing
introspection *n.* 反省 fan sing
intrude *v.t.* 闖入 chorng yap
intrusion *n.* 侵犯 tam fan
intuition *n.* 直覺 jik gok
intuitive *a.* 憑直覺嘅 pang jik gog
geh
invade *v.t.* 侵略 tam leurk
invalid *a.* 無效 mow hao
invalid *a.* 令人退股 ling yan tuy
gu
invalid *n* 病人 beng yan
invalidate *v.t.* 作廢 jok fay
invaluable *a.* 有用嘅 yow yung
geh
invasion *n.* 侵略 tam leurk
invective *n.* 咒 jow
invent *v.t.* 發明 fat ming
invention *n.* 發明 fat ming
inventive *a.* 有創意 yow chorng
yee
inventor *n.* 發明家 fat ming ga
invert *v.t.* 倒轉 dowjoon
invest *v.t.* 投資 tow jee
investigate *v.t.* 調查 tiew ta

investigation *n.* 調查 tiew ta
investment *n.* 投資 tow jee
invigilate *v.t.* 監考 gam hao
invigilation *n.* 監考 gam hao
invigilator *n.* 監考官 gam hao
gwun
invincible *a.* 無敵嘅 mow dik geh
inviolable *a.* 不可侵犯 bat hor
tam fan
invisible *a.* 隱形 yan ying
invitation *v.* 邀請 yiew ting
invite *v.t.* 邀請 yiew ting
invocation *n.* 祈禱 kay tow
invoice *n.* 單 dan
invoke *v.t.* 提及 tay kap
involve *v.t.* 關係到 gwan hay dow
inward *a.* 向內 heurng loy
inwards *adv.* 向內 heurng loy
irate *a.* 好嬲 how low
ire *n.* 憤怒 fan low
Irish *a.* 愛爾蘭嘅 ngoy yee lan
geh
Irish *n.* 愛爾蘭人 ngoy yee lan
yan
irksome *a.* 令人煩惱 ling yan fan
low
iron *n.* 燙斗 torng dow
iron *v.t.* 燙 torng
ironical *a.* 諷刺 fung tee
irony *n.* 反話 fan wah
irradiate *v.i.* 輻照 fuk jiew
irrational *a.* 唔合邏輯 hm hap
lor tap
irreconcilable *a.* 無法化解 mow
fat far gai
irrecoverable *a.* 無法恢復 wu
fat fwuy fuk
irrefutable *a.* 無可否認 mow hor
fow ying
irregular *a.* 唔規則 hm kway jak
irregularity *n.* 唔規則性 hm
kway jak sing

irrelevant *a.* 無關 mow gwan

irrespective *a.* 無關 mow gwan

irresponsible *a.* 不負責任 bat fu jak yam

irrigate *v.t.* 灌水 gwun suy

irrigation *n.* 灌溉 gwun koy

irritable *a.* 容易發嬲 yung yee fat low

irritant *a.* 好煩 ho fan

irritant *n.* 刺激唔 tee gik mat

irritate *v.t.* 煩 fan

irritation *n.* 過敏 gwor man

irruption *n.* 闖入 chorng yap

island *n.* 島 dow

isle *n.* 島 dow

isobar *n.* 等壓線 dang ngat seen

isolate *v.t.* 隔離 gak lay

isolation *n.* 隔絕 gak joot

issue *v.i.* 派 pai

issue *n.* 問題 man tay

it *pron.* 佢 kuy

Italian *a.* 義大利嘅 yee dai lay geh

Italian *n.* 義大利人 yee dai lay yan

italic *a.* 斜體 ter tay

italics *n.* 斜體字 ter tay jee

itch *n.* 癢 yeurng

itch *v.i.* 癢 yeurng

item *n.* 物件 mat geen

ivory *n.* 象牙 jeung ngar

ivy *n* 常春藤 seurng chun tang

J

jab *v.t.* 拮 gat

jabber *v.t.* 急 gap

jack *n.* 千斤頂 teen gan ding

jack *v.t.* 決定放棄 koot ding forng hay

jackal *n.* 豺狼 tai lorng

jacket *n.* 外套 ngoy tow

jade *n.* 玉 yuk

jail *n.* 監牢 garm low

jailer *n.* 獄卒 yuk jut

jam *n.* 果醬 gwor jeurng

jam *v.t.* 塞 sak

jar *n.* 樽 jun

jargon *n.* 專業用詞 joon yeep yung tee

jasmine, jessamine *n.* 茉莉花 mwut lay far

jaundice *n.* 黃疸 worng dan

jaundice *v.t.* 影響 ying heurng

javelin *n.* 標槍 biew cheurng

jaw *n.* 下顎 har ok

jay *n.* 松鴉 chung ngar

jealous *a.* 妒忌 dow gey

jealousy *n.* 妒忌 dow gey

jean *n.* 牛仔褲 ngow jay fu

jeer *v.i.* 嘲笑 jao siew

jelly *n.* 啫哩 jeh lay

jeopardize *v.t.* 損害 shoon hoy

jeopardy *n.* 危險 ngay heem

jerk *n.* 猛烈動作 mang leet dung jok

jerkin *n.* 坎肩 ham geen

jerky *a.* 震 jan

jersey *n.* 運動衫 wan dung sam

jest *n.* 笑話 siew wah

jest *v.i.* 講笑 gorng siew

jet *n.* 噴氣式飛機 pan hay sik fay gey

Jew *n.* 猶太人 yow tai yan

jewel *n.* 寶石 bo sek

jewel *v.t.* 用寶石裝飾 yung bo sek jorng sik

jeweller *n.* 珠寶商 ju bo seurng

jewellery *n.* 首飾 sow sik

jingle *n.* 丁噹聲 ding dorng seng

jingle *v.i.* 丁噹 ding dong

job *n.* 工 gung

jobber *n.* 股票經紀 gu piew ging gey

jobbery *n.* 假公濟私 gar gung jay see

jocular *a.* 幽默 yow mak

jog *v.t.* 慢跑 man pao

join *v.t.* 參加 tam ga

joiner *n.* 木工 muk gung

joint *n.* 關節 gwan jeet

jointly *adv.* 聯合地 loon hap day

joke *n.* 笑話 siew wah

joke *v.i.* 講笑 gorng siew

joker *n.* 鐘意講笑嘅人 jung yee gorng siew geh yan

jollity *n.* 歡樂 fwun lok

jolly *a.* 愉快 yu fai

jolt *n.* 震動 jan dung

jolt *v.t.* 震 jan

jostle *n.* 推開 tuy hoy

jostle *v.t.* 推開 tuy hoy

jot *n.* 一啲 yat dee

jot *v.t.* 寫低 seh day

journal *n.* 日記 yat gey

journalism *n.* 新聞業 san man yeep

journalist *n.* 記者 gey jeh

journey *n.* 旅程 luy ting

journey *v.i.* 去旅行 huy luy hang

jovial *a.* 樂觀 lok gwun

joviality *n.* 快活 fai wut

joy *n.* 喜悅 hay yoot

joyful, joyous *n.* 高興 gow hing

jubilant *a.* 開心 hoy sam

jubilation *n.* 歡騰 fwun tang

jubilee *n.* 五十週年紀念 hm sap jow leen gey leem

judge *n.* 法官 fat gwun

judge *v.i.* 判斷 pwun doon

judgement *n.* 判斷 pwun doon

judicature *n.* 司法 see fat

judicial *a.* 司法 see fat

judiciary *n.* 法官 fat gwun

judicious *a.* 有見地 yow geen day

jug *n.* 壺 wu

juggle *v.t.* 耍雜耍 sa jap sa

juggler *n.* 表演者 biew yeen jeh

juice *n* 汁 jap

juicy *a.* 多汁 dor jap

jumble *n.* 亂堆 loon duy

jumble *v.t.* 整亂 jing loon

jump *n.* 跳 tiew

jump *v.i* 跳 tiew

junction *n.* 交叉路口 gao ta low ho

juncture *n.* 關頭 gwan tow

jungle *n.* 熱帶森林 yeet dai sam lam

junior *a.* 小學生嘅 siew hok sang geh

junior *n.* 小學生 siew hok sang

junk *n.* 垃圾 lap sap

jupiter *n.* 木星 muk sing

jurisdiction *n.* 司法權 see fat koon

jurisprudence *n.* 法律學 fat lut hok

jurist *n.* 法律家 fat lut ga

juror *n.* 陪審員 pwuy sam yoon

jury *n.* 陪審團 pwuy sam toon

juryman *n.* 陪審員 pwuy sam yoon

just *a.* 公正嘅 gung jing geh

just *adv.* 啱啱 ngarm ngarm

justice *n.* 公道 gung dow

justifiable *a.* 有理由嘅 yow lay yow geh

justification *n.* 正當理由 jing dorng lay yow

justify *v.t.* 證明 jing ming

justly *adv.* 公正 gung jing

jute *n.* 黃麻 worng ma

juvenile *a.* 幼稚嘅 yow jee geh

K

keen *a.* 熱心 yeet sam
keenness *n.* 熱情 yeet ting
keep *v.t.* 保管 bo gwun
keeper *n.* 保管人 bo gwun yan
keepsake *n.* 紀念品 gey leem ban
kennel *n.* 狗屋 gow uk
kerchief *n.* 方頭巾 forng tow gan
kernel *n.* 核 wat
kerosene *n.* 煤油 mwuy yow
ketchup *n.* 茄汁 keh jap
kettle *n.* 水壺 suy wu
key *n.* 鎖匙 sor see
key *v.t* 輸入 shu yap
kick *n.* 踢 tek
kick *v.t.* 踢 tek
kid *n.* 細佬仔 say low jay
kidnap *v.t.* 拐 gwai
kidney *n.* 腎 san
kill *v.t.* 殺 sat
kill *n.* 殺 sat
kiln *n.* 窰 yiew
kin *n.* 親戚 tan tik
kind *n.* 種 jung
kind *a* 善良 seen leurng
kindergarten ; *n.* 幼稚園 yow jee yoon
kindle *v.t.* 激起 gik hay
kindly *adv.* 善良咁 seen leurng gam
king *n.* 國王 gwok worng
kingdom *n.* 王國 worng gwok
kinship *n.* 親屬關係 tan suk gwan hay
kiss *n.* 錫 sek
kiss *v.t.* 錫 sek
kit *n.* 裝備 jorng bay
kitchen *n.* 廚房 chu forng
kite *n.* 紙鷂 jee yiew
kith *n.* 親戚朋友 tan tik pang yow

kitten *n.* 細貓 say mao
knave *n.* 無賴 mow lai
knavery *n.* 狡猾 gao wat
knee *n.* 膝頭哥 sat tow gor
kneel *v.i.* 跪 gway
knife *n.* 刀 dow
knight *n.* 騎士 keh see
knight *v.t.* 封...為爵士 fung...way jeurk see
knit *v.t.* 織 jik
knock *v.t.* 敲 hao
knot *n.* 結 geet
knot *v.t.* 打結 da geet
know *v.t.* 知道 jee dow
knowledge *n.* 知識 jee sik

L

label *n.* 標籤 biew teem
label *v.t.* 貼標籤 teep biew teem
labial *a.* 唇音 sun yam
laboratory *n.* 實驗室 sat yeem sat
laborious *a.* 辛苦 san fu
labour *n.* 勞工 low gung
labour *v.i.* 努力做 low lik jow
laboured *a.* 辛苦 san fu
labourer *n.* 勞工 low gung
labyrinth *n.* 迷宮 may gung
lac, lakh *n* 蟲膠 chung gao
lace *n.* 花邊 far been
lace *v.t.* 穿鞋帶 choon hai dai
lacerate *v.t.* 鎅 gai
lachrymose *a.* 易喊 yee harm
lack *n.* 缺乏 koot fat
lack *v.t.* 唔夠 hm gow
lackey *n.* 跟班 gan ban
lacklustre *a.* 無趣味 mow chuy may
laconic *a.* 簡潔嘅 gan geet geh
lactate *v.i.* 哺乳 bo yu

lactometer *n.* 檢乳器 geem yu hay

lactose *n.* 乳糖 yu torng

lacuna *n.* 漏洞 low dung

lacy *a.* 蕾絲嘅 luy see geh

lad *n.* 男仔 larm jay

ladder *n.* 梯 tay

lade *v.t.* 裝載 jorng joy

ladle *n.* 湯殼 torng hok

ladle *v.t.* 不 bat

lady *n.* 女人 luy yan

lag *v.i.* 落後 lok how

laggard *n.* 遲鈍 tee dun

lagoon *n.* 環礁湖 wan jiew wu

lair *n.* 竇 dow

lake *n.* 湖 wu

lama *n.* 喇嘛 la ma

lamb *n.* 羔羊 gow yeurng

lambaste *v.t.* 毒打 duk da

lame *a.* 跛 bay

lame *v.t.* 整跛 jing bay

lament *v.i.* 失望 sat morng

lament *n* 悲歎 bay tan

lamentable *a.* 令人遺憾 ling yan way ham

lamentation *n.* 悲傷 bay seurng

lambkin *n.* 羊皮 yeurng pay

laminate *v.t.* 過塑 gwor sok

lamp *n.* 燈 dang

lampoon *n.* 諷刺文章 fung tee man jeurng

lampoon *v.t.* 諷刺 fung tee

lance *n.* 長矛 cheurng mao

lance *v.t.* 放膿 forng lung

lancer *n.* 槍騎兵 cheurng keh bing

lancet *a.* 柳葉刀 low yeep dow

land *n.* 地 day

land *v.i.* 降落 gorng lok

landing *n.* 降落 gorng lok

landscape *n.* 風景 fung ging

lane *n.* 小路 siew low

language *n.* 語言 yu yeen

languish *v.i.* 長期受苦 cheurng kay sow fu

lank *a.* 又高又瘦 yow gow yow sow

lantern *n.* 燈籠 dang lung

lap *n.* 一圈 yat hoon

lapse *v.i.* 衰弱 suy yeurk

lapse *n* 間隔時間 gan gak see gan

lard *n.* 豬油 ju yow

large *a.* 大 dai

largesse *n.* 贈款 jang fwun

lark *n.* 雲雀 wan jeurk

lascivious *a.* 淫蕩 yam dorng

lash *a.* 好 haow

lash *n* 鞭打 been da

lass *n.* 女仔 luy jay

last1 *a.* 最後 juy ho

last *adv.* 最後 juy ho

last *v.i.* 繼續 gey juk

last *n* 最後嘅人 juy ho geh yan

lastly *adv.* 最後 juy ho

lasting *a.* 繼續 gey juk

latch *n.* 插鎖 tap sor

late *a.* 晚年嘅 man leen geh

late *adv.* 遲 tee

lately 最近 juy gan

latent *a.* 潛伏 teem fuk

lath *n.* 板條 ban tiew

lathe *n.* 車床 cher chorng

lather *n.* 泡沫 pow mwut

latitude *n.* 緯度 way dow

latrine *n.* 坑廁 hang tee

latter *a.* 最後嘅 juy ho geh

lattice *n.* 格仔木架 gak jay muk ga

laud *v.t.* 讚 jan

laud *n* 讚揚 jan yeurng

laudable *a.* 值得讚 jik dak jan

laugh *n.* 笑 siew

laugh *v.i* 笑 siew

laughable *a.* 有趣嘅 yow chuy

geh

laughter n. 笑聲 siew seng

launch v.t. 發行 fat hang

launch n. 發射 fat seh

launder v.t. 洗燙 say torng

laundress n. 洗衣女工 say yee luy gung

laundry n. 洗衫 say sarm

laureate n. 獲獎者 wok jeurng jeh

laureate a. 值得獲獎 jik dak wok jeurng

laurel n 月桂樹 yoot gway shu

lava n. 熔岩 yung ngam

lavatory n. 洗手間 say sow gan

lavender n. 薰衣草 fan yee cho

lavish a. 過度 gwor dow

lavish v.t. 印象深刻 yan jeurng sam hak

law n. 法律 fat lut

lawful a. 合法 hap fat

lawless a. 目無法紀 muk mow fat gey

lawn n. 草地 cho day

lawyer n. 律師 lut see

lax a. 馬虎 mah fu

laxative n. 通便嘅 tung been geh

laxative a 瀉藥 ser yeurk

laxity n. 散漫 san man

lay v.t. 民歌 man gor

lay a. 鋪 pow

lay n 外行嘅 ngoy horng geh

layer n. 層 tang

layman n. 外行 ngoy horng

laze v.i. 偷懶 tow lan

laziness n. 懶散 lan san

lazy n. 懶 lan

lea n. 草原 cho yoon

leach v.t. 過濾 gwor luy

lead n. 領先 ling seen

lead v.t. 帶 dai

lead n. 鉛 yoon

leaden a. 沈悶 tam mwun

leader n. 領隊 ling duy

leadership n. 領導才能 ling dow choy lang

leaf n. 葉 yeep

leaflet n. 傳單 choon dan

leafy a. 多樹葉 dor shu yeep

league n. 聯盟 loon mang

leak n. 漏洞 low dung

leak v.i. 漏 low

leakage n. 漏 low

lean n. 瘦肉 sow yuk

lean v.i. 挨 ai

leap v.i. 跳 tiew

leap n 跳高 tiew gow

learn v.i. 學 hok

learned a. 學咗 hok jor

learner n. 學生 hok sang

learning n. 學習 hok jap

lease n. 租約 jow yeurk

lease v.t. 租用 jow yung

least a. 最少 juy siew

least adv. 至少 jee siew

leather n. 皮 pay

leave n. 離開 lay hoy

leave v.t. 走 jow

lecture n. 演講 yeen gorng

lecture v 講課 gorng for

lecturer n. 講師 gorng see

ledger n. 賬簿 jeurng bo

lee n. 庇護所 bay wu sor

leech n. 水蛭 suy jat

leek n. 西芹 say kan

left a. 左 jor

left n. 左 jor

leftist n 左派分子 jor pai fan jee

leg n. 腳 geurk

legacy n. 遺產 way tan

legal a. 合法嘅 hap fat geh

legality n. 合法性 hap fat sing

legalize v.t. 變合法 been hap fat

legend n. 傳奇 joon kay

legendary *a.* 傳說嘅 choon shoot geh

leghorn *n.* 力行雞 lik horng gey

legible *a.* 清楚 ting chor

legibly *adv.* 易讀 yee duk

legion *n.* 軍團 gwan toon

legionary *n.* 軍團 gwan toon

legislate *v.i.* 立法 lap fat

legislation *n.* 立法 lap fat

legislative *a.* 立法嘅 lap fat geh

legislator *n.* 立法委員 lap fat way yoon

legislature *n.* 立法機關 lap fat gey gwan

legitimacy *n.* 合法性 hap fat sing

legitimate *a.* 合情合理 hap ting hap lay

leisure *n.* 空閒 hung han

leisure *a* 休閒嘅 yow han geh

leisurely *a.* 休閒咁 yow han gam

leisurely *adv.* 慢慢咁 man man gam

lemon *n.* 檸檬 ling mung

lemonade *n.* 檸檬水 ling mung suy

lend *v.t.* 借 jeh

length *n.* 長度 cheurng dow

lengthen *v.t.* 加長 ga cheurng

lengthy *a.* 幾長 gey cheurng

lenience, leniency *n.* 寬大 fwun dai

lenient *a.* 寬容 fwun yung

lens *n.* 鏡片 geng peen

lentil *n.* 扁豆 been dow

Leo *n.* 獅子座 see jee jor

leonine *a* 獅子嘅 see jee geh

leopard *n.* 豹 pao

leper *n.* 痲瘋病患者 ma fung beng wan jeh

leprosy *n.* 痲瘋 ma fung

leprous *a.* 痲瘋嘅 ma fung geh

less *a.* 比較少 bay gao siew

less *n* 少數 siew sow

less *adv.* 比較少 bay gao siew

less *prep.* 扣除 kow chuy

lessee *n.* 租戶 jow wu

lessen *v.t* 變少 been siew

lesser *a.* 更少 gang siew

lesson *n.* 堂 torng

lest *conj.* 費事 fay see

let *v.t.* 畀 bay

lethal *a.* 致命 jee ming

lethargic *a.* 眼瞓 ngan fan

lethargy *n.* 無精打采 mow jing da choy

letter *n* 信 sun

level *n.* 級 kap

level *a* 平嘅 ping geh

level *v.t.* 變平 been ping

lever *n.* 控制桿 hung jay gorn

lever *v.t.* 撬動 giew dung

leverage *n.* 影響力 ying heurng lik

levity *n.* 輕佻 hing tiew

levy *v.t.* 徵收 jing sow

levy *n.* 稅款 suy fwun

lewd *a.* 猥瑣 wuy sor

lexicography *n.* 詞典編纂 tee deen peen mow

lexicon *n.* 詞彙 tee wuy

liability *n.* 責任 jak yam

liable *a.* 信得過嘅 sun dak gwor geh

liaison *n.* 聯繫 loon hay

liar *n.* 講大話嘅人 gorng dai wah geh yan

libel *n.* 誹謗 fay borng

libel *v.t.* 中傷 jung seurng

liberal *a.* 開明 hoy ming

liberalism *n.* 自由主義 jee yow ju yee

liberality *n.* 慷慨 horng koy

liberate *v.t.* 解放 gai forng

liberation *n.* 解放 gai forng

liberator n. 解放者 gai forng jeh

libertine n. 放蕩嘅人 forng dong geh yan

liberty n. 自由 jee yow

librarian n. 圖書館館長 tow shu gwun gwun jeurng

library n. 圖書館 tow shu gwun

licence n. 牌 pai

license v.t. 批准 pay jun

licensee n. 持牌人 tee pai yan

licentious a. 放蕩 forng dong

lick v.t.   lem

lick n 少量 siew leurng

lid n. 蓋 goy

lie v.i. 講大話 gorng dai wah

lie v.i 瞓 fan

lie n 大話 dai wah

lien n. 扣押權 kow ngat koon

lieu n. 代替 doy tay

lieutenant n. 上尉 seurng way

life n 生命 sang ming

lifeless a. 無生氣嘅 mow sang hay geh

lifelong a. 終身嘅 jung sang geh

lift n.   leep

lift v.t. 攞起 lor hay

light n. 光 gwong

light a 輕 heng

light v.t. 點火 deem for

lighten v.i. 減輕 garm heng

lighter n. 打火機 da for gey

lightly adv. 輕輕 heng heng

lightening n. 閃電 seem deen

lignite n. 褐煤 keet mwuy

like a. 似 tee

like n. 喜好 hay ho

like v.t. 鐘意 jung yee

like prep 似 tee

likelihood n. 可能性 hor lang sing

likely a. 幾有可能 gey yow hor lang

liken v.t. 比 bay

likeness n. 相似 seurng tee

likewise adv. 同樣地 tung yeurng day

liking n. 愛好 ngoy ho

lilac n. 丁香 ding heurng

lily n. 百合花 bak hap far

limb n. 肢 tee

limber v.t. 熱身 yeet san

limber n 柔軟 yow yoon

lime n. 青檸 teng ling

lime v.t 傻石灰 sa sek fwuy

lime n. 石灰 sek fwuy

limelight n. 公眾嘅注目 gung jung geh ju muk

limit n. 限制 han jay

limit v.t. 限制 han jay

limitation n. 限制 han jay

limited a. 有限嘅 yow han geh

limitless a. 無限嘅 mow han geh

line n. 線 seen

line v.t. 加層 ga tang

line v.t. 襯 tan

lineage n. 血統 hoot tung

linen n. 亞麻布 ngar mar bo

linger v.i. 徘徊 pwuy wuy

lingo n. 語言 yu yeen

lingua franca n. 通用語 tung yung yu

lingual a. 語言嘅 yu yeen geh

linguist n. 語言學家 yu yeen hok ga

linguistic a. 語言嘅 yu yeen geh

linguistics n. 語言學 yu yeen hok

lining n 內襯 loy tan

link n. 關連 gwan leen

link v.t 連接 leen jeep

linseed n. 亞麻子 ngar mar jee

lintel n. 門框 mwun kwang

lion n 獅子 see jee

lioness n. 母獅 mow see

lip n. 嘴唇 juy sun

liquefy *v.t.* 液化 yik far

liquid *a.* 液體嘅 yik tay geh

liquid *n* 液體 yik tay

liquidate *v.t.* 清盤 ting pwun

liquidation *n.* 清盤 ting pwun

liquor *n.* 酒 jow

lisp *v.t.* 口齒不清 ho tee bat ting

lisp *n* 黐脷根 tee lay gan

list *n.* 清單 ting dan

list *v.t.* 列單 leet dan

listen *v.i.* 聽 teng

listener *n.* 聽者 teng jeh

listless *a.* 無精打采 mow jing da choy

lists *n.* 競技場 ging gey cheurng

literacy *n.* 讀寫能力 duk ser lang lik

literal *a.* 字面意義 jee meen yee yi

literary *a.* 文學嘅 man hok geh

literate *a.* 有文化嘅 yow man far geh

literature *n.* 文學 man hok

litigant *n.* 當事人 dorng see yan

litigate *v.t.* 打官司 da gwun see

litigation *n.* 訴訟 sow jung

litre *n.* 公升 gung sing

litter *n.* 垃圾 lap sap

litter *v.t.* 拋垃圾 pao lap sap

litterateur *n.* 文學家 man hok ga

little *a.* 細 say

little *adv.* 少少 siew siew

little *n.* 少量 siew leurng

littoral *a.* 海岸 hoy ngon

liturgical *a.* 禮拜儀式嘅 lay bai yee sik geh

live *v.i.* 住 ju

live *a.* 生嘅 sang geh

livelihood *n.* 生計 sang gey

lively *a.* 有生氣 yow sang hey

liver *n.* 肝 gorn

livery *n.* 制服 jay fuk

living *a.* 生嘅 sang geh

living *n* 生計 sang gey

lizard *n.* 蜥蜴 sik yik

load *n.* 大堆 dai duy

load *v.t.* 裝 jorng

loadstar *n.* 北極星 bak gik sing

loadstone *n.* 磁石 tee sek

loaf *n.* 一條 yat tiew

loaf *v.i.* 遊手好閒 yow sow ho han

loafer *n.* 拖鞋 tor hai

loan *n.* 貸款 tai fwun

loan *v.t.* 借 jeh

loath *a.* 唔情願 hm ting yoon

loathe *v.t.* 憎 jang

loathsome *a.* 乞人憎 hat yan jang

lobby *n.* 前廳 teen teng

lobe *n.* 耳垂 yee chuy

lobster *n.* 龍蝦 lung har

local *a.* 附近嘅 fu gan geh

locale *n.* 現場 yeen cheurng

locality *n.* 地區 day kuy

localize *v.t.* 局部化 guk bo far

locate *v.t.* 搵出確定位置 wan chut kok ding way jee

location *n.* 地點 day deem

lock *n.* 鎖 sor

lock *v.t* 鎖 sor

lock *n* 頭髮 tow fat

locker *n.* 儲物櫃 chu mat gway

locket *n.* 盒式頸鏈 hap sik geng leen

locomotive *n.* 火車頭 for cher tow

locus *n.* 中心 jung sam

locust *n.* 蝗蟲 worng chung

locution *n.* 語言風格 yu yeen fung gak

lodge *n.* 小屋 siew uk

lodge *v.t.* 寄宿 gey suk

lodging *n.* 租嘅房 jow geh forng

loft *n.* 閣樓 gok low
lofty *a.* 高嘅 gow geh
log *n.* 木頭 muk tow
logarithm *n.* 對數 duy sow
loggerhead *n.* 蠢材 chun choy
logic *n.* 邏輯 lor tap
logical *a.* 合乎邏輯 fu hap lor tap
logician *n.* 邏輯專家 lor tap joon ga
loin *n.* 腰肉 yiew yuk
loiter *v.i.* 徘徊 pwuy wuy
loll *v.i.* 懶散咁坐 lan san gam chor
lollipop *n.* 糖仔棍 tong jay gwan
lone *a.* 單獨嘅 dan duk geh
loneliness *n.* 孤單 gu dan
lonely *a.* 孤單 gu dan
lonesome *a.* 寂寞 jik mok
long *a.* 長 cheurng
long *adv* 長期 cheurng kay
long *v.i* 渴望 hot morng
longevity *n.* 長命 cheurng meng
longing *n.* 渴望 hot morng
longitude *n.* 經度 ging dow
look *v.i* 睇 tay
look *n.* 風格 fung gak
loom *n* 織布機 jik bo gey
loom *v.i.* 逼近 bik kan
loop *n.* 圓圈 yoon hoon
loop-hole *n.* 罅 la
loose *a.* 鬆嘅 sung geh
loose *v.t.* 鬆開 sung hoy
loosen *v.t.* 鬆開 sung hoy
loot *n.* 戰利品 jeen lay ban
loot *v.i.* 打劫 da geep
lop *v.t.* 斬 jam
lop *n.* 跳蚤 tiew sat
lord *n.* 勳爵 fan jeurk
lordly *a.* 宏偉 wang way
lordship *n.* 貴族權利 gway juk koon lay
lore *n.* 傳說 choon shoot
lorry *n.* 大貨車 dai for cher

lose *v.t.* 輸 shu
loss *n.* 損失 shoon sat
lot *n.* 全部 choon bo
lot *n* 一批 yat pay
lotion *n.* 護膚液 wu fuk yik
lottery *n.* 六合彩 luk hap choy
lotus *n.* 蓮花 leen far
loud *a.* 嘈 ccho
lounge *v.i.* 懶散咁坐 lan san gam chor
lounge *n.* 等候室 dang ho sat
louse *n.* 蝨 sat
lovable *a.* 惹人愛 yeh yan ngoy
love *n* 愛情 ngoy ting
love *v.t.* 愛 ngoy
lovely *a.* 好靚 ho leng
lover *n.* 情人 ting yan
loving *a.* 愛緊 ngoy gan
low *a.* 低嘅 day geh
low *adv.* 低 day
low *v.i.* 整低 jing day
low *n.* 低點 day deem
lower *v.t.* 降低 gorng day
lowliness *n.* 卑微 bay may
lowly *a.* 無足輕重 mow juk heng chung
loyal *a.* 忠心 jung sam
loyalist *n.* 忠心嘅人 jung sam geh yan
loyalty *n.* 忠心 jung sam
lubricant *n.* 潤滑油 yun wat yow
lubricate *v.t.* 上油 seurng yow
lubrication *n.* 潤滑 yun wat
lucent *a.* 發光嘅 fat gworng geh
lucerne *n.* 紫苜蓿 jee muk suk
lucid *a.* 易明嘅 yee ming geh
lucidity *n.* 清晰度 ting sik dow
luck *n.* 運氣 wan hay
luckily *adv.* 好彩 how choy
luckless *a.* 唔好彩 hm ho choy
lucky *a.* 好彩 ho choy

lucrative *a.* 賺大錢嘅 jan dai teen geh

lucre *n.* 利益 lay yik

luggage *n.* 行李 hang lay

lukewarm *a.* 暖嘅 loon geh

lull *v.t.* 令人放鬆 ling yan forng sung

lull *n.* 間歇 gan keet

lullaby *n.* 搖籃曲 yiew lam kuk

luminary *n.* 專家 joon ga

luminous *a.* 發光嘅 fat gworng geh

lump *n.* 一嚿 yat gow

lump *v.t.* 將就 jeurng jow

lunacy *n.* 精神錯亂 jing san chor loon

lunar *a.* 月亮嘅 yoot leurng geh

lunatic *n.* 顛佬 deen low

lunatic *a.* 黐線嘅 tee seen geh

lunch *n.* 晏晝 ngan jow

lunch *v.i.* 食晏 sik ngan

lung *n* 肺 fay

lunge *n.* 撲 pok

lunge *v.i* 撲 pok

lurch *n.* 前傾 teen king

lurch *v.i.* 浪下浪下 lorng ha lorng ha

lure *n.* 吸引力 kap yan lik

lure *v.t.* 誘惑 yow wak

lurk *v.i.* 埋伏 mai fuk

luscious *a.* 甜美嘅 teem may geh

lush *a.* 豪華 ho wah

lust *n.* 強烈嘅慾望 keurng leet geh yuk morng

lustful *a.* 貪慾 tam yuk

lustre *n.* 光澤 gworng jak

lustrous *a.* 有光澤 yow gworng jak

lusty *a.* 強壯 keurng jorng

lute *n.* 琵琶 pay pa

luxuriance *n.* 繁茂 fan mow

luxuriant *a.* 豐盛 fung sing

luxurious *a.* 豪華 ho wah

luxury *n.* 奢侈 ter tee

lynch *v.t.* 私刑處死 see ying chu say

lyre *n.* 七弦琴 tat yoon kam

lyric *a.* 抒情嘅 shu ting geh

lyric *n.* 歌詞 gor tee

lyrical *a.* 抒情嘅 shu ting geh

lyricist *n.* 填詞人 teen tee yan

M

magical *a.* 魔幻 mor wan

magician *n.* 魔術師 mor sut see

magisterial *a.* 權威嘅 koon way geh

magistracy *n.* 治安官 jee on gwun

magistrate *n.* 地方官 day forng gwun

magnanimity *n.* 寬大 fwun dai

magnanimous *a.* 寬宏 fwun wang

magnate *n.* 權貴 koon gway

magnet *n.* 磁石 tee sek

magnetic *a.* 有磁力嘅 yow tee lik geh

magnetism *n.* 磁力 tee lik

magnificent *a.* 宏偉 wang way

magnify *v.t.* 放大 forng dai

magnitude *n.* 幅度 fuk dow

magpie *n.* 喜鵲 hay jeurk

mahogany *n.* 桃花木 tow far muk

mahout *n.* 象夫 jeurng fu

maid *n.* 女僕 luy buk

maiden *n.* 處女 chu luy

maiden *a* 首次嘅 sow tee geh

mail *n.* 郵件 yow geen

mail *v.t.* 寄 gey

mail *n* 郵遞 yow day
main *a* 主要嘅 ju yiew geh
main *n* 電源 deen yoon
mainly *adv.* 主要 ju yiew
mainstay *n.* 支柱 jee chu
maintain *v.t.* 維持 way tee
maintenance *n.* 維修 way sow
maize *n.* 粟米 suk may
majestic *a.* 雄偉 hung way
majesty *n.* 陛下 bay ha
major *a.* 主要嘅 ju yiew geh
major *n* 主修課程 ju sow for ting
majority *n.* 大部分 dai bo fan
make *v.t.* 整 jing
make *n* 牌子 pai jee
maker *n.* 製造者 jay jow jeh
mal adjustment *n.* 失調 sat tiew
mal administration *n.* 管理不善 gwun lay bat seen
malady *n.* 病 beng
malaria *n.* 瘧疾 yeurk jat
maladroit *a.* 輪盡 lun jun
malafide *a.* 唔誠實 hm sing sat
malafide *adv* 唔誠實 hm sing sat
malaise *n.* 唔舒服 hm shu fuk
malcontent *a.* 抱不平嘅 pow bat ping geh
malcontent *n* 反叛者 fan pwun jeh
male *a.* 男性嘅 larm sing geh
male *n* 男性 larm sing
malediction *n.* 詛咒 juy jow
malefactor *n.* 罪犯 juy fan
maleficent *a.* 作惡嘅 jok ok geh
malice *n.* 惡意 ok yee
malicious *a.* 惡毒嘅 ok duk geh
malign *v.t.* 誹謗 fay borng
malign *a* 有害嘅 yow hoy geh
malignancy *n.* 惡性 ok sing
malignant *a.* 惡性嘅 ok sing geh
malignity *n.* 惡意 ok yee
malleable *a.* 可塑嘅 hor sok geh

malmsey *n.* 馬姆齊甜酒 ma mow tay teem jow
malnutrition *n.* 營養不良 ying yeurng bat leurng
malpractice *n.* 不法行為 bat fat hang way
malt *n.* 麥芽 mak ngar
mal-treatment *n.* 虐待 yeurk doy
mamma *n.* 媽媽 ma ma
mammal *n.* 哺乳類動物 bo yu luy dung mat
mammary *a.* 乳房嘅 yu forng geh
mammon *n.* 財富 choy fu
mammoth *n.* 毛象 mo jeurng
mammoth *a* 龐大嘅 porng dai geh
man *n.* 男人 larm yan
man *v.t.* 操縱 cho jung
manage *v.t.* 管理 gwun lay
manageable *a.* 可以處理嘅 hor yee chu lay geh
management *n.* 管理 gwun lay
manager *n.* 經理 ging lay
managerial *a.* 經理嘅 ging lay geh
mandate *n.* 命令 ming ling
mandatory *a.* 規定嘅 kway ding geh
mane *n.* 獅鬣 see leep
manes *n.* 鬃毛 jung mow
manful *a.* 陰間嘅諸神 yam gan geh ju san
manganese *n.* 錳 mang
manger *n.* 馬槽 ma cho
mangle *v.t.* 嚴重損壞 yeem jung shoon wai
mango *n* 芒果 morng gwor
manhandle *v.t.* 拉扯 lai ter
manhole *n.* 出入孔 chut yap hung
manhood *n.* 男人 larm yan
mania *n* 狂熱 kworng yeet

maniac *n.* 顛佬 deen low

manicure *n.* 指甲護理 jee gam wu lay

manifest *a.* 明顯嘅 ming heen geh

manifest *v.t.* 表示 biew see

manifestation *n.* 顯示 heen see

manifesto *n.* 宣言 shoon yeen

manifold *a.* 好多嘅 ho dor geh

manipulate *v.t.* 操控 cho hung

manipulation *n.* 操作 cho jok

mankind *n.* 人類 yan luy

manlike *a.* 有男子氣概 yow lam jee hay koy

manliness *n* 男子氣概 larm jee hay koy

manly *a.* 強壯嘅 keurng jorng geh

manna *n.* 及時雨 kap see yu

mannequin *n.* 人體模型 yan tay mow ying

manner *n.* 禮貌 lay mao

mannerism *n.* 言行舉止 yeen han guy jee

mannerly *a.* 客氣嘅 hak hay geh

manoeuvre *n.* 策略 tak leurk

manoeuvre *v.i.* 移動 yee dung

manor *n.* 莊園宅第 jorng yoon jak day

manorial *a.* 莊園嘅 jorng yoon geh

mansion *n.* 豪宅 ho jak

mantel *n.* 壁爐架 bik low ga

mantle *n* 責任 jak yam

mantle *v.t* 覆蓋 fuk koy

manual *a.* 用手嘅 yung sow geh

manual *n* 說明書 shoot ming shu

manufacture *v.t.* 大量生產 dai leurng sang tan

manufacture *n* 大量製造 dai leurng jay jow

manufacturer *n* 製造商 jay jow seurng

manumission *n.* 解放 gai forng

manumit *v.t.* 解放奴隸 gai forng low day

manure *n.* 肥料 fay liew

manure *v.t.* 施肥 see fay

manuscript *n.* 手稿 sow go

many *a.* 好多 ho dor

map *n* 地圖 day tow

map *v.t.* 繪製地圖 kwuy jay day tow

mar *v.t.* 破壞 por wai

marathon *n.* 馬拉松 ma lai chung

maraud *v.i.* 搶劫 cheurng geep

marauder *n.* 搶掠者 cheurng leurk jeh

marble *n.* 雲石 wan sek

march *n* 齊步走 tay bo jow

March *n.* 三月 sam yoot

march *v.i* 遊行 yow hang

mare *n.* 母馬 mow ma

margarine *n.* 人造奶油 yan jow lai yow

margin *n.* 頁邊 yeep been

marginal *a.* 唔重要嘅 hm jung yiew geh

marigold *n.* 萬壽菊 man sow guk

marine *a.* 海嘅 hoy geh

mariner *n.* 水手 suy sow

marionette *n.* 牽線木偶 heen seen muk oh

marital *a.* 婚姻嘅 fan yan geh

maritime *a.* 海嘅 hoy geh

mark *n.* 痕 han

mark *v.t.* 畫記號 wak gey ho

marker *n.* 記號 gey ho

market *n* 街市 gai see

market *v.t* 推銷 tuy siew

marketable *a.* 暢銷嘅 cheurng siew geh

marksman *n.* 神槍手 san cheurng sow

marl *n.* 泥灰 lay fwuy

marmalade *n.* 橘子醬 gat jee jeurng

maroon *n.* 褐紅色 keet hung sik

maroon *a* 褐紅色嘅 keet hung geh

maroon *v.t* 困住 kwan ju

marriage *n.* 婚姻 fan yan

marriageable *a.* 適婚嘅 sik fan geh

marry *v.t.* 嫁 ga

Mars *n* 火星 for sing

marsh *n.* 濕地 sap day

marshal *n* 高級軍官 gow kap gwan gwun

marshal *v.t* 收集 sow jap

marshy *a.* 濕地嘅 sap day geh

marsupial *n.* 有袋類動物 yow doy luy dung mat

mart *n.* 貿易場所 mow yik cheurng sor

marten *n.* 貂 diew

martial *a.* 戰爭嘅 jeen jan geh

martinet *n.* 執法人 jap fat yan

martyr *n.* 烈士 leet see

martyrdom *n.* 殉職 sun jik

marvel *n.* 奇蹟 kay jik

marvel *v.i* 感到驚奇 gam dow ging kay

marvellous *a.* 好好嘅 ho ho geh

mascot *n.* 吉祥物 gat cheurng mat

masculine *a.* 男子漢嘅 larm jee hon geh

mash *n.* 薯仔泥 shu jay lay

mash *v.t* 整碎 jing suy

mask *n.* 面具 meen guy

mask *v.t.* 掩飾 yeem sik

mason *n.* 石匠 sek jeurng

masonry *n.* 磚石建築 joon sek geen juk

masquerade *n.* 掩飾 yeem sik

mass *n.* 一嚿 yat gow

mass *v.i* 聚集 juy jap

massacre *n.* 大屠殺 dai tow sat

massacre *v.t.* 屠殺 tow sat

massage *n.* 按摩 on mor

massage *v.t.* 按摩 on mor

masseur *n.* 按摩師 on mor see

massive *a.* 巨大嘅 guy dai geh

massy *a.* 沈重嘅 tam jung geh

mast *n.* 桅杆 ngay gorn

master *n.* 主人 ju yan

master *v.t.* 掌握 jeurng ak

masterly *a.* 技術精湛 gey sut jing jam

masterpiece *n.* 傑作 geet jok

mastery *n.* 精通 jing tung

masticate *v.t.* jiew

masturbate *v.i.* 手淫 sow yam

mat *n.* 細地氈 say day jeen

matador *n.* 鬥牛士 dow ngow see

match *n.* 比賽 bay choy

match *v.i.* 登對 dang duy

match *n* 火柴 for tai

matchless *a.* 無得比嘅 mow dak bay geh

mate *n.* 朋友 pang yow

mate *v.t.* 交配 gao pwuy

mate *n* 兄弟 hing day

material *a.* 物質嘅 mat jat geh

material *n* 質料 jat liew

materialism *n.* 物質主義 mat jat ju yee

materialize *v.t.* 實現 sat yeen

maternal *a.* 母親嘅 mow tan geh

maternity *n.* 懷孕 wai yan

mathematical *a.* 數學嘅 sow hok geh

mathematician *n.* 數學家 sow hok ga

mathematics *n* 數學 sow hok

matinee *n.* 午後場 hm ho cheurng

matriarch *n.* 女族長 luy juk jeurng

matricidal *a.* 弒母嘅 see mow geh
matricide *n.* 弒母罪 see mow juy
matriculate *v.t.* 正式錄取 jing sik luk chuy
matriculation *n.* 大學註冊 dai hok ju tak
matrimonial *a.* 婚姻嘅 fan yan geh
matrimony *n.* 婚姻 fan yin
matrix *n* 社會環境 ser wuy wan ging
matron *n.* 女護士長 luy wu see jeurng
matter *n.* 事 see
matter *v.i.* 緊要 gan yiew
mattock *n.* 鶴嘴鋤 hok juy chor
mattress *n.* 床褥 chorng yuk
mature *a.* 成熟嘅 sing suk geh
mature *v.i* 成熟 sing suk
maturity *n.* 成熟 sing suk
maudlin *a* 婆婆媽媽 por por ma ma
maul *n.* 大槌 dai chuy
maul *v.t* 打傷 da seurng
maulstick *n.* 腕杖 wun jeurng
maunder *v.t.* 徘徊 pwuy wuy
mausoleum *n.* 陵墓 ling mow
mawkish *a.* 婆婆媽媽 por por ma ma
maxilla *n.* 下顎 har ok
maxim *n.* 格言 gak yeen
maximize *v.t.* 放到最大 forng dow juy dai
maximum *a.* 最大限度 juy dai han dow
maximum *n* 最大限度 juy dai han dow
May *n.* 五月 hm yoot
may *v* 可能 hor lang
mayor *n.* 市長 see jeurng
maze *n.* 迷宮 may gung
me *pron.* 我 ngor

mead *n.* 蜂蜜酒 fung mat jow
meadow *n.* 草地 cho day
meagre *a.* 太少 tai siew
meal *n.* 一餐 yat tan
mealy *a.* 粉狀嘅 fan jorng geh
mean *a.* 衰 suy
mean *n.* 平均數 ping gwan sow
mean *v.t* 表示 biew see
meander *v.i.* 漫步 man bo
meaning *n.* 意思 yee see
meaningful *a.* 有意思 yow yee see
meaningless *a.* 無意思 mow yee see
meanness *n.* 卑鄙 bay pay
means *n* 方法 forng fat
meanwhile *adv.* 期間 kay gan
measles *n* 麻疹 ma tan
measurable *a.* 可以量度嘅 hor yee leurng dok geh
measure *n.* 措施 cho see
measure *v.t* 量度 leurng dok
measureless *a.* 無限嘅 mow han geh
measurement *n.* 長度 cheurng dow
meat *n.* 肉 yuk
mechanic *n.* 機械師 gey hai see
mechanic *a* 機械嘅 gey hai geh
mechanical *a.* 機械嘅 gey hai geh
mechanics *n.* 機械學 gey hai hok
mechanism *n.* 機械裝置 gey hai jorng jee
medal *n.* 獎牌 jeurng pai
medallist *n.* 獎牌獲得者 jeurng pai wok dak jeh
medieval *a.* 中世紀嘅 jung say gey geh
medieval *a.* 落後嘅 lok ho geh
median *a.* 中間嘅 jung gan geh
mediate *v.i.* 調停 tiew ting
mediation *n.* 調解 tiew gai

mediator *n.* 調停者 tiew ting jeh
medical *a.* 醫療嘅 yee liew geh
medicament *n.* 藥 yeurk
medicinal *a.* 藥嘅 yeurk geh
medicine *n.* 藥 yeurk
medico *n.* 醫生 yee sang
mediocre *a.* 普通嘅 pow tung ghe
mediocrity *n.* 普通 pow tung
meditate *v.t.* 冥想 ming seurng
meditation *n.* 冥想 ming seurng
meditative *a.* 深思嘅 sam see geh
medium *n* 形式 ying sik
medium *a* 中號 jung ho
meek *a.* 溫順嘅 wan sun geh
meet *n.* 運動會 wan dung wuy
meet *v.t.* 見 geen
meeting *n.* 會 wuy
megalith *n.* 巨石 guy sek
megalithic *a.* 巨石建造嘅 guy sek geen jow geh
megaphone *n.* 喇叭筒 la ba tung
melancholia *n.* 憂鬱症 yow wat jing
melancholic *a.* 憂鬱嘅 yow wat geh
melancholy *n.* 傷悲 seurng bay
melancholy *adj* 令人悲哀嘅 ling yan bay ngoy
melee *n.* 混亂 wan loon
meliorate *v.t.* 改善 goy seen
mellow *a.* 甘美嘅 gam may geh
melodious *a.* 動聽 dung ting
melodrama *n.* 情節劇 ting jeet kek
melodramatic *a.* 誇大嘅 kwa dai geh
melody *n.* 旋律 shoon lut
melon *n.* 瓜 gwa
melt *v.i.* 溶 yung
member *n.* 會員 wuy yoon

membership *n.* 會員身分 wuy yoon san fan
membrane *n.* 膜 mok
memento *n.* 紀念品 gey leem ban
memoir *n.* 回憶錄 wuy yik luk
memorable *a.* 難忘嘅 lan morng geh
memorandum *n* 備忘錄 bay morng luk
memorial *n.* 紀念碑 gey leem bay
memorial *a* 紀念嘅 gey leem geh
memory *n.* 記憶 gey yik
menace *n* 威脅 way heep
menace *v.t* 威脅到 way heep dow
mend *v.t.* 整 jing
mendacious *a.* 虛假 huy ga
menial *a.* 卑賤嘅 bay jeen geh
menial *n* 僕人 buk yan
meningitis *n.* 腦膜炎 low mok yeem
menopause *n.* 更年期 gang leen kay
menses *n.* 月經 yoot ging
menstrual *a.* 月經嘅 yoot ging geh
menstruation *n.* 經期 ging kay
mental *a.* 智力嘅 jee lik geh
mentality *n.* 心態 sam tai
mention *n.* 提及 tay kap
mention *v.t.* 提及 tay kap
mentor *n.* 導師 dow see
menu *n.* 餐牌 tan pai
mercantile *a.* 商業嘅 seurng yeep geh
mercenary *a.* 只係爲錢嘅 jee hay way teen geh
mercerize *v.t.* 絲光 see gworng
merchandise *n.* 推銷 tuy siew
merchant *n.* 商人 seurng yan
merciful *a.* 寬大嘅 fwun dai geh
merciless *adj.* 無情嘅 mow ting

geh

mercurial *a.* 變幻莫測 been wan mok tak

mercury *n.* 水銀 suy an

mercy *n.* 寬恕 fwun shu

mere *a.* 僅僅 gan gan

merge *v.t.* 合併 hap ping

merger *n.* 合併 hap ping

meridian *a.* 子午線 jee hm seen

merit *n.* 優點 yow deem

merit *v.t* 值得 jik dak

meritorious *a.* 值得讚嘅 jik dak jan geh

mermaid *n.* 美人魚 may yan yu

merman *n.* 雄人魚 hung yan yu

merriment *n.* 歡樂 fwun lok

merry *a* 愉快嘅 yu fai geh

mesh *n.* 網狀物 morng jorng mat

mesh *v.t* 吻合 man hao

mesmerism *n.* 催眠術 chuy meen sut

mesmerize *v.t.* 迷惑 may wak

mess *n.* 亂 loon

mess *v.i* 整亂 jing loon

message *n.* 訊息 sun sik

messenger *n.* 送信人呢 sung sun yan

messiah *n.* 救星 gow sing

Messrs *n.* 先生 seen sang

metabolism *n.* 新陳代謝 san tan doy jeh

metal *n.* 金屬 gam suk

metallic *a.* 金屬嘅 gam suk geh

metallurgy *n.* 治金學 jee gam hok

metamorphosis *n.* 變質 been jat

metaphor *n.* 暗喻 am yu

metaphysical *a.* 玄學嘅 yoon hok geh

metaphysics *n.* 玄學 yoon hok

mete *v.t* 責罰 jak fat

meteor *n.* 隕石 wan sek

meteoric *a.* 流星嘅 low sing geh

meteorologist *n.* 氣象學家 hay jeurng hok ga

meteorology *n.* 氣象學 hay jeurng hok

meter *n.* 計量器 gey leurng hay

method *n.* 方法 forng fat

methodical *a.* 有條理嘅 yow tiew lay geh

metre *n.* 米 may

metric *a.* 公制嘅 gung jay geh

metrical *a.* 格律嘅 gak lut geh

metropolis *n.* 首都 sow dow

metropolitan *a.* 大城市嘅 dai sing see ghe

metropolitan *n.* 大主教 dai ju gao

mettle *n.* 勇氣 yung hay

mettlesome *a.* 勇敢嘅 yung gam geh

mew *v.i.* 喵 miew

mew *n.* 貓叫聲 mao giew seng

mezzanine *n.* 夾樓層 gap low tang

mica *n.* 雲母 wan mow

microfilm *n.* 縮微膠卷 suk may gao gwun

micrology *n.* 微工藝學 may gung ngay hok

micrometer *n.* 千分尺 teen fan tek

microphone *n.* 咪 may

microscope *n.* 顯微鏡 heen may geng

microscopic *a.* 微細嘅 may say geh

microwave *n.* 微波爐 may bor low

mid *a.* 中間嘅 jung gan geh

midday *n.* 中午 jung hm

middle *a.* 中間嘅 jung gan geh

middle *n* 中間 jung gan

middleman *n.* 中間人 jung gan yan

middling *a.* 中等嘅 jung dang geh

midget *n.* 矮人 ngay yan

midland *n.* 中部地區 jung bo day kuy

midnight *n.* 午夜 hm yeh

mid-off *n.* 投球手左後 tow kow sow geh jor ho

mid-on *n.* 投球手嘅前右 tow kow sow geh teen yow

midriff *n.* 腹部 fuk bo

midst *n.* 中間 jung gan

midsummer *n.* 仲夏 jung ha

midwife *n.* 穩婆 wan por

might *n.* 力量 lik leurng

mighty *adj.* 大力嘅 dai lik geh

migraine *n.* 偏頭痛 peen tow tung

migrant *n.* 移民 yee man

migrate *v.i.* 移居 yee guy

migration *n.* 移居 yee guy

milch *a.* 有奶嘅 yow lai geh

mild *a.* 溫和嘅 wan wor geh

mildew *n.* 黴菌 may kwan

mile *n.* 英里 ying lay

mileage *n.* 英里數 ying lay sow

milestone *n.* 里程碑 lay ting bay

milieu *n.* 環境 wan ging

militant *a.* 好戰嘅 ho jeen geh

militant *n* 好戰嘅人 ho jeen geh yan

military *a.* 軍事嘅 gwan see geh

military *n* 軍隊 gwan duy

militate *v.i.* 影響 ying heurng

militia *n.* 民兵 man bing

milk *n.* 奶 lai

milk *v.t.* 揸奶 ja lai

milky *a.* 奶嘅 lai geh

mill *n.* 麵粉廠 meen fan chorng

mill *v.t.* 磨成粉 mor sing fan

millennium *n.* 千禧年 teen hay leen

miller *n.* 磨坊工人 mor forng gung yan

millet *n.* 粟 suk

milliner *n.* 女帽商 luy mow seurng

milliner *n.* 女帽設計師 luy mow teek gey see

millinery *n.* 女帽業 luy mow yeep

million *n.* 百萬 bak man

millionaire *n.* 百萬富翁 bak man fu yung

millipede *n.* 馬陸 ma luk

mime *n.* 啞劇表演 ngar kek biew yeen

mime *v.i* 用啞劇動作 yung ngar kek dung jok

mimesis *n.* 模仿 mow forng

mimic *a.* 模仿嘅 mow forng ghe

mimic *n* 識模仿嘅人 sik mow forng geh yan

mimic *v.t* 模仿 mow forng

mimicry *n* 模仿 mow forng

minaret *n.* 宣禮塔 shoon lay tap

mince *v.t.* 絞碎 gao suy

mind *n.* 頭腦 tow low

mind *v.t.* 介意 gai yee

mindful *a.* 考慮到 hao luy dow

mindless *a.* 盲目嘅 mang muk geh

mine *pron.* 我嘅 ngor geh

mine *n* 礦 kworng

miner *n.* 礦工 kworng gung

mineral *n.* 礦物質 kworng mat jat

mineral *a* 礦物質嘅 kworng mat jat geh

mineralogist *n.* 礦物學家 kworng mat hok ga

mineralogy *n.* 礦物學 kworng mat hok

mingle *v.t.* 混合 wan hap

miniature *n.* 微型畫 may ying

wah

miniature *a.* 小型嘅 siew ying geh

minim *n.* 半音符 bwun yan fu

minimal *a.* 最少嘅 juy siew geh

minimize *v.t.* 縮細 suk say

minimum *n.* 最低限度 juy day han dow

minimum *a* 最少嘅 juy siew geh

minion *n.* 下屬 har suk

minister *n.* 大臣 dai san

minister *v.i.* 服侍 fuk see

ministrant *a.* 服務嘅 fuk mow geh

ministry *n.* 政府部門 jing fu bo mun

mink *n.* 水貂 suy diew

minor *a.* 比較細嘅 bay gao say geh

minor *n* 未成年人 may sing leen yan

minority *n.* 少數 siew sow

minster *n.* 大教堂 dai gao tong

mint *n.* 薄荷 bok hor

mint *n* 鑄幣廠 ju bay chorng

mint *v.t.* 鑄造 ju jow

minus *prep.* 減除 garm chuy

minus *a* 負 fu

minus *n* 負號 fu ho

minuscule *a.* 好細嘅 ho say geh

minute *a.* 好細嘅 ho say geh

minute *n.* 分鐘 fan jung

minutely *adv.* 每分鐘嘅 mwuy fan jung geh

minx *n.* 狡猾嘅女仔 gao wat geh luy jay

miracle *n.* 奇蹟 kay jik

miraculous *a.* 神氣嘅 san kay geh

mirage *n.* 海市蜃樓 hoy see san low

mire *n.* 泥沼 lay jiew

mire *v.t.* 陷入 ham yap

mirror *n* 鏡 geng

mirror *v.t.* 反射 fan she

mirth *n.* 歡笑 fwun siew

mirthful *a.* 高興 gow hing

misadventure *n.* 不幸嘅遭遇 bat hang geh jow yu

misalliance *n.* 錯誤嘅結合 chor hm geh geet hap

misanthrope *n.* 厭世者 yeem say jeh

misapplication *n.* 濫用 larm yung

misapprehend *v.t.* 誤解 hm gai

misapprehension *n* 誤解 hm gai

misappropriate *v.t.* 私吞 see tun

misappropriation *n.* 落格 lok gak

misbehave *v.i.* 行文不端 hang way bat doon

misbehaviour *n.* 行爲不當 hang way bat dorng

misbelief *n.* 誤信 hm sun

miscalculate *v.t.* 算錯 shoon chor

miscalculation *n.* 誤算 hm shoon

miscall *v.t.* 叫錯 giew chor

miscarriage *n.* 小產 siew tan

miscarry *v.i.* 小產 siew tan

miscellaneous *a.* 各種各樣嘅 gok jung gok yeurng geh

miscellany *n.* 雜記 jap gey

mischance *n.* 不幸 bat hang

mischief *n* 惡作劇 ok jok kek

mischievous *a.* 搞鬼嘅 gao gway geh

misconceive *v.t.* 誤會 hm wuy

misconception *n.* 誤解 hm gai

misconduct *n.* 失職 sat jik

misconstrue *v.t.* 誤會 hm wuy

miscreant *n.* 不法之徒 bat fat jee tow

misdeed *n.* 惡行 ok hang

misdemeanour *n.* 行為不當 hang way bat dorng

misdirect *v.t.* 誤導 hm dow

misdirection *n.* 誤導 hm dow

miser *n.* 孤寒 gu horn

miserable *a.* 可憐 hor leen

miserly *a.* 孤寒嘅 gu horn geh

misery *n.* 痛苦 tung fu

misfire *v.i.* 唔起作用 hm hay jok yung

misfit *n.* 行為怪異嘅人 hang way gwai yee geh yan

misfortune *n.* 不幸 bat hang

misgive *v.t.* 令人擔心 ling yan dam sam

misgiving *n.* 疑慮 yee luy

misguide *v.t.* 誤入歧途 hm yap kay tow

mishap *n.* 不幸 bat hang

misjudge *v.t.* 睇錯 tay chor

mislead *v.t.* 誤導 hm dow

mismanagement *n.* 管理不善 gwun lay bat seen

mismatch *v.t.* 錯配 chor pwuy

misnomer *n.* 用詞不當 yung tee bat dorng

misplace *v.t.* 亂放 loon forng

misprint *n.* 印錯 yan chor

misprint *v.t.* 印錯 yan chor

misrepresent *v.t.* 歪曲 wai kuk

misrule *n.* 管治不當 gwun jee bat dorng

miss *n.* 小姐 siew jeh

miss *v.t.* 掛住 gwa ju

missile *n.* 導彈 dow dan

mission *n.* 任務 yam mow

missionary *n.* 傳教士 choon gao see

missis, missus *n..* 老婆 low por

missive *n.* 信 sun

mist *n.* 薄霧 bok mow

mistake *n.* 錯 chor

mistake *v.t.* 搞錯 gao chor

mister *n.* 先生 seen sang

mistletoe *n.* 槲寄生 huk gey sang

mistreat *v.t.* 虐待 yeurk doy

mistress *n.* 二奶 yee lai

mistrust *n.* 疑慮 yee luy

mistrust *v.t.* 唔信 hm sun

misty *a.* 多霧嘅 dor mow geh

misunderstand *v.t.* 誤會 hm wuy

misunderstanding *n.* 誤會 hm wuy

misuse *n.* 濫用 larm yung

misuse *v.t.* 濫用 larm yung

mite *n.* 蟎 mwun

mite *n* 可憐嘅細路 hor leen geh say low

mithridate *n.* 解藥 gai yeurk

mitigate *v.t.* 減輕 garm heng

mitigation *n.* 減輕 garm heng

mitre *n.* 牧冠 muk gwun

mitten *n.* 連指手套 leen jee sow tow

mix *v.i* 溝 kow

mixture *n.* 混合品 wan hap ban

moan *v.i.* 發牢騷 fat low sow

moan *n.* 牢騷 low sow

moat *n.* 護城河 wu sing hor

moat *v.t.* 減 wik

mob *n.* 暴民 bo man

mob *v.t.* 攻擊 gung gik

mobile *a.* 流動嘅 low dung geh

mobility *n.* 流動性 low dung sing

mobilize *v.t.* 調動 diew dung

mock *v.i.* 笑 siew

mock *adj* 虛假嘅 huy ga geh

mockery *n.* 笑柄 siew beng

modality *n.* 情態 ting tai

mode *n.* 方式 forng sik

model *n.* 模特兒 mo dak yee

model *v.t.* 展示 jeen see

moderate *a.* 適量嘅 sik leurng geh

moderate *v.t.* 緩和 wun wor
moderation *n.* 合理 hap lay
modern *a.* 現代嘅 yeen doy geh
modernity *n.* 現代性 yeen doy sing
modernize *v.t.* 現代化 yeen doy far
modest *a.* 謙虛 heem huy
modesty *n* 謙虛 heem huy
modicum *n.* 少量嘅 siew leurng geh
modification *n.* 更改 gang goy
modify *v.t.* 改 goy
modulate *v.t.* 調整 tiew jing
moil *v.i.* 忙 morng
moist *a.* 濕潤嘅 sap yun geh
moisten *v.t.* 整濕 jing sap
moisture *n.* 水分 suy fan
molar *n.* 大牙 dai ngar
molar *a* 大牙嘅 dai ngar geh
molasses *n* 糖漿 torng jeurng
mole *n.* 鼴鼠 yeem shu
molecular *a.* 分子嘅 fan jee geh
molecule *n.* 分子 fan jee
molest *v.t.* 性騷擾 sing sow yiew
molestation *n.* 性騷擾 sing sow yiew
molten *a.* 熔化嘅 yung far geh
moment *n.* 一刻 yat hak
momentary *a.* 一刻 yat hak
momentous *a.* 關鍵嘅 gwan geen geh
momentum *n.* 推動力 tuy dung lik
monarch *n.* 君主 gwan ju
monarchy *n.* 君主制 gwan ju gway
monastery *n.* 寺院 jee yoon
monasticism *n* 修道生活 sow dow sang wut
Monday *n.* 星期一 sing kay yat

monetary *a.* 錢銀嘅 teen ngan geh
money *n.* 錢 teen
monger *n.* 商人 seurng yan
mongoose *n.* 貓鼬 mao yow
mongrel *a* 雜種狗 jap jung gow
monitor *n.* 螢光幕 ying gworng mok
monitory *a.* 監察嘅 gam tat geh
monk *n.* 和尚 wor seurng
monkey *n.* 馬騮 mar low
monochromatic *a.* 單色嘅 dan sik geh
monocle *n.* 單片眼鏡 dan peen ngan geng
monocular *a.* 單眼嘅 dan ngan geh
monody *n.* 輓歌 wan gor
monogamy *n.* 一夫一妻制 yat fu yat tay jay
monogram *n.* 花押字 far ngat jee
monograph *n.* 專論 joon lun
monogynous *a.* 一妻制嘅 yat tay jay geh
monolatry *n.* 一神崇拜 yat san sung bai
monolith *n.* 巨石 guy sek
monologue *n.* 獨白 duk bak
monopolist *n.* 專營者 joon ying jeh
monopolize *v.t.* 獨佔 duk jeem
monopoly *n.* 獨家經營權 duk gar ging ying koon
monosyllable *n.* 單音節詞 dan yam jeet tee
monosyllabic *a.* 單音節嘅 dan yam jeet geh
monotheism *n.* 一神教 yat san gao
monotheist *n.* 一神教信徒 yat san gao sun tow

monotonous *a.* 單調嘅 dan diew geh

monotony *n* 單調 dan diew

monsoon *n.* 雨季 yu gway

monster *n.* 妖怪 yiew gwai

monstrous *a.* 嚇人嘅 hak yan geh

monostrous *n.* 長期單調 cheurng kay dan diew

month *n.* 月 yoot

monthly *a.* 每個月 mwuy gor yoot

monthly *adv* 每個月 mwuy gor yoot

monthly *n* 月刊 yoot hon

monument *n.* 歷史遺跡 lik see way jik

monumental *a.* 重要嘅 jung yiew geh

moo *v.i* 哞 mow

mood *n.* 心情 sam ting

moody *a.* 喜怒無常 hay low mow seurng

moon *n.* 月亮 yoot leurng

moor *n.* 荒野 forng yeh

moor *v.t* 停泊 ting bok

moorings *n.* 停船處 ting shoon chu

moot *n.* 爭論 jang lun

mop *n.* 地拖 day tor

mop *v.t.* 拖 tor

mope *v.i.* 悶悶不樂 mwun mwun bat lok

moral *a.* 道德嘅 dow dak geh

moral *n.* 道德 dow dak

morale *n.* 士氣 see hay

moralist *n.* 道德學家 dow dak hok ga

morality *n.* 道德 dow dak

moralize *v.t.* 訓話 fan wah

morbid *a.* 病態 beng tai

morbidity *n* 病態 beng tai

more *a.* 更多 gang dor

more *adv* 更多 gang dor

moreover *adv.* 而且 yee ter

morganatic *a.* 貴賤通婚嘅 gway jeen tung fan geh

morgue *n.* 殮房 leem forng

moribund *a.* 快頂唔住 fai ding hm ju

morning *n.* 上晝 seurng jow

moron *n.* 蠢材 chun choy

morose *a.* 悶悶不樂嘅 mwun mwun bat lok geh

morphia *n.* 嗎啡 ma feh

morrow *n.* 聽日 ting yat

morsel *n.* 少量 siew leurng

mortal *a.* 會死嘅 wuy say geh

mortal *n* 普通人 pow tung yan

mortality *n.* 死亡率 say morng lut

mortar *v.t.* 灰泥 fwuy lay

mortgage *n.* 貸款 tai fwun

mortgage *v.t.* 抵押 day ngat

mortagagee *n.* 承按人 sing ngon yan

mortgagor *n.* 抵押人 day ngat yan

mortify *v.t.* 難堪 lan ham

mortuary *n.* 殮房 leem forng

mosaic *n.* 馬賽克 ma choy hak

mosque *n.* 清真寺 ting jan jee

mosquito *n.* 蚊 man

moss *n.* 苔蘚 toy seen

most *pron.* 最 juy

most *adv.* 最多 juy dor

most *n* 最多 juy dor

mote *n.* 塵 tan

motel *n.* 旅館 luy gwun

moth *n.* 飛蛾 fay ngor

mother *n* 母親 mow tan

mother *v.t.* 照顧 jiew gu

motherhood *n.* 母性 mow sing

motherlike *a.* 似媽咪 tee ma mi

motherly *a.* 母性嘅 mow sing geh

motif *n.* 主題 ju tay
motion *n.* 動作 dong jok
motion *v.i.* 指示 jee see
motionless *a.* 郁都唔郁下 yuk dow hm yuk ha
motivate *v* 激勵 gik lay
motivation *n.* 推動 tuy dung
motive *n.* 動機 dung gey
motley *a.* 亂嘅 loon geh
motor *n.* 馬達 ma dat
motor *v.i.* 坐車 chor cher
motorist *n.* 駕駛者 ga say jeh
mottle *n.* 斑點 ban deem
motto *n.* 格言 gak yeen
mould *n.* 模具 mow guy
mould *v.t.* 塑造 sok jow
mould *n* 風格 fung gak
mould *n* 黴菌 may kwan
mouldy *a.* 發毛 fat mow
moult *v.i.* 蛻毛 tuy mow
mound *n.* 一堆 yat duy
mount *n.* 山 san
mount *v.t.* 裝 jorng
mount *n* 上馬 seurng ma
mountain *n.* 山 san
mountaineer *n.* 登山家 dang san ga
mountainous *a.* 多山 dor san
mourn *v.i.* 哀悼 oy diew
mourner *n.* 送葬者 sung jorng jeh
mournful *a* 憂傷嘅 yow seurng geh
mourning *n.* 哀悼 oy diew
mouse *n.* 老鼠 low shu
moustache *n.* 鬍鬚 wu sow
mouth *n.* 嘴 juy
mouth *v.t.* 無聲咁講 mow seng gam gorng
mouthful *n.* 成口 sing ho
movable *a.* 可以郁嘅 hor yee yuk geh
movables *n.* 動產 dung tan

move *n.* 搬 bwun
move *v.t.* 郁 yuk
movement *n.* 動作 dung jok
mover *n.* 搬運工 bwun wan gung
movies *n.* 電影 deen ying
mow *v.t.* 割草 got cho
much *a* 幾多 gey dor
much *adv* 更加 gang ga
mucilage *n.* 膠水 gao suy
muck *n.* 糞便 fan been
mucous *a.* 分泌液嘅 fan bay yik geh
mucus *n.* 黏液 leem yik
mud *n.* 泥 lay
muddle *n.* 混亂 wan loon
muddle *v.t.* 搞亂 gao loon
muffle *v.t.* 整細 jing say
muffler *n.* 頸巾 geng gan
mug *n.* 杯 bwuy
muggy *a.* 悶熱 mwun yeet
mulatto *n.* 黑白混血兒 hak bak wan hoot yee
mulberry *n.* 桑樹 sorng shu
mule *n.* 騾子 lor jee
mulish *a.* 騾似嘅 lor jee geh
mull *n.* 思考 see hao
mull *v.t.* 反覆思考 fan fuk see hao
mullah *n.* 毛拉 mo lai
mullion *n.* 豎框 shu kwang
multifarious *a.* 各種各樣嘅 gok jung gok yeurng geh
multiform *a* 多種形式嘅 dor jung ying sik geh
multilateral *a.* 多國嘅 dor gwok geh
multiparous *a.* 多胞胎 dor bao toy
multiple *a.* 多樣嘅 dor yeurng geh
multiple *n* 倍數 pwuy sow
multiped *n.* 多足動物 dor juk dung mat

multiplex *a.* 戲院 hay yoon

multiplicand *n.* 被乘數 bay sing sow

multiplication *n.* 乘數 sing sow

multiplicity *n.* 多重性 dor chung sing

multiply *v.t.* 乘 sing

multitude *n.* 眾多 jung dor

mum *a.* 保持沈默 bo tee tam mak

mum *n* 媽 ma

mumble *v.i.* 口齒不清 ho tee bat ting

mummer *n.* 啞劇演員 ngar kek yeen yoon

mummy *n.* 媽咪 ma mi

mummy *n* 木乃伊 muk lai yee

mumps *n.* 痄腮 ja soy

munch *v.t.* jiew

mundane *a.* 平凡嘅 ping fan geh

municipal *a.* 市政嘅 see jing geh

municipality *n.* 自治區 ji jee kuy

munificent *a.* 慷慨嘅 horng koy geh

muniment *n.* 證書 jing shu

munitions *n.* 軍火 gwan for

mural *a.* 牆嘅 cheurng geh

mural *n.* 壁畫 bik wah

murder *n.* 謀殺 mow sat

murder *v.t.* 謀殺 mow sat

murderer *n.* 殺人兇手 sat yan hung sow

murderous *a.* 兇殘嘅 hung tan geh

murmur *n.* 喃喃聲 am am seng

murmur *v.t.* 發牢騷 fat low sow

muscle *n.* 肌肉 gey yuk

muscovite *n.* 白雲母 bak wan mow

muscular *a.* 強壯嘅 keurng jorng geh

muse *v.i.* 冥想 ming seurng

muse *n* 靈感 ling gam

museum *n.* 博物館 bok mat gwun

mush *n.* 糊狀物 wu jorng mat

mushroom *n.* 蘑菇 mor gu

music *n.* 音樂 yam ok

musical *a.* 音樂嘅 yan ok geh

musician *n.* 音樂家 yam ok ga

musk *n.* 麝香 ser heurng

musket *n.* 火槍 for cheurng

musketeer *n.* 火槍手 for cheurng sow

muslin *n.* 平紋細布 ping man say bo

must *v.* 一定 yat ding

must *n.* 必需 beet suy

must *n* 一定 yat ding

mustache *n.* 鬚鬚 wu sow

mustang *n.* 北美野馬 bak may yeh ma

mustard *n.* 芥末 gai mwut

muster *v.t.* 聚集 juy jap

muster *n* 聚集嘅人群 juy jap geh yan kwun

musty *a.* 有霉味嘅 yow mwuy may geh

mutation *n.* 變化 been far

mutative *a.* 變化嘅 been far geh

mute *a.* 無聲嘅 mow seng geh

mute *n.* 啞巴 ngar ba

mutilate *v.t.* 變殘廢 been tan fay

mutilation *n.* 肢體殘缺 jee tay tan koot

mutinous *a.* 背叛 bwuy bwun

mutiny *n.* 暴動 bo dung

mutiny *v. i* 反抗 fan korng

mutter *v.i.* 發牢騷 fat low sow

mutton *n.* 羊肉 yeurng yuk

mutual *a.* 共同嘅 gung tung geh

muzzle *n.* 口鼻 ho bay

muzzle *v.t* 壓制 ngat jay

my *a.* 我嘅 ngor geh

myalgia *n.* 肌肉痛 gey yuk tung

myopia *n.* 近視 gan see

myopic a. 近視嘅 gan see geh
myosis n. 縮瞳症 suk tung jing
myriad n. 無數 mow sow
myriad a 無數嘅 mow sow geh
myrrh n. 沒藥 mwut yeurk
myrtle n. 香桃木 heurng tow muk
myself pron. 我自己 ngor jee gey
mysterious a. 神祕嘅 san bay geh
mystery n. 迷 may
mystic a. 神祕嘅 san bay geh
mystic n 神祕主義者 san bay ju yee jeh
mysticism n. 神主義意 san bay ju yee
mystify v.t. 故弄玄虛 gu lung yoon huy
myth n. 神話 san wah
mythical a. 神話嘅 san wah geh
mythological a. 神話嘅 san wah geh
mythology n. 神話 san wah

N

nab v.t. 捉住 juk ju
nabob n. 穆斯林官員 muk see lam gwun yoon
nadir n. 最低點 juy day deem
nag n. 馬 ma
nag v.t. 哦 or
nail n. 釘 deng
nail v.t. 釘 deng
naive a. 天真 teen jan
naivete n. 天真 teen jan
naivety n. 天真 teen jan
naked a. 裸體 lor tay
name n. 名 meng
name v.t. 改名 goy meng
namely adv. 就係 jow hay

namesake n. 同名人 tong meng yan
nap v.i. 瞓晏覺 fan ngan gao
nap n. 晏覺 ngan gao
nap n 短絨毛 doon yung mow
nape n. 後頸 how geng
napkin n. 餐巾 tan gan
narcissism n. 自憐 jee loon
narcissus n 水仙花 suy seen far
narcosis n. 麻醉 ma juy
narcotic n. 鎮靜劑 jan jing jay
narrate v.t. 講述 gorng sut
narration n. 旁白 porng bak
narrative n. 描述 miew sut
narrative a. 描述嘅 miew sut geh
narrator n. 旁白者 porng ban jeh
narrow a. 窄 jak
narrow v.t. 縮窄 suk jak
nasal a. 鼻嘅 bay geh
nasal n 鼻音 bay yam
nascent a. 初期嘅 chor kay geh
nasty a. 衰格 suy gak
natal a. 出生嘅 chut sang geh
natant a. 漂嘅 piew geh
nation n. 國家 gwok ga
national a. 全國嘅 choon gwok geh
nationalism n. 國家主義 gwok ga ju yee
nationalist n. 民族主義者 man juk ju yee jeh
nationality n. 國籍 gwok jik
nationalization n. 國有化 gwok yow far
nationalize v.t. 國有化 gwok yow far
native a. 本地嘅 bwun day geh
native n 本地人 bwun day yan
nativity n. 誕生 dan sang
natural a. 天然嘅 teen yeen geh
naturalist n. 博物學家 bok mat hok ga

naturalize v.t. 入籍 yap jik

naturally adv. 自然咁 jee yeen gam

nature n. 大自然 dai jee yeen

naughty a. 拽 yay

nausea n. 作嘔 jok oh

nautic(al) a. 船嘅 shoon geh

naval a. 海軍嘅 hoy gwan geh

nave n. 中殿 jung deen

navigable a. 可以通航嘅 hor yi tung horng geh

navigate v.i. 確定位置 kok ding way jee

navigation n. 導航 dow horng

navigator n. 導航儀 dow horng yee

navy n. 海軍 hoy gwan

nay adv. 唔係 hm hay

neap a. 小潮 siew tiew

near a. 近 kan

near prep. 附近 fu gan

near adv. 附近 fu gan

near v.i. 接近 jeep gan

nearly adv. 差唔多 ta hm dor

neat a. 整齊 jing tay

nebula n. 星雲 sing wan

necessary n. 必要 beet yiew

necessary a 需要嘅 suy yiew geh

necessitate v.t. 變成必要嘅 been sing bat yiew geh

necessity n. 必要 beet yiew

neck n. 頸 geng

necklace n. 頸鏈 geng leen

necklet n. 頸鏈 geng leen

necromancer n. 巫婆 mow por

necropolis n. 問米婆 man may por

nectar n. 花蜜 far mat

need n. 需要 suy yiew

need v.t. 要 yiew

needful a. 需要嘅 suy yiew geh

needle n. 針 jam

needless a. 唔需要嘅 hm suy yiew geh

needs adv. 需要 suy yiew

needy a. 窮嘅 kung geh

nefandous a. 唔似樣 hm tee yeurng

nefarious a. 惡毒 ok duk

negation n. 反面 fan meen

negative a. 有害嘅 yow hoy geh

negative n. 負面 fu meen

negative v.t. 拒絕 kuy joot

neglect v.t. 忽略 fat leurk

neglect n 忽略 fat leurk

negligence n. 疏忽 sor fat

negligent a. 疏忽嘅 sor fat geh

negligible a. 微不足道 may bat juk dow

negotiable a. 有得傾嘅 yow dak king geh

negotiate v.t. 傾 king

nagotiation n. 討論 tow lun

negotiator n. 談判人 tam pwun yan

negress n. 女黑人 luy hak yan

negro n. 黑人 hak yan

neigh v.i. 馬叫聲 ma giew seng

neigh n. 馬叫聲 ma giew seng

neighbour n. 隔籬鄰舍 gak lay lun she

neighbourhood n. 附近 fu gan

neighbourly a. 住附近嘅 ju fu gan geh

neither conj. 亦都唔 yik dow hm

nemesis n. 報應 bo ying

neolithic a. 新石器時代嘅 san sek hay see doy geh

neon n. 氖氣 lai hay

nephew n. 姪仔 jat jay

nepotism n. 裙帶關係 kwan dai gwan hay

Neptune n. 海王星 hoy worng sing

nerve *n.* 神經 san ging
nerveless *a.* 麻木嘅 ma muk geh
nervous *a.* 緊張 gan jeurng
nescience *n.* 無知 mow jee
nest *n.* 雀巢 jeurk chao
nest *v.t.* 築巢 juk chao
nether *a.* 嘅下面 geh ha meen
nestle *v.i.* 抱 pow
nestling *n.* 未離巢嘅雀 may lay chao geh jeurk
net *n.* 網 morng
net *v.t.* 淨賺 jing jan
net *a* 淨低嘅 jing day geh
net *v.t.* 落網 lok morng
nettle *n.* 蕁麻 tam ma
nettle *v.t.* 激嬲 gik low
network *n.* 網絡 morng lok
neurologist *n.* 神經科醫生 san ging for yee sang
neurology *n.* 神經學 san ging hok
neurosis *n.* 恐懼症 hung kuy jing
neuter *a.* 中性嘅 jung sing geh
neuter *n* 閹割 yeem got
neutral *a.* 中立嘅 jung lap geh
neutralize *v.t.* 變無效 been mow hao
neutron *n.* 中子 jung jee
never *adv.* 永遠都唔會 wing yoon dow hm wuy
nevertheless *conj.* 不過 bat gowr
new *a.* 新 san
news *n.* 新聞 san man
next *a.* 隔籬 gak lay
next *adv.* 跟住 gan ju
nib *n.* 筆尖 bat jeem
nibble *v.t.* 細細啖食 say say dam sik
nibble *n* 一細啖 yat say dam
nice *a.* 好 how
nicety *n.* 仔細 jee say

niche *n.* 地位 day way
nick *n.* 監獄 gam yuk
nickel *n.* 鎳 leep
nickname *n.* 花名 far meng
nickname *v.t.* 起花名 hay far meng
nicotine *n.* 尼古丁 lay gu ding
niece *n.* 姪女 jat luy
niggard *n.* 孤寒鬼 gu horn gway
niggardly *a.* 孤寒 gu horn
nigger *n.* 黑鬼 hak gway
nigh *adv.* 差唔多 char hm dor
nigh *prep.* 近 kan
night *n.* 夜晚 yeh man
nightingale *n.* 夜鶯 yeh ang
nightly *adv.* 每晚 mwuy man
nightmare *n.* 惡夢 ok mung
nightie *n.* 睡衣 suy yee
nihilism *n.* 虛無主義 huy mow ju yee
nil *n.* 零 ling
nimble *a.* 靈活 ling wut
nimbus *n.* 雨雲 yu wan
nine *n.* 九 gow
nineteen *n.* 十九 sap gow
nineteenth *a.* 第十九 day sap gow
ninetieth *a.* 第九十 day gow sap
ninth *a.* 第九 day gow
ninety *n.* 九十 gow sap
nip *v.t* 好快去下 how fai huy ha
nipple *n.* 乳頭 yu tow
nitrogen *n.* 氮氣 dam hay
no *a.* 唔係 hm hay
no *adv.* 唔係 hm hay
no *n* 唔係 hm hay
nobility *n.* 貴族 gway juk
noble *a.* 高貴嘅 gow gway geh
noble *n.* 貴族 gway juk
nobleman *n.* 貴族 gway juk
nobody *pron.* 無人 mow yan
nocturnal *.a.* 夜間活動嘅 yeh gan wut dung geh

nod *v.i.* 㞖頭 ngap tow

node *n.* 節點 jeet deem

noise *n.* 聲 seng

noisy *a.* 嘈 cho

nomad *n.* 遊牧民 yow muk man

nomadic *a.* 遊牧嘅 yow muk geh

nomenclature *n.* 命名法 ming ming fat

nominal *a.* 名義上嘅 ming yee seurng geh

nominate *v.t.* 推展 tuy jeen

nomination *n.* 推展 tuy jeen

nominee *n* 被提名人 bay tay ming yan

non-alignment *n.* 唔結盟嘅 hm geeng mang geh

nonchalance *n.* 漠不關心 mok bat gwan sam

nonchalant *a.* 冷靜嘅 lang jing geh

none *pron.* 一啲都無 yat dee dow mow

none *adv.* 一啲都無 yat dee dow mow

nonentity *n.* 無成就嘅人 mow sing jow geh yan

nonetheless *adv.* 就算係咁 jow shoon hai gam

nonpareil *a.* 無得比嘅 mow dak bay geh

nonpareil *n.* 極品 gik ban

nonplus *v.t.* 困擾 kwan yiew

nonsense *n.* 廢話 fay wah

nonsensical *a.* 荒謬嘅 forng mow geh

nook *n.* 角落 gok lok

noon *n.* 正午 jing hm

noose *n.* 繩套 sing tow

noose *v.t.* 捉 juk

nor *conj* 亦都唔 yik dow hm

norm *n.* 正常 jing seurng

norm *n.* 標準 biew jun

normal *a.* 正常 jing seurng

normalcy *n.* 正常 jing seurng

normalize *v.t.* 正常化 jing seurng far

north *n.* 北 bak

north *a* 北方嘅 bak forng geh

north *adv.* 向北 heurng bak

northerly *a.* 北方嘅 bak forng geh

northerly *n.* 北風 bak fung

northern *a.* 北方嘅 bak forng geh

nose *n.* 鼻哥 bay gor

nose *v.t* 聞 man

nosegay *n.* 一細紮花 yat say jat far

nosey *a.* 八卦 bat gwa

nosy *a.* 八卦 bat gwa

nostalgia *n.* 念舊 leem gow

nostril *n.* 鼻 bay

nostrum *n.* 祕方 bay forng

not *adv.* 唔係 hm hay

notability *n.* 知名度 jee ming dow

notable *a.* 值得注意嘅 jing dak ju yee geh

notary *n.* 公證人 gung jing yan

notation *n.* 符號 fu ho

notch *n.* 級 kap

note *n.* 字條 jee tiew

note *v.t.* 寫低 seh day

noteworthy *a.* 值得注意嘅 jik dak ju yee geh

nothing *n.* 無嘢 mow yeh

nothing *adv.* 無嘢 mow yeh

notice *n.* 通知 tung jee

notice *v.t.* 注意 ju yee

notification *n.* 通知 tung jee

notify *v.t.* 通知 tung jee

notion *n.* 信念 sun leem

notional *a.* 理論上 lay lun seurng

notoriety *n.* 惡名 ok ming

notorious *a.* 聲名狼藉嘅 sing ming lorng jik geh

notwithstanding *prep.* 雖然 suy yeen

notwithstanding *adv.* 就算係咁 jow shoon hai gam

notwithstanding *conj.* 不過 bat gwor

nought *n.* 零 ling

noun *n.* 名詞 ming tee

nourish *v.t.* 滋潤 jee yun

nourishment *n.* 營養品 ying yeurng ban

novel *a.* 新穎嘅 san wing geh

novel *n* 小說 siew shoot

novelette *n.* 中篇小說 jung peen siew shoot

novelist *n.* 小說家 siew shoot ga

novelty *n.* 新穎 san wing

November *n.* 十一月 sap yat yoot

novice *n.* 新手 san sow

now *adv.* 而家 yee ga

now *conj.* 既然 gey yeen

nowhere *adv.* 無埞 mow deng

noxious *a.* 有害嘅 yow hoy geh

nozzle *n.* 管口 gwun ho

nuance *n.* 細微差別 say may tar beet

nubile *a.* 性感嘅 sing gam geh

nuclear *a.* 原子能嘅 yoon jee lang geh

nucleus *n.* 原子核 yoon jee wat

nude *a.* 赤裸嘅 tek lor geh

nude` *n* 裸體 lor tay

nudity *n.* 裸體 lor tay

nudge *v.t.* 輕推 heng tuy

nugget *n.* 一細嚿 yat say gow

nuisance *n.* 麻煩事 ma fan see

null *a.* 無效嘅 mow hao geh

nullification *n.* 無效 mow hao

nullify *v.t.* 作廢 jok fay

numb *a.* 無感覺嘅 mo gam gok geh

number *n.* 號碼 ho ma

number *v.t.* 編號 peen ho

numberless *a.* 無數嘅 mow sow geh

numeral *a.* 數字 sow jee

numerator *n.* 分子 fan jee

numerical *a.* 數字嘅 sow jee geh

numerous *a.* 好多嘅 ho dor geh

nun *n.* 修女 sow luy

nunnery *n.* 尼姑庵 lay gu am

nuptial *a.* 婚禮嘅 fan lay geh

nuptials *n.* 婚禮 fan lay

nurse *n.* 護士 wu see

nurse *v.t* 照顧 jiew gu

nursery *n.* 幼稚園 yow jee yoon

nurture *n.* 栽培 joy pwuy

nurture *v.t.* 栽培 joy pwuy

nut *n* 果仁 gwor yan

nutrition *n.* 營養 ying yeurng

nutritious *a.* 有營養 yow ying yeurng

nutritive *a.* 營養嘅 ying yeurng geh

nuzzle *v.* 用鼻摸 yung bay mor

nylon *n.* 尼龍 lay lung

nymph *n.* 仙女 seen luy

O

oak *n.* 橡樹 jeurng shu

oar *n.* 船槳 shoon jeurng

oarsman *n.* 撐艇手 tang teng sow

oasis *n.* 沙漠嘅綠洲 sa mok geh luk jow

oat *n.* 燕麥 yeen mak

oath *n.* 誓言 say yeen

obduracy *n.* 硬頸 ngan geng

obdurate *a.* 硬頸嘅 ngan geng geh

obedience *n.* 服從 fuk chung

obedient *a.* 聽話嘅 teng wah geh

obeisance *n.* 敬仰 ging yeurng

obesity *n.* 肥胖症 fay bwun jing

obey *v.t.* 遵從 jun chung

obituary *a.* 訃告 fu gow

object *n.* 物體 mat tay

object *v.t.* 反對 fan duy

objection *n.* 反對 fan duy

objectionable *a.* 令人反感嘅 ling yan fan gam geh

objective *n.* 目的 muk dik

objective *a.* 客觀嘅 hak gwun geh

oblation *n.* 祭品 jay ban

obligation *n.* 責任 jak yam

obligatory *a.* 一定要嘅 yat ding yiew geh

oblige *v.t.* 逼使 bik say

oblique *a.* 轉彎抹角 joon wan mwut gok

obliterate *v.t.* 消滅 siew meet

obliteration *n.* 消滅 siew meet

oblivion *n.* 無意識 mow yee sik

oblivious *a.* 唔注意嘅 hm ju yee geh

oblong *a.* 長方形嘅 cheurng forng ying geh

oblong *n.* 長方形 cheurng forng ying

obnoxious *a.* 令人作嘔嘅 ling yan jok oh geh

obscene *a.* 下流嘅 ha low geh

obscenity *n.* 下流嘅行為 ha low geh hang way

obscure *a.* 少為人知嘅 siew way yan jee geh

obscure *v.t.* 變模糊 been mow wu

obscurity *n.* 含糊 ham wu

observance *n.* 宗教儀式 jung gao ye sik

observant *a.* 觀察力強 gwun tat lik keurng

observation *n.* 觀察 gwun tat

observatory *n.* 天文台 teen man toy

observe *v.t.* 觀察 gwun tat

obsess *v.t.* 迷戀 may loon

obsession *n.* 沈迷 tam may

obsolete *a.* 淘汰咗嘅 tow tai jor geh

obstacle *n.* 障礙物 jeurng ngoy mat

obstinacy *n.* 固執 gu jap

obstinate *a.* 硬頸 ngan geng

obstruct *v.t.* 阻 jor

obstruction *n.* 阻擋 jor dorng

obstructive *a.* 阻止 jor jee

obtain *v.t.* 得到 dak dow

obtainable *a.* 可以得到嘅 hor yee dak dow geh

obtuse *a.* 遲鈍嘅 tee dun geh

obvious *a.* 明顯 ming heen

occasion *n.* 場合 cheurng hap

occasion *v.t* 導致 dow jee

occasional *a.* 間唔中 gan hm jung

occasionally *adv.* 耐唔中 loy hm jung

occident *n.* 西方 say forng

occidental *a.* 西方嘅 say forng geh

occult *a.* 神祕嘅 san bay geh

occupancy *n.* 佔有 jeem yow

occupant *n.* 佔有人 jeem yow yan

occupation *n.* 職業 jik yeep

occupier *n.* 佔有人 jeem yow yan

occupy *v.t.* 佔用 jeem uimg

occur *v.i.* 發生 fat sang

occurrence *n.* 出現 chut yeen

ocean *n.* 海洋 hoy yeurng

oceanic *a.* 海洋嘅 hoy yeurng geh

octagon *n.* 八角形 bat gok ying

octagonal *a.* 八角形嘅 bat gok ying geh

octave *n.* 八度 bat dow

October *n.* 十月 sap yoot

octogenarian *a.* 八旬老人 bat sun low yan

octroi *n.* 入市稅 yao see suy

ocular *a.* 眼嘅 ngan geh

oculist *n.* 眼科醫生 ngan for yee sang

odd *a.* 怪嘅 gwai geh

oddity *n.* 古怪 gu gwai

odds *n.* 可能性 hor lang sing

ode *n.* 頌歌 jung gor

odious *a.* 令人作嘔嘅 ling yan jok oh geh

odium *n.* 反感 fan gam

odorous *a.* 有味嘅 yow may geh

odour *n.* 臭味 chow may

offence *n.* 罪 juy

offend *v.t.* 得罪 dak juy

offender *n.* 犯罪人 fan juy yan

offensive *a.* 得罪人嘅 dak juy yan geh

offensive *n* 攻擊 gung gik

offer *v.t.* 提供 tay gung

offer *n* 提議 tay yee

offering *n.* 祭品 jay ban

office *n.* 寫字樓 seh jee low

officer *n.* 官員 gwun yoon

official *a.* 正式嘅 jing sik geh

official *n* 官員 gwun yoon

officially *adv.* 正式 jing sik

officiate *v.i.* 主持 ju tee

officious *a.* 多管閒事 dor gwun han see

offing *n.* 即將發生 jik jeurng fat sang

offset *v.t.* 抵消 day siew

offset *n* 抵消 day siew

offshoot *n.* 分枝 fan jee

offspring *n.* 仔女 jay luy

oft *adv.* 通常 tung seurng

often *adv.* 通常 tung seurng

ogle *v.t.* 眼甘甘 ngan gam gam

ogle *n* 凝望 ying morng

oil *n.* 油 yow

oil *v.t* 上油 seurng yow

oily *a.* 好油 ho yow

ointment *n.* 藥膏 yeurk gow

old *a.* 舊嘅 gow geh

oligarchy *n.* 寡頭政治 gwa tow jing jee

olive *n.* 橄欖 gam lam

olympiad *n.* 奧運會 oh wan wuy

omega *n.* 歐米加 oh may ga

omelette *n.* 煎蛋捲 jeen dan goon

omen *n.* 預兆 yu siew

ominous *a.* 唔吉利嘅 hm gat lay geh

omission *n.* 遺漏 way low

omit *v.t.* 發出 fat chut

omnipotence *n.* 全能 choon lang

omnipotent *a.* 無所不能嘅 mow sor bat lang geh

omnipresence *n.* 無所不在 mow sor bat joy

omnipresent *a.* 無所不在嘅 mow sor bat joy geh

omniscience *n.* 全知 choon jee

omniscient *a.* 無所不知嘅 mow sor bat jee geh

on *prep.* 喺...嘅上面 hay...geh seurng meen

on *adv.* 喺...嘅上面 hay...geh seurng meen

once *adv.* 一次 yat tee

one *a.* 一 yat

one *pron.* 一 yat
oneness *n.* 一致 yat jee
onerous *a.* 晒力嘅 sai lik gey
onion *n.* 蔥 chung
on-looker *n.* 旁觀者 porng gwun jeh
only *a.* 只有 jee yow
only *adv.* 只係 jee hay
only *conj.* 不過 bat gwor
onomatopoeia *n.* 象聲詞 jeurng sing tee
onrush *n.* 突如其來 dak yu kay loy
onset *n.* 開始 hoy tee
onslaught *n.* 攻擊 gung gik
onus *n.* 職責 jik jak
onward *a.* 向前 heurng teen
onwards *adv.* 向前 heurng teen
ooze *n.* 泥漿 lay jeurng
ooze *v.i.* 慢慢滲出 man man sam chut
opacity *n.* 透明度 tow ming dow
opal *n.* 貓眼石 mao ngan sek
opaque *a.* 唔透明嘅 hm tow ming geh
open *a.* 打開嘅 da hoy geh
open *v.t.* 打開 da hoy
opening *n.* 開頭 hoy tow
openly *adv.* 公開咁 gung hoy gam
opera *n.* 歌劇 gor kek
operate *v.t.* 操作 cho jok
operation *n.* 手術 sow sut
operative *a.* 用緊嘅 yung gan geh
operator *n.* 操作人 cho jok yan
opine *v.t.* 認爲 ying way
opinion *n.* 意見 yee geen
opium *n.* 鴉片 ngar peen
opponent *n.* 對手 suy sow
opportune *a.* 適合嘅 sik hap geh
opportunism *n.* 機會主義 gey wuy ju yee

opportunity *n.* 機會 gey wuy
oppose *v.t.* 反對 fan duy
opposite *a.* 對住 duy ju
opposition *n.* 對立 duy lap
oppress *v.t.* 壓制 ngat jay
oppression *n.* 壓制 ngat jay
oppressive *a.* 壓制嘅 ngat jay geh
oppressor *n.* 壓迫者 ngat bik jeh
opt *v.i.* 揀 gan
optic *a.* 眼嘅 ngan geh
optician *n.* 眼鏡商 ngan geng seurng
optimism *n.* 樂觀 lok gwun
optimist *n.* 樂觀嘅人 lok gwun geh yan
optimistic *a.* 樂觀 lok gwun
optimum *n.* 最好 juy ho
optimum *a* 最佳嘅 juy gai geh
option *n.* 選擇 shoon jak
optional *a.* 可以揀嘅 hor yee gan geh
opulence *n.* 財富 choy fu
opulent *a.* 豪華嘅 ho wah geh
oracle *n.* 牧師 muk see
oracular *a.* 玄妙嘅 yoon miew geh
oral *a.* 口頭嘅 ho tow geh
orally *adv.* 口述嘅 ho sut geh
orange *n.* 橙 tang
orange *a* 橙色嘅 tang sik geh
oration *n.* 演講 yeen gorng
orator *n.* 演講家 yeen gorng ga
oratorical *a.* 演講嘅 yeen gorng geh
oratory *n.* 演講術 yeen gorng sut
orb *n.* 球體 kow tay
orbit *n.* 軌道 gway dow
orchard *n.* 果園 gwor yoon
orchestra *n.* 管弦樂隊 gwun yoon ok duy

orchestral *a.* 管弦樂嘅 gwun yoon ok geh
ordeal *n.* 折磨 jeet mor
order *n.* 次序 tee juy
order *v.t* 訂 deng
orderly *a.* 有條理嘅 yow tiew lay geh
orderly *n.* 護理員 wu lay yoon
ordinance *n.* 法令 fat ling
ordinarily *adv.* 平時咁 ping see gam
ordinary *a.* 普通 po tung
ordnance *n.* 軍用器材 gwan yung hay choy
ore *n.* 礦石 kworng sek
organ *n.* 器官 hay gwun
organic *a.* 有機嘅 yow gey geh
organism *n.* 生物 sang mat
organization *n.* 組織 jow jik
organize *v.t.* 安排 on pai
orient *n.* 東方 dung forng
orient *v.t.* 適應 sik ying
oriental *a.* 東方嘅 dung forng geh
oriental *n* 東方人 dung forng yan
orientate *v.t.* 面對 meen duy
origin *n.* 源頭 toon tow
original *a.* 原作嘅 yoon jok geh
original *n* 正本 jing bwun
originality *n.* 創意 chorng yee
originate *v.t.* 起源於 hay yoon yu
originator *n.* 創作人 chorng jok yan
ornament *n.* 裝飾品 jorng sik ban
ornament *v.t.* 裝飾 jorng sik
ornamental *a.* 裝飾嘅 jorng sik geh
ornamentation *n.* 裝飾 jorng sik
orphan *n.* 孤兒 gu yee
orphan *v.t* 成爲孤兒 sing way gu yee

orphanage *n.* 孤兒院 gu yee yoon
orthodox *a.* 正統嘅 jing tung geh
orthodoxy *n.* 正統觀念 jing tung gwun leem
oscillate *v.i.* 波動 bor dung
oscillation *n.* 擺動 bai dung
ossify *v.t.* 僵化 geurng far
ostracize *v.t.* 排斥 pai tik
ostrich *n.* 鴕鳥 torliew
other *a.* 其他 kay ta
other *pron.* 另外 ling ngoy
otherwise *adv.* 除此之外 chuy tee jee ngoy
otherwise *conj.* 如果唔係 yu gwor hm hay
otter *n.* 海獺 hoy lai
ottoman *n.* 長軟凳 cheurng yoon dang
ounce *n.* 安士 on see
our *pron.* 我哋 ngor day
oust *v.t.* 罷免 ba meen
out *adv.* 出去 chut huy
out-balance *v.t.* 重過 chung gwor
outbid *v.t.* 出高價 chut go ga
outbreak *n.* 爆發 bao fat
outburst *n.* 爆發 bao fat
outcast *n.* 被排斥者 bay pai tik jeh
outcast *a* 排斥 pai tik
outcome *n.* 結果 geet gwor
outcry *a.* 強烈抗議 keurng leet korng yee
outdated *a.* 過時 gwor see
outdo *v.t.* 勝過 sing gwor
outdoor *a.* 戶外嘅 woo ngoy geh
outer *a.* 外邊嘅 ngoy been geh
outfit *n.* 裝束 jorng chuk
outfit *v.t* 裝備 jorng bay
outgrow *v.t.* 着唔落 jeurk hm lok
outhouse *n.* 外圍建築 ngoy way geen juk

outing *n.* 郊遊 gao yow

outlandish *a.* 唔尋常嘅 hm tam seurng geh

outlaw *n.* 逃犯 tow fan

outlaw *v.t* 變爲非法 been way fay fat

outline *n.* 外型 ngoy ying

outline *v.t.* 講下 gorng har

outlive *v.i.* 比...長命 bay...cheurng meng

outlook *n.* 見解 geen gai

outmoded *a.* 過晒時嘅 gwor sai see geh

outnumber *v.t.* 壓倒 ngat dow

outpatient *n.* 門診病人 mun tan beng yan

outpost *n.* 前哨 teen sao

output *n.* 出產量 chut tan leurng

outrage *n.* 憤怒 fan low

outrage *v.t.* 發晒火 fat sai for

outright *adv.* 毫無保留咁 ho mo bo low gam

outright *a* 徹底嘅 teet day geh

outrun *v.t.* 超越 tiew yoot

outset *n.* 最初 chuy chor

outshine *v.t.* 勝過 sing gwor

outside *a.* 出邊嘅 chut been geh

outside *n* 出邊 chut been

outside *adv* 出邊嘅 chut been geh

outside *prep* 出邊 chut been

outsider *n.* 外來人 ngoy loy yan

outsize *a.* 特大 dak dai

outskirts *n.pl.* 市郊 see gao

outspoken *a.* 率直 sut jik

outstanding *a.* 優秀 yow sow

outward *a.* 向外 heurng ngoy

outward *adv* 外面 ngoy meen

outwards *adv* 向外 heurng ngoy

outwardly *adv.* 表面上 biew meen seurng

outweigh *v.t.* 重過 chung gwor

outwit *v.t.* 智勝 jee sing

oval *a.* 卵形嘅 lun ying geh

oval *n* 卵形 lun ying

ovary *n.* 卵巢 lun tao

ovation *n.* 熱烈歡迎 yeet leet fwun ying

oven *n.* 焗爐 guk low

over *prep.* 上面 seurng meen

over *adv* 過 gwor

over *n* 一輪投球 yat lun tow kow

overact *v.t.* 誇張 kwa jeurng

overall *n.* 外套 ngoy tow

overall *a* 總體嘅 jung tay geh

overawe *v.t.* 敬畏 ging way

overboard *adv.* 船外 shoon ngoy

overburden *v.t.* 負擔過重 fu dam gwor chung

overcast *a.* 多雲 dor wan

overcharge *v.t.* 收多錢 sow dor teen

overcharge *n* 收多錢 sow dor teen

overcoat *n.* 大褸 dai low

overcome *v.t.* 克服 hak fuk

overdo *v.t.* 做得過分 jow dak gwor fan

overdose *n.* 過量 gwor leurng

overdose *v.t.* 過量服用 gwor leung fuk yung

overdraft *n.* 透支 tow jee

overdraw *v.t.* 透支 tow jee

overdue *a.* 過期 gwor kay

overhaul *v.t.* 超越 tiew yoot

overhaul *n.* 改造 goy jow

overhear *v.t.* 無意中聽到 mo yee jung teng dow

overjoyed *a* 非常高興 fay seurng go hing

overlap *v.t.* 重疊 chung deep

overlap *n* 重疊 chung deep

overleaf *adv.* 下一頁 har yat yeep

overload *v.t.* 超載 tiew joy

overload *n* 過多 gwor dor

overlook *v.t.* 忽略 fat leurk

overnight *adv.* 一夜之間 yat yeh jee gan

overnight *a* 一夜之間 yat yeh jee gan

overpower *v.t.* 征服 jing fuk

overrate *v.t.* 高估 gow gu

overrule *v.t.* 駁回 bok wuy

overrun *v.t* 超時 tiew see

oversee *v.t.* 監督 gam duk

overseer *n.* 監工 gam gung

overshadow *v.t.* 掩蓋 yeem koy

oversight *n.* 疏忽 sor fat

overt *a.* 公開嘅 gung hoy geh

overtake *v.t.* 爬頭 pa tow

overthrow *v.t.* 推翻 tuy fan

overthrow *n* 推翻 tuy fan

overtime *adv.* 加班 gar ban

overtime *n* 加班 gar ban

overture *n.* 前奏曲 teen jow kuk

overwhelm *v.t.* 擊敗 gik bai

overwork *v.i.* 工作過度 gung jok gwor dow

overwork *n.* 工作過度 gung jok gwor dow

owe *v.t* 欠 heem

owl *n.* 貓頭鷹 mao tow ying

own *a.* 自己嘅 jee gey geh

own *v.t.* 擁有 yung yow

owner *n.* 物主 mat ju

ownership *n.* 產權 tan koon

ox *n.* 牛 ngow

oxygen *n.* 氧氣 yeurng hay

oyster *n.* 蠔 ho

pace *n* 速度 chuk dow

pace *v.i.* 節奏 jeet jow

pacific *a.* 平靜嘅 ping jing geh

pacify *v.t.* 平息 ping sik

pack *n.* 一包 yat bao

pack *v.t.* 執行李 jap hang lay

package *n.* 包裹 bao gwor

packet *n.* 一包 yat bao

packing *n.* 包裝 bao jorng

pact *n.* 協議 heep yee

pad *n.* 墊 deen

pad *v.t.* 加墊 ga deen

padding *n.* 墊 deen

paddle *v.i.* 撐船 tang shoon

paddle *n* 船槳 shoon jeurng

paddy *n.* 稻田 dow teen

page *n.* 頁 yeep

page *v.t.* 呼叫 fu giew

pageant *n.* 選美比賽 shoon may bay choy

pageantry *n.* 盛況 sing forng

pagoda *n.* 塔 tap

pail *n.* 桶 tung

pain *n.* 痛苦 tung fu

pain *v.t.* 痛 tung

painful *a.* 痛苦 tung fu

painstaking *a.* 辛苦嘅 san fu geh

paint *n.* 漆油 tat yow

paint *v.t.* 油 yow

painter *n.* 畫家 wah gar

painting *n.* 畫 wah

pair *n.* 一對 yat duy

pair *v.t.* 組成一對 jo sing yat duy

pal *n.* 朋友 pang yow

palace *n.* 皇宮 worng gung

palanquin *n.* 轎 kiew

palatable *a.* 好味嘅 ho may geh

palatal *a.* 顎嘅 ok geh

palate *n.* 上顎嘅 色哦口 geh

palatial *a.* 堂皇嘅 torng worng geh

pale *n.* 越軌 yoot gway

pale *a* 淺 teen

pale *v.i.* 變白 been bak

palette *n.* 調色板 tiew sik ban

palm *n.* 手板 sow ban
palm *v.t.* 收埋係手板 sow mai hay sow ban
palm *n.* 棕櫚樹 jung luy shu
palmist *n.* 手相術士 sow seurng sut see
palmistry *n.* 手相術 sow seurng sut
palpable *a.* 明顯嘅 ming heen geh
palpitate *v.i.* 急跳 gap tiew
palpitation *n.* 心悸 sam gway
palsy *n.* 痲痹 ma bay
paltry *a.* 無用嘅 mow yung ghe
pamper *v.t.* 縱容 jung yung
pamphlet *n.* 手冊 sow tak
pamphleteer *n.* 手冊作者 sow tak jok jeh
panacea *n.* 萬能之計 man lang jee gey
pandemonium *n.* 騷動 sow dung
pane *n.* 玻璃窗 bor lay cheurng
panegyric *n.* 頌文 jung man
panel *n.* 鑲板 seurng ban
panel *v.t.* 鑲板 seurng ban
pang *n.* 一陣劇痛 yat jan kek tung
panic *n.* 激動 gik dung
panorama *n.* 全景 choon ging
pant *v.i.* 喘氣 choon hay
pant *n.* 氣喘 hay choon
pantaloon *n.* 傻佬 sor low
pantheism *n.* 泛神論 fan san lun
pantheist *n.* 泛神論者 fan san lun jeh
panther *n.* 黑豹 hak pao
pantomime *n.* 童話劇 tung wah kek
pantry *n.* 食物室 sik mat sat
papacy *n.* 教宗嘅職位 gao jung geh jik way
papal *a.* 教宗嘅 gao jung geh
paper *n.* 紙 jee

par *n.* 標準杆數 biew jun gorn sow
parable *n.* 寓言 yu yeen
parachute *n.* 降落傘 gorng lok sna
parachutist *n.* 跳傘者 tiew san jeh
parade *n.* 遊行 yow hang
parade *v.t.* 遊行 yow hang
paradise *n.* 天堂 teen torng
paradox *n.* 矛盾 mao tun
paradoxical *a.* 自相矛盾嘅 jee seurng mao tun geh
paraffin *n.* 石蠟 sek lap
paragon *n.* 模範 mow fan
paragraph *n.* 段 don
parallel *a.* 平行嘅 ping hang geh
parallel *v.t.* 同時發生 tung see fat sang
parallelism *n.* 相似度 seurng tee dow
parallelogram *n.* 平行四角型 ping hang say gok ying
paralyse *v.t.* 變癱 been tan
paralysis *n.* 癱瘓 tan wun
paralytic *a.* 癱瘓嘅 tan wun geh
paramount *a.* 罪重要嘅 juy jung yiew geh
paramour *n.* 情人 ting yan
paraphernalia *n. pl* 裝備 jorng bay
paraphrase *n.* 解釋 gai sik
paraphrase *v.t.* 解釋 gai sik
parasite *n.* 寄生蟲 gey sang chung
parcel *n.* 包裹 bao gwor
parcel *v.t.* 包 bao
parch *v.t.* 烘 hung
pardon *v.t.* 赦免 ser meen
pardon *n.* 特赦 dak ser
pardonable *a.* 可以原諒嘅 hor yee yoon leurng geh

parent n. 父母 fu mow
parentage n. 出生 chut sang
parental a. 父母嘅 fu mow geh
parenthesis n. 插入語 tap yap yu
parish n. 教區 gao kuy
parity n. 平等 ping dang
park n. 公園 gung yoon
park v.t. 泊 pak
parlance n. 講法 gorng fat
parley n. 對話 duy wah
parley v.i 談判 tam pwun
parliament n. 國會 gwok wuy
parliamentarian n. 議員 yee yoon
parliamentary a. 國會嘅 gwok wuy geh
parlour n. 客廳 hak teng
parody n. 模仿 mow forng
parody v.t. 模仿 mow forng
parole n. 假釋 ga sik
parole v.t. 假釋 ga sik
parricide n. 殺父母罪 sat fu mow juy
parrot n. 鸚鵡 ying mow
parry v.t. 擋開 dorng hoy
parry n. 擋 dorng
parson n. 牧師 muk see
part n. 部份 bo fan
part v.t. 分開 fan hoy
partake v.i. 參與 tarm yu
partial a. 部份嘅 bo fan geh
partiality n. 偏袒 peen tan
participate v.i. 參與 tarm yu
participant n. 參與者 tarm yu jeh
participation n. 參與 tarm yu
particle a. 微粒 may lap
particular a. 特別嘅 dak beet geh
particular n. 細節 say jeet
partisan n. 游擊隊員 yow gik duy yoon
partisan a. 偏袒嘅 peen tan geh

partition n. 分區 fan kuy
partition v.t. 分割 fan got
partner n. 拍檔 pak dorng
partnership n. 合作 hap jok
party n. 派對 pai duy
pass v.i. 通過 tung gowr
pass n 通行證 tung hang jing
passage n. 通到 tung dow
passenger n. 乘客 sing hak
passion n. 熱情 yeet ting
passionate a. 熱情 yeet ting
passive a. 被動嘅 bay dung geh
passport n. 護照 wu jiew
past a. 過去嘅 gwor huy geh
past n. 過去 gwor huy
past prep. 過 gwor
paste n. 肉醬 yuk jeurng
paste v.t. 貼 teep
pastel n. 蠟筆 lap bat
pastime n. 消遣 siew heen
pastoral a. 牧民嘅 muk man geh
pasture n. 牧場 muk cheurng
pasture v.t. 放牧 forng muk
pat v.t. 拍 pak
pat n 拍 pak
pat adv 瞭如指掌 liew yu jee jeurng
patch v.t. 補 bo
patch n 一笪 yat dat
patent a. 明顯嘅 ming heen geh
patent n 專利權 joon lay koon
patent v.t. 申請專利 san ting joon lay
paternal a. 父親嘅 fu tan geh
path n. 小路 siew low
pathetic a. 無用嘅 mow yung geh
pathos n. 感染力 gam yeem lik
patience n. 耐性 loy sing
patient a. 有耐性嘅 yow loy sing geh
patient n 病人 beng yan
patricide n. 弑父罪 see fu juy

patrimony *n.* 遺產 yee tan

patriot *n.* 愛國者 ngoy gwok jeh

patriotic *a.* 愛國嘅 ngoy gwok geh

partiotism *n.* 愛國精神 ngoy gwok jing san

patrol *v.i.* 巡邏 chun lor

patrol *n* 巡邏 chun lor

patron *n.* 贊助人 jan jor yan

patronage *n.* 贊助 jan jor

patronize *v.t.* 扮晒嘢 ban sai yeh

pattern *n.* 花樣 far yeurng

paucity *n.* 少量 siew leurng

pauper *n.* 窮人 kung yan

pause *n.* 暫停 jam ting

pause *v.i.* 暫停 jam ting

pave *v.t.* 鋪 pow

pavement *n.* 行人路 hang yan low

pavilion *n.* 涼亭 leurng ting

paw *n.* 爪 jao

paw *v.t.* 嘟手嘟腳 yuk sow yuk geurk

pay *v.t.* 抓人 jao yan

pay *n* 人工 yan gung

payable *a.* 要畀嘅 yiew bay geh

payee *n.* 收款人 sow fwun yan

payment *n.* 款項 fwun horng

pea *n.* 綠豆 luk dow

peace *n.* 和平 wor ping

peaceable *a.* 和平嘅 wor ping geh

peaceful *a.* 安靜嘅 on jing geh

peach *n.* 桃 tow

peacock *n.* 孔雀 hung jeurk

peahen *n.* 雌孔雀 tee hung jeurk

peak *n.* 頂峰 ding fung

pear *n.* 梨 lay

pearl *n.* 珍珠 jan ju

peasant *n.* 農民 lung man

peasantry *n.* 農民 lung man

pebble *n.* 卵石 lun sek

peck *n.* 錫 sek

peck *v.i.* 啄 deurk

peculiar *a.* 怪嘅 gwai geh

peculiarity *n.* 怪癖 gwai pik

pecuniary *a.* 金錢嘅 gam teen geh

pedagogue *n.* 教師 gao see

pedagogy *n.* 教育學 gao yuk hok

pedal *n.* 踏板 dap ban

pedal *v.t.* 踩 tai

pedant *n.* 講究 gorng gow

pedantic *a.* 太過講究 tai gwor gorng gow

pedantry *n.* 迂腐 yu fu

pedestal *n.* 底座 day jor

pedestrian *n.* 行人 hang yan

pedigree *n.* 族譜 juk pow

peel *v.t.* 搣 meet

peel *n.* 皮 pay

peep *v.i.* 偷睇 tow tay

peep *n* 偷望 tow morng

peer *n.* 同輩 tung pwuy

peerless *a.* 無得比嘅 mow dak bay geh

peg *n.* 夾 geep

peg *v.t.* 夾住 geep ju

pelf *n.* 不義之財 bat yee jee choy

pell-mell *adv.* 趕 gorn

pen *n.* 筆 bat

pen *v.t.* 寫 she

penal *a.* 刑罰嘅 ying fat geh

penalize *v.t.* 懲罰 ting fat

penalty *n.* 懲罰 ting fat

pencil *n.* 鉛筆 yoon bat

pencil *v.t.* 畫 wak

pending *prep.* 等緊 dang gan

pending *a* 待定嘅 doy ding geh

pendulum *n.* 鐘擺 jung bai

penetrate *v.t.* 插入 tap yap

penetration *n.* 插入 tap yap

penis *n.* 陰莖 yam ging

penniless *a.* 仙都唔仙下 seen dow hm seen ha

penny *n.* 便士 been see

pension *n.* 退休金 tuy yow gam

pension *v.t.* 強迫退休 keurng bik tuy yow

pensioner *n.* 退休人士 tuy yow yan see

pensive *a.* 沈思嘅 tam see geh

pentagon *n.* 五角型 hm gok ying

peon *n.* 苦功 fu gung

people *n.* 人 yan

people *v.t.* 住滿人 ju mwun yan

pepper *n.* 胡椒粉 wu jiew fan

pepper *v.t.* 加胡椒粉 ga wu jiew fan

per *prep.* 每 mwuy

perambulator *n.* BB車 bee bee cher

perceive *v.t.* 注意 ju yee

perceptible *adj* 睇得出嘅 tay dak chut geh

per cent *adv.* 百分之 bak fan jee

percentage *n.* 百分率 bak fan lut

perception *n.* 知覺 jee gok

perceptive *a.* 觀察力強嘅 gwun tat lik keurng geh

perch *n.* 棲息處 tay sik chu

perch *v.i.* 坐 chor

perennial *a.* 持續嘅 tee juk geh

perennial *n.* 多年生植物 dor leen sang jik mat

perfect *a.* 完美嘅 yoon may geh

perfect *v.t.* 整完美 jing yoon may

perfection *n.* 完美 yoon may

perfidy *n.* 背叛 bwuy bwun

perforate *v.t.* 大窿 da lung

perforce *adv.* 一定嘅 yat ding geh

perform *v.t.* 表演 biew yeen

performance *n.* 演出 yeen chut

performer *n.* 表演者 biew yeen jeh

perfume *n.* 香水 heurng suy

perfume *v.t.* 搽香水 ta heurng suy

perhaps *adv.* 或者 wak jeh

peril *n.* 危險 ngay heem

peril *v.t.* 禍害 wor hoy

perilous *a.* 危險嘅 ngay heem geh

period *n.* 時期 see kay

periodical *n.* 期刊 kay horn

periodical *a.* 定期嘅 ding kay geh

periphery *n.* 周圍 jow way

perish *v.i.* 死 say

perishable *a.* 易變質嘅 yee been jat geh

perjure *v.i.* 畀假口供 bay ga ho gung

perjury *n.* 偽證罪 ngay jing juy

permanence *n.* 永久性 wing gow sing

permanent *a.* 永久嘅 wing gow geh

permissible *a.* 容許嘅 yung huy geh

permission *n.* 批准 pay jun

permit *v.t.* 允許 wan huy

permit *n.* 許可證 huy hor jing

permutation *n.* 排列方式 pai leet forng sik

pernicious *a.* 有害嘅 yow hoy geh

perpendicular *a.* 垂直嘅 suy jik geh

perpendicular *n.* 垂直線 suy jik seen

perpetual *a.* 不斷嘅 bat doon geh

perpetuate *v.t.* 持續 tee juk

perplex *v.t.* 困擾 kwan yiew

perplexity *n.* 困擾 kwan yiew

persecute *v.t.* 逼害 bik hoy

persecution *n.* 逼害 bik hoy

perseverance *n.* 毅力 ngay lik

persevere *v.i.* 堅持 geen tee

persist *v.i.* 保持 bo tee

persistence *n.* 堅持 geen tee

persistent *a.* 執著嘅 jap jeurk geh

person *n.* 人 yan

personage *n.* 名人 ming yan

personal *a.* 私人嘅 see yan geh

personality *n.* 性格 sing gak

personification *n.* 人格化 yan gak far

personify *v.t.* 擬人化 yee yan far

personnel *n.* 人事部 yan see bo

perspective *n.* 觀點 gwun deem

perspiration *n.* 汗珠 horn ju

perspire *v.i.* 出汗 chut horn

persuade *v.t.* 說服 suy fuk

persuasion *n.* 說服力 suy fuk lik

pertain *v.i.* 關於 gwan yu

pertinent *a.* 有關嘅 yow gwan geh

perturb *v.t.* 感到不安 gam dow bat on

perusal *n.* 讀 duk

peruse *v.t.* 讀 duk

pervade *v.t.* 遍及 peen kap

perverse *a.* 任性嘅 yam sing geh

perversion *n.* 變態 been tai

perversity *n.* 倔強 gwat keurng

pervert *v.t.* 色狼 sik lorng

pessimism *n.* 悲觀 bay gwun

pessimist *n.* 悲觀嘅人 bay gwun geh yan

pessimistic *a.* 悲觀嘅 bay gwun geh

pest *n.* 害蟲 hoy chung

pesticide *n.* 殺蟲劑 sat chung jay

pestilence *n.* 瘟疫 wan yik

pet *n.* 寵物 chung mat

pet *v.t.* 調情 tiew ting

petal *n.* 花瓣 far fan

petition *n.* 請願書 ting yoon shu

petition *v.t.* 請願 ting yoon

petitioner *n.* 請願者 ting yoon jeh

petrol *n.* 汽油 hay yow

petroleum *n.* 石油 sek yow

petticoat *n.* 襯裙 tan kwan

petty *a.* 瑣碎嘅 sor suy geh

petulance *n.* 細路仔脾氣 say low jay pay hay

petulant *a.* 任性嘅 yam sing geh

phantom *n.* 鬼 gway

pharmacy *n.* 藥房 yeurk forng

phase *n.* 階段 gai doon

phenomenal *a.* 非凡嘅 fay fan geh

phenomenon *n.* 非凡嘅人 fay fan geh yan

phial *n.* 細藥樽 say yeurk jun

philanthropic *a.* 慈善嘅 tee seen geh

philanthropist *n.* 慈善家 tee seen ga

philanthropy *n.* 慈善 tee seen

philological *a.* 語言學 yu yeen hok

philologist *n.* 語言學家 yu yeen hok ga

philology *n.* 語言學 yu yeen hok

philosopher *n.* 哲學家 jeet hok ga

philosophical *a.* 哲學嘅 jeet hok geh

philosophy *n.* 哲學 jeet hok

phone *n.* 電話 deen wah

phonetic *a.* 拼音嘅 ping yam geh

phonetics *n.* 語音學 yu yam hok

phosphate *n.* 磷酸鹽 lun shoon yeem

phosphorus *n.* 磷 lun

photo *n* 相 seurng

photograph *v.t.* 影 ying

photograph *n* 相 seurng

photographer *n.* 攝影師 seep ying see

photographic *a.* 攝影嘅 seep ying geh

photography *n.* 攝影 seep ying

phrase *n.* 成語 sing yu

phrase *v.t.* 表達 biew dat

phraseology *n.* 措辭 chotee

physic *n.* 藥 yeurk

physic *v.t.* 醫 yee

physical *a.* 身體嘅 san tay geh

physician *n.* 醫師 yee see

physicist *n.* 物理學家 mat lay hok ga

physics *n.* 物理學 mat lay hok

physiognomy *n.* 容貌 yung mao

physique *n.* 體型 tay ying

pianist *n.* 鋼琴家 gorng kam ga

piano *n.* 鋼琴 gorng kam

pick *v.t.* 揀 gan

pick *n.* 選擇 shoon jak

picket *n.* 糾察人 dow tat yan

picket *v.t.* 抗議 korng yee

pickle *n.* 泡菜 pao choy

pickle *v.t* 醃 yeep

picnic *n.* 野餐 yeh tan

picnic *v.i.* 野餐 yeh tan

pictorical *a.* 圖畫嘅 tow wah geh

picture *n.* 圖畫 tow wah

picture *v.t.* 想像 seurng jeurng

picturesque *a.* 優美嘅 yow may geh

piece *n.* 塊 fai

piece *v.t.* 組合晒 jow hap sai

pierce *v.t.* 穿過 choon gwor

piety *n.* 虔誠 keen sing

pig *n.* 豬 ju

pigeon *n.* 白鴿 bak gap

pigmy *n.* 唔重要嘅人 hm jung yiew geh yan

pile *n.* 一堆 yat duy

pile *v.t.* 堆 duy

piles *n.* 痔瘡 jee chorng

pilfer *v.t.* 偷 tow

pilgrim *n.* 朝聖者 tiew sing jeh

pilgrimage *n.* 朝聖之旅 tiew sing jee luy

pill *n.* 藥丸 yeurk yoon

pillar *n.* 柱 chu

pillow *n* 枕頭 jam tow

pillow *v.t.* 墊住 deen ju

pilot *n.* 飛機師 fay gey see

pilot *v.t.* 揸 ja

pimple *n.* 粉刺 fan tee

pin *n.* 針 jam

pin *v.t.* 釘住 deng ju

pinch *v.t.* 捏 meet

pinch *v.* 捏 meet

pine *n.* 松樹 chung shu

pine *v.i.* 難過 lan gwor

pineapple *n.* 菠蘿 bor lor

pink *n.* 粉紅色 fan hung sik

pink *a* 粉紅色嘅 fan hung sik geh

pinkish *a.* 粉紅嘅 fan hung ghe

pinnacle *n.* 頂峰 ding fung

pioneer *n.* 開拓者 hoy tok jeh

pioneer *v.t.* 做先鋒 jow seen fung

pious *a.* 虔誠嘅 keen sing geh

pipe *n.* 管 gwun

pipe *v.i* 用管輸送 yung gwun shu sung

piquant *a.* 開胃嘅 hoy way geh

piracy *n.* 盜版行為 dow ban hang way

pirate *n.* 海盜 hoy dow

pirate *v.t* 盜印 dow yan

pistol *n.* 手槍 sow cheurng

piston *n.* 活塞 wut sat

pit *n.* 深坑 sam hang

pit *v.t.* 整坑 jing hang

pitch *n.* 球場 kow cheurng

pitch *v.t.* 用力掟 yung lik deng

pitcher *n.* 投球手 tow kow sow

piteous *a.* 可憐嘅 hor leen geh

pitfall *n.* 陷阱 ham jeng

pitiable *a.* 值得同情嘅 jik dak tung ting geh

pitiful *a.* 可憐嘅 hor leen geh

pitiless *a.* 無情嘅 mow ting geh

pitman *n.* 礦工 kworng gung

pittance *n.* 低人工 day yan gung

pity *n.* 同情 tung ting

pity *v.t.* 可憐 hor leen

pivot *n.* 中心點 jung sam deem

pivot *v.t.* 旋轉 shoon joon

placard *n.* 標語牌 biew yu pai

place *n.* 地方 day forng

place *v.t.* 擺 bai

placid *a.* 溫和嘅 wan wo geh

plague *a.* 疫病 yik beng

plague *v.t.* 折磨 jeet mor

plain *a.* 簡單嘅 gan dan geh

plain *n.* 平地 ping day

plaintiff *n.* 原告 yoon gow

plan *n.* 計劃 gey wak

plan *v.t.* 計劃 gey wak

plane *n.* 飛機 fay gey

plane *v.t.* 刨 pao

plane *a.* 平嘅 ping geh

plane *n* 平面 ping meen

planet *n.* 星球 sing kow

planetary *a.* 行星嘅 hang sing geh

plank *n.* 木板 muk ban

plank *v.t.* 用力擺 yung lik bai

plant *n.* 植物 jik mat

plant *v.t.* 種 jung

plantain *n.* 車前草 cher teen cho

plantation *n.* 種植園 jung jik yoon

plaster *n.* 止血貼 jee hoot teep

plaster *v.t.* 用灰泥鋪 yung fwuy lay pow

plate *n.* 碟 deep

plate *v.t.* 電鍍 deen dow

plateau *n.* 高地 gow day

platform *n.* 台 toy

platonic *a.* 純友誼嘅 sun yow yee geh

platoon *n.* 排 pai

play *n.* 戲劇 hay kek

play *v.i.* 玩 wan

player *n.* 玩家 wan ga

plea *n.* 請求 ting kow

plead *v.i.* 懇求 han kow

pleader *n.* 答辯人 dap been yan

pleasant *a.* 愉快嘅 yu fai geh

pleasantry *n.* 客氣說話 hak hay shoot wah

please *v.t.* 令人滿意 ling yan mwun yee

pleasure *n.* 愉快 yu fai

plebiscite *n.* 公民投票 gung man tow piew

pledge *n.* 保證 bo jing

pledge *v.t.* 承諾 sing lok

plenty *n.* 充裕 chung yu

plight *n.* 困難 kwan lan

plod *v.i.* 沈重咁行 tam chung gam hang

plot *n.* 故事情節 gu see ting jeet

plot *v.t.* 密謀 mat mow

plough *n.* 犁 lay

plough *v.i* 耕 gang

ploughman *n.* 農夫 lung fu

pluck *v.t.* 猛 mang

pluck *n* 膽量 dam leurng

plug *n.* 插蘇 tap sow

plug *v.t.* 插 tap

plum *n.* 布冧 bo lam

plumber *n.* 水工 suy gung

plunder *v.t.* 搶劫 cheurng geep

plunder *n* 搶 cheurng

plunge *v.t.* 暴跌 bo deet

plunge *n* 突然跌落 dak yeen deet lok

plural *a.* 複數 fuk sow

plurality *n.* 複數 fuk sow

plus *a.* 多 dor

plus *n* 好處 ho chu
ply *v.t.* 持續 tee juk
ply *n* 層 tang
pneumonia *n.* 肺炎 fay yeem
pocket *n.* 口袋 ho doy
pocket *v.t.* 袋 doy
pod *n.* 豆莢 sow gap
poem *n.* 詩 see
poesy *n.* 詩 see
poet *n.* 詩人 see yan
poetaster *n.* 差嘅詩人 ta geh see yan
poetess *n.* 女詩人 luy see yan
poetic *a.* 詩嘅 see geh
poetics *n.* 詩學 see hok
poetry *n.* 詩集 see jap
poignancy *n.* 悲慘 bay tarm
poignant *a.* 令人悲慘 ling yan bay tarm
point *n.* 點 deem
point *v.t.* 指 jee
poise *v.t.* 捉實 juk sat
poise *n* 儀態 yee tai
poison *n.* 毒 duk
poison *v.t.* 毒 duk
poisonous *a.* 有毒嘅 yow duk geh
poke *v.t.* 篤 duk
poke *n.* 篤 duk
polar *a* 極地嘅 gik day geh
pole *n.* 管 gwun
police *n.* 警察 ging tat
policeman *n.* 警察 ging tat
policy *n.* 方針 forng jam
polish *v.t.* 擦 tat
polish *n* 擦光劑 tat gworng jay
polite *a.* 有禮貌 yow lay mao
politeness *n.* 禮貌 lay mao
politic *a.* 明智嘅 ming jee geh
political *a.* 政治嘅 jing jee geh
politician *n.* 政治家 jing jee ga
politics *n.* 政治 jing jee

polity *n.* 國家組織 gwok ga jow jik
poll *n.* 投票 tow piew
poll *v.t.* 調查 diew ta
pollen *n.* 花粉 far fan
pollute *v.t.* 污染 wu yeem
pollution *n.* 污染 wu yeem
polo *n.* 馬球 ma kow
polygamous *a.* 一夫多妻嘅 yat fu dor tay geh
polygamy *n.* 一夫多妻 yat fu dor tay
polyglot1 *n.* 識多種語言嘅人 sik dor jung yu yeen geh yan
polyglot2 *a.* 多種語言寫成嘅 dor jung yu yeen seh sing geh
polytechnic *a.* 工藝嘅 gung ngay geh
polytechnic *n.* 理工學院 lay gung hok yoon
polytheism *n.* 多神信仰 dor san sun yeurng
polytheist *n.* 多神教徒 dor san gao tow
polytheistic *a.* 多神崇拜嘅 dor san sung bai geh
pomp *n.* 排場 pai cheurng
pomposity *n.* 自大 jee dai
pompous *a.* 誇大嘅 kwa dai geh
pond *n.* 池塘 tee tong
ponder *v.t.* 仔細考慮 jee say hao luy
pony *n.* 細馬 say ma
poor *a.* 窮 kung
pop *v.i.* 爆 bao
pop *n* 流行曲 low hang kuk
pope *n.* 教宗 gao jung
poplar *n.* 楊樹 yeurng shu
poplin *n.* 府綢 fu cho
populace *n.* 平民百姓 ping man bak sing

popular *a.* 受歡迎嘅 sow fwun ying geh

popularity *n.* 收歡迎度 sow fwun ying dow

popularize *v.t.* 宣傳 shoon choon

populate *v.t.* 填充 teen chung

population *n.* 人口 yan ho

populous *a.* 人口眾多嘅 yan ho jung dor geh

porcelain *n.* 瓷器 tee hay

porch *n.* 門廊 mwun lorng

pore *n.* 毛孔 mow hung

pork *n.* 豬肉 ju yuk

porridge *n.* 麥皮 mak pay

port *n.* 港口 gorng ho

portable *a.* 隨手攜帶嘅 chuy sow kway dai geh

portage *n.* 搬運 bwun wan

portal *n.* 入口 yap ho

portend *v.t.* 預兆 yu siew

porter *n.* 行李員 hang lay yoon

portfolio *n.* 文件夾 man geen gap

portico *n.* 柱廊 chu lorng

portion *n* 一份 yat fan

portion *v.t.* 分 fan

portrait *n.* 肖像 tiew jeurng

portraiture *n.* 畫像 wah jeurng

portray *v.t.* 顯得 heen dak

portrayal *n.* 描繪 miew kwuy

pose *v.i.* 擺姿勢 bai jee say

pose *n.* 姿勢 jee say

position *n.* 位置 way jee

position *v.t.* 擺 bai

positive *a.* 正面嘅 jing meen geh

possess *v.t.* 擁有 yung yow

possession *n.* 財物 choy mat

possibility *n.* 可能性 hor lang sing

possible *a.* 可能嘅 hor lang geh

post *n.* 郵政 yow jing

post *v.t.* 寄 gey

post *n* 職位 jik way

post *v.t.* 派人 pai yan

post *adv.* 快嘅 fai geh

postage *n.* 郵費 yow fay

postal *a.* 郵遞嘅 yow day geh

post-date *v.t.* 填遲日期 teen tee yat kay

poster *n.* 海報 hoy bo

posterity *n.* 後代 ho doy

posthumous *a.* 死後嘅 say ho geh

postman *n.* 郵差 yow tai

postmaster *n.* 郵政局長 yow jing guk jeurng

post-mortem *a.* 死後嘅 say ho geh

post-mortem *n.* 驗屍 yeem see

post-office *n.* 郵局 yow guk

postpone *v.t.* 延遲 yeen tee

postponement *n.* 延期 yeen kay

postscript *n.* 附言 fu yeen

posture *n.* 姿勢 jee say

pot *n.* 罐 gwun

pot *v.t.* 裝入盆度 jorng yao pwun dow

potash *n.* 碳酸鉀 tan shoon gap

potassium *n.* 鉀 gap

potato *n.* 薯仔 shu jay

potency *n.* 影響力 ying heurng lik

potent *a.* 有效嘅 yow hao geh

potential *a.* 有潛能 yow teem lang

potential *n.* 潛質 teem jat

potentiality *n.* 潛力 teem lik

potter *n.* 陶工 tow gung

pottery *n.* 陶器 tow hay

pouch *n.* 細袋 say doy

poultry *n.* 家禽肉 ga kam yuk

pounce *v.i.* 突襲 dak jap

pounce *n* 突襲 dak jap

pound *n.* 英鎊 ying borng

pound *v.t.* 怦怦咁跳 bung bung gam tiew
pour *v.i.* 倒 dow
poverty *n.* 貧窮 pan kung
powder *n.* 粉 fan
powder *v.t.* 加粉 ga fan
power *n.* 權力 koon lin
powerful *a.* 有權嘅 yow koon geh
practicability *n.* 實用性 sat yung sing
practicable *a.* 可行嘅 hor hang geh
practical *a.* 實際嘅 sat jay geh
practice *n.* 實際行動 sat jay hang dung
practise *v.t.* 練習 leen jap
practitioner *n.* 從業者 chung yeep jeh
pragmatic *a.* 實用嘅 sat yung geh
pragmatism *n.* 實用主義 sat yung ju yee
praise *n.* 稱讚 ting jan
praise *v.t.* 讚 jan
praiseworthy *a.* 值得讚嘅 jik dak jan geh
prank *n.* 惡作劇 ok jok kek
prattle *v.i.* 講廢話 gorng fay wah
prattle *n.* 廢話 fay wah
pray *v.i.* 祈禱 kay tow
prayer *n.* 禱告 tow gow
preach *v.i.* 宣揚 shoon yeurng
preacher *n.* 傳教者 choon dow jeh
preamble *n.* 開場白 hoy cheurng bak
precaution *n.* 預防 yu forng
precautionary *a.* 預防嘅 yu forng geh
precede *v.* 先於 seen yu
precedence *n.* 優先權 yow seen koon
precedent *n.* 先例 seen lay

precept *n.* 準則 jun jak
preceptor *n.* 訓導人 fan dow yan
precious *a.* 珍貴嘅 jan gway geh
precis *n.* 摘要 jak yiew
precise *a.* 準確嘅 jun kok geh
precision *n.* 準確度 jun kok dow
precursor *n.* 先驅 seen kuy
predecessor *n.* 前任 teen yam
predestination *n.* 宿命論 suk ming lun
predetermine *v.t.* 預先決定 yu seen koot ding
predicament *n.* 困境 kwan ging
predicate *n.* 謂語 way yu
predict *v.t.* 預計 yu gey
prediction *n.* 估計 gu gey
predominance *n.* 優勢 yow say
predominant *a.* 佔優勢嘅 jeem yow say geh
predominate *v.i.* 佔優勢 jeem yow say
pre-eminence *n.* 傑出 geet chut
pre-eminent *a.* 傑出嘅 geet chut geh
preface *n.* 序言 juy yeen
preface *v.t.* 寫序 ser juy
prefect *n.* 學長 hok jeurng
prefer *v.t.* 比較鐘意 bay gao jung yee
preference *n.* 喜好 hay ho
preferential *a.* 優先嘅 yow seen geh
prefix *n.* 前綴 teen juy
prefix *v.t.* 係...前面加 hay...teen meen ga
pregnancy *n.* 懷孕 wai yan
pregnant *a.* 有咗 yow jor
prehistoric *a.* 史前嘅 see teen geh
prejudice *n.* 偏見 peen geen
prelate *n.* 高級教士 gow kap gao see

preliminary *a.* 初步嘅 chor bo geh

preliminary *n* 預備措施 yu bay cho see

prelude *n.* 序曲 juy kuk

prelude *v.t.* 開始 hoy tee

premarital *a.* 婚前嘅 fan teen geh

premature *a.* 早產嘅 jow tan geh

premeditate *v.t.* 預先考慮 yu seen hao luy

premeditation *n.* 預謀 yu mow

premier *a.* 首要嘅 sow yiew geh

premier *n* 首相 sow seurng

premiere *n.* 首映 sow ying

premium *n.* 附加費 fu ga fay

premonition *n.* 預感 yu gam

preoccupation *n.* 盤算 pwun shoon

preoccupy *v.t.* 日夜思考 yat yeh see hao

preparation *n.* 準備 jun bay

preparatory *a.* 準備嘅 jun bay geh

prepare *v.t.* 準備 jun bay

preponderance *n.* 優勢 yow say

preponderate *v.i.* 佔優勢 jeem yow say

preposition *n.* 介詞 gai tee

prerequisite *a.* 必需嘅 beet suy geh

prerequisite *n* 條件 tiew geen

prerogative *n.* 特權 dak koon

prescience *n.* 預知 yu jee

prescribe *v.t.* 開 hoy

prescription *n.* 藥方 yeurk forng

presence *n.* 出現 chut yeen

present *a.* 而家嘅 yee ga geh

present *n.* 禮物 lay mat

present *v.t.* 頒 ban

presentation *n.* 演講 yeen gorng

presently *adv.* 而家 yee ga

preservation *n.* 保護 bo wu

preservative *n.* 防腐劑 forng fu jay

preservative *a.* 保存嘅 bo choon geh

preserve *v.t.* 保存 bo choon

preserve *n.* 果醬 gwor jeurng

preside *v.i.* 主持 ju tee

president *n.* 總統 jung tung

presidential *a.* 總統嘅 jung tung geh

press *v.t.* gam

press *n* 傳媒 choon mwuy

pressure *n.* 壓力 ngat lik

pressurize *v.t.* 施壓 see ngat

prestige *n.* 威信 way sun

prestigious *a.* 有威望嘅 yow way morng geh

presume *v.t.* 估 gu

presumption *n.* 假設 ga teet

presuppose *v.t.* 預料 yu liew

presupposition *n.* 假設 ga teet

pretence *n.* 假象 ga jeurng

pretend *v.t.* 假扮 ga ban

pretension *n.* 自命 jee ming

pretentious *a.* 自命不凡嘅 jee ming bat fan geh

pretext *n* 藉口 jik ho

prettiness *n.* 美麗 may lay

pretty *a* 靚嘅 leng geh

pretty *adv.* 幾 gey

prevail *v.i.* 壓倒 ngat dow

prevalence *n.* 普遍 pow peen

prevalent *a.* 普遍嘅 pow peen geh

prevent *v.t.* 防止 forng jee

prevention *n.* 預防 yu forng

preventive *a.* 預防性嘅 yu forng sing geh

previous *a.* 之前嘅 jee teen geh

prey *n.* 獵物 leep mat

prey *v.i.* 捕食 bo sik

price *n.* 價錢 ga teen

price *v.t.* 定價 ding ga

prick *n.* 針拮 jam gat

prick *v.t.* 拮 gat

pride *n.* 驕傲 giew ow

pride *v.t.* 為...而驕傲 way...yee giew oh

priest *n.* 神父 san fu

priestess *n.* 女祭司 luy jay see

priesthood *n.* 神父職位 san fu jik way

prima facie *adv.* 初步印象 chor bo yan jeurng

primarily *adv.* 主要 ju yiew

primary *a.* 最重要嘅 juy jung yiew geh

prime *a.* 主要嘅 ju yiew geh

prime *n.* 盛年 sing leen

primer *n.* 低 day

primeval *a.* 原始嘅 yoon tee geh

primitive *a.* 落後嘅 lok ho geh

prince *n.* 王子 worng jee

princely *a.* 似王子咁嘅 tee worng jee gam geh

princess *n.* 公主 gung ju

principal *n.* 校長 hao jeurng

principal *a* 最重要嘅 juy jung yiew geh

principle *n.* 原則 yoon jak

print *v.t.* 印 yan

print *n* 複印 fuk yan

printer *n.* 印刷機 yan tat gey

prior *a.* 嘅之前 geh jee teen

prior *n* 會長 wuy jeurng

prioress *n.* 修女院院長 sow luy yoon yoon jeurng

priority *n.* 優先權 yow seen koon

prison *n.* 監獄 gam yuk

prisoner *n.* 囚犯 chow fan

privacy *n.* 私隱 see yan

private *a.* 私人嘅 see yan geh

privation *n.* 貧困 pan kwan

privilege *n.* 特權 dak koon

prize *n.* 獎品 jeurng ban

prize *v.t.* 珍惜 jan sik

probability *n.* 可能性 hor lang sing

probable *a.* 有可能嘅 yow hor lang geh

probably *adv.* 有可能 yow hor lang

probation *n.* 試用期 see yung kay

probationer *n.* 見習生 geen jap sang

probe *v.t.* 盤問 pwun man

probe *n* 探究 tam gow

problem *n.* 問題 man tay

problematic *a.* 有問題嘅 yow man tay geh

procedure *n.* 程序 ting juy

proceed *v.i.* 繼續做 gey juk jow

proceeding *n.* 過程 gwor ting

proceeds *n.* 收入 sow yap

process *n.* 程序 ting juy

procession *n.* 行列 horng leet

proclaim *v.t.* 宣佈 shoon bo

proclamation *n.* 聲名 sing ming

proclivity *n.* 癖好 pik ho

procrastinate *v.i.* 拖延 tor yeen

procrastination *n.* 延遲 yeen tee

proctor *n.* 監考官 garm hao gwun

procure *v.t.* 獲得 wok dak

procurement *n.* 採購 choy gow

prodigal *a.* 敗家嘅 bai ga geh

prodigality *n.* 浪費 lorng fay

produce *v.t.* 生產 sang tan

produce *n.* 產品 tan ban

product *n.* 產品 tan ban

production *n.* 製造 jay jok

productive *a.* 有效率嘅 yow hao lut geh

productivity *n.* 生產率 sang tan lut

profane *a.* 褻瀆神靈嘅 seet juk san ling geh

profane *v.t.* 褻瀆神靈 seet juk san ling

profess *v.t.* 聲稱 sing ting

profession *n.* 職業 jik yeep

professional *a.* 專業嘅 joon yeep geh

professor *n.* 教授 gao sow

proficiency *n.* 精通 jing tung

proficient *a.* 熟手嘅 suk sow geh

profile *n.* 簡介 'gan gai

profile *v.t.* 寫簡介 seh gan gai

profit *n.* 利潤 lay yun

profit *v.t.* 得益 dak yik

profitable *a.* 有利潤嘅 yow lay yun geh

profiteer *n.* 奸商 gan seurng

profiteer *v.i.* 獲取暴利 wok chuy bo lay

profligacy *n.* 浪費 lorng fay

profligate *a.* 嘥嘅 sai geh

profound *a.* 深嘅 sam geh

profundity *n.* 深度 sam dow

profuse *a.* 大量嘅 dai leurng geh

profusion *n.* 大量 dai leurng

progeny *n.* 子孫 jee shoon

programme *n.* 節目 jeetmuk

programme *v.t.* 計劃 gey wak

progress *n.* 進度 jun dow

progress *v.i.* 進步 jun bo

progressive *a.* 有進度嘅 yow jun dow geh

prohibit *v.t.* 禁止 gam jee

prohibition *n.* 禁制令 gam jay ling

prohibitive *a.* 禁止嘅 gam jee geh

prohibitory *a.* 禁止嘅 gam jee geh

project *n.* 計劃 gey wak

project *v.t.* 放映 forng ying

projectile *n.* 投射物 tow she mat

projectile *a* 發射嘅 fat seh geh

projection *n.* 放映嘅影像 forng ying geh ying jeurng

projector *n.* 放映機 forng ying gey

proliferate *v.i.* 激增 gik jang

proliferation *n.* 激增 gik jang

prolific *a.* 多產嘅 dor tan geh

prologue *n.* 序 juy

prolong *v.t.* 延長 yeen cheurng

prolongation *n.* 延長 yeen cheurng

prominence *n.* 突出 dak chut

prominent *a.* 突出嘅 dan chut geh

promise *n* 承諾 sing lok

promise *v.t* 應承 ying sing

promising *a.* 有希望嘅 yow hay morng geh

promissory *a.* 約好嘅 yeurk ho geh

promote *v.t.* 宣傳 shoon choon

promotion *n.* 宣傳 shoon choon

prompt *a.* 即刻 jik hak

prompt *v.t.* 提 tay

prompter *n.* 提示人 tay see yan

prone *a.* 容易感染到 yung yee gam yeem dow

pronoun *n.* 代名詞 doy ming tee

pronounce *v.t.* 發音 fat yam

pronunciation *n.* 發音 fat yam

proof *n.* 證據 jing guy

proof *a* 可以防護 hor yee forng wu

prop *n.* 道具 dow guy

prop *v.t.* 支撐 jee tang

propaganda *n.* 宣傳 shoon choon

propagandist *n.* 宣傳者 shoon choon jeh

propagate *v.t.* 傳播 choon bor

propagation *n.* 宣傳 shoon choon

propel *v.t.* 推動 tuy dung

proper *a.* 真正嘅 tan jing geh

property *n.* 財產 choy tan

prophecy *n.* 預言 yu yeen
prophesy *v.t.* 預告 yu gow
prophet *n.* 預言家 yu yeen ga
prophetic *a.* 預言嘅 yu yeen geh
proportion *n.* 比例 bay lay
proportion *v.t.* 分 fan
proportional *a.* 成比例嘅 sing bay lay geh
proportionate *a.* 成比例嘅 sing bay lay geh
proposal *n.* 計劃 gey wak
propose *v.t.* 求婚 kow fan
proposition *n.* 提議 tay yee
propound *v.t.* 提出 tay chut
proprietary *a.* 專有嘅 joon yow geh
proprietor *n.* 業主 yeep ju
propriety *n.* 得體 dak tay
prorogue *v.t.* 休會 yow wuy
prosaic *a.* 無聊嘅 mow liew geh
prose *n.* 散文 san man
prosecute *v.t.* 起訴 hay sow
prosecution *n.* 訴訟 sow jung
prosecutor *n.* 檢察官 geem tat gwun
prosody *n.* 韻律 wan lut
prospect *n.* 希望 hay morng
prospective *a.* 有望嘅 yow morng geh
prospsectus *n.* 簡介 gan gai
prosper *v.i.* 發達 fat dat
prosperity *n.* 興旺 hing worng
prosperous *a.* 繁榮嘅 fan wing geh
prostitute *n.* 妓女 gey luy
prostitute *v.t.* 賣淫 mai yam
prostitution *n.* 賣淫 mai yam
prostrate *a.* 趴低嘅 par day geh
prostrate *v.t.* 趴低 par day
prostration *n.* 衰竭 suy keet
protagonist *n.* 擁護者 yung wu jeh

protect *v.t.* 保護 bo wu
protection *n.* 保護 bo wu
protective *a.* 保護嘅 bo wu geh
protector *n.* 保護人 bo wu yan
protein *n.* 蛋白質 dan bak jatt
protest *n.* 抗議 korng yee
protest *v.i.* 反對 fan duy
protestation *n.* 鄭重聲明 jeng jung sing ming
prototype *n.* 樣板 yeurng ban
proud *a.* 驕傲嘅 giew oh geh
prove *v.t.* 證明 jing ming
proverb *n.* 格言 gak yeen
proverbial *a.* 眾所周知 jung sor jow jee
provide *v.i.* 提供 tay gung
providence *n.* 上帝 seurng day
provident *a.* 未雨綢繆 may yu tow mow
providential *a.* 及時嘅 kap see geh
province *n.* 省 sang
provincial *a.* 省嘅 sang geh
provincialism *n.* 固執 gu jap
provision *n.* 供應 gung ying
provisional *a.* 暫時嘅 jam see geh
provisonality *n.* 暫時性 jam see sing
provocation *n.* 刺激 tee gik
provocative *a.* 挑釁嘅 tiew yan geh
provoke *v.t.* 惹 yeh
prowess *n.* 威力 way lik
proximate *a.* 最接近嘅 juy jeep gan geh
proximity *n.* 近 kan
proxy *n.* 代理 doy lay
prude *n.* 正經過度嘅人 jing ging gwor dow geh yan
prudence *n.* 審慎 sam san
prudent *a.* 審慎嘅 sam san geh

prudential *a.* 謹慎嘅 gan san geh
prune *v.t.* 修剪 sow jeen
pry *v.i.* 打聽 da ting
psalm *n.* 讚美詩 jan may see
pseudonym *n.* 筆名 bat meng
psyche *n.* 心靈 sam ling
psychiatrist *n.* 精神科醫生 jing san for yee sang
psychiatry *n.* 精神病學 jing san beng hok
psychic *a.* 通靈嘅 tung ling geh
psychological *a.* 心靈嘅 sam ling geh
psychologist *n.* 心理學家 sam lay hok ga
psychology *n.* 心理學 sam lay hok
psychopath *n.* 精神病患者 jing san beng wan jeh
psychosis *n.* 精神病 jing san beng
psychotherapy *n.* 心裡治療 sam lay jee liew
puberty *n.* 青春期 ting chun kay
public *a.* 公眾嘅 gung jung geh
public *n.* 公眾 gung jung
publication *n.* 出版 chut ban
publicity *n.* 宣傳 shoon shoon
publicize *v.t.* 宣傳 shoon choon
publish *v.t.* 刊登 horn dang
publisher *n.* 出版人 chut ban yan
pudding *n.* 布丁 bo ding
puddle *n.* 水窪 suy tam
puddle *v.t.* 踩過水窪 tai gwor suy tam
puerile *a.* 幼稚嘅 yow jee geh
puff *n.* 吸 kap
puff *v.i.* 噴出 pan chut
pull *v.t.* 拉 lai
pull *n.* 拉 lai
pulley *n.* 滑輪 wat lun
pullover *n.* 過頭笠 gwor tow lap

pulp *n.* 紙漿 jee jeurng
pulp *v.t.* 攪成漿 gao sing jeurng
pulpit *a.* 講壇 gorng tan
pulpy *a.* 紙漿狀嘅 jee jeurng jorng geh
pulsate *v.i.* 搏動 bok dung
pulsation *n.* 震動 jan dung
pulse *n.* 脈搏 mak bok
pulse *v.i.* 跳動 tiew dung
pulse *n* 節拍 jeet bak
pump *n.* 泵 bung
pump *v.t.* 泵 bung
pumpkin *n.* 南瓜 lam gwa
pun *n.* 雙關語 seurng gwan yu
pun *v.i.* 用雙關語 yung seurng gwan yu
punch *n.* 拳擊 koon gik
punch *v.t.* 拳打 koon da
punctual *a.* 準時嘅 jun see geh
punctuality *n.* 準時率 jun see lut
punctuate *v.t.* 加標點符號 ga biew deem fu ho
punctuation *n.* 標點符號 biew deem fu ho
puncture *n.* 細窿 say lung
puncture *v.t.* 拮穿 gat choon
pungency *n.* 辛辣 san lat
pungent *a.* 強烈味道 keurng leet may dow
punish *v.t.* 罰 fat
punishment *n.* 懲罰 ting fat
punitive *a.* 懲罰嘅 ting fat geh
puny *a.* 孱弱孱弱 san yeurk geh
pupil *n.* 學生 hok sang
puppet *n.* 扯線公仔 ter seen gung jay
puppy *n.* 幼犬 yow hoon
purblind *n.* 半盲孱弱 bwun mang geh
purchase *n.* 購買 kow mai
purchase *v.t.* 買 mai
pure *a* 純嘅 sun geh

purgation *n.* 淨化 jing far
purgative *n.* 瀉藥 ser yeurk
purgative *a* 淨化嘅 jing far geh
purgatory *n.* 折磨 jeet mor
purge *v.t.* 清除 ting chuy
purification *n.* 淨化 jing far
purify *v.t.* 淨化 jing far
purist *n.* 純粹主義者 sun suy ju yee jeh
puritan *n.* 清教徒 ting gao tow
puritanical *a.* 清教徒式嘅 ting gao tow sik geh
purity *n.* 純潔 sun geet
purple *adj./n.* 紫色 jee sik
purport *n.* 大概意思 dai koy yee see
purport *v.t.* 自稱 jee ting
purpose *n.* 目的 muk dik
purpose *v.t.* 有目的 yow muk dik
purposely *adv.* 特登嘅 dak dang geh
purr *n.* 貓呼嚕聲 mao fu low seng
purr *v.i.* 貓打呼嚕 mao da fu low
purse *n.* 銀包 ngan bao
purse *v.t.* 撮起嘴唇 juy hay juy sun
pursuance *n.* 追求 juy kow
pursue *v.t.* 追求 juy kow
pursuit *n.* 追求 juy kow
purview *n.* 範圍嘅 fan way geh
pus *n.* 膿 lung
push *v.t.* 推 tuy
push *n.* 推 tuy
put *v.t.* 擺 bai
puzzle *n.* 謎 may
puzzle *v.t.* 令人煩嘅 ling yan fan geh
pygmy *n.* 侏儒 ju yu
pyorrhoea *n.* 膿漏 lung low
pyramid *n.* 金字塔 gam jee tap
pyre *n.* 柴堆 tai duy
python *n.* 蟒蛇 morng she

Q

quack *v.i.* 呱呱聲 gwa gwa seng
quack *n* 鴨叫聲 arp giew seng
quackery *n.* 江湖醫術 gorng wu yeet sut
quadrangle *n.* 四方院 say forng yoon
quadrangular *a.* 四角型嘅 say gok ying geh
quadrilateral *a. & n.* 四角型 say gok ying
quadruped *n.* 四足動物 say juk dung mat
quadruple *a.* 四倍嘅 say pwuy geh
quadruple *v.t.* 變為四倍 been way say pwuy
quail *n.* 鵪鶉 am chun
quaint *a.* 古色古香嘅 gu sik gu heurng ghe
quake *v.i.* 發抖 dat dow
quake *n* 地震 day jan
qualification *n.* 學歷 hok lik
qualify *v.i.* 有資格 yow jee gak
qualitative *a.* 質量嘅 jat leurng geh
quality *n.* 質量 jat leurng
quandary *n.* 困惑 kwan wak
quantitative *a.* 數量嘅 sow leurng geh
quantity *n.* 數量 sow leurng
quantum *n.* 量子 leurng jee
quarrel *n.* 嗌交 ai sap
quarrel *v.i.* 頂頸 ding geng
quarrelsome *a.* 成日嗌交 sing yat ai sap
quarry *n.* 採石場 choy sek cheurng
quarry *v.i.* 採 choy
quarter *n.* 四份一 say fan yat

quarter *v.t.* 分為四份一 fan way say fan yat

quarterly *a.* 每季度嘅 mwuy gway dow geh

queen *n.* 女王 luy worng

queer *a.* 奇怪嘅 kay gwai geh

quell *v.t.* 鎮壓 jan ngat

quench *v.t.* 止 jee

query *n.* 疑問 yee man

query *v.t* 懷疑 wai yee

quest *n.* 探索 tam sok

quest *v.t.* 探索 tam sok

question *n.* 問題 man tay

question *v.t.* 質疑 jat yee

questionable *a.* 可疑嘅 hor yee geh

questionnaire *n.* 問卷 man goon

queue *n.* 一條長龍 yat tiew cheurng lung

quibble *n.* 嗌謞 ai sap

quibble *v.i.* 嗌謞 ai sap

quick *a.* 快嘅 fai geh

quick *n* 快 fai

quicksand *n.* 流沙 low sa

quicksilver *n.* 水銀 suy an

quiet *a.* 細聲嘅 say seng geh

quiet *n.* 靜 jing

quiet *v.t.* 平靜 ping jing

quilt *n.* 棉被 meen pay

quinine *n.* 奎寧 fwuy ling

quintessence *n.* 典範 deen fan

quit *v.t.* 退出 tuy chut

quite *adv.* 幾 gey

quiver *n.* 震動 jan dung

quiver *v.i.* 震 jan

quixotic *a.* 唔實際嘅 hm sat jay geh

quiz *n.* 小測驗 siew tak yeem

quiz *v.t.* 問 man

quorum *n.* 法定人數 fat ding yan sow

quota *n.* 配額 pwuy ak

quotation *n.* 報價 bo ga

quote *v.t.* 引用 yan yung

quotient *n.* 商數 seurng sow

R

rabbit *n.* 兔仔 tow jay

rabies *n.* 瘋狗症 fung gow jing

race *n.* 賽跑 choy pao

race *v.i* 比賽 bay choy

racial *a.* 種族嘅 jung juk geh

racialism *n.* 種族歧視 jung juk kay see

rack *v.t.* 受盡折磨 sow jun jeet mor

rack *n.* 架 ga

racket *n.* 吵鬧 tao lao

radiance *n.* 容光煥發 yung gwong wun fat

radiant *a.* 光芒四射 gwong morng say she

radiate *v.t.* 散發出 san fat chut

radiation *n.* 輻射 fuk she

radical *a.* 激進嘅 gik jun geh

radio *n.* 收音機 sow yam gey

radio *v.t.* 播 bor

radish *n.* 蘿蔔 lor bak

radium *n.* 鐳 luy

radius *n.* 半徑 bwun ging

rag *n.* 爛布 lan bo

rag *v.t.* 整蠱 jing gu

rage *n.* 火 for

rage *v.i.* 發火 fat for

raid *n.* 突襲 dak jap

raid *v.t.* 搜查 sow ta

rail *n.* 欄杆 lan gorn

rail *v.t.* 怒斥 low tik

raling *n.* 圍欄 way lan

raillery *n.* 講笑 gorng siew

railway *n.* 鐵路 teet low

rain *v.i.* 落雨 lok yu

rain *n* 雨 yu

rainy *a.* 多雨嘅 dor yu geh

raise *v.t.* 提高 tay gow

raisin *n.* 提子乾 tay jee gon

rally *v.t.* 集合 jap hap

rally *n* 公眾集會 gung jung jap wuy

ram *n.* 公羊 gung yeurng

ram *v.t.* 撞 jorng

ramble *v.t.* 亂講 loon gorng

ramble *n* 散步 san bo

rampage *v.i.* 橫衝直撞 wang chung jik jorng

rampage *n.* 亂鬧 loon lao

rampant *a.* 猖狂 cheurng kwong

rampart *n.* 城牆 sing cheurng

rancour *n.* 怨恨 yoon han

random *a.* 隨意嘅 chuy yee geh

range *v.t.* 變 been

range *n.* 系列 hay leet

ranger *n.* 護林人 wu lam yan

rank *n.* 地位 day way

rank *v.t.* 分級 fan kap

rank *a* 難聞嘅 lan man geh

ransack *v.t.* 洗劫 say geep

ransom *n.* 贖金 suk gam

ransom *v.t.* 交贖金 gao suk gam

rape *n.* 強姦罪 keurng gan juy

rape *v.t.* 強姦 keurng gan

rapid *a.* 快 fai

rapidity *n.* 迅速 sun chuk

rapier *n.* 長劍 cheurng geem

rapport *n.* 默契 mak kay

rapt *a.* 全神貫注 choon san gwun ju

rapture *n.* 歡天喜地 fwun teen hay day

rare *a.* 罕有 hon yow

rascal *n.* 無賴 mow lai

rash *a.* 皮疹 pay tan

rat *n.* 老鼠 low shu

rate *v.t.* 評估 ping gu

rate *n.* 率 lut

rather *adv.* 幾 gey

ratify *v.t.* 證實批准 jing sik pay jun

ratio *n.* 對比率 duy bay lut

ration *n.* 配額 pwuy ak

rational *a.* 理性 lay sing

rationale *n.* 原理 yoon lay

rationality *n.* 合理性 hap lay sing

rationalize *v.t.* 合理化 hap lay far

rattle *v.i.* 搖 yiew

rattle *n* 喀嗒聲 ka ta seng

ravage *n.* 損壞 shoon wai

ravage *v.t.* 毀壞 way wai

rave *v.i.* 亂嗌廿四 loop ap ya say

raven *n.* 渡鴉 dow ngar

ravine *n.* 深谷 sam guk

raw *a.* 生嘅 sang geh

ray *n.* 光線 gworng seen

raze *v.t.* 夷爲平地 yee way ping day

razor *n.* 剃刀 tay dow

reach *v.t.* 到 dow

react *v.i.* 反應 fan ying

reaction *n.* 反應 fan ying

reactinary *a.* 保守嘅 bo sow geh

read *v.t.* 讀 duk

reader *n.* 讀者 duk jeh

readily *adv.* 樂意 lok yee

readiness *n.* 準備 jun bay

ready *a.* 準備 jun bay

real *a.* 真嘅 jan geh

realism *n.* 逼真 bik tan

realist *n.* 現實主義者 yeen sat ju yee jeh

realistic *a.* 逼真嘅 bik tan geh

reality *n.* 現實生活 yeen sat sang wut

realization *n.* 領悟 ling hm

realize *v.t.* 意識到 yee sik dow

really *adv.* 真係 jan hay

realm *a.* 領域 ling wik
ream *n.* 令 ling
reap *v.t.* 收穫 sow wok
reaper *n.* 收割機 sow got gey
rear *n.* 後面 how meen
rear *v.t.* 養 yeurng
reason *n.* 原因 yoon yan
reason *v.i.* 講道理 gorng dow lay
reasonable *a.* 有道理 yow dow lay
reassure *v.t.* 向人保證 heurng yan bo jing
rabate *n.* 退款 tuy fwun
rebel *v.i.* 反 fan
rebel *n.* 作反 jok fan
rebellion *n.* 謀反 mow fan
rebellious *a.* 反叛嘅 fan bwun geh
rebirth *n.* 重生 chung sang
rebound *v.i.* 反彈 fan dan
rebound *n.* 籃板球 lam ban kow
rebuff *n.* 拒絕 kuy joot
rebuff *v.t.* 一口拒絕 yat ho kuy joot
rebuke *v.t.* 批評 pay ping
rebuke *n.* 批評 pay ping
recall *v.t.* 諗返起 lam fan hay
recall *n.* 記性 gey sing
recede *v.i.* 減弱 garm yeurk
receipt *n.* 單 dan
receive *v.t.* 收 sow
receiver *n.* 接收人 jeep sow yan
recent *a.* 近排 gan pai
recently *adv.* 近排 gan pai
reception *n.* 接待處 jeep doy chu
receptive *a.* 願意聆聽嘅 yoon yee ling ting geh
recess *n.* 休會期 yow wuy kay
recession *n.* 經濟衰退 ging jay suy tuy
recipe *n.* 食譜 sik po
recipient *n.* 收件人 sow geen yan

reciprocal *a.* 互惠互利 wu way wu lay
reciprocate *v.t.* 回報 wuy bo
recital *n.* 演奏會 yeen jow wuy
recitation *n.* 朗誦 lorng jung
recite *v.t.* 朗誦 lorng jung
reckless *a.* 不計後果 bat gey how gwor
reckon *v.t.* 認爲 ying way
reclaim *v.t.* 攞返 lor fan
reclamation *n* 開拓 hoy tok
recluse *n.* 隱士 yan see
recognition *n.* 認可 ying hor
recognize *v.t.* 認得 ying dak
recoil *v.i.* 退縮 tuy suk
recoil *adv.* 退縮 tuy suk
recollect *v.t.* 記得 gey dak
recollection *n.* 記憶 gey yik
recommend *v.t.* 推薦 tuy jeen
recommendation *n.* 提議 tay yee
recompense *v.t.* 賠 pwuy
recompense *n.* 賠償 pwuy seurng
reconcile *v.t.* 和解 wor gai
reconciliation *n.* 和解 wor gai
record *v.t.* 錄 luk
record *n.* 紀錄 gey luk
recorder *n.* 錄音機 luk yam gey
recount *v.t.* 講述 gorng sut
recoup *v.t.* 攞返 lor fan
recourse *n.* 依靠 yee kao
recover *v.t.* 恢復 fwuy fuk
recovery *n.* 恢復 fwuy fuk
recreation *n.* 消遣活動 siew heen wut dung
recruit *n.* 新人 san yan
recruit *v.t.* 招募 jiew mow
rectangle *n.* 長方形 cheurng forng ying
rectangular *a.* 長方形嘅 cheurng forng ying geh

rectification *n.* 改正 goy jing
rectify *v.i.* 矯正 giew jing
rectum *n.* 直腸 jik cheurng
recur *v.i.* 再發生 joy fat sang
recurrence *n.* 重現 chung yeen
recurrent *a.* 循環嘅 chun wan geh
red *a.* 紅色嘅 hung sik geh
red *n.* 紅色 hung sik
redden *v.t.* 變紅 been hung
reddish *a.* 紅紅哋 hung hung day
redeem *v.t.* 挽回 wan wuy
redemption *n.* 贖返 suk fan
redouble *v.t.* 加倍 ga pwuy
redress *v.t.* 糾正 gow jing
redress *n* 賠償 pwuy seurng
reduce *v.t.* 減 garm
reduction *n.* 減 garm
redundance *n.* 裁員 choy yoon
redundant *a.* 畀人炒嘅 bay yan tao geh
reel *n.* 捲筒 goon tung
reel *v.i.* 擺下擺下 yiew ha yiew ha
refer *v.t.* 提起 tay hay
referee *n.* 裁判 choy pwun
reference *n.* 提到 tay dow
referendum *n.* 全民投票 choon man tow piew
refine *v.t.* 去除雜質 huy chuy jap jat
refinement *n.* 改善 goy seen
refinery *n.* 提煉廠 tay leen chorng
reflect *v.t.* 反映 fan ying
reflection *n.* 倒映 dow ying
reflective *a.* 反光 fan gwong
reflector *n.* 反射器 fan seh hay
reflex *n.* 反應 fan ying
reflex *a* 反應嘅 fan ying geh
reflexive *a* 反射嘅 fan ser geh
reform *v.t.* 改 goy
reform *n.* 改善 goy seen
reformation *n.* 改革 goy gak

reformatory *n.* 感化院 gam far yoon
reformatory *a* 改革嘅 goy gak geh
reformer *n.* 改革者 goy gak jeh
refrain *v.i.* 克制 hak jay
refrain *n* 副歌 fu gor
refresh *v.t.* 提醒 tay seng
refreshment *n.* 飲品 yam ban
refrigerate *v.t.* 變冷 been lang
refrigeration *n.* 冷凍 lang dung
refrigerator *n.* 雪櫃 shoot gway
refuge *n.* 避難 bay lan
refugee *n.* 難民 lan man
refulgence *n.* 輝煌 fay worng
refulgent *a.* 燦爛嘅 tan lan geh
refund *v.t.* 退 tuy
refund *n.* 退款 tuy fwun
refusal *n.* 拒絕 kuy joot
refuse *v.t.* 拒絕 kuy joot
refuse *n.* 拒絕 kuy joot
refutation *n.* 反駁 fan bok
refute *v.t.* 反駁 fan bok
regal *a.* 豪華嘅 ho wah geh
regard *v.t.* 視為 see way
regard *n.* 問候 man ho
regenerate *v.t.* 再生 jor sang
regeneration *n.* 重生 chung sang
regicide *n.* 弒君罪 see gwan juy
regime *n.* 統治方式 tung jee forng sik
regiment *n.* 軍團 gwan toon
regiment *v.t.* 組團 jow toon
region *n.* 地區 day kuy
regional *a.* 地區嘅 day kuy geh
register *n.* 登記簿 dang gey bo
register *v.t.* 登記 dang gey
registrar *n.* 登記員 dang gey yoon
registration *n.* 登記 dang gey
registry *n.* 註冊處 chu tak chu
regret *v.i.* 後悔 how fwut

regular **regret** *n* 遺憾 way han
regular *a.* 定時嘅 ding see geh
regularity *n.* 規律性 kway lut sing
regulate *v.t.* 約束 yeurk chuk
regulation *n.* 規則 kway jak
regulator *n.* 調節器 tiew jeet hay
rehabilitate *v.t.* 恢復 fwuy fuk
rehabilitation *n.* 復原 fuk yoon
rehearsal *n.* 彩排 choy pai
rehearse *v.t.* 排練 pai leen
reign *v.i.* 統治期 tung jee kay
reign *n* 統治 tung jee
reimburse *v.t.* 補償 bo seurng
rein *n.* 勒繩 lak sing
rein *v.t.* 勒住 lak ju
reinforce *v.t.* 加強 ga keurng
reinforcement *n.* 強化 keurng far
reinstate *v.t.* 復職 fuk jik
reinstatement *n.* 復職 fuk jik
reiterate *v.t.* 重複 chung fuk
reiteration *n.* 重複 chung fuk
reject *v.t.* 拒絕 kuy joot
rejection *n.* 拒絕 kuy joot
rejoice *v.i.* 高興 gow hing
rejoin *v.t.* 返去 fan huy
rejoinder *n.* 反駁 fan bok
rejuvenate *v.t.* 變後生 been ho sang
rejuvenation *n.* 恢復青春 fwuy fuk ting chun
relapse *v.i.* 復發 fuk fat
relapse *n.* 舊病復發 gow beng fuk fat
relate *v.t.* 聯繫 loon hay
relation *n.* 關係 gwan hay
relative *a.* 有關係嘅 yow gwan hay geh
relative *n.* 親戚 tan tik
relax *v.t.* 放鬆 forng sung
relaxation *n.* 放鬆 forng sung
relay *n.* 接力賽 jeep lik choy

relay *v.t.* 轉發 joon fat
release *v.t.* 放 forng
release *n* 發佈 fat bo
relent *v.i.* 終於應承 jung yu ying sing
relentless *a.* 持續嘅 tee juk geh
relevance *n.* 關係 gwan hay
relevant *a.* 有關嘅 yow gwan geh
reliable *a.* 信得過嘅 sun dak gwor geh
reliance *n.* 依賴 yee lai
relic *n.* 遺跡 way jik
relief *n.* 解脫 gai toot
relieve *v.t.* 減輕 garm heng
religion *n.* 宗教 jung gao
religious *a.* 虔誠嘅 keen sing geh
relinquish *v.t.* 放棄 forng hay
relish *v.t.* 享受 heurng sow
relish *n* 樂趣 lok chuy
reluctance *n.* 勉強 meen keurng
reluctant *a.* 勉強嘅 meen keurng geh
rely *v.i.* 依賴 yee lai
remain *v.i.* 保持 bo tee
remainder *n.* 剩低 jing day
remains *n.* 遺跡 way jik
remand *v.t.* 還押候審 wan ngat ho sam
remand *n* 還押 wan ngat
remark *n.* 言論 yeen lun
remark *v.t.* 講 gorng
remarkable *a.* 引人注目嘅 yarn yan ju muk geh
remedial *a.* 補救嘅 bo gow geh
remedy *n.* 藥 yeurk
remedy *v.t* 醫 yee
remember *v.t.* 記得 gey dak
remembrance *n.* 紀念 gey leem
remind *v.t.* 提 tay
reminder *n.* 提醒 tay seng
reminiscence *n.* 回憶 wuy yik
reminiscent *a.* 回憶返 wuy yik

fan

remission *n.* 緩解期 wun gai kay

remit *v.t.* 匯款 wuy fwun

remittance *n.* 匯款金額 wuy fwun gam ak

remorse *n.* 自責 jee jak

remote *a.* 偏遠嘅 peen yoon geh

removable *a.* 可以徐嘅 hor yee chuy geh

removal *n.* 消除 siew chuy

remove *v.t.* 清除 ting chuy

remunerate *v.t.* 出糧 chut leurng

remuneration *n.* 酬勞 chow low

remunerative *a.* 報酬豐厚嘅 bo chow fung ho geh

renaissance *n.* 復興 fuk hing

render *v.t.* 變得 been dak

rendezvous *n.* 約會 yeurk wuy

renew *v.t.* 更新 gang san

renewal *n.* 更新 gang san

renounce *v.t.* 宣佈放棄 shoon bo forng hay

renovate *v.t.* 翻新 fan san

renovation *n.* 翻新 fan san

renown *n.* 名望 ming morng

renowned *a.* 有名嘅 yow meng geh

rent *n.* 租金 jow gam

rent *v.t.* 租 jow

renunciation *n.* 宣佈放棄 shoon bo forng hay

repair *v.t.* 整返 jing fan

repair *n.* 修理 sow lay

raparable *a.* 有得整嘅 yow dak jing geh

repartee *n.* 巧妙嘅答案 hao miew geh dap on

repatriate *v.t.* 遣返 heen fan

repatriate *n* 遣返人 heen fan yan

repatriation *n.* 遣返 heen fan

repay *v.t.* 還返 wan fan

repayment *n.* 賠償 pwuy seurng

repeal *v.t.* 廢除 fay chuy

repeal *n* 廢除 fay chuy

repeat *v.t.* 重複 chung fuk

repel *v.t.* 擊退 gik tuy

repellent *a.* 令人討厭嘅 ling yan tow yeem geh

repellent *n* 殺蟲劑 sat chung jay

repent *v.i.* 後悔 ho fwuy

repentance *n.* 後悔 ho fwuy

repentant *a.* 後悔嘅 ho fwuy geh

repercussion *n.* 反應 fan ying

repetition *n.* 重複 chung fuk

replace *v.t.* 代替 doy tay

replacement *n.* 代替 doy tay

replenish *v.t.* 補充 bo chung

replete *a.* 充滿 chung mwun

replica *n.* 複製品 fuk jay ban

reply *v.i.* 回覆 wuy fuk

reply *n* 回覆 wuy fuk

report *v.t.* 報告 bo gow

report *n.* 報告 bo gow

reporter *n.* 記者 gey jeh

repose *n.* 休息 yow sik

repose *v.i.* 休息 yow sik

repository *n.* 倉庫 chorng fu

represent *v.t.* 代表 doy biew

representation *n.* 代表 doy biew

representative *n.* 代表 doy biew

representative *a.* 有代表性嘅 yow doy biew sing geh

repress *v.t.* 克制 hay jay

repression *n.* 壓制 ngat jay

reprimand *n.* 斥責 tik jak

reprimand *v.t.* 斥責 tik jak

reprint *v.t.* 重印 chung yan

reprint *n.* 重印 chung yan

reproach *v.t.* 指責 jee jak

reproach *n.* 批評 pay ping

reproduce *v.t.* 再造 joy jow

reproduction *n* 繁殖 fan jik

reproductive *a.* 生殖嘅 sang jik geh

reproof *n.* 責備 jay bay

reptile *n.* 爬行動物 pa hang dung mat

republic *n.* 共和國 gung wor gwok

republican *a.* 共和黨嘅 gung wor dorng geh

republican *n* 共和黨黨員 gung wor dorng dorng yoon

repudiate *v.t.* 拒絕 kuy joot

repudiation *n.* 拒絕 kuy joot

repugnance *n.* 反感 fan gam

repugnant *a.* 令人反感嘅 ling yan fan gam geh

repulse *v.t.* 擊退 gik tuy

repulse *n.* 拒絕 kuy joot

repulsion *n.* 反感 fan gam

repulsive *a.* 令人反感嘅 ling yan fan gam geh

reputation *n.* 名譽 ming yu

repute *v.t.* 認為 ying way

repute *n.* 名氣 ming hay

request *v.t.* 要求 yiew kow

request *n* 請求 ting kow

requiem *n.* 安魂曲 on wan kuk

require *v.t.* 需要 suy yiew

requirement *n.* 需要 suy yiew

requisite *a.* 必需嘅 beet suy geh

requisite *n* 必需嘅野 beet suy geh yeh

requisition *n.* 徵用 jing yung

requisition *v.t.* 徵用 jing yung

requite *v.t.* 回報 wuy bo

rescue *v.t.* 救 gow

rescue *n* 搶救 cheurng gow

research *v.i.* 資料收集 jee liew sow jao

research *n* 調查 tiew ta

resemblance *n.* 似 tee

resemble *v.t.* 似 tee

resent *v.t.* 激氣 gik hay

resentment *n.* 怨恨 yoon han

reservation *n.* 預訂 yu deng

reserve *v.t.* 預約 yu yeurk

reservoir *n.* 水庫 suy fu

reside *v.i.* 住 ju

residence *n.* 住所 ju sor

resident *a.* 居住嘅 guy ju geh

resident *n* 居民 guy man

residual *a.* 殘留嘅 tan low geh

residue *n.* 殘留物質 tan low man jat

resign *v.t.* 辭職 tee jik

resignation *n.* 辭職 tee jik

resist *v.t.* 反抗 fan korng

resistance *n.* 反抗力 fan korng lik

resistant *a.* 有抵抗力 yow day korng lik

resolute *a.* 堅決嘅 geen koot geh

resolution *n.* 清晰度 ting sik dow

resolve *v.t.* 解決 gai koot

resonance *n.* 響亮 heurng leurng

resonant *a.* 響亮嘅 heurng leurng geh

resort *v.i.* 依靠 yee kao

resort *n* 旅遊勝地 luy yow sing day

resound *v.i.* 響 heurng

resource *n.* 資源 jee yoon

resourceful *a.* 機智嘅 gey jee geh

respect *v.t.* 尊重 joon jung

respect *n.* 尊重 joon jung

respectful *a.* 尊重嘅 joon jung geh

respective *a.* 分別嘅 fan beet geh

respiration *n.* 呼吸 fu kap

respire *v.i.* 呼吸 fu kap

resplendent *a.* 輝煌嘅 fay worng geh

respond *v.i.* 答 dap

respondent *n.* 回答人 wuy dap yan

response *n.* 答覆 dap fuk
responsibility *n.* 責任 jak yam
responsible *a.* 有責任感 yow jak yam gam
rest *v.i.* 休息 yow sik
rest *n* 其餘 kay yu
restaurant *n.* 餐廳 tan teng
restive *a.* 唔耐煩嘅 hm loy fan geh
restoration *n.* 復原 fuk yoon
restore *v.t.* 恢復 fwuy fuk
restrain *v.t.* 制止 jay jee
restrict *v.t.* 限 han
restriction *n.* 限制 han jay
restrictive *a.* 約束嘅 yeurk chuk geh
result *v.i.* 造成 jow sing
result *n.* 後果 ho gwor
resume *v.t.* 繼續 gey juk
resume *n.* 簡歷 gan lik
resumption *n.* 恢復 fwuy fuk
resurgence *n.* 復現 fuk yeen
resurgent *a.* 復興嘅 fuk hing geh
retail *v.t.* 賣 mai
retail *n.* 零售 ling sow
retail *adv.* 以零售方式 yee ling sow forng sik
retail *a* 零售嘅 ling sow geh
retailer *n.* 零售商 ling sow seurng
retain *v.t.* 保持 bo tee
retaliate *v.i.* 報復 bo fuk
retaliation *n.* 報復 bo fuk
retard *v.t.* 阻礙 jor ngoy
retardation *n.* 延滯 yeen jay
retention *n.* 維持 way tee
retentive *a.* 有記性 yow gey sing
reticence *n.* 沈默寡言 tam mak gwa yeen
reticent *a.* 沈默嘅 tam mak geh
retina *n.* 視網膜 see morng mok
retinue *n.* 隨從 chuy chung
retire *v.i.* 退休 tuy yow

retirement *n.* 退休 tuy yow
retort *v.t.* 駁嘴 bok juy
retort *n.* 駁嘴 bok juy
retouch *v.t.* 執下 jap ha
retrace *v.t.* 返轉頭 fan joon tow
retread *v.t.* 翻抄 fan tao
retread *n.* 翻抄 fan tao
retreat *v.i.* 撤退 teet tuy
retrench *v.t.* 節省開支 jeet sang hoy jee
retrenchment *n.* 節省開支 jeet sang hoy jee
retrieve *v.t.* 攞返 lor fan
retrospect *n.* 回想 wuy seurng
retrospection *n.* 回憶 wuy yik
retrospective *a.* 以前嘅 yee teen geh
return *v.i.* 返嚟 fan lay
return *n.* 回來 wuy loy
revel *v.i.* 陶醉 tow juy
revel *n.* 狂歡 kworng fwun
revelation *n.* 揭露 keet low
reveller *n.* 醉酒佬 juy jow low
revelry *n.* 狂歡作樂 kworng fwun jok lok
revenge *v.t.* 報仇 bo sow
revenge *n.* 報仇 bo sow
revengeful *a.* 報復嘅 bo fuk geh
revenue *n.* 財政收入 choy jing sow yap
revere *v.t.* 尊敬 joon ging
reverence *n.* 尊敬 joon ging
reverend *a.* 尊敬嘅 joon ging geh
reverent *a.* 非常尊敬嘅 fay seurng joon ging geh
reverential *a.* 充滿敬意嘅 chung mwun ging yee geh
reverie *n.* 幻想 wan seurng
reversal *n.* 倒轉 dow joon
reverse *a.* 相反嘅 seurng fan geh
reverse *n* 相反 seurng fan
reverse *v.t.* 倒轉 dow joon

reversible *a.* 可以翻轉嘅 hor yee fan joon geh
revert *v.i.* 回復 wuy fuk
review *v.t.* 回顧 wuy gu
review *n* 評價 ping ga
revise *v.t.* 溫習 wan jap
revision *n.* 溫習 wan jap
revival *n.* 復蘇 fuk sow
revive *v.i.* 復蘇 fuk sow
revocable *a.* 可以撤回嘅 hor yee teet wuy geh
revocation *n.* 廢除 fay chuy
revoke *v.t.* 取消 chuy siew
revolt *v.i.* 反抗 fan korng
revolt *n.* 反抗 fan korng
revolution *n.* 革命 gak ming
revolutionary *a.* 巨變嘅 guy been geh
revolutionary *n* 改革者 goy gak jeh
revolve *v.i.* 環繞 wan yiew
revolver *n.* 左輪槍 jor lun cheurng
reward *n.* 獎勵 jeurng lay
reward *v.t.* 獎 jeurng
rhetoric *n.* 修辭 sow tee
rhetorical *a.* 反問嘅 fan man geh
rheumatic *a.* 風濕病嘅 fung sap beng geh
rheumatism *n.* 風濕 fung sap
rhinoceros *n.* 犀牛 say ngow
rhyme *n.* 押韻 ngat wan
rhyme *v.i.* 押韻 ngat wan
rhymester *n.* 差嘅詩人 ta geh see yan
rhythm *n* 節奏 jeet jow
rhythmic *a.* 有節奏嘅 yow jeet jow geh
rib *n.* 肋骨 lak gwat
ribbon *n.* 絲帶 see dai
rice *n.* 米 may
rich *a.* 有錢嘅 yow teen geh

riches *n.* 財富 choy fu
richness *a.* 豐富 fung fu
rick *n.* 乾草堆 gorn cho duy
rickets *n.* 佝僂病 kuy low beng
rickety *a.* 唔穩固嘅 hm wan gu geh
rickshaw *n.* 人力車 yan lik cher
rid *v.t.* 擺脫 bay toot
riddle *n.* 謎語 may yu
riddle *v.i.* 充滿 chung mwun
ride *v.t.* 騎 keh
ride *n* 旅程 luy ting
rider *n.* 騎手 keh sow
ridge *n.* 山脊 san jek
ridicule *v.t.* 奚落 hai lok
ridicule *n.* 奚落 hai lok
ridiculous *a.* 荒謬嘅 forng mow geh
rifle *v.t.* 偷 tow
rifle *n* 來福槍 loy fuk cheurng
rift *n.* 裂縫 leet fung
right *a.* 啱嘅 ngam geh
right *adv* 向右 heurng yow
right *n* 權 koon
right *v.t.* 糾正 gow jing
righteous *a.* 正當嘅 jing dorng geh
rigid *a.* 死板嘅 say ban geh
rigorous *a.* 嚴格嘅 yeem gak geh
rigour *n.* 嚴厲 yeem lay
rim *n.* 邊緣 been yoon
ring *n.* 戒指 gai jee
ring *v.t.* 打界 da bay
ringlet *n.* 捲髮 goon fat
ringworm *n.* 癬 seen
rinse *v.t.* 沖洗 chung say
riot *n.* 騷亂 sow loon
riot *v.t.* 鬧事 lao see
rip *v.t.* 撕爛 see lan
ripe *a.* 熟嘅 suk geh
ripen *v.i.* 成熟 sing suk
ripple *n.* 波浪 bor long

ripple *v.t.* 蕩漾 dorng yeurng	**roguery** *n.* 惡作劇 ok jok kek
rise *v.* 升 sing	**roguish** *a.* 蠱惑嘅 gu wak geh
rise *n.* 增加 jang ga	**role** *n.* 角色 gok sik
risk *v.t.* 冒險 mow heem	**roll** *n.* 卷 goon
risk *n.* 風險 fung hee,	**roll** *v.i.* 捲 goon
risky *a.* 危險嘅 ngay heem geh	**roll-call** *n.* 點名 deem meng
rite *n.* 儀式 yee sik	**roller** *n.* 滾筒 gwan tung
ritual *n.* 儀式 yee sik	**romance** *n.* 浪漫 lorng man
ritual *a.* 儀式上嘅 yee sik seurng geh	**romantic** *a.* 浪漫嘅 lorng man geh
rival *n.* 競爭對手 ging jang duy sow	**romp** *v.i.* 輕易咁取勝 hing yee gam chuy sing
rival *v.t.* 比得上 bay dak seurng	**romp** *n.* 風流韻事 fung low wan see
rivalry *n.* 競爭 ging jang	**rood** *n.* 十字架 sap jee ga
river *n.* 河 hor	**roof** *n.* 瓦面 ngar meen
rivet *n.* 鍋釘 wor deng	**roof** *v.t.* 整屋頂 jing uk deng
rivet *v.t.* 吸引住 kap yan ju	**rook** *n.* 禿鼻烏鴉 tuk bay wu ngar
rivulet *n.* 溪流 kay low	**rook** *v.t.* 呃 ak
road *n.* 路 low	**room** *n.* 房 forng
roam *v.i.* 漫步 man bo	**roomy** *a.* 寬敞嘅 fwun torng geh
roar *n.* 吼叫 hao giew	**roost** *n.* 棲息處 tay sik chu
roar *v.i.* 吼叫 hao giew	**roost** *v.i.* 棲息 tay sik
roast *v.t.* 烤 hao	**root** *n.* 根 gan
roast *a* 烤嘅 hao geh	**root** *v.i.* 搵 wan
roast *n* 烤肉 hao yuk	**rope** *n.* 繩 sing
rob *v.t.* 偷 tow	**rope** *v.t.* 綁 borng
robber *n.* 賊 tak	**rosary** *n.* 數珠 sow ju
robbery *n.* 搶劫 cheurng geep	**rose** *n.* 玫瑰 mwuy gway
robe *n.* 長袍 cheurng pow	**roseate** *a.* 粉紅色嘅 fan hung sik geh
robe *v.t.* 着長袍 jeurk cheurng pow	**rostrum** *n.* 講台 gorng toy
robot *n.* 機械人 gey hai yan	**rosy** *a.* 紅潤嘅 hung yun geh
robust *a.* 強壯嘅 keurng jorng geh	**rot** *n.* 腐爛 fu lan
rock *v.t.* 搖 yiew	**rot** *v.i.* 腐爛 fu lan
rock *n.* 石頭 sek tow	**rotary** *a.* 轉動嘅 joon dung geh
rocket *n.* 火箭 for jeen	**rotate** *v.i.* 轉 joon
rod *n.* 杆 gorn	**rotation** *n.* 轉動 joon dung
rodent *n.* 齧齒動物 jeet tee dung mat	**rote** *n.* 死記硬背 say gey ngang bwuy
roe *n.* 魚子 yu jee	**rouble** *n.* 盧布 low bo
rogue *n.* 無賴 mow lai	**rough** *a.* 諧雺雺 hai sap sap

round *a.* 圓形嘅 yoon ying geh
round *adv.* 環繞 wan yiew
round *n.* 局 guk
round *v.t.* 繞過 yiew gwor
rouse *v.i.* 叫醒 giew seng
rout *v.t.* 徹底打敗 teet day da bai
rout *n* 徹底打敗 teet day da bai
route *n.* 路線 low seen
routine *n.* 日常事務 yat seurng see mow
routine *a* 日常嘅 yat seurng geh
rove *v.i.* 流浪 low lorng
rover *n.* 流浪者 low lorng jeh
row *n.* 一行 yat horng
row *v.t.* 撑 tang
row *n* 糾紛 gow fan
row *n.* 一排 yat pai
rowdy *a.* 吵嘅 cho geh
royal *a.* 王室嘅 worng sat geh
royalist *n.* 保皇主義者 bo worng ju yee jeh
royalty *n.* 王室成員 worng sat sing yoon
rub *v.t.* 捽 jut
rub *n* 問題 man tay
rubber *n.* 橡膠 jeurng gao
rubbish *n.* 垃圾 lap sap
rubble *n.* 碎石 suy sek
ruby *n.* 紅寶石 hung bo sek
rude *a.* 無禮貌嘅 mow lay mao geh
rudiment *n.* 基礎 gey chor
rudimentary *a.* 基本嘅 gey bwun geh
rue *v.t.* 後悔 ho fwuy
rueful *a.* 後悔嘅 ho fwuy geh
ruffian *n.* 歹徒 dai tow
ruffle *v.t.* 整皺 jing tao
rug *n.* 細地氈 say day jeen
rugged *a.* 崎嶇嘅 kay kuy geh
ruin *n.* 廢墟 fay huy
ruin *v.t.* 破壞 por wai

rule *n.* 規矩 kway guy
rule *v.t.* 統治 tung jee
ruler *n.* 間尺 gan tek
ruling *n.* 裁決 choy koot
rum *n.* 朗姆酒 lorng mow jow
rum *a* 古怪嘅 gu gwai geh
rumble *v.i.* 發隆隆聲 fat lung lung seng
rumble *n.* 隆隆聲 lung lung seng
ruminant *a.* 反芻嘅 fan tow geh
ruminant *n.* 反芻動物 fan tow dung mat
ruminate *v.i.* 認真思考 ying jan see hao
rumination *n.* 思考 see hao
rummage *v.i.* 搜掠 sow leurk
rummage *n* 搜尋 sow tam
rummy *n.* 拉米紙牌 lai may jee pai
rumour *n.* 謠言 yiew yeen
rumour *v.t.* 傳 choon
run *v.i.* 跑 pao
run *n.* 跑步 pao bo
rung *n.* 梯級 tay kap
runner *n.* 跑手 pao sow
rupee *n.* 盧比 low bay
rupture *n.* 破裂 por leet
rupture *v.t.* 破裂 por leet
rural *a.* 鄉下嘅 heurng ha geh
ruse *n.* 詭計 gway gey
rush *n.* 趕時間 gorn see gan
rush *v.t.* 趕 gorn
rush *n* 衝 chung
rust *n.* 鐵鏽 teet sow
rust *v.i* 生鏽 sang sow
rustic *a.* 鄉下嘅 heurng ha geh
rustic *n* 鄉下人 heurng ha yan
rusticate *v.t.* 去鄉下 huy heurng ha
rustication *n.* 鄉村生活 heurng choon sang wut
rusticity *n.* 樸素 pok sow

rusty *a.* 生鏽 sang sow

rut *n.* 刻板生活 hak ban sang wut

ruthless *a.* 冷酷無情 lang huk mo ting

rye *n.* 黑麥 hak mak

S

sabbath *n.* 安息日 on sik yat

sabotage *n.* 蓄意破壞 chuk yee por wai

sabotage *v.t.* 蓄意破壞 chuk yee por wai

sabre *n.* 佩劍 pwuy geem

sabre *v.t.* 殺 sat

saccharin *n.* 糖精 tong jing

saccharine *a.* 情緒化 ting suy far

sack *n.* 麻包袋 ma bao doy

sack *v.t.* 炒 tao

sacrament *n.* 聖禮 sing lay

sacred *a.* 神聖嘅 san sing geh

sacrifice *n.* 祭品 jay ban

sacrifice *v.t.* 犧牲 hay sang

sacrificial *a.* 犧牲嘅 hay sang geh

sacrilege *n.* 褻瀆 seet juk

sacrilegious *a.* 褻瀆 seet juk

sacrosanct *a.* 神聖不可侵犯 san sing bat hor tam fan

sad *a.* 傷心 seurng sam

sadden *v.t.* 令人難過 ling yan lan gwor

saddle *n.* 馬鞍 ma on

saddle *v.t.* 裝馬鞍 jorng ma on

sadism *n.* 虐待狂 yeurk doy kwong

sadist *n.* 虐待狂 yeurk doy kwong

safe *a.* 安全 on choon

safe *n.* 保險箱 bo heem seurng

safeguard *n.* 保護 bo wu

safety *n.* 安全 on choon

saffron *n.* 藏紅花粉 jorng hung far fan

saffron *a* 橙黃色 tang worng sik

sagacious *a.* 精明 jing ming

sagacity *n.* 聰慧 chung way

sage *n.* 智者 jee jeh

sage *a.* 聰明嘅 chung ming geh

sail *n.* 船帆 shoon fan

sail *v.i.* 坐船 chor shoon

sailor *n.* 船員 shoon yoon

saint *n.* 聖人 sing yan

saintly *a.* 聖潔嘅 sing geet geh

sake *n.* 為咗 way jor

salable *a.* 暢銷 cheurng siew

salad *n.* 沙律 sa lut

salary *n.* 糧 leurng

sale *n.* 減價 garm ga

salesman *n.* 售貨員 sow for yoon

salient *a.* 最重要嘅 juy jung yiew geh

saline *a.* 鹽嘅 yeem geh

salinity *n.* 鹽性 yeem sing

saliva *n.* 口水 ho suy

sally *n.* 突襲 dak jap

sally *v.i.* 衝出 chung chut

saloon *n.* 酒吧 jow ba

salt *n.* 鹽 yeem

salt *v.t* 加鹽 ga yeem

salty *a.* 鹹 harm

salutary *a.* 有益嘅 yow yik geh

salutation *n.* 問候 man ho

salute *v.t.* 敬禮 ging lay

salute *n* 敬禮 ging lay

salvage *n.* 搶救 cheurng gow

salvage *v.t.* 搶救 cheurng gow

salvation *n.* 救恩 gow yan

same *a.* 一樣嘅 yat yeurng geh

sample *n.* 樣本 yeurng bwun

sample *v.t.* 試下 see har

sanatorium *n.* 療養院 liew yeurng yoon

sanctification *n.* 神聖化 san sing far

sanctify *v.t.* 神聖化 san sing far

sanction *n.* 制裁 jay choy

sanction *v.t.* 懲罰 ting fat

sanctity *n.* 神聖嘅 san sing geh

sanctuary *n.* 庇護所 bay wu sor

sand *n.* 沙 sa

sandal *n.* 涼鞋 leurng hai

sandalwood *n.* 檀香油 tan heurng yow

sandwich *n.* 三文治 sam man jee

sandwich *v.t.* 夾喺中間 geep hay jung gan

sandy *a.* 沙嘅 sa geh

sane *a.* 理智嘅 lay jee geh

sanguine *a.* 樂觀 lok gwun

sanitary *a.* 衛生嘅 way sang geh

sanity *n.* 理智 lay jee

sap *n.* 液 yik

sap *v.t.* 變虛弱 been huy yeurk

sapling *n.* 幼樹 yow shu

sapphire *n.* 藍寶石 lam bo sek

sarcasm *n.* 諷刺 fung tee

sarcastic *a.* 諷刺嘅 fung tee geh

sardonic *a.* 輕視嘅 hing see geh

satan *n.* 魔鬼 mor gway

satchel *n.* 書包 shu bao

satellite *n.* 衛星 way sing

satiable *a.* 滿足嘅 mun juk geh

satiate *v.t.* 厭 yeem

satiety *n.* 滿足 mun juk

satire *n.* 諷刺 fung tee

satirical *a.* 諷刺嘅 fung tee geh

satirist *n.* 諷刺作家 fung tee jok ga

satirize *v.t.* 諷刺 fung tee

satisfaction *n.* 滿意 mun yee

satisfactory *a.* 滿意嘅 mun yee geh

satisfy *v.t.* 滿足 mun juk

saturate *v.t.* 濕晒 sap sai

saturation *n.* 飽和度 bao wor dow

Saturday *n.* 星期六 sing kay luk

sauce *n.* 醬汁 jeurng jap

saucer *n.* 茶碟 ta deep

saunter *v.t.* 慢慢行 man man hang

savage *a.* 惡嘅 ok geh

savage *n* 野蠻人 yeh man yan

savagery *n.* 殘暴行為 tan bo hang way

save *v.t.* 救 gow

save *prep* 徐咗 chuy jor

saviour *n.* 救星 gow sing

savour *n.* 味道 may dow

savour *v.t.* 品嘗 ban seurng

saw *n.* 鋸 guy

saw *v.t.* 睇到 tay dow

say *v.t.* 講 gorng

say *n.* 發言權 fat yeen koon

scabbard *n.* 鞘 tiew

scabies *n.* 疥癬 gai seen

scaffold *n.* 棚架 pang ga

scale *n.* 規模 kway mo

scale *v.t.* 攀登 pan dang

scalp *n* 頭皮 tow pay

scamper *v.i* 紮紮跳 jat jat tiew

scamper *n* 奔跑 ban pao

scan *v.t.* 掃描 sow miew

scandal *n* 醜聞 tow man

scandalize *v.t.* 令人震驚 ling yan jan ging

scant *a.* 少少 siew siew

scanty *a.* 唔夠 hm gow

scapegoat *n.* 代罪羔羊 doy juy gow yeurng

scar *n* 疤痕 ba han

scar *v.t.* 留疤痕 low ba han

scarce *a.* 稀有嘅 hay yow geh

scarcely *adv.* 勉強 meen keurng

scarcity *n.* 缺乏 koot fat

scare *n.* 嚇 hak

scare *v.t.* 嚇 hak
scarf *n.* 頸巾 geng gan
scatter *v.t.* 灑 sa
scavenger *n.* 食腐肉嘅動物 sik fu yuk geh dung mat
scene *n.* 鏡頭 geng tow
scenery *n.* 風景 fung ging
scenic *a.* 風景優美嘅 fung ging yow may geh
scent *n.* 味道 may dow
scent *v.t.* 聞到 man dow
sceptic *n.* 多疑嘅人 dor yee geh yan
sceptical *a.* 懷疑嘅 wai yee geh
scepticism *n.* 懷疑態度 wai yee tai dow
sceptre *n.* 權仗 koon jeurng
schedule *n.* 節目表 jeet muk biew
schedule *v.t.* 安排 on pai
scheme *n.* 計劃 gey wak
scheme *v.i.* 密謀 mat mow
schism *n.* 分裂 dan leet
scholar *n.* 學者 hok jeh
scholarly *a.* 有學問嘅 yow hok ham geh
scholarship *n.* 獎學金 jeurng hok gam
scholastic *a.* 學校嘅 hok hao geh
school *n.* 學校 hok hao
science *n.* 科學 for hok
scientific *a.* 科學嘅 for hok geh
scientist *n.* 科學家 for hok ga
scintillate *v.i.* 發出火花 fat chut for far
scintillation *n.* 閃 seem
scissors *n.* 鉸剪 gao jeen
scoff *n.* 整 jing
scoff *v.i.* 狼吞虎咽 lorng tun fur yeen
scold *v.t.* 鬧 lao

scooter *n.* 滑板車 wat ban cher
scope *n.* 機會 gey wuy
scorch *v.t.* 燒燶 siew lung
score *n.* 分數 fan sow
score *v.t.* 得分 dak fan
scorer *n.* 得分者 dak fan jeh
scorn *n.* 鄙視 pay see
scorn *v.t.* 鄙視 pay see
scorpion *n.* 蝎子 keet jee
Scot *n.* 蘇格蘭人 sow gak lan yan
scotch *a.* 蘇格蘭嘅 sow gak lan geh
scotch *n.* 蘇格蘭威士忌 sow gak lan way see gey
scot-free *adv.* 逍遙法外 siew yiew fat ngoy
scoundrel *n.* 無賴 mow lai
scourge *n.* 禍害 wor hoy
scourge *v.t.* 折磨 jeet mor
scout *n* 童子軍 tung jee gwan
scout *v.i* 物色 mat sik
scowl *v.i.* 皺眉頭 jow may tow
scowl *n.* 皺眉頭 jow may tow
scramble *v.i.* 爬 pa
scramble *n* 爬 pa
scrap *n.* 碎片 suy peen
scratch *n.* 抓 jao
scratch *v.t.* 抓 jao
scrawl *v.t.* 亂寫 loon she
scrawl *n* 潦草嘅字 liew cho geh jee
scream *v.i.* 叫 giew
scream *n* 叫聲 giew seng
screen *n.* 屏幕 ping mok
screen *v.t.* 檢查 geem ta
screw *n.* 螺絲 lor see
screw *v.t.* 上螺絲 seurng lor see
scribble *v.t.* 亂畫 loon wak
scribble *n.* 潦草嘅字 liew cho geh jee
script *n.* 劇本 kek bwun
scripture *n.* 聖經 sing ging

scroll *n.* 書卷 shu goon

scrutinize *v.t.* 仔細檢查 jee say geem ta

scrutiny *n.* 仔細檢查 jee say geem ta

scuffle *n.* 衝突 chung dat

scuffle *v.i.* 衝突 chung dat

sculptor *n.* 雕刻家 diew hak ga

sculptural *a.* 雕刻嘅 diew hak geh

sculpture *n.* 雕刻 diew hak

scythe *n.* 大鐮刀 dai leem dow

scythe *v.t.* 用大鐮刀割 yung dai leem dow got

sea *n.* 海 hoy

seal *n.* 海豹 hoy pao

seal *n.* 印章 yan jeurng

seal *v.t.* 封 fung

seam *n.* 線縫 色恩 fung

seam *v.t.* 接縫 jeep fung

seamy *a.* 污糟嘅 wu jow ghe

search *n.* 搜索 sow sok

search *v.t.* 搵 wan

season *n.* 季節 gway jeet

season *v.t.* 加調味料 ga iew may liew

seasonable *a.* 當令嘅 dorng ling geh

seasonal *a.* 季節嘅 gway jeet geh

seat *n.* 座位 jor way

seat *v.t.* 坐 chor

secede *v.i.* 脫離 toot lay

secession *n.* 脫離 toot lay

secessionist *n.* 脫離主義者 toot lay ju yee jeh

seclude *v.t.* 隔離 gak lay

secluded *a.* 與世隔絕嘅 yu say gak joot geh

seclusion *n.* 隱居 yan guy

second *a.* 第二嘅 day yee geh

second *n* 秒 miew

second *v.t.* 支持 jee tee

secondary *a.* 次要嘅 tee yiew geh

seconder *n.* 贊成人 jan sing yan

secrecy *n.* 保密 bo mat

secret *a.* 祕密嘅 bay mat geh

secret *n.* 祕密 bay may

secretariat (e) *n.* 秘書處 bay shu chu

secretary *n.* 秘書 bay shu

secrete *v.t.* 分泌 fan bay

secretion *n.* 分泌 fan bay

secretive *a.* 神祕嘅 san bay geh

sect *n.* 派別 pai beet

sectarian *a.* 教派嘅 gao pai geh

section *n.* 部份 bo fan

sector *n.* 部門 bo mwun

secure *a.* 安全嘅 on choon geh

secure *v.t.* 保護 bo wu

security *n.* 保安 bo on

sedan *n.* 轎車 giew cher

sedate *a.* 鎮定嘅 jan ding geh

sedate *v.t.* 畀鎮靜劑 bay jan jing jay

sedative *a.* 鎮靜嘅 jan jing geh

sedative *n* 鎮靜劑 jan jing jay

sedentary *a.* 成日坐嘅 sing yat chor geh

sediment *n.* 沈澱物 tam deen mat

sedition *n.* 煽動叛亂嘅詞 seen dung bwun loon geh tee

seditious *a.* 煽動性嘅 seen dung sing geh

seduce *v* 誘惑 yow wak

seduction *n.* 魅力 may lik

seductive *a* 性感嘅 sing gam geh

see *v.t.* 睇 tay

seed *n.* 種子 jung jee

seed *v.t.* 播種 bor jung

seek *v.t.* 搵 wan

seem *v.i.* 睇來 tay lay

seemly *a.* 得體嘅 dak tay geh

seep *v.i.* 滲入 sam yap

seer *n.* 預言家 yu yeen ga
seethe *v.i.* 激氣 gik hay
segment *n.* 部份 bo fan
segment *v.t.* 分割 fan got
segregate *v.t.* 分 fan
segregation *n.* 隔離措施 gak lay cho see
seismic *a.* 地震嘅 day jan geh
seize *v.t.* 捉住 juk ju
seizure *n.* 起獲 hay wok
seldom *adv.* 難得 lan dak
select *v.t.* 揀 gan
select *a* 精選嘅 jing shoon geh
selection *n.* 選擇 shoon jak
selective *a.* 有選擇嘅 yow shoon jak geh
self *n.* 自己 jee gey
selfish *a.* 自私 jee see
selfless *a.* 無私嘅 mow see geh
sell *v.t.* 賣 mai
seller *n.* 賣家 mai ga
semblance *n.* 假象 ga jeurng
semen *n.* 精液 jing yik
semester *n.* 學期 hok kay
seminal *a.* 影響深遠嘅 ying heurng sam yoon geh
seminar *n.* 研討會 yeen tow wuy
senate *n.* 參議院 tam yee yoon
senator *n.* 參議員 tam yee yoon
senatorial *a.* 參議員嘅 tam yee yoon geh
senatorial *a* 參議員嘅 tam yee yoon geh
send *v.t.* 寄 gey
senile *a.* 老糊塗嘅 low wu tow geh
senility *n.* 高齡 gow ling
senior *a.* 級別高嘅 kap beet gow geh
senior *n.* 上級 seurng kap
seniority *n.* 年長 leen jeurng
sensation *n.* 感覺 gam gok

sensational *a.* 轟動嘅 gwan dung geh
sense *n.* 五官 hm gwun
sense *v.t.* 感覺到 gam gok dow
senseless *a.* 無知覺嘅 mow jee gok geh
sensibility *n.* 敏感性 man gam sing
sensible *a.* 明智嘅 ming jee geh
sensitive *a.* 敏感嘅 man gam geh
sensual *a.* 感官嘅 gam gwun geh
sensualist *n.* 好色者 ho sik jeh
sensuality *n.* 享受 heurng sow
sensuous *a.* 感覺嘅 gam gok geh
sentence *n.* 句子 guy jee
sentence *v.t.* 判決 pwun koot
sentience *n.* 感覺性 gam gok sing
sentient *a.* 有感覺嘅 yow gam gok geh
sentiment *n.* 情緒 ting suy
sentimental *a.* 感情用事嘅 gam ting yung see geh
sentinel *n.* 哨兵 sao bing
sentry *n.* 哨兵 sao bing
separable *a.* 可以分開嘅 hor yee fan hoy geh
separate *v.t.* 分開 fan hoy
separate *a.* 分開嘅 fan hoy geh
separation *n.* 分離 fan lay
sepsis *n.* 膿毒病 lung duk beng
September *n.* 九月 gow yoot
septic *a.* 感染咗嘅 gam yeem jor geh
sepulchre *n.* 墳墓 fan mow
sepulture *n.* 墳墓 fan mow
sequel *n.* 續集 juk jap
sequence *n.* 一系列 yat hay leet
sequester *v.t.* 隔離 gak lay
serene *a.* 平靜嘅 ping jing geh
serenity *n.* 平靜 ping jing
serf *n.* 農奴 lung low

serge *n.* 嗶嘰 bat gey
sergeant *n.* 沙展 sa jeen
serial *a.* 連續嘅 leen juk geh
serial *n.* 連續劇 leen juk kek
series *n.* 系列 hay leet
serious *a* 嚴重嘅 yeem jung geh
sermon *n.* 講道 gorng dow
sermonize *v.i.* 說教 shoot gao
serpent *n.* 蛇 seh
serpentine *a.* 彎彎曲曲 wan wan kuk kuk
servant *n.* 工人 gung yan
serve *v.t.* 接待 jeep doy
serve *n.* 發球 fat kow
service *n.* 服務 fuk mow
service *v.t* 服務 fuk mow
serviceable *a.* 有用嘅 yow yung geh
servile *a.* 太順從嘅 tai sun chung geh
servility *n.* 屈從 wat chung
session *n.* 堂 torng
set *v.t* 設置 teet jee
set *a* 固定嘅 gu ding geh
set *n* 一套 yat tow
settle *v.i.* 解決 gai koot
settlement *n.* 協議 heep yee
settler *n.* 移民 yee man
seven *n.* 七 tat
seven *a* 七 tat
seventeen *n., a* 十七 sap tat
seventeenth *a.* 第十七 day sap tat
seventh *a.* 第七 day tat
seventieth *a.* 第七十 day tat sap
seventy *n., a* 七十 tat sap
sever *v.t.* 切斷 teet toon
several *a* 幾個 gey gor
severance *n.* 斷絕 toon joot
severe *a.* 嚴重嘅 yeem jung geh
severity *n.* 嚴重性 yeem jung sing

sew *v.t.* 聯返 loon fan
sewage *n.* 污水 wu suy
sewer *n* 污水道 wu suy dow
sewerage *n.* 排水系統 pai suy hay tung
sex *n.* 性行爲 sing hang way
sexual *a.* 性嘅 sing geh
sexuality *n.* 性取向 sing chuy heurng
sexy *n.* 性感 sing gam
shabby *a.* 破舊嘅 por gow geh
shackle *n.* 手扣 sow kow
shackle *v.t.* 扣住 kow ju
shade *n.* 陰 yam
shade *v.t.* 遮 jeh
shadow *n.* 影 ying
shadow *v.t* 射影 seh ying
shadowy *a.* 陰暗嘅 yam am geh
shaft *n.* 電梯蹧 deen tay cho
shake *v.i.* 搖 yiew
shake *n* 搖動 yiew dung
shaky *a.* 唔穩陣嘅 hm wan jan geh
shallow *a.* 淺嘅 teen geh
sham *v.i.* 冒充 mo chung
sham *n* 假象 ga jeurng
sham *a* 假嘅 ga geh
shame *n.* 羞恥 sow tee
shame *v.t.* 羞恥 sow tee
shameful *a.* 可恥嘅 hor tee geh
shameless *a.* 無恥嘅 mow tee ghe
shampoo *n.* 洗頭水 say tow suy
shampoo *v.t.* 洗頭 say tow
shanty *n.* 棚屋 pang uk
shape *n.* 形狀 ying jorng
shape *v.t* 塑造 sok jow
shapely *a.* 有曲線嘅 yow kuk seen ghe
share *n.* 股份 gu fan
share *v.t.* 分 fan
share *n* 一份 yat fan

shark *n.* 鯊魚 sa yu

sharp *a.* 尖嘅 jeem geh

sharp *adv.* 正 jing

sharpen *v.t.* 整尖 jing jeem

sharpener *n.* 鉛筆刨 yoon bat pao

sharper *n.* 騙子 peen jee

shatter *v.t.* 粉碎 fan suy

shave *v.t.* 剃 tay

shave *n* 剃 tay

shawl *n.* 被肩 pay geen

she *pron.* 佢 kuy

sheaf *n.* 一沓 yat dap

shear *v.t.* 剪 jeen

shears *n. pl.* 大剪刀 dai jeen dow

shed *v.t.* 落 lok

shed *n* 棚 pang

sheep *n.* 羊 yeurng

sheepish *a.* 唔好意思嘅 hm ho yee see geh

sheer *a.* 完全嘅 yoon choon geh

sheet *n.* 張 jeurng

sheet *v.t.* 罩 jao

shelf *n.* 架 ga

shell *n.* 殼 hok

shell *v.t.* 去殼 huy hok

shelter *n.* 住所 ju sor

shelter *v.t.* 保護 bo wu

shelve *v.t.* 上架 seurng ga

shepherd *n.* 牧羊人 muk yeurng yan

shield *n.* 盾 tun

shield *v.t.* 擋住 dorng ju

shift *v.t.* 轉移 joon yee

shift *n* 班 ban

shifty *a.* 唔可靠嘅 hm hor kao geh

shilling *n.* 先令 seen ling

shilly-shally *v.i.* 猶豫 yow yee

shilly-shally *n.* 猶豫 yow yee

shin *n.* 小腿 siew tuy

shine *v.i.* 發光 fat gworng

shine *n* 光澤 gworng jak

shiny *a.* 閃嘅 seem geh

ship *n.* 船 shoon

ship *v.t.* 運 wan

shipment *n.* 運送嘅貨 wan sung geh for

shire *n.* 郡 gwan

shirk *v.t.* 逃避 tow bay

shirker *n.* 逃避者 tow bay jeh

shirt *n.* 裇衫 sut sam

shiver *v.i.* 打冷震 da lang jan

shoal *n.* 魚群 yu kwan

shoal *n* 淺灘 teen tan

shock *n.* 嚇 hak

shock *v.t.* 嚇 hak

shoe *n.* 鞋 hai

shoe *v.t.* 釘蹄鐵 deng tay teet

shoot *v.t.* 射 she

shoot *n* 幼苗 yow miew

shop *n.* 店 deem

shop *v.i.* 行街 hang gai

shore *n.* 岸 on

short *a.* 短嘅 doon geh

short *adv.* 唔夠 hm gow

shortage *n.* 短缺 doon koot

shortcoming *n.* 短處 doon chu

shorten *v.t.* 整短 jing doon

shortly *adv.* 一陣 yat jan

shorts *n. pl.* 短褲 doon fu

shot *n.* 射擊 seh gik

shoulder *n.* 膊頭 bok tow

shoulder *v.t.* 承擔 sing dam

shout *n.* 大叫 dai giew

shout *v.i.* 大叫 dai giew

shove *v.t.* 推 tuy

shove *n.* 推 tuy

shovel *n.* 鐵鏟 teet tan

shovel *v.t.* 鏟 tan

show *v.t.* 證明 jing ming

show *n.* 表演 biew yeen

shower *n.* 沖涼 chung leurng

shower *v.t.* 沖涼 chung leurng

shrew *n.* 老虎乸 low fu la

shrewd *a.* 精明嘅 jing ming ghe

shriek *n.* 尖叫聲 jeem giew seng

shriek *v.i.* 尖叫 jeem giew

shrill *a.* 尖聲嘅 jeem seng geh

shrine *n.* 聖地 sing day

shrink *v.i* 縮細 suk say

shrinkage *n.* 縮細 suk say

shroud *n.* 壽衣 sow yee

shroud *v.t.* 遮住 jeh ju

shrub *n.* 灌木 gwun muk

shrug *v.t.* 聳膊 sung bok

shrug *n* 聳膊 sung bok

shudder *v.i.* 打震 da jan

shudder *n* 打震 da jan

shuffle *v.i.* 拖住腳行 tor ju geurt hang

shuffle *n.* 洗牌 say pay

shun *v.t.* 避開 bay hoy

shunt *v.t.* 調去 diew huy

shut *v.t.* 閂 san

shutter *n.* 鐵閘 teet jap

shuttle *n.* 梭 sor

shuttle *v.t.* 兩地走 leurng day jow

shuttlecock *n.* 羽毛球 yu mow kow

shy *n.* 怕醜 pa tow

shy *v.i.* 怕醜 pa tow

sick *a.* 有病嘅 yow beng geh

sickle *n.* 鐮刀 leem dow

sickly *a.* 多病嘅 dor beng geh

sickness *n.* 疾病 jat beng

side *n.* 側邊 jat been

side *v.i.* 支持 jee tee

siege *n.* 包圍 bao way

siesta *n.* 晏覺 ngan goa

sieve *n.* 篩 say

sieve *v.t.* 篩 say

sift *v.t.* 篩 say

sigh *n.* 唉聲嘆氣 ai seng tan hay

sigh *v.i.* 唉聲嘆氣 ai seng tan hay

sight *n.* 視力 see lik

sight *v.t.* 見到 geen dow

sightly *a.* 少少 siew siew

sign *n.* 牌 pai

sign *v.t.* 簽 teem

signal *n.* 信號 sun ho

signal *a.* 重大嘅 jung dai geh

signal *v.t.* 發信號 fat sun ho

signatory *n.* 簽署方 teem chu forng

signature *n.* 簽名 teem meng

significance *n.* 重要性 jung yiew sing

significant *a.* 重要嘅 jung yiew geh

signification *n.* 意思 yee see

signify *v.t.* 表示 biew see

silence *n.* 無聲 mow seng

silence *v.t.* 變安靜 been on jing

silencer *n.* 消音器 siew yam hay

silent *a.* 無聲嘅 mow seng geh

silhouette *n.* 影 ying

silk *n.* 絲綢 see tow

silken *a.* 輕柔嘅 hing yow geh

silky *a.* 輕柔嘅 hing yow geh

silly *a.* 傻嘅 sor geh

silt *n.* 泥沙 lay sa

silt *v.t.* 塞 sak

silver *n.* 銀 ngan

silver *a* 銀色嘅 ngan sik geh

silver *v.t.* 鍍銀 dow ngan

similar *a.* 似 tee

similarity *n.* 相似度 seurng tee dow

simile *n.* 明喻 ming yu

similitude *n.* 相似度 seurng tee dow

simmer *v.i.* 燉 dun

simple *a.* 簡單 gan dan

simpleton *n.* 傻瓜 sor gwa

simplicity *n.* 簡單 gan dan

simplification *n.* 簡化 gan far

simplify *v.t.* 簡化 gan far

simultaneous *a.* 同時發生 tung see fat sang

sin *n.* 罪惡 juy ok

sin *v.i.* 犯過失 fan gwor sat

since *prep.* 從 chung

since *conj.* 從 chung

since *adv.* 從 chung

sincere *a.* 衷心 chung sam

sincerity *n.* 真誠 jan sing

sinful *a.* 邪惡嘅 ter ok geh

sing *v.i.* 唱 cheurng

singe *v.t.* 燒燶 siew lung

singe *n* 燒傷 siew seurng

singer *n.* 歌手 gor sow

single *a.* 單一嘅 dan yat geh

single *n.* 單程票 dan ting piew

single *v.t.* 單獨挑出 dan duk tiew chut

singular *a.* 單數嘅 dan sow geh

singularity *n.* 奇特 kay dak

singularly *adv.* 特別 dak beet

sinister *a.* 險惡 heem ok

sink *v.i.* 沈 tam

sink *n* 洗手盤 say sow pwun

sinner *n.* 罪人 juy yan

sinuous *a.* 彎曲嘅 wan kuk geh

sip *v.t.* 細細啖飲 say say dam yam

sip *n.* 一細啖 yat say dam

sir *n.* 先生 seen sang

siren *n.* 警報器 ging bo hay

sister *n.* 家姐 ga jeh

sisterhood *n.* 姐妹情誼 jeh mwuy ting yee

sisterly *a.* 姊妹咁嘅 jee mwuy gam geh

sit *v.i.* 坐 chor

site *n.* 現場 yeen cheurng

situation *n.* 情況 ting forng

six *n., a* 六 luk

sixteen *n., a.* 十六 sap luk

sixteenth *a.* 第十六 day sap luk

sixth *a.* 第六 day luk

sixtieth *a.* 第六十 day luk sap

sixty *n., a.* 六十 luk sap

sizable *a.* 幾大嘅 gey dai geh

size *n.* 大細 dai say

size *v.t.* 調大細 tiew dai say

sizzle *v.i.* 煎 jeen

sizzle *n.* 嚓嚓聲 see see seng

skate *n.* 溜冰鞋 low bing hai

skate *v.t.* 溜冰 low bing

skein *n.* 一紮 yat jat

skeleton *n.* 骸骨 hai gwat

sketch *n.* 描繪 miew kwuy

sketch *v.t.* 描繪 miew kwuy

sketchy *a.* 粗略嘅 cho leurk geh

skid *v.i.* 跣 seen

skid *n* 打滑 da wat

skilful *a.* 有技術嘅 yow gey sut geh

skill *n.* 技能 gey lang

skin *n.* 皮膚 pay fu

skin *v.t* 去皮 huy pay

skip *v.i.* 跳繩 tiew sing

skip *n* 廢料桶 fay liew tung

skipper *n.* 船長 shoon jeurng

skirmish *n.* 爭執 jang jap

skirmish *v.t.* 爭執 jang jap

skirt *n.* 裙 kwan

skirt *v.t.* 環繞 wan yiew

skit *n.* 滑稽短劇 wat kay doon kek

skull *n.* 頭骨 tow gwat

sky *n.* 天 teen

sky *v.t.* 飛 fay

slab *n.* 厚塊 ho fai

slack *a.* 鬆弛嘅 sung tee geh

slacken *v.t.* 放慢 forng man

slacks *n.* 休閒褲 yow han fu

slake *v.t.* 解渴 gai hot

slam *v.t.* 砰 bung

slam *n* 砰 bung

slander *n.* 詆毀 day way

slander *v.t.* 詆毀 day way

slanderous *a.* 中傷嘅 jung seurng geh

slang *n.* 俚語 lay yu

slant *v.t.* 傾斜 king ter

slant *n* 斜坡 ter bor

slap *n.* 一巴掌 yat ba jeurng

slap *v.t.* 摑 gwak

slash *v.t.* 劈 pek

slash *n* 劈 pek

slate *n.* 瓦塊 ngar fai

slattern *n.* 邋遢嘅女人 lat tat geh luy yan

slatternly *a.* 唔檢點嘅 hm geem deem geh

slaughter *n.* 屠殺 tow sat

slaughter *v.t.* 劏 torng

slave *n.* 奴隸 low day

slave *v.i.* 辛苦咁做嘢 san fu gam jow yeh

slavery *n.* 奴隸制 low day jay

slavish *a.* 盲目遵從 mang muk joon chung

slay *v.t.* 殺 sat

sleek *a.* 光滑嘅 gworng wat geh

sleep *v.i.* 瞓覺 fan gao

sleep *n.* 瞓覺 fan gao

sleeper *n.* 瞓得…嘅人 fan dak... geh yan

sleepy *a.* 眼瞓 ngan fan

sleeve *n* 衫袖 sam jow

sleight *n.* 敏捷手法 man jeet sow fat

slender *n.* 苗條 miew tiew

slice *n.* 一塊 yat fai

slice *v.t.* 切塊 teet fai

slick *a* 花言巧語嘅 far yeen hao yu geh

slide *v.i.* sur

slide *n* 滑梯 sur wat tay

slight *a.* 輕微嘅 hing may geh

slight *n.* 輕視 hing see

slight *v.t.* 輕視 hing see

slim *a.* 苗條嘅 miew tiew geh

slim *v.i.* 減肥 gam fay

slime *n.* 黏液 leem yik

slimy *a.* 粘住黏液嘅 tee ju leem yik geh

sling *n.* 吊帶 diew dai

slip *v.i.* 跣跌 seen deet

slip *n.* 跣 seen

slipper *n.* 拖鞋 tor hai

slippery *a.* 跣 seen

slipshod *a.* 馬虎嘅 ma fu geh

slit *n.* 裂縫 leet fung

slit *v.t.* 鎅 gai

slogan *n.* 口號 how ho

slope *n.* 斜坡 ter bor

slope *v.i.* 傾斜 king ter

sloth *n.* 樹懶 shu lan

slothful *n.* 懶散嘅 lan san geh

slough *n.* 蛻皮 tuy pay

slough *n.* 絕望 joot morng

slough *v.t.* 拋棄 pao hay

slovenly *a.* 邋遢嘅 lat tat geh

slow *a* 慢 man

slow *v.i.* 慢 man

slowly *adv.* 慢慢 man man

slowness *n.* 慢度 man dow

sluggard *n.* 遊手好閒嘅人 yow sow ho han geh yan

sluggish *a.* 懶嘅 lan geh

sluice *n.* 水閘 suy jap

slum *n.* 貧民窟 pan man fat

slumber *v.i.* 瞓 fan

slumber *n.* 瞓覺 fan gao

slump *n.* 驟降 jao gorng

slump *v.i.* 驟降 jao gorng

slur *n.* 含糊聲 ham wu seng

slush *n.* 雪泥 shoot lay

slushy *a.* 泥濘嘅 lay ling geh

slut *n.* 淫蕩嘅女人 yam dorng geh luy yan

sly *a.* 狡猾 gao wat

smack *n.* 摑 gwak

smack *v.i.* 摑 gwak	**snap** *a* 倉促嘅 chorng choot geh
smack *n* 一巴掌 yat ba jeurng	**snare** *n.* 陷阱 ham jeng
smack *n.* 啪聲 pak seng	**snare** *v.t.* 設陷阱 teet ham jeng
smack *v.t.* 撞 jorng	**snarl** *n.* 低吼 day hao
small *a.* 細嘅 say geh	**snarl** *v.i.* 低吼 day hao
small *n* 後腰 ho yiew	**snatch** *v.t.* 搶 cheurng
smallness *adv.* 細 say	**snatch** *n.* 搶 cheurng
smallpox *n.* 天花 teen far	**sneak** *v.i.* 偷偷咁走 tow tow gam jow
smart *a.* 聰明嘅 chung ming geh	**sneak** *n* 告狀人 gow jorng yan
smart *v.i* 難過 lan gwor	**sneer** *v.i* 嘲笑 chao siew
smart *a.* 光鮮嘅 gworng seen geh	**sneer** *n* 嘲笑 chao siew
smash *v.t.* 打碎 da suy	**sneeze** *v.i.* 打乞嗤 da hat tee
smash *n* 撞車 jorng cher	**sneeze** *n* 乞嗤 hat tee
smear *v.t.* 搽 ta	**sniff** *v.i.* 聞 man
smear *n.* 污漬 wu jik	**sniff** *n* 聞 man
smell *n.* 氣味 hay may	**snob** *n.* 勢利鬼 say lay gway
smell *v.t.* 聞 man	**snobbery** *n.* 態度勢利 tai dow say lay
smelt *v.t.* 聞到 man dow	**snobbish** *v* 勢利嘅 say lay geh
smile *n.* 笑 siew	**snore** *v.i.* 打鼻鼾 da bay horn
smile *v.i.* 笑 siew	**snore** *n* 鼻鼾聲 bay horn seng
smith *n.* 鐵匠 teet jeurng	**snort** *v.i.* 哼 hang
smock *n.* 罩衣 jao yee	**snort** *n.* 哼 hang
smog *n.* 煙霧 yeen mow	**snout** *n.* 豬鼻 ju bay
smoke *n.* 煙 yeen	**snow** *n.* 雪 shoot
smoke *v.i.* 食煙 sik yeen	**snow** *v.i.* 落雪 lok shoot
smoky *a.* 多煙嘅 dor yeen geh	**snowy** *a.* 多雪嘅 dor shoot geh
smooth *a.* 滑嘅 wat geh	**snub** *v.t.* 冷落 lang lok
smooth *v.t.* 整平 jing ping	**snub** *n.* 冷落 lang lok
smother *v.t.* 焗死人 guk say yan	**snuff** *n.* 鼻煙 bay yeem
smoulder *v.i.* 無明火燒 mow ming for siew	**snug** *n.* 舒服 shu fuk
smug *a.* 得戚 dak tik	**so** *adv.* 所以 sor yee
smuggle *v.t.* 走私 jow see	**so** *conj.* 所以 sor yee
smuggler *n.* 走私者 jow see jeh	**soak** *v.t.* 整濕 jing sap
snack *n.* 零食 ling sik	**soak** *n.* 濕晒 sap sai
snag *n.* 問題 man tay	**soap** *n.* 番梘 fan gan
snail *n.* 蝸牛 wor ngoy	**soap** *v.t.* 用番梘洗 yung fan gan say
snake *n.* 蛇 seh	**soapy** *a.* 多番梘 dor fan gan
snake *v.i.* 曲折前行 kuk jeet teen hang	**soar** *v.i.* 急升 gap sing
snap *v.t.* 整斷 jing toon	**sob** *v.i.* 哭訴 huk sow
snap *n* 相 seurng	

sob *n* 喊 ham
sober *a.* 清醒嘅 ting sing geh
sobriety *n.* 未醉 may juy
sociability *n.* 社交 seh gao
sociable *a.* 合群嘅 hap kwan geh
social *n.* 社會嘅 seh wuy geh
socialism *n* 社會主義 seh wuy ju yee
socialist *n,a* 社會主義者 seh wuy ju yee jeh
society *n.* 社會 seh wuy
sociology *n.* 社會學 seh wuy hok
sock *n.*, 襪 mat
socket *n.* 插座 tap jor
sod *n.* 討厭鬼 tow yeem gway
sodomite *n.* 禽獸 jam sow
sodomy *n.* 雞姦 gey gan
sofa *n.* 梳化 sor fa
soft *n.* 軟 yoon
soften *v.t.* 整軟 jing yoon
soil *n.* 泥 lay
soil *v.t.* 整污糟 jing wu jow
sojourn *v.i.* 逗留 dow low
sojourn *n* 逗留 dow low
solace *v.t.* 安慰 on way
solace *n.* 安慰 on way
solar *a.* 太陽嘅 tai yeurng geh
solder *n.* 焊料 hon liew
solder *v.t.* 焊接 hon jeep
soldier *n.* 士兵 see bing
soldier *v.i.* 堅持 geen tee
sole *n.* 鞋底 hai day
sole *v.t* 換鞋底 wun hai day
sole *a* 唯一嘅 way yat geh
solemn *a.* 嚴肅嘅 yeem suk geh
solemnity *n.* 嚴肅 yeem suk
solemnize *v.t.* 舉行 guy hang
solicit *v.t.* 求 kow
solicitation *n.* 懇請 han ting
solicitor *n.* 律師 lut see
solicitous *a.* 操心 cho sam
solicitude *n.* 牽掛 heen gwa

solid *a.* 硬嘅 ngang geh
solid *n* 固體 gu tay
solidarity *n.* 團結 toon geet
soliloquy *n.* 獨白 duk bak
solitary *a.* 單獨嘅 dan duk geh
solitude *n.* 獨處 duk chu
solo *n* 獨唱 duk cheurng
solo *a.* 單獨嘅 dan duk geh
solo *adv.* 自己一個 jee gey yat gor
soloist *n.* 獨唱者 duk cheurng jeh
solubility *n.* 溶解度 yung gai dow
soluble *a.* 可以溶嘅 hor yee yung geh
solution *n.* 解決辦法 gai koot ban fat
solve *v.t.* 解開 gai hoy
solvency *n.* 付債能力 fu jai lang lik
solvent *a.* 可以溶嘅 hor yee yung geh
solvent *n* 溶劑 yung jay
sombre *a.* 沮喪嘅 juy sorng geh
some *adv.* 有啲 yow dee
some *pron.* 有啲 yow dee
somebody *pron.* 有人 yow yan
somebody *n.* 有人 yow yan
somehow *adv.* 唔知點解就 hm jee deem gai jow
someone *pron.* 有人 yow yan
somersault *n.* 空翻 hung fan
somersault *v.i.* 打空翻 da hung fan
something *pron.* 一啲嘢 yat dee yeh
something *adv.* 一啲嘢 yat dee yeh
sometime *adv.* 有時 yow see
sometimes *adv.* 有時 yow see
somewhat *adv.* 有啲 yow dee
somewhere *adv.* 某個地方 mow gor day forng

somnambulism *n.* 夢遊病 mung yow beng

somnambulist *n.* 夢遊病患者 mung yow beng wan jeh

somnolence *n.* 眼瞓 ngan fan

somnolent *n.* 眼瞓 ngan fan

son *n.* 仔 jay

song *n.* 歌 gor

songster *n.* 歌手 gor sow

sonic *a.* 聲音嘅 sing yam geh

sonnet *n.* 十四行詩 sap say horng see

sonority *n.* 響亮 heurng leurng

soon *adv.* 好快 ho fai

soot *n.* 油煙 yow yeen

soot *v.t.* 鋪滿油煙 pow mwun yow yeen

soothe *v.t.* 減輕 garm heng

sophism *n.* 詭辯 gway been

sophist *n.* 智者 jee jeh

sophisticate *v.t.* 複雜化 fuk jap far

sophisticated *a.* 複雜 fuk jap

sophistication *n.* 複雜 fuk jap

sorcerer *n.* 術士 sut see

sorcery *n.* 巫術 mow sut

sordid *a.* 卑鄙 bay pay

sore *a.* 痛嘅 tung geh

sore *n* 腫 jung

sorrow *n.* 悲傷 bay seurng

sorrow *v.i.* 悲傷 bay seurng

sorry *a.* 對唔住 duy hm ju

sort *n.* 種類 jung luy

sort *v.t* 整 jing

soul *n.* 心靈 sam ling

sound *a.* 合理嘅 hap lay geh

sound *v.i.* 聽起嚟 teng hay lay

sound *n* 聲 seng

soup *n.* 湯 torng

sour *a.* 酸 shoon

sour *v.t.* 惡化 ok far

source *n.* 來源 loy yoon

south *n.* 南 larm

south *a.* 南方嘅 larm forng geh

south *adv* 向南 heurng larm

southerly *a.* 南方嘅 larm forng geh

southern *a.* 南方嘅 larm forng geh

souvenir *n.* 手信 sow sun

sovereign *n.* 君主 gwan ju

sovereign *a* 獨立嘅 duk lap geh

sovereignty *n.* 主權 ju koon

sow *v.t.* 種 jung

sow *n.* 母豬 mow ju

space *n.* 空間 hung gan

space *v.t.* 隔開 gak hoy

spacious *a.* 寬敞 fwun torng

spade *n.* 鏟 tan

spade *v.t.* 鏟 tan

span *n.* 範圍 fan way

span *v.t.* 持續 tee juk

Spaniard *n.* 西班牙人 say ban ngar yan

spaniel *n.* 西班牙獵狗 say ban ngar leep gow

Spanish *a.* 西班牙嘅 say ban ngar geh

Spanish *n.* 西班牙人 say ban ngar yan

spanner *n.* 士巴拿 see ba la

spare *v.t.* 抽出 tow chut

spare *a* 多咗嘅 dor jor geh

spare *n.* 備用品 bay yung bam

spark *n.* 火花 for far

spark *v.i.* 引發 yan fat

spark *n.* 星火 sing for

sparkle *v.i.* 閃 seem

sparkle *n.* 閃 seem

sparrow *n.* 麻雀 ma jeurk

sparse *a.* 罕有嘅 hon yow geh

spasm *n.* 抽搐 tow chuk

spasmodic *a.* 斷斷續續 toon toon juk juk

spate *n.* 一連串 yat leen choon
spatial *a.* 空間 hung gan
spawn *n.* 卵 lun
spawn *v.i.* 造成 jow sing
speak *v.i.* 講 gorng
speaker *n.* 喇叭 la ba
spear *n.* 矛 mao
spear *v.t.* 用矛揾 yung mao gat
spearhead *n.* 領隊 ling duy
spearhead *v.t.* 帶頭 dai tow
special *a.* 特別 dak beet
specialist *n.* 專家 joon gar
speciality *n.* 專長 joon cheurng
specialization *n.* 專門化 joon mwun far
specialize *v.i.* 專攻 joon gung
species *n.* 種類 jung luy
specific *a.* 特定嘅 dak ding geh
specification *n.* 規範 kway fan
specify *v.t.* 詳述 cheurng sut
specimen *n.* 種類 jung luy
speck *n.* 一細點 yat say deem
spectacle *n.* 眼鏡 ngan geng
spectacular *a.* 壯觀 jorng gwun
spectator *n.* 觀眾 gwun jung
spectre *n.* 恐懼 hung guy
speculate *v.i.* 推測 tuy tak
speculation *n.* 推測 tuy tak
speech *n.* 台詞 toy tee
speed *n.* 速度 chuk dow
speed *v.i.* 加速 ga chuk
speedily *adv.* 快 fai
speedy *a.* 快 fai
spell *n.* 咒語 jow yu
spell *v.t.* 串 choon
spell *n* 魅力 may lik
spend *v.t.* 使 say
spendthrift *n.* 大使嘅人 dai say geh yan
sperm *n.* 精子 jing jee
sphere *n.* 球形 kow ying
spherical *a.* 球形嘅 kow ying geh

spice *n.* 香料 heurng liew
spice *v.t.* 加香料 ga heurng liew
spicy *a.* 辣 lat
spider *n.* 蜘蛛 jee ju
spike *n.* 尖頭 jeem tow
spike *v.t.* 插 tap
spill *v.i.* 倒瀉 dow seh
spill *n* 瀉 seh
spin *v.i.* 轉 joon
spin *n.* 轉 joon
spinach *n.* 菠菜 bor choy
spinal *a.* 脊骨嘅 jek gwat geh
spindle *n.* 繞線杆 yiew seen gorn
spine *n.* 脊骨 jek gwat
spinner *n.* 紡紗工 forng sa gung
spinster *n.* 老姑婆 low gu por
spiral *n.* 螺旋型 lor shoon ying
spiral *a.* 螺旋形嘅 lor shoon ying geh
spirit *n.* 精心 jing san
spirited *a.* 堅定嘅 geen ding geh
spiritual *a.* 心靈嘅 sam ling geh
spiritualism *n.* 招魂術 jiew wan sut
spiritualist *n.* 信招魂嘅人 sun jiew wan geh yan
spirituality *n.* 精神性 jing san sing
spit *v.i.* 吐 tow
spit *n* 口水 ho suy
spite *n.* 怨恨 yoon han
spittle *n* 口水 ho suy
spittoon *n.* 痰罐 tam gwun
splash *v.i.* 潑 pwut
splash *n* 落水聲 lok suy seng
spleen *n.* 脾 pay
splendid *a.* 非常好嘅 fay seurng ho geh
splendour *n.* 華麗 wah lay
splinter *n.* 木刺 muk tee
splinter *v.t.* 碎 suy
split *v.i.* 分 fan

split *n* 裂口 leet ho
spoil *v.t.* 破壞 por wai
spoil *n* 賊物 jorng mat
spoke *n.* 講 gorng
spokesman *n.* 發言人 fat yeen yan
sponge *n.* 海綿 hoy meen
sponge *v.t.* 用海綿抹 yung hoy meen mat
sponsor *n.* 贊助商 jan jor seurng
sponsor *v.t.* 贊助 jan jor
spontaneity *n.* 衝動 chung dung
spontaneous *a.* 衝動 chung dung
spoon *n.* 匙羹 tee gang
spoon *v.t.* 不 bat
spoonful *n.* 一匙羹 yat tee gang
sporadic *a.* 斷斷續續 toon toon juk juk
sport *n.* 運動 wan dung
sport *v.i.* 曬 sai
sportive *a.* 運動細胞 wan dung say bao
sportsman *n.* 運動員 wan dung yoon
spot *n.* 斑點 ban deem
spot *v.t.* 見到 geen dow
spotless *a.* 一塵不染 yat tan bat yeem
spousal *n.* 婚禮 fan lay
spouse *n.* 配偶 pwuy oh
spout *n.* 嘴 juy
spout *v.i.* 噴 pan
sprain *n.* 扭傷 low seurng
sprain *v.t.* 扭嘅 low tan
spray *n.* 噴劑 pan jay
spray *n* 水花 suy far
spray *v.t.* 噴 pan
spread *v.i.* 傳開 choon hoy
spread *n.* 傳播 choon bor
spree *n.* 歡狂 fwun kworng
sprig *n.* 帶葉嘅細枝 dai yeep geh

say jee
sprightly *a.* 精力充沛 jing lik chung pwuy
spring *v.i.* 彈 dan
spring *n* 春天 chun teen
sprinkle *v. t.* 灑 sa
sprint *v.i.* 快跑 fai pao
sprint *n* 短距離賽跑 doon kuy lay choy pao
sprout *v.i.* 發芽 fat ngar
sprout *n* 新芽 san ngar
spur *n.* 馬刺 ma tee
spur *v.t.* 鞭策 been tak
spurious *a.* 偽造嘅 ngay jow geh
spurn *v.t.* 拒絕 kuy joot
spurt *v.i.* 噴 pan
spurt *n* 湧出嘅 yung chut geh
sputnik *n.* 人造衛星 yan jow way sing
sputum *n.* 痰 tam
spy *n.* 間諜 gan deep
spy *v.i.* 監視 gam see
squad *n.* 小隊 siew duy
squadron *n.* 中隊 jung duy
squalid *a.* 邋遢 lat tat
squalor *n.* 邋遢 lat tat
squander *v.t.* 嘥 sai
square *n.* 四方形 say forng ying
square *a* 四方形嘅 say forng ying geh
square *v.t.* 平方 ping forng
squash *v.t.* 壓扁 ngat been
squash *n* 壁球 bik kow
squat *v.i.* 踎低 mow day
squeak *v.i.* 吱吱叫 jeet jeet giew
squeak *n* 吱吱聲 jeet jeet seng
squeeze *v.t.* 搾 ja
squint *v.i.*
squint *n* 斜視 ter see
squire *n.* 鄉紳 heurng san
squirrel *n.* 松鼠 chung shu
stab *v.t.* 捅 tung

stab *n.* 捅 tung
stability *n.* 穩定性 wan ding sing
stabilization *n.* 穩定 wan ding
stabilize *v.t.* 穩定 wan ding
stable *a.* 穩定嘅 wan ding geh
stable *n* 馬房 ma forng
stable *v.t.* 穩固嘅 wan gu geh
stadium *n.* 體育場 tay yuk ch- eurng
staff *n.* 工作人員 gung jok yan yoon
staff *n.* 職員 jik yoon
stag *n.* 雄鹿 hung luk
stage *n.* 舞台 mow toy
stage *v.t.* 上演 seurng yeen
stagger *v.i.* 搖搖擺擺 yiew yiew bai bai
stagger *n.* 搖晃 yiew forng
stagnant *a.* 無變化 mow been far
stagnate *v.i.* 停滯 ting jay
stagnation *n.* 停滯 ting jay
staid *a.* 古板嘅 gu ban geh
stain *n.* 污漬 wu jik
stain *v.t.* 整污糟 jing wu jow
stainless *a.* 無瑕疵 mow ha tee
stair *n.* 樓梯 low tay
stake *n* 股份 gu fan
stake *v.t.* 冒險 mow heem
stale *a.* 唔新鮮嘅 hm san seen geh
stale *v.t.* 過時 gwor see
stalemate *n.* 僵局 geurng guk
stalk *n.* 花梗 far gang
stalk *v.i.* 跟蹤 gan jung
stalk *n* 葉柄 yeep beng
stall *n.* 攤位 tan way
stall *v.t.* 死火 say for
stallion *n.* 種馬 jung ma
stalwart *a.* 忠實嘅 jung sat geh
stalwart *n* 忠實擁護者 jung sat yung wu jeh
stamina *n.* 耐力 loy lik

stammer *v.i.* 嘍口 low ho
stammer *n* 嘍口 low ho
stamp *n.* 郵票 yow piew
stamp *v.i.* 印 yan
stampede *n.* 風氣 fung hay
stampede *v.i* 狂跑 kworng pao
stand *v.i.* 企 kay
stand *n.* 貨攤 for tan
standard *n.* 標準 biew jun
standard *a* 普通嘅 pow tung geh
standardization *n.* 統一 tung yat
standardize *v.t.* 統一 tung yat
standing *n.* 地位 day way
standpoint *n.* 立場 lap cheurng
standstill *n.* 停滯 ting jay
stanza *n.* 節 jeet
staple *n.* 釘書釘 deng shu deng
staple *a* 基本嘅 gey bwun geh
star *n.* 星星 sing sing
star *v.t.* 主演 ju yeen
starch *n.* 澱粉 deen fan
starch *v.t.* 槳 jeurng
stare *v.i.* 瞪 dang
stare *n.* 凝視 ying see
stark *n.* 嚴厲 yeem lay
stark *adv.* 絕對 joot duy
starry *a.* 佈滿星星 bow mwun sing sing
start *v.t.* 開始 hoy tee
start *n* 開始 hoy tee
startle *v.t.* 嚇 hak
starvation *n.* 飢餓 gey or
starve *v.i.* 挨餓 ai or
state *n.* 狀況 jorng forng
state *v.t* 講明 gorng ming
stateliness *n.* 威嚴 way yeem
stately *a.* 壯觀嘅 jorng gwun geh
statement *n.* 銀行單 an horng dan
statesman *n.* 政治家 jing jee ga
static *n.* 干擾 gorn yiew
statics *n.* 靜力學 jing lik hok

station *n.* 車站 cher jam

station *v.t.* 派駐 pai ju

stationary *a.* 唔郁嘅 hm yuk geh

stationer *n.* 文具商 man guy seurng

stationery *n.* 文具 man guy

statistical *a.* 統計嘅 tung gey geh

statistician *n.* 統計學家 tung gey hok ga

statistics *n.* 統計 tung gey

statue *n.* 石像 sek jeurng

stature *n.* 身高 san gow

status *n.* 地位 day way

statute *n.* 法令 fat ling

statutory *a.* 法定嘅 fat ding geh

staunch *a.* 堅定嘅 geen ding geh

stay *v.i.* 留 low

stay *n* 逗留 dow low

steadfast *a.* 堅定嘅 geen ding geh

steadiness *n.* 穩定性 wan ding sing

steady *a.* 穩陣嘅 wan jan geh

steady *v.t.* 固定 gu ding

steal *v.i.* 偷 tow

stealthily *adv.* 暗地裡 am day luy

steam *n* 蒸氣 jing hay

steam *v.i.* 蒸 jing

steamer *n.* 蒸籠 jing lung

steed *n.* 駿馬 jun ma

steel *n.* 鋼 gorng

steep *a.* 斜 ter

steep *v.t.* 沈迷 tam may

steeple *n.* 尖塔 jeem tap

steer *v.t.* 揸 ja

stellar *a.* 星嘅 sing geh

stem *n.* 莖 ging

stem *v.i.* 封住 fung ju

stench *n.* 惡臭 ok tow

stencil *n.* 模板 mow ban

stencil *v.i.* 用模板印 yung mow ban yan

stenographer *n.* 速記員 chuk gey yoon

stenography *n.* 速記 chuk gey

step *n.* 腳步 geurt bo

step *v.i.* 行 hang

steppe *n.* 大草原 dai cho yoon

stereotype *n.* 刻板印象 hak ban yan jeurng

stereotype *v.t.* 類型化睇法 luy ying far tay fat

stereotyped *a.* 定型 ding ying

sterile *a.* 無菌嘅 mow kwan geh

sterility *n.* 不孕 bat yan

sterilization *n.* 消毒 siew duk

sterilize *v.t.* 消毒 siew duk

sterling *a.* 優秀嘅 yow sow geh

sterling *n.* 英鎊 ying borng

stern *a.* 嚴厲嘅 yeem lay geh

stern *n.* 嚴厲 yeem lay

stethoscope *n.* 聽筒 teng tung

stew *n.* 燜嘅菜 man geh choy

stew *v.t.* 燜 man

steward *n.* 服務員 fuk mow yoon

stick *n.* 棍 gwan

stick *v.t.* 黐 tee

sticker *n.* 貼紙 teep jee

stickler *n.* 堅持嘅人 geen tee geh yan

sticky *a.* 黐 tee

stiff *n.* 僵硬 geurng ang

stiffen *v.t.* 變僵硬 been geurng ang

stifle *v.t.* 壓制 ngat jay

stigma *n.* 恥辱 tee yuk

still *a.* 靜止 jing jee

still *adv.* 仲 jung

still *v.t.* 變平靜 been ping jing

still *n.* 劇照 kek jiew

stillness *n.* 靜止 jing jee

stilt *n.* 高蹺 gow kiew

stimulant *n.* 興奮劑 hing fan jay

stimulate *v.t.* 激發 gik fat

stimulus *n.* 刺激 tee gik

sting *v.t.* 刺 tee

sting *n.* 叮 deng

stingy *a.* 小器嘅 siew hay geh

stink *v.i.* 臭 tow

stink *n* 惡臭 ok tow

stipend *n.* 生活津貼 sang wut jun teep

stipulate *v.t.* 規定 kway ding

stipulation *n.* 規定 kway ding

stir *v.i.* 攪 gao

stirrup *n.* 馬鐙 ma dang

stitch *n.* 針腳 jam geurt

stitch *v.t.* 聯 loon

stock *n.* 存貨 choon for

stock *v.t.* 存貨 choon for

stock *a.* 成日有 sing yat yow

stocking *n.* 絲襪 see mat

stoic *n.* 堅強 geen keurng

stoke *v.t.* 激起 gik hay

stoker *n.* 司爐 see low

stomach *n.* 肚 tow

stomach *v.t.* 食得 sik dak

stone *n.* 石頭 sek tow

stone *v.t.* 掟石 deng sek

stony *a.* 多石頭 dor sek tow

stool *n.* 褶凳 jeep dang

stoop *v.i.* 彎腰 wan yiew

stoop *n* 駝背 tor bwuy

stop *v.t.* 停 ting

stop *n* 車站 cher jam

stoppage *n* 罷工 ba gung

storage *n.* 存放 choon forng

store *n.* 士多 see dor

store *v.t.* 保存 bo choon

storey *n.* 樓層 low tang

stork *n.* 鸛 gwun

storm *n.* 暴風雨 bo fung yu

storm *v.i.* 突襲 dak jap

stormy *a.* 暴風雨嘅 bow fung yu geh

story *n.* 故事 gu see

stout *a.* 肥嘅 fay geh

stove *n.* 爐頭 low tow

stow *v.t.* 收好 sow ho

straggle *v.i.* 散佈 san bow

straggler *n.* 落後嘅人 lok ho geh yan

straight *a.* 直嘅 jik geh

straight *adv.* 直 jik

straighten *v.t.* 整直 jing jik

straightforward *a.* 率直 sut jik

straightway *adv.* 即刻 jik hak

strain *v.t.* 拉傷 lai seurng

strain *n* 拉傷 lai seurng

strait *n.* 海峽 hoy hap

straiten *v.t.* 變窄 been jak

strand *v.i.* 滯留 jay low

strand *n* 一串 yat choon

strange *a.* 古怪 gu gwai

stranger *n.* 陌生人 mak sang yan

strangle *v.t.* 勒死 lak say

strangulation *n.* 勒死 lak say

strap *n.* 帶 dai

strap *v.t.* 綁 borng

stratagem *n.* 策略 tak leurk

strategic *a.* 戰略嘅 jeen leurk geh

strategist *n.* 軍事家 gwan see ga

strategy *n.* 方法 fong fat

stratum *n.* 層 tang

straw *n.* 吸管 kap gwun

strawberry *n.* 士多啤梨 see dor beh lay

stray *v.i.* 蕩失路 dorng sat low

stray *a* 走失嘅 jow sat geh

stray *n* 走散嘅動物 jow san geh dung mat

stream *n.* 小溪 siew kay

stream *v.i.* 流 low

streamer *n.* 彩帶 choy dai

streamlet *n.* 小溪 siew kay

street *n.* 街 gai

strength *n.* 力氣 lik hay

strengthen *v.t.* 加強 ga keurng

strenuous *a.* 辛苦嘅 san fu geh
stress *n.* 壓力 ngat lik
stress *v.t* 強調 keurng diew
stretch *v.t.* 拉 lai
stretch *n* 彈性 dan sing
stretcher *n.* 擔架 dam ga
strew *v.t.* 佈滿 bo mwun
strict *a.* 嚴格 yeem gak
stricture *n.* 限制 han jay
stride *v.i.* 大步行 dai bo hang
stride *n* 大步 dai bo
strident *a.* 刺耳嘅 tee yee geh
strife *n.* 衝突 chung dat
strike *v.t.* 打 da
strike *n* 罷工 ba gung
striker *n.* 前鋒 teen fung
string *n.* 繩 sing
string *v.t.* 串 choon
stringency *n.* 緊縮 gan suk
stringent *a.* 嚴厲嘅 yeem lay geh
strip *n.* 一條 yat tiew
strip *v.t.* 徐衫 chuy sam
stripe *n.* 條紋 tiew man
stripe *v.t.* 加條紋 ga tiew man
strive *v.i.* 奮鬥 fan dow
stroke *n.* 一劃 yat wak
stroke *v.t.* 輕摸 heng mor
stroke *n* 擊球 gik kow
stroll *v.i.* 散步 san bo
stroll *n* 散步 san bo
strong *a.* 大力 dai lik
stronghold *n.* 堡壘 bo luy
structural *a.* 結構嘅 geet kow geh
structure *n.* 結構 geet kow
struggle *v.i.* 掙扎 jang jat
struggle *n* 難題 lan tay
strumpet *n.* 妓女 gey luy
strut *v.i.* 抬頭挺胸行 toy tow ting hung hang
strut *n* 支柱 jee chu
stub *n.* 煙頭 yeen tow

stubble *n.* 茬 ta
stubborn *a.* 硬頸 ngang geng
stud *n.* 釘 deng
stud *v.t.* 加釘 ga deng
student *n.* 學生 hok sang
studio *n.* 錄音室 luk yam sat
studious *a.* 好學嘅 ho hok geh
study *v.i.* 讀書 duk shu
study *n.* 書房 shu forng
stuff *n.* 嘢 yeh
stuff *2 v.t.* 塞滿 sat mun
stuffy *a.* 焗 guk
stumble *v.i.* 棘嘅 kik tan
stumble *n.* 跌 deet
stump *n.* 樹墩 shu dun
stump *v.t* 難倒 lan dow
stun *v.t.* 打暈 da wan
stunt *v.t.* 阻礙生長 jor ngoy sang jeurng
stunt *n* 特技 dak gey
stupefy *v.t.* 令人驚訝 ling yan ging ngar
stupendous *a.* 極大嘅 gik dai geh
stupid *a* 蠢 chun
stupidity *n.* 蠢 chun
sturdy *a.* 紮實 jat sat
sty *n.* 豬場 ju cheurng
stye *n.* 麥粒腫 mak lap jung
style *n.* 風格 fung gak
subdue *v.t.* 制服 jay fuk
subject *n.* 主題 ju tay
subject *a* 影響嘅 ying heurng geh
subject *v.t.* 臣服 san fuk
subjection *n.* 制服 jay fuk
subjective *a.* 主觀 ju gwun
subjudice *n.* 懸案 yoon on
subjugate *v.t.* 征服 jing fuk
subjugation *n.* 制服 jay fuk
sublet *v.t.* 轉租 joon jow
sublimate *v.t.* 昇華 sing wah
sublime *a.* 崇高嘅 sung gow geh

sublime *n* 崇高嘅事 sung gow geh see

sublimity *n.* 高尚 gow seurng

submarine *n.* 潛艇 teem suy teng

submarine *a* 海底嘅 hoy day geh

submerge *v.i.* 潛入水裡度 teem yap suy dow

submission *n.* 屈服 wat fuk

submissive *a.* 聽話嘅 teng wah geh

submit *v.t.* 交 gao

subordinate *a.* 隸屬 day suk

subordinate *n* 部屬 bow suk

subordinate *v.t.* 屬於 suk yu

subordination *n.* 附屬 fu suk

subscribe *v.t.* 報名 bow meng

subscription *n.* 訂閱 deng yoot

subsequent *a.* 後嚟 ho lay

subservience *n.* 從屬 chung suk

subservient *a.* 次要 tee yiew

subside *v.i.* 減弱 garm yeurk

subsidiary *a.* 附帶嘅 fu dai geh

subsidize *v.t.* 資助 jee jor

subsidy *n.* 津貼 jun teep

subsist *v.i.* 維持生活 way tee sang wut

subsistence *n.* 勉強維持生活 meen keurng way tee sang wut

substance *n.* 物質 mat jat

substantial *a.* 大量嘅 dai leurng geh

substantially *adv.* 基本上 gey bwun seurng

substantiate *v.t.* 證明 jing ming

substantiation *n.* 證實 jing sat

substitute *n.* 代替人 doy tay yan

substitute *v.t.* 代替 doy tay

substitution *n.* 代替 doy tay

subterranean *a.* 地下嘅 day ha geh

subtle *n.* 唔明顯嘅 hm ming heen geh

subtlety *n.* 巧妙 hao miew

subtract *v.t.* 減 garm

subtraction *n.* 減 garm

suburb *n.* 郊區 gao kuy

suburban *a.* 郊區嘅 gao kuy geh

subversion *n.* 顛覆 deen fuk

subversive *a.* 破壞嘅 por wai geh

subvert *v.t.* 推翻 tuy fan

succeed *v.i.* 成功 sing gung

success *n.* 成就 sing jow

successful *a* 成功 sing gung

succession *n.* 繼承 gey sing

successive *a.* 連續嘅 leen juk geh

successor *n.* 繼承人 gey sing yan

succour *n.* 幫助 borng jor

succour *v.t.* 幫 borng

succumb *v.i.* 屈服 wat fuk

such *a.* 似 tee

such *pron.* 非常之 fay seurng jee

suck *v.t.* 啜 joot

suck *n.* 吸 kap

suckle *v.t.* 餵奶 way lai

sudden *n.* 突然 dat yeen

suddenly *adv.* 突然間 dat yeen gan

sue *v.t.* 告 go

suffer *v.t.* 受苦 so fu

suffice *v.i.* 足夠 juk gow

sufficiency *n.* 充足 chung juk

sufficient *a.* 足夠 juk go

suffix *n.* 後綴 ho joot

suffix *v.t.* 加後綴 ga ho joot

suffocate *v.t* 窒息 jat sik

suffocation *n.* 窒息 jat sik

suffrage *n.* 投票權 tow piew koon

sugar *n.* 糖 tong

sugar *v.t.* 加糖 ga torng

suggest *v.t.* 提議 tey yee

suggestion *n.* 提議 tay yee

suggestive *a.* 暗示嘅 am see geh

suicidal *a.* 有自殺傾向 yow jee sat king heurng

suicide *n.* 自殺 jee sat

suit *n.* 西裝 say jorng

suit *v.t.* 襯 tan

suitability *n.* 適合性 sik hap sing

suitable *a.* 適合 sik hap

suite *n.* 套房 tow forng

suitor *n.* 收購者 sow kow jeh

sullen *a.* 悶悶不樂 mun mun bat lok

sulphur *n.* 硫磺 low wong

sulphuric *a.* 硫酸 low shoon

sultry *a.* 悶熱 mun yeet

sum *n.* 總數 jung so

sum *v.t.* 總結 jung geet

summarily *adv.* 概要 koy yiew

summarize *v.t.* 總結 jung geet

summary *n.* 總結 jung geet

summary *a* 總結性嘅 jung geet sing geh

summer *n.* 夏天 har teen

summit *n.* 山頂 san deng

summon *v.t.* 呼喚 fu wun

summons *n.* 傳票 choon piew

sumptuous *a.* 奢侈嘅 ter tee geh

sun *n.* 太陽 tai yeurng

sun *v.t.* 曬太陽 sai tai yeurng

Sunday *n.* 星期日 sing kay yat

sunder *v.t.* 分開 fan hoy

sundry *a.* 雜項嘅 jap horng ghe

sunny *a.* 好太陽 ho tai yeurng

sup *v.i.* 細細啖飲 say say dam yam

superabundance *n.* 過多 gwor dor

superabundant *a.* 大量嘅 dai leurng geh

superb *a.* 好極嘅 ho gik geh

superficial *a.* 粗枝大葉 cho jee dai yeep

superficiality *n.* 表面性 biew meen sing

superfine *a.* 精製嘅 jing jay geh

superfluity *n.* 奢侈品 ter tee ban

superfluous *a.* 過多嘅 gwor dor geh

superhuman *a.* 超出常人嘅 tiew chut seurng yan geh

superintend *v.t.* 主管 ju gwun

superintendence *n.* 監督 gam duk

superintendent *n.* 監管人 gam gwun yan

superior *a.* 優越 yow yoot

superiority *n.* 優越 yow yoot

superlative *a.* 卓越嘅 cheurk yoot geh

superlative *n.* 最高級 juy gow kap

superman *n.* 超人 tiew yan

supernatural *a.* 超自然嘅 tiew jee yeen geh

supersede *v.t.* 取代 chuy doy

supersonic *a.* 超音波嘅 tiew yam bor geh

superstition *n.* 迷信 mey sun

superstitious *a.* 迷信 mey sun

supertax *n.* 附加稅 fu ga suy

supervise *v.t.* 監督 gam duk

supervision *n.* 監督 gam duk

supervisor *n.* 主管 ju gwun

supper *n.* 宵夜 siew yeh

supple *a.* 柔軟 yow yoon

supplement *n.* 補充 bo chung

supplement *v.t.* 補充 bo chung

supplementary *a.* 額外嘅 ak ngoy geh

supplier *n.* 供應者 gung ying jeh

supply *v.t.* 提供 tey gung

supply *n* 供應量 gung ying leurng

support v.t. 支持 jee tee
support n. 支持 jee tee
suppose v.t. 估 gu
supposition n. 推測 tuy tak
suppress v.t. 鎮壓 jan ngat
suppression n. 鎮壓 jan ngat
supremacy n. 最大權利 juy dai koon lik
supreme a. 最高嘅 juy gow geh
surcharge n. 附加肥 fu ga fay
surcharge v.t. 收額外費 sow ak ngoy fay
sure a. 肯定 hang ding
surely adv. 想必 seurng beet
surety n. 擔保人 dam bo yan
surf n. 激浪 gik lorng
surface n. 表面 biew meen
surface v.i 露面 low meen
surfeit n. 過量 gwor leurng
surge n. 激增 gik jang
surge v.i. 湧 yung
surgeon n. 外科醫生 ngoy for yee sang
surgery n. 手術 sow sut
surmise n. 推測 tuy tak
surmise v.t. 推測 tuy tak
surmount v.t. 克服 hak fuk
surname n. 姓 sing
surpass v.t. 超過 tiew gwor
surplus n. 剩餘 jing yu
surprise n. 驚喜 ging hey
surprise v.t. 令人驚喜 ling yan ging hay
surrender v.t. 投降 tow horng
surrender n 投降 tow horng
surround v.t. 圍住 way ju
surroundings n. 周圍 jow way
surtax n. 附加稅 fu ga suy
surveillance n. 監視 gam see
survey n. 調查 tiew ta
survey v.t. 調查 tiew ta
survival n. 生存 sang choon

survive v.i. 生存 sang choon
suspect v.t. 懷疑 wai yee
suspect a. 唔可信嘅 hm hor sun geh
suspect n 嫌疑犯 yeem yee fan
suspend v.t. 暫停 jam ting
suspense n. 懸念 yoon leem
suspension n. 暫停職務 jam ting jik mow
suspicion n. 嫌疑 yeem yee
suspicious a. 可疑 hor yee
sustain v.t. 維持 way tee
sustenance n. 事務 sik mat
swagger v.i. 大搖大擺行 dai yiew dai bai hang
swagger n 大搖大擺 dai yiew dai bai
swallow v.t. 吞 tun
swallow n. 燕子 yeen jee
swallow n. 啖 dam
swamp n. 沼地 jiew day
swamp v.t. 浸 jam
swan n. 天鵝 teen ngor
swarm n. 一大群 yat dai kwan
swarm v.i. 飛嚟飛去 fay lay fay huy f
swarthy a. 皮膚黑嘅 pay fu hak geh
sway v.i. 搖擺 yiew bai
sway n 搖擺 yiew bai
swear v.t. 發誓 fat say
sweat n. 汗 horn
sweat v.i. 流汗 low horn
sweater n. 冷衫 larng sam
sweep v.i. 掃 sow
sweep n. 掃 sow
sweeper n. 清潔工 ting geet gung
sweet a. 甜 teem
sweet n 糖 tong
sweeten v.t. 整甜 jing teem
sweetmeat n. 糖 torng
sweetness n. 甜味 teem may

swell *v.i.* 腫 jung
swell *n* 腫 jung
swift *a.* 迅速嘅 sun chuk geh
swim *v.i.* 游水 yow suy
swim *n* 游水 yow suy
swimmer *n.* 游泳者 yow wing jeh
swindle *v.t.* 呃 ak
swindle *n.* 呃 ak
swindler *n.* 騙子 peen jeh
swine *n.* 豬 ju
swing *v.i.* 搖 yiew
swing *n* 鞦韆 teen tow
Swiss *n.* 瑞士人 suy see yan
Swiss *a* 瑞士嘅 suy see geh
switch *n.* 掣 jay
switch *v.t.* 轉 joon
swoon *n.* 暈 wan
swoon *v.i* 迷戀 may loon
swoop *v.i.* 向下猛衝 heurng ha mang chung
swoop *n* 突擊搜查 dak gik sow ta
sword *n.* 劍 geem
sycamore *n.* 西卡莫 say ka mok
sycophancy *n.* 誹謗 fay borng
sycophant *n.* 擦鞋仔 tat hai jay
syllabic *a.* 音節嘅 yam jeet geh
syllable *n.* 音節 yam jeet
syllabus *n.* 教學大綱 gao hok dai gorng
sylph *n.* 窈窕淑女 miew tiew suk luy
sylvan *a.* 森林嘅 sam lam geh
symbol *n.* 標誌 biew jee
symbolic *a.* 代表性 doy biew sing
symbolism *n.* 象徵手法 jeurng jik sow fat
symbolize *v.t.* 象徵 jeurng jing
symmetrical *a.* 對稱嘅 duy ting ghe
symmetry *n.* 對稱 duy ting
sympathetic *a.* 同情嘅 tung ting geh

sympathize *v.i.* 同情 tong ting
sympathy *n.* 同情心 tung ting sam
symphony *n.* 交響曲 gao heurng kuk
symposium *n.* 討論會 tow lun wuy
symptom *n.* 症狀 jing jorng
symptomatic *a.* 症狀嘅 jing jorng geh
synonym *n.* 同義詞 tung yee tee
synonymous *a.* 等同於 dang tung yu
synopsis *n.* 概要 koy yiew
syntax *n.* 句法 guy fat
synthesis *n.* 綜合 jung hap
synthetic *a.* 人造嘅 yan jow geh
synthetic *n* 合成物 hap sing mat
syringe *n.* 注射器 ju seh hay
syringe *v.t.* 用注射器洗 yung ju seh hay say
syrup *n.* 糖漿 tong jeurng
system *n.* 系統 hay tung
systematic *a.* 有條理嘅 yow tiew lay geh
systematize *v.t.* 系統化 hay tung far

T

table *n.* 枱 toy
table *v.t.* 擱置 gok jee
tablet *n.* 藥 yeurk
taboo *n.* 禁忌 gam gey
taboo *a* 禁忌 gam gey
taboo *v.t.* 禁止 gam jee
tabular *a.* 表格式 biew gak sik
tabulate *v.t.* 列成表格 leet sing biew gak
tabulation *n.* 列表 leet biew

tabulator *n.* 製表員 jay biew yoon

tacit *a.* 默示 mak see

taciturn *a.* 沈默寡言 tam mak gwa yeen

tackle *n.* 應付 ying fu

tackle *v.t.* 阻截 jor jeet

tact *n.* 得體 dak tay

tactful *a.* 機智嘅 gey jee geh

tactician *n.* 策士 tak see

tactics *n.* 策略 tak leurk

tactile *a.* 觸覺 juk gok

tag *n.* 牌 pai

tag *v.t.* 標籤 biew teem

tail *n.* 尾 mey

tailor *n.* 裁縫 choy fung

tailor *v.t.* 訂做 deng jow

taint *n.* 污染 wu yeem

taint *v.t.* 污染 wu yeem

take *v.t* 攞 lor

tale *n.* 故事 gu see

talent *n.* 才華 choy wah

talisman *n.* 護身符 wu san fu

talk *v.i.* 講 gong

talk *n* 講座 gong jor

talkative *a.* 健談 geen tam

tall *a.* 高 go

tallow *n.* 動物油脂 dung mat yow jee

tally *n.* 紀錄 gey luk

tally *v.t.* 吻合 man hap

tamarind *n.* 羅望子 lor morng jee

tame *a.* 溫順 wan sun

tame *v.t.* 馴服 suk fuk

tamper *v.i.* 破壞 por wai

tan *v.i.* 曬黑 sai hak

tan *n., a.* 棕黃色 jung worng sik

tangent *n.* 切線 teet seen

tangible *a.* 實在嘅 sat joy geh

tangle *n.* 打結 da geet

tangle *v.t.* 打晒結 da sai geet

tank *n.* 缸 gong

tanker *n.* 油槽車 yow cho cher

tanner *n.* 製革工人 jay gak gung yan

tannery *n.* 皮革廠 pay gak chorng

tantalize *v.t.* 引 yan

tantamount *a.* 等於 dang yu

tap *n.* 水候 suy ho

tap *v.t.* 輕拍 heng pak

tape *n.* 錄影帶 luk ying dai

tape *v.t* 錄 luk

taper *v.i.* 變窄 been jak

taper *n* 木條 muk tiew

tapestry *n.* 織錦 jik gam

tar *n.* 瀝青 lik teng

tar *v.t.* 用瀝青鋪 yung lik teng pow

target *n.* 目標 muk biew

tariff *n.* 收費表 sow fay biew

tarnish *v.t.* 失去光澤 sat huy gworng jak

task *n.* 任務 yam mo

task *v.t.* 派任務 pai yam mow

taste *n.* 試 see

taste *v.t.* 試 see

tasteful *a.* 高雅嘅 gow ngar geh

tasty *a.* 好味 ho may

tatter *n.* 碎布 suy bo

tatter *v.t* 撕爛 see lan

tattoo *n.* 紋身 man san

tattoo *v.i.* 紋身 man san

taunt *v.t.* 辱罵 yuk ma

taunt *n* 嘲笑 jao siew

tavern *n.* 酒館 jow gwun

tax *n.* 稅 suy

tax *v.t.* 收稅 sow suy

taxable *a.* 應納稅嘅 ying lap suy geh

taxation *n.* 稅 suy

taxi *n.* 的士 dik see

taxi *v.i.* 滑行 wat hang

tea *n* 茶 ta

teach *v.t.* 教 gao

teacher *n.* 老師 lo see

teak *n.* 柚木 yow muk

team *n.* 隊 duy

tear *v.t.* 撕開 see hoy

tear *n.* 裂痕 leet han

tear *n.* 眼淚 ngan luy

tearful *a.* 眼濕濕 ngan sap sap

tease *v.t.* 整蠱 jing gu

teat *n.* 乳頭 yu tow

technical *a.* 技術嘅 gey sut geh

technicality *n.* 技術性細節 gey sut sing say jeet

technician *n.* 技師 gey see

technique *n.* 技巧 gey hao

technological *a.* 技術嘅 gey sut geh

technologist *n.* 技術專家 gey sut joon ga

technology *n.* 科技 for gey

tedious *a.* 囉唆 lor sor

tedium *n.* 囉唆 lor sor

teem *v.i.* 充滿 chung mun

teenager *n.* 青少年 ting siew leen

teens *n. pl.* 十幾歲 sap gey suy

teethe *v.i.* 生牙 sang ngar

teetotal *a.* 滴酒不沾 dik jow bat jeem

teetotaller *n.* 唔飲酒嘅人 hm yam jow geh yan

telecast *n.* 電視廣播 deen see gworng bor

telecast *v.t.* 廣播 gworng bor

telecommunications *n.* 電訊 deen sun

telegram *n.* 電報 deen bo

telegraph *n.* 電報 deen bo

telegraph *v.t.* 打電報 da deen bo

telegraphic *a.* 電報嘅 deen bo geh

telegraphist *n.* 電報員 deen bo yoon

telegraphy *n.* 電報學 deen bo hok

telepathic *a.* 心靈感應嘅 sam ling gam ying geh

telepathist *n.* 心靈感應者 sam ling gam ying jeh

telepathy *n.* 心靈感應 sam ling gam ying

telephone *n.* 電話 deem wah

telephone *v.t.* 打電話 da deen wah

telescope *n.* 望遠鏡 morng yoon geng

telescopic *a.* 放大嘅 forng dai geh

televise *v.t.* 廣播 gworng bor

television *n.* 電視 deen see

tell *v.t.* 講 gong

teller *n.* 出納員 chut lap yoon

temper *n.* 脾氣 pay hay

temper *v.t.* 變溫和 been wan wor

temperament *n.* 氣質 hay jat

temperamental *a.* 喜怒無常 hay low mow seurng

temperance *n.* 滴酒不沾 dik jow bat jeem

temperate *a.* 溫和嘅 wan wor geh

temperature *n.* 溫度 wan dow

tempest *n.* 暴風雨 bo fung yu

tempestuous *a.* 劇烈 kek leet

temple *n.* 太陽穴 tai yeurng yoot

temple *n* 廟 miew

temporal *a.* 世間嘅 say gan geh

temporary *a.* 暫時嘅 jam see geh

tempt *v.t.* 誘惑 yow wak

temptation *n.* 誘惑 yow wak

tempter *n.* 誘惑者 yow wak jeh

ten *n., a* 十 sap

tenable *a.* 講得過嘅 gorng dak gwor geh

tenacious *a.* 堅持嘅 geen tee geh

tenacity *n.* 固執 gu jap

tenancy *n.* 租期 jow kay

tenant *n.* 租戶 jow wu
tend *v.i.* 通常會 tung seurng wuy
tendency *n.* 傾向 king heurng
tender *n* 供應船 gung ying shoon
tender *v.t.* 提議 tay yee
tender *n* 投票 tow biew
tender *a* 溫柔 wan yow
tenet *n.* 原則 yoon jak
tennis *n.* 網球 mong kow
tense *n.* 時態 see tai
tense *a.* 緊張 gan jeurng
tension *n.* 緊張 gan jeurng
tent *n.* 帳篷 jeurng fung
tentative *a.* 唔肯定嘅 hm hang ding geh
tenure *n.* 任期 yam kay
term *n.* 學期 hok kay
term *v.t.* 叫做 giew jow
terminable *a.* 可以終止嘅 hor yee jung jee geh
terminal *a.* 末期嘅 mwut kay geh
terminal *n* 機場 gey cheurng
terminate *v.t.* 終止 jung jee
termination *n.* 終止 jung jee
terminological *a.* 專門名詞嘅 joon mun ming tee geh
terminology *n.* 術語 sut yu
terminus *n.* 終點站 jung deem jam
terrace *n.* 排屋 派uk
terrible *a.* 可怕 hor pa
terrier *n.* 小獵犬 siew leep hoon
terrific *a.* 好好 ho ho
terrify *v.t.* 嚇 hak
territorial *a.* 地盤 day pwun
territory *n.* 地盤 day pwun
terror *n.* 驚恐 ging hung
terrorism *n.* 恐怖主義 hung bo ju yee
terrorist *n.* 恐怖份子 hung bo fan jee
terrorize *v.t.* 恐嚇 hung hak

terse *a.* 簡要嘅 gan yiew geh
test *v.t.* 試 see
test *n* 測試 tak see
testament *n.* 證據 jing guy
testicle *n.* 睪丸 gow yoon
testify *v.i.* 證實 jing sat
testimonial *n.* 推薦信 tuy jeen sun
testimony *n.* 證據 jing guy
tete-a-tete *n.* 面對面 meen duy meen
tether *n.* 拴 san
tether *v.t.* 拴繩 san sing
text *n.* 字 jee
textile *a.* 紡織嘅 forng jik geh
textile *n* 紡織品 forng jik ban
textual *a.* 正文嘅 jing man geh
texture *n.* 質感 jat gam
thank *v.t.* 多謝 dor jeh
thanks *n* 多謝 dor jeh
thankful *a.* 感謝 gam jeh
thankless *a.* 吃力不討好 hek lik bat tow ho
that *a.* 嗰個 gor gor
that *dem. pron.* 嗰個 gor gor
that *rel. pron.* 嗰 gor
that *adv.* 咁 gam
that *conj.* 以致 yee jee
thatch *n.* 稻草 dow cho
thatch *v.t.* 用茅草整屋頂 yung mao cho jing uk deng
thaw *v.i* 解凍 gai dung
thaw *n* 熔化季節 yung far gway jeet
theatre *n.* 劇院 kek yoon
theatrical *a.* 戲劇嘅 hay kek geh
theft *n.* 偷竊 tow seet
their *a.* 佢哋 kuy dey
theirs *pron.* 佢哋 kuy dey
theism *n.* 有神論 yow san lun
theist *n.* 有神論者 yow san lun jeh

them *pron.* 佢哋 kuy day
thematic *a.* 主題嘅 ju tay geh
theme *n.* 主題 ju tay
then *adv.* 跟住 gan ju
then *a* 當時 dorng see
thence *adv.* 然後 yeen ho
theocracy *n.* 神權政治 san koon jing jee
theologian *n.* 神學家 san hok ga
theological *a.* 神學嘅 san hok geh
theology *n.* 宗教學 jung gao hok
theorem *n.* 定理 ding lay
theoretical *a.* 理論上 lay lun seurng
theorist *n.* 理論家 lay lun ga
theorize *v.i.* 理論化 lay lun far
theory *n.* 理論 lay lun
therapy *n.* 治療 jee liew
there *adv.* 嗰度 gor dow
thereabouts *adv.* 嗰度附近 gor dow fu gan
thereafter *adv.* 之後 jee ho
thereby *adv.* 因此 yan tee
therefore *adv.* 所以 sor yi
thermal *a.* 保暖嘅 bo loon geh
thermometer *n.* 探熱針 tam yeet jam
thermos (flask) *n.* 暖水壺 loon suy wu
thesis *n.* 論文 lun man
thick *a.* 厚 ho
thick *n.* 艱難 gan lan
thick *adv.* 厚厚咁 ho ho gam
thicken *v.i.* 整厚 jing ho
thicket *n.* 樹叢 shu chung
thief *n.* 賊 tak
thigh *n.* 大髀 dai bay
thimble *n.* 頂針 ding jam
thin *a.* 瘦 so
thin *v.t.* 稀釋 hay sik
thing *n.* 嘢 yeh

think *v.t.* 諗 lum
thinker *n.* 思想家 see seurng ga
third *a.* 第三 day sam
third *n.* 第三 day sam
thirdly *adv.* 第三 day sam
thirst *n.* 渴 hot
thirst *v.i.* 渴 hot
thirsty *a.* 口渴 ho hot
thirteen *n.* 十三 sap sam
thirteen *a* 十三 sap sam
thirteenth *a.* 第十三 day sap sam
thirtieth *a.* 第三十 day sam sap
thirtieth *n* 第三十 day sam sap
thirty *n.* 三十 sam sap
thirty *a* 三十 sam sap
thistle *n.* 薊 gey
thither *adv.* 向嗰度 heurng gor dow
thorn *n.* 刺 tee
thorny *a.* 多刺 dor tee
thorough *a* 仔細 jee say
thoroughfare *n.* 大街 dai gai
though *conj.* 雖然 suy yeen
though *adv.* 不過 bat gwor
thought *n* 諗 lum
thoughtful *a.* 體貼 tay teep
thousand *n.* 一千 yat teen
thousand *a* 一千 teen
thrall *n.* 影響 ying heurng
thralldom *n.* 奴隸 low day
thrash *v.t.* 連續打 leen juk da
thread *n.* 線 seen
thread *v.t* 穿 choon
threadbare *a.* 破舊 por gow
threat *n.* 威脅 way heep
threaten *v.t.* 恐嚇 hung hak
three *n.* 三 sam
three *a* 三 sam
thresh *v.t.* 脫粒 toot lap
thresher *n.* 打穀者 da guk jeh
threshold *n.* 門口 mun ho
thrice *adv.* 三次 sam tee

thrift *n.* 慳家 han ga
thrifty *a.* 慳 han
thrill *n.* 刺激 tee gik
thrill *v.t.* 刺激 tee gik
thrive *v.i.* 興旺 hing worng
throat *n.* 喉嚨 ho lung
throaty *a.* 嘶啞嘅 see ngar geh
throb *v.i.* 抽搐 tow chuk
throb *n.* 跳動 tiew dung
throe *n.* 劇痛 kek tung
throne *n.* 王位 worng way
throne *v.t.* 登位 dang way
throng *n.* 一大班人 yat dai ban yan
throng *v.t.* 群集 kwan jap
throttle *n.* 油門 yow mun
throttle *v.t.* 勒死 lak say
through *prep.* 穿過 choon gwor
through *adv.* 通過 tung gwor
through *a* 全程嘅 choon ting geh
throughout *adv.* 遍及 peen kap
throughout *prep.* 由始至終 yow tee jee jung
throw *v.t.* 掟 deng
throw *n.* 掟 deng
thrust *v.t.* 猛推 mang tuy
thrust *n* 插 tap
thud *n.* 砰聲 pung seng
thud *v.i.* 砰 pung
thug *n.* 死仔 say leng jay
thumb *n.* 手指公 sow jee gung
thumb *v.t.* 用手指公評 yung sow jee gung ping
thump *n.* 重擊 chung gik
thump *v.t.* 重擊 chung gik
thunder *n.* 雷 luy
thunder *v.i.* 打雷 da luy
thunderous *a.* 大聲 dai seng
Thursday *n.* 星期四 sing kay say
thus *adv.* 所以 sor yi
thwart *v.t.* 阻止 jor jee
tiara *n.* 皇冠 worng gwun

tick *n.* 剔 tik
tick *v.i.* 剔 tik
ticket *n.* 票 piew
tickle *v.t.* 擳 jeet
ticklish *a.* 怕擳 pa jee
tidal *a.* 潮嘅 tiew geh
tide *n.* 潮 tiew
tidings *n. pl.* 消息 siew sik
tidiness *n.* 整齊 jing tay
tidy *a.* 整齊 jing tay
tidy *v.t.* 執 jap
tie *v.t.* 綁 borng
tie *n* 呔 tai
tier *n.* 級 kap
tiger *n.* 老虎 lo fu
tight *a.* 緊 gan
tighten *v.t.* 整緊 jing gan
tigress *n.* 老虎乸 low fu la
tile *n.* 瓷磚 tee joon
tile *v.t.* 鋪瓷磚 po tee joon
till *prep.* 直到 jik dow
till *n. conj.* 直到 jik dow
till *v.t.* 耕 gang
tilt *v.i.* 斜 ter
tilt *n.* 斜 ter
timber *n.* 木 muk
time *n.* 時間 see gan
time *v.t.* 計時 gey see
timely *a.* 及時 kap see
timid *a.* 細膽 say dam
timidity *n.* 無膽 mow dam
timorous *a.* 細膽 say dam
tin *n.* 罐 gwun
tin *v.t.* 裝罐 jorng gwun
tincture *n.* 藥酒 yeurk jow
tincture *v.t.* 染 yeem
tinge *n.* 少少 siew siew
tinge *v.t.* 染少少 yeem siew siew
tinker *n.* 修補匠 sow bo jeurng
tinsel *n.* 金屬絲 gam suk see
tint *n.* 淺色 teen sik
tint *v.t.* 稍微染 sao may yeem

tiny *a.* 細粒 say lap
tip *n.* 貼士 teep see
tip *v.t.* 畀貼士 bay teep see
tip *n.* 一堆垃圾 yat duy lap sap
tip *v.t.* 倒 dow
tip *n.* 頭 tow
tip *v.t.* 輕輕咁掂 heng heng gam deem
tipsy *a.* 少少醉 siew siew juy
tirade *n.* 長篇大論 cheurng peen dai lun
tire *v.t.* 攰 gwuy
tiresome *a.* 好煩 ho fan
tissue *n.* 紙巾 jee gan
Titanic *a.* 鐵達尼號 teet dat nay ho
tithe *n.* 捐稅 goon sut
title *n.* 名 meng
titular *a.* 有名無實 yow ming mow sat
toad *n.* 蟾蜍 siem chuy
toast *n.* 多士 dor see
toast *v.t.* 乾杯 gorn bwuy
tobacco *n.* 煙草 yeem cho
today *adv.* 今日 gam yat
today *n.* 今日 gam yat
toe *n.* 腳趾 geurt jee
toe *v.t.* 順從 sun chung
toffee *n.* 太妃糖 tai fay torng
toga *n.* 闊外袍 fwut ngoy pow
together *adv.* 一齊 yat chay
toil *n.* 苦工 fu gung
toil *v.i.* 辛苦做 san fu jow
toilet *n.* 廁所 tee sor
toils *n. pl.* 陷阱 ham jing
token *n.* 代幣 doy bay
tolerable *a.* 仲可以 jung hor yee
tolerance *n.* 耐力 loy lik
tolerant *a.* 忍受到嘅 yan sow dow geh
tolerate *v.t.* 忍 yan
toleration *n.* 容忍 yung yan
toll *n.* 通行費 tung hang fay

toll *n* 數目 sow muk
toll *v.t.* 敲 hao
tomato *n.* 番茄 fan keh
tomb *n.* 墓 mo
tomboy *n.* 男人婆 larm yan por
tomcat *n.* 公貓 gung mao
tome *n.* 厚書 ho shu
tomorrow *n.* 聽日 ting yat
tomorrow *adv.* 聽日 ting yat
ton *n.* 噸 dun
tone *n.* 語氣 yu hay
tone *v.t.* 變結實 been geet sat
tongs *n. pl.* 鉗 keem
tongue *n.* 脷 lay
tonic *a.* 補嘅 bo geh
tonic *n.* 湯力水 torng lik suy
tonight *n.* 今晚 gam man
tonight *adv.* 今晚 gam man
tonne *n.* 噸 dun
tonsil *n.* 扁桃體 been tow tay
tonsure *n.* 剃度 tay dow
too *adv.* 太過 tai gwor
tool *n.* 工具 gung guy
tooth *n.* 牙 ngar
toothache *n.* 牙痛 ngar tung
toothsome *a.* 好味嘅 ho may geh
top *n.* 頂 deng
top *v.t.* 超過 tiew gwor
top *n.* 上面 seurng meen
topaz *n.* 黃寶石 worng bo seng
topic *n.* 題目 tay muk
topical *a.* 有關嘅 yow gwan geh
topographer *n.* 地形學家 day ying hok ga
topographical *a.* 地形嘅 day ying geh
topography *n.* 地形 day ying
topple *v.i.* 倒塌 dow tap
topsy turvy *a.* 亂七八糟嘅 loon tat bat jow geh
topsy turvy *adv* 顛三倒四 deen sam dow say

torch *n.* 電筒 deen tung
torment *n.* 折磨 jeet mor
torment *v.t.* 折磨 jeet mor
tornado *n.* 龍捲風 lung goon fung
torpedo *n.* 魚雷 yu luy
torpedo *v.t.* 用魚雷襲擊 yung yu luy jap gik
torrent *n.* 急流 gap low
torrential *a.* 傾瀉嘅 king seh geh
torrid *a.* 乾燥嘅 gorn cho geh
tortoise *n.* 龜 gway
tortuous *a.* 彎彎曲曲嘅 wan wan kuk kuk geh
torture *n.* 折磨 jeet mor
torture *v.t.* 折磨 jeet mor
toss *v.t.* 掟 deng
toss *n* 擲銀決定 jak ngan koot ding
total *a.* 總計嘅 jung gey geh
total *n.* 總數 jung sow
total *v.t.* 計 gey
totality *n.* 全部 choon bo
touch *v.t.* 掂 deem
touch *n* 觸覺 juk gok
touchy *a.* 易嬲 yee low
tough *a.* 艱難 gan lan
toughen *v.t.* 強化 keurng far
tour *n.* 旅行 luy hang
tour *v.i.* 遊覽 yow lam
tourism *n.* 旅遊業 luy yow yeep
tourist *n.* 旅客 luy hak
tournament *n.* 錦標賽 gam biew choy
towards *prep.* 向 heurng
towel *n.* 毛巾 mo gan
towel *v.t.* 用毛巾抹 yung mo gan mat
tower *n.* 塔 tap
tower *v.i.* 超過 tiew gwor
town *n.* 市鎮 see jan
township *a.* 鎮區 jan kuy
toy *n.* 玩具 wun guy

toy *v.i.* 玩 wan
trace *n.* 痕跡 han jik
trace *v.t.* 跟蹤 gan jung
traceable *a.* 可以追溯嘅 hor yee juy sok geh
track *n.* 軌道 gway dow
track *v.t.* 追蹤 juy jung
tract *n.* 大片土地 dai peen tow day
tract *n* 宗教短文 jung gao doon man
traction *n.* 拉力 lai lik
tractor *n.* 拖拉機 tor lai gey
trade *n.* 買賣 mai mai
trade *v.i* 交易 gao yik
trader *n.* 商人 seurng yan
tradesman *n.* 商人 seurng yan
tradition *n.* 傳統 choon tung
traditional *a.* 傳統嘅 choon tung geh
traffic *n.* 交通 gao tung
traffic *v.i.* 非法做買賣 fay fat jow mai mai
tragedian *n.* 悲劇作家 bay kek jok ga
tragedy *n.* 悲劇 bay kek
tragic *a.* 悲慘嘅 bay tarm geh
trail *n.* 痕跡 han jik
trail *v.t.* 拉 lai
trailer *n.* 預告 yu go
train *n.* 火車 for cher
train *v.t.* 訓練 fan leen
trainee *n.* 練習生 leen jap sang
training *n.* 訓練 fan leen
trait *n.* 特徵 dak jing
traitor *n.* 叛徒 bwun tow
tram *n.* 電車 deen cher
trample *v.t.* 踩碎 tai suy
trance *n.* 發呆 fat oy
tranquil *a.* 安靜 on jing
tranquility *n.* 平靜 ping jing

tranquillize *v.t.* 變平靜 been ping jing
transact *v.t.* 辦理 ban lay
transaction *n.* 交易 gao yik
transcend *v.t.* 超越 tiew yoot
transcendent *a.* 傑出嘅 geet chut geh
transcribe *v.t.* 記錄 gey luk
transcription *n.* 抄寫 tao seh
transfer *n.* 轉 joon
transfer *v.t.* 轉 joon
transferable *a.* 可以轉嘅 hor yee joon geh
transfiguration *n.* 變形 been ying
transfigure *v.t.* 變形 been ying
transform *v.* 改變形態 goy been ying tai
transformation *n.* 變化 been far
transgress *v.t.* 越軌 yoot gway
transgression *n.* 違反 way fan
transit *n.* 運輸 wan shu
transition *n.* 轉變 joon been
transitive *n.* 轉遞 joon day
transitory *a.* 暫時 jam see
translate *v.t.* 翻譯 fan yik
translation *n.* 翻譯 fan yik
transmigration *n.* 轉世 joon say
transmission *n.* 傳染 choon yeem
transmit *v.t.* 傳送 choon sung
transmitter *n.* 發射機 fat seh gey
transparent *a.* 透明 tow ming
transplant *v.t.* 移植 yee jik
transport *v.t.* 運送 wan sung
transport *n.* 交通工具 gao tung gung guy
transportation *n.* 交通工具 gao tung gung guy
trap *n.* 陷阱 ham jeng
trap *v.t.* 捉 juk
trash *n.* 垃圾 lap sap

travel *v.i.* 旅遊 luy yow
travel *n* 旅行 luy hang
traveller *n.* 旅客 luy hao
tray *n.* 盤 pwun
treacherous *a.* 奸嘅 gan geh
treachery *n.* 背叛 bwuy bun
tread *v.t.* 踩 tai
tread *n* 步法 bo fat
treason *n.* 叛國罪 pwun gwok juy
treasure *n.* 寶藏 bo jorng
treasure *v.t.* 珍惜 jan sik
treasurer *n.* 財物主管 choy mow ju gwun
treasury *n.* 財政部 choy jing bo
treat *v.t.* 對待 duy doy
treat *n* 款待 fwun doy
treatise *n.* 論文 lun man
treatment *n.* 治療 jee liew
treaty *n.* 協定 heep ding
tree *n.* 樹 shu
trek *v.i.* 長途跋涉 cheurng tow bat seet
trek *n.* 長途跋涉 cheurng tow bat seet
tremble *v.i.* 震 jan
tremendous *a.* 巨大嘅 guy dai geh
tremor *n.* 微震 may jan
trench *n.* 溝 kow
trench *v.t.* 掘 gwat
trend *n.* 潮流 tiew lo
trespass *v.i.* 擅自侵入 seen jee tam yap
trespass *n.* 非法侵入 fay fat tam yap
trial *n.* 審訊 sam sun
triangle *n.* 三角形 sam gok ying
triangular *a.* 三角形 sam gok ying
tribal *a.* 部族嘅 bo juk geh
tribe *n.* 族 juk
tribulation *n.* 痛苦 tung fu

tribunal *n.* 法庭 fat ting
tributary *n.* 支流 jee low
tributary *a.* 支流嘅 jee low geh
trick *n* 騙局 peen guk
trick *v.t.* 呃 ak
trickery *n.* 花招 far jiew
trickle *v.i.* 滴 dik
trickster *n.* 騙子 peen jee
tricky *a.* 難嘅 lan geh
tricolour *a.* 三色嘅 sam sik geh
tricolour *n* 三色旗 sam sik kay
tricycle *n.* 三輪車 sam lun cher
trifle *n.* 鬆糕 sung go
trifle *v.i* 睇小 tay siew
trigger *n.* 板機 ban gey
trim *a.* 苗條 miew tiew
trim *n* 修剪 sow jeen
trim *v.t.* 修剪 sow jeen
trinity *n.* 三位一體 sam way yat tay
trio *n.* 三個人 sam gor yam
trip *v.t.* 棘嘅 kik tan
trip *n.* 旅行 luy hang
tripartite *a.* 有三個部份 yow sam gor bo fan geh
triple *a.* 三個部份 sam gor bo fan
triple *v.t.,* 三倍 sam pwuy
triplicate *a.* 三個 sam gor
triplicate *n* 一式三份 yat sik sam fan
triplicate *v.t.* 三倍 sam pwuy
triplication *n.* 分成三份 fan sing sam fan
tripod *n.* 三腳架 sam geurt ga
triumph *n.* 成就 sing jow
triumph *v.i.* 打敗 da bai
triumphal *a.* 凱旋嘅 hoy shoon geh
triumphant *a.* 大獲全勝 dai wok choon sing
trivial *a.* 瑣碎 sor suy
troop *n.* 士兵 see bing

troop *v.i* 列隊行 leet duy hang
trooper *n.* 騎兵 keh bing
trophy *n.* 獎座 jeurng jor
tropic *n.* 熱帶 yeet dai
tropical *a.* 熱帶 yeet dai
trot *v.i.* 快步行 fai bao hang
trot *n* 小步快跑 siew bo fai pao
trouble *n.* 問題 man tay
trouble *v.t.* 煩 fan
troublesome *a.* 令人煩惱 ling yan fan low
troupe *n.* 戲團 hay toon
trousers *n. pl* 褲 fu
trowel *n.* 細鏟 say tan
truce *n.* 停戰協定 ting jeen heep ding
truck *n.* 卡車 ka cher
true *a.* 啱 ngarm
trump *n.* 王牌 worng pai
trump *v.t.* 打敗 da bai
trumpet *n.* 喇叭 la ba
trumpet *v.i.* 宣揚 shoon yeurng
trunk *n.* 車尾箱 cher may seurng
trust *n.* 信任 sun yam
trust *v.t* 信 sun
trustee *n.* 受託人 sow tok yan
trustful *a.* 信得過 sun dak gwor
trustworthy *a.* 信得過 sun dak gwor
trusty *n.* 模範囚犯 mo fan tow fan
truth *n.* 真相 tan seurng
truthful *a.* 誠實 sing sat
try *v.i.* 試 see
try *n* 嘗試 seurng see
trying *a.* 麻煩 ma fan
tryst *n.* 幽會 yow wuy
tub *n.* 罐 gwun
tube *n.* 管 gwun
tuberculosis *n.* 肺癆 fay lo
tubular *a.* 管狀 gwun jorng
tug *v.t.* 拉 lai
tuition *n.* 指導 jee dow

tumble *v.i.* 跌倒 deet dow
tumble *n.* 跌 deet
tumbler *n.* 玻璃杯 bor lay bwuy
tumour *n.* 腫瘤 jung lo
tumult *n.* 騷亂 sow loon
tumultuous *a.* 熱烈 yeet leet
tune *n.* 曲 kuk
tune *v.t.* 調音 tiew yam
tunnel *n.* 地下通到 day ha tung dow
tunnel *v.i.* 挖地道 gwat day dow
turban *n.* 包頭巾 bao tow gan
turbine *n.* 渦輪機 wor lun gey
turbulence *n.* 氣流 hay low
turbulent *a.* 混亂嘅 wan loon geh
turf *n.* 草皮 cho pay
turkey *n.* 火雞 for gey
turmeric *n.* 薑黃根粉 geurng worng gan fan
turmoil *n.* 騷動 sow dung
turn *v.i.* 轉 joon
turn *n* 彎 wan
turner *n.* 車工 cher gung
turnip *n.* 蘿蔔 lor bak
turpentine *n.* 松節油 chung jeet yow
turtle *n.* 烏龜 wu gway
tusk *n.* 象牙 jeurng ngar
tussle *n.* 爭鬥 jang dow
tussle *v.i.* 掙 jang
tutor *n.* 教師 gao see
tutorial *a.* 導師嘅 dow see geh
tutorial *n.* 輔導課 fu dow for
twelfth *a.* 第十二 day sap yee
twelfth *n.* 第十二 day sap yee
twelve *n.* 十二 sap yeet
twelve *a.* 十二 sup yee
twentieth *a.* 第二十 day yee sap
twentieth *n* 第二十 day yee sap
twenty *a.* 二十 yee sap
twenty *n* 二十 yee sup
twice *adv.* 兩次 leurng tee

twig *n.* 樹枝 shu jee
twilight *n* 暮色 mow sik
twin *n.* 雙胞胎之一 seurng bao toy jee yat
twin *a* 相連 seurng leen
twinkle *v.i.* 閃 seem
twinkle *n.* 閃亮 seem leurng
twist *v.t.* 扭 low
twist *n.* 轉變 joon been
twitter *n.* 吱吱聲 jee jee seng
twitter *v.i.* 吱喳 jee ja
two *n.* 二 yee
two *a.* 兩 leurng
twofold *a.* 有兩個部份 yow leurng gor bo fan
type *n.* 類型 luy ying
type *v.t.* 打字 da jee
typhoid *n* 傷寒 seurng hon
typhoon *n.* 颱風 toy fung
typhus *n.* 斑疹傷寒 ban tan seurng hon
typical *a.* 典型嘅 deen ying geh
typify *v.t.* 做...嘅典範 jow...geh deen fa
typist *n.* 打字員 da jee yoon
tyranny *n.* 苛政 hor jing
tyrant *n.* 暴君 bo gwan
tyre *n.* 車胎 cher tai

U

udder *n.* 乳房 yu forng
uglify *v.t.* 醜化 tow far
ugliness *n.* 醜陋 tow low
ugly *a.* 醜 tow
ulcer *n.* 潰瘍 kwuy yeurng
ulcerous *a.* 潰瘍嘅 kwuy yeurng geh
ulterior *a.* 不可告人嘅 bat hor gow yan geh

ultimate *a.* 終極嘅 jung gik geh

ultimately *adv.* 最後 juy ho

ultimatum *n.* 最後通牒 juy ho tung deep

umbrella *n.* 遮 jeh

umpire *n.* 裁判員 choy pwun yoon

umpire *v.t.,* 做裁判 jow choy pwun

unable *a.* 唔可以 hm hor yi

unanimity *n.* 一致同意 yat jee tung yee

unanimous *a.* 一致嘅 yat jee geh

unaware *a.* 唔在意 hm joy yee

unawares *adv.* 未主義到 may ju yee dow

unburden *v.t.* 傾訴 king sow

uncanny *a.* 異常嘅 yee seurng geh

uncertain *a.* 唔肯定 hm han ding

uncle *n.* 阿叔 ah suk

uncouth *a.* 粗魯 cho low

under *prep.* 喺...嘅下面 hay...geh ha meen

under *adv* 少於 siew yu

under *a* 喺...嘅下面 hay...geh ha meen

undercurrent *n.* 暗流 am low

underdog *n* 唔被睇好嘅人 hm bay tay ho geh yan

undergo *v.t.* 經歷 ging lik

undergraduate *n.* 大學生 dai hok sang

underhand *a.* 祕密嘅 bay mat geh

underline *v.t.* 畫線 wak seen

undermine *v.t.* 逐漸減弱 juk jeen garm yeurk

underneath *adv.* 喺...嘅下面 hay...geh ha meen

underneath *prep.* 喺...嘅下面 hay...geh ha meen

understand *v.t.* 明白 ming bak

undertake *v.t.* 負責 fu jak

undertone *n.* 細聲 say seng

underwear *n.* 內衣 loy yee

underworld *n.* 陰曹地府 yam cho day fu

undo *v.t.* 解開 gai hoy

undue *a.* 過分 gwor fan

undulate *v.i.* 起伏 hay fuk

undulation *n.* 波浪形 bor lorng ying

unearth *v.t.* 發掘 fat gwat

uneasy *a.* 擔心 dam sam

unfair *a* 唔公平 hm gung ping

unfold *v.t.* 打開 da hoy

unfortunate *a.* 不幸 bat han

ungainly *a.* 笨手笨腳 ban sow ban geurt

unhappy *a.* 唔開心 hm hoy sam

unification *n.* 統一 tung yat

union *n.* 協會 heep wuy

unionist *n.* 聯合主義者 loon hap ju yee jeh

unique *a.* 獨特 duk tak

unison *n.* 一齊 yat tay

unit *n.* 單位 dan way

unite *v.t.* 團結 toon geet

unity *n.* 聯合 loon hap

universal *a.* 全世界嘅 choon say gai geh

universality *n.* 普遍性 pow peen sing

universe *n.* 宇宙 yu jow

university *n.* 大學 dai hok

unjust *a.* 唔公平嘅 hm gung ping geh

unless *conj.* 徐非 chuy fay

unlike *a* 唔同 hm tung

unlike *prep* 唔似 hm tee

unlikely *a.* 無咩可能 mow meh hor lang

unmanned *a.* 無人操作嘅 mow yan cho jok geh

unmannerly *a* 無禮貌嘅 mow lay moa geh

unprincipled *a.* 不道德嘅 bat dow dak geh

unreliable *a.* 唔信得過嘅 hm sun dak gwor geh

unrest *n* 騷動 sow dung

unruly *a.* 難控制嘅 lan hung jay geh

unsettle *v.t.* 擔憂 dam yow

unsheathe *v.t.* 拔出 bat chut

until *prep.* 直到 jik dow

until *conj* 直到 jik dow

untoward *a.* 意外嘅 yee ngoy geh

unwell *a.* 唔舒服 hm shu fuk

unwittingly *adv.* 無意咁 mow yee gam

up *adv.* 向上 heurng seurng

up *prep.* 沿着 yoon ju

upbraid *v.t* 鬧 lao

upheaval *n.* 劇變 kek been

uphold *v.t* 支持 jee tee

upkeep *n* 保養 bow yeurng

uplift *v.t.* 激勵 gik lay

uplift *n* 提高 tay gow

upon *prep* 上 seurng

upper *a.* 上嘅 seurng geh

upright *a.* 挺直嘅 ting jik geh

uprising *n.* 起義 hay yee

uproar *n.* 騷動 sow dung

uproarious *a.* 熱烈 yeet leet

uproot *v.t.* 連根拔起 leen gan bat hay

upset *v.t.* 令到唔開心 ling dow hm hoy sam

upshot *n.* 結果 geet gwor

upstart *n.* 暴發戶 bo fat wu

up-to-date *a.* 最新嘅 juy san geh

upward *a.* 向上嘅 heurng seurng geh

upwards *adv.* 上面 seurng meen

urban *a.* 城市嘅 sing see geh

urbane *a.* 彬彬有禮嘅 ban ban yow lay geh

urbanity *n.* 文雅 man ngar

urchin *n.* 頑童 wan tung

urge *v.t* 催 chuy

urge *n* 衝動 chung dung

urgency *n.* 急事 gap see

urgent *a.* 緊急 gan gap

urinal *n.* 尿兜 liew dow

urinary *a.* 尿嘅 liew geh

urinate *v.i.* 屙尿 or liew

urination *n.* 屙尿 or liew

urine *n.* 尿 liew

urn *n* 骨灰甕 gwat fwuy ang

usage *n.* 用法 yung fat

use *n.* 用處 yung chu

use *v.t.* 用 yung

useful *a.* 有用 yow yung

usher *n.* 門衛 mun way

usher *v.t.* 引導 yan dow

usual *a.* 平時 ping see

usually *adv.* 通常 tung seurng

usurer *n.* 大耳窿 dai yee lung

usurp *v.t.* 侵權 tam koon

usurpation *n.* 侵佔 tam jeem

usury *n.* 放貴利 forng gway lay

utensil *n.* 用具 yung guy

uterus *n.* 子宮 jee gung

utilitarian *a.* 實用嘅 sat yung geh

utility *n.* 效用 hao yung

utilization *n.* 利用 lay yung

utilize *v.t.* 用 yung

utmost *a.* 最大嘅 juy dai geh

utmost *n* 最大量 juy dai leurng

utopia *n* . 理想國 lay seurng gwok

utopian *a.* 不切實際 bat teet sat jay

utter *v.t.* 講 gorng

utter *a* 徹底 teet day

utterance *n.* 言論 yeen lun

utterly *adv.* 徹底咁 teet day gam

vacancy *n.* 空缺 hung koot
vacant *a.* 空嘅 hung geh
vacate *v.t.* 搬出 bwun chut
vacation *n.* 假期 ga kay
vaccinate *v.t.* 打疫苗 da yik miew
vaccination *n.* 接種 jeep jung
vaccinator *n.* 接種員 jeep jung yoon
vaccine *n.* 疫苗 yik miew
vacillate *v.i.* 成日轉軚 sing yat joon tai
vacuum *n.* 真空 jan hung
vagabond *n.* 流浪漢 low lorng hon
vagabond *a* 流浪嘅 low lorng geh
vagary *n.* 難測 lan tak
vagina *n.* 陰道 yam dow
vague *a.* 粗略嘅 cho leurk geh
vagueness *n.* 含糊度 ham wu dow
vain *a.* 自負 jee fu
vainglorious *a.* 自負 jee fu
vainglory *n.* 虛榮 huy wing
vainly *adv.* 嘥氣嘅 sai hay geh
vale *n.* 山谷 san guk
valiant *a.* 勇敢嘅 yung gam geh
valid *a.* 有效 yow hao
validate *v.t.* 證實 jing sat
validity *n.* 合法性 hap fat sing
valley *n.* 山谷 san guk
valour *n.* 勇氣 yung hay
valuable *a.* 有價值 yow ga jik
valuation *n.* 估價 gu ga
value *n.* 價值 ga jik
value *v.t.* 珍惜 jan sik
valve *n.* 氣門 hay mun
van *n.* 貨車 for cher
vanish *v.i.* 消失 siew sat

vanity *n.* 自負 jee fu
vanquish *v.t.* 徹底擊敗 teet day gik bai
vaporize *v.t.* 蒸發 jing fat
vaporous *a.* 充滿蒸氣 chung mwun jing hay
vapour *n.* 蒸氣 jing hay
variable *a.* 多變嘅 dor been geh
variance *n.* 差額 ta ak
variation *n.* 變化 been far
varied *a.* 不同嘅 bat tung geh
variety *n.* 不同類型 bat tug luy ying
various *a.* 幾種嘅 gey jung geh
varnish *n.* 清漆 ting tat
varnish *v.t.* 上清漆 seurng ting tat
vary *v.t.* 有唔同嘅 yow hm tung geh
vasectomy *n.* 輸精管切除手術 shu jing gwun teet chuy sow sut
vaseline *n.* 礦脂 kworng jee
vast *a.* 巨大嘅 guy dai geh
vault *n.* 保險庫 bo heem fu
vault *n.* 墓穴 mow yoot
vault *v.i.* 跳 tiew
vegetable *n.* 蔬菜 sor choy
vegetable *a.* 青菜 teng choy
vegetarian *n.* 素食者 sow sik jeh
vegetarian *a* 素食嘅 sow sik geh
vegetation *n.* 草木 cho muk
vehemence *n.* 強烈 keurng leet
vehement *a.* 強烈 keurng leet
vehicle *n.* 交通工具 gao tubg gung guy
vehicular *a.* 車輛嘅 cher leurng geh
veil *n.* 棉紗 meen sa
veil *v.t.* 遮 jeh
vein *n.* 靜脈 jing mak
velocity *n.* 速度 chuk dow
velvet *n.* 絲絨 see yung
velvety *a.* 絲絨嘅 see yung geh

venal *a.* 見利忘義 geen lay morng yee

venality *n.* 腐敗 fu bai

vendor *n.* 小販 siew fan

venerable *a.* 值得尊重嘅 jik dak joon jung geh

venerate *n.* 敬重 ging jung

veneration *n.* 尊敬 joon ging

vengeance *n.* 報復 bo fuk

venial *a.* 可以寬恕嘅 hor yee wun shu geh

venom *n.* 毒液 duk yik

venomous *a.* 有毒嘅 yow duk geh

vent *n.* 風口 fung ho

ventilate *v.t.* 通風 tung fung

ventilation *n.* 通風 tung fung

ventilator *n.* 通風口 tung fung ho

venture *n.* 企業 kay yeep

venture *v.t.* 敢去 gam huy

venturesome *a.* 大膽嘅 dai dam geh

venturous *a.* 大膽嘅 dai dam geh

venue *n.* 地點 dey deem

veracity *n.* 誠實 sing sat

veranda *n.* 陽台 yeurng tow

verb *n.* 動詞 dung tee

verbal *a.* 口講嘅 ho gorng geh

verbally *adv.* 口頭上嘅 ho tow seurng geh

verbatim *a.* 逐個字 juk gor jee

verbatim *adv.* 逐個字 juk gor jee

verbose *a.* 囉唆 lor sor

verbosity *n.* 囉唆 lor sor

verdant *a.* 碧綠嘅 bik luk geh

verdict *n.* 裁決 choy koot

verge *n.* 邊緣 been yoon

verification *n.* 確認 kok ying

verify *v.t.* 證實 ting sat

verisimilitude *n.* 逼真 bik jan

veritable *a.* 名副其實嘅 ming fu kay sat geh

vermillion *n.* 鮮紅色 seen hung sik

vermillion *a.* 鮮紅色嘅 seen hung sik geh

vernacular *n.* 本地話 bwun day wah

vernacular *a.* 本地嘅 bwun day geh

vernal *a.* 春天嘅 chun teen geh

versatile *a.* 多才多藝嘅 dor choy dor ngay geh

versatility *n.* 多用途 dor yung tow

verse *n.* 詩節 see jeet

versed *a.* 熟練嘅 suk leen geh

versification *n.* 詩律 see lut

versify *v.t.* 作詩 jok see

version *n.* 版本 ban bwun

versus *prep.* 對 duy

vertical *a.* 打直 da jik

verve *n.* 精力 jing lik

very *a.* 非常 fay seurng

vessel *n.* 大船 dai shoon

vest *n.* 背心 bwuy sam

vest *v.t.* 屬於 suk yu

vestige *n.* 遺跡 way jik

vestment *n.* 祭衣 jay yee

veteran *n.* 退伍軍人 tuy hm gwan yan

veteran *a.* 經驗豐富嘅 ging yeem fung fu geh

veterinary *a.* 獸醫嘅 sow yee geh

veto *n.* 否決 fow koot

veto *v.t.* 否決 for koot

vex *v.t.* 煩 fan

vexation *n* 煩惱 fan low

via *prep.* 經 ging

viable *a.* 可行嘅 hor hang ghe

vial *n.* 管形樽 gwun ying jun

vibrate *v.i.* 震 jan

vibration *n.* 震動 jan dung

vicar *n.* 牧師 muk see

vicarious a. 代替嘅 doy tay geh
vice n. 罪行 juy hang
viceroy n. 總督 jung duk
vice-versa adv. 反之亦然 fan jee yik yeen
vicinity n. 附近 fun gan
vicious a. 狠 han
vicissitude n. 變遷 been teen
victim n. 受害者 sow hoy jeh
victimize v.t. 令人受苦 ling yan sow fu
victor n. 勝利者 sing lay jeh
victorious a. 勝利嘅 sing lay geh
victory n. 勝利 sing lay
victuals n. pl 飲食 yam sik
vie v.i. 爭 jang
view n. 風景 fung ging
view v.t. 睇 tay
vigil n. 守夜 sow yeh
vigilance n. 警戒 ging gai
vigilant a. 警覺嘅 ging gok geh
vigorous a. 精力充沛 jing lik chung pwuy
vile a. 邪惡嘅 ter ok geh
vilify v.t. 中傷 jung seurng
villa n. 別墅 beet suy
village n. 村 choon
villager n. 村民 choon man
villain n. 衰人 suy yan
vindicate v.t. 證實 jing sat
vindication n. 證明無罪 jing ming mow juy
vine n. 葡萄藤 pow tow tang
vinegar n. 醋 cho
vintage n. 釀造年份 yeurng jow leen fan
violate v.t. 違反 way fan
violation n. 違反 way fan
violence n. 暴力 bo lik
violent a. 劇烈嘅 kek leet geh
violet n. 紫羅蘭 jee lor lan
violin n. 小提琴 siew tay kam

violinist n. 小提琴家 siew tay kam ga
virgin n. 處女 chu luy
virgin n 處男 chu larm
virginity n. 貞潔 jing geet
virile a. 強壯嘅 keurng jorng geh
virility n. 力量 lik leurng
virtual a 虛擬 huy yee
virtue n. 美德 may dak
virtuous a. 品德高 ban dak gow
virulence n. 毒性 duk sing
virulent a. 狠毒嘅 han duk geh
virus n. 病毒 beng duk
visage n. 面 meen
visibility n. 能見度 lang geen dow
visible a. 見到嘅 geen dow geh
vision n. 視力 see lik
visionary a. 有創意 yow chorng yee
visionary n. 有眼力嘅人 yow ngan lik geh yan
visit n. 參觀 tam gwun
visit v.t. 探 tarm
visitor n. 客人 hak yan
vista n. 景色 ging sik
visual a. 視覺嘅 see gok geh
visualize v.t. 想像 seurng jeurng
vital a. 好重要嘅 ho jung yiew geh
vitality n. 活力 wut lik
vitalize v.t. 激勵 gik lay
vitamin n. 維他命 way ta ming
vitiate v.t. 失效 sat hao
vivacious a. 活潑嘅 wut pwut geh
vivacity n. 活潑 wut pwut
viva-voce adv. 口頭上嘅 ho tow seurng geh
viva-voce a 口嘅嘅 ho tow geh
viva-voce n 口試 ho see
vivid a. 清晰嘅 ting sik geh
vixen n. 雌狐 tee wu

vocabulary *n.* 單詞 dan tee
vocal *a.* 聲嘅 seng geh
vocalist *n.* 歌手 gor sow
vocation *n.* 使命感 see ming gam
vogue *n.* 流行 low hang
voice *n.* 聲 seng
voice *v.t.* 表示 biew see
void *a.* 缺乏 koot fat
void *v.t.* 變無效 been mow hao
void *n.* 空間 hung gan
volcanic *a.* 火山嘅 for san geh
volcano *n.* 火山 for san
volition *n.* 意志力 yee jee lik
volley *n.* 擊球 gik kow
volley *v.t* 攔球 lan kow
volt *n.* 伏特 fuk dak
voltage *n.* 伏特 fuk dak
volume *n.* 音量 yam leurng
voluminous *a.* 肥大嘅 fay dai ghe
voluntarily *adv.* 自願咁 jee yoon gam
voluntary *a.* 自願 jee yoon
volunteer *n.* 志願者 jee yoon jeh
volunteer *v.t.* 主動建議 ju dung geen yee
voluptuary *n.* 沈迷酒色嘅 tam may jow sik geh
voluptuous *a.* 豐滿嘅 fung mun geh
vomit *v.t.* 嘔 oh
vomit *n* 嘔 oh
voracious *a.* 大食嘅 dai sik geh
votary *n.* 信徒 sun tow
vote *n.* 選舉 shoon guy
vote *v.i.* 投票 tow piew
voter *n.* 投票人 tow piew yan
vouch *v.i.* 擔保 dam bow
voucher *n.* 優惠券 yow way goon
vouchsafe *v.t.* 允許 wan huy
vow *n.* 承諾 sing lok
vow *v.t.* 許下諾言 huy ha lok yeen

vowel *n.* 元音 yoon yam
voyage *n.* 航行 horng hang
voyage *v.i.* 遠行 yoon hang
voyager *n.* 航行者 horng hang jeh
vulgar *a.* 粗魯嘅 cho low geh
vulgarity *n.* 粗魯 cho low
vulnerable *a.* 脆弱 chuy yeurk
vulture *n.* 禿鷲 tuk jow

wade *v.i.* 跋涉 pa seep
waddle *v.i.* 搖擺 yiew bai
waft *v.t.* 漂蕩 piew dorng
waft *n* 一股 yat gu
wag *v.i.* 搖 yiew
wag *n* 搖擺 yiew bai
wage *v.t.* 發動 fat dung
wage *n.* 糧 leurng
wager *n.* 打賭 da dow
wager *v.i.* 打賭 da dow
wagon *n.* 馬車 ma cher
wail *v.i.* 痛哭 tung huk
wail *n* 尖叫聲 jeem giew seng
wain *n.* 運貨馬車 wan for ma cher
waist *n.* 腰 yiew
waistband *n.* 腰頭 yiew tow
waistcoat *n.* 背心 bwuy sam
wait *v.i.* 等 dang
wait *n.* 等 dang
waiter *n.* 侍應 see ying
waitress *n.* 女侍應 luy see ying
waive *v.t.* 放棄 forng hay
wake *v.t.* 醒 seng
wake *n* 守靈 sow ling
wake *n* 船跡 shoon jik
wakeful *a.* 失眠 sat meen
walk *v.i.* 行 han
walk *n* 散步 san bo

wall *n.* 牆 cheurng
wall *v.t.* 圍住 way ju
wallet *n.* 銀包 an bao
wallop *v.t.* 猛擊 mang gik
wallow *v.i.* 翻滾 fan gwun
walnut *n.* 核桃 hat tow
walrus *n.* 海象 hoy jeurng
wan *a.* 憔悴 tiew suy
wand *n.* 魔法棒 mor fat pang
wander *v.i.* 遊蕩 yow dorng
wane *v.i.* 衰落 suy lok
wane *n* 變細 been say
want *v.t.* 想要 seurng yiew
want *n* 想要 seurng yiew
wanton *a.* 惡意嘅 ok yee geh
war *n.* 仗 jeurng
war *v.i.* 對抗 duy korng
warble *v.i.* 唱 cheurng
warble *n* 鳥鳴 liew ming
warbler *n.* 鶯 ang
ward *n.* 病房 beng forng
ward *v.t.* 防止 forng jee
warden *n.* 管理人 gwun lay yan
warder *n.* 守衛 sow way
wardrobe *n.* 衣櫃 yee gway
wardship *n.* 監護 gam wu
ware *n.* 物品 mat ban
warehouse *v.t* 倉庫 chorngfu
warfare *n.* 戰爭 jeen jang
warlike *a.* 好戰嘅 ho jeen geh
warm *a.* 暖 loon
warm *v.t.* 暖返 loon fan
warmth *n.* 溫暖 wan look
warn *v.t.* 警告 ging gow
warning *n.* 警告 ging gow
warrant *n.* 執行令 jap hang ling
warrant *v.t.* 保證 bo jing
warrantee *n.* 被保證人 bay bo jing yn
warrantor *n.* 保證人 bo jing yan
warranty *n.* 保養期 bo yeurng kay

warren *n.* 養兔場 yeurng tow cheurng
warrior *n.* 武士 mo see
wart *n.* 疣 yow
wary *a.* 謹慎 gan san
wash *v.t.* 洗 say
wash *n* 洗 say
washable *a.* 可以洗嘅 hor yi say geh
washer *n.* 洗衣機 say yee gey
wasp *n.* 黃蜂 worng fung
waspish *a.* 暴躁嘅 bo cho geh
wassail *n.* 酒宴 jow yeem
wastage *n.* 損耗 shoon ho
waste *a.* 無用嘅 mo yung geh
waste *n.* 垃圾 lap sap
waste *v.t.* 嘥 sai
wasteful *a.* 浪費 lorng fay
watch *v.t.* 睇 tay
watch *n.* 手錶 sow biew
watchful *a.* 眼利 ngan lay
watchword *n.* 口號 how ho
water *n.* 水 suy
water *v.t.* 淋水 lam suy
waterfall *n.* 瀑布 buk bo
water-melon *n.* 西瓜 say gwa
waterproof *a.* 防水嘅 forng suy geh
waterproof *n* 防水 forng suy
waterproof *v.t.* 變防水 been forng suy
watertight *a.* 水密嘅 suy mat geh
watery *a.* 似水嘅 tee suy geh
watt *n.* 瓦 ngar
wave *n.* 海浪 hoy lorng
wave *v.t.* 揮手 fay sow
waver *v.i.* 動搖 dung yiew
wax *n.* 蠟 lap
wax *v.t.* 打蠟 da lap
way *n.* 路 low
wayfarer *n.* 旅客 luy hak
waylay *v.t.* 攔住 lan ju

wayward *a.* 任性 yam sing
weak *a.* 弱 yeurk
weaken *v.t. & i* 削弱 seurk yeurk
weakling *n.* 弱者 yeurk jeh
weakness *n.* 弱點 yeurk deem
weal *n.* 紅腫 hung jung
wealth *n.* 富裕 fu yu
wealthy *a.* 有錢 yow teen
wean *v.t.* 戒奶 gai lai
weapon *n.* 武器 mo hey
wear *v.t.* 着 jeurk
weary *a.* 攰 gwuy
weary *v.t. & i* 攰 gwuy
weary *a.* 無興趣 mo hing chuy
weary *v.t.* 無興趣 mo hing chuy
weather *n* 天氣 teen hey
weather *v.t.* 變 been
weave *v.t.* 織 jik
weaver *n.* 織布工 jik bo gung
web *n.* 蜘蛛網 jee ju mong
webby *a.* 網狀嘅 morng jorng geh
wed *v.t.* 結婚 geet fan
wedding *n.* 婚禮 fan lay
wedge *n.* 楔 seet
wedge *v.t.* 楔位 seep way
wedlock *n.* 婚姻 fan yan
Wednesday *n.* 星期三 sing kay sam
weed *n.* 雜草 jap cho
weed *v.t.* 請雜草 ting jap cho
week *n.* 禮拜 lay bai
weekly *a.* 每個禮拜嘅 mwuy gor lay bai geh
weekly *adv.* 每個禮拜 mwuy gor lay bai
weekly *n.* 週刊 jow horn
weep *v.i.* 流淚 low luy
weevil *n.* 象鼻蟲 jeurng bay chung
weigh *v.t.* 磅 bong
weight *n.* 體重 tay chung
weightage *n.* 權重 koon chung

weighty *a.* 重 chung
weir *n.* 堤壩 tay bar
weird *a.* 奇怪 kay gwai
welcome *a.* 歡迎 fwun ying
welcome *n* 歡迎 fwun ying
welcome *v.t* 歡迎 fwun ying
weld *v.t.* 焊接 horn jeep
weld *n* 焊接點 horn jeep deem
welfare *n.* 幸福 hang fuk
well *a.* 健康 geen horng
well *adv.* 好 ho
well *n.* 水井 suy jeng
well *v.i.* 流出 low chut
wellington *n.* 膝膠靴 tat gao hur
well-known *a.* 出名 chut meng
well-read *a.* 博學 bok hok
well-timed *a.* 及時 kap see
well-to-do *a.* 有錢 yow teen
welt *n.* 紅腫 hung jung
welter *n.* 一大堆 yat dai duy
wen *n.* 粉瘤 fan low
wench *n.* 少女 siew luy
west *n.* 西 say
west *a.* 西方嘅 say forng geh
west *adv.* 向西 heurng say
westerly *a.* 西方嘅 say forng geh
westerly *adv.* 向西嘅 heurng say geh
western *a.* 西方 say forng
wet *a.* 濕 sap
wet *v.t.* 濕 sap
wetness *n.* 濕度 sap dow
whack *v.t.* 拍 pak
whale *n.* 鯨魚 king yu
wharfage *n.* 碼頭費 ma tow fay
what *a.* 咩 meh
what *pron.* 咩 meh
what *interj.* 咩 meh
whatever *pron.* 無論 mo lun
wheat *n.* 小麥 siew mak
wheedle *v.t.* 氹 tam
wheel *a.* 轆 luk

wheel *v.t.* 推 tuy

whelm *v.t.* 淹沒 yeem mwut

whelp *n.* 狗仔 gow jay

when *adv.* 幾時 gey see

when *conj.* 幾時 gey see

whence *adv.* 從邊度 chung been dow

whenever *adv. conj* 隨時 chuy see

where *adv.* 邊度 been dow

where *conj.* 喺 hay

whereabout *adv.* 喺邊度 hay been dow

whereas *conj.* 而 yee

whereat *conj.* 於是 yu see

wherein *adv.* 喺邊度 hay been dow

whereupon *conj.* 於是 yu see

wherever *adv.* 邊度 been dow

whet *v.t.* 增強興趣 jang keurng hing chuy

whether *conj.* 無論...定係 mo lun...ding hay

which *pron.* 邊個 been gor

which *a* 邊個 been gor

whichever *pron* 無論邊個 mo lun been gor

whiff *n.* 少少味 siew siew may

while *n.* 一陣 yat jan

while *conj.* 當...嘅時候 dong...geh see ho

while *v.t.* 消磨時間 siew mor see gan

whim *n.* 心血來潮 sam hoot loy tiew

whimper *v.i.* 抽泣 chow yap

whimsical *a.* 異想天開嘅 yee seurng teen hoy geh

whine *v.i.* 發牢騷 fat low sow

whine *n* 喊聲 ham seng

whip *v.t.* 鞭打 been da

whip *n.* 鞭 been

whipcord *n.* 鞭 been

whir *n.* 嗡嗡聲 wung wung seng

whirl *n.i.* 轉 joon

whirl *n* 旋轉 shoon joon

whirligig *n.* 旋轉木馬 shoon joon muk ma

whirlpool *n.* 旋渦 shoon wor

whirlwind *n.* 旋風 shoon fung

whisk *v.t.* 發 fat

whisk *n* 攪機 gao gey

whisker *n.* 鬚 sow

whisky *n.* 威士忌 way see gey

whisper *v.t.* 耳邊講 yee been gorng

whisper *n* 細聲講 say seng gorng

whistle *v.i.* 吹口哨 chuy ho sao

whistle *n* 口哨 ho sao

white *a.* 白色嘅 bak sik geh

white *n* 白色 bak sik

whiten *v.t.* 變白 been bak

whitewash *n.* 石灰水 sek fwuy suy

whitewash *v.t.* 掩飾 yeem sik

whither *adv.* 到邊度 dow been dow

whitish *a.* 白白嘅 bak bak geh

whittle *v.t.* 雕 diew

whiz *v.i.* 掠過 leurk gwor

who *pron.* 邊個 been gor

whoever *pron.* 邊個 been gor

whole *a.* 全部 choon bo

whole *n* 整個 jing gor

whole-hearted *a.* 全心全意 choon sam choon yee

wholesale *n.* 批發 pay fat

wholesale *a* 批發 pay fat

wholesale *adv.* 批發 pay fat

wholesaler *n.* 批發商 pay fat seurng

wholesome *a.* 有益 yow yik

wholly *adv.* 完全 yoon choon

whom *pron.* 邊個 been gor

whore *n.* 妓女 gey luy	**windlass** *v.t.* 降低 gorng day
whose *pron.* 邊個嘅 been gor geh	**windmill** *n.* 風車 fung ter
why *adv.* 點解 deem gai	**window** *n.* 窗 cheurng
wick *n.* 燭芯 juk sam	**windy** *a.* 大風 dai fung
wicked *a.* 邪惡嘅 ter ok geh	**wine** *n.* 酒 jow
wicker *n.* 柳條 low tiew	**wing** *n.* 翼 yik
wicket *n.* 板球 ban kow	**wink** *v.i.* 眨眼 jam ngan
wide *a.* 闊 fwut	**wink** *n* 眼色 ngan sik
wide *adv.* 闊 fwut	**winner** *n.* 贏家 yeng ga
widen *v.t.* 整闊 jing fwut	**winnow** *v.t.* 篩選 撒野shoon
widespread *a.* 普遍 po poeen	**winsome** *a.* 有魅力 yow may lik
widow *n.* 寡婦 gwa fu	**winter** *n.* 冬天 dung teen
widow *v.t.* 喪偶 song ow	**winter** *v.i* 過冬 gwor dung
widower *n.* 寡佬 gwa low	**wintry** *a.* 寒冷嘅 hon lang geh
width *n.* 闊度 fwut dow	**wipe** *v.t.* 抹 mat
wield *v.t.* 運用 wan yung	**wipe** *n.* 濕紙巾 sap jee gan
wife *n.* 老婆 lo por	**wire** *n.* 電線 deen seen
wig *n.* 假髮 ga fat	**wire** *v.t.* 接駁電線 jeep bok deen seen
wight *n.* 生物 sang mat	
wigwam *n.* 棚屋 pang uk	**wireless** *a.* 無線 mo seen
wild *a.* 野生嘅 yeh sang geh	**wireless** *n* 無線 mo seen
wilderness *n.* 荒野 forng yeh	**wiring** *n.* 線路 seen low
wile *n.* 詭計 gway gey	**wisdom** *n.* 智慧 jee way
will *n.* 遺囑 way juk	**wisdom-tooth** *n.* 智慧齒 jee way tee
will *v.t.* 會 wuy	
willing *a.* 樂意 lok yee	**wise** *a.* 有智慧 yow jee wey
willingness *n.* 自願 jee yoon	**wish** *n.* 願望 yoon mong
willow *n.* 柳樹 low shu	**wish** *v.t.* 許願 huy yoon
wily *a.* 狡猾嘅 gao wat geh	**wishful** *a.* 渴望嘅 hot morng geh
wimble *n.* 手搖鑽 sow yiew joon	**wisp** *n.* 一細紮 yat say jat
wimple *n.* 頭巾 tow gan	**wistful** *a.* 傷感 seurng gam
win *v.t.* 贏 yeng	**wit** *n.* 智慧 jee way
win *n* 贏 yeng	**witch** *n.* 女巫 luy mo
wince *v.i.* 畏縮 way suk	**witchcraft** *n.* 魔法 mor fat
winch *n.* 絞車 gao cher	**witchery** *n.* 巫術 mo sut
wind *n.* 風 fung	**with** *prep.* 同 tung
wind *v.t.* 上鏈 seurng leen	**withal** *adv.* 而且 yee ter
wind *v.t.* 環繞 wan yiew	**withdraw** *v.t.* 退出 tuy chut
windbag *n.* 多嘢講嘅人 dor yeh gorng geh yan	**withdrawal** *n.* 退出 tuy chut
	withe *n.* 枝 jee
winder *n.* 上鏈柄 seurng leen beng	**wither** *v.i.* 凋謝 diew jeh
	withhold *v.t.* 抑壓 yik at

within *prep.* 之內 jee loy	**word** *v.t* 話太多 wah tai dor
within *adv.* 裡面 luy meen	**wordy** *a.* 話太多 wah tai dor
within *n.* 入邊 yap been	**work** *n.* 工作 gung jok
without *prep.* 缺乏 koot fat	**work** *v.t.* 做嘢 jow yeh
without *adv.* 無 mo	**workable** *a.* 可行嘅 hor hang geh
without *n* 出邊 chut been	**workaday** *a.* 普通嘅 po tung geh
withstand *v.t.* 頂住 ding ju	**worker** *n.* 工人 gung yan
witless *a.* 唔明白事理 hm ming bak see lay	**workman** *n.* 工匠 gung jeurng
witness *n.* 目擊證人 muk gik ting yan	**workmanship** *n.* 手藝 sow ngay
witness *v.i.* 目擊 muk gik	**workshop** *n.* 工場 gung cheurng
witticism *n.* 妙語 miew yu	**world** *n.* 世界 sey gai
witty *a.* 機智 gey jee	**worldling** *n.* 俗人 juk yan
wizard *n.* 魔法師 mor fat see	**worldly** *a.* 世事嘅 sai see geh
wobble *v.i* 搖 yiew	**worm** *n.* 蚯蚓 yow yan
woe *n.* 痛苦 tung fu	**wormwood** *n.* 蒿 ho
woebegone *a.* 悲傷 bay seurng	**worn** *a.* 殘晒 tan sai
woeful *n.* 悲哀 bay ngoy	**worry** *n.* 擔憂 dam yow
wolf *n.* 狼 long	**worry** *v.i.* 擔心 dam sam
woman *n.* 女人 luy yan	**worsen** *v.t.* 變得更壞 been dak gang wai
womanhood *n.* 女人 luy yan	**worship** *n.* 信奉 sun fung
womanish *n.* 女人嘅 luy yan geh	**worship** *v.t.* 拜 bai
womanise *v.t.* 女性化 luy sing far	**worshipper** *n.* 崇拜者 sun bai jeh
womb *n.* 子宮 jee gung	**worst** *n.* 最壞 juy wai
wonder *n* 驚訝 ging ngar	**worst** *a* 最壞嘅 juy wai geh
wonder *v.i.* 想知 seurng jee	**worst** *v.t.* 戰勝 jeen sing
wonderful *a.* 好好嘅 ho ho geh	**worsted** *n.* 精紡毛料 jing forng mo liew
wondrous *a.* 奇異咗 kay yee geh	**worth** *n.* 價值 gah jik
wont *a.* 習慣咗 jap gwan jor	**worth** *a* 值得 jik dak
wont *n* 習慣 jap gwan	**worthless** *a.* 唔值得 hm jik dak
wonted *a.* 習慣嘅 jap gwan geh	**worthy** *a.* 值得 jik dak
woo *v.t.* 追求 juy kow	**would-be** *a.* 未來 may loy
wood *n.* 木 muk	**wound** *n.* 傷 seurng
woods *n.* 樹林 shu lam	**wound** *v.t.* 傷害 seurng hoy
wooden *a.* 木造嘅 muk jow geh	**wrack** *n.* 破壞 por wai
woodland *n.* 樹林 shu lam	**wraith** *n.* 鬼魂 gway wan
woof *n.* 狗吠聲 gow fay seng	**wrangle** *v.i.* 嘈 cho
wool *n.* 毛冷 mo larn	**wrangle** *n.* 爭論 jang lun
woollen *a.* 毛嘅 mo geh	**wrap** *v.t.* 包 bao
woollen *n* 冷衫 larn sam	**wrap** *n* 包裝料 bao jorng liew
word *n.* 字 jee	**wrapper** *n.* 包裝紙 bao jorng jee

wrath *n.* 怒火 low for
wreath *n.* 花圈 far hoon
wreathe *v.t.* 圍繞 way yiew
wreck *n.* 沈船 tam shoon
wreck *v.t.* 破壞 por wai
wreckage *n.* 殘骸 tan hai
wrecker *n.* 破壞者 por wai jeh
wren *n.* 鷦鷯 jiew liew
wrench *n.* 扳鉗 ban keem
wrench *v.t.* 大力擰 dai lik ling
wrest *v.t.* 搶 cheurng
wrestle *v.i.* 摔跤 sut gao
wrestler *n.* 摔跤選手 sut gao shoonsow
wretch *n.* 不幸嘅人 bat hang geh yan
wretched *a.* 難受 larn sow
wrick *n* 扭傷 low seurng
wriggle *v.i.* 扭嚟扭去 low lay low huy
wriggle *n* 扭動 low dung
wring *v.t* 擰出 ling chut
wrinkle *n.* 皺紋 jow man
wrinkle *v.t.* 皺 jow
wrist *n.* 手腕 sow wun
writ *n.* 書面命令 shu meen ming ling
write *v.t.* 寫 ser
writer *n.* 作者 jok jeh
writhe *v.i.* 扭動 low dung
wrong *a.* 錯嘅 chor geh
wrong *adv.* 錯嘅 chor geh
wrong *v.t.* 唔公正 hm gung jing
wrongful *a.* 唔正當嘅 hm jing dong geh
wry *a.* 諷刺 fung tee

xerox *n.* 影印機 ying yan gey
xerox *v.t.* 複印 fuk yan
Xmas *n.* 聖誕節 sing dan jeet
x-ray *n.* X光 ex gwong
x-ray *a.* X光嘅 ex gwong geh
x-ray *v.t.* X光檢查 ex gwong geem ta
xylophagous *a.* 蝕木嘅 sik muk geh
xylophilous *a.* 木生嘅 muk sang geh
xylophone *n.* 木琴 muk kam

yacht *n.* 遊艇 yow teng
yacht *v.i* 揸遊艇 ja yow teng
yak *n.* 犛牛 mo ngow
yap *v.i.* 講嘢 gorng yeh
yap *n* 狗吠聲 gow fay seng
yard *n.* 碼 ma
yarn *n.* 冷線 larn seen
yawn *v.i.* 打喊路 da ham low
yawn *n.* 喊路 ham low
year *n.* 年 leen
yearly *a.* 每年嘅 mwuy leen geh
yearly *adv.* 一年一度嘅 yat leen yat dow geh
yearn *v.i.* 渴望 hot morng
yearning *n.* 渴望 hot morng
yeast *n.* 酵母菌 hao mo kwan
yell *v.i.* 嗌 ai

yell *n* 嗌 ai
yellow *a.* 黃色嘅 wong sik geh
yellow *n* 黃色 wong sik
yellow *v.t.* 變黃 been wong
yellowish *a.* 黃黃地 wong wong day
Yen *n.* 日元 yat yoon
yeoman *n.* 自由民 jee yow man
yes *adv.* 係 hay
yesterday *n.* 尋日 tam yat
yesterday *adv.* 尋日 tam yat
yet *adv.* 仲 jung
yet *conj.* 但係 dan hay
yield *v.t.* 屈服 wat fuk
yield *n* 產量 tan leurng
yoke *n.* 軛
yoke *v.t.* 上軛 seurng ak
yolk *n.* 蛋黃 dan worng
yonder *a.* 嗰邊 gor been
yonder *adv.* 嗰邊 gor been
young *a.* 後生 ho sang
young *n* 青年人 ting leen yan
youngster *n.* 細路仔 say low jay
youth *n.* 少年 siew leen
youthful *a.* 後生嘅 ho sang geh

zephyr *n.* 微風 may fung
zero *n.* 零 ling
zest *n.* 熱情 yeet ting
zigzag *n.* 彎曲 wan kuk
zigzag *a.* 鋸齒形 guy chee ying
zigzag *v.i.* 曲折前進 kuk jeet teen jun
zinc *n.* 鋅 san
zip *n.* 拉鍊 lai leen
zip *v.t.* 拉 lai
zodiac *n* 生肖 sang chiew
zonal *a.* 區域嘅··· kuy wik geh
zone *n.* 地區 day kuy
zoo *n.* 動物園 dung mat yoon
zoological *a.* 動物學嘅 dung mat hok geh
zoologist *n.* 動物學家 dung mat hok ga
zoology *n.* 動物學 dung mat hok
zoom *n.* 縮放 suk fong
zoom *v.i.* 快速 fai chuk

Z

zany *a.* 古怪嘅 gu gwai geh
zeal *n.* 熱情 yeet ting
zealot *n.* 發燒友 fat siew yow
zealous *a.* 熱情嘅 yeet ting geh
zebra *n.* 斑馬 ban ma
zenith *n.* 頂峰 ding fung

CANTONESE-ENGLISH

A

ah ay shu jee 阿魏樹脂 n. asafoetida
ah mun 阿門 interj. amen
ah suk 阿叔 n. uncle
ah yee fat 阿爾法 n alpha
ai 拗 v. t bicker
ai 挨 v.i. lean
ai 嗌 v.i. yell
ai 嗌 n yell
ai gao 嗌交 v. t brangle
ai man 挨晚 n evening
ai or 挨餓 v.i. starve
ai sap 嗌謔 n. quarrel
ai sap 嗌謔 n. quibble
ai sap 嗌謔 v.i. quibble
ai seng tan hay 唉聲嘆氣 n. sigh
ai seng tan hay 唉聲嘆氣 v.i. sigh
ai yan 矮人 n dwarf
ak 呃 v. t beguile
ak 呃 v. t. bilk
ak 呃 v. t deceive
ak 呃 v.t gull
ak 呃 v.t. hoodwink
ak 呃 v.t. rook
ak 呃 v.t. swindle
ak 呃 n. swindle
ak 呃 v.t. trick
ak 軛 n. yoke
ak fat 額髮 n forelock
ak ngoy 額外 adv extra
ak ngoy geh 額外嘅 a extra
ak ngoy geh 額外嘅 a. supplementary
ak tow 額頭 n brow
ak tow 額頭 n forehead
ak wan 厄運 n doom
ak yan 呃人 n deceit
am 暗 a dim
am am seng 喃喃聲 n. murmur
am chun 鵪鶉 n. quail
am day luy 暗地裡 adv. stealthily
am gwong 暗光 n glow
am ho 暗號 n. cipher, cipher
am jee 暗指 a. allusive
am low 暗流 n. undercurrent
am san 喑身 v.t fit
am see 暗示 v.i. allude
am see 暗示 n allusion
am see 暗示 v.i hint
am see 暗示 v.t. imply
am see 暗示 v.t. insinuate
am see 暗示 v.t. intimate
am see 暗示 n. intimation
am see geh 暗示嘅 a. suggestive
am yu 暗喻 n. metaphor
an bao 銀包 n. wallet
an hong 銀行 n. bank
an hong ga 銀行家 n. banker
an horng dan 銀行單 n. statement
an jai 銀仔 n coin
ang 鶯 n. warbler
ang bay 硬幣 n coinage
ang far 硬化 v.t. harden
ang geng 硬頸 a. headstrong
ang lorn 硬朗 a. hale
ao 咬 v. t. bite
ap 鴨 n. duck
arp giew seng 鴨叫聲 n quack
at 壓 v. t crush
at 呃 n.t. delude
at ho 押後 v.t. adjourn
at mo 壓模 n die
at suk 壓縮 v. t. compress
at suk 壓縮 v. t condense
at suk geh 壓縮嘅 a. compact
at tow wan 押頭韻 v. alliterate
at tow wan 押頭韻 n. alliteration
ay 唉 interj. alas
ay 蟻 n ant
ay gao 嗌交 v.t. argue
ay jow 偽造 a. counterfeit

ay jow jeh 偽造者 *n. counterfeiter*
ay lam 矮林 *n. coppice*

B

B B B B *n. baby*
ba dow 霸道 *a. aggressive*
ba gung 罷工 *n stoppage*
ba gung 罷工 *n strike*
ba han 疤痕 *n scar*
ba luy mo 芭蕾舞 *sn. ballet*
ba meen 罷免 *v. t depose*
ba meen 罷免 *v. t dethrone*
ba meen 罷免 *v.t. oust*
ba sam 靶心 *n bull's eye*
ba see 巴士 *n bus*
bai 擺 *v.t. place*
bai 擺 *v.t. position*
bai 擺 *v.t. put*
bai 拜 *v.t. worship*
bai bai 拜拜 *interj. bye-bye*
bai dung 擺動 *n. oscillation*
bai ga geh 敗家嘅 *a. prodigal*
bai jee say 擺姿勢 *v.i. pose*
bai ping 擺平 *v. t even*
bak 北 *n. north*
bak bak geh 白白嘅 *a. whitish*
bak fan jee 百分之 *adv. per cent*
bak fan lut 百分率 *n. percentage*
bak for choon shu 百科全書 *n. encyclopaedia*
bak forng geh 北方嘅 *a north*
bak forng geh 北方嘅 *a. northerly*
bak forng geh 北方嘅 *a. northern*
bak fung 北風 *n. northerly*
bak gap 白鴿 *n. pigeon*
bak gik sing 北極星 *n. loadstar*
bak gwat ding 白骨頂 *n. coot*
bak hap far 百合花 *n. lily*

bak jeurk fu yan 伯爵夫人 *n. countess*
bak lan day 白蘭地 *n brandy*
bak lo 白鷺 *n aigrette*
bak man 百萬 *n. million*
bak man fu yung 百萬富翁 *n. millionaire*
bak may yeh ma 北美野馬 *n. mustang*
bak pwuy 百倍 *n. & adj centuple*
bak sik 白色 *n white*
bak sik geh 白色嘅 *a. white*
bak tee 白癡 *n. idiot*
bak wan mow 白雲母 *n. muscovite*
ban 板 *n board*
ban 班 *n class*
ban 版 *n edition*
ban 扮 *v.t feign*
ban 頒 *v.t. present*
ban 班 *n shift*
ban ban yow lay geh 彬彬有禮嘅 *a. urbane*
ban bwun 版本 *n. version*
ban dak gow 品德高 *a. virtuous*
ban deem 斑點 *n. mottle*
ban deem 斑點 *n. spot*
ban gak go seurng 品加高尚 *a. honourable*
ban gey 班機 *n flight*
ban gey 板機 *n. trigger*
ban gung sat geh 辦公室嘅 *a clerical*
ban jeurk kam 班卓琴 *n. banjo*
ban jung 品種 *n breed*
ban keem 扳鉗 *n. wrench*
ban kow 板球 *n cricket*
ban kow 板球 *n. wicket*
ban lay 辦理 *v.t. transact*
ban long shu 檳榔樹 *n areca*
ban long yeep 檳榔葉 *n betel*
ban ma 斑馬 *n. zebra*
ban pao 奔跑 *v.t. gallop*
ban pao 奔跑 *n scamper*

ban sai yeh 扮晒嘢 *n affectation*
ban sai yeh 扮晒嘢 *v.t. patronize*
ban seurng 品嘗 *v.t. savour*
ban sow ban geurt 笨手笨腳 *a. ungainly*
ban tan seurng hon 斑疹傷寒 *n. typhus*
ban tiew 板條 *n. lath*
ban tiew seurng 板條箱 *n. crate*
bang dai 繃帶 *~n. bandage*
bao 爆 *v. i. burst*
bao 包 *v. t envelop*
bao 包 *v.t. parcel*
bao 爆 *v.i. pop*
bao 包 *v.t. wrap*
bao 包 *n bundle*
bao fat 爆發 *v. i erupt*
bao fat 爆發 *n eruption*
bao fat 爆發 *n. outbreak*
bao fat 爆發 *n. outburst*
bao fuk 包袱 *n burden*
bao gwor 包裹 *n. package*
bao gwor 包裹 *n. parcel*
bao ham 包含 *v. i consist*
bao ham 包含 *v. t encompass*
bao ja 爆炸 *n blast*
bao ja 爆炸 *v. t. explode*
bao ja 爆炸 *n. explosion*
bao ja sing 爆炸性 *a explosive*
bao jat 包紮 *v.t bandage*
bao jorng 包裝 *n. packing*
bao jorng jee 包裝紙 *n. wrapper*
bao jorng liew 包裝料 *n wrap*
bao kwut 包括 *v.t. include*
bao kwut 包括 *n. inclusion*
bao kwut 包括 *a. inclusive*
bao liew 爆料 *v. t divulge*
bao por 爆破 *n burst*
bao tow gan 包頭巾 *n. turban*
bao way 包圍 *n. siege*
bao wor dow 飽和度 *n. saturation*
barn jeurng 頒獎 *v.t. award*

bat 八 *n eight*
bat 不 *v.t. ladle*
bat 筆 *n. pen*
bat 不 *v.t. spoon*
bat cheurng geh 不祥嘅 *a. inauspicious*
bat chut 拔出 *v.t. unsheathe*
bat doon geh 不斷嘅 *a continuous*
bat doon geh 不斷嘅 *a. perpetual*
bat dorng 不當 *a. injudicious*
bat dow 八度 *n. octave*
bat dow dak 不道德 *a. immoral*
bat dow dak geh 不道德嘅 *a. unprincipled*
bat fat hang way 不法行為 *n. malpractice*
bat fat jee tow 不法之徒 *n. miscreant*
bat fu jak yam 不負責任 *a. irresponsible*
bat ga shoon jak 不加選擇 *a. indiscriminate*
bat gey 嗶嘰 *n. serge*
bat gey how gwor 不計後果 *a. reckless*
bat gik 北極 *n Arctic*
bat ging 不敬 *a. impertinent*
bat gok ying 八角形 *n. octagon*
bat gok ying geh 八角形嘅 *a. octagonal*
bat gowr 不過 *conj. nevertheless*
bat gwa 八卦 *a. inquisitive*
bat gwa 八卦 *a. nosey*
bat gwa 八卦 *a. nosy*
bat gwor 不過 *conj. but*
bat gwor 不過 *adv. however*
bat gwor 不過 *conj. notwithstanding*
bat gwor 不過 *conj. only*
bat gwor 不過 *adv. though*
bat han 不幸 *a. unfortunate*
bat hang 不幸 *n. mischance*
bat hang 不幸 *n. misfortune*

bat hang 不幸 *n. mishap*
bat hang geh jow yu 不幸嘅遭遇 *n. misadventure*
bat hang geh yan 不幸嘅人 *n. wretch*
bat hor gow yan geh 不可告人嘅 *a. ulterior*
bat hor koot fat geh 不可缺乏嘅 *a. indispensable*
bat hor tam fan 不可侵犯 *a. inviolable*
bat jeem 筆尖 *n. nib*
bat joy cheurng jing guy 不在場證據 *n. alibi*
bat kap mat 不及物 *a. (verb) intransitive*
bat lay 不利 *a adverse*
bat lay 不利 *a. inimical*
bat lay yan so 不利因素 *n disadvantage*
bat meng 筆名 *n. pseudonym*
bat mun 不滿 *n discontent*
bat mun 不滿 *n displeasure*
bat mun 不滿 *n dissatisfaction*
bat ngar hang way 不雅行爲 *n. indecency*
bat on 不安 *n disquiet*
bat sap 八十 *n eighty*
bat say geh 不死嘅 *a. immortal*
bat say geh 不死嘅 *a. imperishable*
bat sing yan see 不省人事 *n. insensibility*
bat sun low yan 八旬老人 *a. octogenarian*
bat teet sat jay 不切實際 *a. utopian*
bat teet sat jay geh 不切實際嘅 *a. impracticable*
bat ting geh 不停嘅 *~a. ceaseless*
bat tug luy ying 不同類型 *n. variety*
bat tung geh 不同嘅 *a dissimilar*
bat tung geh 不同嘅 *a. varied*
bat yan 不孕 *n. sterility*

bat yee jee choy 不義之財 *n. pelf*
bat yeep 畢業 *v.i. graduate*
bat yeep sang 畢業生 *n graduate*
bat yoot 八月 *n. August*
bat yuk 不育 *n barren*
bay 跛 *n cripple*
bay 避 *v. t dodge*
bay 畀 *prep for*
bay 畀 *v.t. give*
bay 畀 *v.t. grant*
bay 畀 *v.t hand*
bay 跛 *a. lame*
bay 畀 *v.t. let*
bay 比 *v.t. liken*
bay 鼻 *n. nostril*
bay bo jing yn 被保證人 *n. warrantee*
bay bo sik geh 畀保釋嘅 *a. bailable*
bay choon 臂釧 *a armlet*
bay choy 比賽 *n. competition*
bay choy 比賽 *n. contest*
bay choy 比賽 *n. match*
bay choy 比賽 *v.i race*
bay dak seurng 比得上 *v.t. rival*
bay dung geh 被動嘅 *a. passive*
bay forng 祕方 *n. nostrum*
bay ga ho gung 畀假口供 *v.i. perjure*
bay gao 比較 *v. t compare*
bay gao 比較 *n comparison*
bay gao jung yee 比較鐘意 *v.t favour*
bay gao jung yee 比較鐘意 *v.t. prefer*
bay gao say geh 比較細嘅 *a. minor*
bay gao siew 比較少 *a. less*
bay gao siew 比較少 *adv. less*
bay garm gum 被監禁 *a. captive*
bay geh 鼻嘅 *a. nasal*
bay go 被告 *n defendant*
bay gor 鼻哥 *n. nose*
bay gwun 悲觀 *n. pessimism*
bay gwun geh 悲觀嘅 *a. pessimistic*

bay gwun geh yan 悲觀嘅人 *n.* pessimist

bay ha 陛下 *n. majesty*

bay horn seng 鼻鼾聲 *n snore*

bay hoy 避開 *v.t. avoid*

bay hoy 避開 *n. avoidance*

bay hoy 避開 *v. t elude*

bay hoy 避開 *v. t evade*

bay hoy 避開 *v.t. shun*

bay jan jing jay 畀鎮靜劑 *v.t. sedate*

bay jeen geh 卑賤嘅 *a. menial*

bay juy jow geh 被詛咒嘅 *a. accursed*

bay kap yan dow 被吸引到 *v.i. gravitate*

bay kek 悲劇 *n. tragedy*

bay kek jok ga 悲劇作家 *n. tragedian*

bay lan 避難 *n. refuge*

bay lan sor 避難所 *n. haven*

bay lay 比例 *n. proportion*

bay ma yow 蓖麻油 *n. castor oil*

bay man 碑文 *n epitaph*

bay mat geh 秘密嘅 *adj. clandestine*

bay mat geh 祕密嘅 *a. secret*

bay mat geh 祕密嘅 *a. underhand*

bay may 卑微 *n. lowliness*

bay may 祕密 *n. secret*

bay meen 避免 *v.t. avert*

bay morng luk 備忘錄 *n memorandum*

bay ngoy 悲哀 *n. woeful*

bay pai tik jeh 被排斥者 *n. outcast*

bay pay 卑鄙 *a. base*

bay pay 卑鄙 *a despicable*

bay pay 卑鄙 *n. meanness*

bay pay 卑鄙 *a. sordid*

bay pwun mow juy 被判無罪 *n. acquittal*

bay seurng 悲傷 *n. lamentation*

bay seurng 悲傷 *n. sorrow*

bay seurng 悲傷 *v.i. sorrow*

bay seurng 悲傷 *a. woebegone*

bay shu 秘書 *n. secretary*

bay shu chu 秘書處 *n. secretariat (e)*

bay sing sow 被乘數 *n. multiplicand*

bay sow 匕首 *n. dagger*

bay tan 悲歎 *n lament*

bay tarm 悲慘 *n. poignancy*

bay tarm geh 悲慘嘅 *a. tragic*

bay tay ming yan 被提名人 *n nominee*

bay teep see 畀貼士 *v.t. tip*

bay toot 擺脫 *v.t. rid*

bay tung 悲痛 *n. grief*

bay wu sor 庇護所 *n. lee*

bay wu sor 庇護所 *n. sanctuary*

bay yam 鼻音 *n nasal*

bay yan 避孕 *n. contraception*

bay yan gow 被人告 *n. accused*

bay yan tao geh 畀人炒嘅 *a. redundant*

bay yee geen 畀意見 *v.t. advise*

bay yeem 鼻煙 *n. snuff*

bay ying way 被認爲 *v. t constitute*

bay yu geh 比如嘅 *a figurative*

bay yung bam 備用品 *n. spare*

bay...cheurng meng 比...長命 *v.i. outlive*

bee bee cher BB車 *n. perambulator*

been 邊 *n edge*

been 變 *v.t. range*

been 變 *v.t. weather*

been 鞭 *n. whip*

been 鞭 *n. whipcord*

been am 變暗 *v. t dim*

been bak 變白 *v. t. & i blanch*

been bak 變白 *v.i. pale*

been bak 變白 *v.t. whiten*

been bay 便秘 *n. constipation*

been da 鞭打 *n lash*

been da 鞭打 *v.t. whip*

been dai darm 變大膽 *v. t embolden*

been dak 變得 *v.t. render*

been dak gang wai 變得更壞 v.t. worsen

been dak sik hap yan 變得適合人 v.t. humanize

been dow 扁豆 n. lentil

been dow 邊度 adv. where

been dow 邊度 adv. wherever

been far 變化 n. mutation

been far 變化 n. transformation

been far 變化 n. variation

been far geh 變化嘅 a. mutative

been forng lut see 辯方律師 n advocate

been forng suy 變防水 v.t. waterproof

been fung fu 變豐富 v. t enrich

been ga 貶價 v.t. depredate

been gai 邊界 n border

been gai 邊界 n boundary

been gai 邊界 n. frontier

been geet sat 變結實 v.t. tone

been geurng ang 變僵硬 v.t. stiffen

been gor 邊個 pron. which

been gor 邊個 a which

been gor 邊個 pron. who

been gor 邊個 pron. whoever

been gor 邊個 pron. whom

been gor geh 邊個嘅 pron. whose

been gwong dee 變光啲 v. t brighten

been hap fat 變合法 v.t. legalize

been ho sang 變後生 v.t. rejuvenate

been hung 變紅 v.t. redden

been huy yeurk 變虛弱 v. t. enfeeble

been huy yeurk 變虛弱 v.t. sap

been jak 變窄 v.t. straiten

been jak 變窄 v.i. taper

been jat 變質 n. metamorphosis

been jiew tan 變焦炭 v. t coke

been kung 變窮 v.t. depauperate

been kung 變窮 v.t. impoverish

been lang 變冷 v.t. refrigerate

been leurng 變涼 v. i. cool

been mar muk 變麻木 v. t. dull

been mor sut 變魔術 v.i. conjure

been mow hao 變無效 v.t. neutralize

been mow hao 變無效 v.t. void

been mow wu 變模糊 v.t. obscure

been on jing 變安靜 n hush

been on jing 變安靜 v.t. silence

been ping 變平 v.t. level

been ping dang 變平等 v. t. equalize

been ping jing 變平靜 v.t. still

been ping jing 變平靜 v.t. tranquillize

been say 變細 n wane

been see 便士 n. penny

been siew 變少 v.t lessen

been sing 變成 v. i become

been sing bat yiew geh 變成必要嘅 v.t. necessitate

been tai 變態 n. perversion

been tak 鞭策 v.t. spur

been tan 變癱 v.t. paralyse

been tan fay 變殘廢 v.t. mutilate

been teen 變遷 n. vicissitude

been ting chor 變清楚 v. i. dawn

been tow tay 扁桃體 n. tonsil

been wan mok tak 變幻莫測 a. mercurial

been wan wor 變溫和 v.t. temper

been way fay fat 變為非法 v.t outlaw

been way say pwuy 變為四倍 v.t. quadruple

been wong 變黃 v.t. yellow

been wut yeurk 變活躍 a. animate

been ying 辨認 v.t. identify

been ying 變形 n. transfiguration

been ying 變形 v.t. transfigure

been yoon 邊沿 n brim

been yoon 邊緣 n. brink

been yoon 邊緣 n. rim

been yoon 邊緣 n. verge

beet suy 必需 n. must

beet suy 別墅 n. villa

beet suy geh 必需嘅 *a essential*
beet suy geh 必需嘅 *a. integral*
beet suy geh 必需嘅 *a. prerequisite*
beet suy geh 必需嘅 *a. requisite*
beet suy geh yeh 必需嘅嘢 *n requisite*
beet suy jun so geh 必需遵守嘅 *a binding*
beet yiew 必要 *n. necessary*
beet yiew 必要 *n. necessity*
beh jow 啤酒 *n beer*
beh jow chorng 啤酒廠 *n brewery*
bei yu 比喻 *n. analogy*
beng 病 *n disease*
beng 病 *a. ill*
beng 病 *n ill*
beng 病 *n. illness*
beng 病 *n. malady*
beng deem 餅店 *n bakery*
beng duk 病毒 *n. virus*
beng forng 病房 *n. ward*
beng gon 餅乾 *n biscuit*
beng kwan 病菌 *n. germ*
beng lik 病歷 *n anamnesis*
beng tai 病態 *a. morbid*
beng tai 病態 *n morbidity*
beng yan 病人 *n invalid*
beng yan 病人 *n patient*
biew bak 表白 *n confession*
biew cheurng 標槍 *n. javelin*
biew dat 表達 *v. t. convey*
biew dat 表達 *v. t. express*
biew dat 表達 *v.t. phrase*
biew dat yee geen 表達意見 *v. i comment*
biew deem fu ho 標點符號 *n. punctuation*
biew gak 表格 *n form*
biew gak sik 表格式 *a. tabular*
biew jee 標誌 *n. symbol*
biew jun 標準 *n criterion*
biew jun 標準 *n. norm*

biew jun 標準 *n. standard*
biew jun gorn sow 標準杆數 *n. par*
biew meen 表面 *a. cosmetic*
biew meen 表面 *n. surface*
biew meen seurng 表面上 *adv. outwardly*
biew meen sing 表面性 *n. superficiality*
biew pwun 錶盤 *n dialogue*
biew see 表示 *a. expressive*
biew see 表示 *a. indicative*
biew see 表示 *v.t. manifest*
biew see 表示 *v.t mean*
biew see 表示 *v.t. signify*
biew see 表示 *v.t. voice*
biew tan 表親 *n. cousin*
biew tay 標題 *n. heading*
biew teem 標籤 *n. label*
biew teem 標籤 *v.t. tag*
biew ting 表情 *n. expression*
biew yeem 表現 *v. i. behave*
biew yeen 表演 *v.t. perform*
biew yeen 表演 *n. show*
biew yeen jeh 表演者 *n. juggler*
biew yeen jeh 表演者 *n. performer*
biew yeurng 表揚 *v. t commend*
biew yu pai 標語牌 *n. placard*
bik gway 壁櫃 *n. closet*
bik hoy 逼害 *v.t. persecute*
bik hoy 逼害 *n. persecution*
bik jan 逼真 *n. verisimilitude*
bik kan 逼近 *v.i. loom*
bik kow 壁球 *n squash*
bik low ga 壁爐架 *n. mantel*
bik luk geh 碧綠嘅 *a. verdant*
bik say 逼使 *v.t. oblige*
bik tan 逼真 *n. realism*
bik tan geh 逼真嘅 *a. realistic*
bik wah 壁畫 *n. mural*
bing 冰 *n. ice*
bing 冰 *a. icy*
bing geen 並肩 *adv abreast*

bing hor 冰河 n. glacier
bing ju 冰柱 n. icicle
bing pao 冰雹 n. hail
bing san 冰山 n. iceberg
bing toon 兵團 n corps
bing ying 兵營 n. barrack
bing ying 兵營 n. cantonment
bo 布 n cloth
bo 補 v.t. patch
bo biew 保鏢 n. bodyguard
bo biew 保鏢 n bouncer
bo bwuy 寶貝 n. babe
bo bwuy 寶貝 n darling
bo cho 暴躁 a fiery
bo cho geh 暴躁嘅 a. waspish
bo choon 保存 v. t conserve
bo choon 保存 v.t. preserve
bo choon 保存 v.t. store
bo choon geh 保存嘅 a. preservative
bo chow fung ho geh 報酬豐厚嘅 a.
  remunerative
bo chu 部署 v.t. deploy
bo chung 補充 v.t. replenish
bo chung 補充 n. supplement
bo chung 補充 v.t. supplement
bo chung mat 補充物 n complement
bo deet 暴跌 v.t. plunge
bo ding 布丁 n. pudding
bo dung 暴動 n. mutiny
bo fan 部份 n. part
bo fan 部份 n. section
bo fan 部份 n. segment
bo fan geh 部份嘅 a. partial
bo fat 步法 n tread
bo fat wu 暴發戶 n. upstart
bo fuk 報復 v.i. retaliate
bo fuk 報復 n. retaliation
bo fuk 報復 n. vengeance
bo fuk geh 報復嘅 a. revengeful
bo fung shoot 暴風雪 n blizzard
bo fung yu 暴風雨 n. storm
bo fung yu 暴風雨 n. tempest

bo ga 報價 n. quotation
bo geh 補嘅 a. tonic
bo gow 報告 v.t. report
bo gow 報告 n. report
bo gow geh 補救嘅 a. remedial
bo gwan 暴君 n despot
bo gwan 暴君 n. tyrant
bo gwun 保管 v.t. keep
bo gwun yan 保管人 n. keeper
bo heem 保險 n. insurance
bo heem fu 保險庫 n. vault
bo heem gong 保險槓 n. bumper
bo heem see 保險絲 n fuse
bo heem seurng 保險箱 n. safe
bo jee 佈置 n. array
bo jee 佈置 v. t deck
bo jee 佈置 v.t. furnish
bo jeurng 保障 n. indemnity
bo jing 保證 n. assurance
bo jing 保證 v.t. assure
bo jing 保證 v. t ensure
bo jing 保證 n. pledge
bo jing 保證 v.t. warrant
bo jing yan 保證人 n. warrantor
bo jorng 寶藏 n. treasure
bo juk geh 部族嘅 a. tribal
bo lam 布冧 n. plum
bo liew 布料 n fabric
bo lik 暴力 n force
bo lik 暴力 n. violence
bo lo 暴露 v. t expose
bo loon geh 保暖嘅 a. thermal
bo luy 堡壘 n bulwark
bo luy 堡壘 n. citadel
bo luy 堡壘 n. fort
bo luy 堡壘 n. stronghold
bo man 暴民 n. mob
bo mat 保密 n. secrecy
bo mun 部門 n department
bo mwun 部門 n. sector
bo mwun 佈滿 v.t. strew
bo on 保安 n. security

bo ping 步兵 *n. infantry*
bo sek 寶石 *n gem*
bo sek 寶石 *n. jewel*
bo seurng 補償 *n. atonement*
bo seurng 布商 *n draper*
bo seurng 補償 *v.t. reimburse*
bo shoon 補選 *n by-election*
bo sik 保釋 *n. bail*
bo sik 保釋 *v. t. bail*
bo sik 捕食 *v.i. prey*
bo so 保守 *a conservative*
bo so dong jee tee jeh 保守黨支持者 *n conservative*
bo sow 報仇 *v.t. avenge*
bo sow 保守 *a. insular*
bo sow 報仇 *v.t. revenge*
bo sow 報仇 *n. revenge*
bo sow geh 保守嘅 *a. reactinary*
bo tee 保持 *v.i. persist*
bo tee 保持 *v.i. remain*
bo tee 保持 *v.t. retain*
bo tee tam mak 保持沈默 *a. mum*
bo worng ju yee jeh 保皇主義者 *n. royalist*
bo wu 保護 *n. preservation*
bo wu 保護 *v.t. protect*
bo wu 保護 *n. protection*
bo wu 保護 *n. safeguard*
bo wu 保護 *v.t. secure*
bo wu 保護 *v.t. shelter*
bo wu geh 保護嘅 *a. protective*
bo wu yan 保護人 *n. protector*
bo yam bo sik 暴飲暴食 *n. gluttony*
bo yeurng 保養 *n. guarantee*
bo yeurng kay 保養期 *n. warranty*
bo ying 報應 *n. nemesis*
bo yu 哺乳 *v.i. lactate*
bo yu luy dung mat 哺乳類動物 *n. mammal*
bok 駁 *v.t. confute*
bok chuy beng gon 薄脆餅乾 *n cracker*

bok dow 搏鬥 *v. i. battle*
bok dow 搏鬥 *n combat1*
bok dung 搏動 *v.i. pulsate*
bok hok 博學 *a. well-read*
bok hor 薄荷 *n. mint*
bok juy 駁嘴 *v.t. retort*
bok juy 駁嘴 *n. retort*
bok mat gwun 博物館 *n. museum*
bok mat hok ga 博物學家 *n. naturalist*
bok mo 薄霧 *n. haze*
bok mow 薄霧 *n. mist*
bok see hok way 博士學位 *n doctorate*
bok shoon 駁船 *n. barge*
bok tow 膞頭 *n. shoulder*
bok wuy 駁回 *v.t. overrule*
bong 綁 *v.t bind*
bong 磅 *v.t. weigh*
bong jor 幫助 *v.t aid*
bong jor 幫助 *v.t. assist*
bong jor 幫助 *n. assistance*
bor 波 *n. ball*
bor 播 *v.t. radio*
bor choy 菠菜 *n. spinach*
bor dung 波動 *v.i. oscillate*
bor jung 播種 *v.t. seed*
bor lay bwuy 玻璃杯 *n. tumbler*
bor lay cheurng 玻璃窗 *n. pane*
bor lay gung yan 玻璃工人 *n. glazier*
bor long 波浪 *n. ripple*
bor lor 菠蘿 *n. pineapple*
bor lorng ying 波浪形 *n. undulation*
borng 幫 *n boost*
borng 幫 *v.t facilitate*
borng 幫 *v.t. help*
borng 綁 *v.t. rope*
borng 綁 *v.t. strap*
borng 幫 *v.t. succour*
borng 綁 *v.t. tie*
borng ga 綁架 *n abduction*

borng jor 幫助 n help
borng jor 幫助 n. succour
bow fung yu geh 暴風雨嘅 a. stormy
bow meng 報名 v.t. subscribe
bow mwun sing sing 佈滿星星 a. starry
bow suk 部屬 n subordinate
bow yeurng 保養 n upkeep
buk bo 瀑布 n. waterfall
buk yan 僕人 n menial
bun hoy 半開 adv. ajar
bung 泵 n. pump
bung 泵 v.t. pump
bung 砰 v.t. slam
bung 砰 n slam
bung bung gam tiew 怦怦咁跳 v.t. pound
bwun 伴 v.t. accompany
bwun 伴 n accomplice
bwun 伴 n. companion
bwun 半 a half
bwun 搬 v.i. heave
bwun 搬 n. move
bwun cheurng fu 半長褲 n. breeches
bwun chut 搬出 v.t. vacate
bwun day 本地 a aboriginal
bwun day geh 本地嘅 a. native
bwun day geh 本地嘅 a. vernacular
bwun day wah 本地話 n. vernacular
bwun day yan 本地人 n native
bwun geurt sek 絆腳石 n drag
bwun ging 半徑 n. radius
bwun jow 伴奏 n accompaniment
bwun jow 搬走 v. t clear
bwun kow 半球 n. hemisphere
bwun luy 伴侶 n. helpmate
bwun mang geh 半盲屌弱 n. purblind
bwun tow 叛徒 n. traitor
bwun wan 搬運 n. portage
bwun wan gung 搬運工 n. mover
bwun yan fu 半音符 n. minim

bwuy 杯 n. cup
bwuy 杯 n. mug
bwuy bun 背叛 v.t. betray
bwuy bun 背叛 n betrayal
bwuy bun 背叛 n. treachery
bwuy bwun 背叛 a. mutinous
bwuy bwun 背叛 n. perfidy
bwuy ging 背景 n. background
bwuy jek 背脊 n. back
bwuy sam 背心 n. vest
bwuy sam 背心 n. waistcoat
bwuy toy 胚胎 n embryo
bwuy yee dak 貝爾德 n. bayard

C

ccho 嘈 a. loud
cha hm dor 差唔多 adv alike
cha hm dor 差唔多 adv. almost
cha ming 查明 v.t. ascertain
cha yow 搽油 v.t. anoint
chan teen geh 產前嘅 adj. antenatal
chao siew 嘲笑 v.i sneer
chao siew 嘲笑 n sneer
char hm dor 差唔多 adv. nigh
chee yan geh yoon 似人嘅猿 adj. anthropoid
cher 車 n. automobile
cher 車 n. car
cher chorng 車床 n. lathe
cher forng 車房 n. garage
cher gung 車工 n. turner
cher jam 車站 n. station
cher jam 車站 n stop
cher kuk 車軸 n. axle
cher leurng geh 車輛嘅 a. vehicular
cher may seurng 車尾箱 n. trunk
cher seurng 車廂 n. carriage
cher tai 車胎 n. tyre

cher teen cho 車前草 n. plantain

cheurk yoot geh 卓越嘅 a. superlative

cheurng 腸 n. bowel

cheurng 槍 n. gun

cheurng 腸 n. intestine

cheurng 長 a. long

cheurng 搶 n plunder

cheurng 唱 v.i. sing

cheurng 搶 v.t. snatch

cheurng 搶 n. snatch

cheurng 牆 n. wall

cheurng 唱 v.i. warble

cheurng 窗 n. window

cheurng 搶 v.t. wrest

cheurng bay yoon 長臂猿 n. gibbon

cheurng dang 長凳 n bench

cheurng dek 長笛 n flute

cheurng dow 長度 n. length

cheurng dow 長度 n. measurement

cheurng forng ying 長方形 n. oblong

cheurng forng ying 長方形 n. rectangle

cheurng forng ying geh 長方形嘅 a. oblong

cheurng forng ying geh 長方形嘅 a. rectangular

cheurng geem 長劍 n. rapier

cheurng geep 搶劫 n. dacoity

cheurng geep 搶劫 v.i. maraud

cheurng geep 搶劫 v.t. plunder

cheurng geep 搶劫 n. robbery

cheurng geh 腸嘅 adj. alvine

cheurng geh 腸嘅 a. intestinal

cheurng geh 牆嘅 a. mural

cheurng geng luk 長頸鹿 n. giraffe

cheurng gow 搶救 n rescue

cheurng gow 搶救 n. salvage

cheurng gow 搶救 v.t. salvage

cheurng hap 場合 n. occasion

cheurng kay 長期 adv long

cheurng kay dan diew 長期單調 n.

monostrous

cheurng kay sow fu 長期受苦 v.i. languish

cheurng keh bing 槍騎兵 n. lancer

cheurng key kwan yiew 長期困擾 v. t bedevil

cheurng kwong 猖狂 a. rampant

cheurng leem 窗簾 n curtain

cheurng leurk jeh 搶掠者 n. marauder

cheurng mao 長矛 n. lance

cheurng meng 長命 n. longevity

cheurng peen dai lun 長篇大論 n. tirade

cheurng pow 長袍 n. robe

cheurng say geh 詳細嘅 a elaborate

cheurng say miew sut 詳細描述 v. t elaborate

cheurng siew 暢銷 a. salable

cheurng siew geh 暢銷嘅 a. marketable

cheurng sut 詳述 v. t detail

cheurng sut 詳述 v.t. specify

cheurng tow bat seet 長途跋涉 v.i. trek

cheurng tow bat seet 長途跋涉 n. trek

cheurng yoon dang 長軟凳 n. ottoman

chiew v. t chew

chiew so 招手 v. t beckon

cho 粗 a coarse

cho 草 n. glass

cho 草 n grass

cho 嘈 a. noisy

cho 醋 n. vinegar

cho 嘈 v.i. wrangle

cho day 草地 n. lawn

cho day 草地 n. meadow

cho far 醋化 v. acetify

cho geh 吵嘅 a. rowdy

cho go 草稿 n draft

cho hung 操控 v.t. manipulate
cho jap seng 嘈雜聲 n babel
cho jap seng 嘈雜聲 n din
cho jap seng 嘈雜聲 n. hubbub
cho jee dai yeep 粗枝大葉 a. superficial
cho jok 操作 n. manipulation
cho jok 操作 v.t. operate
cho jok yan 操作人 n. operator
cho jung 操縱 v.t. man
cho leurk geh 粗略嘅 a. sketchy
cho leurk geh 粗略嘅 a. vague
cho lo 粗魯 adj. crass
cho low 粗魯 a. uncouth
cho low 粗魯 n. vulgarity
cho low geh 粗魯嘅 a. vulgar
cho lut 醋栗 n. gooseberry
cho muk 草木 n. vegetation
cho pay 草皮 n. turf
cho sam 操心 a. solicitous
cho see 措施 n. measure
cho sut 草率 a. hasty
cho teem 草簽 v.t initial
cho yan 粗人 n boor
cho yan 粗人 n carl
cho yee 草擬 v. t draft
cho yoon 草原 n. lea
choo koot 處決 n execution
choo see 廚師 n cook
choon 寸 n. inch
choon 傳 v.t. rumour
choon 串 v.t. spell
choon 串 v.t. string
choon 穿 v.t thread
choon 村 n. village
choon bo 全部 a. all
choon bo 全部 a entire
choon bo 全部 n. lot
choon bo 全部 n. totality
choon bo 全部 a. whole
choon bo geh 全部嘅 a comprehensive

choon bor 傳播 v.t. propagate
choon bor 傳播 n. spread
choon dan 傳單 n. circular
choon dan 傳單 n. handbill
choon dan 傳單 n. leaflet
choon dong 存檔 n.pl. archives
choon dow jeh 傳教者 n. preacher
choon for 存貨 n. stock
choon for 存貨 v.t. stock
choon forng 存放 n. storage
choon gao see 傳教士 n. missionary
choon ging 全景 n. panorama
choon gwok geh 全國嘅 a. national
choon gwor 穿過 v.t. pierce
choon gwor 穿過 prep. through
choon hai dai 穿鞋帶 v.t. lace
choon hay 喘氣 v.i gasp
choon hay 喘氣 v.i. pant
choon hm gwor geh 穿唔過嘅 a. impenetrable
choon hoy 傳開 v.i. spread
choon jan 傳真 n facsimile
choon jee 全知 n. omniscience
choon jor seen gwor 存在先過 v.t. antecede
choon joy 存在 v.t. be
choon joy 存在 v.i exist
choon joy 存在 n existence
choon kow geh 全球嘅 a. global
choon lang 全能 n. omnipotence
choon lang geh 全能嘅 a. almighty
choon man 傳聞 n. hearsay
choon man 村民 n. villager
choon man tow piew 全民投票 n. referendum
choon mwuy 傳媒 n press
choon piew 傳票 n. summons
choon sam choon yee 全心全意 a. whole-hearted
choon san geh 全身嘅 adv. bodily
choon san gwun ju 全神貫注 v.t engross

choon san gwun ju 全神貫注 *a. rapt*

choon say gai geh 全世界嘅 *a. universal*

choon shoot 傳說 *n. lore*

choon shoot geh 傳說嘅 *a. legendary*

choon sung 傳送 *n conveyance*

choon sung 傳送 *v.t. transmit*

choon tay shoon man 全體選民 *n electorate*

choon teen 存錢 *v.t. bank*

choon tey yeen yoon 全體演員 *n. cast*

choon ting geh 全程嘅 *a through*

choon tung 串通 *n collusion*

choon tung 傳統 *n. tradition*

choon tung geh 傳統嘅 *a. traditional*

choon yan 串人 *v.i. gibe*

choon yeem 傳染 *a contagious*

choon yeem 傳染 *v.t. infect*

choon yeem 傳染 *n. transmission*

choon yeem sing 傳染性 *a. infectious*

chor 錯 *n blunder*

chor 銼 *v.t file*

chor 錯 *a. incorrect*

chor 錯 *n. mistake*

chor 坐 *v.i. perch*

chor 坐 *v.t. seat*

chor 坐 *v.i. sit*

chor bo geh 初步嘅 *a. introductory*

chor bo geh 初步嘅 *a. preliminary*

chor bo yan jeurng 初步印象 *adv. prima facie*

chor cher 坐車 *v.i. motor*

chor geh 錯嘅 *a erroneous*

chor geh 錯嘅 *a. wrong*

chor geh 錯嘅 *adv. wrong*

chor gok 錯覺 *n. delusion*

chor gok 錯覺 *n. illusion*

chor guk 雛菊 *n daisy*

chor hm geh geet hap 錯誤嘅結合 *n. misalliance*

chor kay 初期 *n. infancy*

chor kay geh 初期嘅 *a. nascent*

chor ng 錯誤 *n error*

chor pwuy 錯配 *v.t. mismatch*

chor seurng 挫傷 *v.t. contuse*

chor shoon 坐船 *v.i. sail*

chorng 床 *n bed*

chorng yuk 床褥 *n. mattress*

chorng choot 倉促 *a cursory*

chorng choot geh 倉促嘅 *a snap*

chorng fu 倉庫 *n. godown*

chorng fu 倉庫 *n. repository*

chorng jao 床罩 *n. coverlet*

chorng jok jeh 創作者 *n creator*

chorng jok yan 創作人 *n. originator*

chorng lap 創立 *v. t erect*

chorng lap yan 創立人 *n. founder*

chorng mat chu 隱藏物 *n cache*

chorng san chu 藏身處 *n. hide*

chorng san jeh 創新者 *n. innovator*

chorng yap 闖入 *v.t. intrude*

chorng yap 闖入 *n. irruption*

chorng yee 創意 *adj. creative*

chorng yee 創意 *n. originality*

chorngfu 倉庫 *v.t warehouse*

chotee 措辭 *n. phraseology*

chow 臭 *a. foul*

chow fan 囚犯 *n. prisoner*

chow gam 酬金 *n. honorarium*

chow low 酬勞 *n. remuneration*

chow may 臭味 *n. odour*

chow teen 秋天 *n. autumn*

chow yap 抽泣 *v.i. whimper*

choy 探 *v.i. quarry*

choy dai 彩帶 *n. streamer*

choy ding 裁定 *v.t. adjudge*

choy ding 裁定 *v. i decree*

choy fu 財富 *n. mammon*

choy fu 財富 *n. opulence*

choy fu 財富 *n. riches*

choy fung 裁縫 *n. tailor*

choy garm gwan bay 裁減軍備 *n. disarmament*

choy gow 採購 n. procurement
choy jing 財政 n finance
choy jing bo 財政部 n. treasury
choy jing geh 財政嘅 a financial
choy jing geh 財政嘅 a fiscal
choy jing sow yap 財政收入 n. revenue
choy koot 裁決 n decree
choy koot 裁決 n. ruling
choy koot 裁決 n. verdict
choy liew 材料 n. ingredient
choy mat 財物 n. belongings
choy mat 財物 n. possession
choy mow ju gwun 財物主管 n. treasurer
choy pai 彩排 n. rehearsal
choy pao 賽跑 n. race
choy poon 裁判 v.t. arbitrate
choy pwun 裁判 n. arbiter
choy pwun 裁判 n. referee
choy pwun yoon 裁判員 n. umpire
choy sek cheurng 採石場 n. quarry
choy tan 財產 n. fortune
choy tan 財產 n. property
choy wah 才華 n. talent
choy yoon 裁員 n. redundance
chu 柱 n. pillar
chu forng 廚房 n. kitchen
chu gway 櫥櫃 n. cabinet
chu larm 處男 n virgin
chu lay 處理 n. dealing
chu lay 處理 n disposal
chu lay 處理 v.t handle
chu lorng 柱廊 n. portico
chu luy 處女 n. maiden
chu luy 處女 n. virgin
chu mat gway 儲物櫃 n. locker
chu tak chu 註冊處 n. registry
chuk 捉 v. t. catch
chuk bok 束縛 n bondage
chuk bok 束縛 n fetter
chuk day 速遞 n delivery

chuk dow 速度 n pace
chuk dow 速度 n. speed
chuk dow 速度 n. velocity
chuk gey 速記 n. stenography
chuk gey yoon 速記員 n. stenographer
chuk jun 促進 v.i. hasten
chuk yee por wai 蓄意破壞 n. sabotage
chuk yee por wai 蓄意破壞 v.t. sabotage
chun 蠢 adj. asinine
chun 蠢 adj. daft
chun 蠢 a dumb
chun 蠢 n folly
chun 蠢 a stupid
chun 蠢 n. stupidity
chun choy 蠢材 n blockhead
chun choy 蠢材 v. t burk
chun choy 蠢材 n fool
chun choy 蠢材 n. loggerhead
chun choy 蠢材 n. moron
chun geh 蠢嘅 a foolish
chun geh 蠢嘅 a. idiotic
chun lor 巡邏 v.i. patrol
chun lor 巡邏 n patrol
chun teen 春天 n spring
chun teen geh 春天嘅 a. vernal
chun wan 循環 n circulation
chun wan 循環 n cycle
chun wan geh 循環嘅 a cyclic
chun wan geh 循環嘅 a. recurrent
chun yan 蠢人 n. clot
chun yeurng larm 巡洋艦 n cruiser
chung 從 prep. from
chung 重 a. hefty
chung 蔥 n. onion
chung 衝 n rush
chung 從 prep. since
chung 從 conj. since
chung 從 adv. since
chung 重 a. weighty

chung been dow 從邊度 adv. whence
chung cha 沖茶 v. t. brew
chung chut 衝出 v.i. sally
chung dat 衝突 v. i conflict
chung dat 衝突 n. scuffle
chung dat 衝突 v.i. scuffle
chung dat 衝突 n. strife
chung deep 重疊 v.t. overlap
chung deep 重疊 n overlap
chung dung 衝動 n. impetuosity
chung dung 衝動 n. impulse
chung dung 衝動 a. impulsive
chung dung 衝動 n. spontaneity
chung dung 衝動 a. spontaneous
chung dung 衝動 n urge
chung fan juy 重婚罪 n bigamy
chung fuk 重複 v.t. reiterate
chung fuk 重複 n. reiteration
chung fuk 重複 v.t. repeat
chung fuk 重複 n. repetition
chung gam yee ho 從今以後 adv. henceforward
chung gao 蟲膠 n lac, lakh
chung gik 重擊 n. thump
chung gik 重擊 v.t. thump
chung gung 充公 v. t confiscate
chung gwor 重過 v.t. out-balance
chung gwor 重過 v.t. outweigh
chung ho yee chut 衝口而出 v. t blurt
chung jeet yow 松節油 n. turpentine
chung juk 充足 n abundance
chung juk 充足 n. sufficiency
chung juk geh 充足嘅 a abundant
chung leurng 沖涼 v. t bathe
chung leurng 沖涼 n. shower
chung leurng 沖涼 v.t. shower
chung mat 寵物 n. pet
chung ming 聰明 a. intelligent
chung ming choy jee 聰明才智 n. intelligence
chung ming geh 聰明嘅 a. sage
chung ming geh 聰明嘅 a. smart

chung morng 匆忙 n. haste
chung mun 充滿 v.i. teem
chung mun 充滿 a. fraught
chung mwun 充滿 a. replete
chung mwun 充滿 v.i. riddle
chung mwun ging yee geh 充滿敬意嘅 a. reverential
chung mwun jing hay 充滿蒸氣 a. vaporous
chung ngar 松鴉 n. jay
chung sam 衷心 a. sincere
chung san 重新 adv. afresh
chung san 重新 adv. anew
chung sang 重生 n. rebirth
chung sang 重生 n. regeneration
chung say 沖洗 v.i flush
chung say 沖洗 v.t. rinse
chung shu 松樹 n. pine
chung shu 松鼠 n. squirrel
chung suk 從屬 n. subservience
chung tee yee ho 從此以後 adv. henceforth
chung tee yee ho 從此以後 adv. hereafter
chung way 聰慧 n. sagacity
chung yan 重印 v.t. reprint
chung yan 重印 n. reprint
chung yeen 重現 n. recurrence
chung yeep jeh 從業者 n. practitioner
chung yu 充裕 n. plenty
chut ban 出版 n. publication
chut ban yan 出版人 n. publisher
chut been 出邊 n outside
chut been 出邊 prep outside
chut been 出邊 n without
chut been geh 出邊嘅 a. outside
chut been geh 出邊嘅 adv outside
chut ga 出價 v.t bid
chut go ga 出高價 v.t. outbid
chut gway 出軌 v. t. derail
chut gwok 出國 adv abroad

chut ho 出口 *n. exit*
chut ho 出口 *n export*
chut ho 出口 *v. t. export*
chut horn 出汗 *v.i. perspire*
chut huy 出去 *adv. out*
chut jik 出席 *v.t. attend*
chut jik lut 出席率 *n. attendance*
chut lap yoon 出納員 *n. teller*
chut leurng 出糧 *v.t. remunerate*
chut mao 出貓 *v. t. cheat*
chut meng 出名 *a famous*
chut meng 出名 *a. well-known*
chut sang 出生 *n. birth*
chut sang 出生 *v. born*
chut sang 出生 *n. parentage*
chut sang fu yu 出生富裕 *adj. born rich*
chut sang geh 出生嘅 *a. natal*
chut siew jee gak 取消資格 *n disqualification*
chut siew jee gak 取消資格 *v. t. disqualify*
chut tan leurng 出產量 *n. output*
chut yap hung 出入孔 *n. manhole*
chut yeen 出現 *n. advent*
chut yeen 出現 *v.i. appear*
chut yeen 出現 *v.i. arise*
chut yeen 出現 *v. i emerge*
chut yeen 出現 *n. occurrence*
chut yeen 出現 *n. presence*
chuy 除 *v.t. bare*
chuy 吹 *v.i. blow*
chuy 脆 *a. brittle*
chuy 催 *v. t bustle*
chuy 脆 *a crisp*
chuy 脆 *adj. crump*
chuy 催 *v.t urge*
chuy ho sao 吹口哨 *v.i. whistle*
chuy chor 最初 *n. outset*
chuy chung 隨從 *n. retinue*
chuy dak jun 徐得盡 *n. aliquot*
chuy dek 吹笛 *v.i flute*

chuy doy 取代 *v. t displace*
chuy doy 取代 *v.t. supersede*
chuy fat 除法 *n division*
chuy fay 徐非 *conj. unless*
chuy huy 除去 *v. t eliminate*
chuy huy 除去 *n elimination*
chuy jay 槌仔 *n. hammer*
chuy jor 徐咗 *prep besides*
chuy jor 徐咗 *prep except*
chuy jor 徐咗 *prep save*
chuy meen 催眠 *v.t. hypnotize*
chuy meen sut 催眠術 *n. mesmerism*
chuy meen suy 催眠術 *n. hypnotism*
chuy pung 吹捧 *v.t. glorify*
chuy sam 徐衫 *v.t. strip*
chuy see 隨時 *adv. conj whenever*
chuy siew 取消 *v. t. cancel*
chuy siew 取消 *n cancellation*
chuy siew 取消 *v.t. revoke*
chuy sow kway dai geh 隨手攜帶嘅 *a. portable*
chuy suy 吹水 *v. i brag*
chuy tee jee ngoy 除此之外 *adv. otherwise*
chuy yee geh 隨意嘅 *a. random*
chuy yeurk 脆弱 *a delicate*
chuy yeurk 脆弱 *a. fragile*
chuy yeurk 脆弱 *a. vulnerable*

D

da 打 *v. t. beat*
da 打 *n. dial*
da 打 *v.t fight*
da 打 *v.t. hit*
da 打 *v.t. strike*
da bai 打敗 *v.i. triumph*
da bai 打敗 *v.t. trump*
da ban 打扮 *v.t. attire*

da ban 打扮 *n. garb*
da bay 打界 *v.t. ring*
da bay horn 打鼻鼾 *v.i. snore*
da deen bo 打電報 *v. t. cable*
da deen bo 打電報 *v.t. telegraph*
da deen wah 打電話 *v.t. telephone*
da dow 打鬥 *v. i. & n brawl*
da dow 打賭 *n. wager*
da dow 打賭 *v.i. wager*
da ert 打嗝 *v. t belch*
da ert seng 打嗝聲 *n belch*
da fat 打發 *v. t. consign*
da for gey 打火機 *n. lighter*
da gao 打交 *n fight*
da geep 打劫 *v.i. loot*
da geet 打結 *v.t. knot*
da geet 打結 *n. tangle*
da gik 打擊 *n blow*
da gik 打擊 *n hit*
da gu 打鼓 *v.i. drum*
da guk jeh 打穀者 *n. thresher*
da gut 打嗝 *n. hiccup*
da gwun see 打官司 *v.t. litigate*
da ham low 打喊路 *v.i. yawn*
da hat tee 打乞嚏 *v.i. sneeze*
da hoy 打開 *v.t. open*
da hoy 打開 *v.t. unfold*
da hoy geh 打開嘅 *a. open*
da hung fan 打空翻 *v.i. somersault*
da jam 打針 *n. injection*
da jan 打震 *v.i. shudder*
da jan 打震 *n shudder*
da jee 打字 *v.t. type*
da jee yoon 打字員 *n. typist*
da jiew fu 打招呼 *v.t. greet*
da jik 打直 *a. vertical*
da lang jan 打冷震 *v.i. shiver*
da lap 打蠟 *v.t. wax*
da leep 打獵 *v.t. hunt*
da lung 打窿 *v.t hole*
da lung 大窿 *v.t. perforate*
da luy 打雷 *v.i. thunder*

da sai geet 打晒結 *v.t. tangle*
da seurng 打傷 *v.t maul*
da shoon 打算 *v.t. intend*
da sing dai bao 打成大包 *v.t. bale*
da suy 打碎 *v.t. smash*
da ting 打聽 *v.t. inquire*
da ting 打聽 *v.i. pry*
da toon 打斷 *v. t disrupt*
da wan 打暈 *v.t. stun*
da wat 打滑 *n skid*
da wor 打和 *n draw*
da yiew 打擾 *n. interruption*
da yik miew 打疫苗 *v.t. vaccinate*
da yu forng jam 打預防針 *v.t. inoculate*
dai 大 *a big*
dai 帶 *v. t bring*
dai 大 *a. large*
dai 帶 *v.t. lead*
dai 帶 *n. strap*
dai ba 大巴 *n coach*
dai ban jeurng 大笨象 *n elephant*
dai bao 大包 *n. bale*
dai bay 大髀 *n. thigh*
dai bo 大步 *n stride*
dai bo fan 大部分 *n bulk*
dai bo fan 大部分 *n. majority*
dai bo hang 大步行 *v.i. stride*
dai buk bo 大瀑布 *n. cataract*
dai cho yoon 大草原 *n. steppe*
dai chuy 大槌 *n. maul*
dai dam 大膽 *a. adventurous*
dai dam 大膽 *a. bold*
dai dam 大膽 *a brave*
dai dam 大膽 *n. daring*
dai dam 大膽 *n. hardihood*
dai dam 大膽 *n. intrepidity*
dai dam geh 大膽嘅 *a. venturesome*
dai dam geh 大膽嘅 *a. venturous*
dai duy 大堆 *v.t. array*
dai duy 大堆 *n. load*
dai far gwun 戴花冠 *v.t. garland*

dai for cher 大貨車 *n. lorry*
dai for duy 大火堆 *n bonfire*
dai forng 大方 *a bountiful*
dai forng 大方 *a. generous*
dai fu yung 大富豪 *n. croesus*
dai fuk teen day 大幅田地 *n. acreage*
dai fung 大風 *a. windy*
dai gai 大街 *n. avenue*
dai gai 大街 *n. thoroughfare*
dai gao tong 大教堂 *n. cathedral*
dai gao tong 大教堂 *n. minster*
dai geng siew gwai 大驚小怪 *v.i fuss*
dai geng siew gwai 大驚小怪 *n. hysteria*
dai giew 大叫 *n. shout*
dai giew 大叫 *v.i. shout*
dai gung see 大公司 *n corporation*
dai har 大廈 *n edifice*
dai harm 大喊 *n.i. bawl*
dai hok 大學 *n. university*
dai hok ju tak 大學註冊 *n. matriculation*
dai hok sang 大學生 *n. undergraduate*
dai jee yeen 大自然 *n. nature*
dai jeen dow 大剪刀 *n. pl. shears*
dai jeurk lung 大雀籠 *n. aviary*
dai ju gao 大主教 *n. archbishop*
dai ju gao 大主教 *n. metropolitan*
dai koy 大概 *adv about*
dai koy 大概 *a. approximate*
dai koy yee see 大概意思 *n. purport*
dai leem dow 大鐮刀 *n. scythe*
dai leurng 大梁 *n. girder*
dai leurng 大量 *n. profusion*
dai leurng geh 大量嘅 *a. profuse*
dai leurng geh 大量嘅 *a. substantial*
dai leurng geh 大量嘅 *a. superabundant*
dai leurng jay jow 大量製造 *n manufacture*

dai leurng mo chut 大量冒出 *v.i billow*
dai leurng sang tan 大量生產 *v.t. manufacture*
dai lik 大力 *a. strong*
dai lik gam deng 大力咁掟 *v.t. hurl*
dai lik geh 大力嘅 *adj. mighty*
dai lik ling 大力擰 *v.t. wrench*
dai lo geh 大腦嘅 *adj cerebral*
dai low 大路 *n. highway*
dai low 大褸 *n. overcoat*
dai luk mo geh yan 戴綠帽嘅人 *n. cuckold*
dai lut see 大律師 *n. barrister*
dai ma 大麻 *n. hemp*
dai mak 大麥 *n. barley*
dai morng 大網 *n. conspectus*
dai ngar 大牙 *n. molar*
dai ngar geh 大牙嘅 *a molar*
dai pao 大炮 *n. artillery*
dai pao 大炮 *n. cannon*
dai peen tow day 大片土地 *n. tract*
dai san 大臣 *n. minister*
dai san dung 大山洞 *n. cavern*
dai say 大使 *n extravagance*
dai say 大細 *n. size*
dai say geh 大使嘅 *a extravagant*
dai say geh yan 大使嘅人 *n. spendthrift*
dai see 大使 *n. ambassador*
dai sek 大石 *n boulder*
dai seng 大聲 *adv. aloud*
dai seng 大聲 *a. thunderous*
dai seng giew 大聲叫 *v.t. howl*
dai seng yiew kow 大聲要求 *v. i. clamour*
dai she 大赦 *n. amnesty*
dai shoon 大船 *n. vessel*
dai shu jee 大樹枝 *n bough*
dai sik geh 大食嘅 *a. voracious*
dai sing see ghe 大城市嘅 *a. metropolitan*

dai tow 歹徒 n. ruffian
dai tow 帶頭 v.t. spearhead
dai tow sat 大屠殺 n carnage
dai tow sat 大屠殺 n. holocaust
dai tow sat 大屠殺 n. massacre
dai wah 大話 n lie
dai wok choon sing 大獲全勝 a. triumphant
dai wong fung 大黃峰 n. hornet
dai yat gor jee mow 第一個字母 n. initial
dai yee 大意 a. careless
dai yee lung 大耳窿 n. usurer
dai yeep geh say jee 帶葉嘅細枝 n. sprig
dai yeep jee 大頁紙 n foolscap
dai yiew dai bai 大搖大擺 n swagger
dai yiew dai bai hang 大搖大擺行 v.i. swagger
dai yu 大雨 n downpour
dak beet 特別 adv. singularly
dak beet 特別 a. special
dak beet geh 特別嘅 a especial
dak beet geh 特別嘅 a. particular
dak chut 突出 n. prominence
dak dai 特大 a. outsize
dak dang 特登 a deliberate
dak dang geh 特登嘅 adv. purposely
dak deem 特點 n feature
dak ding 特定 a certain
dak ding geh 特定嘅 a. specific
dak dow 得到 n. acquisition
dak dow 得到 v. t. derive
dak dow 得到 v.t. obtain
dak fai leet cher 特快列車 n express
dak fan 得分 v.t. score
dak fan jeh 得分者 n. scorer
dak gey 特技 n stunt
dak gik sow ta 突擊搜查 n swoop
dak harn 得閒 a available
dak huy ging ying koon 特許經營權 n. frachise

dak jap 突襲 v.i. pounce
dak jap 突襲 n pounce
dak jap 突襲 n. raid
dak jap 突襲 n. sally
dak jap 突襲 v.i. storm
dak jing 特徵 n. hallmark
dak jing 特徵 n. trait
dak juy 得罪 v. t displease
dak juy 得罪 v.t. offend
dak juy yan geh 得罪人嘅 a. offensive
dak koon 特權 n. prerogative
dak koon 特權 n. privilege
dak ser 特赦 n. pardon
dak tay 得體 n decorum
dak tay 得體 n. propriety
dak tay 得體 n. tact
dak tay geh 得體嘅 a. seemly
dak tik 得戚 adj. complacent
dak tik 得戚 v. i crow
dak tik 得戚 a. smug
dak yeen deet lok 突然跌落 n plunge
dak yeen gan 突然間 a abrupt
dak yik 得益 v.t. profit
dak yu kay loy 突如其來 n. onrush
dam 啖 n. swallow
dam bo yan 擔保人 n. surety
dam bow 擔保 v.i. vouch
dam ga 擔架 n. stretcher
dam hay 氮氣 n. nitrogen
dam jap 膽汁 n bile
dam leurng 膽量 n boldness
dam leurng 膽量 n bravery
dam leurng 膽量 n pluck
dam sam 擔心 n. apprehension
dam sam 擔心 v.t dread
dam sam 擔心 a. uneasy
dam sam 擔心 v.i. worry
dam sam geh 擔心嘅 a. apprehensive
dam siew gway 膽小鬼 n. coward
dam yow 擔憂 v.t. unsettle
dam yow 擔憂 n. worry

dan 單 n bill
dan 單 n. invoice
dan 單 n. receipt
dan 彈 v.i. spring
dan bak 蛋白 n albumen
dan bak jatt 蛋白質 n. protein
dan bo 擔保 v.t guarantee
dan cher 單車 n. bicycle
dan cher sow 單車手 n cyclist
dan chut geh 突出嘅 a. prominent
dan diew 單調 a. humdrum
dan diew 單調 n monotony
dan diew geh 單調嘅 a. monotonous
dan duk geh 單獨嘅 a. lone
dan duk geh 單獨嘅 a. solitary
dan duk geh 單獨嘅 a. solo
dan duk tiew chut 單獨挑出 v.t. single
dan forng 單方 adv ex-parte
dan forng meen geh 單方面嘅 a ex-parte
dan geurt tiew 單腳跳 v. i hop
dan geurt tiew 單腳跳 n hop
dan go 蛋糕 n. cake
dan hay 但係 prep but
dan hay 但係 conj however
dan hay 但係 conj. yet
dan leet 分裂 n. schism
dan mok she gik 彈幕射擊 n. barrage
dan ngan geh 單眼嘅 a. monocular
dan peen ngan geng 單片眼鏡 n. monocle
dan san larm yan 單身男人 n. bachelor
dan sang 誕生 n. nativity
dan seurng 犯上 n. insubordination
dan sik geh 單色嘅 a. monochromatic
dan sing 彈性 n stretch
dan sow geh 單數嘅 a. singular
dan tee 單詞 n. vocabulary

dan ting piew 單程票 n. single
dan way 單位 n. apartment
dan way 單位 n. unit
dan worng 蛋黃 n. yolk
dan yam jeet geh 單音節嘅 a. monosyllabic
dan yam jeet tee 單音節詞 n. monosyllable
dan yat geh 單一嘅 a. single
dan yeurk 彈藥 n. ammunition
dang 等 v. t bide
dang 凳 n. chair
dang 燈 n. lamp
dang 等 v.i. wait
dang 等 n. wait
dang 瞪 v.i. stare
dang been geh 等邊嘅 a equilateral
dang dang 等等 adv. etcetera
dang duy 登對 v.i. match
dang gak yeet 登革熱 n. dengue
dang gan 等緊 v.t. await
dang gan 等緊 prep. pending
dang gey 登記 v.t. register
dang gey 登記 n. registration
dang gey bo 登記簿 n. register
dang gey yoon 登記員 n. registrar
dang ho sat 等候室 n. lounge
dang kap jay dow 等級制度 n. hierarchy
dang lung 燈籠 n. lantern
dang ngat seen 等壓線 n. isobar
dang pao 燈泡 n. bulb
dang san ga 登山家 n. mountaineer
dang tap 燈塔 n beacon
dang tung yu 等同於 a. synonymous
dang way 登位 v. t enthrone
dang way 登位 v.t. throne
dang yu 等於 v. amount
dang yu 等於 v. t equal
dang yu 等於 a. tantamount
dap 搥 v.t hammer
dap 答 v.i. respond

dap ban 踏板 *n. pedal*
dap been yan 答辯人 *n. pleader*
dap fuk 答覆 *n. response*
dap on 答案 *n answer*
dap shoon yow larm 搭船遊覽 *v.i. cruise*
dat chut 突出 *n. hernia*
dat dow 發抖 *v.i. quake*
dat sing 達成 *v. t concert2*
dat sing 達成 *v.t. fulfil*
dat yeen 突然 *n. sudden*
dat yeen gan 突然間 *adv. suddenly*
day 低 *n bottom*
day 地 *n. ground*
day 地 *n. land*
day 低 *adv. low*
day 低 *n. primer*
day bo 地堡 *n bunker*
day deem 地點 *n. location*
day deem 低點 *n. low*
day dorng 抵擋 *v.t fend*
day dow geh 地道嘅 *a. idiomatic*
day forng 地方 *n area*
day forng 地方 *n. place*
day forng fat 地方法 *n bylaw, bye-law*
day forng gwun 地方官 *n. magistrate*
day gao 地窖 *n cellar*
day geh 低嘅 *a. low*
day gow 第九 *a. ninth*
day gow sap 第九十 *a. ninetieth*
day gwok 帝國 *n empire*
day gwok tung jee 帝國統治 *n. imperialism*
day ha geh 地下嘅 *a. subterranean*
day ha tung dow 地下通到 *n. tunnel*
day hao 低吼 *n. snarl*
day hao 低吼 *v.i. snarl*
day har sat 地下室 *n. basement*
day jan 地震 *n quake*
day jan geh 地震嘅 *a. seismic*

day jat geh 地質嘅 *a. geological*
day jat hok 地質學 *n. geology*
day jat hok ga 地質學家 *n. geologist*
day jay 抵制 *v. t. boycott*
day jay 抵制 *n boycott*
day jee 地址 *n. address*
day jor 底座 *n. pedestal*
day kow 地球 *n. globe*
day kuy 地區 *n district*
day kuy 地區 *n. locality*
day kuy 地區 *n. region*
day kuy 地區 *n. zone*
day kuy geh 地區嘅 *a. regional*
day lay geh 地理嘅 *a. geographical*
day lay hok 地理學 *n. geography*
day lay hok ga 地理學家 *n. geographer*
day luk 第六 *a. sixth*
day luk sap 第六十 *a. sixtieth*
day ngat 抵押 *v.t. mortgage*
day ngat yan 抵押人 *n. mortgagor*
day ping seen 地平線 *n. horizon*
day pwun 地盤 *a. territorial*
day pwun 地盤 *n. territory*
day sam 第三 *a. third*
day sam 第三 *n. third*
day sam 第三 *adv. thirdly*
day sam kap yan lik 地心吸引力 *n. gravity*
day sam sap 第三十 *a. thirtieth*
day sam sap 第三十 *n thirtieth*
day sap gow 第十九 *a. nineteenth*
day sap luk 第十六 *a. sixteenth*
day sap sam 第十三 *a. thirteenth*
day sap tat 第十七 *a. seventeenth*
day sap yee 第十二 *a. twelfth*
day sap yee 第十二 *n. twelfth*
day say 抵死 *v. t. damn*
day siew 抵消 *v.t. counteract*
day siew 抵消 *v.t. offset*
day siew 抵消 *n offset*
day suk 隸屬 *a. subordinate*

day tat 第七 *a. seventh*
day tat sap 第七十 *a. seventieth*
day tor 地拖 *n. mop*
day tow 地圖 *n. atlas*
day tow 地圖 *n map*
day way 地位 *n. niche*
day way 地位 *n. rank*
day way 詆毀 *n. slander*
day way 詆毀 *v.t. slander*
day way 地位 *n. standing*
day way 地位 *n. status*
day yan gung 低人工 *n. pittance*
day yat gor 第一個 *a first*
day yat gor 第一個 *n first*
day yee geh 第二嘅 *a. second*
day yee sap 第二十 *a. twentieth*
day yee sap 第二十 *n twentieth*
day ying 地形 *n. topography*
day ying geh 地形嘅 *a. topographical*
day ying hok ga 地形學家 *n. topographer*
deem 點 *v. t dip*
deem 點 *n dot*
deem 點 *n. point*
deem 店 *n. shop*
deem 掂 *v.t. touch*
deem dow ho 點都好 *adv. anyhow*
deem for 點火 *v.t. light*
deem gai 點解 *adv. why*
deem gik 點擊 *n. click*
deem kwong 癲狂 *adv. amuck*
deem meng 點名 *n. roll-call*
deem so 點數 *n. count*
deem tee 電池 *n battery*
deem wah 電話 *n. telephone*
deem yeurng 點樣 *adv. how*
deen 電 *a electric*
deen 電 *n electricity*
deen 墊 *n. pad*
deen 墊 *n. padding*
deen bo 電報 *n. telegram*

deen bo 電報 *n. telegraph*
deen bo geh 電報嘅 *a. telegraphic*
deen bo hok 電報學 *n. telegraphy*
deen bo yoon 電報員 *n. telegraphist*
deen cher 電車 *n. tram*
deen dow 電鍍 *v.t. plate*
deen fan 典範 *n. quintessence*
deen fan 澱粉 *n. starch*
deen fuk 顛覆 *n. subversion*
deen ha 殿下 *n. Highness*
deen hoon 墊圈 *n. gasket*
deen ju 墊住 *v.t. pillow*
deen larm 電纜 *n. cable*
deen larm 靛藍 *n. indigo*
deen low 顛佬 *n. lunatic*
deen low 顛佬 *n. maniac*
deen sam dow say 顛三倒四 *adv topsy turvy*
deen see 電視 *n. television*
deen see gworng bor 電視廣播 *n. telecast*
deen seen 電線 *n. wire*
deen sun 電訊 *n. telecommunications*
deen tay cho 電梯蹭 *n. shaft*
deen tung 電筒 *n. torch*
deen wah 電話 *n. call*
deen wah 電話 *n. phone*
deen wah bo 電話簿 *n directory*
deen ying 典型 *a classic*
deen ying 典型 *n embodiment*
deen ying 電影 *n film*
deen ying 電影 *n. movies*
deen ying geh 典型嘅 *a. typical*
deen yoon 電源 *n main*
deep 碟 *n dish*
deep 碟 *n. plate*
deet 跌 *v. i drop*
deet 跌 *v.i. fall*
deet 跌 *n fall*
deet 跌 *v.t fell*
deet 跌 *n. stumble*
deet 跌 *n. tumble*

deet dow 跌倒 *v.i. tumble*
deet ga 跌價 *v.t.i. depreciate*
deh dee 爹地 *n dad, daddy*
deh dee 爹地 *n father*
deng 訂 *v. t. book*
deng 掟 *v. t discard*
deng 掟 *v.t fling*
deng 釘 *n. nail*
deng 釘 *v.t. nail*
deng 訂 *v.t order*
deng 叮 *n. sting*
deng 釘 *n. stud*
deng 掟 *v.t. throw*
deng 掟 *n. throw*
deng 頂 *n. top*
deng 掟 *v.t. toss*
deng jow 訂做 *v.t. tailor*
deng ju 釘住 *v.t. pin*
deng sek 掟石 *v.t. stone*
deng shu deng 釘書釘 *n. staple*
deng tay teet 釘蹄鐵 *v.t. shoe*
deng yoot 訂閱 *n. subscription*
deurk 啄 *v.i. peck*
dey deem 地點 *n. venue*
dey ha 地下 *n floor*
dey jan 地震 *n earthquake*
dey jeen 地氈 *n. carpet*
dey kow 地球 *n earth*
dey yuk 地獄 *a. hell*
diew 雕 *v. t. chisel*
diew 吊 *v. t dangle*
diew 貂 *n. marten*
diew 雕 *v.t. whittle*
diew cher 吊車 *n crane*
diew dai 吊帶 *n. sling*
diew dung 調動 *v.t. mobilize*
diew hak 雕刻 *n. sculpture*
diew hak ga 雕刻家 *n. sculptor*
diew hak geh 雕刻嘅 *a. sculptural*
diew hay 吊起 *v.t. hoist*
diew huy 調去 *v.t. shunt*
diew jeh 凋謝 *v.i. wither*

diew jeurng 雕像 *n effigy*
diew mat dai 吊襪帶 *n. garter .*
diew ta 調查 *v.t. poll*
diew yu 釣魚 *v.i fish*
dik 滴 *n drip*
dik 滴 *v. i drip*
dik 滴 *n drop*
dik 滴 *v.i. trickle*
dik jow bat jeem 滴酒不沾 *a. teetotal*
dik jow bat jeem 滴酒不沾 *n. temperance*
dik kok 的確 *adv. indeed*
dik see 的士 *n. cab*
dik see 的士 *n. taxi*
dik yan 敵人 *n. antagonist*
dik yan 敵人 *n enemy*
dik yan 敵人 *n foe*
dik yee 敵意 *n animus*
dik yee 敵意 *n antagonism*
ding dong 丁噹 *v.i. jingle*
ding dong seng 丁噹聲 *n. clink*
ding dorng seng 丁噹聲 *n. jingle*
ding fan 訂婚 *n. betrothal*
ding fan 訂婚 *n. engagement*
ding fung 頂峰 *n. peak*
ding fung 頂峰 *n. pinnacle*
ding fung 頂峰 *n. zenith*
ding ga 定價 *v.t. price*
ding geng 頂頸 *v.i. quarrel*
ding heurng 丁香 *n clove*
ding heurng 丁香 *n. lilac*
ding hm sun geh 頂唔順嘅 *a. intolerable*
ding jam 頂針 *n. thimble*
ding ju 頂住 *v.t. withstand*
ding kay geh 定期嘅 *a. periodical*
ding lay 定理 *n. theorem*
ding see geh 定時嘅 *a. regular*
ding ying 定型 *a. stereotyped*
don 段 *n. paragraph*
dong jok 動作 *n. motion*

dong on sat 檔案室 n chancery

dong sat lo 當失路 adv., astray

dong yeen 當然 adv. certainly

dong...geh see ho 當...嘅時候 conj. while

doon chu 短處 n. shortcoming

doon fu 短褲 n. pl. shorts

doon geh 短嘅 a. short

doon geurt gey 矮腳雞 n. bantam

doon gu see 短故事 n. anecdote

doon ho 短號 n. cornet

doon jam geh kwong yeet 短暫嘅狂熱 n fad

doon koot 短缺 n. shortage

doon kuy lay choy pao 短距離賽跑 n sprint

doon leen 鍛鍊 v. t exercise

doon yee ngan geh mo 短而硬嘅毛 n bristle

doon yung mow 短絨毛 n nap

dor 多 a. plus

dor bao toy 多胞胎 a. multiparous

dor been geh 多變嘅 a. variable

dor beng geh 多病嘅 a. sickly

dor choy dor ngay geh 多才多藝嘅 a. versatile

dor chung sing 多重性 n. multiplicity

dor fan gan 多番梘 a. soapy

dor gwok geh 多國嘅 a. multilateral

dor gwun han see 多管閒事 a. officious

dor hay tay 多氣體 a. gassy

dor jap 多汁 a. juicy

dor jeh 多謝 v.t. thank

dor jeh 多謝 n. thanks

dor jor geh 多咗嘅 a spare

dor juk dung mat 多足動物 n. multiped

dor jung ying sik geh 多種形式嘅 a multiform

dor jung yu yeen seh sing geh 多種語言寫成嘅 a. polyglot2

dor leen sang jik mat 多年生植物 n. perennial

dor mow geh 多霧嘅 a. misty

dor san 多山 a. mountainous

dor san gao tow 多神教徒 n. polytheist

dor san sun yeurng 多神信仰 n. polytheism

dor san sung bai geh 多神崇拜嘅 a. polytheistic

dor see 多士 n. toast

dor sek tow 多石頭 a. stony

dor shoot geh 多雪嘅 a. snowy

dor shu yeep 多樹葉 a. leafy

dor sing 惰性 a. inert

dor tan geh 多產嘅 a. prolific

dor tee 多刺 a. thorny

dor toy 墮胎 n abortion

dor wan 多雲 a cloudy

dor wan 多雲 a. overcast

dor yee geh yan 多疑嘅人 n. sceptic

dor yeen geh 多煙嘅 a. smoky

dor yeh gorng geh yan 多嘢講嘅人 n. windbag

dor yeurng geh 多樣嘅 a. multiple

dor yow 多油 a. greasy

dor yu geh 多餘嘅 a excess

dor yu geh 多雨嘅 a. rainy

dor yung tow 多用途 n. versatility

dorlok 墮落 a decadent

dorng 檔 n. gear

dorng 擋 n. parry

dorng day geh 當地嘅 a. indigenous

dorng hoy 擋開 v.t. parry

dorng ju 擋住 v.t. shield

dorng ling geh 當令嘅 a. seasonable

dorng sat low 蕩失路 v.i. stray

dorng see 當時 a then

dorng see yan 當事人 n. litigant

dorng yeurng 蕩漾 v.t. ripple

doryu 多餘 n excess

dow 到 v.i. arrive

dow 刀 n. baslard
dow 豆 n. bean
dow 賭 v.i bet
dow 竇 n den
dow 倒 v empty
dow 賭 v.i. gamble
dow 賭 v.i game
dow 島 n. island
dow 島 n. isle
dow 刀 n. knife
dow 竇 n. lair
dow 倒 v.i. pour
dow 到 v.t. reach
dow 倒 v.t. tip
dow ban hang way 盜版行爲 n. piracy
dow been dow 到邊度 adv. whither
dow bok 賭博 n gamble
dow cho 稻草 n. thatch
dow chu 到處 adv around
dow dak 道德 a ethical
dow dak 道德 n. moral
dow dak 道德 n. morality
dow dak biew jun 道德標準 n. ethics
dow dak geh 道德嘅 a. moral
dow dak hok ga 道德學家 n. moralist
dow dan 導彈 n. missile
dow dat 到達 n. arrival
dow fung 斗篷 n. cloak
dow ga ying 度假營 n. camp
dow gam 鍍金 v.t. gild
dow gam 鍍金 a. gilt
dow gey 妒忌 a envious
dow gey 妒忌 v. t envy
dow gey 妒忌 a. jealous
dow gey 妒忌 n. jealousy
dow goon liew 杜鵑鳥 n cuckoo
dow guy 道具 n. prop
dow heep 道歉 v.i. apologize
dow heep 道歉 n. apology
dow ho 逗號 n comma

dow horng 導航 n. navigation
dow horng yee 導航儀 n. navigator
dow jang 鬥爭 n crusade
dow jay 賭仔 n. gambler
dow jee 導致 v.t occasion
dow joon 倒轉 n. reversal
dow joon 倒轉 v.t. reverse
dow kay 到期 n expiry
dow kow 豆蔻 n. cardamom
dow lee dow 到呢度 adv. hither
dow low 逗留 v.i. sojourn
dow low 逗留 n sojourn
dow low 逗留 n stay
dow may yoot 度蜜月 n. honeymoon
dow ngan 鍍銀 v.t. silver
dow ngar 渡鴉 n. raven
dow ngow see 鬥牛士 n . matador
dow oh 倒鈎 n. barb
dow peen 刀片 n. blade
dow see 導師 n. mentor
dow see geh 導師嘅 a. tutorial
dow seh 倒瀉 v.i. spill
dow tap 倒塌 v.i. topple
dow tat yan 糾察人 n. picket
dow teen 稻田 n. paddy
dow yan 盜印 v.t pirate
dow yeen 導演 n. director
dow ying 倒映 n. reflection
dow yung 盜用 v.t. appropriate
dowjoon 倒轉 v.t. invert
doy 袋 n. bag
doy 袋 v.t. pocket
doy bay 代幣 n. token
doy biew 代表 n behalf
doy biew 代表 n deligate1
doy biew 代表 v. t. embody
doy biew 代表 v.t. represent
doy biew 代表 n. representation
doy biew 代表 n. representative
doy biew sing 代表性 a. symbolic
doy biew toon 代表團 n delegation
doy biew toon 代表團 n deputation

doy ding geh 待定嘅 *a pending*

doy juy gow yeurng 代罪羔羊 *n. scapegoat*

doy lay 代理 *n. proxy*

doy lay chu 代理處 *n. agency*

doy ming tee 代名詞 *n. pronoun*

doy sing 代數 *n. algebra*

doy tay 代替 *a. alternative*

doy tay 代替 *n. lieu*

doy tay 代替 *v.t. replace*

doy tay 代替 *n. replacement*

doy tay 代替 *v.t. substitute*

doy tay 代替 *n. substitution*

doy tay ban 代替品 *n. alternative*

doy tay geh 代替嘅 *a. vicarious*

doy tay yan 代替人 *n. substitute*

duk 讀 *n. perusal*

duk 讀 *v.t. peruse*

duk 毒 *n. poison*

duk 毒 *v.t. poison*

duk 篤 *v.t. poke*

duk 篤 *n. poke*

duk 讀 *v.t. read*

duk bak 獨白 *n. monologue*

duk bak 獨白 *n. soliloquy*

duk ban 毒品 *n drug*

duk cheurng 獨唱 *n solo*

duk cheurng jeh 獨唱者 *n. soloist*

duk choy jeh 獨裁者 *n autocrat*

duk choy jeh 獨裁者 *n dictator*

duk choy jing ji 獨裁政治 *n autocracy*

duk chu 獨處 *n. solitude*

duk da 毒打 *v.t. lambaste*

duk dak geh 獨特嘅 *a. inimitable*

duk gar ging ying koon 獨家經營權 *n. monopoly*

duk jeem 獨佔 *v.t. monopolize*

duk jeh 讀者 *n. reader*

duk lap 獨立 *n. independence*

duk lap 獨立 *a. independent*

duk lap geh 獨立嘅 *a sovereign*

duk san 獨身 *n. celibacy*

duk san sang wut 獨身生活 *n. celibacy*

duk ser lang lik 讀寫能力 *n. literacy*

duk shu 讀書 *v.i. study*

duk sing 毒性 *n. virulence*

duk tak 獨特 *a. unique*

duk yik 毒液 *n. venom*

duk yow geh 獨有嘅 *a exclusive*

dum 揼 *v. t dispose*

dun 鈍 *a blunt*

dun 燉 *v.i. simmer*

dun 噸 *n. ton*

dun 噸 *n. tonne*

dun man ok 鈍吻鱷 *n alligator*

dung 凍 *a chilly*

dung 凍 *a cold*

dung 東 *n east*

dung 洞 *n. hollow*

dung fong 東方 *a eastern*

dung forng 東方 *n. orient*

dung forng geh 東方嘅 *a east*

dung forng geh 東方嘅 *a. oriental*

dung forng yan 東方人 *n oriental*

dung geet 凍結 *v.i. freeze*

dung gey 動機 *n. motive*

dung jok 動作 *n. action*

dung jok 動作 *n. movement*

dung mak 動脈 *n. artery*

dung mat 動物 *n. animal*

dung mat fan 動物糞 *n dung*

dung mat hok 動物學 *n. zoology*

dung mat hok ga 動物學家 *n. zoologist*

dung mat hok geh 動物學嘅 *a. zoological*

dung mat kwan 動物群 *n fauna*

dung mat yoon 動物園 *n. zoo*

dung mat yow jee 動物油脂 *n. tallow*

dung meen 冬眠 *n. hibernation*

dung ming tee 動名詞 *n. gerund*

dung tai 動態 *n. dynamics*
dung tan 動產 *n. movables*
dung tee 動詞 *n. verb*
dung tee been fa 動詞變化 *v.t. & i. conjugate*
dung teen 冬天 *n. winter*
dung ting 動聽 *a. melodious*
dung wah 動畫 *n animation*
dung wah 動畫 *n. cartoon*
dung yiew 動搖 *v.i. waver*
duy 堆 *v.t. pile*
duy 隊 *n. team*
duy 對 *prep. versus*
duy bay 對比 *v. t contrast*
duy bay lut 對比率 *n. ratio*
duy chay 對齊 *v.t. align*
duy doy 對待 *v.t. treat*
duy hm ju 對唔住 *a. sorry*
duy jat 對質 *n. confrontation*
duy jeurng 隊長 *n. captain*
duy jeurng jik way 隊長職位 *n. captaincy*
duy jiew 對照 *v.t. contrapose*
duy jiew 對照 *n contrast*
duy jik 堆積 *v.t heap*
duy jik geh 堆積嘅 *adv aheap*
duy ju 對住 *a. opposite*
duy kong 對抗 *v.t. antagonize*
duy korng 對抗 *n. hostility*
duy korng 對抗 *v.i. war*
duy lap 對立 *n. antithesis*
duy lap 對立 *n. opposition*
duy loon 對聯 *n. couplet*
duy meen 對面 *prep. across*
duy sow 對手 *n. adversary*
duy sow 對數 *n. logarithm*
duy ting 對稱 *n. symmetry*
duy ting ghe 對稱嘅 *a. symmetrical*
duy wah 對話 *n. parley*
duy wan yow hay 對韻遊戲 *n. crambo*
duy yeen jee piew 兌現支票 *v. t. cash*

duy ying 隊形 *n formation*
duy ying see mat 對應事物 *n. counterpart*

E

ex gwong X光 *n. x-ray*
ex gwong geem ta X光檢查 *v.t. x-ray*
ex gwong geh X光嘅 *a. x-ray*

F

fa 花 *n bloom*
fa choy 花彩 *n festoon*
fa fa gung jee 花花公子 *n dandy*
fa fay 花費 *v. t expend*
fa hap mat 化合物 *n compound*
fa jorng ban 化妝品 *n. cosmetic*
fa luy 花蕾 *n bud*
fa sek 化石 *n. fossil*
fai 快 *adv. apace*
fai 快 *adj brisk*
fai 快 *a express*
fai 快 *a fast*
fai 快 *adv fast*
fai 塊 *n. piece*
fai 快 *n quick*
fai 快 *a. rapid*
fai 快 *adv. speedily*
fai 快 *a. speedy*
fai bao hang 快步行 *v.i. trot*
fai chuk 快速 *v.i. zoom*
fai ding hm ju 快頂唔住 *a. moribund*
fai geh 快嘅 *adv. post*
fai geh 快嘅 *a. quick*
fai lok 快樂 *n. happiness*

fai pao 快跑 *v.i. sprint*
fai seem 快閃 *n dash*
fai wut 快活 *n. joviality*
fan 份 *n. allotment*
fan 煩 *v.t. annoy*
fan 反 *pref. anti*
fan 翻 *v. i. capsize*
fan 飯 *n dinner*
fan 分 *v. t divide*
fan 煩 *v.t. fret*
fan 煩 *v.t. frustrate*
fan 瞓 *v.i lie*
fan 分 *v.t. portion*
fan 粉 *n. powder*
fan 分 *v.t. proportion*
fan 反 *v.i. rebel*
fan 分 *v.t. segregate*
fan 分 *v.t. share*
fan 瞓 *v.i. slumber*
fan 分 *v.i. split*
fan 煩 *v.t. trouble*
fan 煩 *v.t. vex*
fan 煩 *v.t. irritate*
fan bay 分泌 *v.t. secrete*
fan bay 分泌 *n. secretion*
fan bay yik geh 分泌液嘅 *a. mucous*
fan been 糞便 *n. muck*
fan beet 分別 *v. i distinguish*
fan beet geh 分別嘅 *a. respective*
fan bo 帆布 *n. canvas*
fan bo 分佈 *n distribution*
fan bok 反駁 *v. t contradict*
fan bok 反駁 *v. t counter*
fan bok 反駁 *v. t disprove*
fan bok 反駁 *n. refutation*
fan bok 反駁 *v.t. refute*
fan bok 反駁 *n. rejoinder*
fan bwun 分半 *v.t. halve*
fan bwun geh 反叛嘅 *a. rebellious*
fan chor 犯錯 *v. i err*
fan dak...geh yan 瞓得…嘅人 *n. sleeper*

fan dan 反彈 *v.i. rebound*
fan dow 奮鬥 *v.i. strive*
fan dow yan 訓導人 *n. preceptor*
fan duy 反對 *prep. against*
fan duy 反對 *n disapproval*
fan duy 反對 *v. t disapprove*
fan duy 反對 *v.t. object*
fan duy 反對 *n. objection*
fan duy 反對 *v.t. oppose*
fan duy 反對 *v.i. protest*
fan duy jo 反對做 *a. averse*
fan fat 犯法 *a. illegal*
fan fat geh 犯法嘅 *a criminal*
fan fuk fu giew 反覆呼叫 *n chant*
fan fuk see hao 反覆思考 *v.t. mull*
fan gai 分解 *v. t. decompose*
fan gai 分解 *n. decomposition*
fan gam 反感 *n. antipathy*
fan gam 反感 *n. aversion*
fan gam 反感 *n dislike*
fan gam 反感 *n. odium*
fan gam 反感 *n. repugnance*
fan gam 反感 *n. repulsion*
fan gan 番梘 *n. soap*
fan gao 瞓覺 *v.i. sleep*
fan gao 瞓覺 *n. sleep*
fan gao 瞓覺 *n. slumber*
fan gao see gan 瞓覺時間 *n. bed-time*
fan got 分割 *v.t. partition*
fan got 分割 *v.t. segment*
fan gwong 反光 *a. reflective*
fan gwor sat 犯過失 *v.i. sin*
fan gwun 翻滾 *v.i. wallow*
fan heen duy 分遣隊 *n detachment*
fan heurng jee ging 焚香致敬 *v. t cense*
fan hm dow 分唔到 *a. indivisible*
fan hm hoy 分唔開 *a. inseparable*
fan hoy 分開 *adv. apart*
fan hoy 分開 *v. t detach*
fan hoy 分開 *v.t. part*
fan hoy 分開 *v.t. separate*

fan hoy 分開 *v.t. sunder*
fan hoy geh 分開嘅 *a. separate*
fan hung 反控 *n. countercharge*
fan hung ghe 粉紅嘅 *a. pinkish*
fan hung sik 粉紅色 *n. pink*
fan hung sik geh 粉紅色嘅 *a pink*
fan hung sik geh 粉紅色嘅 *a. roseate*
fan huy 返去 *v.t. rejoin*
fan jan 瞓陣 *n. doze*
fan jang 紛爭 *n discord*
fan jee 分子 *n. molecule*
fan jee 分子 *n. numerator*
fan jee 分枝 *n. offshoot*
fan jee geh 分子嘅 *a. molecular*
fan jee yik yeen 反之亦然 *adv. vice-versa*
fan jeurk 勳爵 *n. lord*
fan jik 繁殖 *n reproduction*
fan joon tow 返轉頭 *v.t. retrace*
fan jor gao 瞓咗覺 *adv. asleep*
fan jorng geh 粉狀嘅 *a. mealy*
fan jung 分鐘 *n. minute*
fan juy yan 犯罪人 *n. offender*
fan kap 分級 *v.t. rank*
fan kay 分歧 *n. clash*
fan kay 分歧 *n. disagreement*
fan keh 番茄 *n. tomato*
fan korng 反抗 *v. i mutiny*
fan korng 反抗 *v.t. resist*
fan korng 反抗 *v.i. revolt*
fan korng 反抗 *n. revolt*
fan korng lik 反抗力 *n. resistance*
fan koy 憤慨 *a. indignant*
fan koy 憤慨 *n. indignation*
fan kuy 分區 *n. partition*
fan lay 婚禮 *n. nuptials*
fan lay 返嚟 *v.i. return*
fan lay 分離 *n. separation*
fan lay 婚禮 *n. spousal*
fan lay 婚禮 *n. wedding*
fan lay geh 婚禮嘅 *a. nuptial*

fan leen 訓練 *v.t. train*
fan leen 訓練 *n. training*
fan lo 煩惱 *n. annoyance*
fan lo 煩惱 *n botheration*
fan lo 煩惱 *n. fret*
fan lo 煩惱 *n. frustration*
fan low 憤怒 *n. ire*
fan low 憤怒 *n. outrage*
fan low 煩惱 *n vexation*
fan low 粉瘤 *n. wen*
fan luy 分類 *v.t. assort*
fan luy 分類 *v. t classify*
fan man geh 反問嘅 *a. rhetorical*
fan may 昏迷 *n. coma*
fan meen 反面 *n. negation*
fan mow 繁茂 *n. luxuriance*
fan mow 墳墓 *n. sepulchre*
fan mow 墳墓 *n. sepulture*
fan ngan gao 瞓晏覺 *v.i. nap*
fan ngoy ting 婚外情 *n. affair*
fan puy 分配 *v.t. allocate*
fan puy 分配 *v.t. allot*
fan puy 分配 *v.t. apportion*
fan puy dow geh yeh 分配到嘅嘢 *n. allocation*
fan pwun jeh 反叛者 *n malcontent*
fan pwuy 分配 *v. t distribute*
fan san 分散 *v. t disperse*
fan san 翻新 *v.t. renovate*
fan san 翻新 *n. renovation*
fan san lun 泛神論 *n. pantheism*
fan san lun jeh 泛神論者 *n. pantheist*
fan say jat juk jeh 憤世嫉俗者 *n cynic*
fan seh hay 反射器 *n. reflector*
fan sek hok 糞石學 *n. coprology*
fan sek low 番石榴 *n. guava*
fan ser geh 反射嘅 *a reflexive*
fan she 反射 *v.t. mirror*
fan sik 分析 *v.t. analyse*

fan sik geet gwor 分析結果 *n. analysis*

fan sik geh 分析嘅 *a analytical*

fan sik yoon 分析員 *n analyst*

fan sing 反省 *v.i. introspect*

fan sing 反省 *n. introspection*

fan sing sam fan 分成三份 *n. triplication*

fan sow 反手 *n. backhand*

fan sow 分數 *n. score*

fan suy 粉碎 *v.t. shatter*

fan tao 翻抄 *v.t. retread*

fan tao 翻抄 *n. retread*

fan tee 粉刺 *n acne*

fan tee 粉刺 *n. pimple*

fan teen geh 婚前嘅 *a. premarital*

fan tow 墳頭 *n. grave*

fan tow dung mat 反芻動物 *n. ruminant*

fan tow geh 反芻嘅 *a. ruminant*

fan wah 反話 *n. irony*

fan wah 訓話 *v.t. moralize*

fan way 範圍 *n. span*

fan way geh 範圍嘅 *n. purview*

fan way say fan yat 分爲四份一 *v.t. quarter*

fan wing geh 繁榮嘅 *a. prosperous*

fan yan 煩人 *n bore*

fan yan 婚姻 *n. marriage*

fan yan 婚姻 *n. wedlock*

fan yan geh 婚姻嘅 *a. marital*

fan yan geh 婚姻嘅 *a. matrimonial*

fan yee cho 薰衣草 *n. lavender*

fan yee tee 反義詞 *n. antonym*

fan yik 翻譯 *v.t. interpret*

fan yik 翻譯 *n. interpreter*

fan yik 翻譯 *v.t. translate*

fan yik 翻譯 *n. translation*

fan yin 婚姻 *n. matrimony*

fan ying 反應 *v.i. react*

fan ying 反應 *n. reaction*

fan ying 反映 *v.t. reflect*

fan ying 反應 *n. reflex*

fan ying 反應 *n. repercussion*

fan ying geh 反應嘅 *a reflex*

far 花 *n flower*

far been 花邊 *n. lace*

far dor 花朵 *n blossom*

far fan 花瓣 *n. petal*

far fan 花粉 *n. pollen*

far gang 花梗 *n. stalk*

far geh 花嘅 *a flowery*

far gwun 花冠 *n anadem*

far hok 化學 *n. chemistry*

far hok ga 化學家 *n. chemist*

far hok geh 化學嘅 *a. chemical*

far hok mat ban 化學物品 *n. chemical*

far hoon 花圈 *n. wreath*

far jiew 花招 *n. trickery*

far mat 花蜜 *n. nectar*

far meng 化名 *n. alias*

far meng 化名 *adv. alias*

far meng 花名 *n. nickname*

far ngat jee 花押字 *n. monogram*

far san 化身 *n. incarnation*

far seurng 花商 *n florist*

far wan 花環 *n. garland*

far yeen hao yu geh 花言巧語嘅 *a slick*

far yeurng 花樣 *n. pattern*

far yoon 花園 *n. garden*

farn duy 反對 *v. t demur*

fat 罰 *v.t. punish*

fat 發 *v.t. whisk*

fat bo 發佈 *n release*

fat chut 發出 *v.t. omit*

fat chut for far 發出火花 *v.i. scintillate*

fat dat 發達 *v.i. prosper*

fat deen 發顛 *v.t dement*

fat deen gey 發電機 *n dynamo*

fat deen hay 發電器 *n. generator*

fat ding geh 法定嘅 *a. statutory*

fat ding yan sow 法定人數 *n. quorum*

fat dung 發動 *v.t. wage*

fat for 發火 *v.i. rage*

fat fwun 罰款 *n fine*

fat fwun 罰款 *v.t fine*

fat gam 罰金 *n forfeit*

fat gwat 發掘 *v.t. unearth*

fat gwok geh 法國嘅 *a. French*

fat gwok yan 法國人 *n French*

fat gwong 發光 *adv. aglow*

fat gwong 發光 *v.i. glow*

fat gworng 發光 *v.i. shine*

fat gworng geh 發光嘅 *a. lucent*

fat gworng geh 發光嘅 *a. luminous*

fat gwun 法官 *n. judge*

fat gwun 法官 *n. judiciary*

fat hang 發行 *v.t. launch*

fat hao 發酵 *v.t ferment*

fat hao 發酵 *n fermentation*

fat hay 發起 *v.t. initiate*

fat jok 發作 *n fit*

fat kow 發球 *n. serve*

fat lan yung 法蘭絨 *n flannel*

fat lang 發冷 *n ague*

fat leurk 忽略 *v.t. neglect*

fat leurk 忽略 *n neglect*

fat leurk 忽略 *v.t. overlook*

fat ling 法令 *n. ordinance*

fat ling 法令 *n. statute*

fat lonrg jat 珐瑯質 *n enamel*

fat low sow 發牢騷 *v.i. grumble*

fat low sow 發牢騷 *v.i. moan*

fat low sow 發牢騷 *v.t. murmur*

fat low sow 發牢騷 *v.i. mutter*

fat low sow 發牢騷 *v.i. whine*

fat lung lung seng 發隆隆聲 *v.i. rumble*

fat lut 法律 *n. law*

fat lut ga 法律家 *n. jurist*

fat lut hok 法律學 *n. jurisprudence*

fat ming 發明 *v.t devise*

fat ming 發明 *v.t. invent*

fat ming 發明 *n. invention*

fat ming ga 發明家 *n. inventor*

fat mow 發毛 *a. mouldy*

fat ngar 發芽 *v.i. germinate*

fat ngar 發芽 *v.i. sprout*

fat ngoy 發呆 *v.t. glaze*

fat oy 發呆 *n. trance*

fat pai 發牌 *v. i deal*

fat sai for 發晒火 *v.t. outrage*

fat sang 發生 *v.t. happen*

fat sang 發生 *v.i. occur*

fat say 發誓 *v.t. swear*

fat see 忽視 *n disregard*

fat see 忽視 *v.t. ignore*

fat see see seng 發嘶嘶聲 *v.i hiss*

fat seh 發射 *v.t fire*

fat seh 發射 *n. launch*

fat seh geh 發射嘅 *a projectile*

fat seh gey 發射機 *n. transmitter*

fat siew 發燒 *n fever*

fat siew yow 發燒友 *n. zealot*

fat sun ho 發信號 *v.t. signal*

fat ting 法庭 *n. court*

fat ting 法庭 *n. tribunal*

fat yam 發音 *v.t. pronounce*

fat yam 發音 *n. pronunciation*

fat yeem 發炎 *n. inflammation*

fat yeem 發炎 *a. inflammatory*

fat yeen 發現 *v. t discover*

fat yeen 發現 *n. discovery*

fat yeen koon 發言權 *n. say*

fat yeen yan 發言人 *n. spokesman*

fat yuk 發育 *n. growth*

fay 飛 *v.t flutter*

fay 飛 *v.i fly*

fay 肺 *n lung*

fay 飛 *v.t. sky*

fay ban 飛奔 *n. gallop*

fay biew 飛鏢 *n. dart*

fay borng 誹謗 *v. t. calumniate*

fay borng 誹謗 *n defamation*

fay borng 誹謗 *n. libel*

fay borng 誹謗 *v.t. malign*

fay borng 誹謗 *n. sycophancy*

fay bwun jing 肥胖症 *n. obesity*

fay chuk 飛速 *n breakneck*

fay chuy 廢除 *v.t abolish*

fay chuy 廢除 *v abolition*

fay chuy 廢除 *v. t. abrogate*

fay chuy 廢除 *v.t. annul*

fay chuy 廢除 *v.t. repeal*

fay chuy 廢除 *n repeal*

fay chuy 廢除 *n. revocation*

fay dai ghe 肥大嘅 *a. voluminous*

fay fan geh 非凡嘅 *a. phenomenal*

fay fan geh yan 非凡嘅人 *n. phenomenon*

fay fat geh 非法嘅 *a. illicit*

fay fat jow mai mai 非法做買賣 *v.i. traffic*

fay fat tam yap 非法侵入 *n. trespass*

fay geh 肥嘅 *a. stout*

fay gey 飛機 *n. aeroplane*

fay gey 飛機 *n. aircraft*

fay gey 飛機 *n. plane*

fay gey see 飛機師 *n. pilot*

fay huy 廢墟 *n. ruin*

fay jay 飛仔 *n. hooligan*

fay jeurng 徽章 *n. badge*

fay jeurng 徽章 *n crest*

fay lay fay huy 飛嚟飛去 *v.i. swarm*

fay liew 肥料 *n compost*

fay liew 肥料 *n fertilizer*

fay liew 肥料 *n. manure*

fay liew tung 廢料桶 *n skip*

fay lo 肺癆 *n. tuberculosis*

fay ngor 飛蛾 *n. moth*

fay see 費事 *conj. lest*

fay seurng 非常 *adv. highly*

fay seurng 非常 *a. very*

fay seurng go hing 非常高興 *a overjoyed*

fay seurng ho geh 非常好嘅 *a. splendid*

fay seurng jee 非常之 *pron. such*

fay seurng joon ging geh 非常尊敬嘅 *a. reverent*

fay seurng ok duk geh 非常惡毒嘅 *a. heinous*

fay sow 揮手 *v.t. wave*

fay wah 廢話 *n. nonsense*

fay wah 廢話 *n. prattle*

fay worng 輝煌 *n. refulgence*

fay worng geh 輝煌嘅 *a. resplendent*

fay yeem 肺炎 *n. pneumonia*

fay yu 鯡魚 *n. herring*

fay yuk 肥沃 *a fertile*

fei 肥 *a fat*

fey bong 誹謗 *v. asperse*

fey gey see 飛機師 *n. aviator*

fok loon 霍亂 *n. cholera*

fong dai 放大 *v.t. amplify*

fong fat 方法 *n. strategy*

fong meen 方面 *n. aspect*

fong sik 方式 *n. approach*

fong so 防守 *v. t defend*

fong ting sik 方程式 *n equation*

fong yeen 方言 *n dialect*

fong yu 防禦 *n defence*

for 貨 *n. cargo*

for 貨 *n. commodity*

for 火 *n fire*

for 貨 *n. freight*

for 火 *n. rage*

for bay 貨幣 *n currency*

for cher 火車 *n. train*

for cher 貨車 *n. van*

for cher tow 火車頭 *n. locomotive*

for cheurng 火槍 *n. musket*

for cheurng sow 火槍手 *n. musketeer*

for chorng 貨倉 *n depot*

for far 火化 *v. t cremate*

for far 火化 *n cremation*

for far 火花 *n. spark*

for gey 科技 n. technology
for gey 火雞 n. turkey
for gwong 火光 n flare
for hay 科系 n faculty
for hok 科學 n. science
for hok ga 科學家 n. scientist
for hok geh 科學嘅 a. scientific
for jeen 火箭 n. rocket
for koot 否決 v.t. veto
for low 火爐 n. furnace
for san 火山 n. volcano
for san geh 火山嘅 a. volcanic
for see lam 科林斯 n. Corinth
for sing 火星 n Mars
for tai 火柴 n match
for tan 貨攤 n. stand
for ting 課程 n. course
for ting 課程 n curriculum
for yeem 火焰 n blaze
for yeem 火焰 n flame
forng 放 v.t free
forng 放 v.t. release
forng 房 n. room
forng been 方便 n. convenience
forng been 方便 a convenient
forng been 方便 a. handy
forng dai 放大 v. t enlarge
forng dai 放大 v.t. magnify
forng dai geh 放大嘅 a. telescopic
forng day 放低 v. t deposit
forng deen 放電 v.i flirt
forng dong 放蕩 n debauch
forng dong 放蕩 n debauchery
forng dong 放蕩 a. licentious
forng dong geh yan 放蕩嘅人 n. libertine
forng dow juy dai 放到最大 v.t. maximize
forng fat 方法 n means
forng fat 方法 n. method
forng fu 防腐 v. t embalm
forng fu jay 防腐劑 n. antiseptic

forng fu jay 防腐劑 n. preservative
forng gway lay 放貴利 n. usury
forng hay 放棄 v.t, abdicate
forng hay 放棄 n abdication
forng hay 放棄 v.t forgo
forng hay 放棄 v.t. forswear
forng hay 放棄 v.t. relinquish
forng hay 放棄 v.t. waive
forng heurng 方向 n direction
forng hung 防空 a. anti-aircraft
forng ja dan geh yan 放炸彈嘅人 n bomber
forng jam 方針 n. policy
forng jee 防止 v. t. combat
forng jee 防止 v.t. prevent
forng jee 防止 v.t. ward
forng jik ban 紡織品 n textile
forng jik geh 紡織嘅 a. textile
forng jow 方舟 n ark
forng juk 放逐 v. t exile
forng lay 放餌 v.t. bait
forng lung 放膿 v.t. lance
forng man 訪問 v.t. interview
forng man 放慢 v.t. slacken
forng meen 方面 n facet
forng mo geh 荒謬嘅 a. grotesque
forng mow 荒謬 a absurd
forng mow 荒謬 n absurdity
forng mow geh 荒謬嘅 a. nonsensical
forng mow geh 荒謬嘅 a. ridiculous
forng muk 放牧 v.t. pasture
forng ngoy 防礙 n. hindrance
forng sa gung 紡紗工 n. spinner
forng sik 方式 n. mode
forng sung 放鬆 v.t. relax
forng sung 放鬆 n. relaxation
forng suy 防水 n waterproof
forng suy geh 防水嘅 a. waterproof
forng tow gan 方頭巾 n. kerchief
forng way 方位 n bearing

forng yap san am 放入神龕 v. t enshrine

forng yeh 荒野 n. moor

forng yeh 荒野 n. wilderness

forng ying 放映 v.t. project

forng ying geh ying jeurng 放映嘅影像 n. projection

forng ying gey 放映機 n bioscope

forng ying gey 放映機 n. projector

fow biew 浮標 n buoy

fow ju 浮住 adv. afloat

fow koot 否決 n. veto

fow lik 浮力 n buoyancy

fow ying 否認 v. t abnegate

fow ying 否認 n abnegation

fow ying 否認 n denial

fow ying 否認 v. t. deny

fu 苦 a bitter

fu 附 v. t enclose

fu 孵 v.i. incubate

fu 負 a minus

fu 褲 n. pl trousers

fu bai 腐敗 n. venality

fu bwun 副本 n duplicate

fu cho 府綢 n. poplin

fu dai geh 附帶嘅 a. subsidiary

fu dai tiew geen 附帶條件 a conditional

fu dam 負擔 v.t. afford

fu dam 負擔 v. t burden

fu dam gwor chung 負擔過重 v.t. overburden

fu dow for 輔導課 n. tutorial

fu ga 附加 v.t. append

fu ga fay 附加費 n. premium

fu ga fay 附加肥 n. surcharge

fu ga suy 附加稅 n. supertax

fu ga suy 附加稅 n. surtax

fu gan 附近 prep. near

fu gan 附近 adv. near

fu gan 附近 n. neighbourhood

fu gan geh 附近嘅 a. local

fu gar 附加 v.t. attach

fu geen 附件 n. appendage

fu geen 附件 n. attachment

fu geen 附件 n. enclosure

fu giew 呼叫 v.t. page

fu gor 副歌 n. chorus

fu gor 副歌 n refrain

fu gow 訃告 a. obituary

fu gung 苦功 n. peon

fu gung 苦工 n. toil

fu hap 符合 v.t. accord

fu hap 符合 v. i correspond

fu hap lor tap 合乎邏輯 a. logical

fu ho 負號 n minus

fu ho 符號 n. notation

fu hot 呼喝 v. i bellow

fu jai lang lik 付債能力 n. solvency

fu jak 負責 a. answerable

fu jak 負責 v.t. undertake

fu jor geh 輔助嘅 a. auxiliary

fu jor yan yoon 輔助人員 n. auxiliary

fu ju 副署 v. t. countersign

fu kap 呼吸 n. respiration

fu kap 呼吸 v.i. respire

fu lan 腐爛 adj carious

fu lan 腐爛 n. decay

fu lan 腐爛 v. i decay

fu lan 腐爛 n. rot

fu lan 腐爛 v.i. rot

fu lik 苦力 n coolie

fu lo 苦惱 n. anguish

fu lo 俘虜 n. captive

fu low 呼嚕 n. grunt

fu low seng 呼嚕聲 v.i. grunt

fu luk 附錄 n. appendix

fu meen 負面 n. negative

fu mor 撫摩 v. t. caress

fu mor 撫摸 v.t fondle

fu mow 父母 n. parent

fu mow geh 父母嘅 a. parental

fu mun 苦悶 v.t. agonize

fu pak ja yeurk 琥珀炸藥 n. amberite

fu sik 膚色 n complexion
fu sik sing 腐蝕性 a. caustic
fu sik sing geh 腐蝕性嘅 adj. corrosive
fu sow 副手 n deputy
fu suk 附屬 n. adjunct
fu suk 附屬 n. subordination
fu suk mat 附屬物 n appurtenance
fu tan ban 副產品 n by-product
fu tan geh 父親嘅 a. paternal
fu tay gan geh 夫妻間嘅 a conjugal
fu tee 副詞 n. adverb
fu tee geh 副詞嘅 a. adverbial
fu tow 斧頭 n. axe
fu tow 斧頭 n. hatchet
fu wun 呼喚 v.t. conjure
fu wun 呼喚 v.t. summon
fu yam 輔音 n. consonant
fu yeen 附言 n. postscript
fu yu 富裕 n. affluence
fu yu 富裕 n. wealth
fuk bo 腹部 n abdomen
fuk bo 腹部 n. midriff
fuk bo geh 腹部嘅 a. abdominal
fuk chung 服從 v. i comply
fuk chung 服從 n. obedience
fuk dak 伏特 n. volt
fuk dak 伏特 n. voltage
fuk dow 幅度 n. magnitude
fuk fat 復發 v.i. relapse
fuk gwun 腹管 n. cornicle
fuk hap tee 復合詞 n compound
fuk hing 復興 n. renaissance
fuk hing geh 復興嘅 a. resurgent
fuk jap 複雜 a complex
fuk jap 複雜 a. intricate
fuk jap 複雜 a. sophisticated
fuk jap 複雜 n. sophistication
fuk jap fa 複雜化 v. t complicate
fuk jap fa 複雜化 n. complication
fuk jap far 複雜化 v.t. sophisticate
fuk jay 複製 v. t copy

fuk jay 複製 v. t duplicate
fuk jay ban 複製品 n copy
fuk jay ban 複製品 n. replica
fuk jay ghe 複製嘅 a duplicate
fuk jiew 輻照 v.i. irradiate
fuk jik 復職 v.t. reinstate
fuk jik 復職 n. reinstatement
fuk jorng 服裝 n. apparel
fuk jorng 服裝 n. costume
fuk koy 覆蓋 v.t mantle
fuk koy tang 覆蓋層 n coating
fuk mo yoon 服務員 n. attendant
fuk mow 服務 n. service
fuk mow 服務 v.t service
fuk mow geh 服務嘅 a. ministrant
fuk mow yoon 服務員 n. steward
fuk see 服侍 v.i. minister
fuk seurng bo 腹上部 n anticardium
fuk she 輻射 n. radiation
fuk sow 複數 a. plural
fuk sow 複數 n. plurality
fuk sow 復蘇 n. revival
fuk sow 復蘇 v.i. revive
fuk wut jeet 復活節 n easter
fuk yam 福音 n. gospel
fuk yan 複印 v. t cyclostyle
fuk yan 複印 n print
fuk yan 複印 v.t. xerox
fuk yan gey 復印機 n cyclostyle
fuk yeen 復現 n. resurgence
fuk yoon 復原 n. rehabilitation
fuk yoon 復原 n. restoration
fun gan 附近 n. vicinity
fung 封 v.t. seal
fung 風 n. wind
fung chee hey kek fung 諷刺喜劇風 adj aristophanic
fung chuk gey 風速計 n anemometer
fung dek 風笛 n. bagpipe
fung dow 蜂竇 n alveary
fung dow 峰竇 n. beehive
fung forng 蜂房 n. hive

fung fu 豐富 *a. richness*
fung gak 風格 *n. look*
fung gak 風格 *n mould*
fung gak 風格 *n. style*
fung geen 封建 *a feudal*
fung ging 風景 *n. landscape*
fung ging 風景 *n. scenery*
fung ging 風景 *n. view*
fung ging yow may geh 風景優美嘅 *a. scenic*
fung gow jing 瘋狗症 *n. rabies*
fung hay 風氣 *n. stampede*
fung hee, 風險 *n. risk*
fung heen 奉獻 *v. t. dedicate*
fung heen 奉獻 *n dedication*
fung ho 風口 *n. vent*
fung ju 封住 *v.t bar*
fung ju 封住 *v.i. stem*
fung kam 風琴 *n. harmonium*
fung kwong 瘋狂 *a. frantic*
fung low wan see 風流韻事 *n. romp*
fung mat jow 蜂蜜酒 *n. mead*
fung may 風味 *n. cuisine*
fung meen 封面 *n. cover*
fung mun dow 豐滿度 *n. fullness*
fung mun geh 豐滿嘅 *a. voluptuous*
fung sap 風濕 *n. rheumatism*
fung sap beng geh 風濕病嘅 *a. rheumatic*
fung seen 風扇 *n fan*
fung sing 奉承 *n adulation*
fung sing 奉承 *n flattery*
fung sing 豐盛 *a. luxuriant*
fung sor 封鎖 *n blockade*
fung tao 蜂巢 *n. honeycomb*
fung tee 諷刺 *a. ironical*
fung tee 諷刺 *v.t. lampoon*
fung tee 諷刺 *n. sarcasm*
fung tee 諷刺 *n. satire*
fung tee 諷刺 *v.t. satirize*
fung tee 諷刺 *a. wry*
fung tee geh 諷刺嘅 *a. sarcastic*

fung tee geh 諷刺嘅 *a. satirical*
fung tee jok ga 諷刺作家 *n. satirist*
fung tee man jeurng 諷刺文章 *n. lampoon*
fung tee wah 諷刺畫 *n. caricature*
fung ter 風車 *n. windmill*
fung way gway juk 封爲貴族 *v. t. ennoble*
fung...way jeurk see 封...爲爵士 *v.t. knight*
fut fut 狒狒 *n. baboon*
fut lung 弗隆 *n. furlong*
fuy 灰 *n. ash*
fwun dai 寬大 *n. lenience, leniency*
fwun dai 寬大 *n. magnanimity*
fwun dai geh 寬大嘅 *a. merciful*
fwun doy 款待 *n treat*
fwun fu 歡呼 *n acclamation*
fwun fu seng 歡呼聲 *n. cheer*
fwun horng 款項 *n. payment*
fwun kworng 歡狂 *n. spree*
fwun lok 歡樂 *n. frolic*
fwun lok 歡樂 *n. jollity*
fwun lok 歡樂 *n. merriment*
fwun shu 寬恕 *n. condonation*
fwun shu 寬恕 *n. mercy*
fwun siew 歡笑 *n. mirth*
fwun tang 歡騰 *n. jubilation*
fwun teen hay day 歡天喜地 *n. rapture*
fwun torng 寬敞 *a. capacious*
fwun torng 寬敞 *a. spacious*
fwun torng geh 寬敞嘅 *a. roomy*
fwun wang 寬宏 *a. magnanimous*
fwun wang dai leurng 寬宏大量 *n. generosity*
fwun ying 歡迎 *a. welcome*
fwun ying 歡迎 *n welcome*
fwun ying 歡迎 *v.t welcome*
fwun yung 寬容 *a. lenient*
fwut 闊 *a broad*
fwut 闊 *a. wide*

fwut 闊 *adv. wide*
fwut dow 闊度 *n breadth*
fwut dow 闊度 *n. width*
fwut ngoy pow 闊外袍 *n. toga*
fwuy fuk 恢復 *v.t. recover*
fwuy fuk 恢復 *n. recovery*
fwuy fuk 恢復 *v.t. rehabilitate*
fwuy fuk 恢復 *v.t. restore*
fwuy fuk 恢復 *n. resumption*
fwuy fuk ting chun 恢復青春 *n. rejuvenation*
fwuy hai doon see 詼諧短詩 *n epigram*
fwuy lay 灰泥 *v.t. mortar*
fwuy ling 奎寧 *n. quinine*
fwuy sam 灰心 *v. t deject*
fwuy sik geh 灰色嘅 *a. grey*

G

ga 加 *v.t. add*
ga 嫁 *v.t. marry*
ga 架 *n. rack*
ga 架 *n. shelf*
ga ban 假扮 *v.t. pretend*
ga biew deem fu ho 加標點符號 *v.t. punctuate*
ga cheet 假設 *v.t. assume*
ga cheet 假設 *n. assumption*
ga cheurng 加長 *v.t. lengthen*
ga chuk 加速 *v.t accelerate*
ga chuk 加速 *n acceleration*
ga chuk 加速 *v.i. speed*
ga deen 加墊 *v.t. pad*
ga deng 加釘 *v.t. stud*
ga fan 加粉 *v.t. powder*
ga fat 假髮 *n. wig*
ga feh 咖啡 *n coffee*
ga feh deem 咖啡店 *n. cafe*

ga ga seng siew 嘎嘎聲笑 *v. i cackle*
ga gak tung jeurng 價格通脹 *n. inflation*
ga geh 假嘅 *a sham*
ga heurng liew 加香料 *v.t. spice*
ga ho joot 加後綴 *v.t. suffix*
ga hoy 加害 *v.t. inflict*
ga huy 嘉許 *n commendation*
ga iew may liew 加調味料 *v.t. season*
ga jee seng 嘎吱聲 *v. i creak*
ga jee seng 嘎吱聲 *n creak*
ga jeh 家姐 *n. sister*
ga jeurng 假象 *n. pretence*
ga jeurng 假象 *n. semblance*
ga jeurng 假象 *n sham*
ga jik 價值 *n. value*
ga kam 家禽 *n. fowl*
ga kam yuk 家禽肉 *n. poultry*
ga kay 假期 *n. vacation*
ga keurng 加強 *v. t. cement*
ga keurng 加強 *v. t. consolidate*
ga keurng 加強 *v.t. intensify*
ga keurng 加強 *v.t. reinforce*
ga keurng 加強 *v.t. strengthen*
ga lun 加侖 *n. gallon*
ga meen 加冕 *v. t crown*
ga meen deen lay 加冕典禮 *n coronation*
ga mow hang peen 假冒行騙 *n. imposture*
ga pwuy 加倍 *v. t. double*
ga pwuy 加倍 *v.t. redouble*
ga san man 假新聞 *n canard*
ga say chorng 駕駛艙 *n. cock-pit*
ga say jeh 駕駛者 *n. motorist*
ga see 家私 *n. furniture*
ga seurng 加上 *n. addition*
ga seurng 加上 *a. additional*
ga sik 假釋 *n. parole*
ga sik 假釋 *v.t. parole*
ga tang 加層 *v.t. line*
ga teen 價錢 *n. price*

ga teet 假設 *n. hypothesis*
ga teet 假設 *a. hypothetical*
ga teet 假設 *n. presumption*
ga teet 假設 *n. presupposition*
ga tiew man 加條紋 *v.t. stripe*
ga ting luy gao see 家庭女教師 *n. governess*
ga torng 加糖 *v.t. sugar*
ga tow 加圖 *v.t. illustrate*
ga wu jiew fan 加胡椒粉 *v.t. pepper*
ga yap 加入 *v.t. incorporate*
ga yat jee larm 假日指南 *n brochure*
ga yeem 加鹽 *v.t salt*
ga yeet 加熱 *v.t heat*
ga yoon sik 加緣飾 *v.t fringe*
gah jik 價值 *n. worth*
gai 戒 *v.i. abstain*
gai 鉬 *v.t groove*
gai 鉬 *v.t. lacerate*
gai 鉬 *v.t. slit*
gai 街 *n. street*
gai chuy 解除 *v.t absolve*
gai doon 階段 *n. gradation*
gai doon 階段 *n. phase*
gai dung 解凍 *v.i thaw*
gai fo hook 解剖學 *n. anatomy*
gai forng 解放 *n. emancipation*
gai forng 解放 *v.t. liberate*
gai forng 解放 *n. liberation*
gai forng 解放 *n. manumission*
gai forng jeh 解放者 *n. liberator*
gai forng low day 解放奴隸 *v.t. manumit*
gai fow 解剖 *v.t dissect*
gai fow 解剖 *n dissection*
gai gu 解雇 *n dismissal*
gai hot 解渴 *v.t. slake*
gai hoy 解開 *v.t. solve*
gai hoy 解開 *v.t. undo*
gai jee 戒指 *n. ring*
gai koot 解決 *v.t. resolve*
gai koot 解決 *v.i. settle*

gai koot ban fat 解決辦法 *n. solution*
gai lai 戒奶 *v.t ablactate*
gai lai 戒奶 *n ablactation*
gai lai 戒奶 *v.t. wean*
gai mwut 芥末 *n. mustard*
gai san 解散 *v.t. dismiss*
gai see 街市 *n market*
gai seen 界線 *n. demarcation*
gai seen 疥癬 *n. scabies*
gai siew 介紹 *v.t. introduce*
gai siew 介紹 *n. introduction*
gai sik 解釋 *v.t define*
gai sik 解釋 *n definition*
gai sik 解釋 *v.t. explain*
gai sik 解釋 *n explanation*
gai sik 解釋 *n. paraphrase*
gai sik 解釋 *v.t. paraphrase*
gai tee 介詞 *n. preposition*
gai toot 解脫 *n. relief*
gai yap 介入 *v.i. intervene*
gai yap 介入 *n. intervention*
gai yee 介意 *v.t. mind*
gai yeurk 解藥 *n. antidote*
gai yeurk 解藥 *n. mithridate*
gak 鎘 *n cadmium*
gak dow 格鬥 *n. grapple*
gak gak siew 格格笑 *v.i. giggle*
gak gor yoot geh 隔個月嘅 *adj. bimonthly*
gak hoy 隔開 *v.t. space*
gak jay muk ga 格仔木架 *n. lattice*
gak joot 隔絕 *n. isolation*
gak lay 隔籬 *a. adjacent*
gak lay 隔籬 *n. insulation*
gak lay 隔籬 *v.t. isolate*
gak lay 隔籬 *a. next*
gak lay 隔籬 *v.t. seclude*
gak lay 隔籬 *v.t. sequester*
gak lay cho see 隔離措施 *n. segregation*

gak lay lun she 隔籬鄰舍 *n.* *neighbour*

gak lut geh 格律嘅 *a. metrical*

gak ming 革命 *n. revolution*

gak sik 格式 *n format*

gak yeen 格言 *n. adage*

gak yeen 格言 *n aphorism*

gak yeen 格言 *n dictum*

gak yeen 格言 *n. maxim*

gak yeen 格言 *n. motto*

gak yeen 格言 *n. proverb*

gak yeet 隔熱 *v.t. insulate*

gam 金 *n. gold*

gam *v.t. press*

gam 咁 *adv. that*

gam biew choy 錦標賽 *n. tournament*

gam doon 錦緞 *n brocade*

gam dow bat on 感到不安 *v.t. perturb*

gam dow ging kay 感到驚奇 *v.i marvel*

gam duk 監督 *v.t. oversee*

gam duk 監督 *n. superintendence*

gam duk 監督 *v.t. supervise*

gam duk 監督 *n. supervision*

gam far yoon 感化院 *n. reformatory*

gam fay 減肥 *v.i. slim*

gam gai 尷尬 *a. awkward*

gam gai 尷尬 *v. t embarrass*

gam gey 禁忌 *n. taboo*

gam gey 禁忌 *a taboo*

gam gik 感激 *n. appreciation*

gam gik 感激 *a. grateful*

gam gik 感激 *n. gratitude*

gam gik 感激 *a. indebted*

gam gok 感覺 *n feeling*

gam gok 感覺 *n. sensation*

gam gok dow 感覺到 *a. appreciable*

gam gok dow 感覺到 *v.t. sense*

gam gok geh 感覺嘅 *a. sensuous*

gam gok sing 感覺性 *n. sentience*

gam gung 監工 *n. overseer*

gam gwun geh 感官嘅 *a. sensual*

gam gwun yan 監管人 *n. superintendent*

gam hao 監考 *v.t. invigilate*

gam hao 監考 *n. invigilation*

gam hao gwun 監考官 *n. invigilator*

gam heng 減輕 *v.t. alleviate*

gam heng 減輕 *n. alleviation*

gam huy 敢去 *v.t. venture*

gam jay ling 禁制令 *n. injunction*

gam jay ling 禁制令 *n. prohibition*

gam jee 禁止 *n. ban*

gam jee 禁止 *v. t. debar*

gam jee 禁止 *v.t forbid*

gam jee 禁止 *v.t. prohibit*

gam jee 禁止 *v.t. taboo*

gam jee geh 禁止嘅 *a. prohibitive*

gam jee geh 禁止嘅 *a. prohibitory*

gam jee tap 金字塔 *n. pyramid*

gam jeh 感謝 *a. thankful*

gam jeurng 金匠 *n. goldsmith*

gam lam 橄欖 *n. olive*

gam ling 禁令 *n ban*

gam man 今晚 *n. tonight*

gam man 今晚 *adv. tonight*

gam may geh 甘美嘅 *a. mellow*

gam mo 感冒 *n cold*

gam see 監視 *v.i. spy*

gam see 監視 *n. surveillance*

gam sik geh 金色嘅 *a. golden*

gam suk 金屬 *n. metal*

gam suk geh 金屬嘅 *a. metallic*

gam suk see 金屬絲 *n. tinsel*

gam tan tee 感歎詞 *n exclamation*

gam tan tee 感歎詞 *n. interjection*

gam tat geh 監察嘅 *a. monitory*

gam teen geh 金錢嘅 *a. pecuniary*

gam ting 感情 *n. affection*

gam ting 感情 *n emotion*

gam ting fung fu 感情豐富 *a emotional*

gam ting yung see geh 感情用事嘅 *a.* sentimental

gam wu 監護 *n.* wardship

gam yat 今日 *adv.* today

gam yat 今日 *n.* today

gam yeem 感染 *n.* infection

gam yeem jor geh 感染咗嘅 *a.* septic

gam yeem lik 感染力 *n.* pathos

gam yow 甘油 *n.* glycerine

gam yuk 禁慾 *n.* ascetic

gam yuk 禁慾 *a.* ascetic

gam yuk 監獄 *n.* nick

gam yuk 監獄 *n.* prison

gam yung ga 金融家 *n financier*

gan 鹼 *n alkali*

gan 揀 *v. t.* choose

gan 揀 *v.i.* opt

gan 揀 *v.t.* pick

gan 根 *n.* root

gan 揀 *v.t.* select

gan 緊 *a.* tight

gan ban 跟班 *n.* lackey

gan dan 簡單 *a.* brief

gan dan 簡單 *a.* simple

gan dan 簡單 *n.* simplicity

gan dan geh 簡單嘅 *a.* plain

gan deep 間諜 *n.* spy

gan doon yee mo lay 簡短而無禮 *a* curt

gan far 簡化 *n.* simplification

gan far 簡化 *v.t.* simplify

gan gai 簡介 *n.* profile

gan gai 簡介 *n.* prospsectus

gan gak 間隔 *n.* compartment

gan gak 間隔 *n.* interval

gan gak see gan 間隔時間 *n lapse*

gan gan 僅僅 *adv.* barely

gan gan 僅僅 *a.* mere

gan gao gwan tow 緊急關頭 *n.* conjuncture

gan gap 緊急 *n emergency*

gan gap 緊急 *a.* urgent

gan geet 簡潔 *n brevity*

gan geet 簡潔 *a concise*

gan geet geh 簡潔嘅 *a.* laconic

gan geh 奸嘅 *a.* treacherous

gan gey 根基 *n.* base

gan hm jung 間唔中 *a.* occasional

gan ja hang way 奸詐行爲 *n* duplicity

gan jeep 間接 *a.* indirect

gan jeurng 緊張 *a.* intense

gan jeurng 緊張 *a.* nervous

gan jeurng 緊張 *a.* tense

gan jeurng 緊張 *n.* tension

gan ju 跟住 *v.t follow*

gan ju 跟住 *adv.* next

gan ju 跟住 *adv.* then

gan jung 跟蹤 *v.i.* stalk

gan jung 跟蹤 *v.t.* trace

gan kap 分級 *v.t grade*

gan keet 間歇 *n.* interim

gan keet 間歇 *n.* interlude

gan keet 間歇 *n.* lull

gan lan 艱難 *n.* hardship

gan lan 艱難 *n.* thick

gan lan 艱難 *a.* tough

gan leurk 簡略 *a crude*

gan lik 簡歷 *n.* resume

gan pai 近排 *a.* recent

gan pai 近排 *adv.* recently

gan pay lik jun 筋疲力盡 *v. t.* exhaust

gan san 謹慎 *a.* cautious

gan san 謹慎 *n discretion*

gan san 謹慎 *a.* wary

gan san geh 謹慎嘅 *a.* prudential

gan see 近視 *n.* myopia

gan see geh 近視嘅 *a.* myopic

gan seurng 奸商 *n.* profiteer

gan suk 緊縮 *n.* stringency

gan tek 間尺 *n.* ruler

gan ting 簡稱 *v.t.* abbreviate

gan ting 簡稱 *n abbreviation*
gan yiew 緊要 *v.i. matter*
gan yiew geh 簡要嘅 *a. terse*
gang 耕 *v. t cultivate*
gang 耕 *v.i plough*
gang 耕 *v.t. till*
gang dor 更多 *a. more*
gang dor 更多 *adv more*
gang ga 更加 *adv much*
gang goy 更改 *v. t correct*
gang goy 更改 *n. modification*
gang ho 更好 *adv. better*
gang jun yat bo 更進一步 *a further*
gang leen kay 更年期 *n. menopause*
gang san 更新 *v.t. renew*
gang san 更新 *n. renewal*
gang shu sik 更舒適 *n. cosier*
gang siew 更少 *a. lesser*
gang yoon 更遠 *adv. beyond*
gang yoon geh 更遠嘅 *adv. further*
gao 攪 *v. t. & i. churn*
gao 教 *v. t educate*
gao 攪 *v.i. stir*
gao 交 *v.t. submit*
gao 教 *v.t. teach*
gao bay 交畀 *v.t. consign*
gao cher 絞車 *n. winch*
gao chor 搞錯 *v.t. mistake*
gao deem 搞掂 *v.t. accomplish*
gao deem 交點 *n. intersection*
gao deem jor 搞掂咗 *a accomplished*
gao fwuy 教誨 *a didactic*
gao gey 攪機 *n whisk*
gao gway geh 搞鬼嘅 *a. mischievous*
gao heurng kuk 交響曲 *n. symphony*
gao ho 較好 *a better*
gao hok dai gorng 教學大綱 *n. syllabus*
gao jay ban 救濟品 *n. alms*
gao jeen 交戰 *n belligerency*
gao jeen 鉸剪 *n. scissors*
gao jeen gwok 交戰國 *n belligerent*

gao jung 教宗 *n. pope*
gao jung geh 教宗嘅 *a. papal*
gao jung geh jik way 教宗嘅職位 *n. papacy*
gao kuy 教區 *n. parish*
gao kuy 郊區 *n. suburb*
gao kuy geh 郊區嘅 *a. suburban*
gao leen 教練 *n. instructor*
gao loon 搞亂 *v.t. muddle*
gao lorng jorng 膠囊狀 *adj capsular*
gao low 交流 *n. intercourse*
gao pai geh 教派嘅 *a. sectarian*
gao pwuy 交配 *v.i. copulate*
gao pwuy 交配 *v.t. mate*
gao pwuy fan jik 交配繁殖 *v.t breed*
gao sang 搞生 *v. t. enliven*
gao see 教師 *n. pedagogue*
gao see 教師 *n. tutor*
gao siew 搞笑 *n. funny*
gao sing jeurng 攪成漿 *v.t. pulp*
gao sor fan 教唆犯 *ns. barrator*
gao sow 教授 *n. professor*
gao suk gam 交贖金 *v.t. ransom*
gao suy 膠水 *n. adhesive*
gao suy 膠水 *n. glue*
gao suy 絞碎 *v.t. mince*
gao suy 膠水 *n. mucilage*
gao ta 較差 *a. inferior*
gao ta 交叉 *v.t. intersect*
gao ta low ho 交叉路口 *n. junction*
gao tiew 教條 *n dogma*
gao tong 教堂 *n. church*
gao tong mo day 教堂墓地 *n. churchyard*
gao tubg gung guy 交通工具 *n. vehicle*
gao tung 交通 *n. traffic*
gao tung gung guy 交通工具 *n. transport*
gao tung gung guy 交通工具 *n. transportation*
gao wat 狡猾 *a crafty*

gao wat 狡猾 *n cunning*
gao wat 狡猾 *n. knavery*
gao wat 狡猾 *a. sly*
gao wat geh 狡猾嘅 *a cunning*
gao wat geh 狡猾嘅 *a. wily*
gao wat geh luy jay 狡猾嘅女仔 *n. minx*
gao wu cher 救護車 *n. ambulance*
gao wun 交換 *n. barter2*
gao wun 交換 *n exchange*
gao wun 交換 *v. t exchange*
gao wun 交換 *n. interchange*
gao wun 交換 *v. interchange*
gao yik 交易 *n deal*
gao yik 交易 *v.i trade*
gao yik 交易 *n. transaction*
gao ying ga 絞刑架 *n. . gallows*
gao yow 郊遊 *n. outing*
gao yu gey 攪乳機 *n. churn*
gao yuk 教育 *n education*
gao yuk hok 教育學 *n. pedagogy*
gap 急 *a desperate*
gap 鴿 *n dove*
gap 急 *v.t. jabber*
gap 鉀 *n. potassium*
gap ban 甲板 *n deck*
gap chung 甲蟲 *n beetle*
gap geh 急嘅 *a. imperative*
gap ju 急住 *n hurry*
gap low 急流 *n. torrent*
gap low tang 夾樓層 *n. mezzanine*
gap see 急事 *n. urgency*
gap sing 急升 *v.i. soar*
gap tiew 急跳 *v.i. palpitate*
gar 假 *a false*
gar ban 假扮 *v. t disguise*
gar ban 嘉賓 *n. guest*
gar ban 加班 *adv. overtime*
gar ban 加班 *n overtime*
gar chuk 加速 *v. t. expedite*
gar deem 加點 *v. t dot*
gar gak 價格 *n. cost*

gar geh 假嘅 *a bogus*
gar gung jay see 假公濟私 *n. jobbery*
gar jorng 嫁妝 *n dowry*
gar ting geh 家庭嘅 *a domestic*
garm 減 *v.t. reduce*
garm 減 *v.t. subtract*
garm 減 *n. subtraction*
garm 減 *n. reduction*
garm chuy 減除 *prep. minus*
garm day 減低 *v.t. abate*
garm day 減低 *n. abatement*
garm ga 減價 *n. sale*
garm gam 監禁 *n. confinement*
garm gum 監禁 *n. captivity*
garm hao gwun 監考官 *n. proctor*
garm heng 減輕 *v.t. allay*
garm heng 減輕 *v.t. assuage*
garm heng 減輕 *v.i. lighten*
garm heng 減輕 *v.t. mitigate*
garm heng 減輕 *n. mitigation*
garm heng 減輕 *v.t. relieve*
garm heng 減輕 *v.t. soothe*
garm low 監牢 *n. jail*
garm siew 減少 *v. t decrease*
garm siew 減少 *v. t dwindle*
garm wu koon 監護權 *v custody*
garm wu yan 監護人 *n custodian*
garm yeurk 減弱 *v.i. recede*
garm yeurk 減弱 *v.i. subside*
garm ying 減刑 *v. t commute*
garn lan 艱難 *a. arduous*
garn siew 減少 *v. t diminish*
gat 拮 *v.t. jab*
gat 拮 *v.t. prick*
gat cheurng mat 吉祥物 *n. mascot*
gat choon 拮穿 *v.t. puncture*
gat jat 甲由 *n cockroach*
gat jee jeurng 橘子醬 *n. marmalade*
gat lay geh 吉利嘅 *a. auspicious*
geem 劍 *n. sword*
geem cha 檢查 *v. t. check*

geem cha 檢查 n check
geem cha 檢查 v. t examine
geem ta 檢查 n. inspection
geem ta 檢查 v.t. screen
geem tat gwun 檢察官 n. inspector
geem tat gwun 檢察官 n. prosecutor
geem yu hay 檢乳器 n. lactometer
geen 見 v.t. meet
geen ding geh 堅定嘅 a. spirited
geen ding geh 堅定嘅 a. staunch
geen ding geh 堅定嘅 a. steadfast
geen dow 見到 v.t. sight
geen dow 見到 v.t. spot
geen dow geh 見到嘅 a. visible
geen gai 見解 n. outlook
geen horng 健康 a fit
geen horng 健康 n. health
geen horng 健康 a. healthy
geen horng 健康 a. well
geen jap sang 見習生 n. probationer
geen juk 建築 n building
geen juk hok 建築學 n. architecture
geen juk kwan 建築群 n complex
geen juk see 建築師 n. architect
geen keurng 堅強 n. stoic
geen keurng geh 堅強嘅 a forceful
geen koot 堅決 a. adamant
geen koot 堅決 n. adamant
geen koot 堅決 a. insistent
geen koot geh 堅決嘅 a. resolute
geen lap 建立 n erection
geen lay morng yee 見利忘義 a. venal
geen ngay bat wat 堅毅不屈 a. indomitable
geen tam 健談 a. talkative
geen tee 堅持 v.t. insist
geen tee 堅持 n. insistence
geen tee 堅持 v.i. persevere
geen tee 堅持 n. persistence
geen tee 堅持 v.i. soldier
geen tee geh 堅持嘅 a. tenacious

geen tee geh yan 堅持嘅人 n. stickler
geen yee 建議 n. counsel
geep 夾 n. peg
geep hay jung gan 夾喺中間 v.t. sandwich
geep ju 夾住 v.t. peg
geep keem 夾鉗 n clamp
geet 結 n. knot
geet cheurng 結腸 n colon
geet chuk 結束 v. t conclude
geet chuk 結束 v. t end
geet chut 傑出 n. pre-eminence
geet chut geh 傑出嘅 a. pre-eminent
geet chut geh 傑出嘅 a. transcendent
geet fan 結婚 v.t. wed
geet fan teen geh 結婚前嘅 adj. antenuptial
geet guk 結局 n finish
geet gwor 結果 n. outcome
geet gwor 結果 n. upshot
geet hap 結合 v. t combine
geet hap 結合 adj. conjunct
geet hap 結合 v.t. fuse
geet hap 結合 n. fusion
geet jok 傑作 n. masterpiece
geet kow 結構 n construction
geet kow 結構 n. structure
geet kow geh 結構嘅 a. structural
geet lun 結論 n. conclusion
geet lun 結論 n. inference
geet mang 結盟 v.t. ally
geet mok 結膜 n. conjunctiva
geet sat 結實 a firm
geet ta 結他 n. guitar
geh ha meen 嘅下面 a. nether
geh jee teen 嘅之前 a. prior
geng 驚 a. afraid
geng 驚 a dread
geng 驚 v.i fear
geng 驚 a. fearful
geng 鏡 n mirror

geng 頸 *n. neck*
geng gan 頸巾 *n. muffler*
geng gan 頸巾 *n. scarf*
geng leen 頸鏈 *n. necklace*
geng leen 頸鏈 *n. necklet*
geng peen 鏡片 *n. lens*
geng tow 鏡頭 *n. scene*
geurk 腳 *n. leg*
geurng 姜 *n. ginger*
geurng ang 僵硬 *n. stiff*
geurng far 僵化 *v.t. ossify*
geurng guk 僵局 *n deadlock*
geurng guk 僵局 *n. stalemate*
geurng worng gan fan 薑黃根粉 *n. turmeric*
geurt 腳 *n foot*
geurt bo 腳步 *n. step*
geurt jang 腳踭 *n. heel*
geurt jee 腳趾 *n. toe*
geurt leen 腳鍊 *n anklet*
geurt ngan 腳踝 *n. ankle*
gey 計 *v. t. calculate*
gey 雞 *n. chicken*
gey 寄 *v.t. mail*
gey 寄 *v.t. post*
gey 幾 *adv. pretty*
gey 幾 *adv. quite*
gey 幾 *adv. rather*
gey 寄 *v.t. send*
gey 薊 *n. thistle*
gey 計 *v.t. total*
gey bun geh 基本嘅… *a elementary*
gey bwun 基本 *a. basic*
gey bwun geh 基本嘅 *a. fundamental*
gey bwun geh 基本嘅 *a. rudimentary*
gey bwun geh 基本嘅 *a staple*
gey bwun seurng 基本上 *adv. substantially*
gey cheurng 機場 *n aerodrome*
gey cheurng 幾長 *a. lengthy*
gey cheurng 機場 *n terminal*
gey chor 基礎 *adj. basal*

gey chor 基礎 *n. basis*
gey chor 基礎 *n. foundation*
gey chor 基礎 *n. rudiment*
gey dai geh 幾大嘅 *a. sizable*
gey dak 記得 *v.t. recollect*
gey dak 記得 *v.t. remember*
gey dan 雞蛋 *n egg*
gey dor 幾多 *a much*
gey duk gao 基督教 *n. Christianity*
gey duk gao tow 基督教徒 *n. Christendom*
gey duk tow 基督徒 *n Christian*
gey duk tow 基督徒 *a. Christian*
gey forng 飢荒 *n famine*
gey fu mow 幾乎無 *adv. hardly*
gey gan 雞姦 *n. sodomy*
gey gor 幾個 *a few*
gey gor 幾個 *a several*
gey gow 機構 *n. institute*
gey gow 機構 *n. institution*
gey hai geh 機械嘅 *a mechanic*
gey hai geh 機械嘅 *a. mechanical*
gey hai hok 機械學 *n. mechanics*
gey hai jorng jee 機械裝置 *n. mechanism*
gey hai see 機械師 *n. mechanic*
gey hai yan 機械人 *n. robot*
gey hao 技巧 *n. technique*
gey hm dow geh 計唔到嘅 *a. incalculable*
gey ho 記號 *n. marker*
gey hor hok 幾何學 *n. geometry*
gey hor hok geh 幾何學嘅 *a. geometrical*
gey jee 機智 *a. witty*
gey jee geh 機智嘅 *a. resourceful*
gey jee geh 機智嘅 *a. tactful*
gey jeh 記者 *n. correspondent*
gey jeh 記者 *n. journalist*
gey jeh 記者 *n. reporter*
gey jeurng yan 記帳人 *n book-keeper*
gey juk 繼續 *v. i. continue*

gey juk 繼續 *v.i. last*
gey juk 繼續 *a. lasting*
gey juk 繼續 *v.t. resume*
gey juk jow 繼續做 *v.i. proceed*
gey jung geh 幾種嘅 *a. various*
gey lang 技能 *n. skill*
gey leem 紀念 *v. t. commemorate*
gey leem 紀念 *n. commemoration*
gey leem 紀念 *n. remembrance*
gey leem ban 紀念品 *n. keepsake*
gey leem ban 紀念品 *n. memento*
gey leem bay 紀念碑 *n. memorial*
gey leem geh 紀念嘅 *a memorial*
gey leem yat 紀念日 *n. anniversary*
gey leurng hay 計量器 *n. meter*
gey luk 紀錄 *n. record*
gey luk 紀錄 *n. tally*
gey luk 記錄 *v.t. transcribe*
gey lut 紀律 *n discipline*
gey luy 妓女 *n. bawd*
gey luy 妓女 *n. prostitute*
gey luy 妓女 *n. strumpet*
gey luy 妓女 *n. whore*
gey mat 機密 *a. confidential*
gey or 飢餓 *n. starvation*
gey sang 寄生 *adj. adnascent*
gey sang chung 寄生蟲 *n. parasite*
gey see 技師 *n. technician*
gey see 計時 *v.t. time*
gey see 幾時 *adv. when*
gey see 幾時 *conj. when*
gey see hay 記時器 *n chronograph*
gey shoon 計算 *n. calculation*
gey shoon 計算 *n. computation*
gey shoon 計算 *v.t. compute*
gey sing 繼承 *v.t. inherit*
gey sing 記性 *n. recall*
gey sing 繼承 *n. succession*
gey sing yan 繼承人 *n. heir*
gey sing yan 繼承人 *n. successor*
gey so gey 計數機 *n calculator*
gey suk 寄宿 *v.t. lodge*

gey sut geh 技術嘅 *a. technical*
gey sut geh 技術嘅 *a. technological*
gey sut jing jam 技術精湛 *a. masterly*
gey sut joon ga 技術專家 *n. technologist*
gey sut sing say jeet 技術性細節 *n. technicality*
gey wak 計劃 *n. plan*
gey wak 計劃 *v.t. plan*
gey wak 計劃 *v.t. programme*
gey wak 計劃 *n. project*
gey wak 計劃 *n. proposal*
gey wak 計劃 *n. scheme*
gey wuy 機會 *n. chance*
gey wuy 機會 *n. opportunity*
gey wuy 機會 *n. scope*
gey wuy ju yee 機會主義 *n. opportunism*
gey yap jeurng wu 記入賬戶 *v. t debit*
gey yee hay 計議器 *n. gauge*
gey yeen 既然 *conj. now*
gey yik 記憶 *n. memory*
gey yik 記憶 *n. recollection*
gey yoon 妓院 *n brothel*
gey yow hor lang 幾有可能 *a. likely*
gey yuk 肌肉 *n. muscle*
gey yuk tung 肌肉痛 *n. myalgia*
giew 叫 *v. t. call*
giew 叫 *v.i exclaim*
giew 叫 *v.i. scream*
giew cher 轎車 *n. sedan*
giew chor 叫錯 *v.t. miscall*
giew dung 撬動 *v.t. lever*
giew hai 繳械 *v. t disarm*
giew jing 矯正 *v.i. rectify*
giew jow 叫做 *v.t. term*
giew oh 驕傲 *n conceit*
giew oh geh 驕傲嘅 *a. proud*
giew ow 驕傲 *n. pride*
giew seng 叫聲 *n. bellows*

giew seng 叫聲 *n cry*
giew seng 叫醒 *v.i. rouse*
giew seng 叫聲 *n scream*
giew siew 嬌小 *a. dainty*
giew yeurng 嬌養 *v. t cocker*
gik 激 *v. t enrage*
gik 激 *v.t. infuriate*
gik bai 擊敗 *v. t. defeat*
gik bai 擊敗 *v.t. overwhelm*
gik ban 極品 *n. nonpareil*
gik dai geh 極大嘅 *a. stupendous*
gik day geh 極地嘅 *a polar*
gik doon 極端 *a drastic*
gik doon 極端 *n extreme*
gik doon fan jee 極端分子 *n extremist*
gik dung 激動 *v.t. agitate*
gik dung 激動 *v. t commove*
gik dung 激動 *a. giddy*
gik dung 激動 *n. panic*
gik fat 激發 *v.t. incite*
gik fat 激發 *v.t. stimulate*
gik gwong 極光 *n aurora*
gik hay 激起 *v.t. inflame*
gik hay 激起 *v.t. kindle*
gik hay 激氣 *v.t. resent*
gik hay 激氣 *v.i. seethe*
gik hay 激起 *v.t. stoke*
gik hay hing chuy 激起興趣 *v.t. intrigue*
gik hey 激起 *v.t. arouse*
gik jang 激增 *v.i. proliferate*
gik jang 激增 *n. proliferation*
gik jang 激增 *n. surge*
gik jun geh 激進嘅 *a. radical*
gik kow 擊球 *n stroke*
gik kow 擊球 *n. volley*
gik kow so 擊球手 *n. batsman*
gik lay 激勵 *n. goad*
gik lay 激勵 *v motivate*
gik lay 激勵 *v.t. uplift*
gik lay 激勵 *v.t. vitalize*

gik lo 激嬲 *v.t. aggravate*
gik lo 激嬲 *n. aggravation*
gik lorng 激浪 *n. surf*
gik low 激嬲 *v.t. nettle*
gik ta 極差 *a disastrous*
gik tuy 擊退 *v.t. repel*
gik tuy 擊退 *v.t. repulse*
gik wut 激活 *v. t enable*
giklay 激勵 *v.t. galvanize*
gikyan 激人 *v.t. incense*
ging 莖 *n. stem*
ging 經 *prep. via*
ging bo 警報 *n alarm*
ging bo hay 警報器 *n. siren*
ging deen 經典 *n classic*
ging dow 經度 *n. longitude*
ging dung 驚動 *v.t alarm*
ging fay 經費 *n. appropriation*
ging gai 警戒 *n. vigilance*
ging gey cheurng 競技場 *n. lists*
ging gey yan 經紀人 *n agent*
ging gey yan 經紀人 *n broker*
ging go 警告 *n. caution*
ging gok 警覺 *a. alert*
ging gok geh 警覺嘅 *a. vigilant*
ging gok sing 警覺性 *n. alertness*
ging gow 警告 *n. admonition*
ging gow 警告 *v.t. warn*
ging gow 警告 *n. warning*
ging gwor 經過 *adv by*
ging hak 驚嚇 *n. fright*
ging hay 驚喜 *v.t. impress*
ging hey 驚喜 *n. surprise*
ging hung 驚恐 *n. terror*
ging jang 競爭 *v. i compete*
ging jang 競爭 *n. rivalry*
ging jang duy sow 競爭對手 *n. rival*
ging jang lik 競爭力 *a competitive*
ging jay 經濟 *n economy*
ging jay geh 經濟嘅 *a economic*
ging jay geh 經濟嘅 *a economical*
ging jay hok 經濟學 *n. economics*

ging jay suy tuy 經濟衰退 *n. recession*

ging jung 敬重 *n. venerate*

ging kay 驚奇 *v.t. amaze*

ging kay 驚奇 *n. amazement*

ging kay 經期 *n. menstruation*

ging lay 經理 *n. manager*

ging lay 敬禮 *v.t. salute*

ging lay 敬禮 *n salute*

ging lay geh 經理嘅 *a. managerial*

ging lik 經歷 *v. t. experience*

ging lik 經歷 *v.t. undergo*

ging ngar 驚訝 *v.t. astonish*

ging ngar 驚訝 *n. astonishment*

ging ngar 驚訝 *n wonder*

ging sik 景色 *n. vista*

ging tat 警察 *n constable*

ging tat 警察 *n. police*

ging tat 警察 *n. policeman*

ging way 敬畏 *n. awe*

ging way 敬畏 *v.t. overawe*

ging yee 敬意 *n. homage*

ging yeem 經驗 *n experience*

ging yeem fung fu 經驗豐富 *a expert*

ging yeem fung fu geh 經驗豐富嘅 *a. veteran*

ging yeurng 敬仰 *n. obeisance*

go 告 *n. charge*

go 高 *a. high*

go 告 *v.t. sue*

go 高 *a. tall*

go beet 告別 *n farewell*

go dow 高度 *n. height*

go dow gey 高度計 *n altimeter*

go dow jan yeurng 高度讚揚 *v. t exalt*

go fung 高峰 *n. apotheosis*

go fung see kay 高峰時期 *n. heyday*

go hing 高興 *a. cheerful*

go hing 高興 *n delight*

go hing 高興 *v. t. delight*

go hing 高興 *n. gaiety*

go hing 高興 *a. glad*

go hing 高興 *v.t. gladden*

go hing 高興 *n. glee*

go hing 高興 *n. hilarity*

go jat leurng 高質量 *a fine*

go jung 告終 *v.i. culminate*

go san 高山 *n. alp*

go tiew 高潮 *n. climax*

go yee fu kow 高爾夫球 *n. golf*

gok 鉻 *n chrome*

gok 角 *n. horn*

gok dow 角度 *n. angle*

gok jee 各自 *pron. each*

gok jee 擱置 *v.t. table*

gok ji 擱置 *n. abeyance*

gok jung gok yeurng geh 各種各樣嘅 *a. miscellaneous*

gok jung gok yeurng geh 各種各樣嘅 *a. multifarious*

gok lok 角落 *n corner*

gok lok 角落 *n. nook*

gok low 閣樓 *n. loft*

gok mok 角膜 *n cornea*

gok sik 角色 *n. character*

gok sik 角色 *n. role*

gok sik fan pwuy 角色分配 *n casting*

gon 乾 *n arefaction*

gon 乾 *a dry*

gon 趕 *v.t. hurry*

gon cho 乾草 *n. hay*

gon jeng 乾淨 *n. clean*

gon jeng 乾淨 *n cleanliness*

gong 講 *v.i. talk*

gong 缸 *n. tank*

gong 講 *v.t. tell*

gong ga 講價 *v.t. bargain*

gong go lay yee 講究禮儀 *a. ceremonious*

gong gong seurng fan 剛剛相反 *n. antipodes*

gong jor 講座 *n talk*

gong lam dow 降臨到 *v. t befall*

gong mun 肛門 *n. anus*
gong siew 講笑 *v.t. banter*
goon 捐 *v. t contribute*
goon 捲 *v.t. convolve*
goon 捲 *n. curl*
goon 捐 *v. t donate*
goon 卷 *n. roll*
goon 捲 *v.i. roll*
goon fat 捲髮 *n. ringlet*
goon fwun 捐款 *n. benefaction*
goon fwun 捐款 *n. donation*
goon jang jeh 捐贈者 *n donor*
goon kuk 蜷曲 *v.t. crimple*
goon mai 捲埋 *v.t. furl*
goon sut 捐稅 *n. tithe*
goon tung 捲筒 *n. reel*
goon yap 捲入 *v. t entangle*
gor 歌 *n. song*
gor 嗰 *rel. pron. that*
gor been 嗰邊 *a. yonder*
gor been 嗰邊 *adv. yonder*
gor beet geh 個別嘅 *a. individual*
gor dow 嗰度 *adv. there*
gor dow fu gan 嗰度附近 *adv. thereabouts*
gor gor 嗰個 *a. that*
gor gor 嗰個 *dem. pron. that*
gor kek 歌劇 *n. opera*
gor mo biew yeen 歌舞表演 *n. cabaret*
gor sing 個性 *n. individualism*
gor sing 個性 *n. individuality*
gor sow 歌手 *n. singer*
gor sow 歌手 *n. songster*
gor sow 歌手 *n. vocalist*
gor tee 歌詞 *n. lyric*
gorn 肝 *n. liver*
gorn 趕 *adv. pell-mell*
gorn 杆 *n. rod*
gorn 趕 *v.t. rush*
gorn bwuy 乾杯 *v.t. toast*
gorn cho 乾燥 *adj. arid*

gorn cho duy 乾草堆 *n. rick*
gorn cho geh 乾燥嘅 *a. torrid*
gorn chut 趕出 *v. t. expel*
gorn hon 乾旱 *n drought*
gorn see gan 趕時間 *n. rush*
gorn yiew 干擾 *n. static*
gorn yu 干預 *v.i. interfere*
gorn yu 干預 *n. interference*
gorng 港 *n. harbour*
gorng 講 *v.t. remark*
gorng 講 *v.t. say*
gorng 講 *v.i. speak*
gorng 講 *n. spoke*
gorng 鋼 *n. steel*
gorng 講 *v.t. utter*
gorng dai wah 講大話 *v.i. lie*
gorng dai wah geh yan 講大話嘅人 *n. liar*
gorng dak gwor geh 講得過嘅 *a. tenable*
gorng day 降低 *n decrease*
gorng day 降低 *n. decrement*
gorng day 降低 *v.t. lower*
gorng day 降低 *v.t. windlass*
gorng day san fan 降低身分 *v. t degrade*
gorng dow 講道 *n. sermon*
gorng dow lay 講道理 *v.i. reason*
gorng fat 講法 *n. parlance*
gorng fay wah 講廢話 *v.i. prattle*
gorng for 講課 *v lecture*
gorng ga 降價 *v. t. cheapen*
gorng ga 降價 *v. t. debase*
gorng ga 講價 *v.i. haggle*
gorng gow 講究 *n. pedant*
gorng har 講下 *v.t. outline*
gorng ho 港口 *n. port*
gorng kam 鋼琴 *n. piano*
gorng kam ga 鋼琴家 *n. pianist*
gorng lok 降落 *v. i. descend*
gorng lok 降落 *n. descent*
gorng lok 降落 *v.i. land*

gorng lok 降落 *n. landing*
gorng lok sna 降落傘 *n. parachute*
gorng ming 講明 *v.t. account*
gorng ming 講明 *v.t state*
gorng see 講師 *n. lecturer*
gorng siew 講笑 *v.i. jest*
gorng siew 講笑 *v.i. joke*
gorng siew 講笑 *n. raillery*
gorng sut 講述 *v.t. narrate*
gorng sut 講述 *v.t. recount*
gorng tan 講壇 *a. pulpit*
gorng ting chor 講清楚 *v. t elucidate*
gorng toy 講台 *n. rostrum*
gorng wu yeet sut 江湖醫術 *n. quackery*
gorng yeh 講嘢 *v.i. yap*
got cho 割草 *v.t. mow*
gow 狗 *n dog*
gow 夠 *a enough*
gow 告 *v.t. impeach*
gow 告 *n. impeachment*
gow 九 *n. nine*
gow 救 *v.t. rescue*
gow 救 *v.t. save*
gow beng fuk fat 舊病復發 *n. relapse*
gow dam 夠膽 *v. i. dare*
gow day 高地 *n. plateau*
gow fan 糾紛 *n row*
gow fay seng 狗吠聲 *n. woof*
gow fay seng 狗吠聲 *n yap*
gow geh 高嘅 *a. lofty*
gow geh 舊嘅 *a. old*
gow gu 高估 *v.t. overrate*
gow gway geh 高貴嘅 *a. noble*
gow hing 高興 *n. joyful, joyous*
gow hing 高興 *a. mirthful*
gow hing 高興 *v.i. rejoice*
gow jay 狗仔 *n. whelp*
gow jing 糾正 *v.t. redress*
gow jing 糾正 *v.t. right*
gow jorng yan 告狀人 *n sneak*

gow kap gao see 高級教士 *n. prelate*
gow kap gwan gwun 高級軍官 *n marshal*
gow kiew 高蹺 *n. stilt*
gow kuk sap sam wan 九曲十三彎 *adj anfractuous*
gow ling 高齡 *n. senility*
gow mat jeh 告密者 *n. informer*
gow ngar geh 高雅嘅 *a. tasteful*
gow oh jee dai geh 高傲自大嘅 *a. haughty*
gow sap 九十 *n. ninety*
gow seurng 高尚 *n. sublimity*
gow sing 救星 *n. messiah*
gow sing 救星 *n. saviour*
gow sow 高手 *n ace*
gow uk 狗屋 *n. kennel*
gow yan 救恩 *n. salvation*
gow yeurng 羔羊 *n. lamb*
gow yoon 睪丸 *n. testicle*
gow yoot 九月 *n. September*
goy 改 *v.t. alter*
goy 蓋 *n. lid*
goy 改 *v.t. modify*
goy 改 *v.t. reform*
goy been 改變 *v. t. change*
goy been 改變 *n. change*
goy been ying tai 改變形態 *v. transform*
goy gak 改革 *n. reformation*
goy gak geh 改革嘅 *a reformatory*
goy gak jeh 改革者 *n. reformer*
goy gak jeh 改革者 *n revolutionary*
goy jing 改正 *n correction*
goy jing 改正 *n. rectification*
goy jow 改造 *n. overhaul*
goy leurng 改良 *v.t. ameliorate*
goy leurng 改良 *n. amelioration*
goy meng 改名 *v.t. name*
goy peen geh 改編嘅 *n. adaptation*
goy seen 改善 *n betterment*
goy seen 改善 *v.t. meliorate*

goy seen 改善 *n. refinement*
goy seen 改善 *n. reform*
gu 鈷 *n cobalt*
gu 鼓 *n drum*
gu 估 *v. t estimate*
gu 估 *v.i guess*
gu 估 *v.t. presume*
gu 估 *v.t. suppose*
gu ban geh 古板嘅 *a. staid*
gu dan 孤單 *n. loneliness*
gu dan 孤單 *a. lonely*
gu deen 古典 *a classical*
gu ding 固定 *v.t. steady*
gu ding geh 固定嘅 *a. immovable*
gu ding geh 固定嘅 *a set*
gu doy 古代 *n. antiquity*
gu doy geh 古代嘅 *a. archaic*
gu dung 古董 *a. antique*
gu fan 股份 *n. share*
gu fan 股份 *n stake*
gu fu ling ding 孤苦伶仃 *a forlorn*
gu ga 估價 *n. valuation*
gu gey 估計 *n. estimate*
gu gey 估計 *n. prediction*
gu gu giew 咕咕叫 *v. i coo*
gu gwai 古怪 *n. oddity*
gu gwai 古怪 *a. strange*
gu gwai geh 古怪嘅 *a rum*
gu gwai geh 古怪嘅 *a. zany*
gu horn 孤寒 *n. miser*
gu horn 孤寒 *a. niggardly*
gu horn geh 孤寒嘅 *a. miserly*
gu horn gway 孤寒鬼 *n. niggard*
gu jap 固執 *n. obstinacy*
gu jap 固執 *n. provincialism*
gu jap 固執 *n. tenacity*
gu jeurng 鼓掌 *v.t. applaud*
gu jeurng 故障 *n breakdown*
gu jeurng 鼓掌 *n clap*
gu jeurng 故障 *n. hitch*
gu joo 僱主 *n employer*
gu lap 孤立 *n. insularity*

gu lay 鼓勵 *v. t encourage*
gu lay 鼓勵 *n. incentive*
gu lor ma kek cheurng 古羅馬劇場 *n amphitheatre*
gu low 古老 *a. ancient*
gu low geh 古老嘅 *a. immemorial*
gu lung yoon huy 故弄玄虛 *v.t. mystify*
gu man 顧問 *n. counsellor*
gu man mat geh 古文物嘅 *a. antiquarian*
gu mat sow chong gar 古物收藏家 *n antiquarian*
gu mat sow chong gar 古物收藏家 *n. antiquary*
gu piew ging gey 股票經紀 *n. jobber*
gu see 故事 *n. story*
gu see 故事 *n. tale*
gu see ting jeet 故事情節 *n. plot*
gu sik gu heurng ghe 古色古香嘅 *a. quaint*
gu tay 固體 *n solid*
gu wak 蠱惑 *n antic*
gu wak 蠱惑 *n. guile*
gu wak geh 蠱惑嘅 *a. roguish*
gu wak jay 蠱惑仔 *n. gangster*
gu yee 故意 *a. intentional*
gu yee 孤兒 *n. orphan*
gu yee yoon 孤兒院 *n. orphanage*
gu yoon 僱員 *n employee*
gu yow geh 固有嘅 *a. inherent*
guk 焗 *v.t. bake*
guk 焗 *a. humid*
guk 局 *n. innings*
guk 局 *n. round*
guk 焗 *a. stuffy*
guk bo far 局部化 *v.t. localize*
guk chorng 穀倉 *n. barn*
guk gung 鞠躬 *v. t bow*
guk gung 鞠躬 *n bow*
guk low 焗爐 *n. oven*
guk luy 穀類 *a cereal*

guk mat 穀物 *n. cereal*
guk say yan 焗死人 *v.t. smother*
gung 拱 *n. arch*
gung 工 *n. job*
gung bo 公報 *n. communiqué*
gung bo 公報 *n. gazette*
gung cheurng 工場 *n. workshop*
gung choon 共存 *v. i co-exist*
gung choon 共存 *n co-existence*
gung chorng 工廠 *n factory*
gung dow 公道 *n. justice*
gung gey 公雞 *n cock*
gung gik 攻擊 *v. assail*
gung gik 攻擊 *v.t. mob*
gung gik 攻擊 *n offensive*
gung gik 攻擊 *n. onslaught*
gung gik sing 攻擊性 *n aggression*
gung go 公告 *n bulletin*
gung guy 工具 *n. implement*
gung guy 工具 *n. tool*
gung gwor yu kow 供過於求 *n glut*
gung hao 功效 *n efficacy*
gung heen 貢獻 *n contribution*
gung heurng geh 共享嘅 *a communal*
gung hey 恭喜 *v. t congratulate*
gung hoy gam 公開咁 *adv. openly*
gung hoy geh 公開嘅 *a. overt*
gung jay 公仔 *n doll*
gung jay geh 公制嘅 *a. metric*
gung jeen sow 弓箭手 *n archer*
gung jeurk 公爵 *n duke*
gung jeurng 工匠 *n. artisan*
gung jeurng 工匠 *n craftsman*
gung jeurng 工匠 *n. workman*
gung jik 功績 *n feat*
gung jing 公正 *a. candid*
gung jing 公正 *adv. justly*
gung jing geh 公正嘅 *a. just*
gung jing yan 公證人 *n. notary*
gung jok 工作 *n employment*
gung jok 工作 *n. work*
gung jok gwor dow 工作過度 *v.i.*

gung jok gwor dow 工作過度 *n.*
overwork
gung jok yan yoon 工作人員 *n. crew*
gung jok yan yoon 工作人員 *n. staff*
gung ju 公主 *n. princess*
gung jung 公眾 *n. public*
gung jung geh 公眾嘅 *a. public*
gung jung geh ju muk 公眾嘅注目 *n. limelight*
gung jung jap wuy 公眾集會 *n rally*
gung lang 功能 *n. function*
gung long 拱廊 *n arcade*
gung man hok 公民學 *n civics*
gung man koon lay 公民權利 *n citizenship*
gung man tow piew 公民投票 *n. plebiscite*
gung mao 公貓 *n. tomcat*
gung mo jeh 共謀者 *n. conspirator*
gung muk 肱木 *n ancon*
gung ngay geh 工藝嘅 *a. polytechnic*
gung ping 公平 *a fair*
gung ping 公平 *adv. fairly*
gung ping 公平 *n. impartiality*
gung ping geh 公平嘅 *a equitable*
gung see 公司 *n. company*
gung see 公司 *n. firm*
gung see geh 公司嘅 *adj. corporate*
gung sik 共識 *n. consensus*
gung sik 公式 *n formula*
gung sing 公升 *n. litre*
gung tan ju yee 共產主義 *n communism*
gung ting see 工程師 *n engineer*
gung tow 工頭 *n foreman*
gung tung geh 共同嘅 *a. mutual*
gung wor dorng dorng yoon 共和黨黨員 *n republican*
gung wor dorng geh 共和黨嘅 *a. republican*
gung wor gwok 共和國 *n. republic*

gung yan 工人 n domestic
gung yan 工人 n. hireling
gung yan 工人 n. servant
gung yan 工人 n. worker
gung yeep geh 工業嘅 a. industrial
gung yeurng 公羊 n. ram
gung ying 供應 n. provision
gung ying jeh 供應者 n. supplier
gung ying leurng 供應量 n supply
gung ying shoon 供應船 n tender
gung yoon 公園 n. park
guy 鋸 n. saw
guy been geh 巨變嘅 a. revolutionary
guy chee ying 鋸齒形 a. zigzag
guy chut 舉出 v. t cite
guy dai 巨大 n. immensity
guy dai geh 巨大嘅 a. gigantic
guy dai geh 巨大嘅 a. immense
guy dai geh 巨大嘅 a. massive
guy dai geh 巨大嘅 a. tremendous
guy dai geh 巨大嘅 a. vast
guy fat 句法 n. syntax
guy hang 舉行 v.t. solemnize
guy heurng 巨響 n. bang
guy jee 句子 n. sentence
guy ju 居住 n. habitation
guy ju geh 居住嘅 a. resident
guy ju yu 居住於 v.t. inhabit
guy kwong jing 懼曠症 n. agoraphobia
guy lorng 巨浪 n billow
guy man 居民 n. inhabitant
guy man 居民 n resident
guy sek 巨石 n. megalith
guy sek 巨石 n. monolith
guy sek geen jow geh 巨石建造嘅 a. megalithic
guy tay far 具體化 v.t. incarnate
guy yan 巨人 n. giant
gwa 掛 v.t. hang
gwa 瓜 n. melon

gwa fu 寡婦 n. widow
gwa gwa seng 呱呱聲 v.i. quack
gwa ju 掛住 v.t. miss
gwa low 寡佬 n. widower
gwa tow jing jee 寡頭政治 n. oligarchy
gwai 拐 v.t. kidnap
gwai geh 怪嘅 a. odd
gwai geh 怪嘅 a. peculiar
gwai jow 拐走 v.t. abduct
gwai pik 怪癖 n. peculiarity
gwak 摑 v.t. slap
gwak 摑 n. smack
gwak 摑 v.i. smack
gwan 郡 n. shire
gwan 棍 n. stick
gwan bay 軍備 n. armament
gwan dung geh 轟動嘅 a. sensational
gwan duy 軍隊 n. army
gwan duy 軍隊 n battalion
gwan duy 軍隊 n military
gwan for 軍火 n. munitions
gwan geen geh 關鍵嘅 a decisive
gwan geen geh 關鍵嘅 a. momentous
gwan hai fu 軍械庫 n. armoury
gwan hao sang 軍校生 n. cadet
gwan hay 關係 n. affiliation
gwan hay 關係 n bond
gwan hay 關係 n. relation
gwan hay 關係 n. relevance
gwan hay dow 關係到 v.t. involve
gwan jeet 關節 n. joint
gwan jeet yeem 關節炎 n arthritis
gwan jor 慣咗 a. accustomed
gwan ju 君主 n. monarch
gwan ju 君主 n. sovereign
gwan ju gway 君主制 n. monarchy
gwan leen 關連 n connection
gwan leen 關連 n. link
gwan sam 關心 v. i. care
gwan see ga 軍事家 n. strategist

gwan see geh 軍事嘅 a. military
gwan sing 慣性 n. inertia
gwan sum 關心 n concern
gwan toon 軍團 n. legion
gwan toon 軍團 n. legionary
gwan toon 軍團 n. regiment
gwan tow 關頭 n. juncture
gwan tung 滾筒 n. roller
gwan yu 關於 prep about
gwan yu 關於 v.i. pertain
gwan yung hay choy 軍用器材 n. ordnance
gwat 骨 n. bone
gwat 掘 v.t. dig
gwat 掘 v.t. trench
gwat day dow 挖地道 v.i. tunnel
gwat fwuy ang 骨灰甕 n urn
gwat jeet 骨折 n. fracture
gwat keurng 倔強 n. perversity
gwat tow horng 掘頭巷 n. close
gway 櫃 n. ambry
gway 貴 a. costly
gway 櫃 n cupboard
gway 鬼 n. ghost
gway 跪 v.i. kneel
gway 鬼 n. phantom
gway 龜 n. tortoise
gway been 詭辯 n. sophism
gway dow 軌道 n. orbit
gway dow 軌道 n. track
gway gey 詭計 n dodge
gway gey 詭計 n. ruse
gway gey 詭計 n. wile
gway gow yu 歸咎於 v.t. impute
gway jeen tung fan geh 貴賤通婚嘅 a. morganatic
gway jeet 季節 n. season
gway jeet geh 季節嘅 a. seasonal
gway juk 貴族 n. aristocracy
gway juk 貴族 n. nobility
gway juk 貴族 n. noble
gway juk 貴族 n. nobleman

gway juk koon lay 貴族權利 n. lordship
gway toy 櫃台 n. counter
gway tung 櫃桶 n drawer
gway wan 鬼魂 n. wraith
gway wan chut mwut 鬼魂出沒 v.t. haunt
gway yan yu 歸因於 v.t. ascribe
gway yan yu 歸因於 v.t. attribute
gwey 貴 a expensive
gwok ga 國家 n. country
gwok ga 國家 n. nation
gwok ga jap toon 國家集團 n bloc
gwok ga jow jik 國家組織 n. polity
gwok ga ju yee 國家主義 n. nationalism
gwok gor 國歌 n anthem
gwok jay 國際 a. international
gwok jay jeurng kay 國際象棋 n. chess
gwok jik 國籍 n. nationality
gwok worng 國王 n. king
gwok wuy 國會 n congress
gwok wuy 國會 n. parliament
gwok wuy geh 國會嘅 a. parliamentary
gwok yow far 國有化 n. nationalization
gwok yow far 國有化 v.t. nationalize
gwong 光 a bright
gwong 光 n. light
gwong bor 廣播 n broadcast
gwong bor 廣播 v. t broadcast
gwong choy 光彩 n brilliance
gwong jak 光澤 n. gloss
gwong morng say she 光芒四射 a. radiant
gwong seen 光線 n beam
gwong tow 光頭 a. bald
gwong wat geh 光滑嘅 a. glossy
gwong wing geh 光榮嘅 a. glorious
gwong yoon 光源 n. illumination

gwoon choy ga 棺材架 *n bier*
gwoon deem 觀點 *n angle*
gwoon jung 觀眾 *n. audience*
gwor 過 *v. t cross*
gwor 過 *adv over*
gwor 過 *prep. past*
gwor chor 過錯 *n fault*
gwor dor 過多 *n overload*
gwor dor 過多 *n. superabundance*
gwor dor geh 過多嘅 *a. superfluous*
gwor dow 過度 *a. lavish*
gwor dung 過冬 *v.i winter*
gwor fan 過分 *a. undue*
gwor hm dow 過唔到 *a. impassable*
gwor huy 過去 *n. past*
gwor huy geh 過去嘅 *a. past*
gwor jeurng 果醬 *n. jam*
gwor jeurng 果醬 *n. preserve*
gwor kay 過期 *v.i. expire*
gwor kay 過期 *a. overdue*
gwor leung fuk yung 過量服用 *v.t. overdose*
gwor leurng 過量 *n. overdose*
gwor leurng 過量 *n. surfeit*
gwor luy 過濾 *v.t filter*
gwor luy 過濾 *v.t. leach*
gwor luy hay 過濾器 *n filter*
gwor man 過敏 *n. irritation*
gwor sai see 過晒時 *n anachronism*
gwor sai see 過晒時 *a. antiquated*
gwor sai see geh 過晒時嘅 *a. outmoded*
gwor sam 果心 *n. core*
gwor sat 過失 *n demerit*
gwor see 過時 *a. outdated*
gwor see 過時 *v.t. stale*
gwor sok 過塑 *v.t. laminate*
gwor ting 過程 *n. proceeding*
gwor tow lap 過頭笠 *n. pullover*
gwor yan 果仁 *n nut*
gwor yoon 果園 *n. orchard*
gworng bor 廣播 *v.t. telecast*

gworng bor 廣播 *v.t. televise*
gworng gow 廣告 *v. advert*
gworng gow 廣告 *n advertisement*
gworng jak 光澤 *n. lustre*
gworng jak 光澤 *n shine*
gworng seen 光線 *n. ray*
gworng seen geh 光鮮嘅 *a. smart*
gworng wat geh 光滑嘅 *a. sleek*
gwun 獾 *n. badger*
gwun 滾 *v.i. boil*
gwun 罐 *n. can*
gwun 管 *n. pipe*
gwun 管 *n. pole*
gwun 罐 *n. pot*
gwun 鸛 *n. stork*
gwun 罐 *n. tin*
gwun 罐 *n. tub*
gwun 管 *n. tube*
gwun choy 棺材 *n coffin*
gwun deem 觀點 *n contention*
gwun deem 觀點 *n. perspective*
gwun dung 轟動 *adv. astir*
gwun ga 管家 *n chamberlain*
gwun gwan 冠軍 *n. champion*
gwun ho 管口 *n. nozzle*
gwun ja 轟炸 *v. t bombard*
gwun ja 轟炸 *n bombardment*
gwun jee bat dorng 管治不當 *n. misrule*
gwun jorng 管狀 *a. tubular*
gwun jung 觀眾 *n. spectator*
gwun jung jik 觀眾席 *n. auditorium*
gwun koy 灌溉 *n. irrigation*
gwun lay 管理 *v.t. manage*
gwun lay 管理 *n. management*
gwun lay bat seen 管理不善 *n. mismanagement*
gwun lay bat seen 管理不善 *n. mal administration*
gwun lay yan 管理人 *n. warden*
gwun liew 官僚 *n bureaucrat*

gwun liew ju yee 官僚主義 *n.*
Bureacuracy
gwun meen 冠冕 *n. coronet*
gwun muk 灌木 *n. shrub*
gwun pang 棍棒 *n cudgel*
gwun shu 灌輸 *v.t. inculcate*
gwun shu 灌輸 *n. infusion*
gwun suy 灌水 *v.t. irrigate*
gwun tat 觀察 *n. observation*
gwun tat 觀察 *v.t. observe*
gwun tat lik keurng 觀察力強 *a.*
observant
gwun tat lik keurng geh 觀察力強嘅
a. perceptive
gwun ying jun 管形樽 *n. vial*
gwun yoon 官員 *n. functionary*
gwun yoon 官員 *n. officer*
gwun yoon 官員 *n official*
gwun yoon ok duy 管弦樂隊 *n.*
orchestra
gwun yoon ok geh 管弦樂嘅 *a.*
orchestral
gwuy 劾 *v.t. tire*
gwuy 劾 *a. weary*
gwuy 劾 *v.t. & i weary*
gwuy gow 灰狗 *n. greyhound*

H

ha gong 下降 *n decline*
ha jeen geh yan 下賤嘅人 *n churl*
ha low geh 下流嘅 *a. obscene*
ha low geh hang way 下流嘅行爲 *n.*
obscenity
ha meen 下面 *adv below*
ha meen 下面 *adv beneath*
ha meen 下面 *prep beneath*
ha pa 下巴 *n. chin*
hai 蟹 *n crab*

hai 鞋 *n. shoe*
hai day 鞋底 *n. sole*
hai gwat 骸骨 *n. skeleton*
hai jeurng 鞋匠 *n cobbler*
hai lok 奚落 *v.t. ridicule*
hai lok 奚落 *n. ridicule*
hai sap sap 諧霎霎 *a. rough*
hak 刻 *v. t. carve*
hak 客 *n.. client*
hak 客 *n customer*
hak 黑 *a dark*
hak 嚇 *v. t daunt*
hak 刻 *v. t engrave*
hak 克 *n. gramme*
hak 嚇 *v.t. horrify*
hak 嚇 *n. scare*
hak 嚇 *v.t. scare*
hak 嚇 *n. shock*
hak 嚇 *v.t. shock*
hak 嚇 *v.t. startle*
hak 嚇 *v.t. terrify*
hak am 黑暗 *n dark*
hak bak wan hoot yee 黑白混血兒 *n.*
mulatto
hak ban sang wut 刻板生活 *n. rut*
hak ban yan jeurng 刻板印象 *n.*
stereotype
hak bok 刻薄 *a. harsh*
hak dow sor jor 嚇到傻咗 *a. aghast*
hak fuk 克服 *v.t. overcome*
hak fuk 克服 *v.t. surmount*
hak fuk hm dow geh 克服唔到嘅 *a.*
insurmountable
hak gway 黑鬼 *n. nigger*
hak gwun geh 客觀嘅 *a. objective*
hak hay geh 客氣嘅 *a. mannerly*
hak hay shoot wah 客氣說話 *n.*
pleasantry
hak jay 克制 *v.i. refrain*
hak loy jeurng 黑內障 *n amaurosis*
hak mak 黑麥 *n. rye*
hak pao 黑豹 *n. panther*

hak sik 黑色 *a black*
hak sing sing 黑猩猩 *n. chimpanzee*
hak tan 嚇 *v.t. frighten*
hak teng 客廳 *n drawing-room*
hak teng 客廳 *n. parlour*
hak yan 嚇人 *n bluff*
hak yan 黑人 *n. negro*
hak yan 客人 *n. visitor*
hak yan geh 嚇人嘅 *a. monstrous*
ham 喊 *n sob*
ham geen 坎肩 *n. jerkin*
ham giew seng 喊叫聲 *n howl*
ham jeng 陷阱 *n. pitfall*
ham jeng 陷阱 *n. snare*
ham jeng 陷阱 *n. trap*
ham jing 陷阱 *n. pl. toils*
ham low 喊路 *n. yawn*
ham seng 喊聲 *n whine*
ham tat 勘察 *n exploration*
ham wu 含糊 *n. obscurity*
ham wu bat ting 含糊不清 *v.i. gabble*
ham wu dow 含糊度 *n. vagueness*
ham wu seng 含糊聲 *n. slur*
ham yap 陷入 *v.t. mire*
ham yap heem ging 陷入險境 *v.t. imperil*
han 痕 *n. mark*
han 限 *v.t. restrict*
han 慳 *a. thrifty*
han 狠 *a. vicious*
han 行 *v.i. walk*
han dow 限度 *n. extent*
han duk geh 狠毒嘅 *a. virulent*
han ga 慳家 *a. frugal*
han ga 慳家 *n. thrift*
han jay 限制 *v. t confine*
han jay 限制 *v. t curtail*
han jay 限制 *v.t fetter*
han jay 限制 *n. limit*
han jay 限制 *v.t. limit*
han jay 限制 *n. limitation*

han jay 限制 *n. restriction*
han jay 限制 *n. stricture*
han jik 痕跡 *n. trace*
han jik 痕跡 *n. trail*
han ko 懇求 *n adjuration*
han kow 懇求 *n. entreaty*
han kow 懇求 *v.i. plead*
han san 閒散 *n. idleness*
han ting 懇請 *n. solicitation*
han wah 閒話 *n. gossip*
hang 行 *v.t ambulate*
hang 哼 *v. i hum*
hang 哼 *v.i. snort*
hang 哼 *n. snort*
hang 行 *v.i. step*
hang dak tung geh 行得通嘅 *a feasible*
hang ding 肯定 *v.t. affirm*
hang ding 肯定 *v.t. assert*
hang ding 肯定 *a. sure*
hang ding geh 肯定嘅 *a affirmative*
hang ding geh 肯定嘅 *a definite*
hang fat 行法 *n. gait*
hang fuk 幸福 *n felicity*
hang fuk 幸福 *n. welfare*
hang gai 行街 *v.i. shop*
hang jee 杏子 *n. apricot*
hang jing 行政 *n. administration*
hang jing geh 行政嘅 *a. administrative*
hang jing kuy 行政區 *n canton*
hang jing yan yoon 行政人員 *n. administrator*
hang lay 行李 *n. baggage*
hang lay 行李 *n. luggage*
hang lay yoon 行李員 *n. porter*
hang sam 恆心 *a. ambitious*
hang sing geh 行星嘅 *a. planetary*
hang tee 行刺 *v.t. assassinate*
hang tee 坑廁 *n. latrine*
hang way 行爲 *n. act*
hang way 行爲 *n behaviour*

hang way 行爲 n deed

hang way bat doon 行文不端 v.i. misbehave

hang way bat dorng 行爲不當 n. misbehaviour

hang way bat dorng 行爲不當 n. misdemeanour

hang way guy jee 行爲舉止 n conduct

hang way gwai yee geh yan 行爲怪異嘅人 n. misfit

hang yan 杏仁 n. almond

hang yan 行人 n. pedestrian

hang yan low 行人路 n. pavement

hang ying jeh 行刑者 n. executioner

hao 敲 v.t. knock

hao 烤 v.t. roast

hao 敲 v.t. toll

hao choon 哮喘 n. asthma

hao geh 烤嘅 a roast

hao giew 吼叫 n. roar

hao giew 吼叫 v.i. roar

hao gwor 效果 n effect

hao gwun 考官 n examiner

hao ja 敲詐 v.t fleece

hao jeurng 校長 n. principal

hao lut 效率 n efficiency

hao lut go 效率高 a efficient

hao luy 考慮 v. t consider

hao luy 考慮 v. t contemplate

hao luy dow 考慮到 prep. considering

hao luy dow 考慮到 a. mindful

hao luy gan 考慮緊 n contemplation

hao miew 巧妙 a. artful

hao miew 巧妙 n. subtlety

hao miew geh dap on 巧妙嘅答案 n. repartee

hao mo kwan 酵母菌 n. yeast

hao sang 考生 n examinee

hao see 考試 n. examination

hao yuk 烤肉 n roast

hao yung 效用 n. utility

haow 好 a. lash

hap 盒 n carton

hap 盒 n. cartridge

hap cheurng toon 合唱團 n choir

hap dong 恰當 n. adequacy

hap dong 恰當 a. apposite

hap fat 合法 a. lawful

hap fat geh 合法嘅 a. legal

hap fat sing 合法性 n. legality

hap fat sing 合法性 n. legitimacy

hap fat sing 合法性 n. validity

hap fu lor tap 合乎邏輯 a coherent

hap gam 合金 n. alloy

hap goy 盒蓋 v. t. cap

hap jok 合作 v. i collaborate

hap jok 合作 n collaboration

hap jok 合作 v. i co-operate

hap jok 合作 n co-operation

hap jok 合作 n. partnership

hap kwan geh 合群嘅 a. sociable

hap lay 合理 n. moderation

hap lay far 合理化 v.t. rationalize

hap lay geh 合理嘅 a. sound

hap lay sing 合理性 n. rationality

hap ngan gan 瞌眼瞓 v. i doze

hap ping 合併 v.t. amalgamate

hap ping 合併 n amalgamation

hap ping 合併 a. incorporate

hap ping 合併 v.t. merge

hap ping 合併 n. merger

hap sik 合適 a becoming

hap sik geng leen 盒式頸鏈 n. locket

hap sing mat 合成物 n synthetic

hap ting hap lay 合情合理 a. legitimate

hap tung 合同 n. compact

hap tung 合同 n. covenant

hap yeurk 合約 n contract

har chee 瑕疵 n flaw

har gong 下降 v.t. avale

har gorng 下降 a downward

har meen 下面 *prep down*
har ok 下顎 *n. jaw*
har ok 下顎 *n. maxilla*
har suk 下屬 *n. minion*
har tee 瑕疵 *n blemish*
har tee 瑕疵 *n. imperfection*
har teen 夏天 *n. summer*
har teen geh 夏天嘅 *adj aestival*
har wat 下滑 *n downfall*
har yan 蝦人 *v. t. bully*
har yat yeep 下一頁 *adv. overleaf*
harm 喊 *v. i cry*
harm 鹹 *a. salty*
hat 乞 *v. i cadge*
hat tee 乞嚏 *n sneeze*
hat tow 核桃 *n. walnut*
hat yan jang 乞人憎 *a. disagreeable*
hat yan jang 乞人憎 *a. loathsome*
hat yee 乞兒 *n beggar*
hay 係 *am*
hay 喺 *prep. at*
hay 喺 *pref. be*
hay 起 *v. t. construct*
hay 喺 *prep during*
hay 喺 *prep. in*
hay 喺 *conj. where*
hay 係 *adv. yes*
hay been dow 喺邊度 *adv. whereabout*
hay been dow 喺邊度 *adv. wherein*
hay cho jeh 起草者 *n draftsman*
hay choon 氣喘 *n. pant*
hay chorng dow 喺床度 *adv. abed*
hay far meng 起花名 *v.t. nickname*
hay fuk 起伏 *v.i. undulate*
hay guy 器具 *n. appliance*
hay gwun 器官 *n. organ*
hay hing geh 喜慶嘅 *a festive*
hay ho 氣候 *n. climate*
hay ho 喜好 *n. like*
hay ho 喜好 *n. preference*
hay ja geh 欺詐嘅 *a. fraudulent*

hay jat 氣質 *n. temperament*
hay jay 克制 *v.t. repress*
hay jeurk 喜鵲 *n. magpie*
hay jeurng hok 氣象學 *n. meteorology*
hay jeurng hok ga 氣象學家 *n. meteorologist*
hay jow 起皺 *n crimp*
hay kek 喜劇 *n. comedy*
hay kek 戲劇 *n drama*
hay kek 戲劇 *n. play*
hay kek fa 戲劇化 *a dramatic*
hay kek ga 喜劇家 *n. comedian*
hay kek geh 戲劇嘅 *a comic*
hay kek geh 戲劇嘅 *a. theatrical*
hay lap man 希臘文 *a Greek*
hay lap yan 希臘人 *n. Greek*
hay leet 系列 *n collection*
hay leet 系列 *n. range*
hay leet 系列 *n. series*
hay low 氣流 *n. turbulence*
hay low mow seurng 喜怒無常 *a. moody*
hay low mow seurng 喜怒無常 *a. temperamental*
hay may 氣味 *n. smell*
hay morng 希望 *a desirous*
hay morng 希望 *v.t. hope*
hay morng 希望 *n hope*
hay morng 希望 *n. prospect*
hay mun 氣門 *n. valve*
hay ngat gey 氣壓計 *n barometer*
hay po 起泡 *v.t foam*
hay sang 犧牲 *v.t. sacrifice*
hay sang geh 犧牲嘅 *a. sacrificial*
hay seurng meen 喺上面 *adv. aloft*
hay sik 稀釋 *v.t. thin*
hay so 係數 *n. coefficient*
hay sow 起訴 *v.t. indict*
hay sow 起訴 *v.t. prosecute*
hay toon 戲團 *n. troupe*
hay tung 系統 *n. system*

hay tung far 系統化 *v.t. systematize*
hay wok 起獲 *n. seizure*
hay yee 起義 *n. uprising*
hay yoon 戲院 *a. multiplex*
hay yoon yu 起源於 *v.t. originate*
hay yoot 喜悅 *n bliss*
hay yoot 喜悅 *n. joy*
hay yow 汽油 *n. petrol*
hay yow geh 稀有嘅 *a. scarce*
hay...geh ha meen 喺...嘅下面 *prep. under*
hay...geh ha meen 喺...嘅下面 *a under*
hay...geh ha meen 喺...嘅下面 *adv. underneath*
hay...geh ha meen 喺...嘅下面 *prep. underneath*
hay...geh seurng meen 喺...嘅上面 *prep. on*
hay...geh seurng meen 喺...嘅上面 *adv. on*
hay...teen meen ga 係...前面加 *v.t. prefix*
heem 欠 *v.t owe*
heem dan 欠單 *n. chit*
heem huy 謙虛 *a. humble*
heem huy 謙虛 *n. humility*
heem huy 謙虛 *a. modest*
heem huy 謙虛 *n modesty*
heem ok 險惡 *a. sinister*
heen dak 顯得 *v.t. portray*
heen fan 遣返 *v.t. repatriate*
heen fan 遣返 *n. repatriation*
heen fan yan 遣返人 *n repatriate*
heen fat 憲法 *n constitution*
heen gwa 牽掛 *n. solicitude*
heen hak 顯赫 *n eminance*
heen jak 譴責 *v. t. censure*
heen jak 譴責 *n condemnation*
heen jeurng 憲章 *n charter*
heen ju geh 顯著嘅 *a dominant*
heen leen 牽連 *n. implication*

heen leen 牽連 *v.t. incriminate*
heen may geng 顯微鏡 *n. microscope*
heen see 顯示 *n. indication*
heen see 顯示 *n. manifestation*
heen seen muk oh 牽線木偶 *n. marionette*
heen seep 牽涉 *v.t. implicate*
heep ding 協定 *n. treaty*
heep tiew 協調 *a. co-ordinate*
heep tiew 協調 *v. t co-ordinate*
heep tiew 協調 *n co-ordination*
heep wuy 協會 *n. association*
heep wuy 協會 *n. guild*
heep wuy 協會 *n. union*
heep yee 協議 *n. pact*
heep yee 協議 *n. settlement*
heep yee shu 協議書 *n. agreement*
hek lik bat tow ho 吃力不討好 *a. thankless*
heng 輕 *a light*
heng heng 輕輕 *adv. lightly*
heng heng gam deem 輕輕咁掂 *v.t. tip*
heng mor 輕摸 *v.t. stroke*
heng pak 輕拍 *v.t. tap*
heng tuy 輕推 *v.t. nudge*
heurng 響 *v.i hoot*
heurng 香 *n. incense*
heurng 響 *v.i. resound*
heurng 向 *prep. towards*
heurng bak 向北 *adv. north*
heurng choon sang wut 鄉村生活 *n. rustication*
heurng dung 向東 *adv east*
heurng geh 香嘅 *a. fragrant*
heurng gor dow 向嗰度 *adv. thither*
heurng ha geh 鄉下嘅 *a. rural*
heurng ha geh 鄉下嘅 *a. rustic*
heurng ha mang chung 向下猛衝 *v.i. swoop*
heurng ha yan 鄉下人 *n rustic*
heurng har 向下 *adv down*

heurng har 向下 *adv downward*
heurng har 向下 *adv downwards*
heurng ho 向後 *adv. aback*
heurng ho 向後 *adv. backward*
heurng jee 香脂 *n. balsam*
heurng jiew 香蕉 *n. banana*
heurng larm 向南 *adv south*
heurng leurng 響亮 *n. resonance*
heurng leurng 響亮 *n. sonority*
heurng leurng geh 響亮嘅 *a. resonant*
heurng liew 香料 *n. spice*
heurng lo 香爐 *n censer*
heurng loy 向內 *a. inward*
heurng loy 向內 *adv. inwards*
heurng mey 香味 *n. fragrance*
heurng ngoy 向外 *a. outward*
heurng ngoy 向外 *adv outwards*
heurng san 鄉紳 *n. squire*
heurng say 向西 *adv. west*
heurng say geh 向西嘅 *adv. westerly*
heurng seurng 向上 *adv. up*
heurng seurng geh 向上嘅 *a. upward*
heurng so 享受 *v. t enjoy*
heurng sow 享受 *v.t. relish*
heurng sow 享受 *n. sensuality*
heurng suy 香水 *n. perfume*
heurng teen 向前 *adv. forth*
heurng teen 向前 *adv forward*
heurng teen 向前 *a. onward*
heurng teen 向前 *adv. onwards*
heurng tow muk 香桃木 *n. myrtle*
heurng yan bo jing 向人保證 *v.t. reassure*
heurng yow 香油 *n. balm*
heurng yow 向右 *adv right*
hey 氣 *n breath*
hey 起 *v. t build*
hey choy 器材 *n equipment*
hey fan 氣氛 *n. atmosphere*
hey kow 氣球 *n. balloon*

hey sik 稀釋 *v. t dilute*
hey sik 稀釋 *a dilute*
hey tay far 氣體化 *v.t. aerify*
hey yan 起因 *n. cause*
hey yoon 戲院 *n. cinema*
hiew cheurng 囂張 *a. arrogant*
hing chuy 興趣 *n. interest*
hing day 兄弟 *n brother*
hing day 兄弟 *n mate*
hing day geh 兄弟嘅 *a. fraternal*
hing fan 興奮 *adj alacrious*
hing fan 興奮 *v. t electrify*
hing fan 興奮 *v. t excite*
hing fan 興奮 *v. i exult*
hing fan jay 興奮劑 *n agonist*
hing fan jay 興奮劑 *n. stimulant*
hing hay 氫氣 *n. hydrogen*
hing jorng 輕撞 *n dig*
hing juk 慶祝 *v. t. & i. celebrate*
hing juk wut dung 慶祝活動 *n. celebration*
hing juk wut dung 慶祝活動 *n festivity*
hing may geh 輕微嘅 *a. slight*
hing see 輕視 *a contemptuous*
hing see 輕視 *n. slight*
hing see 輕視 *v.t. slight*
hing see geh 輕視嘅 *a. sardonic*
hing sut 輕率 *a facile*
hing sut 輕率 *n flippancy*
hing sut 輕率 *adv. headlong*
hing sut 輕率 *a. impetuous*
hing sut 輕率 *n. imprudence*
hing tiew 輕佻 *a. frivolous*
hing tiew 輕佻 *n. levity*
hing worng 興旺 *v.i flourish*
hing worng 興旺 *n. prosperity*
hing worng 興旺 *v.i. thrive*
hing yee 輕易 *n ease*
hing yee gam chuy sing 輕易咁取勝 *v.i. romp*

hing yee seurng sun 輕易相信 *adj.* *credulity*

hing yow geh 輕柔嘅 *a.* *silken*

hing yow geh 輕柔嘅 *a.* *silky*

hm bao kwut 唔包括 *v. t except*

hm bay tay ho geh yan 唔被睇好嘅人 *n underdog*

hm dow 誤導 *v.t. misdirect*

hm dow 誤導 *n. misdirection*

hm dow 誤導 *v.t. mislead*

hm forng been 唔方便 *a.* *inconvenient*

hm gai 誤解 *v.t. misapprehend*

hm gai 誤解 *n misapprehension*

hm gai 誤解 *n. misconception*

hm gan san 唔謹慎 *a. indiscreet*

hm gan yiew 唔緊要 *a. immaterial*

hm gat lay geh 唔吉利嘅 *a. ominous*

hm geem deem geh 唔檢點嘅 *a.* *slatternly*

hm geem deem hang way 唔檢點行為 *n. indiscretion*

hm geeng mang geh 唔結盟嘅 *n. non-alignment*

hm gey dak 唔記得 *v.t forget*

hm gok ying 五角型 *n. pentagon*

hm gow 唔夠 *a. insufficient*

hm gow 唔夠 *v.t. lack*

hm gow 唔夠 *a. scanty*

hm gow 唔夠 *adv. short*

hm gung 蜈蚣 *n. centipede*

hm gung jing 唔公正 *n. injustice*

hm gung jing 唔公正 *v.t. wrong*

hm gung ping 唔公平 *a unfair*

hm gung ping geh 唔公平嘅 *a.* *unjust*

hm gway 唔貴 *a. inexpensive*

hm gwong choy geh 唔光彩嘅 *a.* *ignoble*

hm gwun 五官 *n. sense*

hm han ding 唔肯定 *a. uncertain*

hm hang ding geh 唔肯定嘅 *a.* *tentative*

hm hap dong 唔恰當 *a. indecent*

hm hap lor tap 唔合邏輯 *a.* *irrational*

hm hap lor tap geh 唔合邏輯嘅 *a.* *illogical*

hm hap see 唔合時 *a. inopportune*

hm hap sik geh hang way 唔合適嘅行為 *n. impropriety*

hm hay 唔係 *adv. nay*

hm hay 唔係 *a. no*

hm hay 唔係 *adv. no*

hm hay 唔係 *n no*

hm hay 唔係 *adv. not*

hm hay jok yung 唔起作用 *v.i. misfire*

hm heem huy 唔謙虛 *a. immodest*

hm heem huy 唔謙虛 *n. immodesty*

hm ho cheurng 午後場 *n. matinee*

hm ho choy 唔好彩 *a. luckless*

hm ho gorng yeh 唔好講嘢 *v.i hush*

hm ho yee see geh 唔好意思嘅 *a.* *sheepish*

hm hor kao geh 唔可靠嘅 *a. shifty*

hm hor sun geh 唔可信嘅 *a. suspect*

hm hor yi 唔可以 *a. unable*

hm how 唔好 *a. indifferent*

hm hoy sam 唔開心 *a. unhappy*

hm jee deem gai jow 唔知點解就 *adv. somehow*

hm jee juk geh 唔知足嘅 *a.* *insatiable*

hm jik dak 唔值得 *a. worthless*

hm jing dong geh 唔正當嘅 *a.* *improper*

hm jing dong geh 唔正當嘅 *a.* *wrongful*

hm jing seurng 唔正常 *n. aberrance*

hm jing seurng 唔正常 *a abnormal*

hm jing seurng 唔正常 *adj acentric*

hm jing seurng 唔正常 *adv. amiss*

hm joon ging 唔尊敬 n disrespect
hm jow yeh 唔做嘢 n. inaction
hm joy yee 唔在意 a. unaware
hm ju yee geh 唔注意嘅 a. oblivious
hm jun kok 唔準確 a. inaccurate
hm jun kok 唔準確 a. inexact
hm jun sow dow dak 唔遵守道德 a.
 amoral
hm jung sam 唔忠心 a disloyal
hm jung yee 唔鐘意 v. t dislike
hm jung yiew 唔重要 n.
 insignificance
hm jung yiew 唔重要 a. insignificant
hm jung yiew geh 唔重要嘅 a.
 incidental
hm jung yiew geh 唔重要嘅 a.
 marginal
hm jung yiew geh yan 唔重要嘅人 n.
 pigmy
hm kway jak 唔規則 a. irregular
hm kway jak sing 唔規則性 n.
 irregularity
hm lay 唔理 v. t disregard
hm loy fan geh 唔耐煩嘅 a. restive
hm ming bak see lay 唔明白事理 a.
 witless
hm ming heen geh 唔明顯嘅 n.
 subtle
hm ming jee geh 唔明智嘅 a.
 imprudent
hm mun yee 唔滿意 v. t. dissatisfy
hm on choon 唔安全 a. insecure
hm san seen geh 唔新鮮嘅 a. stale
hm sap jow leen gey leem 五十週年
 紀念 n. jubilee
hm sat jay geh 唔實際嘅 a. quixotic
hm shoon 誤算 n. miscalculation
hm shu fuk 唔舒服 a crook
hm shu fuk 唔舒服 n discomfort
hm shu fuk 唔舒服 a. indisposed
hm shu fuk 唔舒服 n. malaise
hm shu fuk 唔舒服 a. unwell

hm siew sam 唔小心 a accidental
hm sik hap geh 唔適合 a.
 inapplicable
hm sik hap ju geh 唔適合住嘅 a.
 inhospitable
hm sing sat 唔誠實 a. corrupt
hm sing sat 唔誠實 a dishonest
hm sing sat 唔誠實 n. dishonesty
hm sing sat 唔誠實 a. insincere
hm sing sat 唔誠實 a. malafide
hm sing sat 唔誠實 adv malafide
hm sun 唔信 n distrust
hm sun 唔信 v. t. distrust
hm sun 誤信 n. misbelief
hm sun 唔信 v.t. mistrust
hm sun chung geh 唔順從嘅 a.
 insubordinate
hm sun dak gwor geh 唔信得過嘅 a.
 unreliable
hm sun geet geh 唔純潔嘅 a. impure
hm suy yiew geh 唔需要嘅 a.
 needless
hm tam seurng geh 唔尋常嘅 a.
 outlandish
hm tay leurng 唔體諒 a.
 inconsiderate
hm tee 唔似 prep unlike
hm tee yeurng 唔似樣 a. nefandous
hm ting hm chor 唔清唔楚 a.
 incoherent
hm ting yoon 唔情願 a. loath
hm tow ming geh 唔透明嘅 a.
 opaque
hm tung 唔同 a different
hm tung 唔同 a unlike
hm tung geh 唔同嘅 a diverse
hm tung geh 唔同嘅 a else
hm tung yee 唔同意 v. i disagree
hm wai yee 唔懷疑 a. implicit
hm wan ding 唔穩定 adj. astatic
hm wan ding 唔穩定 a critical

hm wan ding sing 唔穩定性 *n. instability*

hm wan gu geh 唔穩固嘅 *a. rickety*

hm wan huy 唔允許 *a. inadmissible*

hm wan jan geh 唔穩陣嘅 *a. shaky*

hm wut yeurk 唔活躍 *a. inactive*

hm wuy 誤會 *v.t. misconceive*

hm wuy 誤會 *v.t. misconstrue*

hm wuy 誤會 *v.t. misunderstand*

hm wuy 誤會 *n. misunderstanding*

hm yam jow geh yan 唔飲酒嘅人 *n. teetotaller*

hm yap kay tow 誤入歧途 *v.t. misguide*

hm yat jee 唔一致 *adj absonant*

hm yeh 午夜 *n. midnight*

hm ying tung 唔認同 *v.t. gainsay*

hm yoon may 唔完美 *a. imperfect*

hm yoot 五月 *n. May*

hm yuk geh 唔郁嘅 *a. stationary*

hm yung 唔溶 *n. insoluble*

hm yung yan 唔容忍 *a. intolerant*

ho 後 *a after*

ho 蠔 *n. oyster*

ho 厚 *a. thick*

ho 好 *adv. well*

ho 蒿 *n. wormwood*

ho ah 好啊 *interj. hurrah*

ho bay 口鼻 *n. muzzle*

ho chee yoon gam 好似猿咁 *a. apish*

ho choy 口才 *n eloquence*

ho choy 好彩 *a. fortunate*

ho choy 好彩 *a. lucky*

ho chu 好處 *n. advantage*

ho chu 好處 *n gain*

ho chu 好處 *n good*

ho chu 好處 *n plus*

ho dai geh 好大嘅 *a enormous*

ho dai geh 好大嘅 *a. huge*

ho dor 好多 *adv. galore*

ho dor 好多 *a. many*

ho dor geh 好多嘅 *a. manifold*

ho dor geh 好多嘅 *a. numerous*

ho dow 好鬥 *a belligerent*

ho doy 口袋 *n. pocket*

ho doy 後代 *n. posterity*

ho fai 好快 *adv. anon*

ho fai 厚塊 *n. slab*

ho fai 好快 *adv. soon*

ho fan 好煩 *a. irritant*

ho fan 好煩 *a. tiresome*

ho fwuy 後悔 *v.i. repent*

ho fwuy 後悔 *n. repentance*

ho fwuy 後悔 *v.t. rue*

ho fwuy geh 後悔嘅 *a. repentant*

ho fwuy geh 後悔嘅 *a. rueful*

ho gao siew 好搞笑 *a. hilarious*

ho geep 浩劫 *n. havoc*

ho geh 好嘅 *a. good*

ho gey 後記 *n epilogue*

ho gik geh 好極嘅 *a. superb*

ho gok 號角 *n bugle*

ho gorng geh 口講嘅 *a. verbal*

ho gwor 後果 *n consequence*

ho gwor 後果 *a consequent*

ho gwor 後果 *n. result*

ho hak 好客 *n. hospitality*

ho hak geh 好客嘅 *a. hospitable*

ho ho 好好 *a great*

ho ho 好好 *a. terrific*

ho ho gam 厚厚咁 *adv. thick*

ho ho geh 好好嘅 *a. marvellous*

ho ho geh 好好嘅 *a. wonderful*

ho ho yan 好好人 *a cordial*

ho ho yan see 好好人士 *a. affable*

ho hok geh 好學嘅 *a. studious*

ho hot 口渴 *a. thirsty*

ho jak 豪宅 *n. mansion*

ho jeen geh 好戰嘅 *a. militant*

ho jeen geh 好戰嘅 *a. warlike*

ho jeen geh yan 好戰嘅人 *n militant*

ho joot 後綴 *n. suffix*

ho jung yiew geh 好重要嘅 *a. vital*

ho kay 好奇 *a curious*

ho kay sam 好奇心 *n curiosity*
ho la 好嬶 *a effeminate*
ho lay 後來 *adv after*
ho lay 後嚟 *a. subsequent*
ho leng 好靚 *a. attractive*
ho leng 好靚 *a. gorgeous*
ho leng 好靚 *a. lovely*
ho lung 喉嚨 *n. throat*
ho lung geh 喉嚨嘅 *a. guttural*
ho ma 號碼 *n. number*
ho may 好味 *a. tasty*
ho may geh 好味嘅 *a. palatable*
ho may geh 好味嘅 *a. toothsome*
ho meen 後面 *adv behind*
ho meen 後面 *prep behind*
ho mo bo low gam 毫無保留咁 *adv.*
  outright
ho pang yow 好朋友 *n chum*
ho sang 後生 *a. young*
ho sang geh 後生嘅 *a. youthful*
ho sao 口哨 *n whistle*
ho say geh 好細嘅 *a. minuscule*
ho say geh 好細嘅 *a. minute*
ho see 口試 *n viva-voce*
ho seh 後寫 *adj. adscript*
ho shu 厚書 *n. tome*
ho siew geh 好笑嘅 *a comical*
ho sik jeh 好色者 *n. sensualist*
ho sut 口述 *v. t dictate*
ho sut 口述 *n dictation*
ho sut geh 口述嘅 *adv. orally*
ho suy 好衰 *a. awful*
ho suy 口水 *n. saliva*
ho suy 口水 *n spit*
ho suy 口水 *n spittle*
ho tai yeurng 好太陽 *a. sunny*
ho tee bat ting 口齒不清 *v.t. lisp*
ho tee bat ting 口齒不清 *v.i. mumble*
ho teen sing 後天性 *adj adscititious*
ho tow geh 口頭嘅 *a. oral*
ho tow geh 口嘅嘅 *a viva-voce*
ho tow seurng geh 口頭上嘅 *adv.*

ho tow seurng geh 口頭上嘅 *adv.*
  verbally
ho tow yeem geh 好討厭嘅 *a.*
  infernal
ho wah 豪華 *a. lush*
ho wah 豪華 *a. luxurious*
ho wah geh 豪華嘅 *a. opulent*
ho wah geh 豪華嘅 *a. regal*
ho wan 好玩 *n. fun*
ho yam 口音 *n accent*
ho yiew 後腰 *n small*
ho yow 好油 *a. oily*
hok 學 *v.i. learn*
hok 殼 *n. shell*
hok hao 學校 *n. school*
hok hao geh 學校嘅 *a. scholastic*
hok jap 學習 *n. learning*
hok jeh 學者 *n. scholar*
hok jeurng 學長 *n. prefect*
hok jor 學咗 *a. learned*
hok juy chor 鶴嘴鋤 *n. mattock*
hok kay 學期 *n. semester*
hok kay 學期 *n. term*
hok lik 學歷 *n. qualification*
hok sang 學生 *n. learner*
hok sang 學生 *n. pupil*
hok sang 學生 *n. student*
hok sut geh 學術嘅 *a academic*
hok way 學位 *n degree*
hok yoon 學院 *n academy*
hok yoon 學院 *n college*
hon jeep 焊接 *v.t. solder*
hon koy 慷慨 *n bounty*
hon lang 寒冷 *n. chill*
hon lang geh 寒冷嘅 *a. wintry*
hon liew 焊料 *n. solder*
hon yow 罕有 *a. rare*
hon yow geh 罕有嘅 *a. sparse*
hong hung 航空 *n. aviation*
hoon 勸 *v. t. counsel*
hoon 勸 *v. t dissuade*

hoon giew seng 吠叫聲 *v.t. bark*
hoon jor 勸阻 *v.i. dehort*
hoot 血 *n blood*
hoot lum lum 血淋淋 *a bloody*
hoot tung 血統 *n. lineage*
hor 河 *n. river*
hor bay 可悲 *a deplorable*
hor hang geh 可行嘅 *a. practicable*
hor hang geh 可行嘅 *a. workable*
hor hang ghe 可行嘅 *a. viable*
hor jing 苛政 *n. tyranny*
hor ka yan 可卡因 *n cocaine*
hor kao geh 可靠嘅 *a credible*
hor lang 可能 *v may*
hor lang fat sang geh see 可能發生嘅
　事 *n. contingency*
hor lang geh 可能嘅 *a. possible*
hor lang sing 可能性 *n. likelihood*
hor lang sing 可能性 *n. odds*
hor lang sing 可能性 *n. possibility*
hor lang sing 可能性 *n. probability*
hor leen 可憐 *a. miserable*
hor leen 可憐 *v.t. pity*
hor leen geh 可憐嘅 *a. piteous*
hor leen geh 可憐嘅 *a. pitiful*
hor leen geh say low 可憐嘅細路 *n
mite*
hor ngoy 可愛 *a. adorable*
hor ngoy geh 可愛嘅 *a darling*
hor pa 可怕 *a formidable*
hor pa 可怕 *a. terrible*
hor sok geh 可塑嘅 *a. malleable*
hor tee geh 可恥嘅 *a. shameful*
hor yee 可疑 *a. suspicious*
hor yee chu lay geh 可以處理嘅 *a.
manageable*
hor yee chuy geh 可以徐嘅 *a.
removable*
hor yee dak dow geh 可以得到嘅 *a.
obtainable*
hor yee fan hoy geh 可以分開嘅 *a.
separable*

hor yee fan joon geh 可以翻轉嘅 *a.
reversible*
hor yee forng wu 可以防護 *a proof*
hor yee gan geh 可以揀嘅 *a.
optional*
hor yee geh 可疑嘅 *a. questionable*
hor yee joon geh 可以轉嘅 *a.
transferable*
hor yee jung jee geh 可以終止嘅 *a.
terminable*
hor yee juy sok geh 可以追溯嘅 *a.
traceable*
hor yee leurng dok geh 可以量度嘅
a. measurable
hor yee teet wuy geh 可以撤回嘅 *a.
revocable*
hor yee way choon geh 可以遺傳嘅
a. heritable
hor yee wun shu geh 可以寬恕嘅 *a.
venial*
hor yee yoon leurng geh 可以原諒嘅
a. pardonable
hor yee yuk 可以喐 *adj ambulant*
hor yee yuk geh 可以喐嘅 *a.
movable*
hor yee yung geh 可以溶嘅 *a.
soluble*
hor yee yung geh 可以溶嘅 *a.
solvent*
hor yi 可以 *a able*
hor yi 可以 *v. t. can*
hor yi jeep sow 可以接受 *a
acceptable*
hor yi jeep sow 可以接受 *a.
admissible*
hor yi jeep sow 可以接受 *a.
agreeable*
hor yi say geh 可以洗嘅 *a. washable*
hor yi sik geh 可以食嘅 *a eatable*
hor yi sik geh 可以食嘅 *a edible*
hor yi tung horng geh 可以通航嘅 *a.
navigable*

hor yi yee geh 可以醫嘅 *a curable*
horn 汗 *n. sweat*
horn dang 刊登 *v.t. publish*
horn hung hok 航空學 *n.pl. aeronautics*
horn jeep 焊接 *v.t. weld*
horn jeep deem 焊接點 *n weld*
horn ju 汗珠 *n. perspiration*
horng hang 航行 *n. voyage*
horng hang jeh 航行者 *n. voyager*
horng koy 慷慨 *n. liberality*
horng koy geh 慷慨嘅 *a. munificent*
horng leet 行列 *n. procession*
horng yeep 行業 *n. industry*
hot 渴 *n. thirst*
hot 渴 *v.i. thirst*
hot choy 喝彩 *v. t. cheer*
hot mong 渴望 *adj. agog*
hot mong 渴望 *adj. appetent*
hot mong 渴望 *adj. athirst*
hot morn gam 渴望咁 *adv avidly*
hot morng 渴望 *v.t. covet*
hot morng 渴望 *v.t. crave*
hot morng 渴望 *n desire*
hot morng 渴望 *v.t desire*
hot morng 渴望 *v.i. hanker*
hot morng 渴望 *n hunger*
hot morng 渴望 *v.i long*
hot morng 渴望 *n. longing*
hot morng 渴望 *v.i. yearn*
hot morng 渴望 *n. yearning*
hot morng geh 渴望嘅 *a. wishful*
how 好 *a. nice*
how choy 好彩 *adv. luckily*
how doy 後代 *n descendant*
how fai huy ha 好快去下 *v.t nip*
how fwut 後悔 *v.i. regret*
how geng 後頸 *n. nape*
how ho 口號 *n. slogan*
how ho 口號 *n. watchword*
how low 好嬲 *a. irate*
how meen 後面 *adv. back*

how meen 後面 *n. rear*
hoy 開 *v.t. prescribe*
hoy 海 *n. sea*
hoy bat 海拔 *n elevation*
hoy bat 海拔 *n. altitude*
hoy bo 海報 *n. poster*
hoy cheurng bak 開場白 *n. preamble*
hoy chorng geh 開創嘅 *a. inaugural*
hoy chung 害蟲 *n. pest*
hoy day geh 海底嘅 *a submarine*
hoy dow 海盜 *n. pirate*
hoy dung 開動 *v.t. activate*
hoy fa 開花 *v.i. bloom*
hoy fa 開花 *v.i blossom*
hoy far 開化 *v. t civilize*
hoy geh 海嘅 *a. marine*
hoy geh 海嘅 *a. maritime*
hoy gwan 海軍 *n. navy*
hoy gwan geh 海軍嘅 *a. naval*
hoy hap 海峽 *n. strait*
hoy jee 開支 *n. expense*
hoy jeurng 海象 *n. walrus*
hoy lai 海獺 *n. otter*
hoy lay 海狸 *n beaver*
hoy lor hok 海螺殼 *n. conch*
hoy lorng 海浪 *n. wave*
hoy meen 海綿 *n. sponge*
hoy ming 開明 *a. liberal*
hoy ngon 海岸 *n coast*
hoy ngon 海岸 *a. littoral*
hoy ow 海鷗 *n. gull*
hoy pao 海豹 *n. seal*
hoy sam 開心 *a. happy*
hoy sam 開心 *a. jubilant*
hoy see san low 海市蜃樓 *n. mirage*
hoy shoon geh 凱旋嘅 *a. triumphal*
hoy tee 開始 *n begin*
hoy tee 開始 *n. beginning*
hoy tee 開始 *v. t commence*
hoy tee 開始 *n commencement*
hoy tee 開始 *v. t embark*
hoy tee 開始 *n. inception*

hoy tee 開始 n. onset
hoy tee 開始 v.t. prelude
hoy tee 開始 v.t. start
hoy tee 開始 n start
hoy tok 開拓 n reclamation
hoy tok jeh 開拓者 n. pioneer
hoy tow 開頭 n. opening
hoy wan 海灣 n bay
hoy wan 海灣 n bight
hoy wan 海灣 n. gulf
hoy way geh 開胃嘅 a. piquant
hoy worng sing 海王星 n. Neptune
hoy yeurng 海洋 n. ocean
hoy yeurng geh 海洋嘅 a. oceanic
huk gey sang 槲寄生 n. mistletoe
huk sow 哭訴 v.i. sob
hung 空 a. bare
hung 熊 n bear
hung 胸 n breast
hung 空 a empty
hung 烘 v.t. parch
hung bak 空白 a blank
hung bo 胸部 n bosom
hung bo 恐怖 a. ghastly
hung bo 恐怖 n. horror
hung bo fan jee 恐怖份子 n. terrorist
hung bo geh 恐怖嘅 a. horrible
hung bo ju yee 恐怖主義 n. terrorism
hung bo sek 紅寶石 n. ruby
hung fan 空翻 n. somersault
hung gak 空格 n blank
hung gan 空間 n. space
hung gan 空間 a. spatial
hung gan 空間 n. void
hung geh 空嘅 a. vacant
hung giew 吼叫 v.i. growl
hung giew seng 吼叫聲 n growl
hung ging 孔徑 n. aperture
hung gow 控告 n accusation
hung gow 控告 v.t. accuse
hung gow 控告 n. indictment

hung guy 恐懼 n dread
hung guy 恐懼 n fear
hung guy 恐懼 n. spectre
hung hak 恐嚇 v.t. cow
hung hak 恐嚇 n. intimidation
hung hak 恐嚇 v.t. terrorize
hung hak 恐嚇 v.t. threaten
hung han 空閒 n. leisure
hung hey 空氣 n air
hung hey low tung 空氣流通 a. airy
hung hung day 紅紅哋 a. reddish
hung jay 控制 v.t control
hung jay 控制 n curb
hung jay 控制 v.t curb
hung jay 控制 v.t dominate
hung jay 控制 n domination
hung jay 控制 n grip
hung jay 控制 v.t harness
hung jay 控制 n. hold
hung jay gorn 控制桿 n. lever
hung jay koon 控制權 n control
hung jeurk 孔雀 n. peacock
hung jung 紅腫 n. weal
hung jung 紅腫 n. welt
hung jung geh 空中嘅 a. aerial
hung koot 空缺 n. vacancy
hung kuy jing 恐懼症 n. neurosis
hung lor bak 紅蘿蔔 n. carrot
hung luk 雄鹿 n. stag
hung or 雄鵝 n. gander
hung sam geh 空心嘅 a. hollow
hung sik 紅色 n. red
hung sik geh 紅色嘅 a. red
hung tan geh 兇殘嘅 a. murderous
hung way 雄偉 a. majestic
hung yan yu 雄人魚 n. merman
hung yun geh 紅潤嘅 a. rosy
hur 靴 n boot
huy 去 v.i. go
huy 去 v.t head
huy chuy jap jat 去除雜質 v.t. refine
huy ga 虛假 a. mendacious

huy ga geh 虛假嘅 *adj mock*
huy gou 虛構 *n figment*
huy ha lok yeen 許下諾言 *v.t. vow*
huy heurng ha 去鄉下 *v.t. rusticate*
huy hok 去殼 *v.t. shell*
huy hor jing 許可證 *n. permit*
huy jeurng sing say 虛張聲勢 *v. t bluff*
huy kow 虛構 *v.t fabricate*
huy kow geh 虛構嘅 *a fictitious*
huy luy hang 去旅行 *v.i. journey*
huy mow ju yee 虛無主義 *n. nihilism*
huy ngay 虛偽 *n. hypocrisy*
huy ngay 虛偽 *n. insincerity*
huy ngay geh 虛偽嘅 *a. hypocritical*
huy pay 去皮 *v.t skin*
huy pwuy 許配 *v. t betroth*
huy sey 去死 *adj. alamort*
huy wing 虛榮 *n. vainglory*
huy yee 虛擬 *a virtual*
huy yeurk 虛弱 *n debility*
huy yeurk 虛弱 *a feeble*
huy yoon 許願 *v.t. wish*

J

ja 揸 *v.t. pilot*
ja 搾 *v.t. squeeze*
ja 揸 *v.t. steer*
ja 炸 *v. t bomb*
ja cher 揸車 *v. t drive*
ja dan 炸彈 *n bomb*
ja ju 揸住 *v.t hold*
ja lai 揸奶 *v.t. milk*
ja lan 炸爛 *v.i blast*
ja soy 痄腮 *n. mumps*
ja yeurk 炸藥 *n dynamite*
ja yeurk 炸藥 *n. explosive*

ja yow teng 揸遊艇 *v.i yacht*
jai 債 *n.pl. arrears*
jai 債 *n debt*
jai gai 齋戒 *v.i fast*
jai gai kay 齋戒期 *n fast*
jai jok sing dung wah peen 製作成動畫片 *v.t. animate*
jai ju 債主 *n creditor*
jai mo yan 債務人 *n debtor*
jak 窄 *a. narrow*
jak been 側邊 *prep. beside*
jak fat 責罰 *v.t mete*
jak gwai 責怪 *v.t. admonish*
jak gwai 責怪 *v. t blame*
jak ngan koot ding 擲銀決定 *n toss*
jak yam 責任 *n blame*
jak yam 責任 *n duty*
jak yam 責任 *n. liability*
jak yam 責任 *n mantle*
jak yam 責任 *n. obligation*
jak yam 責任 *n. responsibility*
jak yiew 摘要 *n abridgement*
jak yiew 摘要 *n abstract*
jak yiew 摘要 *n. breviary*
jak yiew 摘要 *n. digest*
jak yiew 摘要 *n. precis*
jam 斬 *v. t chop*
jam 浸 *v.t flood*
jam 浸 *v.t. immerse*
jam 浸 *n. immersion*
jam 斬 *v.t. lop*
jam 針 *n. needle*
jam 針 *n. pin*
jam 浸 *v.t. swamp*
jam gat 針拮 *n. prick*
jam geurt 針腳 *n. stitch*
jam ngan 眨眼 *v. t. & i blink*
jam ngan 眨眼 *v.i. wink*
jam see 暫時 *a. transitory*
jam see geh 暫時嘅 *a. provisional*
jam see geh 暫時嘅 *a. temporary*
jam see sing 暫時性 *n. provisonality*

jam sow 禽獸 *n. sodomite*
jam ting 暫停 *n. pause*
jam ting 暫停 *v.i. pause*
jam ting 暫停 *v.t. suspend*
jam ting jik mow 暫停職務 *n. suspension*
jam tow 斬頭 *v. t. behead*
jam tow 枕頭 *n pillow*
jan 讚 *v.t acclaim*
jan 讚 *n acclaim*
jan 讚 *v. t compliment*
jan 賺 *v. t earn*
jan 讚 *v. t. extol*
jan 讚 *v.i hail*
jan 震 *a. jerky*
jan 震 *v.t. jolt*
jan 讚 *v.t. laud*
jan 讚 *v.t. praise*
jan 震 *v.i. quiver*
jan 震 *v.i. tremble*
jan 震 *v.i. vibrate*
jan dai teen geh 賺大錢嘅 *a. lucrative*
jan ding 鎮定 *n. composure*
jan ding geh 鎮定嘅 *a. sedate*
jan dung 震動 *n. jolt*
jan dung 震動 *n. pulsation*
jan dung 震動 *n. quiver*
jan dung 震動 *n. vibration*
jan geh 真嘅 *a. real*
jan gway geh 珍貴嘅 *a. precious*
jan hay 真係 *adv. really*
jan hung 真空 *n. vacuum*
jan jing 鎮靜 *v. t. calm*
jan jing geh 真正嘅 *a bonafide*
jan jing geh 鎮靜嘅 *adj calmative*
jan jing geh 鎮靜嘅 *a. sedative*
jan jing jay 鎮靜劑 *n. narcotic*
jan jing jay 鎮靜劑 *n sedative*
jan jor 贊助 *n. patronage*
jan jor 贊助 *v.t. sponsor*
jan jor seurng 贊助商 *n. sponsor*

jan jor yan 贊助人 *n. patron*
jan ju 珍珠 *n. pearl*
jan kuy 鎮區 *a. township*
jan kwan 真菌 *n. fungus*
jan may see 讚美詩 *n. psalm*
jan ngat 鎮壓 *v.t. quell*
jan ngat 鎮壓 *v.t. suppress*
jan ngat 鎮壓 *n. suppression*
jan sik 珍惜 *v. t. cherish*
jan sik 珍惜 *v.t. prize*
jan sik 珍惜 *v.t. treasure*
jan sik 珍惜 *v.t. value*
jan sing 贊成 *v.i. assent*
jan sing 真誠 *n. sincerity*
jan sing yan 贊成人 *n. seconder*
jan yeurng 讚揚 *n. compliment*
jan yeurng 讚揚 *n. glorification*
jan yeurng 讚揚 *n laud*
jang 憎 *v.t. abhor*
jang 憎 *v. t despise*
jang 憎 *v.t. hate*
jang 憎 *v.t. loathe*
jang 挣 *v.i. tussle*
jang 爭 *v.i. vie*
jang 增 *v.t. gain*
jang been 爭辯 *v. t contest*
jang dow 爭鬥 *n. tussle*
jang fwun 贈款 *n. largesse*
jang ga 增加 *v.t. accrete*
jang ga 增加 *v.t. augment*
jang ga 增加 *n. augmentation*
jang ga 增加 *v.t. increase*
jang ga 增加 *n increase*
jang ga 增加 *n. rise*
jang gow 增高 *v.t. heighten*
jang jap 爭執 *n affray*
jang jap 爭執 *n. skirmish*
jang jap 爭執 *v.t. skirmish*
jang jat 挣扎 *v.i. struggle*
jang jeurng 增長 *n accrementition*
jang jik 增值 *v.i. accrue*
jang jik 增值 *n. increment*

jang jun 增進 *v.t further*
jang keurng 增強 *v.t. fortify*
jang keurng hing chuy 增強興趣 *v.t. whet*
jang lun 爭論 *n. altercation*
jang lun 爭論 *n. conflict*
jang lun 爭論 *n controversy*
jang lun 爭論 *n. debate*
jang lun 爭論 *n dispute*
jang lun 爭論 *n. moot*
jang lun 爭論 *n. wrangle*
jao 爪 *n claw*
jao 爪 *n. paw*
jao 抓 *n. scratch*
jao 抓 *v.t. scratch*
jao 罩 *v.t. sheet*
jao fung 罩篷 *n. canopy*
jao gorng 驟降 *n. slump*
jao gorng 驟降 *v.i. slump*
jao siew 嘲笑 *v.i. jeer*
jao siew 嘲笑 *n taunt*
jao yan 抓人 *v.t. pay*
jao yee 罩衣 *n. smock*
jap 集 *n episode*
jap 閘 *n. gate*
jap 汁 *n juice*
jap 執 *v.t. tidy*
jap cho 雜草 *n. weed*
jap dat yoon 執達員 *n. bailiff*
jap fat yan 執法人 *n. martinet*
jap for deem 雜貨店 *n. grocer*
jap for deem 雜貨店 *n. grocery*
jap gey 雜記 *n. miscellany*
jap gey see 雜技師 *n. acrobat*
jap gik 襲擊 *n. assault*
jap gik 襲擊 *n. attack*
jap gik 襲擊 *v.t. attack*
jap gwan 習慣 *v.t. accustom*
jap gwan 習慣 *n. habit*
jap gwan 習慣 *n wont*
jap gwan geh 習慣嘅 *a. wonted*
jap gwan jor 習慣咗 *v. t. habituate*

jap gwan jor 習慣咗 *a. wont*
jap ha 執下 *v.t. retouch*
jap hang 執行 *v. t. enforce*
jap hang 執行 *v. t execute*
jap hang 執行 *v.t. implement*
jap hang lay 執行李 *v.t. pack*
jap hang ling 執行令 *n. warrant*
jap hap 集合 *v.t. rally*
jap horng ghe 雜項嘅 *a. sundry*
jap jat 雜質 *n. impurity*
jap jeurk geh 執著嘅 *a. persistent*
jap juk 習俗 *n. custom*
jap juk 習俗 *a customary*
jap jung 雜種 *n hybrid*
jap jung geh 雜種嘅 *a. hybrid*
jap jung gow 雜種狗 *a mongrel*
jap see 執事 *n. deacon*
jap tay 集體 *a collective*
jap wuy 集會 *n. convention*
jap wuy 集會 *n. convocation*
jar 炸 *v.t. fry*
jat 紮 *n bunch*
jat been 側邊 *n. side*
jat beng 疾病 *n. sickness*
jat day ta 質地差 *a flimsy*
jat gam 質感 *n. texture*
jat jat tiew 紮紮跳 *v.i scamper*
jat jay 姪仔 *n. nephew*
jat leurng 質量 *n. quality*
jat leurng geh 質量嘅 *a. qualitative*
jat liew 質料 *n material*
jat luy 姪女 *n. niece*
jat sat 紮實 *a. sturdy*
jat sik 窒息 *n apnoea*
jat sik 窒息 *v.t suffocate*
jat sik 窒息 *n. suffocation*
jat yee 質疑 *v. i dispute*
jat yee 質疑 *v.t. question*
jay 仔 *n. son*
jay 掣 *n. switch*
jay ban 祭品 *n. oblation*
jay ban 祭品 *n. offering*

jay ban 祭品 *n. sacrifice*
jay bay 責備 *n. reproof*
jay biew yoon 製表員 *n. tabulator*
jay choy 制裁 *n. sanction*
jay fuk 制服 *n. livery*
jay fuk 制服 *v.t. subdue*
jay fuk 制服 *n. subjection*
jay fuk 制服 *n. subjugation*
jay gak gung yan 製革工人 *n. tanner*
jay jee 制止 *v.t foil*
jay jee 制止 *v.t. restrain*
jay jok 製作 *n fabrication*
jay jok 製造 *n. production*
jay jow jeh 製造者 *n. maker*
jay jow seurng 製造商 *n manufacturer*
jay low 滯留 *v.i. strand*
jay low fay 滯留費 *n. demurrage*
jay luy 仔女 *n. offspring*
jay tan 祭壇 *n. altar*
jay yee 祭衣 *n. vestment*
jay yeurk gung see 製藥公司 *n. compounder*
jee 紙 *n. paper*
jee 指 *v.t. point*
jee 止 *v.t. quench*
jee 字 *n. text*
jee 枝 *n. withe*
jee 字 *n. word*
jee bay gam 自卑感 *n. inferiority*
jee bun ju yee jeh 資本主義者 *n. capitalist*
jee chan 資產 *n. asset*
jee chorng 痔瘡 *n. piles*
jee chu 支柱 *n. mainstay*
jee chu 支柱 *n strut*
jee chut 指出 *v.t. indicate*
jee dai 自大 *n. pomposity*
jee dan 子彈 *n bullet*
jee day 自大 *n. arrogance*
jee deen 字典 *n dictionary*

jee dow 知道 *a. aware*
jee dow 指導 *v. t direct*
jee dow 指導 *n. guidance*
jee dow 知道 *v.t. know*
jee dow 指導 *n. tuition*
jee fay gwun 指揮官 *n commander*
jee fey ga 指揮家 *n conductor*
jee forng 脂肪 *n fat*
jee fu 自負 *n egotism*
jee fu 自負 *a. vain*
jee fu 自負 *a. vainglorious*
jee fu 自負 *n. vanity*
jee gam 資金 *n. fund*
jee gam hok 治金學 *n. metallurgy*
jee gam wu lay 指甲護理 *n. manicure*
jee gan 之間 *prep between*
jee gan 紙巾 *n. tissue*
jee gap chor 指甲銼 *n file*
jee gey 自己 *a. alone*
jee gey 知己 *n confidant*
jee gey 自己 *n. self*
jee gey geh 自己嘅 *a. own*
jee gey yat gor 自己一個 *adv. solo*
jee gok 知覺 *n. perception*
jee gung 子宮 *n. uterus*
jee gung 子宮 *n. womb*
jee hay 只係 *adv. only*
jee hay way teen geh 只係爲錢嘅 *a. mercenary*
jee heurng 志向 *n. aspiration*
jee hm seen 子午線 *a. meridian*
jee ho 之後 *prep. after*
jee ho 之後 *adv. thereafter*
jee hoot teep 止血貼 *n. plaster*
jee hung 指控 *n. allegation*
jee ja 吱喳 *v.i. twitter*
jee ja giew 吱喳叫 *v.i. chirp*
jee ja giew seng 吱喳叫聲 *n chirp*
jee jak 指責 *v. t. chide*
jee jak 指責 *v. t. condemn*
jee jak 指責 *v. t denounce*

jee jak 指責 *n. denunciation*
jee jak 自責 *n. remorse*
jee jak 指責 *v.t. reproach*
jee jee giew 吱吱叫 *v. i cheep*
jee jee seng 吱吱聲 *n. twitter*
jee jeh 智者 *n. sage*
jee jeh 智者 *n. sophist*
jee jeurng 紙漿 *n. pulp*
jee jeurng jorng geh 紙漿狀嘅 *a. pulpy*
jee ji 自治 *a autonomous*
jee joon 自傳 *n. autobiography*
jee jor 資助 *v. t endow*
jee jor 資助 *v.t. subsidize*
jee ju 蜘蛛 *n. spider*
jee ju mong 蜘蛛網 *n. web*
jee ju morng 蜘蛛網 *n cobweb*
jee juk 知足 *v. t content*
jee jung 之中 *prep. among*
jee jung 之中 *prep. amongst*
jee lam 指南 *n. guide*
jee larm jam 指南針 *n compass*
jee liew 飼料 *n fodder*
jee liew 資料 *n. information*
jee liew 治療 *n. therapy*
jee liew 治療 *n. treatment*
jee liew sow jao 資料收集 *v.i. research*
jee lik 智力 *n. intellect*
jee lik geh 智力嘅 *a. mental*
jee loon 自憐 *n. narcissism*
jee lor lan 紫羅蘭 *n. violet*
jee low 支流 *n. tributary*
jee low geh 支流嘅 *a. tributary*
jee loy 之內 *prep. within*
jee meen yee yi 字面意義 *a. literal*
jee ming 致命 *a deadly*
jee ming 致命 *a. lethal*
jee ming 自命 *n. pretension*
jee ming bat fan geh 自命不凡嘅 *a. pretentious*
jee ming dow 知名度 *n. notability*

jee ming geh 致命嘅 *a fatal*
jee mo 字母 *n. alphabet*
jee mo sun juy 字母順序 *a. alphabetical*
jee muk suk 紫苜蓿 *n. lucerne*
jee mwuy gam geh 姊妹咁嘅 *a. sisterly*
jee ngor 自我 *n ego*
jee on gwun 治安官 *n. magistracy*
jee pay 指派 *v.t. assign*
jee pay 紙皮 *n. cardboard*
jee piew 支票 *n. cheque*
jee sat 自殺 *n. suicide*
jee say 仔細 *n. nicety*
jee say 姿勢 *n. pose*
jee say 姿勢 *n. posture*
jee say 仔細 *a thorough*
jee say geem ta 仔細檢查 *v.t. scrutinize*
jee say geem ta 仔細檢查 *n. scrutiny*
jee say hao luy 仔細考慮 *n consideration*
jee say hao luy 仔細考慮 *v. i deliberate*
jee say hao luy 仔細考慮 *v.t. ponder*
jee see 芝士 *n. cheese*
jee see 指示 *v.t. instruct*
jee see 指示 *n. instruction*
jee see 指示 *v.i. motion*
jee see 自私 *a. selfish*
jee seurng mao tun geh 自相矛盾嘅 *a. paradoxical*
jee shoon 子孫 *n. progeny*
jee siew 至少 *adv. least*
jee sik 知識 *n. knowledge*
jee sik 紫色 *adj./n. purple*
jee sik fan jee 知識分子 *n. intellectual*
jee sik fan jee 知識分子 *n. intelligentsia*
jee sing 智勝 *v.t. outwit*
jee tang 支撐 *v.t. prop*

jee tay tan koot 肢體殘缺 *n. mutilation*
jee tee 支持 *n. advocacy*
jee tee 支持 *v.t. advocate*
jee tee 支持 *v.t. second*
jee tee 支持 *v.i. side*
jee tee 支持 *v.t. support*
jee tee 支持 *n. support*
jee tee 支持 *v.t uphold*
jee teen 之前 *prep. afore*
jee teen 之前 *adv. ago*
jee teen 之前 *prep before*
jee teen 之前 *conj before*
jee teen geh 之前嘅 *a. antecedent*
jee teen geh 之前嘅 *a. previous*
jee tiew 字條 *n. note*
jee ting 自稱 *v.t. purport*
jee way 智慧 *n. wisdom*
jee way 智慧 *n. wit*
jee way geh 自衛嘅 *adv. defensive*
jee way tee 智慧齒 *n. wisdom-tooth*
jee yan 指引 *v.t. guide*
jee yee way see 自以爲是 *a dogmatic*
jee yeen gam 自然咁 *adv. naturally*
jee yeen san lun jeh 自然神論者 *n. deist*
jee yiew 紙鷂 *n. kite*
jee yoon 寺院 *n. monastery*
jee yoon 資源 *n. resource*
jee yoon 自願 *a. voluntary*
jee yoon 自願 *n. willingness*
jee yoon gam 自願咁 *adv. voluntarily*
jee yoon jeh 志願者 *n. volunteer*
jee yow 自由 *a. free*
jee yow 自由 *n. freedom*
jee yow 自由 *n. liberty*
jee yow 只有 *a. only*
jee yow ju yee 自由主義 *n. liberalism*
jee yow man 自由民 *n. yeoman*
jee yun 滋潤 *v.t. nourish*
jeem am 漸暗 *v.i. darkle*

jeem geh 尖嘅 *a. sharp*
jeem giew 尖叫 *adj argute*
jeem giew 尖叫 *v.i. shriek*
jeem giew seng 尖叫聲 *n. shriek*
jeem giew seng 尖叫聲 *n wail*
jeem hak geh shoot wah 尖刻嘅說話 *n acrimony*
jeem seng geh 尖聲嘅 *a. shrill*
jeem sing hok 占星學 *n. astrology*
jeem sing see 占星師 *n. astrologer*
jeem tap 尖塔 *n. steeple*
jeem tow 尖頭 *n. spike*
jeem uimg 佔用 *v.t. occupy*
jeem yow 佔有 *n. occupancy*
jeem yow say 佔優勢 *v.i. predominate*
jeem yow say 佔優勢 *v.i. preponderate*
jeem yow say geh 佔優勢嘅 *a. predominant*
jeem yow yan 佔有人 *n. occupant*
jeem yow yan 佔有人 *n. occupier*
jeem yu 尖銳 *adj. cultrate*
jeen 箭 *n arrow*
jeen 墊 *n cushion*
jeen 剪 *v. t cut*
jeen 剪 *v.t. shear*
jeen 煎 *v.i. sizzle*
jeen cher 戰車 *n chariot*
jeen chut 展出 *v. t exhibit*
jeen dan goon 煎蛋捲 *n. omelette*
jeen dow 戰鬥 *n battle*
jeen dow 戰鬥 *a. combatant*
jeen gak 賤格 *a. abject*
jeen jan geh 戰爭嘅 *a. martial*
jeen jang 戰爭 *n. warfare*
jeen lam 展覽 *n. exhibition*
jeen lam ban 展覽品 *n. exhibit*
jeen lan 展覽 *n display*
jeen lay ban 戰利品 *n. loot*
jeen leurk geh 戰略嘅 *a. strategic*
jeen luy yan 賤女人 *n bitch*

jeen see 戰士 *n combatant1*
jeen see 展示 *v. t display*
jeen see 展示 *v.t. model*
jeen sing 戰勝 *v.t. worst*
jeen yow 戰友 *n. comrade*
jeep 接 *n. catch*
jeep 摺 *n fold*
jeep 摺 *v.t fold*
jeep been 褶邊 *n. frill*
jeep bok deen seen 接駁電線 *v.t. wire*
jeep dang 褶凳 *n. stool*
jeep doy 接待 *v.t. serve*
jeep doy chu 接待處 *n. reception*
jeep fung 接縫 *v.t. seam*
jeep gan 接近 *v.t. approach*
jeep gan 接近 *v.i. near*
jeep han 摺痕 *n crease*
jeep hap chu 接合處 *n. commissure*
jeep juk 接觸 *n. contact*
jeep jung 接種 *n. vaccination*
jeep jung yoon 接種員 *n. vaccinator*
jeep lik choy 接力賽 *n. relay*
jeep lik pang 接力棒 *n baton*
jeep sow 接受 *& accept*
jeep sow 接受 *n acceptance*
jeep sow 接受 *n embrace*
jeep sow yan 接收人 *n. receiver*
jeet 節 *n. stanza*
jeet 搔 *v.t. tickle*
jeet bak 節拍 *n pulse*
jeet deem 節點 *n. node*
jeet hok 哲學 *n. philosophy*
jeet hok ga 哲學家 *n. philosopher*
jeet hok geh 哲學嘅 *a. philosophical*
jeet jeet giew 吱吱叫 *v.i. squeak*
jeet jeet seng 吱吱聲 *n squeak*
jeet jow 節奏 *v.i. pace*
jeet jow 節奏 *n rhythm*
jeet ju 截住 *v.t. intercept*
jeet mor 折磨 *v.t. afflict*
jeet mor 折磨 *v. t dog*

jeet mor 折磨 *n. ordeal*
jeet mor 折磨 *v.t. plague*
jeet mor 折磨 *n. purgatory*
jeet mor 折磨 *v.t. scourge*
jeet mor 折磨 *n. torment*
jeet mor 折磨 *v.t. torment*
jeet mor 折磨 *n. torture*
jeet mor 折磨 *v.t. torture*
jeet muk biew 節目表 *n. schedule*
jeet sang hoy jee 節省開支 *v.t. retrench*
jeet sang hoy jee 節省開支 *n. retrenchment*
jeet tee dung mat 齧齒動物 *n. rodent*
jeet toon 折斷 *v.t fracture*
jeet tow 折頭 *n discount*
jeet yat 節日 *n festival*
jeetmuk 節目 *n. programme*
jeh 借 *v. t borrow*
jeh 借 *v.t. lend*
jeh 借 *v.t. loan*
jeh 遮 *v.t. shade*
jeh 遮 *n. umbrella*
jeh 遮 *v.t. veil*
jeh gey 借記 *n debit*
jeh ju 遮住 *v. t. cover*
jeh ju 遮住 *v.t. shroud*
jeh lay 啫哩 *n. jelly*
jeh mwuy ting yee 姐妹情誼 *n. sisterhood*
jek gwat 脊骨 *n. spine*
jek gwat geh 脊骨嘅 *a. spinal*
jek gwut 脊骨 *n. backbone*
jeng jung sing ming 鄭重聲明 *n. protestation*
jerk sow 着數 *a. advantageous*
jeung gwun 掌管 *v.t. administer*
jeung ngar 象牙 *n. ivory*
jeurk 雀 *n bird*
jeurk 着 *v. t clothe*
jeurk 着 *v. t dress*

jeurk 着 v.t garb

jeurk 着 v.t. wear

jeurk chao 雀巢 n. nest

jeurk cheurng pow 着長袍 v.t. robe

jeurk for 着火 adv. ablaze

jeurk hm lok 着唔落 v.t. outgrow

jeurk may 着迷 v. t enchant

jeurk may 着迷 v. t enrapture

jeurk may 著迷 n. infatuation

jeurng 獎 n. award

jeurng 章 n. chapter

jeurng 獎 v.t. reward

jeurng 張 n. sheet

jeurng 槳 v.t. starch

jeurng 仗 n. war

jeurng ak 掌握 n grasp

jeurng ak 掌握 v.t. master

jeurng ban 獎品 n. prize

jeurng bay chung 象鼻蟲 n. weevil

jeurng bo 賬簿 n. ledger

jeurng fu 象夫 n. mahout

jeurng fung 帳篷 n. tent

jeurng gao 橡膠 n. rubber

jeurng gwan 將軍 n checkmate

jeurng gwor 橡果 n. acorn

jeurng hok gam 獎學金 n. scholarship

jeurng jap 醬汁 n. sauce

jeurng jeh 長者 n elder

jeurng jik sow fat 象徵手法 n. symbolism

jeurng jing 象徵 v. i denote

jeurng jing 象徵 n emblem

jeurng jing 象徵 v.t. symbolize

jeurng jor 獎座 n. trophy

jeurng jorng 獎狀 n. certificate

jeurng jow 將就 v.t. lump

jeurng lay 獎勵 n. reward

jeurng lo 樟腦 n. camphor

jeurng loy 將來 n future

jeurng ngar 象牙 n. tusk

jeurng ngoy 障礙 n. barrier

jeurng ngoy 障礙 n. impediment

jeurng ngoy mat 障礙物 n. obstacle

jeurng pai 獎牌 n. medal

jeurng pai wok dak jeh 獎牌獲得者 n. medallist

jeurng shu 橡樹 n. oak

jeurng sing 掌聲 n. applause

jeurng sing tee 象聲詞 n. onomatopoeia

ji dung 自動 a. automatic

ji ho 之後 adv. afterwards

ji jee kuy 自治區 n. municipality

ji yoon 寺院 n. abbey

jiew 照 v.t. illuminate

jiew v.t. masticate

jiew v.t. munch

jiew day 沼地 n. swamp

jiew deem 焦點 n focus

jiew gu 照顧 n. care

jiew gu 照顧 v.t. mother

jiew gu 照顧 v.t nurse

jiew gu ma pat 照顧馬匹 v.t. agist

jiew jak 沼澤 n bog

jiew jap 招集 v.t. assemble

jiew jap 召集 v. t convene

jiew jap 召集 v.t. convoke

jiew jap yan 召集人 n convener

jiew liew 鷦鷯 n. wren

jiew mow 招募 v.t. recruit

jiew sow 招手 v.t hail

jiew wan sut 招魂術 n. spiritualism

jik 織 v.t. knit

jik 直 adv. straight

jik 織 v.t. weave

jik bo gey 織布機 n loom

jik bo gung 織布工 n. weaver

jik cheurng 直腸 n. rectum

jik dak 值得 v.t merit

jik dak 值得 a worth

jik dak 值得 a. worthy

jik dak jan 值得讚 a. laudable

jik dak jan geh 值得讚嘅 a. commendable

jik dak jan geh 值得讚嘅 a creditable

jik dak jan geh 值得讚嘅 a. meritorious

jik dak jan geh 值得讚嘅 a. praiseworthy

jik dak joon jung geh 值得尊重嘅 a. venerable

jik dak jow geh 值得做嘅 a desirable

jik dak ju yee geh 值得注意嘅 a. noteworthy

jik dak tung ting geh 值得同情嘅 a. pitiable

jik dak wok jeurng 值得獲獎 a. laureate

jik dow 直到 prep. till

jik dow 直到 n. conj. till

jik dow 直到 prep. until

jik dow 直到 conj until

jik dow yee ga 直到而家 adv. hitherto

jik gam 織錦 n. tapestry

jik geh 直嘅 a. straight

jik ging 直徑 n diameter

jik gok 直覺 n. hunch

jik gok 直覺 n. instinct

jik gok 直覺 n. intuition

jik gok geh 直覺嘅 a. instinctive

jik hak 即刻 a immediate

jik hak 即刻 a. instant

jik hak 即刻 adv. instantly

jik hak 即刻 a. prompt

jik hak 即刻 adv. straightway

jik ho 藉口 n excuse

jik ho 藉口 n pretext

jik jak 職責 n. onus

jik jeep 直接 a direct

jik jeurng 跡象 n. indicator

jik jeurng fat sang 即將發生 a. imminent

jik jeurng fat sang 即將發生 n. offing

jik jeurng fat sang geh 即將發生嘅 a. forthcoming

jik lap geh 直立嘅 a erect

jik luy 積累 v.t. accumulate

jik luy gan 積累緊 n accumulation

jik man day 殖民地 n colony

jik man geh 殖民嘅 a colonial

jik mat 植物 n. plant

jik mat hok 植物學 n botany

jik mat kwan 植物群 n flora

jik mok 寂寞 a. lonesome

jik way 職位 n post

jik yeep 職業 n. occupation

jik yeep 職業 n. profession

jik yeep sang ngai 職業生涯 n. career

jik yoon 職員 n. staff

jing 整 v. t create

jing 整 v.t. make

jing 靜 n. quiet

jing 整 n. scoff

jing 正 adv. sharp

jing 整 v.t sort

jing 蒸 v.i. steam

jing 整 v.t. mend

jing bay 整跛 v.t. lame

jing been 政變 n. coup

jing bwun 正本 n original

jing choy 精彩 a brilliant

jing dak ju yee geh 值得注意嘅 a. notable

jing day 整低 v.i. low

jing day 剩低 n. remainder

jing day geh 淨低嘅 a net

jing doon 整短 v.t. shorten

jing dorng geh 正當嘅 a. righteous

jing dorng lay yow 正當理由 n. justification

jing dow sing san lay 整到成身泥 v. t bemire

jing fan 整返 v.t. repair
jing far 淨化 n. purgation
jing far 淨化 n. purification
jing far 淨化 v.t. purify
jing far geh 淨化嘅 a purgative
jing fat 蒸發 v. i evaporate
jing fat 蒸發 v.t. vaporize
jing forng mo liew 精紡毛料 n. worsted
jing fu 政府 n. government
jing fu bo mun 政府部門 n. ministry
jing fuk 征服 v. t conquer
jing fuk 征服 n conquest
jing fuk 征服 v.t. overpower
jing fuk 征服 v.t. subjugate
jing fwut 整闊 v.t. widen
jing gan 整緊 v.t. tighten
jing geet 貞潔 n. virginity
jing ging gwor dow geh yan 正經過度嘅人 n. prude
jing gon 整乾 v. i. dry
jing gor 整個 n whole
jing gu 整蠱 v.t hoax
jing gu 整蠱 v.t. rag
jing gu 整蠱 v.t. tease
jing guy 證據 n evidence
jing guy 證據 n. proof
jing guy 證據 n. testament
jing guy 證據 n. testimony
jing hak 整黑 v. t. blacken
jing hang 整坑 v.t. pit
jing hay 蒸氣 n steam
jing hay 蒸氣 n. vapour
jing heurng 正向 adv due
jing hm 正午 n. noon
jing ho 整好 v.t fix
jing ho 整厚 v.i. thicken
jing jan 淨賺 v.t. net
jing jay geh 精製嘅 a. superfine
jing jee 政治 n. politics
jing jee 精子 n. sperm
jing jee 靜止 a. still

jing jee 靜止 n. stillness
jing jee ga 政治家 n. politician
jing jee ga 政治家 n. statesman
jing jee geh 政治嘅 a. political
jing jee so dung 政治騷動 n ferment
jing jeem 整尖 v.t. sharpen
jing jik 整直 v.t. straighten
jing jorng 症狀 n. symptom
jing jorng geh 症狀嘅 a. symptomatic
jing kok 正確 adv aright
jing kok 正確 a correct
jing lap 整凹 v.t hollow
jing lik 精力 n. verve
jing lik chung pwuy 精力充沛 a. sprightly
jing lik chung pwuy 精力充沛 a. vigorous
jing lik hok 靜力學 n. statics
jing ling 精靈 n elf
jing loon 整亂 v.t. jumble
jing loon 整亂 v.i mess
jing low 蒸餾 v. t distil
jing lung 蒸籠 n. steamer
jing mak 靜脈 n. vein
jing man geh 正文嘅 n. textual
jing meen 正面 n facade
jing meen geh 正面嘅 a. positive
jing ming 證明 v.t. justify
jing ming 證明 v.t. prove
jing ming 精明 a. sagacious
jing ming 證明 v.t. show
jing ming 證明 v.t. substantiate
jing ming ghe 精明嘅 a. shrewd
jing ming mow juy 證明無罪 n. vindication
jing mo way yoon wuy 政務委員會 n. council
jing ping 整平 v.t. smooth
jing san 精心 n. spirit
jing san beng 精神病 n. insanity
jing san beng 精神病 n. psychosis

jing san beng hok 精神病學 *n.* *psychiatry*

jing san beng wan jeh 精神病患者 *n.* *psychopath*

jing san beng yoon 精神病院 *n* *asylum*

jing san chor loon 精神錯亂 *n.* *lunacy*

jing san for yee sang 精神科醫生 *n.* *psychiatrist*

jing san sing 精神性 *n.* *spirituality*

jing sap 整濕 *v. t. damp*

jing sap 整濕 *v.t. moisten*

jing sap 整濕 *v.t. soak*

jing sat 證實 *v.t. attest*

jing sat 證實 *v. t. certify*

jing sat 證實 *v.t. corroborate*

jing sat 證實 *n. substantiation*

jing sat 證實 *v.i. testify*

jing sat 證實 *v.t. validate*

jing sat 證實 *v.t. vindicate*

jing say 整細 *v.t. muffle*

jing seurng 正常 *n. norm*

jing seurng 正常 *a. normal*

jing seurng 正常 *n. normalcy*

jing seurng fan 正相反 *pref. contra*

jing seurng far 正常化 *v.t. normalize*

jing shoon geh 精選嘅 *a select*

jing shu 證書 *n. muniment*

jing sik 正式 *a formal*

jing sik 正式 *adv. officially*

jing sik geh 正式嘅 *a. official*

jing sik jow jik 正式就職 *v.t. induct*

jing sik luk chuy 正式錄取 *v.t. matriculate*

jing sik pay jun 證實批准 *v.t. ratify*

jing sow 徵收 *v.t. levy*

jing suy 精髓 *n essence*

jing suy 整碎 *v.t mash*

jing tak 政策 *n doctrine*

jing tam 偵探 *n. detective*

jing tam geh 偵探嘅 *a detective*

jing tao 整皺 *v.t. ruffle*

jing tay 整齊 *a. neat*

jing tay 整齊 *n. tidiness*

jing tay 整齊 *a. tidy*

jing teem 整甜 *v.t. sweeten*

jing toon 整斷 *v.t. snap*

jing tung 精通 *n. mastery*

jing tung 精通 *n. proficiency*

jing tung geh 正統嘅 *a. orthodox*

jing tung gwun leem 正統觀念 *n. orthodoxy*

jing uk deng 整屋頂 *v.t. roof*

jing wu jow 整污糟 *v.t. soil*

jing wu jow 整污糟 *v.t. stain*

jing yan 證人 *n. deponent*

jing yik 精液 *n. semen*

jing yoon 整軟 *v.t. soften*

jing yoon may 整完美 *v.t. perfect*

jing yu 剩餘 *n. surplus*

jing yung 徵用 *n. requisition*

jing yung 徵用 *v.t. requisition*

jo 做 *v. t do*

jo geen 組件 *n. component*

jo hap 組合 *n combination*

jo ho yee tow geh yeh 做好意頭嘅嘢 *v.t. auspicate*

jo pang yow 做朋友 *v. t. befriend*

jo seen 祖先 *n. ancestor*

jo seen 祖先 *n. ancestry*

jo seen 祖先 *n forefather*

jo seen geh 祖先嘅 *a. ancestral*

jo sing yat duy 組成一對 *v.t. pair*

jo tan 早餐 *n breakfast*

jo yu 遭遇 *n. encounter*

jok 鑿 *n chisel*

jok 作 *v. t compose*

jok ban 作品 *n composition*

jok ban 作品 *n creation*

jok fan 作反 *n. rebel*

jok fan jeh 作反者 *n. insurgent*

jok fay 作廢 *v.t. invalidate*

jok fay 作廢 *v.t. nullify*

jok jeh 作者 n. author
jok jeh 作者 n. writer
jok oh 作嘔 v.t. gag
jok oh 作嘔 n. nausea
jok ok geh 作惡嘅 a. maleficent
jok see 作詩 v.t. versify
jong 撞 v.t. bang
joo 煮 v. t cook
joon 磚 n brick
joon 鑽 n drill
joon 鑽 v. t. drill
joon 轉 v.i. rotate
joon 轉 v.i. spin
joon 轉 n. spin
joon 轉 v.t. switch
joon 轉 n. transfer
joon 轉 v.t. transfer
joon 轉 v.i. turn
joon 轉 n.i. whirl
joon been 轉變 n. transition
joon been 轉變 n. twist
joon cheurng 專長 n. forte
joon cheurng 專長 n. speciality
joon day 轉遞 n. transitive
joon day gung see 專遞公司 n. courier
joon dung 轉動 n. rotation
joon dung geh 轉動嘅 a. rotary
joon fat 轉發 v.t. relay
joon ga 專家 n expert
joon ga 專家 n. luminary
joon gar 專家 n. specialist
joon gey 轉寄 v.t forward
joon gey 傳記 n biography
joon gey jok ga 傳記作家 n biographer
joon ging 尊敬 n esteem
joon ging 尊敬 v. t esteem
joon ging 尊敬 v. t honour
joon ging 尊敬 v.t. revere
joon ging 尊敬 n. reverence
joon ging 尊敬 n. veneration
joon ging geh 尊敬嘅 a. reverend
joon gung 專攻 v.i. specialize
joon jee 轉子 n. armature
joon jow 轉租 v.t. sublet
joon ju 專注 v.t focus
joon jung 尊重 n deference
joon jung 尊重 v.t. respect
joon jung 尊重 n. respect
joon jung gao geh yan 轉宗教嘅人 n convert
joon jung geh 尊重嘅 a. respectful
joon kay 傳奇 n. legend
joon lay koon 專利權 n patent
joon lun 專論 n. monograph
joon mun ming tee geh 專門名詞嘅 a. terminological
joon mwun far 專門化 n. specialization
joon sam 專心 v. t concentrate
joon sam 專心 n. concentration
joon sam 專心 v. t devote
joon say 轉世 n. transmigration
joon sek 鑽石 n diamond
joon sek geen juk 磚石建築 n. masonry
joon tap 專輯 n. album
joon wan mwut gok 轉彎抹角 a. oblique
joon wan mwut got 轉彎抹角 v.t hedge
joon wang 專橫 a autocratic
joon wun 轉換 n conversion
joon yee 轉移 v.t. & i. deflect
joon yee 轉移 v. t divert
joon yee 轉移 v.t. shift
joon yeem 尊嚴 n dignity
joon yeep geh 專業嘅 a. professional
joon yeep yung tee 專業用詞 n. jargon
joon ying jeh 專營者 n. monopolist
joon yow geh 專有嘅 a. proprietary
joot 啜 v.t. suck

joot dow 決鬥 v. i duel
joot duy 絕對 a absolute
joot duy 絕對 adv absolutely
joot duy 絕對 a. categorical
joot duy 絕對 adv. stark
joot jung geh 絕種嘅 a extinct
joot morng 絕望 n despair
joot morng 絕望 v. i despair
joot morng 絕望 n. slough
jor 左 a. left
jor 左 n. left
jor 阻 v.t. obstruct
jor dorng 阻擋 n. obstruction
jor jee 阻止 v.i bog
jor jee 阻止 v. t. discourage
jor jee 阻止 v.t. impede
jor jee 阻止 v.t. inhibit
jor jee 阻止 a. obstructive
jor jee 阻止 v.t. thwart
jor jeet 阻截 v.t. tackle
jor lan 災難 n disaster
jor larn 災難 n. calamity
jor lun cheurng 左輪槍 n. revolver
jor ngoy 阻礙 v. t. encumber
jor ngoy 阻礙 v.t. handicap
jor ngoy 阻礙 v.t. hinder
jor ngoy 阻礙 v.t. retard
jor ngoy sang jeurng 阻礙生長 v.t. stunt
jor pai fan jee 左派分子 n leftist
jor sang 再生 v.t. regenerate
jor sat 阻塞 v.t block
jor sow 助手 n. assistant
jor way 座位 n. seat
jorng 撞 v. t. clash
jorng 撞 v. i crash
jorng 裝 v.t. load
jorng 裝 v.t. mount
jorng 撞 v.t. smack
jorng 撞 v.t. ram
jorng ban 裝扮 v.t. adorn
jorng bay 裝備 v.t. arm

jorng bay 裝備 v. t equip
jorng bay 裝備 n. kit
jorng bay 裝備 v.t outfit
jorng bay 裝備 n. pl paraphernalia
jorng cher 撞車 n smash
jorng chuk 裝束 n. outfit
jorng forng 狀況 n. state
jorng gwun 裝罐 v. can
jorng gwun 壯觀 a. spectacular
jorng gwun 裝罐 v.t. tin
jorng gwun geh 壯觀嘅 a. stately
jorng hung far fan 藏紅花粉 n. saffron
jorng joy 裝載 v.t. lade
jorng jun gey 裝樽機 n bottler
jorng lay 葬禮 n burial
jorng lay geh 壯麗嘅 a. grand
jorng ma on 裝馬鞍 v.t. saddle
jorng mat 贓物 n booty
jorng mat 贓物 n spoil
jorng mun 裝滿 v.t fill
jorng sik 裝飾 v.t. apparel
jorng sik 裝飾 v.t. bedight
jorng sik 裝飾 n decoration
jorng sik 裝飾 v.t. grace
jorng sik 裝飾 v.t. ornament
jorng sik 裝飾 n. ornamentation
jorng sik ban 裝飾品 n. ornament
jorng sik geh 裝飾嘅 a. ornamental
jorng sow 裝修 v. t decorate
jorng yao pwun dow 裝入盆度 v.t. pot
jorng yoon geh 莊園嘅 a. manorial
jorng yoon jak day 莊園宅第 n. manor
jow 做 prep.. as
jow 走 adv. away
jow 做 v. t. commit
jow 洲 n continent
jow 咒 n curse
jow 早 adv early
jow 早 a early

jow 租 *v.t* hire
jow 咒 *n. invective*
jow 走 *v.t. leave*
jow 酒 *n. liquor*
jow 租 *v.t. rent*
jow 酒 *n. wine*
jow 皺 *v.t. wrinkle*
jow ba 酒吧 *n. saloon*
jow ba 酒吧 *n. bar*
jow bwuy 酒杯 *n. goblet*
jow chor 做錯 *v.i blunder*
jow choy pwun 做裁判 *v.t., umpire*
jow dak gwor fan 做得過分 *v.t. overdo*
jow deem 酒店 *n. hotel*
jow gam 租金 *n. rent*
jow geh forng 租嘅房 *n. lodging*
jow gway 酒鬼 *n bibber*
jow gwun 酒館 *n. tavern*
jow hap sai 組合晒 *v.t. piece*
jow hay 就係 *adv. namely*
jow ho 袖口 *n cuff*
jow horn 週刊 *n. weekly*
jow jeurng 州長 *n. governor*
jow jik 就職 *n. inauguration*
jow jik 組織 *n. organization*
jow jing 酒精 *n alcohol*
jow kay 租期 *n. tenancy*
jow lo geh 走佬嘅 *a. fugitive*
jow long 走廊 *n. corridor*
jow luy yam ban 酒類飲品 *n. intoxicant*
jow man 皺紋 *n. furrow*
jow man 皺紋 *n. wrinkle*
jow may tow 皺眉頭 *v.i. scowl*
jow may tow 皺眉頭 *n. scowl*
jow mey 皺眉 *n. frown*
jow mey 皺眉 *v.i frown*
jow san geh dung mat 走散嘅動物 *n stray*
jow sat 酒塞 *n. cork*
jow sat geh 走失嘅 *a stray*

jow see 走私 *v.t. smuggle*
jow see jeh 走私者 *n. smuggler*
jow seen fung 做先鋒 *v.t. pioneer*
jow shoon 就算 *conj. albeit*
jow shoon hai gam 就算係咁 *adv. nonetheless*
jow shoon hai gam 就算係咁 *adv. notwithstanding*
jow sing 組成 *adj. constituent*
jow sing 組成 *v.t. group*
jow sing 造成 *v.i. result*
jow sing 造成 *v.i. spawn*
jow tan geh 早產嘅 *a. premature*
jow toon 組團 *v.t. regiment*
jow way 周圍 *n. periphery*
jow way 周圍 *n. surroundings*
jow way geh 周圍嘅 *adj. ambient*
jow wey 周圍 *prep. around*
jow wu 租戶 *n. lessee*
jow wu 租戶 *n. tenant*
jow yam 就任 *n accession*
jow yam 就任 *n. induction*
jow yeem 酒宴 *n. wassail*
jow yeh 做嘢 *v.t. work*
jow yeurk 租約 *n. lease*
jow yu 咒語 *n. spell*
jow yung 租用 *n. hire*
jow yung 租用 *v.t. lease*
jow...geh deen fa 做...嘅典範 *v.t. typify*
joy 再 *adv. again*
joy fat sang 再發生 *v.i. recur*
joy geen 再見 *n. adieu*
joy geen 再見 *interj. adieu*
joy geen 再見 *interj. good-bye*
joy jow 再造 *v.t. reproduce*
joy pwuy 栽培 *n. nurture*
joy pwuy 栽培 *v.t. nurture*
joy sang 在生 *a alive*
joy say lay 再洗禮 *n anabaptism*
joy tee ying sing 再次形成 *adj anamorphous*

ju 珠 *n bead*
ju 住 *v. i dwell*
ju 住 *v.i. live*
ju 豬 *n. pig*
ju 住 *v.i. reside*
ju 豬 *n. swine*
ju bay 豬鼻 *n. snout*
ju bay chorng 鑄幣廠 *n mint*
ju bo seurng 珠寶商 *n. jeweller*
ju cheurng 豬場 *n. sty*
ju ding sat bai 注定失敗 *v. t. doom*
ju dung geen yee 主動建議 *v.t. volunteer*
ju dung sing 主動性 *n. initiative*
ju fu gan geh 住附近嘅 *a. neighbourly*
ju gao 主教 *n bishop*
ju gu lik 朱古力 *n chocolate*
ju gwun 主觀 *a. subjective*
ju gwun 主管 *v.t. superintend*
ju gwun 主管 *n. supervisor*
ju jak kuy 住宅區 *n estate*
ju jik 主席 *n chairman*
ju jow 鑄造 *v.t. mint*
ju jow chorng 鑄造廠 *n. foundry*
ju jung siew see 注重小事 *adj. anal*
ju koon 主權 *n. sovereignty*
ju ming geh 著名嘅 *a eminent*
ju mwun yan 住滿人 *v.t. people*
ju sar 朱砂 *n cinnabar*
ju seh hay 注射器 *n. syringe*
ju she 注射 *v.t. inject*
ju shu chung 蛀書蟲 *n. bookish*
ju sor 住所 *n abode*
ju sor 住所 *n domicile*
ju sor 住所 *n dwelling*
ju sor 住所 *n. residence*
ju sor 住所 *n. shelter*
ju sow for ting 主修課程 *n major*
ju suk 住宿 *n. accommodation*
ju tay 主題 *n. motif*
ju tay 主題 *n. subject*

ju tay 主題 *n. theme*
ju tay geh 主題嘅 *a. thematic*
ju tee 主持 *n. host*
ju tee 主持 *v.i. officiate*
ju tee 主持 *v.i. preside*
ju teet 鑄鐵 *n cast-iron*
ju yam 主任 *n. dean*
ju yan 主人 *n. master*
ju yap 注入 *v.t. infuse*
ju yee 注意 *n. attention*
ju yee 注意 *v.t. heed*
ju yee 注意 *v.t. notice*
ju yee 注意 *v.t. perceive*
ju yeen 主演 *v.t. star*
ju yiew 主要 *adv. mainly*
ju yiew 主要 *adv. primarily*
ju yiew geh 主要嘅 *a main*
ju yiew geh 主要嘅 *a. major*
ju yiew geh 主要嘅 *a. prime*
ju yow 豬油 *n. lard*
ju yu 侏儒 *n. pygmy*
ju yuk 豬肉 *n. pork*
juk 竹 *n. bamboo*
juk 捉 *v. t. capture*
juk 捉 *n. capture*
juk 俗 *a. gaudy*
juk 捉 *v.t. noose*
juk 捉 *v.t. trap*
juk 族 *n. tribe*
juk chao 築巢 *v.t. nest*
juk chut 逐出 *v. t evict*
juk chut 逐出 *n eviction*
juk chut gao wuy 逐出教會 *v. t. excommunicate*
juk chut gao wuy 逐出 *n. expulsion*
juk fuk 祝福 *n benison*
juk fuk 祝福 *v. t bless*
juk gan 捉緊 *n clasp*
juk gan 捉緊 *v. i. cling*
juk go 足夠 *a. sufficient*
juk gok 觸覺 *a. tactile*
juk gok 觸覺 *n touch*

juk gor jee 逐個字 *a. verbatim*
juk gor jee 逐個字 *adv. verbatim*
juk gow 足夠 *a. ample*
juk gow 足夠 *adv enough*
juk gow 足夠 *v.i. suffice*
juk hor 祝賀 *n congratulation*
juk hor 祝賀 *v.t felicitate*
juk jap 續集 *n. sequel*
juk jeem 逐漸 *a. gradual*
juk jeen garm yeurk 逐漸減弱 *v.t. undermine*
juk ju 捉住 *v.t. grab*
juk ju 捉住 *v.t. grasp*
juk ju 捉住 *v.t. nab*
juk ju 捉住 *v.t. seize*
juk pow 族譜 *n. pedigree*
juk sam 燭芯 *n. wick*
juk sat 捉實 *v.t. grip*
juk sat 捉實 *v.t. poise*
juk so 觸鬚 *n. antennae*
juk yan 俗人 *n. worldling*
juk yu 竹芋 *n. arrowroot*
juk yu 俗語 *n byword*
jun 準 *v.t. allow*
jun 樽 *n bottle*
jun 樽 *n. jar*
jun bay 準備 *v.t. gird*
jun bay 準備 *n. preparation*
jun bay 準備 *v.t. prepare*
jun bay 準備 *n. readiness*
jun bay 準備 *a. ready*
jun bay geh 準備嘅 *a. preparatory*
jun bo 進步 *v.t. improve*
jun bo 進步 *n. improvement*
jun bo 進步 *v.i. progress*
jun chung 遵從 *v.t. obey*
jun dow 進度 *n. progress*
jun far 進化 *n evolution*
jun far 進化 *v.t evolve*
jun gung 進攻 *v.t. advance*
jun hang gan 進行緊 *adv. afoot*
jun jak 準則 *n. precept*

jun jik geh 盡職嘅 *a dutiful*
jun kok 準確 *a. accurate*
jun kok dow 準確度 *n. precision*
jun kok geh 準確嘅 *a exact*
jun kok geh 準確嘅 *a. precise*
jun kok sing 準確性 *n. accuracy*
jun lik 盡力 *v.i endeavour*
jun ma 駿馬 *n. steed*
jun see geh 準時嘅 *a. punctual*
jun see lut 準時率 *n. punctuality*
jun sing 晉升 *n. advancement*
jun sow 遵守 *v.i. adhere*
jun sow 遵守 *n. adherence*
jun sow 遵守 *n. conformity*
jun teep 津貼 *n. allowance*
jun teep 津貼 *n benefit*
jun teep 津貼 *n. subsidy*
jun ting gam 盡情咁 *adv. heartily*
jun yap 進入 *v.t. import*
jung 中 *prep. amid*
jung 鐘 *n. clock*
jung 種 *n. kind*
jung 種 *v.t. plant*
jung 腫 *n sore*
jung 種 *v.t. sow*
jung 仲 *adv. still*
jung 腫 *v.i. swell*
jung 腫 *n swell*
jung 仲 *adv. yet*
jung bai 鐘擺 *n. pendulum*
jung bo day kuy 中部地區 *n. midland*
jung choy 仲裁 *n. arbitration*
jung choy yan 仲裁人 *n. arbitrator*
jung dai geh 重大嘅 *a. signal*
jung dang geh 中等嘅 *a. middling*
jung deem jam 終點站 *n. terminus*
jung deen 中殿 *n. nave*
jung dor 眾多 *n. multitude*
jung duk 總督 *n. viceroy*
jung duy 中隊 *n. squadron*
jung for juy 縱火罪 *n arson*

jung gan 中間 n middle
jung gan 中間 n. midst
jung gan geh 中間嘅 a. intermediate
jung gan geh 中間嘅 a. median
jung gan geh 中間嘅 a. mid
jung gan geh 中間嘅 a. middle
jung gan yan 中間人 n. intermediary
jung gan yan 中間人 n. middleman
jung gao 宗教 n. religion
jung gao doon man 宗教短文 n tract
jung gao hok 宗教學 n. theology
jung gao ye sik 宗教儀式 n. observance
jung geet 總結 v.t. sum
jung geet 總結 v.t. summarize
jung geet 總結 n. summary
jung geet sing geh 總結性嘅 a summary
jung gey 總計 v.i amount
jung gey geh 總計嘅 a. total
jung gik geh 終極嘅 a. ultimate
jung gor 頌歌 n carol
jung gor 頌歌 n. ode
jung ha 仲夏 n. midsummer
jung hap 綜合 n. synthesis
jung hm 中午 n. midday
jung ho 中號 a medium
jung hor yee 仲可以 a. tolerable
jung jee 終止 v.i abort
jung jee 終止 v. i. cease
jung jee 中子 n. neutron
jung jee 種子 n. seed
jung jee 終止 v.t. terminate
jung jee 終止 n. termination
jung jik jeh 種植者 n. grower
jung jik yoon 種植園 n. plantation
jung jing 忠貞 n. chastity
jung juk geh 種族嘅 a. racial
jung juk kay see 種族歧視 n. racialism
jung lap geh 中立嘅 a. impartial
jung lap geh 中立嘅 a. neutral

jung lay 總理 n. chancellor
jung lo 腫瘤 n. tumour
jung luy 種類 n. category
jung luy 種類 n classification
jung luy 種類 n. sort
jung luy 種類 n. species
jung luy 種類 n. specimen
jung luy shu 棕櫚樹 n. palm
jung ma 種馬 n. stallion
jung man 頌文 n. panegyric
jung mow 鬃毛 n. manes
jung peen siew shoot 中篇小說 n. novelette
jung sam 中心 n center
jung sam 中心 a. central
jung sam 中心 n centre
jung sam 中心 n. locus
jung sam 忠心 a. loyal
jung sam 忠心 n. loyalty
jung sam deem 中心點 n. pivot
jung sam geh yan 忠心嘅人 n. loyalist
jung sang geh 終身嘅 a. lifelong
jung sao yap 總收入 n. gross
jung sat 忠實 n fidelity
jung sat geh 忠實嘅 a. stalwart
jung sat yung wu jeh 忠實擁護者 n stalwart
jung say gey geh 中世紀嘅 a. medieval
jung seurng 中傷 v.t. backbite
jung seurng 中傷 v. t. defame
jung seurng 中傷 v.t. vilify
jung seurng 中傷 v.t. libel
jung seurng geh 中傷嘅 a. slanderous
jung sik 棕色 a brown
jung sik 棕色 n brown
jung sing 忠誠 n. allegiance
jung sing geh 忠誠嘅 a faithful
jung sing geh 中性嘅 a. neuter
jung so 總數 v.t. aggregate

jung so 總數 n. sum

jung sor jow jee 眾所周知 a. proverbial

jung sow 總數 n. total

jung tay geh 總體嘅 a overall

jung ting heurng yung 盡情享用 v.i feast

jung toon 中斷 n abrupt on

jung tow 鐘頭 n. hour

jung tung 總統 n. president

jung tung geh 總統嘅 a. presidential

jung worng sik 棕黃色 n., a. tan

jung yee 鐘意 v.t fancy

jung yee 鐘意 a fond

jung yee 鐘意 v.t. like

jung yee gorng siew geh yan 鐘意講笑嘅人 n. joker

jung yew geh 重要嘅 a focal

jung yiew 重要 a. important

jung yiew geh 重要嘅 a. monumental

jung yiew geh 重要嘅 a. significant

jung yiew sing 重要性 n. importance

jung yiew sing 重要性 n. significance

jung yu ying sing 終於應承 v.i. relent

jung yung 縱容 n. connivance

jung yung 縱容 n. indulgence

jung yung 縱容 a. indulgent

jung yung 縱容 v.t. pamper

jut 捽 v.t. rub

juy 追 v. t. chase1

juy 罪 n crime

juy 序 n foreword

juy 最 pron. most

juy 嘴 n. mouth

juy 罪 n. offence

juy 序 n. prologue

juy 嘴 n. spout

juy 醉 n. intoxication

juy bo 追捕 n. chase2

juy chor 最初 a. initial

juy chuy jeh 追隨者 n follower

juy dai geh 最大嘅 a. utmost

juy dai han dow 最大限度 a. maximum

juy dai han dow 最大限度 n maximum

juy dai koon lik 最大權利 n. supremacy

juy dai leurng 最大量 n utmost

juy day deem 最低點 n. nadir

juy day han dow 最低限度 n. minimum

juy dor 最多 adv. most

juy dor 最多 n most

juy fan 罪犯 n convict

juy fan 罪犯 n criminal

juy fan 罪犯 n culprit

juy fan 罪犯 n. malefactor

juy gai geh 最佳嘅 a optimum

juy gan 最近 lately

juy gow geh 最高嘅 a. supreme

juy gow kap 最高級 n. superlative

juy hang 罪行 n. vice

juy hay juy sun 撮起嘴唇 v.t. purse

juy ho 最後 a final

juy ho 最後 a. last1

juy ho 最後 adv. last

juy ho 最後 adv. lastly

juy ho 最好 n. optimum

juy ho 最後 adv. ultimately

juy ho geh 最後嘅 a. latter

juy ho geh yan 最後嘅人 n last

juy ho tung deep 最後通牒 n. ultimatum

juy jap 聚集 v. i. cluster

juy jap 聚集 v.i mass

juy jap 聚集 v.t. muster

juy jap geh yan kwan 聚集嘅人群 n muster

juy jeep gan geh 最接近嘅 a. proximate

juy jow 詛咒 v. t curse

juy jow 詛咒 n. malediction

juy jow low 醉酒佬 n drunkard
juy jow low 醉酒佬 n. reveller
juy jung 最終 adv. eventually
juy jung 追蹤 v.t. track
juy jung yee geh 最鐘意嘅 a favourite
juy jung yee geh yan 最鐘意嘅人 n favourite
juy jung yiew 最重要 a. cardinal
juy jung yiew geh 最重要嘅 a foremost
juy jung yiew geh 罪重要嘅 a. paramount
juy jung yiew geh 最重要嘅 a. primary
juy jung yiew geh 最重要嘅 a principal
juy jung yiew geh 最重要嘅 a. salient
juy kow 追求 n. pursuance
juy kow 追求 v.t. pursue
juy kow 追求 n. pursuit
juy kow 追求 v.t. woo
juy kuk 序曲 n. prelude
juy ok 罪惡 n. sin
juy san geh 最新嘅 a. up-to-date
juy siew 最少 a. least
juy siew geh 最少嘅 a. minimal
juy siew geh 最少嘅 a minimum
juy sorng 沮喪 n dejection
juy sorng 沮喪 v. t dishearten
juy sorng 沮喪 v. t embitter
juy sorng geh 沮喪嘅 a. sombre
juy sun 嘴唇 n. lip
juy wai 最壞 n. worst
juy wai geh 最壞嘅 a worst
juy yan 罪人 n. sinner
juy yeen 序言 n. preface

K

ka 卡 n. carat
ka 卡 n. card
ka cher 卡車 n. truck
ka leen wah 嘉年華 n carnival
ka lo lay 卡路里 n. calorie
ka ta seng 喀嗒聲 n rattle
ka way 卡位 n booth
kam so 禽獸 n brute
kan 近 adv. anigh
kan 近 a. close
kan 近 a. near
kan 近 prep. nigh
kan 近 n. proximity
kan lik 勤力 a diligent
kan lik 勤力 a. industrious
kang 哽 v. t. choke
kao gan 靠近 prep by
kap 級 n. grade
kap 級 n. level
kap 級 n. notch
kap 吸 n. puff
kap 吸 n. suck
kap 級 n. tier
kap beet gow geh 級別高嘅 a. senior
kap gorn 吸乾 v. t blot
kap gwun 吸管 n. straw
kap see 及時 a. timely
kap see 及時 a. well-timed
kap see geh 及時嘅 a. providential
kap see yu 及時雨 n. manna
kap sow 吸收 v.t absorb
kap sow 吸收 v. assimilate
kap sow 吸收 n assimilation
kap yan 吸引 v.t. appeal
kap yan 吸引 v.t. attract
kap yan 吸引 n. attraction
kap yan 吸引 v.t. beckon
kap yan 吸引 v. t. charm2

kap yan 吸引 *v. t engage*
kap yan ik 吸引力 *n. glamour*
kap yan ju 吸引住 *v.t. rivet*
kap yan lik 吸引力 *n. fascination*
kap yan lik 吸引力 *n. lure*
kap yap 吸引 *v.t fascinate*
kap yap 吸入 *v.i. inhale*
kat 咳 *n. cough*
kat 咳 *v. i. cough*
kay 鰭 *n fin*
kay 旗 *n flag*
kay 企 *v.i. stand*
kay dak 奇特 *n. singularity*
kay fat 啓發 *v. t. enlighten*
kay fat 啓發 *v.t. inspire*
kay gan 期間 *n duration*
kay gan 期間 *adv. meanwhile*
kay gwai 奇怪 *adj bizarre*
kay gwai 奇怪 *a. weird*
kay gwai geh 奇怪嘅 *a. queer*
kay horn 期刊 *n. periodical*
kay jik 奇蹟 *n. marvel*
kay jik 奇蹟 *n. miracle*
kay jung yat gor 其中一個 *a., either*
kay kuy 崎嶇 *adj bumpy*
kay kuy geh 崎嶇嘅 *a. rugged*
kay low 溪流 *n. rivulet*
kay see 歧視 *v. t. discriminate*
kay see 歧視 *n discrimination*
kay ta 其他 *adv else*
kay ta 其他 *a. other*
kay tow 企圖 *v. t. essay*
kay tow 祈禱 *n. invocation*
kay tow 祈禱 *v.i. pray*
kay yee geh 奇異咗 *a. wondrous*
kay yeep 企業 *n enterprise*
kay yeep 企業 *n. venture*
kay yu 其餘 *n rest*
keem 鉗 *n. pl. tongs*
keen sing 虔誠 *n. piety*
keen sing geh 虔誠嘅 *a. godly*
keen sing geh 虔誠嘅 *a. pious*

keen sing geh 虔誠嘅 *a. religious*
keet hung geh 褐紅色嘅 *a maroon*
keet hung sik 褐紅色 *n. maroon*
keet jee 蝎子 *n. scorpion*
keet low 揭露 *n. revelation*
keet mwuy 褐煤 *n. lignite*
keh 騎 *v.t. ride*
keh bing 騎兵 *n. cavalry*
keh bing 騎兵 *n. trooper*
keh jap 茄汁 *n. ketchup*
keh jee 茄子 *n brinjal*
keh mah man pao 騎馬慢跑 *n canter*
keh see 騎士 *n chevalier*
keh see 騎士 *n. knight*
keh sow 騎手 *n. rider*
kek been 劇變 *n. upheaval*
kek bwun 劇本 *n. script*
kek jiew 劇照 *n. still*
kek leet 劇烈 *a. tempestuous*
kek leet geh 劇烈嘅 *a. violent*
kek tung 劇痛 *n. throe*
kek yoon 劇院 *n. theatre*
keurng bik 強迫 *v. t compel*
keurng bik 強迫 *n compulsion*
keurng bik 強迫 *v.t force*
keurng bik tuy yow 強迫退休 *v.t. pension*
keurng cheurng 強搶 *n abaction*
keurng cheurng jeh 強搶者 *n abactor*
keurng diew 強調 *v.t accent*
keurng diew 強調 *v. t belabour*
keurng diew 強調 *n emphasis*
keurng diew 強調 *v. t emphasize*
keurng diew 強調 *v.t stress*
keurng diew geh 強調嘅 *a emphatic*
keurng dow 強盜 *n. bandit*
keurng dow 強度 *n. intensity*
keurng fa 強化 *n consolidation*
keurng far 強化 *n. reinforcement*
keurng far 強化 *v.t. toughen*
keurng gan 強姦 *v.t. rape*

keurng gan juy 強姦罪 *n. rape*
keurng hang geh 強行嘅 *a forcible*
keurng jorng 強壯 *a. lusty*
keurng jorng geh 強壯嘅 *a. manly*
keurng jorng geh 強壯嘅 *a. muscular*
keurng jorng geh 強壯嘅 *a. robust*
keurng jorng geh 強壯嘅 *a. virile*
keurng leet 強烈 *n. vehemence*
keurng leet 強烈 *a. vehement*
keurng leet fan duy 強烈反對 *a. hostile*
keurng leet geh yuk morng 強烈嘅慾望 *n. lust*
keurng leet korng yee 強烈抗議 *a. outcry*
keurng leet may dow 強烈味道 *a. pungent*
keurng leet yiew kow 強烈要求 *v. t demand*
key morng 期望 *n. expectation*
key sat 其實 *adv. actually*
kiew 橋 *n bridge*
kiew 轎 *n. palanquin*
kik tan 棘嘅 *v.i. stumble*
kik tan 棘嘅 *v.t. trip*
king 傾 *v.t. converse*
king 傾 *v.t. negotiate*
king gey 傾偈 *n. chat1*
king gey 傾偈 *v. i. chat2*
king gey 傾偈 *n conversation*
king heurng 傾向 *v.i. incline*
king heurng 傾向 *n. tendency*
king sam 傾心 *v. t enamour*
king seh geh 傾瀉嘅 *a. torrential*
king so 鯨鬚 *n. baleen*
king sow 傾訴 *v.t. unburden*
king ter 傾斜 *v.t. slant*
king ter 傾斜 *v.i. slope*
king ter geh 傾斜嘅 *adj. declivous*
king yu 鯨魚 *n. whale*
kok ding 確定 *n confirmation*

kok ding sing 確定性 *n. certainty*
kok ding way jee 確定位置 *v.i. navigate*
kok jok geh 確鑿嘅 *a conclusive*
kok sat geh 確實嘅 *a concrete*
kok ying 確認 *v. t confirm*
kok ying 確認 *n. verification*
kong shoon jay 抗酸劑 *adj. antacid*
koon 權 *n right*
koon chung 權重 *n. weightage*
koon da 拳打 *v.t. punch*
koon gik 拳擊 *n boxing*
koon gik 拳擊 *n. punch*
koon gway 權貴 *n. magnate*
koon jeurng 權仗 *n. sceptre*
koon lik 權力 *n. authority*
koon lin 權力 *n. power*
koon tow 拳頭 *n fist*
koon way geh 權威嘅 *a. magisterial*
koon yee jee gey 權宜之計 *a expedient*
koot deem 缺點 *n defect*
koot deem 缺點 *n drawback*
koot ding 決定 *v. t decide*
koot ding 決定 *n decision*
koot ding 決定 *v. t determine*
koot ding forng hay 決定放棄 *v.t. jack*
koot ding sing 決定性 *adj. crucial*
koot dow 決鬥 *n duel*
koot fat 缺乏 *n dearth*
koot fat 缺乏 *n. lack*
koot fat 缺乏 *n. scarcity*
koot fat 缺乏 *a. void*
koot fat 缺乏 *prep. without*
koot ham 缺陷 *n disability*
koot sam 決心 *n. determination*
koot tik 缺席 *n absence*
koot tik 缺席 *a absent*
koot tik 缺席 *v.t absent*
korng yee 抗議 *v.t. picket*
korng yee 抗議 *n. protest*

kow 求 *v. t. beg*
kow 求 *v. t. entreat*
kow 扣 *v.t fasten*
kow 求 *v.t. implore*
kow 溝 *v.i mix*
kow 求 *v.t. solicit*
kow 溝 *n. trench*
kow cheurng 球場 *n. pitch*
kow chuy 扣除 *v.t. deduct*
kow chuy 扣除 *prep. less*
kow fan 求婚 *v.t. propose*
kow jor yeh 溝咗嘢 *v.t. adulterate*
kow ju 扣住 *v.t. shackle*
kow low 扣鈕 *v. t. button*
kow low 扣留 *v. t detain*
kow low 扣留 *v.t. intern*
kow mai 購買 *n. purchase*
kow ngat koon 扣押權 *n. lien*
kow ngoy kay 求愛期 *n. courtship*
kow pak 球拍 *n bat*
kow see 構思 *n conception*
kow tay 球體 *n. orb*
kow tung 溝通 *v. t communicate*
kow wan 溝勻 *v. t blend*
kow yeh 溝嘢 *n. adulteration*
kow ying 球形 *n. sphere*
kow ying geh 球形嘅 *a. spherical*
kowju 扣住 *n buckle*
koy 鈣 *n calcium*
koy leem 概念 *n concept*
koy yiew 概要 *adv. summarily*
koy yiew 概要 *n. synopsis*
kuk 軸 *n. axis*
kuk 曲 *n. tune*
kuk jeet teen hang 曲折前行 *v.i. snake*
kuk jeet teen jun 曲折前進 *v.i. zigzag*
kuk seen 曲線 *n curve*
kun gwan kow 曲棍球 *n. hockey*
kung 窮 *a. poor*
kung geh 窮嘅 *a. needy*

kung yan 窮人 *n. pauper*
kuy 渠 *n ditch*
kuy 佢 *pron. he*
kuy 佢 *pron. her*
kuy 佢 *pron. him*
kuy 佢 *pron. it*
kuy 佢 *pron. she*
kuy chut 舉出 *v.t. adduce*
kuy day 佢哋 *pron. them*
kuy dey 佢哋 *a. their*
kuy dey 佢哋 *pron. theirs*
kuy gan 拘謹 *n. inhibition*
kuy geh 佢嘅 *a her*
kuy geh 佢嘅 *pron. his*
kuy joot 拒絕 *v. t. decline*
kuy joot 拒絕 *v.t. negative*
kuy joot 拒絕 *n. rebuff*
kuy joot 拒絕 *n. refusal*
kuy joot 拒絕 *v.t. refuse*
kuy joot 拒絕 *n. refuse*
kuy joot 拒絕 *v.t. reject*
kuy joot 拒絕 *n. rejection*
kuy joot 拒絕 *v.t. repudiate*
kuy joot 拒絕 *n. repudiation*
kuy joot 拒絕 *n. repulse*
kuy joot 拒絕 *v.t. spurn*
kuy juk 驅逐 *v.t. banish*
kuy juk 驅逐 *n. banishment*
kuy lay 距離 *n distance*
kuy low 拘留 *n. arrest*
kuy low beng 佝僂病 *n. rickets*
kuy wik geh 區域嘅… *a. zonal*
kwa dai 誇大 *v. t. exaggerate*
kwa dai geh 誇大嘅 *a. melodramatic*
kwa dai geh 誇大嘅 *a. pompous*
kwa jeurng 誇張 *n. exaggeration*
kwa jeurng 誇張 *n. hyperbole*
kwa jeurng 誇張 *v.t. overact*
kwa lan 跨欄 *n. hurdle1*
kwan 裙 *n dress*
kwan 群 *n flock*
kwan 裙 *n. skirt*

kwan chung 昆蟲 n. insect

kwan chung hok 昆蟲學 n. entomology

kwan dai gwan hay 裙帶關係 n. nepotism

kwan ging 困境 n dilemma

kwan ging 困境 n. predicament

kwan jap 群集 v.t. throng

kwan ju 困住 v.t maroon

kwan lan 困難 n. plight

kwan tay 群體 v. t commune

kwan tay 群體 n. fraternity

kwan wak 困惑 n. quandary

kwan yiew 困擾 v. t. baffle

kwan yiew 困擾 v. t bemuse

kwan yiew 困擾 v.t. nonplus

kwan yiew 困擾 v.t. perplex

kwan yiew 困擾 n. perplexity

kwang 框 n frame

kway dai 攜帶 adj. borne

kway ding 規定 v.t. stipulate

kway ding 規定 n. stipulation

kway ding geh 規定嘅 a. mandatory

kway fan 規範 n. specification

kway gap 盔甲 n. armour

kway guy 規矩 n. rule

kway jak 規則 n. regulation

kway lut sing 規律性 n. regularity

kway mo 規模 n. scale

kway wak 規劃 v.t formulate

kwong dai 擴大 n amplification

kwong dai 擴大 v.t. expand

kwong jeurng 擴張 n. expansion

kwong may 狂迷 n fanatic

kwong yam hey 擴音器 n amplifier

kwong yam jow 狂飲酒 v. i booze

kwong yeet 狂熱 n. frenzy

kworng 礦 n mine

kworng fwun 狂歡 n. revel

kworng fwun jok lok 狂歡作樂 n. revelry

kworng gung 礦工 n. miner

kworng gung 礦工 n. pitman

kworng jee 礦脂 n. vaseline

kworng mat hok 礦物學 n. mineralogy

kworng mat hok ga 礦物學家 n. mineralogist

kworng mat jat 礦物質 n. mineral

kworng mat jat geh 礦物質嘅 a mineral

kworng pao 狂跑 v.i stampede

kworng sek 礦石 n. ore

kworng yeet 狂熱 n mania

kwun 群 n cluster

kwun 裙 n. frock

kwun chung 昆蟲 n. bug

kwun ging 困境 n. adversity

kwun ging 困境 n fix

kwun yiew 困擾 v.t. ail

kwuy jay day tow 繪製地圖 v.t. map

kwuy lo 賄賂 n bribe

kwuy lo 賄賂 v. t. bribe

kwuy wah geh 繪畫嘅 a. graphic

kwuy yeurng 潰瘍 n. ulcer

kwuy yeurng geh 潰瘍嘅 a. ulcerous

L

la 罅 n gap

la 罅 n. loop-hole

la ba 喇叭 n. clarion

la ba 喇叭 n. speaker

la ba 喇叭 n. trumpet

la ba seng 喇叭聲 n. hoot

la ba tung 喇叭筒 n. megaphone

la ma 喇嘛 n. lama

lai 拉 v.t. apprehend

lai 拉 v.t. arrest

lai 拉 v. t drag

lai 奶 n. milk

lai 拉 *v.t. pull*
lai 拉 *n. pull*
lai 拉 *v.t. stretch*
lai 拉 *v.t. trail*
lai 拉 *v.t. tug*
lai 拉 *v.t. zip*
lai geh 奶嘅 *a. milky*
lai hay 氖氣 *n. neon*
lai leen 拉鍊 *n. zip*
lai lik 拉力 *n. traction*
lai luy 奶類 *n dairy*
lai may jee pai 拉米紙牌 *n. rummy*
lai piew 拉票 *v. t. canvass*
lai seurng 拉傷 *v.t. strain*
lai seurng 拉傷 *n strain*
lai ter 拉扯 *v.t. manhandle*
lai yow 奶油 *n cream*
lai yow dung 奶油凍 *n custard*
lak gwat 肋骨 *n. rib*
lak gwat geh 肋骨嘅 *adj. costal*
lak ju 勒住 *v.t. rein*
lak say 勒死 *v.t. strangle*
lak say 勒死 *n. strangulation*
lak say 勒死 *v.t. throttle*
lak sing 勒繩 *n. rein*
lak sok 勒索 *n blackmail*
lak sok 勒索 *v.t blackmail*
lam ban kow 籃板球 *n. rebound*
lam bo sek 藍寶石 *n. sapphire*
lam duy 艦隊 *n. armada*
lam fan hay 諗返起 *v.t. recall*
lam gwa 南瓜 *n. pumpkin*
lam mo gwun 林務官 *n forester*
lam suy 淋水 *v.t. water*
lam yeep 林業 *n forestry*
lan 欄 *n column*
lan 難 *a. hard*
lan 懶 *a. indolent*
lan 懶 *n. lazy*
lan bo 爛布 *n. rag*
lan dak 難得 *adv. seldom*
lan dow 難倒 *v.t stump*

lan duk 難讀 *a. illegible*
lan geh 懶嘅 *a. sluggish*
lan geh 難嘅 *a. tricky*
lan gorn 欄杆 *n. rail*
lan gwor 難過 *v.i. pine*
lan gwor 難過 *v.i smart*
lan ham 難堪 *v.t. mortify*
lan hung jay geh 難控制嘅 *a. unruly*
lan jeet 攔截 *n. interception*
lan ju 攔住 *v.t. waylay*
lan kow 攔球 *v.t volley*
lan man 難民 *n. refugee*
lan man geh 難聞嘅 *a rank*
lan may 闌尾 *n. appendix*
lan morng geh 難忘嘅 *a. memorable*
lan san 懶散 *n. laziness*
lan san gam chor 懶散咁坐 *v.i. loll*
lan san gam chor 懶散咁坐 *v.i. lounge*
lan san geh 懶散嘅 *n. slothful*
lan siew far 難消化 *a. indigestible*
lan tak 難測 *n. vagary*
lan tay 難題 *n. conundrum*
lan tay 難題 *n struggle*
lan tee kay gow 難辭其咎 *a culpable*
lan yee jee sun 難以置信 *a. incredible*
lan yee jeep sow 難以接收 *a. insupportable*
lan yee ying yung 難以形容 *a. indescribable*
lan yee ying yung 難以形容 *a. intangible*
lang dam 冷淡 *adv. aloof*
lang dam 冷淡 *a. frigid*
lang dam 冷淡 *a. impersonal*
lang dung 冷凍 *n. refrigeration*
lang geen dow 能見度 *n. visibility*
lang huk mo ting 冷酷無情 *a. callous*
lang huk mo ting 冷酷無情 *a. inhuman*

lang huk mo ting 冷酷無情 a. ruthless
lang jing 冷靜 n. calm
lang jing geh 冷靜嘅 a. nonchalant
lang keurk hay 冷卻器 n cooler
lang lik 能力 n ability
lang lik 能力 n. capability
lang lik 能力 n competence
lang lok 冷落 v.t. snub
lang lok 冷落 n. snub
lang mok 冷漠 n. apathy
lang tam 冷杉 n fir
lao 鬧 v.t. scold
lao 鬧 v.t upbraid
lao gao 鬧交 n. argument
lao kek 鬧劇 n farce
lao see 鬧事 v.t. riot
lap 蠟 n. wax
lap bat 蠟筆 n. pastel
lap cheurng 立場 n. standpoint
lap fat 立法 v.i. legislate
lap fat 立法 n. legislation
lap fat geh 立法嘅 a. legislative
lap fat gey gwan 立法機關 n. legislature
lap fat way yoon 立法委員 n. legislator
lap forng tay 立方體 a cubical
lap forng ying 立方形 n cube
lap forng ying 立方形 adj. cubiform
lap hak 立刻 adv. forthwith
lap jee jo 立志做 v.t. aspire
lap jik 立即 a. instantaneous
lap juk 蠟燭 n. candle
lap sap 垃圾 n. garbage
lap sap 垃圾 n. junk
lap sap 垃圾 n. litter
lap sap 垃圾 n. rubbish
lap sap 垃圾 n. trash
lap sap 垃圾 n. waste
lap sap hang 垃圾坑 n. cesspool
lap yap 納入 n. incorporation

larm 籃 n. basket
larm 南 n. south
larm day yam 男低音 n. bass
larm duy 艦隊 n fleet
larm fay ling yeurng 南非羚羊 n bontebok
larm forng geh 南方嘅 a. south
larm forng geh 南方嘅 a. southerly
larm forng geh 南方嘅 a. southern
larm gik 南極 a. antarctic
larm jai 男仔 n boy
larm jay 男仔 n. lad
larm jee hay koy 男子氣概 n manliness
larm jee hon geh 男子漢嘅 a. masculine
larm luy tung hao 男女同校 n. co-education
larm sik 藍色 n blue
larm sing 男性 n male
larm sing geh 男性嘅 a. male
larm yan 男人 n. man
larm yan 男人 n. manhood
larm yan por 男人婆 n. tomboy
larm yung 濫用 n abuse
larm yung 濫用 n. misapplication
larm yung 濫用 n. misuse
larm yung 濫用 v.t. misuse
larn 難 a difficult
larn dow 難度 n difficulty
larn sam 冷衫 n woollen
larn seen 冷線 n. yarn
larn sow 難受 a. wretched
larn yee juk mor 難以捉摸 a elusive
larn yee sing dam 難以承擔 a burdensome
larng sam 冷衫 n. sweater
lat 辣 a. spicy
lat jiew 辣椒 n capsicum
lat jiew 辣椒 n. chilli
lat tat 邋遢 a. squalid
lat tat 邋遢 n. squalor

lat tat geh 邋遢嘅 *a. slovenly*

lat tat geh luy yan 邋遢嘅女人 *n. slattern*

lay 嚟 *v. i. come*

lay 泥 *n dirt*

lay 泥 *n. mud*

lay 梨 *n. pear*

lay 犁 *n. plough*

lay 泥 *n. soil*

lay 脷 *n. tongue*

lay bai 禮拜 *n. week*

lay bai yee sik geh 禮拜儀式嘅 *a. liturgical*

lay bo 彌補 *v.i. atone*

lay dow 犁刀 *n colter*

lay fai 泥塊 *n. clod*

lay fan 離婚 *n divorce*

lay fan 離婚 *v. t divorce*

lay fat see 理髮師 *n. barber*

lay fwuy 泥灰 *n. marl*

lay gai 理解 *v. t comprehend*

lay gai 理解 *v.t fathom*

lay ging 離境 *v.t. deport*

lay gu am 尼姑庵 *n. nunnery*

lay gu ding 尼古丁 *n. nicotine*

lay gung hok yoon 理工學院 *n. polytechnic*

lay hap 離合 *n clutch*

lay hay 離棄 *v.t. forsake*

lay hoy 離開 *v. i. depart*

lay hoy 離開 *n departure*

lay hoy 離開 *n. leave*

lay jat 痢疾 *n dysentery*

lay jee 例子 *n example*

lay jee 例子 *n. instance*

lay jee 理智 *a. intellectual*

lay jee 理智 *n. sanity*

lay jee geh 理智嘅 *a. sane*

lay jeet 禮節 *n etiquette*

lay jeurng 泥漿 *n. ooze*

lay jiew 泥沼 *n. mire*

lay ling geh 泥濘嘅 *a. slushy*

lay lun 理論 *n. theory*

lay lun far 理論化 *v.i. theorize*

lay lun ga 理論家 *n. theorist*

lay lun seurng 理論上 *a. notional*

lay lun seurng 理論上 *a. theoretical*

lay lung 尼龍 *n. nylon*

lay mao 禮貌 *n. courtesy*

lay mao 禮貌 *n. manner*

lay mao 禮貌 *n. politeness*

lay mat 禮物 *n. gift*

lay mat 禮物 *n. present*

lay ming 黎明 *n dawn*

lay ngoy 例外 *n exception*

lay sa 泥沙 *n. silt*

lay sam 離心 *adj. centrifugal*

lay seurng 理想 *n. ambition*

lay seurng 理想 *n ideal*

lay seurng far 理想化 *v.t. idealize*

lay seurng geh 理想嘅 *a. ideal*

lay seurng gwok 理想國 *n . utopia*

lay seurng ju yee 理想主義 *n. idealism*

lay seurng ju yee 理想主義 *a. idealistic*

lay seurng ju yee jeh 理想主義者 *n. idealist*

lay sing 理性 *a. rational*

lay ting bay 里程碑 *n. milestone*

lay tong 禮堂 *n. hall*

lay tow 泥土 *n clay*

lay yee 禮儀 *a. ceremonial*

lay yee 禮儀 *n decency*

lay yik 利益 *n. lucre*

lay yu 俚語 *n. slang*

lay yun 利潤 *n. profit*

lay yung 利用 *v. t exploit*

lay yung 利用 *n. utilization*

leay 餌 *n bait*

lee dow 呢度 *adv. here*

lee tow fu gan 呢頭附近 *adv. hereabouts*

leem dow 鐮刀 *n. sickle*

leem forng 殮房 *n. morgue*
leem forng 殮房 *n. mortuary*
leem gow 念舊 *n. nostalgia*
leem tow 黏土 *n. adobe*
leem yik 黏液 *n. mucus*
leem yik 黏液 *n. slime*
leen 鍊 *n chain*
leen 年 *n. year*
leen biew 年表 *n. chronology*
leen far 蓮花 *n. lotus*
leen gam sut 煉金術 *n. alchemy*
leen gan bat hay 連根拔起 *v.t. uproot*
leen gwan sing 連貫性 *n. consistence,-cy*
leen jap 練習 *v.t. practise*
leen jap sang 練習生 *n. trainee*
leen jee sow tow 連指手套 *n. mitten*
leen jeep 連接 *v. t. connect*
leen jeep 連接 *v. t couple*
leen jeep 連接 *v.t link*
leen jeep gen 連接緊 *adj. annectant*
leen jeep ju 連接住 *v abutted*
leen jeurng 年長 *a elder*
leen jeurng 年長 *n. seniority*
leen juk 連續 *adj. consecutive*
leen juk 連續 *adj. continual*
leen juk da 連續打 *v.t. thrash*
leen juk gam 連續咁 *adv consecutively*
leen juk geh 連續嘅 *a. serial*
leen juk geh 連續嘅 *a. successive*
leen juk kek 連續劇 *n. serial*
leen juk pao gwun 連續炮轟 *n. v. & t cannonade*
leen juk sing 連續性 *n continuity*
leen ling 年齡 *n. age*
leen lo 煉爐 *n forge*
leen mai 連埋 *v.t. adjoin*
leep *n. lift*
leep 鎳 *n. nickel*
leep gow 鬣狗 *n. hyaena, hyena*
leep hoon 獵犬 *n. hound*

leep mat 獵物 *n. prey*
leep yan 獵人 *n. fowler*
leep yan 獵人 *n. hunter*__
leep yan 獵人 *n. huntsman*
leep ying 獵鷹 *n falcon*
leet biew 列表 *n. tabulation*
leet dan 列單 *v.t. list*
leet duy hang 列隊行 *v.i troop*
leet fung 裂縫 *n. rift*
leet fung 裂縫 *n. slit*
leet guy 列舉 *v. t. enumerate*
leet han 裂痕 *n crack*
leet han 裂痕 *n fissure*
leet han 裂痕 *n. tear*
leet ho 裂口 *n cleft*
leet ho 裂口 *n split*
leet hoy 裂開 *v. i crack*
leet see 烈士 *n. martyr*
leet sing biew gak 列成表格 *v.t. tabulate*
lek 叻 *a. clever*
lek gwor 叻過 *v. t better*
lem *v.t. lick*
leng 靚 *a beautiful*
leng 領 *n collar*
leng geh 靚嘅 *a pretty*
leng jay 靚仔 *a. handsome*
leng luy 靚女 *n belle*
leurk gwor 掠過 *v.i. whiz*
leurk jee 略知 *n. inkling*
leurng 涼 *a cool*
leurng 糧 *n emolument*
leurng 糧 *n. salary*
leurng 兩 *a. two*
leurng 糧 *n. wage*
leurng chorng 糧倉 *n. granary*
leurng day jow 兩地走 *v.t. shuttle*
leurng dok 量度 *v.t measure*
leurng gor 兩個 *pron both*
leurng gor jee mo geh 兩個字母嘅 *adj biliteral*
leurng gor lay bai 兩個禮拜 *n. fort-*

night
leurng hai 涼鞋 *n. sandal*
leurng jee 量子 *n. quantum*
leurng juk dung mat 兩足動物 *n biped*
leurng leen yat chi geh 兩年一次嘅 *adj biennial*
leurng pwuy 兩倍 *n double*
leurng sam 良心 *n conscience*
leurng sing kay yat tee 兩星期一次 *adj bi-weekly*
leurng tee 兩次 *adv. twice*
leurng ting 涼亭 *n bower*
leurng ting 涼亭 *n. pavilion*
leurng tok 梁托 *n. corbel*
liew 尿 *n. urine*
liew cho geh jee 潦草嘅字 *n scrawl*
liew cho geh jee 潦草嘅字 *n. scribble*
liew dow 尿兜 *n. urinal*
liew fwuy 鳥喙 *n beak*
liew gai 瞭解 *v.t. acquaint*
liew gai 瞭解 *n. insight*
liew gao 鳥膠 *n birdlime*
liew geh 尿嘅 *a. urinary*
liew ha 鳥蛤 *v. i cockle*
liew ming 鳥鳴 *n warble*
liew yeurng yoon 療養院 *n. sanatorium*
liew yu jee jeurng 瞭如指掌 *adv pat*
lik dai mo bay geh 力大無比嘅 *a. herculean*
lik hay 力氣 *n. strength*
lik horng gey 力行雞 *n. leghorn*
lik leurng 力量 *n. energy*
lik leurng 力量 *n. might*
lik leurng 力量 *n. virility*
lik ming 匿名 *n. anonymity*
lik ming 匿名 *a. anonymous*
lik see 歷史 *n. history*
lik see geh 歷史嘅 *a. historical*
lik see gey joy 歷史記載 *n.pl. annals*

lik see hok ga 歷史學家 *n. historian*
lik see sing geh 歷史性嘅 *a . historic*
lik see way jik 歷史遺跡 *n. monument*
lik teng 瀝青 *n. tar*
ling 鈴 *n bell*
ling 零 *n. nil*
ling 零 *n. nought*
ling 令 *n. ream*
ling 零 *n. zero*
ling chut 擰出 *v.t wring*
ling dow 令到 *v.t cause*
ling dow choy lang 領導才能 *n. leadership*
ling dow hm hoy sam 令到唔開心 *v.t. upset*
ling dow mow hao 令到無效 *v. t disable*
ling dow...ging ngar 令到...驚訝 *v.t astound*
ling duy 領隊 *n. leader*
ling duy 領隊 *n. spearhead*
ling gam 靈感 *n. inspiration*
ling gam 靈感 *n muse*
ling hao 靈巧 *adj. deft*
ling hm 同族 *n cognizance*
ling hm 領悟 *n. realization*
ling hm lik 領悟力 *n comprehension*
ling mow 陵墓 *n. mausoleum*
ling mung 檸檬 *adj. citric*
ling mung 檸檬 *n. lemon*
ling mung suy 檸檬水 *n. lemonade*
ling ngoy 另外 *a another*
ling ngoy 另外 *pron. other*
ling seen 領先 *n. lead*
ling sik 零食 *n. snack*
ling sow 零售 *n. retail*
ling sow geh 零售嘅 *a retail*
ling sow seurng 零售商 *n. retailer*
ling wik 領域 *n domain*
ling wik 領域 *a. realm*
ling wut 靈活 *a. nimble*

ling yan bay ngoy 令人悲哀嘅 *adj* melancholy

ling yan bay tarm 令人悲慘 *a.* poignant

ling yan dam sam 令人擔心 *v.t.* misgive

ling yan dor lok 令人墮落 *v. t.* debauch

ling yan fan gam geh 令人反感嘅 *a.* objectionable

ling yan fan gam geh 令人反感嘅 *a.* repugnant

ling yan fan gam geh 令人反感嘅 *a.* repulsive

ling yan fan geh 令人煩嘅 *v.t.* puzzle

ling yan fan low 令人煩惱 *a.* irksome

ling yan fan low 令人煩惱 *a.* troublesome

ling yan forng sung 令人放鬆 *v.t.* lull

ling yan ging hay 令人驚喜 *v.t.* surprise

ling yan ging ngar 令人驚訝 *v.t.* stupefy

ling yan jan ging 令人震驚 *v.t.* scandalize

ling yan jok oh geh 令人作嘔嘅 *a.* obnoxious

ling yan jok oh geh 令人作嘔嘅 *a.* odious

ling yan lan gwor 令人難過 *v.t.* sadden

ling yan mwun yee 令人滿意 *v.t.* please

ling yan seen mo 令人羨慕 *a* enviable

ling yan sow fu 令人受苦 *v.t.* victimize

ling yan tow yeem geh 令人討厭嘅 *a.* repellent

ling yan tung fu 令人痛苦 *a.* grievous

ling yan tuy gu 令人退股 *a. invalid*

ling yan way ham 令人遺憾 *a.* lamentable

ling yan yam juy 令人飲醉 *v.t.* intoxicate

ling yan yan jeurng sam hak 令人印象深刻 *a. imposing*

ling yan yan seurng 令人欣賞 *a.* admirable

ling yeurng 羚羊 *n. antelope*

ling yeurng 領養 *v.t. foster*

ling yeurng low gam yam 領養老金人 *n annuitant*

lo 驢 *n. ass*

lo 腦 *n brain*

lo 褸 *n coat*

lo 爐 *n cooker*

lo day 爐低 *n. hearth*

lo fu 老虎 *n. tiger*

lo giew seng 驢叫聲 *n bray*

lo gung 老公 *n husband*

lo jeurng 路障 *n. barricade*

lo jor 老咗 *a. aged*

lo lik 努力 *n effort*

lo por 老婆 *n. wife*

lo say 老細 *n boss*

lo see 老師 *n. teacher*

lo suy 露水 *n. dew*

lo tee 鸕鶿 *n. cormorant*

lo teen yow lok cheurng 露天遊樂場 *n. fair*

lo tiew 爐條 *n. grate*

lo ting 路程 *n drive*

lo yan 老人 *a elderly*

lo yik 奴役 *v.t. enslave*

lo ying 露營 *v. i. camp*

lok 落 *v.t. shed*

lok chuy 樂趣 *n relish*

lok gak 落格 *n. misappropriation*

lok gwun 樂觀 *a. jovial*

lok gwun 樂觀 *n. optimism*

lok gwun 樂觀 *a. optimistic*

lok gwun 樂觀 *a. sanguine*

lok gwun geh yan 樂觀嘅人 *n. optimist*

lok ho 落後 *v. t benight*

lok ho geh 落後嘅 *a. medieval*

lok ho geh 落後嘅 *a. primitive*

lok ho geh yan 落後嘅人 *n. straggler*

lok how 落後 *v.i. lag*

lok meen 落面 *v.t. humiliate*

lok morng 落網 *v.t. net*

lok sai yu 落細雨 *v. i drizzle*

lok shoot 落雪 *v.i. snow*

lok suy seng 落水聲 *n splash*

lok tor 駱駝 *n. camel*

lok yee 樂意 *adv. readily*

lok yee 樂意 *a. willing*

lok yu 落雨 *v.i. rain*

lok yu jor yan 樂於助人 *a. helpful*

long 狼 *n. wolf*

look ap 亂嗡 *v. t. chatter*

loon 亂 *v. t clutter*

loon 亂 *n. mess*

loon 聯 *v.t. stitch*

loon 暖 *a. warm*

loon ap 亂嗡 *v. t. & i blab*

loon borng 聯邦 *n federation*

loon borng geh 聯邦嘅 *a federal*

loon duy 亂堆 *n. jumble*

loon fan 聯返 *v.t. sew*

loon fan 暖返 *v.t. warm*

loon forng 亂放 *v.t. misplace*

loon gao 亂搞 *v.i fiddle*

loon geh 暖嘅 *a. lukewarm*

loon geh 亂嘅 *a. motley*

loon gorng 亂講 *v.t. ramble*

loon hap 聯合 *n. unity*

loon hap day 聯合地 *adv. jointly*

loon hap jing fu 聯合政府 *n coalition*

loon hap ju yee jeh 聯合主義者 *n. unionist*

loon hay 聯繫 *n. liaison*

loon hay 聯繫 *v.t. relate*

loon lao 亂鬧 *n. rampage*

loon lok 聯絡 *v. t contact*

loon mang 聯盟 *n. alliance*

loon mang 聯盟 *n. league*

loon mor 亂摸 *v.i. fumble*

loon ngoy geh 戀愛嘅 *adj amatory*

loon seurng 聯想 *v.t. associate*

loon she 亂寫 *v.t. scrawl*

loon suy wu 暖水壺 *n. thermos (flask)*

loon tat bat jow geh 亂七八糟嘅 *a. topsy turvy*

loon wak 亂畫 *v.t. scribble*

loop ap ya say 亂嗡廿四 *v.i. rave*

lor 攞 *v. t. carry*

lor 攞 *v.t fetch*

lor 攞 *v.t. get*

lor 鑼 *n. gong*

lor 攞 *v.t take*

lor bak 蘿蔔 *n. radish*

lor bak 蘿蔔 *n. turnip*

lor dow 攞到 *n acquest*

lor fan 攞返 *v.t. reclaim*

lor fan 攞返 *v.t. recoup*

lor fan 攞返 *v.t. retrieve*

lor hay 攞起 *v.t. lift*

lor jee 騾子 *n. mule*

lor jee geh 騾似嘅 *a. mulish*

lor lak 羅勒 *n. basil*

lor morng jee 羅望子 *n. tamarind*

lor see 螺絲 *n. screw*

lor shoon ying 螺旋型 *n. spiral*

lor shoon ying geh 螺旋形嘅 *a. spiral*

lor sor 囉唆 *v. i blether*

lor sor 囉唆 *n. tedium*

lor sor 囉唆 *a. verbose*

lor sor 囉唆 *n. verbosity*

lor sor 囉唆 *a. tedious*

lor tap 邏輯 *n. logic*

lor tap joon ga 邏輯專家 *n. logician*

lor tay 裸體 *a. naked*

lor tay 裸體 *n nude`*
lor tay 裸體 *n. nudity*
lorng dong jeh 浪蕩者 *n debauchee*
lorng fay 浪費 *n. prodigality*
lorng fay 浪費 *n. profligacy*
lorng fay 浪費 *a. wasteful*
lorng ha lorng ha 浪下浪下 *v.i. lurch*
lorng ho 　口 *v.i. gargle*
lorng jung 朗誦 *n. recitation*
lorng jung 朗誦 *v.t. recite*
lorng kang 狼哽 *v. t devour*
lorng man 浪漫 *n. romance*
lorng man geh 浪漫嘅 *a. romantic*
lorng mow jow 朗姆酒 *n. rum*
lorng tun fu yeen 狼吞虎嚥 *n. gobble*
lorng tun fur yeen 狼吞虎咽 *v.i. scoff*
low 嬲 *a. angry*
low 鈕 *n button*
low 嬲 *a cross*
low 驢 *n donkey*
low 流 *v. t drain*
low 流 *v.i flow*
low 漏 *v.i. leak*
low 漏 *n. leakage*
low 路 *n. road*
low 留 *v.i. stay*
low 流 *v.i. stream*
low 扭 *v.t. twist*
low 路 *n. way*
low ba han 留疤痕 *v.t. scar*
low bay 盧比 *n. rupee*
low bing 溜冰 *v.t. skate*
low bing hai 溜冰鞋 *n. skate*
low bo 盧布 *n. rouble*
low cheurng 流暢 *a fluid*
low chut 流出 *v.i. well*
low da 扭打 *v.i. grapple*
low day 奴隸 *n. slave*
low day 奴隸 *n. thralldom*
low day jay 奴隸制 *n. slavery*
low dung 流動 *n flow*

low dung 漏洞 *n. lacuna*
low dung 漏洞 *n. leak*
low dung 扭動 *n wriggle*
low dung 扭動 *v.i. writhe*
low dung geh 流動嘅 *a. mobile*
low dung sing 流動性 *n. mobility*
low for 怒火 *n. anger*
low for 怒火 *n. fury*
low for 怒火 *n. wrath*
low forng 流放 *n. exile*
low fu la 老虎乸 *n. shrew*
low fu la 老虎乸 *n. tigress*
low gam 流感 *n. influenza*
low gu por 老姑婆 *n. spinster*
low gung 勞工 *n. labour*
low gung 勞工 *n. labourer*
low gwun 瘺管 *n fistula*
low hang 流行 *n. vogue*
low hang beng 流行病 *n epidemic*
low hang geh 流行嘅 *a current*
low hang geh 流行嘅 *a fashionable*
low hang kuk 流行曲 *n pop*
low ho 嘍口 *v.i. stammer*
low ho 嘍口 *n stammer*
low hoot 流血 *v. i bleed*
low horn 流汗 *v.i. sweat*
low kuk 扭曲 *v. t distort*
low lay 流利 *a eloquent*
low lay 流利 *a fluent*
low lay low huy 扭嚟扭去 *v.i. wriggle*
low lik 努力 *n diligence*
low lik jow 努力做 *v.i. labour*
low lorng 流浪 *v.i. rove*
low lorng geh 流浪嘅 *a vagabond*
low lorng hon 流浪漢 *n. vagabond*
low lorng jeh 流浪者 *n. rover*
low luy 流淚 *v.i. weep*
low meen 露面 *v.i surface*
low mok yeem 腦膜炎 *n. meningitis*
low por 老婆 *n.. missis, missus*
low sa 流沙 *n. quicksand*

low sam 留心 a. attentive
low sam 留心 n heed
low seen 路線 n. route
low seng gey 留聲機 n. gramophone
low seurng 扭傷 n. sprain
low seurng 扭傷 n wrick
low shoon 硫酸 a. sulphuric
low shu 老鼠 n. mouse
low shu 老鼠 n. rat
low shu 柳樹 n. willow
low sing geh 流星嘅 a. meteoric
low sow 牢騷 n. moan
low tan 扭嚦 v.t. sprain
low tang 樓層 n. storey
low tay 樓梯 n. stair
low tiew 柳條 n. wicker
low tik 怒斥 v.t. rail
low tow 爐頭 n. stove
low wong 硫磺 n. sulphur
low wu tow geh 老糊塗嘅 a. senile
low yeep dow 柳葉刀 a. lancet
loy bo geh 內部嘅 a. internal
loy deen jeh 來電者 n caller
loy fuk cheurng 來福槍 n rifle
loy gow 內疚 n. compunction
loy gow 內疚 n. guilt
loy gow 內疚 a. guilty
loy hm jung 耐唔中 adv. occasionally
loy jak 內側 n. inside
loy jorng 內臟 n. entrails
loy joy geh 內在嘅 a. intrinsic
loy lik 耐力 n. endurance
loy lik 耐力 n. fortitude
loy lik 耐力 n. stamina
loy lik 耐力 n. tolerance
loy sam sam chu 內心深處 a. inmost
loy sam sam chu 內心深處 a. innermost
loy sing 耐性 n. patience
loy tan 內襯 n lining
loy yee 內衣 n. underwear

loy yeurk 懦弱 n. cowardice
loy yoon 來源 n. source
loy yung 內容 n content
loy yung 耐用 a durable
loy yung geh 耐用嘅 a endurable
luk 鹿 n deer
luk 錄 v.t. record
luk 六 n., a six
luk 錄 v.t tape
luk 轆 a. wheel
luk bo sek 綠寶石 n emerald
luk day 陸地 a. inland
luk day 陸地 adv. inland
luk dow 綠豆 n. pea
luk far 綠化 v.t. afforest
luk forng 氯仿 n chloroform
luk gok 鹿角 n. antler
luk gwan 陸軍 n. brigade
luk gwan jun jeurng 陸軍準將 n brigadier
luk hap choy 六合彩 n. lottery
luk hay 氯氣 n chlorine
luk sap 六十 n., a. sixty
luk sik 綠色 n green
luk sik geh 綠色嘅 a. green
luk sik jik mat 綠色植物 n. greenery
luk yam dai 錄音帶 n. cassette
luk yam gey 錄音機 n. recorder
luk yam sat 錄音室 n. studio
luk ying 錄影 v.t film
luk ying dai 錄影帶 n. tape
lum 諗 v.t. think
lum 諗 n thought
lun 磷 n. phosphorus
lun 卵 n. spawn
lun ju cheurng 輪住唱 n. antiphony
lun jun 輪盡 v. t botch
lun jun 輪盡 a clumsy
lun jun 輪盡 a. maladroit
lun kok 輪廓 n contour
lun low 輪流 a. alternate
lun low 輪流 v.t. alternate

lun man 論文 n discourse
lun man 論文 n. essay
lun man 論文 n. thesis
lun man 論文 n. treatise
lun sek 卵石 n. pebble
lun shoon yeem 磷酸鹽 n. phosphate
lun tan 論壇 n. forum
lun tao 卵巢 n. ovary
lun tee 輪齒 n cog
lun ying 卵形 n oval
lun ying geh 卵形嘅 a. oval
lung 籠 n. cage
lung 窿 n. cavity
lung 聾 a deaf
lung 龍 n dragon
lung 窿 n hole
lung 膿 n. pus
lung 窿 n. apex
lung cheurng 農場 n. barton
lung cheurng 農場 n farm
lung duk beng 膿毒病 n. sepsis
lung fu 農夫 n farmer
lung fu 農夫 n. ploughman
lung goon fung 龍捲風 n. tornado
lung har 龍蝦 n. lobster
lung hok 農學 n. agronomy
lung jok mat 農作物 n crop
lung jung 膿腫 n abscess
lung low 膿漏 n. pyorrhoea
lung low 農奴 n. serf
lung lung seng 隆隆聲 n. rumble
lung man 農民 n. peasant
lung man 農民 n. peasantry
lung mat 濃密 a dense
lung muk yeep 農牧業 n. husbandry
lung tong 濃湯 n bisque
lung yeep 農業 n agriculture
lung yeep ga 農業家 n. agriculturist
lung yeep geh 農業嘅 a. agrarian
lung yeep geh 農業嘅 a agricultural
lup 凹 adj. concave
lut 率 n. rate

lut jee 栗子 n. chestnut
lut see 律師 n. lawyer
lut see 律師 n. solicitor
lut sik 甩色 v.i fade
luy 鋁 n. aluminium
luy 女 n daughter
luy 鐳 n. radium
luy 雷 n. thunder
luy bat yeep sang 女畢業生 n alumna
luy buk 女僕 n. maid
luy day yam 女低音 n alto
luy gwun 旅館 n. motel
luy hak 旅客 n. tourist
luy hak 旅客 n. wayfarer
luy hak yan 女黑人 n. negress
luy hang 旅行 n. holiday
luy hang 旅行 n. tour
luy hang 旅行 n travel
luy hang 旅行 n. trip
luy hang tor cher 旅行拖車 n. caravan
luy hao 旅客 n. traveller
luy jay 女仔 n. girl
luy jay 女仔 n. lass
luy jay see 女祭司 n. priestess
luy jeurk see 女爵士 n. dame
luy jik 累積 v.t. amass
luy ju gok 女主角 n. heroine
luy juk jeurng 女族長 n. matriarch
luy lay fuk 女禮服 n. gown
luy meen 裡面 adv. within
luy meen geh 裡面嘅 a. inner
luy mo 女巫 n. witch
luy mow seurng 女帽商 n. milliner
luy mow teek gey see 女帽設計師 n. milliner
luy mow yeep 女帽業 n. millinery
luy san 女神 n. goddess
luy see geh 蕾絲嘅 a. lacy
luy see joon 螺絲鑽 n. auger
luy see yan 女詩人 n. poetess
luy see ying 女侍應 n. waitress

luy she 旅舍 *n. hostel*
luy shoon yeem 鋁酸鹽 *n. aluminate*
luy sing fa 女性化 *a. girlish*
luy sing far 女性化 *v.t. womanise*
luy sing geh 女性嘅 *a female*
luy sing geh 女性嘅 *a feminine*
luy sow dow yoon 女修道院 *n convent*
luy tee 類似 *a. akin*
luy ting 旅程 *n. journey*
luy ting 旅程 *n ride*
luy worng 女王 *n. queen*
luy wu see jeurng 女護士長 *n. matron*
luy xing 女性 *n female*
luy yan 女人 *n. lady*
luy yan 女人 *n. woman*
luy yan 女人 *n. womanhood*
luy yan geh 女人嘅 *n. womanish*
luy yeen yoon 女演員 *n. actress*
luy ying 類型 *n. type*
luy ying far tay fat 類型化睇法 *v.t. stereotype*
luy yow 旅遊 *v.i. travel*
luy yow sing day 旅遊勝地 *n resort*
luy yow yeep 旅遊業 *n. tourism*

M

ma 馬 *n. horse*
ma 媽 *n mum*
ma 馬 *n. nag*
ma 碼 *n. yard*
ma bao doy 麻包袋 *n. sack*
ma bay 麻痹 *n. palsy*
ma cher 馬車 *n. barouche*
ma cher 馬車 *n. cart*
ma cher 馬車 *n chaise*
ma cher 馬車 *n. wagon*

ma cher fu 馬車夫 *n coachman*
ma cho 馬槽 *n. manger*
ma choy hak 馬賽克 *n. mosaic*
ma dang 馬鐙 *n. stirrup*
ma dat 馬達 *n. motor*
ma fan 麻煩 *v. t bother*
ma fan 馬販 *n. coper*
ma fan 麻煩 *n. fuss*
ma fan 麻煩 *a. trying*
ma fan see 麻煩事 *n. nuisance*
ma fan yan 麻煩人 *n. gadfly*
ma feh 嗎啡 *n. morphia*
ma forng 馬房 *n stable*
ma fu geh 馬虎嘅 *a. slipshod*
ma fung 痲瘋 *n. leprosy*
ma fung beng wan jeh 痲瘋病患者 *n. leper*
ma fung geh 痲瘋嘅 *a. leprous*
ma giew seng 馬叫聲 *v.i. neigh*
ma giew seng 馬叫聲 *n. neigh*
ma guy 馬具 *n. harness*
ma hay toon 馬戲團 *n. circus*
ma jeurk 麻雀 *n. sparrow*
ma juy 麻醉 *n anaesthesia*
ma juy 麻醉 *n. narcosis*
ma juy yeurk 麻醉藥 *n. anaesthetic*
ma kow 馬球 *n. polo*
ma lai chung 馬拉松 *n. marathon*
ma luk 馬陸 *n. millipede*
ma ma 媽媽 *n. mamma*
ma mi 媽咪 *n. mummy*
ma mow tay teem jow 馬姆齊甜酒 *n. malmsey*
ma muk geh 麻木嘅 *a. nerveless*
ma on 馬鞍 *n. saddle*
ma tan 麻疹 *n measles*
ma tee 馬刺 *n. spur*
ma tow 碼頭 *n. dock*
ma tow fay 碼頭費 *n. wharfage*
mah fu 馬虎 *a. lax*
mah lak 馬勒 *n bridle*
mai 埋 *v. t bury*

mai 買 *v. t. buy*
mai 賣 *v.t flog*
mai 買 *v.t. purchase*
mai 賣 *v.t. retail*
mai 賣 *v.t. sell*
mai fuk 埋伏 *n. ambush*
mai fuk 埋伏 *v.i. lurk*
mai ga 買家 *n. buyer*
mai ga 賣家 *n. seller*
mai mai 買賣 *n. trade*
mai yam 賣淫 *v.t. prostitute*
mai yam 賣淫 *n. prostitution*
mak 墨 *n. ink*
mak bok 脈搏 *n. pulse*
mak dai gor ho 擘大個口 *adv., agape*
mak kay 默契 *n. rapport*
mak lap jung 麥粒腫 *n. stye*
mak lok mok 脈絡膜 *n choroid*
mak ngar 麥芽 *n. malt*
mak ngar beh jow 麥芽啤酒 *n ale*
mak ngar cho 麥芽醋 *n alegar*
mak pay 麥皮 *n. porridge*
mak sang yan 陌生人 *n. stranger*
mak see 默示 *a. tacit*
mak yeen jeep sow 默然接受 *n. acquiescence*
man 問 *v.t. ask*
man 蚊 *n dollar*
man 紋 *n. groove*
man 蚊 *n. mosquito*
man 聞 *v.t nose*
man 問 *v.t. quiz*
man 慢 *a slow*
man 慢 *v.i. slow*
man 聞 *v.t. smell*
man 聞 *v.i. sniff*
man 聞 *n sniff*
man 燜 *v.t. stew*
man bing 民兵 *n. militia*
man bo 漫步 *v.i. meander*
man bo 漫步 *v.i. roam*
man chuk 慢速 *n crawl*

man dow 聞到 *v.t. scent*
man dow 慢度 *n. slowness*
man dow 聞到 *v.t. smelt*
man far 文化 *n culture*
man far geh 文化嘅 *a cultural*
man fat 文法 *n. grammar*
man fat ga 文法家 *n. grammarian*
man gam 敏感 *n. allergy*
man gam geh 敏感嘅 *a. sensitive*
man gam sing 敏感性 *n. sensibility*
man geen 文件 *n document*
man geen gap 文件夾 *n. portfolio*
man geh choy 燜嘅菜 *n. stew*
man gene 文件 *n file*
man goon 問卷 *n. questionnaire*
man gor 民歌 *v.t. lay*
man guy 文具 *n. stationery*
man guy seurng 文具商 *n. stationer*
man hao 吻合 *v.t mesh*
man hap 吻合 *v.t. tally*
man ho 問候 *n. regard*
man ho 問候 *n. salutation*
man hok 文學 *n. literature*
man hok ga 文學家 *n. litterateur*
man hok geh 文學嘅 *a. literary*
man jeet 敏捷 *a. agile*
man jeet dow 敏捷度 *n. agility*
man jeet sow fat 敏捷手法 *n. sleight*
man jeurng 文章 *n article*
man ju 民主 *n democracy*
man ju 民主 *a democratic*
man juk ju yee jeh 民族主義者 *n. nationalist*
man lang jee gey 萬能之計 *n. panacea*
man leen geh 晚年嘅 *a. late*
man man 慢慢 *adv. slowly*
man man gam 慢慢咁 *adv. leisurely*
man man gwun shu 慢慢灌輸 *v.t. instil*
man man hang 慢慢行 *v.t. saunter*

man man sam chut 慢慢滲出 v.i. ooze

man mang 文盲 n. illiteracy

man mang 文盲 a. illiterate

man may por 問米婆 n. necropolis

man ming seh wuy 文明社會 n. civilization

man mow yat sat 萬無一失 a. infallible

man ngar 文雅 n. urbanity

man pang for ting 文憑課程 n diploma

man pao 慢跑 v.t. jog

man san 紋身 n. tattoo

man san 紋身 v.i. tattoo

man sing 慢性 a. chronic

man sow guk 萬壽菊 n. marigold

man tay 問題 n. issue

man tay 問題 n. question

man tay 問題 n rub

man tay 問題 n. snag

man tay 問題 n. trouble

man tay 問題 n. problem

man tun tun 慢吞吞 v.i. dawdle

man wah 漫畫 n comic

man yoon 文員 n clerk

man yuy 敏銳 n. acumen

mang 盲 n ablepsy

mang 盲 a blind

mang 錳 n. manganese

mang 猛 v.t. pluck

mang cheurng yeem 盲腸炎 n. appendicitis

mang gik 猛擊 v.t. wallop

mang gwok 盟國 n. ally

mang leet dung jok 猛烈動作 n. jerk

mang man 盲文 n braille

mang muk geh 盲目嘅 a. mindless

mang muk joon chung 盲目遵從 a. slavish

mang tuy 猛推 v.t. thrust

mao 錨 n. anchor

mao 貓 n. cat

mao 矛 n. spear

mao da fu low 貓打呼嚕 v.i. purr

mao fu low seng 貓呼嚕聲 n. purr

mao giew seng 貓叫聲 n. mew

mao ngan sek 貓眼石 n. opal

mao tow ying 貓頭鷹 n. owl

mao tun 矛盾 n. antinomy

mao tun 矛盾 n contradiction

mao tun 矛盾 n. paradox

mao uk 茅屋 n. hut

mao yow 貓鼬 n. mongoose

mar low 馬騮 n. monkey

mat 抹 v.t. dust

mat 密 a. frequent

mat 襪 n. sock

mat 抹 v.t. wipe

mat ban 物品 n. ware

mat dow 密度 n density

mat fung 蜜蜂 n. bee

mat geen 物件 n. item

mat jap geh 密集嘅 a. intensive

mat jat 物質 n. substance

mat jat geh 物質嘅 a. material

mat jat ju yee 物質主義 n. materialism

mat ju 物主 n. owner

mat lay hok 物理學 n. physics

mat lay hok ga 物理學家 n. physicist

mat luy 襪類 n. hosiery

mat ma 密碼 n code

mat ma hok 密碼學 n. cryptography

mat mo 密謀 v. i. conspire

mat mow 密謀 v.t. plot

mat mow 密謀 v.i. scheme

mat see 密使 n emissary

mat sik 物色 v.i scout

mat tay 物體 n. object

mat teet 密切 a. intimate

mat teet geh gwan hay 密切嘅關係 n affinity

mat torng 蜜糖 n. honey

may 謎 n enigma
may 醚 n ether
may 米 n. metre
may 咪 n. microphone
may 迷 n. mystery
may 謎 n. puzzle
may 米 n. rice
may bat juk dow 微不足道 a. negligible
may bor low 微波爐 n. microwave
may dak 美德 n. goodness
may dak 美德 n. virtue
may dow 味道 n. savour
may dow 味道 n. scent
may fan yan see 未婚人世 n agamist
may far 美化 v. t beautify
may fung 微風 n breeze
may fung 微風 n. zephyr
may gam 美感 n.pl. aesthetics
may gung 迷宮 n. labyrinth
may gung 迷宮 n. maze
may gung ngay hok 微工藝學 n. micrology
may hok geh 美學嘅 a. aesthetic
may jan 微震 n. tremor
may ju 迷住 v. t. captivate
may ju yee dow 未主義到 adv. unawares
may juy 未醉 n. sobriety
may kwan 黴菌 n. mildew
may kwan 黴菌 n mould
may lap 微粒 a. particle
may lay 美麗 n. prettiness
may lay chao geh jeurk 未離巢嘅雀 n. nestling
may lik 魅力 n. charm1
may lik 魅力 n. seduction
may lik 魅力 n spell
may loon 迷戀 v.t. infatuate
may loon 迷戀 v.t. obsess
may loon 迷戀 v.i swoon
may loy 未來 a. would-be

may loy geh 未來嘅 a. future
may morng 迷茫 n daze
may say geh 微細嘅 a. microscopic
may sik 美食 n. dainty
may sing leen 未成年 n. immaturity
may sing leen yan 未成年人 n minor
may wak 迷惑 v.t bewitch
may wak 迷惑 n dazzle
may wak 迷惑 v. t. dazzle
may wak 迷惑 v.t. mesmerize
may yan yu 美人魚 n. mermaid
may yeurk 微弱 a faint
may ying wah 微型畫 n. miniature
may yoon sing 未完成 a incomplete
may yu 謎語 n. riddle
may yu tow mow 未雨綢繆 a. provident
meen 棉 n. cotton
meen 面 n face
meen 面 n. visage
meen bao 麵包 n bread
meen bao jing geh 麵包整嘅 v. t. & i breaden
meen bao pay 麵包皮 n. crust
meen bao see 麵包師 n. baker
meen bo geh 面部嘅 a facial
meen chuy 免除 v. t. exempt
meen chuy 免除 a. exempt
meen duy 面對 v.t face
meen duy 面對 v.t. orientate
meen duy meen 面對面 n. tete-a-tete
meen fan 麵粉 n flour
meen fan chorng 麵粉廠 n. mill
meen fay geh 免費嘅 adv. gratis
meen guy 面具 n. mask
meen heurng 面向 v.t front
meen hung 面紅 adv ablush
meen hung 面紅 n blush
meen hung 面紅 v.i blush
meen hung 面紅 n flush
meen jak 免責 n. impunity

meen ju 面珠 n cheek
meen keurng 勉強 n. reluctance
meen keurng 勉強 adv. scarcely
meen keurng geh 勉強嘅 a. reluctant
meen keurng jo 勉強做 v.t. grudge
meen keurng way tee sang wut 勉強維持生活 n. subsistence
meen pay 棉被 n. quilt
meen sa 棉紗 n. veil
meen see 面試 n. interview
meen sik 面色 n. countenance
meen toon 麵團 n dough
meen yik 免疫 v.t. immunize
meen yik lik 免疫力 n. immunity
meet 摵 v.t. peel
meet 捏 v.t. pinch
meet 捏 v. pinch
meh 咩 a. what
meh 咩 pron. what
meh 咩 interj. what
meh meh giew 咩咩叫 v. i bleat
meng 名 n. name
meng 名 n. title
mey 尾 n. tail
mey dow 味道 n flavour
mey lay 美麗 n beauty
mey mey 美味 a delicious
mey sun 迷信 n. superstition
mey sun 迷信 a. superstitious
miew 喵 v.i. mew
miew 秒 n second
miew 廟 n temple
miew jun 瞄準 v.i. aim
miew kwuy 描繪 v. t. depict
miew kwuy 描繪 n. portrayal
miew kwuy 描繪 n. sketch
miew kwuy 描繪 v.t. sketch
miew see 藐視 v. t. disdain
miew sut 描述 n description
miew sut 描述 a descriptive
miew sut 描述 n. narrative
miew sut geh 描述嘅 a. narrative

miew tiew 苗條 n. slender
miew tiew 苗條 a. trim
miew tiew geh 苗條嘅 a. slim
miew tiew suk luy 窈窕淑女 n. sylph
miew yu 妙語 n. witticism
ming bak 明白 v.t. understand
ming fu kay sat geh 名副其實嘅 a. veritable
ming hay 名氣 n fame
ming hay 名氣 n. repute
ming heen 明顯 a. apparent
ming heen 明顯 adv clearly
ming heen 明顯 a. conspicuous
ming heen 明顯 a distinct
ming heen 明顯 a. obvious
ming heen geh 明顯嘅 a. manifest
ming heen geh 明顯嘅 a. palpable
ming heen geh 明顯嘅 a. patent
ming jee geh 明智嘅 a. politic
ming jee geh 明智嘅 a. sensible
ming ling 命令 v.t. adjure
ming ling 命令 n command
ming ling 命令 v. t command
ming ling 命令 n. mandate
ming ming fat 命名法 n. nomenclature
ming morng 名望 n. renown
ming muk jeurng darm 明目張膽 a flagrant
ming seurng 冥想 v.t. meditate
ming seurng 冥想 n. meditation
ming seurng 冥想 v.i. muse
ming suy teen gu 名垂千古 v.t. immortalize
ming tee 名詞 n. noun
ming wan 命運 n destiny
ming yan 名人 n celebrity
ming yan 名人 n. personage
ming yee seurng geh 名義上嘅 a. nominal
ming yu 名譽 n. reputation
ming yu 明喻 n. simile

mo 帽 n. cap
mo 舞 n dance
mo 霧 n fog
mo 毛 n. fur
mo 帽 n. hat
mo 墓 n. tomb
mo 無 adv. without
mo chung 毛蟲 n caterpillar
mo chung 冒充 v.i. sham
mo dak ao 無得拗 a. indisputable
mo dak bay 無得比 a. incomparable
mo dak yee 無得醫 a. incurable
mo dak yee 模特兒 n. model
mo dan sing 無彈性 a. inflexible
mo day 無低 a. baseless
mo day 跕低 v. i. crouch
mo day 跕低 v.i. duck
mo deet juy 無秩序 a. haphazard
mo doon 武斷 a. arbitrary
mo fa gwor 無花果 n fig
mo fan tow fan 模範囚犯 n. trusty
mo fat forng sow 無法防守 a. indefensible
mo fat sat see 無法事實 n. impracticability
mo fat yan sow 無法忍受 n. intolerance
mo fong 模仿 v.t. ape
mo forng 模仿 v. t emulate
mo forng 模仿 v.t. imitate
mo forng 模仿 n. imitation
mo forng 模仿 v.t. impersonate
mo forng 模仿 n. impersonation
mo forng jeh 模仿者 n. imitator
mo gam gok geh 無感覺嘅 a. numb
mo gan 毛巾 n. towel
mo geh 毛嘅 a. woollen
mo gey 母雞 n. hen
mo gey meng tow piew 無記名投票 v.i. ballot
mo gey sing 無記性 a forgetful

mo ging yeem 無經驗 n. inexperience
mo han geh 無限嘅 a. immeasurable
mo han kay 無限期 a. indefinite
mo heem 冒險 n adventure
mo heem 冒險 v.t hazard
mo hey 武器 n. weapon
mo hing chuy 無興趣 a. weary
mo hing chuy 無興趣 v.t. weary
mo ho 冒號 n colon
mo jee 無知 n. ignorance
mo jee 無知 a. ignorant
mo jeen 毛氈 n blanket
mo jeurng 毛象 n. mammoth
mo jing fu 無政府 n anarchy
mo jing fu juu yee jeh 無政府主義者 n anarchist
mo jow leen yee kwan 無袖連衣裙 n chemise
mo lai 無賴 n cad
mo lai 毛拉 n. mullah
mo lang 無能 n. impotence
mo lang lik 無能力 n. inability
mo lang lik 無能力 a. incapable
mo lang lik 無能力 n. incapacity
mo lang lik 無能力 a. incompetent
mo larn 毛冷 n. wool
mo liew 無聊 a dull
mo loy sing 無耐性 n. impatience
mo loy sing 無耐性 a. impatient
mo lun 謬論 n fallacy
mo lun 無論 pron. whatever
mo lun been gor 無論邊個 pron whichever
mo lun...ding hay 無論...定係 conj. whether
mo may 無味 adj. bland
mo morng 無望 a. hopeless
mo ngow 犛牛 n. yak
mo sam jorng joy 無心裝載 a. inattentive
mo san lun 無神論 n atheism

mo san lun jeh 無神論者 n atheist

mo see 武士 n. warrior

mo seen 無線 a. wireless

mo seen 無線 n wireless

mo sik geh 無色嘅 adj achromatic

mo so 無數 a. countless

mo sow ling geh 無首領嘅 adj. acephalous

mo sut 巫術 n. witchery

mo ting fu ju yee 無政府主義 n. anarchism

mo tow 無頭 n. acephalus

mo toy 舞台 n arena

mo wu 模糊 v. t blear

mo wu 模糊 n blur

mo wu 模糊 a. hazy

mo yee jung teng dow 無意中聽到 v.t. overhear

mo yeh jow 無嘢做 a. idle

mo yeurk hor gow 無藥可救 a. incorrigible

mo yeurng 母羊 n ewe

mo yik 貿易 n commerce

mo yik 無益 n. futility

mo yik seurng 貿易商 n dealer

mo ying geh 無形嘅 adj. aeriform

mo yoon 墓園 n. cemetery

mo yuk 侮辱 v.t. affront

mo yuk 侮辱 n affront

mo yuk 侮辱 n gibe

mo yung 無用 a. futile

mo yung geh 無用嘅 a. helpless

mo yung geh 無用嘅 a. waste

mok 膜 n. membrane

mok doot 剝奪 v. t deprive

mok bat gwan sam 漠不關心 n. indifference

mok bat gwan sam 漠不關心 n. nonchalance

mok gwong 剝光 v.t. denude

mong 忙 a busy

mong ju 望住 adv agaze

mong kow 網球 n. tennis

mong yoon geng 望遠鏡 n. binocular

mor 摸 v.t feel

mor chat lik 摩擦力 n. friction

mor fat 魔法 n. witchcraft

mor fat pang 魔法棒 n. wand

mor fat see 魔法師 n. wizard

mor forng gung yan 磨坊工人 n. miller

mor gu 蘑菇 n. mushroom

mor gway 魔鬼 n. demon

mor gway 魔鬼 n devil

mor gway 魔鬼 n. satan

mor keet jor 魔羯座 n Capricorn

mor shoon 磨損 n fray

mor sing fan 磨成粉 v.t. mill

mor sut see 魔術師 n. magician

mor suy 磨碎 v.t grate

mor suy 磨碎 v.i. grind

mor suy gey 磨碎機 n. grinder

mor tat 摩擦 v. t brustle

mor wan 魔幻 a. magical

morng 望 v.i. glance

morng 忙 v.i. moil

morng 網 n. net

morng ging low 望景樓 n belvedere

morng gwor 芒果 n mango

morng jorng geh 網狀嘅 a. webby

morng jorng mat 網狀物 n. mesh

morng ju 望住 v.t. gaze

morng lok 網絡 n. network

morng she 蟒蛇 n. python

morng yan fu yee 忘恩負義 n. ingratitude

morng yoon geng 望遠鏡 n. telescope

mow 帽 n. hood

mow 哞 v.i moo

mow ban 模板 n. stencil

mow been far 無變化 a. stagnant

mow chuy may 無趣味 a. lacklustre

mow dak bay geh 無得比嘅 *a. matchless*
mow dak bay geh 無得比嘅 *a. nonpareil*
mow dak bay geh 無得比嘅 *a. peerless*
mow dam 無膽 *n. timidity*
mow day 跍低 *v.i. squat*
mow deng 無埞 *adv. nowhere*
mow dik geh 無敵嘅 *a. invincible*
mow fan 模範 *n. paragon*
mow fan 謀反 *n. rebellion*
mow fan ying 無反應 *a. insensible*
mow fat far gai 無法化解 *a. irreconcilable*
mow fat gai sik 無法解釋 *a. inexplicable*
mow forng 模仿 *n. mimesis*
mow forng 模仿 *v.t mimic*
mow forng 模仿 *n mimicry*
mow forng 模仿 *n. parody*
mow forng 模仿 *v.t. parody*
mow forng ghe 模仿嘅 *a. mimic*
mow gey lut 無紀律 *n. indiscipline*
mow gor day forng 某個地方 *adv. somewhere*
mow gu 無辜 *a. innocent*
mow guy 模具 *n. mould*
mow gwan 無關 *a. irrelevant*
mow gwan 無關 *a. irrespective*
mow gwor geh jik mat 無果嘅植物 *adj. acarpous*
mow ha tee 無瑕疵 *a. stainless*
mow han 無限 *n. infinity*
mow han geh 無限嘅 *a. infinite*
mow han geh 無限嘅 *a. limitless*
mow han geh 無限嘅 *a. measureless*
mow hao 無效 *a. ineffective*
mow hao 無效 *a. inoperative*
mow hao 無效 *a. invalid*
mow hao 無效 *n. nullification*
mow hao geh 無效嘅 *a. null*

mow hay 武器 *n. arsenal*
mow heem 冒險 *v.t. risk*
mow heem 冒險 *v.t. stake*
mow hor bay meen 無可避免 *a. inevitable*
mow hor fow ying 無可否認 *a. irrefutable*
mow hor lang 無可能 *a. impossible*
mow hor lang sing 無可能性 *n. impossibility*
mow hung 毛孔 *n. pore*
mow jee 無知 *n. nescience*
mow jee gok geh 無知覺嘅 *a. senseless*
mow jing da choy 無精打采 *n. lethargy*
mow jing da choy 無精打采 *a. listless*
mow ju 母豬 *n. sow*
mow juk heng chung 無足輕重 *a. lowly*
mow kwan geh 無菌嘅 *a. sterile*
mow lai 無賴 *n. knave*
mow lai 無賴 *n. rascal*
mow lai 無賴 *n. rogue*
mow lai 無賴 *n. scoundrel*
mow lay 無禮 *n. insolence*
mow lay 無禮 *a. insolent*
mow lay geh 無禮嘅 *n. impertinence*
mow lay mao 無禮貌 *a. impolite*
mow lay mao geh 無禮貌嘅 *a. rude*
mow lay moa geh 無禮貌嘅 *a unmannerly*
mow liew geh 無聊嘅 *a. prosaic*
mow lik wan 無力還 *a. insolvent*
mow ma 母馬 *n. mare*
mow may 無味 *a. insipid*
mow may 無味 *n. insipidity*
mow meh hor lang 無咩可能 *a. unlikely*
mow ming for siew 無明火燒 *v.i. smoulder*

mow por 巫婆 n. necromancer

mow san lun jeh 無神論者 n antitheist

mow sang hay geh 無生氣嘅 a. lifeless

mow sang ming geh 無生命嘅 a. inanimate

mow sat 謀殺 n. murder

mow sat 謀殺 v.t. murder

mow see 母獅 n. lioness

mow see geh 無私嘅 a. selfless

mow seng 無聲 n. silence

mow seng gam gorng 無聲咁講 v.t. mouth

mow seng geh 無聲嘅 a. mute

mow seng geh 無聲嘅 a. silent

mow sik 暮色 n twilight

mow sing 母性 n. motherhood

mow sing geh 母性嘅 a. motherly

mow sing jow geh yan 無成就嘅人 n. nonentity

mow sor bat jee geh 無所不知嘅 a. omniscient

mow sor bat joy 無所不在 n. omnipresence

mow sor bat joy geh 無所不在嘅 a. omnipresent

mow sor bat lang geh 無所不能嘅 a. omnipotent

mow sow 無數 n. myriad

mow sow geh 無數嘅 a. innumerable

mow sow geh 無數嘅 a myriad

mow sow geh 無數嘅 a. numberless

mow sut 巫術 n. sorcery

mow tan 母親 n mother

mow tan geh 母親嘅 a. maternal

mow tee ghe 無恥嘅 a. shameless

mow ting geh 無情嘅 adj. merciless

mow ting geh 無情嘅 a. pitiless

mow toy 舞台 n. stage

mow wu 模糊 n. ambiguity

mow wu 模糊 a. ambiguous

mow wu 模糊 a. indistinct

mow wu bat ting 模糊不清 n. illegibility

mow yan 無人 pron. nobody

mow yan cho jok geh 無人操作嘅 a. unmanned

mow yee gam 無意咁 adv. unwittingly

mow yee see 無意思 a. meaningless

mow yee sik 無意識 n. oblivion

mow yeh 無嘢 n. nothing

mow yeh 無嘢 adv. nothing

mow yik cheurng sor 貿易場所 n. mart

mow yoot 墓穴 n. vault

mow yuk 侮辱 n. insult

mow yuk 侮辱 v.t. insult

mow yuk geh 侮辱嘅 a abusive

mow yung geh 無用嘅 a. pathetic

mow yung ghe 無用嘅 a. paltry

muk 木 n. timber

muk 木 n. wood

muk ban 木板 n. plank

muk biew 目標 n. aim

muk biew 目標 n. goal

muk biew 目標 n. target

muk cheurng 牧場 n. pasture

muk di dey 目的地 n destination

muk dik 目的 n. intent

muk dik 目的 n. intention

muk dik 目的 n. objective

muk dik 目的 n. purpose

muk ding ho ngoy 目定口呆 v.i. gape

muk gik 目擊 v.i. witness

muk gik ting yan 目擊證人 n. witness

muk gung 木工 n. carpentry

muk gung 木工 n. joiner

muk gwun 牧冠 n. mitre

muk jeurng 木匠 n. carpenter

muk jow geh 木造嘅 a. wooden

muk kam 木琴 n. xylophone
muk lai yee 木乃伊 n mummy
muk luk 目錄 n. catalogue
muk luk 目錄 n. content
muk mah 木馬 n. hobby-horse
muk man geh 牧民嘅 a. pastoral
muk mow fat gey 目無法紀 a. lawless
muk sang geh 木生嘅 a. xylophilous
muk see 牧師 n clergy
muk see 牧師 n. oracle
muk see 牧師 n. parson
muk see 牧師 n. vicar
muk see lam gwun yoon 穆斯林官員 n. nabob
muk sing 木星 n. jupiter
muk tee 木刺 n. splinter
muk tiew 木條 n taper
muk tow 木頭 n. log
muk tung 木桶 n cask
muk yan 牧人 n. herdsman
muk yeurng jor 牡羊座 n aries
muk yeurng yan 牧羊人 n. shepherd
muk yuk 沐浴 n ablution
mun 悶 v. t bore
mun 門 n door
mun 滿 a. full
mun geh 滿嘅 adv. full
mun ho 門口 n. threshold
mun juk 滿足 a. content
mun juk 滿足 n. satiety
mun juk 滿足 v.t. satisfy
mun juk gam 滿足感 n. gratification
mun juk geh 滿足嘅 a. satiable
mun mun bat lok 悶悶不樂 a. sullen
mun san 門閂 n bolt
mun tan beng yan 門診病人 n. outpatient
mun wai hay morng 滿懷希望 a. hopeful
mun way 門衛 n. usher
mun yee 滿意 n contentment

mun yee 滿意 n. satisfaction
mun yee geh 滿意嘅 a. satisfactory
mun yeet 悶熱 a. sultry
mung 夢 n dream
mung 夢 v. i. dream
mung ju ngan 蒙住眼 v. t blindfold
mung yow beng 夢遊病 n. somnambulism
mung yow beng wan jeh 夢遊病患者 n. somnambulist
mut so 沒收 n confiscation
mwun 蟎 n. mite
mwun kwang 門框 n. lintel
mwun lorng 門廊 n. porch
mwun mwun bat lok 悶悶不樂 v.i. mope
mwun mwun bat lok geh 悶悶不樂嘅 a. morose
mwun yeet 悶熱 a. muggy
mwut kay geh 末期嘅 a. terminal
mwut lay far 茉莉花 n. jasmine, jessamine
mwut sow 沒收 v.t forfeit
mwut yeurk 沒藥 n. myrrh
mwuy 每 prep. per
mwuy fan jung geh 每分鐘嘅 adv. minutely
mwuy gor 每個 a each
mwuy gor 每個 a every
mwuy gor lay bai 每個禮拜 adv. weekly
mwuy gor lay bai geh 每個禮拜嘅 a. weekly
mwuy gor yoot 每個月 a. monthly
mwuy gor yoot 每個月 adv monthly
mwuy gway 玫瑰 n. rose
mwuy gway dow geh 每季度嘅 a. quarterly
mwuy hay 煤氣 n. gas
mwuy leen geh 每年嘅 a. yearly
mwuy leurng gor yoot 每兩個月 adj bimensal

mwuy man 每晚 *adv. nightly*
mwuy yat 每日 *adv. daily*
mwuy yat geh 每日嘅 *a daily*
mwuy yow 煤油 *n. kerosene*

N

ng 五 *n five*
ng sap 五十 *n. fifty*
ngai shu 矮樹 *n bush*
ngam 啱 *adv. aright*
ngam geh 啱嘅 *a. right*
ngam jing 癌症 *n. cancer*
ngan 眼 *n eye*
ngan 銀 *n. silver*
ngan bao 銀包 *n. purse*
ngan fan 眼瞓 *a. lethargic*
ngan fan 眼瞓 *a. sleepy*
ngan fan 眼瞓 *n. somnolence*
ngan fan 眼瞓 *n. somnolent*
ngan for yee sang 眼科醫生 *n. oculist*
ngan gam gam 眼甘甘 *v.t. ogle*
ngan gao 晏覺 *n. nap*
ngan geh 眼嘅 *a. ocular*
ngan geh 眼嘅 *a. optic*
ngan geng 硬頸 *n. obduracy*
ngan geng 硬頸 *a. obstinate*
ngan geng 眼鏡 *n. spectacle*
ngan geng geh 硬頸嘅 *a. obdurate*
ngan geng seh 眼睛蛇 *n cobra*
ngan geng seurng 眼鏡商 *n. optician*
ngan goa 晏覺 *n. siesta*
ngan gwat gwat 眼倔倔 *n. glare*
ngan gwat gwat gam morng 眼倔倔咁望 *v.i glare*
ngan hung 眼孔 *n eyelet*
ngan jeet mo 眼睫毛 *n eyelash*
ngan jow 晏晝 *n. lunch*

ngan kow 眼球 *n eyeball*
ngan lay 眼利 *a. watchful*
ngan luy 眼淚 *n. tear*
ngan sap sap 眼濕濕 *a. tearful*
ngan sik 顏色 *n colour*
ngan sik 眼色 *n wink*
ngan sik geh 銀色嘅 *a silver*
ngang geh 硬嘅 *a. solid*
ngang geng 硬頸 *a. stubborn*
ngap tow 岌頭 *v.i. nod*
ngar 牙 *n. tooth*
ngar 瓦 *n. watt*
ngar ba 啞巴 *n. mute*
ngar fai 瓦塊 *n. slate*
ngar giew 鴉叫 *v. i. caw*
ngar giew seng 鴉叫聲 *n. caw*
ngar kek biew yeen 啞劇表演 *n. mime*
ngar kek yeen yoon 啞劇演員 *n. mummer*
ngar ku 牙箍 *n brace*
ngar mar bo 亞麻布 *n. linen*
ngar mar jee 亞麻子 *n. linseed*
ngar meen 瓦面 *n. roof*
ngar peen 鴉片 *n. opium*
ngar tung 牙痛 *n. toothache*
ngar yee 牙醫 *n dentist*
ngar yuk 牙肉 *n. gum*
ngarm 啱 *a. true*
ngarm ngarm 啱啱 *adv. just*
ngat been 壓扁 *v.t. squash*
ngat bik jeh 壓迫者 *n. oppressor*
ngat dow 壓倒 *v.t. outnumber*
ngat dow 壓倒 *v.i. prevail*
ngat jay 壓制 *v.t muzzle*
ngat jay 壓制 *v.t. oppress*
ngat jay 壓制 *n. oppression*
ngat jay 壓制 *n. repression*
ngat jay 壓制 *v.t. stifle*
ngat jay geh 壓制嘅 *a. oppressive*
ngat lik 壓力 *n. pressure*
ngat lik 壓力 *n. stress*

ngat wan 押韻 n. rhyme
ngat wan 押韻 v.i. rhyme
ngat yan 壓印 n. imprint
ngay gey 危機 n crisis
ngay gorn 桅杆 n. mast
ngay gwan jee 偽君子 n. hypocrite
ngay heem 危險 n. danger
ngay heem 危險 a dangerous
ngay heem 危險 n. hazard
ngay heem 危險 n. insecurity
ngay heem 危險 n. jeopardy
ngay heem 危險 n. peril
ngay heem geh 危險嘅 a. perilous
ngay heem geh 危險嘅 a. risky
ngay jing juy 偽證罪 n. perjury
ngay jo 偽造 v.t forge
ngay jo ban 偽造品 n forgery
ngay jorng 偽裝 n disguise
ngay jow geh 偽造嘅 a. spurious
ngay kap 危及 v. t. endanger
ngay lik 毅力 n. perseverance
ngay sut 藝術 n. art
ngay sut ga 藝術家 n. artist
ngay sut geh 藝術嘅 a. artistic
ngay yan 矮人 n. midget
ngok toon 樂團 n. band
ngor 我 pron. I
ngor 我 pron. me
ngor day 我哋 pron. our
ngor geh 我嘅 pron. mine
ngor geh 我嘅 a. my
ngor jee gey 我自己 pron. myself
ngor po 臥鋪 n bunk
ngow 牛 n bull
ngow 牛 n. cattle
ngow 牛 n. cow
ngow 牛 n. ox
ngow jay fu 牛仔褲 n. jean
ngow pang 牛棚 n byre
ngow tow hoon 牛頭犬 n bulldog
ngow yow 牛油 n butter
ngow yuk 牛肉 n beef

ngoy 愛 v.t. adore
ngoy 愛 n. endearment
ngoy 愛 v.t. love
ngoy been geh 外邊嘅 a. outer
ngoy biew 外表 n appearance
ngoy biew 外表 n. guise
ngoy for yee sang 外科醫生 n. surgeon
ngoy gan 愛緊 a. loving
ngoy gao 外交 n diplomacy
ngoy gao geh 外交嘅 a diplomatic
ngoy gao gwun 外交官 n diplomat
ngoy gwok geh 外國嘅 a foreign
ngoy gwok geh 愛國嘅 a. patriotic
ngoy gwok jeh 愛國者 n. patriot
ngoy gwok jing san 愛國精神 n. partiotism
ngoy gwok yan 外國人 a. alien
ngoy gwok yan 外國人 n foreigner
ngoy ho 愛好 n. liking
ngoy ho jeh 愛好者 n buff
ngoy ho jeh 愛好者 n devotee
ngoy hok 外殼 n. husk
ngoy horng 外行 n. layman
ngoy horng geh 外行嘅 n lay
ngoy loy yan 外來人 n. outsider
ngoy meen 外面 adv outward
ngoy meen geh 外面嘅 a external
ngoy mo 愛慕 n. adoration
ngoy ting 愛情 n love
ngoy tow 外套 n. jacket
ngoy tow 外套 n. overall
ngoy way geen juk 外圍建築 n. outhouse
ngoy yee lan geh 愛爾蘭嘅 a. Irish
ngoy yee lan yan 愛爾蘭人 n. Irish
ngoy ying 外型 n. outline

O

oh 鉤 n. hook

oh 嘔 v.t. vomit

oh 嘔 n vomit

oh jeurng 偶像 n. idol

oh jow dai luk geh 歐洲大陸嘅 a continental

oh may ga 歐米加 n. omega

oh wan wuy 奧運會 n. olympiad

oi dow 哀悼 v. i. condole

ok 惡 a ferocious

ok 惡 a fierce

ok ba 惡霸 n bully

ok duk 惡毒 a. nefarious

ok duk geh 惡毒嘅 a evil

ok duk geh 惡毒嘅 a. malicious

ok fa 惡化 v. i compound

ok far 惡化 v.t. sour

ok geh 顎嘅 a. palatal

ok geh 惡嘅 a. savage

ok hang 惡行 n. infamy

ok hang 惡行 n. misdeed

ok hay 樂器 n. instrument

ok hay ga 樂器家 n. instrumentalist

ok hay yeen jow 樂器演奏 a. instrumental

ok jok kek 惡作劇 n. hoax

ok jok kek 惡作劇 n mischief

ok jok kek 惡作劇 n. prank

ok jok kek 惡作劇 n. roguery

ok ming 惡名 n. notoriety

ok mor 惡魔 n fiend

ok mung 惡夢 n. nightmare

ok sing 惡性 n. malignancy

ok sing geh 惡性嘅 a. malignant

ok tow 惡臭 n. stench

ok tow 惡臭 n stink

ok yee 惡意 n. malice

ok yee 惡意 n. malignity

ok yee geh 惡意嘅 a. wanton

ok yu 鱷魚 n crocodile

on 岸 n. shore

on (puy) 安(培) n ampere

on choon 安全 a. safe

on choon 安全 n. safety

on choon geh 安全嘅 a. secure

on fu 安撫 v.t. appease

on fu 安撫 v.t. conciliate

on gam 按金 n. deposit

on jiew 按照 adv. accordingly

on jing 安靜 a. tranquil

on jing geh 安靜嘅 a. peaceful

on jorng 安裝 v.t. install

on jorng 安裝 n. installation

on jorng see fu 安裝師傅 n fitter

on mor 按摩 n. massage

on mor 按摩 v.t. massage

on mor see 按摩師 n. masseur

on pai 安排 v.t. arrange

on pai 安排 n. arrangement

on pai 安排 v. t conduct

on pai 安排 v.t. organize

on pai 安排 v.t. schedule

on see 安士 n. ounce

on sik yat 安息日 n. sabbath

on wan kuk 安魂曲 n. requiem

on way 安慰 v. t comfort

on way 安慰 n consolation

on way 安慰 v. t console

on way 安慰 v.t. solace

on way 安慰 n. solace

or 鵝 n. goose

or 哦 v.t. nag

or liew 屙尿 v.i. urinate

or liew 屙尿 n. urination

ow da 毆打 v.t. assault

oy diew 哀悼 v.i. mourn

oy diew 哀悼 n. mourning

P

pa 爬 v.i climb
pa 爬 v. t crawl
pa 爬 v. i creep
pa 爬 v.i. scramble
pa 爬 n scramble
pa cho 怕醜 a. bashful
pa go 爬高 n. ascent
pa hang dung mat 爬行動物 n. reptile
pa jee 怕擳 a. ticklish
pa lo por 怕老婆 a. henpecked
pa san ga 爬山家 n alpinist
pa seep 跋涉 v.i. wade
pa tow 爬頭 v.t. overtake
pa tow 怕醜 n. shy
pa tow 怕醜 v.i. shy
pai 派 n faction
pai 派 v.i. issue
pai 排 n. platoon
pai 牌 n. sign
pai 牌 n. tag
pai 牌 n. licence
pai ban see 排版師 n. compositor
pai beet 派別 n. sect
pai beet geh 派別嘅 a factious
pai cheurng 排場 n. pomp
pai duy 派對 n. party
pai jee 牌子 n brand
pai jee 牌子 n make
pai ju 派駐 v.t. station
pai leen 排練 v.t. rehearse
pai leet forng sik 排列方式 n. permutation
pai sing yat horng 排成一行 v.i. file
pai suy 排水 n drainage
pai suy gwun 排水管 n. culvert
pai suy gwun 排水管 n drain
pai suy hay tung 排水系統 n. sewerage
pai tik 排斥 v.t. ostracize
pai tik 排斥 a outcast
pai yam mow 派任務 v.t. task
pai yan 派人 v.t. post
pak 拍 v. i bat
pak 拍 v. t cuff
pak 泊 v.t. park
pak 拍 v.t. pat
pak 拍 n pat
pak 拍 v.t. whack
pak dong 拍檔 n co-partner
pak dorng 拍檔 n. partner
pak jee 拍子 n beat
pak mai 拍賣 n auction
pak mai 拍賣 v.t. auction
pak seng 啪聲 n. smack
pak shu 柏樹 n cypress
pak sow 拍手 v. i. clap
pak tor 拍拖 v. t date
pan 噴 v.i. spout
pan 噴 v.t. spray
pan 噴 v.i. spurt
pan chut 噴出 v. t. eject
pan chut 噴出 v.i. puff
pan dang 攀登 v. i clamber
pan dang 攀登 n. climb
pan dang 攀登 v.t. scale
pan hay sik fay gey 噴氣式飛機 n. jet
pan ho suy 噴口水 v. t beslaver
pan hoot 貧血 n anaemia
pan jay 噴劑 n. spray
pan kung 貧窮 n. poverty
pan kwan 貧困 n. privation
pan lut 頻率 n. frequency
pan man fat 貧民窟 n. slum
pan suy tee 噴水池 n. fountain
pan yoon jik mat 攀緣植物 n creeper
pang 嘭 n. bam
pang 棚 n shed
pang ga 棚架 n. scaffold

pang jik gog geh 憑直覺嘅 a. intuitive
pang uk 棚屋 a. shanty
pang uk 棚屋 n. wigwam
pang yow 朋友 n. friend
pang yow 朋友 n. mate
pang yow 朋友 n. pal
pao 豹 n. leopard
pao 刨 v.t. plane
pao 跑 v.i. run
pao bo 跑步 n. run
pao choy 泡菜 n. pickle
pao hay 拋棄 v. t. desert
pao hay 拋棄 v.t. slough
pao lap sap 拋垃圾 v.t. litter
pao pao 泡泡 n bubble
pao sow 跑手 n. runner
par day 趴低 v.t. prostrate
par day geh 趴低嘅 a. prostrate
pay 批 n batch
pay 皮 n. leather
pay 皮 n. peel
pay 脾 n. spleen
pay dai 皮帶 n belt
pay fat 批發 n. wholesale
pay fat 批發 a wholesale
pay fat 批發 adv. wholesale
pay fat seurng 批發商 n. wholesaler
pay fu 皮膚 n. cutis
pay fu 皮膚 n. skin
pay fu hak geh 皮膚黑嘅 a. swarthy
pay gak chorng 皮革廠 n. tannery
pay geen 披肩 n. cape
pay geen 被肩 n. shawl
pay gu 屁股 n buttock
pay hay 脾氣 n. temper
pay jun 批准 v.t approbate
pay jun 批准 n. approval
pay jun 批准 v.t. approve
pay jun 批准 v.t. authorize
pay jun 批准 v.t. license
pay jun 批准 n. permission

pay lo 疲勞 n fatigue
pay pa 琵琶 n. lute
pay ping 批評 n. censure
pay ping 批評 n criticism
pay ping 批評 v. t criticize
pay ping 批評 v.t. rebuke
pay ping 批評 n. rebuke
pay ping 批評 n. reproach
pay ping ga 批評家 n critic
pay see 鄙視 n contempt
pay see 鄙視 n disdain
pay see 鄙視 n. scorn
pay see 鄙視 v.t. scorn
pay seurng 砒霜 n arsenic
pay tan 皮疹 a. rash
peen fuk 蝙蝠 n bat
peen geen 偏見 n. prejudice
peen gik 偏激 a extreme
peen guk 騙局 n deception
peen guk 騙局 n fiddle
peen guk 騙局 n trick
peen ho 編號 v.t. number
peen jee 騙子 n. cheat
peen jee 騙子 n. fraud
peen jee 騙子 n. impostor
peen jee 騙子 n. sharper
peen jee 騙子 n. trickster
peen jeh 騙子 n. swindler
peen kap 遍及 v.t. pervade
peen kap 遍及 adv. throughout
peen kek 編劇 n dramatist
peen lay 偏離 v. i deviate
peen lay 偏離 n deviation
peen leen see 編年史 n. chronicle
peen sam 偏心 n bias
peen she 編寫 v. t compile
peen tan 偏祖 n. partiality
peen tan geh 偏祖嘅 a. partisan
peen top 編輯 n editor
peen top geh 編輯嘅 a editorial
peen tow tung 偏頭痛 n. migraine
peen yoon geh 偏遠嘅 a. remote

peet chuy 撤除 v. t exclude
peet ho 撤號 n. apostrophe
pek 劈 v.t. hew
pek 劈 v.t. slash
pek 劈 n slash
peng 平 a cheap
peng for 平貨 n. bargain
pi lee pa la 劈里啪啦 v.t. crackle
piew 漂 v.i float
piew 票 n. ticket
piew bak suy 漂白水 v. t bleach
piew dorng 漂蕩 v.t. waft
piew dung 飄動 n flutter
piew ga 票價 n fare
piew ga 票價 n fee
piew geh 漂嘅 a. natant
pik ho 癖好 n. proclivity
pik pak 噼拍 n. & v. i clack
ping dang 平等 n equality
ping dang 平等 n. parity
ping day 平地 n. plain
ping fan 平凡 a. banal
ping fan 平分 v. t bisect
ping fan geh 平凡嘅 a. mundane
ping forng 平房 n bungalow
ping forng 平方 v.t. square
ping ga 評價 v.t. appraise
ping ga 評價 n. assessment
ping ga 評價 n review
ping geh 平嘅 a even
ping geh 平嘅 a flat
ping geh 平嘅 n flat
ping geh 平嘅 a level
ping geh 平嘅 a. plane
ping gu 評估 v.t. assess
ping gu 評估 v. t evaluate
ping gu 評估 v.t. rate
ping gwan sow 平均數 n. mean
ping gwor 蘋果 n. apple
ping gwun 平均 a. average
ping gwun so 平均數 n. average
ping gwun way 平均為 v.t. average

ping hang 平衡 v.t. balance
ping hang geh 平行嘅 a. parallel
ping hang say gok ying 平行四角型 n. parallelogram
ping jing 平靜 n. calm
ping jing 平靜 v.t. quiet
ping jing 平靜 n. serenity
ping jing 平靜 n. tranquility
ping jing geh 平靜嘅 a. pacific
ping jing geh 平靜嘅 a. serene
ping lun 評論 n comment
ping lun 評論 n commentary
ping lun 評論 n editorial
ping lun yoon 評論員 n commentator
ping man 平民 n civilian
ping man 平民 n. commoner
ping man bak sing 平民百姓 n. populace
ping man geh 平民嘅 a civil
ping man say bo 平紋細布 n. muslin
ping meen 平面 n plane
ping mok 屏幕 n. screen
ping see 平時 a. usual
ping see gam 平時咁 adv. ordinarily
ping seurng 平常 a. casual
ping sik 平息 v.t. pacify
ping yam geh 拼音嘅 a. phonetic
ping yee gan yan 平易近人 a. amiable
po 抱 v. t embrace
po day ban 鋪地板 v.t floor
po gung ying 蒲公英 n. dandelion
po mut 泡沫 n foam
po peen geh 普遍嘅 a. commonplace
po peen geh 普遍嘅 a. general
po poeen 普遍 a. widespread
po tee joon 鋪瓷磚 v.t. tile
po tow tong 葡萄糖 n. glucose
po tung 普通 a. ordinary
po tung geh 普通嘅 a. workaday
po way 鋪位 n berth
po yoon 抱怨 v. t cavil

pok 撲 *n. lunge*
pok 撲 *v.i lunge*
pok sik 撲熄 *v.t extinguish*
pok so 樸素 *a. austere*
pok sow 樸素 *n. rusticity*
pong been 旁邊 *n. aside*
pong dai 龐大 *a bulky*
pong gwong 膀胱 *n bladder*
pong lo 旁路 *n bypass*
por gow 破舊 *a. threadbare*
por gow geh 破舊嘅 *a. shabby*
por leet 破裂 *n. rupture*
por leet 破裂 *v.t. rupture*
por por ma ma 婆婆媽媽 *a maudlin*
por por ma ma 婆婆媽媽 *a. mawkish*
por shoon 破損 *n breakage*
por tan 破產 *n. bankrupt*
por tan 破產 *n. bankruptcy*
por tan 破產 *n. insolvency*
por wai 破壞 *v. t. corrupt*
por wai 破壞 *v. t. damage*
por wai 破壞 *v. t destroy*
por wai 破壞 *v.t. mar*
por wai 破壞 *v.t. ruin*
por wai 破壞 *v.t. spoil*
por wai 破壞 *v.i. tamper*
por wai 破壞 *n. wrack*
por wai 破壞 *v.t. wreck*
por wai geh 破壞嘅 *a. subversive*
por wai jeh 破壞者 *n. wrecker*
porng bak 旁白 *n. narration*
porng ban jeh 旁白者 *n. narrator*
porng dai geh 龐大嘅 *a mammoth*
porng gwun jeh 旁觀者 *n. on-looker*
pow 鋪 *a. lay*
pow 抱 *v.i. nestle*
pow 鋪 *v.t. pave*
pow bat ping geh 抱不平嘅 *a. malcontent*
pow mwun yow yeen 鋪滿油煙 *v.t. soot*

pow mwut 泡沫 *n. lather*
pow peen 普遍 *n. prevalence*
pow peen geh 普遍嘅 *a. prevalent*
pow peen sing 普遍性 *n. universality*
pow tow tang 葡萄藤 *n. vine*
pow tung 普通 *n. mediocrity*
pow tung geh 普通嘅 *a standard*
pow tung ghe 普通嘅 *a. mediocre*
pow tung yan 普通人 *n mortal*
pung 砰 *v.i. thud*
pung jorng 碰撞 *v. i. collide*
pung jorng 碰撞 *n collision*
pung jorng 碰撞 *n crash*
pung seng 砰聲 *n. thud*
pwun 盆 *n. basin*
pwun 盤 *n. tray*
pwun doon 判斷 *n estimation*
pwun doon 判斷 *v.i. judge*
pwun doon 判斷 *n. judgement*
pwun gwok juy 叛國罪 *n. treason*
pwun juy 判罪 *n conviction*
pwun koot 判決 *v.t. sentence*
pwun loon 叛亂 *n. insurrection*
pwun loon geh 叛亂嘅 *a. insurgent*
pwun man 盤問 *n. inquisition*
pwun man 盤問 *v.t. probe*
pwun mow juy 判無罪 *v.t. acquit*
pwun shoon 盤算 *n. preoccupation*
pwut 潑 *v.i. splash*
pwut fwun 撥款 *n grant*
pwuy 賠 *v.t. recompense*
pwuy ak 配額 *n. quota*
pwuy ak 配額 *n. ration*
pwuy geem 佩劍 *n. sabre*
pwuy hap 配合 *a co-operative*
pwuy oh 配偶 *n. consort*
pwuy oh 配偶 *n. spouse*
pwuy sam toon 陪審團 *n. jury*
pwuy sam yoon 陪審員 *n. juror*
pwuy sam yoon 陪審員 *n. juryman*
pwuy seurng 賠償 *v.t compensate*
pwuy seurng 賠償 *n compensation*

pwuy seurng 賠償 *n. recompense*
pwuy seurng 賠償 *n redress*
pwuy seurng 賠償 *n. repayment*
pwuy sow 倍數 *n multiple*
pwuy wuy 徘徊 *v.i. linger*
pwuy wuy 徘徊 *v.i. loiter*
pwuy wuy 徘徊 *v.t. maunder*

S

sa 沙 *n. sand*
sa 灑 *v.t. scatter*
sa 灑 *v. t. sprinkle*
sa geh 沙嘅 *a. sandy*
sa jap sa 耍雜耍 *v.t. juggle*
sa jeen 沙展 *n. sergeant*
sa lut 沙律 *n. salad*
sa mok 沙漠 *n desert*
sa mok geh luk jow 沙漠嘅綠洲 *n. oasis*
sa ngar 沙啞 *a. husky*
sa sek fwuy 傻石灰 *v.t lime*
sa tan 沙灘 *n beach*
sa yu 鯊魚 *n. shark*
sai 曬 *n brag*
sai 曬 *v.i. sport*
sai 嘥 *v.t. squander*
sai 嘥 *v.t. waste*
sai choon jorng 細村莊 *n. hamlet*
sai geh 嘥嘅 *a. profligate*
sai hak 曬黑 *v.i. tan*
sai hay geh 嘥氣嘅 *adv. vainly*
sai lik gey 晒力嘅 *a. onerous*
sai meng 曬命 *v.i boast*
sai meng 曬命 *n boast*
sai see geh 世事嘅 *a. worldly*
sai tai yeurng 曬太陽 *v.i. bask*
sai tai yeurng 曬太陽 *v.t. sun*
sai yu 細雨 *n drizzle*

sak 塞 *v.t. jam*
sak 塞 *v.t. silt*
sam 衫 *n. attire*
sam 衫 *n. clothes*
sam 衫 *n clothing*
sam 深 *a. deep*
sam 衫 *n. garment*
sam 心 *n. heart*
sam 三 *n. three*
sam 三 *a three*
sam cha 審查 *n. censorship*
sam cha gwun 審查官 *n. censor*
sam chu 深處 *n abyss*
sam dow 深度 *n depth*
sam dow 深度 *n. profundity*
sam fu kap 深呼吸 *n. gasp*
sam gao tung 心絞痛 *n angina*
sam gap 心急 *a eager*
sam geh 深嘅 *a. profound*
sam geurt ga 三腳架 *n. tripod*
sam gey 審計 *v.t. audit*
sam gey yoon 審計員 *n. auditor*
sam gok jow 三角洲 *n delta*
sam gok ying 三角形 *n. triangle*
sam gok ying 三角形 *a. triangular*
sam gor 三個 *a. triplicate*
sam gor bo fan 三個部份 *a. triple*
sam gor yam 三個人 *n. trio*
sam guk 深谷 *n. ravine*
sam gway 心悸 *n. palpitation*
sam hang 深坑 *n. pit*
sam ho 心口 *n chest*
sam hoot loy tiew 心血來潮 *n. whim*
sam hung sik 深紅色 *n crimson*
sam jee leen 甚至連 *adv even*
sam jorng geh 心臟嘅 *adjs cardiacal*
sam jow 衫袖 *n sleeve*
sam lam 森林 *n forest*
sam lam geh 森林嘅 *a. sylvan*
sam lay hok 心理學 *n. psychology*
sam lay hok ga 心理學家 *n. psychologist*

sam lay jee liew 心裡治療 n. psychotherapy

sam ling 心靈 n. psyche

sam ling 心靈 n. soul

sam ling gam ying 心靈感應 n. telepathy

sam ling gam ying geh 心靈感應嘅 a. telepathic

sam ling gam ying jeh 心靈感應者 n. telepathist

sam ling geh 心靈嘅 a. psychological

sam ling geh 心靈嘅 a. spiritual

sam lun cher 三輪車 n. tricycle

sam man 審問 v.t. interrogate

sam man 審問 n. interrogation

sam man jee 三文治 n. sandwich

sam ngoy geh 深愛嘅 a beloved

sam ngoy geh yan 心愛嘅人 n beloved

sam ping hay wor 心平氣和 adj. amicable

sam pwuy 三倍 v.t., triple

sam pwuy 三倍 v.t. triplicate

sam san 審慎 n. prudence

sam san geh 審慎嘅 a. prudent

sam sap 三十 n. thirty

sam sap 三十 a thirty

sam see geh 深思嘅 a. meditative

sam see suk luy 深思熟慮 n deliberation

sam sik geh 三色嘅 a. tricolour

sam sik kay 三色旗 n tricolour

sam sun 審訊 n. inquest

sam sun 審訊 n. trial

sam ta 審查 n. audit

sam tai 心態 n. mentality

sam tee 三次 adv. thrice

sam ting 心情 n. mood

sam ting geh 深情嘅 a. affectionate

sam way yat tay 三位一體 n. trinity

sam yap 滲入 v.i. seep

sam ying 心形 adj. cordate

sam yoot 三月 n. March

san 身 n body

san 門 v. t close

san 神 n. deity

san 山 n. hill

san 腎 n. kidney

san 山 n. mount

san 山 n. mountain

san 新 a. new

san 門 v.t. shut

san 拴 n. tether

san 鋅 n. zinc

san bay geh 神祕嘅 a. mysterious

san bay geh 神祕嘅 a. mystic

san bay geh 神祕嘅 a. occult

san bay geh 神祕嘅 a. secretive

san bay ju yee 神主義意 n. mysticism

san bay ju yee jeh 神祕主義者 n mystic

san bo 散佈 v. t bestrew

san bo 散步 n ramble

san bo 散步 v.i. stroll

san bo 散步 n stroll

san bo 散步 n walk

san bor 散播 n bruit

san bow 散佈 v.i. straggle

san cheurng sow 神槍手 n. marksman

san chuy 刪除 v. t delete

san chuy 刪除 v. t erase

san deng 山頂 n. summit

san dung 山洞 n. cave

san fan 身分 n. identity

san fan jing ming 身分證明 n. indentification

san fat chut 散發出 v. t emit

san fat chut 散發出 v.t. radiate

san fu 辛苦 a. laborious

san fu 辛苦 a. laboured

san fu 神父 n. priest

san fu gam jow yeh 辛苦咁做嘢 *v.i. slave*

san fu geh 辛苦嘅 *a. painstaking*

san fu geh 辛苦嘅 *a. strenuous*

san fu jik way 神父職位 *n. priesthood*

san fu jow 辛苦做 *v.i. toil*

san fuk 臣服 *v.t. subject*

san ging 神經 *n. nerve*

san ging for yee sang 神經科醫生 *n. neurologist*

san ging hok 神經學 *n. neurology*

san gow 身高 *n. stature*

san guk 山谷 *n dale*

san guk 山谷 *n. vale*

san guk 山谷 *n. valley*

san hok 神學 *n divinity*

san hok ga 神學家 *n. theologian*

san hok geh 神學嘅 *a. theological*

san ja shu 山楂樹 *n. hawthorn*

san jeen 刪剪 *v. t. censor*

san jek 山脊 *n. ridge*

san jung 慎重 *adj. circumspect*

san kay geh 神氣嘅 *a. miraculous*

san koon jing jee 神權政治 *n. theocracy*

san lat 辛辣 *n. pungency*

san leurng 新娘 *n bride*

san lo 山路 *n. defile*

san long 新郎 *n. bridegroom*

san lorng 新郎 *n. groom*

san man 散漫 *n. laxity*

san man 新聞 *n. news*

san man 散文 *n. prose*

san man ga 散文家 *n essayist*

san man yeep 新聞業 *n. journalism*

san mo guy 山毛櫸 *n. beech*

san ngar 新芽 *n sprout*

san see 紳士 *n. gentleman*

san see seurng 新思想 *n. innovation*

san seen 新鮮 *a. fresh*

san sek hay see doy geh 新石器時代

嘅 *a. neolithic*

san sing 拴繩 *v.t. tether*

san sing bat hor tam fan 神聖不可侵犯 *a. sacrosanct*

san sing far 神聖化 *n. sanctification*

san sing far 神聖化 *v.t. sanctify*

san sing geh 神聖嘅 *a divine*

san sing geh 神聖嘅 *a. holy*

san sing geh 神聖嘅 *a. sacred*

san sing geh 神聖嘅 *n. sanctity*

san sow 新手 *n. novice*

san suk 伸縮 *v. t contract*

san tan doy jeh 新陳代謝 *n. metabolism*

san tay geh 身體嘅 *a bodily*

san tay geh 身體嘅 *a corporal*

san tay geh 身體嘅 *a. physical*

san ting 申請 *v.t. apply*

san ting biew 申請表 *n. application*

san ting joon lay 申請專利 *v.t. patent*

san ting yan 申請人 *n. applicant*

san ting yan 申請人 *n. candidate*

san wah 神話 *n. myth*

san wah 神話 *n. mythology*

san wah geh 神話嘅 *a. mythical*

san wah geh 神話嘅 *a. mythological*

san wing 新穎 *n. novelty*

san wing geh 新穎嘅 *a. novel*

san wu 珊瑚 *n coral*

san wuy 晨會 *n. assembly*

san yam seng 呻吟聲 *n groan*

san yan 新人 *n. recruit*

san yeurk geh 孱弱孱弱 *a. puny*

san yeurng 山羊 *n. goat*

san ying 身形 *n figure*

sang 生 *v.t. grow*

sang 省 *n. province*

sang chiew 生肖 *n zodiac*

sang choon 生存 *n. survival*

sang choon 生存 *v.i. survive*

sang choy 生菜 *n. cabbage*

sang geh 生嘅 a. live
sang geh 生嘅 a. living
sang geh 省嘅 a. provincial
sang geh 生嘅 a. raw
sang gey 生計 n. livelihood
sang gey 生計 n living
sang gwór 生果 n. fruit
sang jik geh 生殖嘅 a. reproductive
sang mat 生物 n being
sang mat 生物 n creature
sang mat 生物 n. organism
sang mat 生物 n. wight
sang mat hok 生物學 n biology
sang mat hok ga 生物學家 n biologist
sang ming 生命 n life
sang ngar 生牙 v.i. teethe
sang sow 生鏽 v.i rust
sang sow 生鏽 a. rusty
sang tan 生產 v.t. produce
sang tan lut 生產率 n. productivity
sang wut jun teep 生活津貼 n. stipend
sang yee 生意 n business
sang yee yan 生意人 n businessman
sang yuk lik 生育力 n fertility
sao bing 哨兵 n. sentinel
sao bing 哨兵 n. sentry
sao may yeem 稍微染 v.t. tint
sap 濕 a damp
sap 十 n., a ten
sap 濕 a. wet
sap 濕 v.t. wet
sap bat 十八 a eighteen
sap day 濕地 n. marsh
sap day geh 濕地嘅 a. marshy
sap dow 濕度 n. humidity
sap dow 濕度 n. wetness
sap gey suy 十幾歲 n. pl. teens
sap gow 十九 n. nineteen
sap jee ga 十字架 n cross
sap jee ga 十字架 n. rood

sap jee gan 濕紙巾 n. wipe
sap jun way 十進位 a decimal
sap leen 十年 n decade
sap leep 十年 n. decennary
sap luk 十六 n., a. sixteen
sap ng 十五 n fifteen
sap sai 濕晒 v.t drench
sap sai 濕晒 v.t. saturate
sap sai 濕晒 n. soak
sap sam 十三 n. thirteen
sap sam 十三 a thirteen
sap say horng see 十四行詩 n. sonnet
sap sey 十四 n. fourteen
sap tat 十七 n., a seventeen
sap yat 十一 n eleven
sap yat yoot 十一月 n. November
sap yee yoot 十二月 n december
sap yeet 十二 n. twelve
sap yik 十億 n billion
sap yoot 十月 n. October
sap yun geh 濕潤嘅 a. moist
sar ngar 沙啞 a. hoarse
sat 塞 v.t cram
sat 蚤 n. flea
sat 殺 v.t. kill
sat 殺 n. kill
sat 蝨 n. louse
sat 殺 v.t. sabre
sat 殺 v.t. slay
sat bai 失敗 adv abortive
sat bai 失敗 v.t bungle
sat bai 失敗 n defeat
sat bai 失敗 v.i fail
sat bai 失敗 n failure
sat chung jay 殺蟲劑 n. insecticide
sat chung jay 殺蟲劑 n. pesticide
sat chung jay 殺蟲劑 n repellent
sat fu mow juy 殺父母罪 n. parricide
sat hao 失效 v.t. vitiate

sat hing day jee mwuy juy 殺兄弟姊妹罪 *n. fratricide*

sat hing day jeh 殺兄弟者 *n cain*

sat hm 失誤 *n bungle*

sat huy gworng jak 失去光澤 *v.t. tarnish*

sat jay geh 實際嘅 *a. practical*

sat jay hang dung 實際行動 *n. practice*

sat jik 失職 *n. misconduct*

sat joy geh 實在嘅 *a. tangible*

sat jung 失蹤 *n disappearance*

sat kwan jay 殺菌劑 *n. germicide*

sat lay 失禮 *a discourteous*

sat loy 室內 *adv. indoors*

sat loy 室內 *n. interior*

sat loy geh 室內嘅 *a. indoor*

sat loy geh 室內嘅 *a. interior*

sat meen 失眠 *a. wakeful*

sat ming 失明 *n blindness*

sat morng 失望 *v. t. disappoint*

sat morng 失望 *v.i. lament*

sat mun 塞滿 2 *v.t. stuff*

sat see 實施 *n. imposition*

sat tay 實體 *n entity*

sat ter 剎車 *n brake*

sat ter 剎車 *v. t brake*

sat tiew 失調 *n disorder*

sat tiew 失調 *n. mal adjustment*

sat tow gor 膝頭哥 *n. knee*

sat yan hung sow 殺人兇手 *n. murderer*

sat yan juy 殺人罪 *n. homicide*

sat yeem 實驗 *n experiment*

sat yeem sat 實驗室 *n. laboratory*

sat yeen 實現 *v.t. materialize*

sat yik 失憶 *n amnesia*

sat ying juy 殺嬰罪 *n. infanticide*

sat yung geh 實用嘅 *a. pragmatic*

sat yung geh 實用嘅 *a. utilitarian*

sat yung ju yee 實用主義 *n. pragmatism*

sat yung sing 實用性 *n. practicability*

say 死 *a dead*

say 死 *v. i decease*

say 細 *a. little*

say 死 *v.i. perish*

say 篩 *n. sieve*

say 篩 *v.t. sieve*

say 篩 *v.t. sift*

say 細 *adv. smallness*

say 洗 *v.t. wash*

say 洗 *n wash*

say 西 *n. west*

say 使 *v.t. spend*

say ban geh 死板嘅 *a. rigid*

say ban ngar geh 西班牙嘅 *a. Spanish*

say ban ngar leep gow 西班牙獵狗 *n. spaniel*

say ban ngar yan 西班牙人 *n. Spaniard*

say ban ngar yan 西班牙人 *n. Spanish*

say bao 細胞 *n. cell*

say bao geh 細胞嘅 *adj cellular*

say bo lay gwun 細玻璃管 *n. cuvette*

say dam 細膽 *a. timid*

say dam 細膽 *a. timorous*

say day jeen 細地氈 *n. mat*

say day jeen 細地氈 *n. rug*

say doy 細袋 *n. pouch*

say fan yam fu 四分音符 *n. crotchet*

say fan yat 四份一 *n. quarter*

say for 死火 *v.t. stall*

say forng 西方 *n. occident*

say forng 西方 *a. western*

say forng geh 西方嘅 *a. occidental*

say forng geh 西方嘅 *a. west*

say forng geh 西方嘅 *a. westerly*

say forng ying 四方形 *n. square*

say forng ying geh 四方形嘅 *a square*

say forng yoon 四方院 *n. quadrangle*
say gan geh 世間嘅 *a. temporal*
say gao tong 細教堂 *n. chapel*
say geep 洗劫 *v.t. ransack*
say geh 細嘅 *a. small*
say gey 世紀 *n. century*
say gey ngang bwuy 死記硬背 *n. rote*
say gok ying 四角型 *a. & n. quadrilateral*
say gok ying geh 四角型嘅 *a. quadrangular*
say gwa 西瓜 *n. water-melon*
say hap 細盒 *n casket*
say ho geh 死後嘅 *a. posthumous*
say ho geh 死後嘅 *a. post-mortem*
say jeet 細節 *n detail*
say jeet 細節 *n. particular*
say jeurng 誓章 *n affidavit*
say jorng 西裝 *n. suit*
say juk dung mat 四足動物 *n. quadruped*
say ka mok 西卡莫 *n. sycamore*
say kan 西芹 *n. leek*
say lan far 西蘭花 *n. broccoli*
say lap 細粒 *a. tiny*
say lay 洗禮 *n. baptism*
say lay geh 勢利嘅 *v snobbish*
say lay gway 勢利鬼 *n. snob*
say leng jay 死仔 *n. thug*
say lo 細路 *n. bantling*
say lo jai 細路仔 *n child*
say low 死路 *n. impasse*
say low jay 細路仔 *n. infant*
say low jay 細佬仔 *a. infantile*
say low jay 細佬仔 *n. kid*
say low jay 細路仔 *n. youngster*
say low jay pay hay 細路仔脾氣 *n. petulance*
say lung 細窿 *n. puncture*
say luy gwun 細旅館 *n. inn*
say ma 細馬 *n. pony*

say mao 細貓 *n. kitten*
say may tar beet 細微差別 *n. nuance*
say morng 死亡 *n death*
say morng 死亡 *n decease*
say morng lut 死亡率 *n. mortality*
say ngan yik 洗眼液 *n eyewash*
say ngow 犀牛 *n. rhinoceros*
say pay 洗牌 *n. shuffle*
say pwuy geh 四倍嘅 *a. quadruple*
say sarm 洗衫 *n. laundry*
say say dam sik 細細啖食 *v.t. nibble*
say say dam yam 細細啖飲 *v.t. sip*
say say dam yam 細細啖飲 *v.i. sup*
say seng 細聲 *n coo*
say seng 細聲 *n. undertone*
say seng geh 細聲嘅 *a. quiet*
say seng gorng 細聲講 *n whisper*
say sing 細繩 *n cord*
say sow 世仇 *n. feud*
say sow gan 洗手間 *n. lavatory*
say sow pwun 洗手盤 *n sink*
say tan 細鏟 *n. trowel*
say torng 洗燙 *v.t. launder*
say tow 洗頭 *v.t. shampoo*
say tow suy 洗頭水 *n. shampoo*
say yee gey 洗衣機 *n. washer*
say yee hay 洗耳器 *n. aurilave*
say yee luy gung 洗衣女工 *n. laundress*
say yeen 誓言 *n. oath*
say yeurk jun 細藥樽 *n. phial*
say ying geh 死刑嘅 *a. capital*
see 事 *n. ado*
see 試 *v.t. delibate*
see 事 *n favour1*
see 事 *n. happening*
see 事 *n. incident*
see 事 *n. matter*
see 詩 *n. poem*
see 詩 *n. poesy*
see 試 *n. taste*

see 試 *v.t. taste*
see 試 *v.t. test*
see 試 *v.i. try*
see ba la 士巴拿 *n. spanner*
see ban 私奔 *v. i elope*
see bing 士兵 *n. soldier*
see bing 士兵 *n. troop*
see dai 絲帶 *n. ribbon*
see dor 士多 *n. store*
see dor beh lay 士多啤梨 *n. strawberry*
see doy 時代 *n epoch*
see doy 時代 *n era*
see fan 示範 *v. t demonstrate*
see fan 示範 *n. demonstration*
see fat 司法 *n. judicature*
see fat 司法 *a. judicial*
see fat koon 司法權 *n. jurisdiction*
see fay 施肥 *v.t. manure*
see fu juy 弒父罪 *n. patricide*
see gan 時間 *n. time*
see gao 市郊 *n.pl. outskirts*
see geh 詩嘅 *a. poetic*
see gey 司機 *n. chauffeur*
see gey 司機 *n driver*
see gok geh 視覺嘅 *a. visual*
see gwan juy 弒君罪 *n. regicide*
see gworng 絲光 *v.t. mercerize*
see gwun 史官 *n. annalist*
see gwun 使館 *n embassy*
see gwun gwun yoon 使館館員 *n. attache*
see hao 思考 *n. mull*
see hao 思考 *n. rumination*
see har 試下 *v.t. sample*
see hay 士氣 *n. morale*
see ho 嗜好 *n. hobby*
see hok 詩學 *n. poetics*
see hoy 撕開 *v.t. tear*
see jan 市鎮 *n. town*
see jap 詩集 *n. poetry*
see jee 獅子 *n lion*

see jee geh 獅子嘅 *a leonine*
see jee jor 獅子座 *n. Leo*
see jeet 詩節 *n. verse*
see jeurng 市長 *n. mayor*
see jing geh 市政嘅 *a. municipal*
see jorng 時裝 *n fashion*
see kay 時期 *n. period*
see lan 撕爛 *v.t. rip*
see lan 撕爛 *v.t tatter*
see leep 獅鬣 *n. mane*
see leet 撕裂 *n. avulsion*
see lik 視力 *n. sight*
see lik 視力 *n. vision*
see ling 司令 *n. admiral*
see ling 司令 *n commandant*
see low 司爐 *n. stoker*
see lut 詩律 *n. versification*
see man 市民 *n citizen*
see mat 絲襪 *n. stocking*
see ming gam 使命感 *n. calling*
see ming gam 使命感 *n. vocation*
see mo chu 事務處 *n. bureau*
see morng mok 視網膜 *n. retina*
see mow geh 弒母嘅 *a. matricidal*
see mow juy 弒母罪 *n. matricide*
see ngar geh 嘶啞嘅 *a. throaty*
see ngat 施壓 *v.t. pressurize*
see sang geh 私生嘅 *a. illegitimate*
see sang jee 私生子 *n. bastard*
see sat 事實 *n fact*
see see seng 嘶嘶聲 *n hiss*
see see seng 嘶嘶聲 *n. sizzle*
see seen 事先 *adv. beforehand*
see seurng ga 思想家 *n. thinker*
see sseurng 時尚 *n cult*
see tai 時態 *n. tense*
see tat 視察 *v.t. inspect*
see tay 屍體 *n corpse*
see teen geh 史前嘅 *a. prehistoric*
see ting 私情 *n amour*
see tow 絲綢 *n. silk*
see tun 私吞 *v.t. misappropriate*

see way 視爲 *v.t. regard*
see yan 時人 *n. bard*
see yan 詩人 *n. poet*
see yan 私隱 *n. privacy*
see yan geh 私人嘅 *a. personal*
see yan geh 私人嘅 *a. private*
see yee yoon 市議員 *n. councillor*
see ying 侍應 *n. waiter*
see ying chu say 私刑處死 *v.t. lynch*
see yung 絲絨 *n. velvet*
see yung geh 絲絨嘅 *a. velvety*
see yung kay 試用期 *n. probation*
seem 閃 *v. i. dash*
seem 閃 *v.t flash*
seem 閃 *n flicker*
seem 閃 *v.i. glitter*
seem 閃 *n. scintillation*
seem 閃 *v.i. sparkle*
seem 閃 *n. sparkle*
seem 閃 *v.i. twinkle*
seem deen 閃電 *n. lightening*
seem geh 閃嘅 *a. shiny*
seem gwong 閃光 *n flash*
seem ha 閃閃下 *v.t flicker*
seem lap 閃粒 *n glitter*
seem leurng 閃亮 *n. twinkle*
seem yam 閃人 *v.i flee*
seen 仙 *n cent*
seen 腺 *n. gland*
seen 線 *n. line*
seen 癬 *n. ringworm*
seen 跣 *v.i. skid*
seen 跣 *n. slip*
seen 跣 *a. slippery*
seen 線 *n. thread*
seen been 善變 *a. capricious*
seen cheurng 擅長 *n. adept*
seen deet 跣跌 *v.i. slip*
seen dow hm seen ha 仙都唔仙下 *a. penniless*
seen dung 煽動 *v.t. instigate*
seen dung 煽動 *n. instigation*

seen dung bwun loon geh tee 煽動叛亂嘅詞 *n. sedition*
seen dung sing geh 煽動性嘅 *a. seditious*
seen fat jay yan 先發制人 *v.t forestall*
seen geen jee ming 先見之明 *n foresight*
seen hung sik 鮮紅色 *n. vermillion*
seen hung sik geh 鮮紅色嘅 *a. vermillion*
seen jee tam yap 擅自侵入 *v.i. trespass*
seen kow 線毯 *n. clew*
seen kuy 先驅 *n. precursor*
seen lay 先例 *n. precedent*
seen leurng 善良 *adj benign*
seen leurng 善良 *a kind*
seen leurng gam 善良咁 *adv benignly*
seen leurng gam 善良咁 *adv. kindly*
seen ling 先令 *n. shilling*
seen lo 線路 *n. circuit*
seen low 線路 *n. wiring*
seen luy 仙女 *n. nymph*
seen mo 羨慕 *v envy*
seen sam 善心 *n benevolence*
seen sang 先生 *n. Messrs*
seen sang 先生 *n. mister*
seen sang 先生 *n. sir*
seen yan jeurng 仙人掌 *n. cactus*
seen yee 善意 *n. goodwill*
seen yeurng fey 贍養費 *n. alimony*
seen yu 先於 *v. precede*
seep kap 涉及 *v. t concern*
seep see 攝氏 *a. centigrade*
seep way 楔位 *v.t. wedge*
seep ying 攝影 *n. photography*
seep ying geh 攝影嘅 *a. photographic*
seep ying see 攝影師 *n. photographer*
seet 楔 *n. wedge*
seet juk 褻瀆 *n. sacrilege*
seet juk 褻瀆 *a. sacrilegious*

seet juk san ling 褻瀆神靈 v.t. profane

seet juk san ling geh 褻瀆神靈嘅 a. profane

seh 蛇 n. serpent

seh 蛇 n. snake

seh 瀉 n spill

seh day 寫低 v.t. jot

seh day 寫低 v.t. note

seh gan gai 寫簡介 v.t. profile

seh gao 社交 n. sociability

seh gik 射擊 n. shot

seh jee low 寫字樓 n. office

seh meen 赦免 v.t. assoil

seh wuy 社會 n. community

seh wuy 社會 n. society

seh wuy day way 社會地位 n caste

seh wuy geh 社會嘅 n. social

seh wuy hok 社會學 n. sociology

seh wuy ju yee 社會主義 n socialism

seh wuy ju yee jeh 社會主義者 n,a socialist

seh ying 射影 v.t shadow

sek 錫 n. kiss

sek 錫 v.t. kiss

sek 錫 n. peck

sek fwuy 石灰 n. lime

sek fwuy suy 石灰水 n. whitewash

sek gwun 石棺 n cist

sek jeurng 石匠 n. mason

sek jeurng 石像 n. statue

sek lap 石蠟 n. paraffin

sek meen 石棉 n. asbestos

sek tow 石頭 n. rock

sek tow 石頭 n. stone

sek yow 石油 n. petroleum

seng 醒 v.t. awake

seng 醒 a awake

seng 聲 n. noise

seng 聲 n sound

seng 聲 n. voice

seng 醒 v.t. wake

seng geh 聲嘅 a. vocal

ser 寫 v.t. write

ser heurng 麝香 n. musk

ser juy 寫序 v.t. preface

ser meen 赦免 v.t. pardon

ser wuy wan ging 社會環境 n matrix

ser yeurk 瀉藥 a laxative

ser yeurk 瀉藥 n. purgative

seurk yeurk 削弱 v.t. & i weaken

seurng 雙 pref bi

seurng 上 v. t. board

seurng 箱 n box

seurng 箱 n. case

seurng 箱 n. casing

seurng 雙 a dual

seurng 鑲 v.t. frame

seurng 霜 n. frost

seurng 傷 n. injury

seurng 相 n photo

seurng 相 n photograph

seurng 相 n snap

seurng 上 prep upon

seurng 傷 n. wound

seurng ak 上軛 v.t. yoke

seurng ban 鑲板 n. panel

seurng ban 鑲板 v.t. panel

seurng bao toy jee yat 雙胞胎之一 n. twin

seurng bay 相比 a comparative

seurng bay 傷悲 n. melancholy

seurng been 鑲邊 v.t border

seurng beet 想必 adv. surely

seurng chun tang 常春藤 n ivy

seurng dang yan 上等人 n. gentry

seurng dang yu 相等於 v. t equate

seurng dang yu 相等於 a equivalent

seurng day 上帝 n. god

seurng day 上帝 n. godhead

seurng day 上帝 n. providence

seurng dong dai geh 相當大嘅 a considerable

seurng dow 想鬥 a bellicose

seurng fan 相反 *a contrary*
seurng fan 相反 *n reverse*
seurng fan geh 相反嘅 *a. reverse*
seurng fat 想法 *n. idea*
seurng forng 雙方 *a both*
seurng ga 上架 *v.t. shelve*
seurng gam 傷感 *a. wistful*
seurng gao 上校 *n. colonel*
seurng geen 常見 *a. common*
seurng geh 上嘅 *a. upper*
seurng gey 相機 *n. camera*
seurng gok 雙角嘅 *adj. biangular*
seurng gwan 相關 *n. correlation*
seurng gwan yu 雙關語 *n. pun*
seurng har man 上下文 *n context*
seurng hm 上午 *n forenoon*
seurng ho 傷口 *n cut*
seurng hon 傷寒 *n. typhoid*
seurng hoy 傷害 *v.t harm*
seurng hoy 傷害 *v.t. injure*
seurng hoy 傷害 *v.t. wound*
seurng jee 想知 *v.i. wonder*
seurng jeurng 想像 *v. t conceive*
seurng jeurng 想像 *v.t. picture*
seurng jeurng 想像 *v.t. visualize*
seurng jeurng ha 想像下 *v.t. imagine*
seurng jeurng lik 想像力 *n. imagination*
seurng jor 上咗 *adv aboard*
seurng jow 上昼 *n. morning*
seurng kap 上級 *n. senior*
seurng kuk geh 雙軸嘅 *adj biaxial*
seurng leen 相連 *v.t. interlock*
seurng leen 相連 *a twin*
seurng leen 上鏈 *v.t. wind*
seurng leen beng 上鏈柄 *n. winder*
seurng lor see 上螺絲 *v.t. screw*
seurng luk geh 常綠嘅 *a evergreen*
seurng luk shu 常綠樹 *n evergreen*
seurng ma 上馬 *n mount*
seurng meen 上面 *prep. above*
seurng meen 上面 *prep. over*

seurng meen 上面 *n. top*
seurng meen 上面 *adv. upwards*
seurng mong 傷亡 *n bloodshed*
seurng ngon 上岸 *adv. ashore*
seurng pwuy geh 雙倍嘅 *a double*
seurng sam 傷心 *v.t. grieve*
seurng sam 傷心 *a. sad*
seurng san 上身 *n bodice*
seurng see 嘗試 *v.t. attempt*
seurng see 嘗試 *n. attempt*
seurng see 嘗試 *n endeavour*
seurng see 嘗試 *n try*
seurng sing loon 雙性戀 *adj. bisexual*
seurng so 上訴 *n. appeal*
seurng so yan 上訴人 *n. appellant*
seurng sow 商數 *n. quotient*
seurng tee 相似 *a. analogous*
seurng tee 相似 *n. likeness*
seurng tee dow 相似度 *n. parallelism*
seurng tee dow 相似度 *n. similarity*
seurng tee dow 相似度 *n. similitude*
seurng ting tat 上清漆 *v.t. varnish*
seurng tow 商討 *v. i confer*
seurng tow wuy 商討會 *n consultation*
seurng tung 相同 *a. alike*
seurng tung geh 相同嘅 *a equal*
seurng way 上尉 *n. lieutenant*
seurng yan 上癮 *v.t. addict*
seurng yan 商人 *n. merchant*
seurng yan 商人 *n. monger*
seurng yan 商人 *n. trader*
seurng yan 商人 *n. tradesman*
seurng yan jeh 上癮者 *n. addict*
seurng yeen 上演 *v.t. stage*
seurng yeep geh 商業嘅 *a commercial*
seurng yeep geh 商業嘅 *a. mercantile*
seurng yiew 想要 *v.t. want*
seurng yiew 想要 *n want*

seurng yow 上油 *v.t.* *lubricate*
seurng yow 上油 *v.t* *oil*
seurng yu 雙語 *a* *bilingual*
seurng yu 相遇 *v. t* *encounter*
sey 死 *v. i* *die*
sey 四 *n.* *four*
sey gai 世界 *n.* *world*
sey kwun 細菌 *n.* *bacteria*
sey sap 四十 *n.* *forty*
she 寫 *v.t.* *pen*
she 射 *v.t.* *shoot*
shoon 酸 *n* *acid*
shoon 船 *n* *boat*
shoon 選 *v. t* *elect*
shoon 船 *n.* *ship*
shoon 酸 *a.* *sour*
shoon bo 宣佈 *v.t.* *announce*
shoon bo 宣佈 *n.* *announcement*
shoon bo 宣佈 *v. t.* *declare*
shoon bo 宣佈 *v.t.* *proclaim*
shoon bo 宣佈 *n.* *herald*
shoon bo forng hay 宣佈放棄 *v.t.* *renounce*
shoon bo forng hay 宣佈放棄 *n.* *renunciation*
shoon choon 宣傳 *v. t.* *endorse*
shoon choon 宣傳 *v.t.* *popularize*
shoon choon 宣傳 *v.t.* *promote*
shoon choon 宣傳 *n.* *promotion*
shoon choon 宣傳 *n.* *propaganda*
shoon choon 宣傳 *n.* *propagation*
shoon choon 宣傳 *v.t.* *publicize*
shoon choon jeh 宣傳者 *n.* *propagandist*
shoon chor 算錯 *v.t.* *miscalculate*
shoon chorng 船艙 *n.* *cabin*
shoon fan 船帆 *n.* *sail*
shoon fung 旋風 *n.* *cyclone*
shoon fung 旋風 *n.* *whirlwind*
shoon geh 船嘅 *a.* *nautic(al)*
shoon guy 選舉 *n.* *vote*
shoon ho 損耗 *n.* *wastage*

shoon hoy 損害 *n* *blight*
shoon hoy 損害 *n.* *harm*
shoon hoy 損害 *v.t.* *jeopardize*
shoon jak 選擇 *n.* *choice*
shoon jak 選擇 *n.* *option*
shoon jak 選擇 *n.* *pick*
shoon jak 選擇 *n.* *selection*
shoon jap 選集 *n.* *anthology*
shoon jeurng 船槳 *n.* *oar*
shoon jeurng 船槳 *n* *paddle*
shoon jeurng 船長 *n.* *skipper*
shoon jik 船跡 *n* *wake*
shoon joon 旋轉 *v.t.* *pivot*
shoon joon 旋轉 *n* *whirl*
shoon joon muk ma 旋轉木馬 *n.* *whirligig*
shoon kuy 選區 *n* *constituency*
shoon kuy 選舉 *n* *election*
shoon lay tap 宣禮塔 *n.* *minaret*
shoon man 選民 *n.* *constituent*
shoon may 酸味 *a* *acid*
shoon may bay choy 選美比賽 *n.* *pageant*
shoon ngoy 船外 *adv.* *overboard*
shoon piew 選票 *n* *ballot*
shoon pwun yow juy 宣判有罪 *v. t.* *convict*
shoon sat 損失 *v.t.* *cost*
shoon sat 損失 *n.* *loss*
shoon shoon 宣傳 *n.* *publicity*
shoon sing 酸性 *n.* *acidity*
shoon sut 算術 *n.* *arithmetic*
shoon sut geh 算術嘅 *a.* *arithmetical*
shoon ting 宣稱 *n* *claim*
shoon wai 損壞 *n.* *damage*
shoon wai 損壞 *n.* *ravage*
shoon wor 旋渦 *n.* *whirlpool*
shoon yeen 宣言 *n.* *manifesto*
shoon yeurng 宣揚 *v.i.* *preach*
shoon yeurng 宣揚 *v.i.* *trumpet*
shoon yoon 船員 *n.* *sailor*

shoon yung 蒜蓉 *n. garlic*
shoot 雪 *n. snow*
shoot gao 說教 *v.i. sermonize*
shoot gway 雪櫃 *n. fridge*
shoot gway 雪櫃 *n. refrigerator*
shoot ka 雪茄 *n. cigar*
shoot ka yeen 雪茄煙 *n cheroot*
shoot lay 雪泥 *n. slush*
shoot ming shu 說明書 *n manual*
shoot wah mo wu 說話模糊 *a equivocal*
shu 書 *n book*
shu 輸 *v.t. lose*
shu 樹 *n. tree*
shu bao 書包 *n. satchel*
shu chung 書蟲 *n book-worm*
shu chung 雪松 *n. cedar*
shu chung 樹叢 *n. thicket*
shu dun 樹墩 *n. stump*
shu fat 書法 *n calligraphy*
shu forng 書房 *n. study*
shu fuk 舒服 *n. comfort1*
shu fuk 舒服 *a comfortable*
shu fuk 舒服 *n. snug*
shu gey ju gao 樞機主教 *n. cardinal*
shu goon 書卷 *n. scroll*
shu jay 薯仔 *n. potato*
shu jay lay 薯仔泥 *n. mash*
shu jee 樹枝 *n branch*
shu jee 樹枝 *n. twig*
shu jing gwun teet chuy sow sut 輸精管切除手術 *n. vasectomy*
shu kam 豎琴 *n. harp*
shu kwang 豎框 *n. mullion*
shu lam 樹林 *n. woods*
shu lam 樹林 *n. woodland*
shu lan 樹懶 *n. sloth*
shu lay 樹籬 *n. hedge*
shu meen ming ling 書面命令 *n. writ*
shu muk peen ju jeh 書目編著者 *n bibliographer*

shu pay 樹皮 *n. bark*
shu seurng 書商 *n book-seller*
shu sik 舒適 *a. cosy*
shu sik 舒適 *a. cozy*
shu teem 書籤 *n. book-mark*
shu ting geh 抒情嘅 *a. lyric*
shu ting geh 抒情嘅 *a. lyrical*
shu toy 書枱 *n desk*
shu wun 舒緩 *v. t ease*
shu yap 輸入 *v.t key*
shuy suy gwun 輸水管 *n aqueduct*
si see 史詩 *n epic*
siem chuy 蟾蜍 *n. toad*
siew 燒 *v. t burn*
siew 燒 *n burn*
siew 笑 *v. i chuckle*
siew 燒 *v.i flare*
siew 笑 *n. laugh*
siew 笑 *v.i laugh*
siew 笑 *v.i. mock*
siew 笑 *v.i. smile*
siew 笑 *n. smile*
siew beng 小病 *n. ailment*
siew beng 笑柄 *n. mockery*
siew bo fai pao 小步快跑 *n trot*
siew bo fan 小部份 *n. fraction*
siew buk bo 小瀑布 *n. cascade*
siew bwuy 燒杯 *n beaker*
siew cho 小丑 *n buffoon*
siew cho 小丑 *n clown*
siew chuy 消除 *v. t efface*
siew chuy 消除 *n. removal*
siew duk 消毒 *n. sterilization*
siew duk 消毒 *v.t. sterilize*
siew duy 小隊 *n. squad*
siew fan 小販 *n hawker*
siew fan 小販 *n. vendor*
siew far 消化 *v. t. digest*
siew far 消化 *n digestion*
siew far bat leurng 消化不良 *n. indigestion*
siew fay 消費 *n consumption*

siew fay 消費 n expenditure
siew fay suy 消費稅 n excise
siew gam ling 宵禁令 n curfew
siew gan 燒緊 adv. aflame
siew gan 燒緊 v.i. alight
siew gwor duk geh 消過毒嘅 a. antiseptic
siew gwun 小罐 n. canister
siew hay geh 小器嘅 a. stingy
siew heen 消遣 n. pastime
siew heen wut dung 消遣活動 n. recreation
siew ho 消耗 v. t consume
siew ho leurng 消耗量 n consumption
siew hok sang 小學生 n. junior
siew hok sang geh 小學生嘅 a. junior
siew hong 小巷 n. alley
siew jeh 小姐 n. miss
siew kay 小溪 n. beck
siew kay 小溪 n. brook
siew kay 小溪 n. creek
siew kay 小溪 n. stream
siew kay 小溪 n. streamlet
siew leen 少年 n. youth
siew leep hoon 小獵犬 n. terrier
siew leurng 少量 n lick
siew leurng 少量 n. little
siew leurng 少量 n. morsel
siew leurng 少量 n. paucity
siew leurng geh 少量嘅 n. modicum
siew leurng geh jow 少量嘅酒 n dram
siew low 小路 n. lane
siew low 小路 n. path
siew lung 燒燶 v.t. scorch
siew lung 燒燶 v.t. singe
siew luy 少女 n. damsel
siew luy 少女 n. wench
siew mak 小麥 n far
siew mak 小麥 n. wheat
siew meet 消滅 v.t. obliterate

siew meet 消滅 n. obliteration
siew mor see gan 消磨時間 v.t. while
siew ping 燒瓶 n flask
siew sam 小心 a careful
siew sat 消失 v. i disappear
siew sat 消失 v.i. vanish
siew say 消逝 v. t elapse
siew seen luy 小仙女 n fairy
siew seng 笑聲 n. laughter
siew seurng 燒傷 n singe
siew shoot 小說 n fiction
siew shoot 小說 n novel
siew shoot ga 小說家 n. novelist
siew siew 少少 adv. little
siew siew 少少 a. scant
siew siew 少少 a. sightly
siew siew 少少 n. tinge
siew siew juy 少少醉 a. tipsy
siew siew may 少少味 n. whiff
siew sik 消息 n. pl. tidings
siew sow 少數 n. handful
siew sow 少數 n less
siew sow 少數 n. minority
siew tak jee 小冊子 n booklet
siew tak yeem 小測驗 n. quiz
siew tan 小產 n. miscarriage
siew tan 小產 v.i. miscarry
siew tay kam 小提琴 n. violin
siew tay kam ga 小提琴家 n. violinist
siew tiew 小潮 a. neap
siew tuy 小腿 n. calf
siew tuy 小腿 n. shin
siew uk 小屋 n. cote
siew uk 小屋 n cottage
siew uk 小屋 n. lodge
siew wah 笑話 n. gag
siew wah 笑話 n. jest
siew wah 笑話 n. joke
siew wan 小環 n annulet
siew way yan jee geh 少為人知嘅 a. obscure

siew yam hay 消音器 *n. silencer*
siew yeh 宵夜 *n. supper*
siew yiew fat ngoy 逍遙法外 *adv. scot-free*
siew ying geh 小型嘅 *a. miniature*
siew yow 小丘 *n. hillock*
siew yu 少於 *prep below*
siew yu 少於 *adv under*
sik 骰 *n. dice*
sik 食 *v. t eat*
sik cho 食草 *v.i. graze*
sik dak 食得 *v.t. stomach*
sik dong 適當 *a. appropriate*
sik dong geh 適當嘅 *a. apt*
sik dong sing 適當性 *n advisability*
sik dor jung yu yeen geh yan 識多種 語言嘅人 *n. polyglot1*
sik dorng geh 適當嘅 *adv duly*
sik fan 食飯 *v. t. dine*
sik fan geh 適婚嘅 *a. marriageable*
sik forng 釋放 *v. t discharge*
sik fu yuk geh dung mat 食腐肉嘅動 物 *n. scavenger*
sik geh yan 識嘅人 *n. acquaintance*
sik hap 適合 *a. adequate*
sik hap 適合 *a. applicable*
sik hap 適合 *adj apposite*
sik hap 適合 *a congenial*
sik hap 適合 *a. suitable*
sik hap gang jung geh 適合耕種嘅 *adj arable*
sik hap geh 適合嘅 *a. opportune*
sik hap ju geh 適合住嘅 *a. habitable*
sik hap ju geh 適合住嘅 *a. inhabitable*
sik hap sing 適合性 *n. suitability*
sik jee 食指 *n forefinger*
sik leurng geh 適量嘅 *a. moderate*
sik lorng 色狼 *v.t. pervert*
sik mat 飾物 *n accessory*
sik mat 食物 *n food*
sik mat 事務 *n. sustenance*

sik mat sat 食物室 *n. pantry*
sik mow forng geh yan 識模仿嘅人 *n mimic*
sik muk geh 蝕木嘅 *a. xylophagous*
sik ngan 食晏 *v.i. lunch*
sik po 食譜 *n. recipe*
sik tong 食堂 *n. canteen*
sik yan juk 食人族 *n. androphagi*
sik yat geh 昔日嘅 *a former*
sik yee 適宜 *a. advisable*
sik yeen 食煙 *v.i. smoke*
sik yik 蜥蜴 *n. lizard*
sik ying 適應 *v.t acclimatise*
sik ying 適應 *v.t. adapt*
sik ying 適應 *v.t. orient*
sik ying lik keurng 適應力強 *adj. hardy*
sik yung 食用 *n. eatable*
sing 升 *v.t. ascend*
sing 乘 *v.t. multiply*
sing 升 *v. rise*
sing 繩 *n. rope*
sing 繩 *n. string*
sing 姓 *n. surname*
sing ban seurng 承辦商 *n contractor*
sing bay lay geh 成比例嘅 *a. proportional*
sing bay lay geh 成比例嘅 *a. proportionate*
sing beet 性別 *n. gender*
sing bo 城堡 *n. castle*
sing bo 城堡 *n. fortress*
sing cheurng 城牆 *n. rampart*
sing chuy heurng 性取向 *n. sexuality*
sing dam 承擔 *v.t. shoulder*
sing dan jeet 聖誕節 *n Christmas*
sing dan jeet 聖誕節 *n. Xmas*
sing day 聖地 *n. shrine*
sing fa 聖化 *v.t. consecrate*
sing for 星火 *n. spark*
sing forng 盛況 *n. pageantry*
sing fung 聖俸 *n benefice*

sing gak 性格 n. *personality*
sing gam 性感 n. *sexy*
sing gam geh 性感嘅 a. *nubile*
sing gam geh 性感嘅 a *seductive*
sing geet geh 聖潔嘅 a. *saintly*
sing geh 性嘅 a. *sexual*
sing geh 星嘅 a. *stellar*
sing ging 聖經 n *bible*
sing ging 聖經 n. *scripture*
sing gor 聖歌 n. *hymn*
sing gung 成功 v.i. *succeed*
sing gung 成功 a *successful*
sing gwor 勝過 v.t. *outdo*
sing gwor 勝過 v.t. *outshine*
sing hak 乘客 n. *passenger*
sing han 誠懇 n. *candour*
sing hang way 性行為 n. *sex*
sing hay 星系 n. *galaxy*
sing ho 星號 n. *asterisk*
sing ho 成口 n. *mouthful*
sing jeurng 成長 n. *development*
sing jeurng 成長 n. *germination*
sing jow 成就 n. *accomplishment*
sing jow 成就 n. *achievement*
sing jow 成就 n. *attainment*
sing jow 成就 n. *success*
sing jow 成就 n. *triumph*
sing jow gam 成就感 n. *fulfilment*
sing kay luk 星期六 n. *Saturday*
sing kay ng 星期五 n. *Friday*
sing kay sam 星期三 n. *Wednesday*
sing kay say 星期四 n. *Thursday*
sing kay yat 星期一 n. *Monday*
sing kay yat 星期日 n. *Sunday*
sing kow 星球 n. *planet*
sing kwan 星群 n. *constellation*
sing kwun 星群 n. *asterism*
sing lap 成立 v. t. *establish*
sing lap 成立 n *establishment*
sing lay 聖禮 n. *sacrament*
sing lay 勝利 n. *victory*
sing lay geh 勝利嘅 a. *victorious*

sing lay jeh 勝利者 n. *victor*
sing leen 盛年 n. *prime*
sing leen yan 成年人 n. *adult*
sing lok 承諾 v.t. *pledge*
sing lok 承諾 n *promise*
sing lok 承諾 n. *vow*
sing ming 聲明 v.t. *avow*
sing ming 聲明 n *declaration*
sing ming 聲名 n. *proclamation*
sing ming lorng jik 聲名狼藉 a. *infamous*
sing ming lorng jik geh 聲名狼藉嘅 a. *notorious*
sing mo lang geh 性無能嘅 a. *impotent*
sing ngon yan 承按人 n. *mortagagee*
sing ngoy geh 性愛嘅 a *erotic*
sing sat 誠實 a. *honest*
sing sat 誠實 n. *honesty*
sing sat 誠實 a. *truthful*
sing sat 誠實 n. *veracity*
sing sat geh 誠實嘅 adv *bonafide*
sing see 城市 n *city*
sing see geh 城市嘅 a *civic*
sing see geh 城市嘅 a. *urban*
sing sing 猩猩 n. *gorilla*
sing sing 星星 n. *star*
sing sow 承受 v.t *bear*
sing sow 乘數 n. *multiplication*
sing sow yiew 性騷擾 v.t. *molest*
sing sow yiew 性騷擾 n. *molestation*
sing suk 成熟 a *adult*
sing suk 成熟 v.i *mature*
sing suk 成熟 n. *maturity*
sing suk 成熟 v.i. *ripen*
sing suk geh 成熟嘅 a. *mature*
sing ting 聲稱 v.t. *allege*
sing ting 聲稱 v. t *claim*
sing ting 聲稱 v. i *contend*
sing ting 聲稱 v.t. *profess*
sing tow 繩套 n. *noose*
sing wah 昇華 v.t. *sublimate*

sing wan 星雲 n. nebula
sing way gu yee 成爲孤兒 v.t orphan
sing wun 聲援 v. t. champion
sing yam geh 聲音嘅 a. sonic
sing yan 承認 v.t. admit
sing yan 承認 v. t. confess
sing yan 聖人 n. saint
sing yat 成日 adv always
sing yat ai sap 成日嗌謔 a. quarrelsome
sing yat chor geh 成日坐嘅 a. sedentary
sing yat huy geh day forng 成日去嘅地方 n haunt
sing yat joon tai 成日轉軚 v.i. vacillate
sing yat yow 成日有 a. stock
sing ying 承認 v. acknowledge
sing ying 承認 n. acknowledgement
sing ying 承認 v.t. concede
sing yu 成語 n. idiom
sing yu 成語 n. phrase
sing yuk 性慾 a. amorous
siu hang sing 小行星 adj. asteroid
so 掃 n brush
so 數 v. t. count
so 瘦 a. thin
so bar 掃把 n broom
so fay 收費 v. t. charge
so fu 受苦 v.t. suffer
so jang 手踭 n elbow
so jap 收集 v. t collect
so jap ga 收集家 n collector
so jee 手指 n finger
so long 嗉囊 n. craw
so loon 騷亂 n commotion
so top 修葺 v. t edit
so way 數位 n digit
so yiew 騷擾 v. t disturb
sok jow 塑造 v.t. mould
sok jow 塑造 v.t shape
sok yan 索引 n. index

song fai 爽快 n. alacrity
song lay 喪禮 n. funeral
song ow 喪偶 v.t. widow
song sat 喪失 v. t. bereave
song sat tan yow 喪失親友 n bereavement
sor 梳 n comb
sor 鎖 v.t handcuff
sor 鎖 n. lock
sor 鎖 v.t lock
sor 梭 n. shuttle
sor bai 唆擺 v.t. abet
sor bai 唆擺 n. abetment
sor choy 蔬菜 n. vegetable
sor fa 梳化 n. couch
sor fa 梳化 n. sofa
sor fat 疏忽 n. negligence
sor fat 疏忽 n. oversight
sor fat geh 疏忽嘅 a. negligent
sor geh 傻嘅 a. silly
sor gwa 傻瓜 n. simpleton
sor low 傻佬 n. pantaloon
sor mun 鎖門 v. t bolt
sor san 疏散 v. t evacuate
sor san 疏散 n evacuation
sor see 鎖匙 n. key
sor suy 瑣碎 a. trivial
sor suy geh 瑣碎嘅 a. petty
sor yee 所以 adv. so
sor yee 所以 conj. so
sor yi 所以 adv. therefore
sor yi 所以 adv. thus
sor yoon 疏遠 v.t. alienate
sor yow 所有 pron all
sormo 梳毛 v.t groom
sorng sat 喪失 n forfeiture
sorng sat ming yu 喪失名譽 n disrepute
sorng shu 桑樹 n. mulberry
sow 收 n. admission
sow 手 n hand
sow 收 v.t. receive

sow 掃 v.i. sweep
sow 掃 n. sweep
sow 鬚 n. whisker
sow ak 數額 n amount
sow ak 手鈪 n. bangle
sow ak ngoy fay 收額外費 v.t. surcharge
sow an yoon 收銀員 n. cashier
sow ban 手板 n. palm
sow bay 手臂 n. arm
sow beng 手柄 n. handle
sow biew 手錶 n. watch
sow bo jeurng 修補匠 n. tinker
sow cheurng 手槍 n. pistol
sow doon 手段 n. artifice
sow dor teen 收多錢 v.t. overcharge
sow dor teen 收多錢 n overcharge
sow dow 首都 n. capital
sow dow 首都 n. metropolis
sow dow sang wut 修道生活 n monasticism
sow dung 騷動 n. pandemonium
sow dung 騷動 n. turmoil
sow dung 騷動 n unrest
sow dung 騷動 n. uproar
sow fay biew 收費表 n. tariff
sow for yoon 售貨員 n. salesman
sow fwun yan 收款人 n. payee
sow fwun ying 受歡迎 v.t endear
sow fwun ying dow 收歡迎度 n. popularity
sow fwun ying geh 受歡迎嘅 a. popular
sow gak lan geh 蘇格蘭嘅 a. scotch
sow gak lan way see gey 蘇格蘭威士忌 n. scotch
sow gak lan yan 蘇格蘭人 n. Scot
sow gan 手巾 n. handkerchief
sow gap 豆莢 n. pod
sow geen yan 收件人 n. addressee
sow geen yan 收件人 n. recipient
sow go 手稿 n. manuscript

sow got gey 收割機 n. havester
sow got gey 收割機 n. reaper
sow goy 修改 n alteration
sow goy 修改 v.t. amend
sow goy 修改 n. amendment
sow goy 修改 n.pl. amends
sow gung 手工 n. handiwork
sow gung ngay 手工藝 n. handicraft
sow han 仇恨 n animosity
sow han 仇恨 n enmity
sow han 仇恨 n. hate
sow ho 收好 v.t. stow
sow hok 數學 n mathematics
sow hok ga 數學家 n. mathematician
sow hok geh 數學嘅 a. mathematical
sow hoy jeh 受害者 n. victim
sow jap 收集 v.t. gather
sow jap 收集 v.t marshal
sow jee 數字 a. numeral
sow jee geh 數字嘅 a. numerical
sow jee gung 手指公 n. thumb
sow jeen 修剪 v.t. prune
sow jeen 修剪 n trim
sow jeen 修剪 v.t. trim
sow jing 受精 v.t fertilize
sow ju 數珠 n. rosary
sow juk jee ting 手足之情 n brotherhood
sow jun jeet mor 受盡折磨 v.t. rack
sow jung 訴訟 n. litigation
sow jung 訴訟 n. prosecution
sow koon 授權 v. t depute
sow koon 授權 v. t empower
sow koon tow piew 授權投票 v.t. enfranchise
sow koon yan 受權人 n. attorney
sow kow 手扣 n. handcuff
sow kow 手扣 n. shackle
sow kow jeh 收購者 n. suitor
sow lay 修理 n. repair
sow leen 手鏈 n bracelet
sow leurk 搜掠 v.i. rummage

sow leurng 數量 *n. quantity*

sow leurng geh 數量嘅 *a. quantitative*

sow ling 首領 *n. chieftain*

sow ling 守靈 *n wake*

sow loon 騷亂 *n.t. riot*

sow loon 騷亂 *n. tumult*

sow low dan 手榴彈 *n. grenade*

sow luy 修女 *n. nun*

sow luy yoon yoon jeurng 修女院院長 *n. prioress*

sow mai 收埋 *v.t hide*

sow mai hay sow ban 收埋係手板 *v.t. palm*

sow miew 掃描 *v.t. scan*

sow muk 數目 *n toll*

sow ngay 手藝 *n craft*

sow ngay 手藝 *n. workmanship*

sow peen jeh 受騙者 *n gull*

sow say 手勢 *n. gesture*

sow say 受洗 +*v.t. baptize*

sow seen 首先 *adv first*

sow seurng 受傷 *v.t. hurt*

sow seurng 首相 *n premier*

sow seurng sut 手相術 *n. palmistry*

sow seurng sut see 手相術士 *n. palmist*

sow sik 首飾 *n. jewellery*

sow sik geh 素食嘅 *a vegetarian*

sow sik jeh 素食者 *n. vegetarian*

sow sing 收成 *n. harvest*

sow sok 搜索 *n browse*

sow sok 搜索 *n. search*

sow sun 手信 *n. souvenir*

sow sut 手術 *n. operation*

sow sut 手術 *n. surgery*

sow suy 收稅 *v.t. tax*

sow ta 搜查 *v.t. raid*

sow tak 手冊 *n brochure*

sow tak 手冊 *n. handbook*

sow tak 手冊 *n. pamphlet*

sow tak jok jeh 手冊作者 *n. pamphleteer*

sow tam 搜尋 *n rummage*

sow tee 修辭 *n. rhetoric*

sow tee 羞恥 *n. shame*

sow tee 羞恥 *v.t. shame*

sow tee geh 首次嘅 *a maiden*

sow tok yan 受託人 *n. assignee*

sow tok yan 受託人 *n. trustee*

sow tow 手套 *n. glove*

sow way 守衛 *v.i. guard*

sow way 守衛 *n. warder*

sow way wat 受委屈 *v.t. aggrieve*

sow wok 收穫 *v.t. reap*

sow wu jeh 守護者 *n. guardian*

sow wun 手腕 *n. wrist*

sow yam 手淫 *v.i. masturbate*

sow yam gey 收音機 *n. radio*

sow yap 收入 *n. income*

sow yap 收入 *n. proceeds*

sow yee 壽衣 *n. shroud*

sow yee geh 獸醫嘅 *a. veterinary*

sow yeh 守夜 *n. vigil*

sow yeurng 收養 *v.t. adopt*

sow yeurng 收養 *n adoption*

sow yeurng yan 受養人 *n dependant*

sow yiew 騷擾 *v.t. harass*

sow yiew 騷擾 *n. harassment*

sow yiew geh 首要嘅 *a. chief*

sow yiew geh 首要嘅 *a. premier*

sow yiew joon 手搖鑽 *n. wimble*

sow ying 首映 *n. premiere*

sow yoon 修院 *n. cloister*

sow yuk 瘦肉 *n. lean*

sow yung 收容 *v.t house*

suk 熟 *adj. conversant*

suk 熟 *a familiar*

suk 粟 *n. millet*

suk doon 縮短 *v.t abridge*

suk fan 贖返 *n. redemption*

suk fong 縮放 *n. zoom*

suk fuk 馴服 *v.t. tame*

suk gam 贖金 n. ransom
suk geh 熟嘅 a ripe
suk jak 縮窄 v.t. constrict
suk jak 縮窄 v.t. narrow
suk leen 熟練 a. adept
suk leen geh 熟練嘅 a. versed
suk may 粟米 n corn
suk may 粟米 n. maize
suk may gao gwun 縮微膠卷 n. microfilm
suk ming lun 宿命論 n. predestination
suk say 縮細 v.t. minimize
suk say 縮細 v.i shrink
suk say 縮細 n. shrinkage
suk sik 熟悉 a conversant
suk sing 屬性 n. attribute
suk sow geh 熟手嘅 a. proficient
suk tung jing 縮瞳症 n. myosis
suk yu 屬於 v. i belong
suk yu 屬於 v.t. subordinate
suk yu 屬於 v.t. vest
sun 信 v. t believe
sun 信 n letter
sun 信 n. missive
sun 信 v.t trust
sun bai jeh 崇拜者 n. worshipper
sun chuk 迅速 n. rapidity
sun chuk geh 迅速嘅 a. swift
sun chung 順從 a amenable
sun chung 順從 adj. complaisant
sun chung 順從 n. compliance
sun chung 順從 adj. compliant
sun chung 順從 v.t. toe
sun chuung 順從 v.i. acquiesce
sun dak gwor 信得過 a. trustful
sun dak gwor 信得過 a. trustworthy
sun dak gwor geh 信得過嘅 a. liable
sun dak gwor geh 信得過嘅 a. reliable
sun fung 信封 n envelope
sun fung 信奉 n. worship

sun geet 純潔 a. chaste
sun geet 純潔 n. purity
sun geh 純嘅 a pure
sun ho 信號 n. signal
sun jiew wan geh yan 信招魂嘅人 n. spiritualist
sun jik 殉職 n. martyrdom
sun ju 順住 prep. along
sun leem 信念 n creed
sun leem 信念 n faith
sun leem 信念 n. notion
sun man 詢問 v. t consult
sun man 詢問 n. inquiry
sun sam 信心 n confidence
sun sik 訊息 n. message
sun suy ju yee jeh 純粹主義者 n. purist
sun tow 信徒 n. apostle
sun tow 信徒 n disciple
sun tow 信徒 n. votary
sun yam 唇音 a. labial
sun yam 信任 n. trust
sun yeurng 信仰 n belief
sun yow yee geh 純友誼嘅 a. platonic
sun yu 信譽 n credit
sung 送 v. t deliver
sung bai jeh 崇拜者 n. idolater
sung beet 送別 interj. farewell
sung bok 聳膊 v.t. shrug
sung bok 聳膊 n shrug
sung geh 鬆嘅 a. loose
sung ging 崇敬 v.t. hallow
sung go 鬆糕 n. trifle
sung gow geh 崇高嘅 a. sublime
sung gow geh see 崇高嘅事 n sublime
sung hoy 鬆開 v.t. loose
sung hoy 鬆開 v.t. loosen
sung jorng jeh 送葬者 n. mourner
sung sun yan 送信人呢 n. messenger
sung tee 鬆弛 a flabby
sung tee geh 鬆弛嘅 a. slack

sup yee 十二 *a. twelve*
sur *v.i. slide*
sur wat tay 滑梯 *n slide*
sut gao 摔跤 *v.i. wrestle*
sut gao shoonsow 摔跤選手 *n. wrestler*
sut jik 率直 *a. outspoken*
sut jik 率直 *a. straightforward*
sut sam 袖衫 *n. shirt*
sut see 術士 *n. sorcerer*
sut yu 術語 *n. terminology*
suy 碎 *adv. asunder*
suy 碎 *n crumb*
suy 碎 *v. t crumble*
suy 衰 *a. mean*
suy 碎 *v.t. splinter*
suy 稅 *n. tax*
suy 稅 *n. taxation*
suy 水 *n. water*
suy an 水銀 *n. mercury*
suy an 水銀 *n. quicksilver*
suy ba 水壩 *n dam*
suy bo 碎布 *n. tatter*
suy bo lay 碎玻璃 *n. cullet*
suy cho 水槽 *n. gutter*
suy diew 水貂 *n. mink*
suy dow cheet mey 衰到徹尾 *n. arrant*
suy fan 水分 *n. moisture*
suy far 水花 *n spray*
suy fu 水庫 *n. reservoir*
suy fuk 說服 *v. t convince*
suy fuk 說服 *v.t. persuade*
suy fuk lik 說服力 *n. persuasion*
suy fwun 稅款 *n. levy*
suy gak 衰格 *a. nasty*
suy gung 水工 *n. plumber*
suy gwun 水管 *n. hose*
suy ho 水候 *n. tap*
suy jam 水浸 *n flood*
suy jap 水閘 *n. sluice*
suy jat 水蛭 *n. leech*

suy jeng 水井 *n. well*
suy jik geh 垂直嘅 *a. perpendicular*
suy jik seen 垂直線 *n. perpendicular*
suy jing 水晶 *n crystal*
suy juk gwun 水族館 *n. aquarium*
suy keet 衰竭 *n. prostration*
suy kow 需求 *n demand*
suy lay 水泥 *n. cement*
suy lok 衰落 *v.i. wane*
suy low 水流 *n current*
suy luk leurng chay 水陸兩棲 *adj amphibious*
suy mat geh 水密嘅 *a. watertight*
suy ngow 水牛 *n. buffalo*
suy pao 水泡 *n blain*
suy pao 水泡 *n bleb*
suy pao 水泡 *n blister*
suy peen 碎片 *n. fragment*
suy peen 碎片 *n. scrap*
suy ping jor 水瓶座 *n. aquarius*
suy see geh 瑞士嘅 *a Swiss*
suy see yan 瑞士人 *n. Swiss*
suy seen far 水仙花 *n narcissus*
suy sek 碎石 *n. rubble*
suy sow 水手 *n. mariner*
suy sow 對手 *n. opponent*
suy tam 水漤 *n. puddle*
suy tung 水桶 *n bucket*
suy tuy 衰退 *v.i falter*
suy wu 水壺 *n. kettle*
suy yan 衰人 *a bastard*
suy yan 衰人 *n. villain*
suy yee 睡衣 *n. nightie*
suy yeen 雖然 *conj. although*
suy yeen 雖然 *prep. notwithstanding*
suy yeen 雖然 *conj. though*
suy yeurk 衰弱 *v. i ebb*
suy yeurk 衰弱 *v.i. lapse*
suy yiew 需要 *n. need*
suy yiew 需要 *adv. needs*
suy yiew 需要 *v.t. require*
suy yiew 需要 *n. requirement*

suy yiew geh 需要嘅 *a necessary*
suy yiew geh 需要嘅 *a. needful*
suy yiew geh yeh 需要嘅嘢 *n. acquirement*

T

ta 差 *a. bad*
ta 差 *adv. badly*
ta 搽 *v. t. daub*
ta 差 *adv. ill*
ta 搽 *v.t. smear*
ta 茬 *n. stubble*
ta 茶 *n tea*
ta ak 差額 *n. variance*
ta beet 差別 *n distinction*
ta deep 茶碟 *n. saucer*
ta geh see yan 差嘅詩人 *n. poetaster*
ta geh see yan 差嘅詩人 *n. rhymester*
ta heurng suy 搽香水 *v.t. perfume*
ta hm dor 差唔多 *adv. nearly*
ta ngow yow 搽牛油 *v. t butter*
ta yee 差異 *n disparity*
tai 踩 *v.t. conculcate*
tai 踩 *v.t. pedal*
tai 呔 *n tie*
tai 踩 *v.t. tread*
tai ba 柴把 *n faggot*
tai cheurng 太長 *a. interminable*
tai day 踩低 *v.t. abase*
tai day 踩低 *n abasement*
tai dow 態度 *n. attitude*
tai dow say lay 態度勢利 *n. snobbery*
tai duy 柴堆 *n. pyre*
tai fay torng 太妃糖 *n. toffee*
tai fwun 貸款 *n. loan*
tai fwun 貸款 *n. mortgage*

tai garm 太監 *n eunuch*
tai gwor 太過 *adv. too*
tai gwor gorng gow 太過講究 *a. pedantic*
tai gwor suy tam 踩過水淦 *v.t. puddle*
tai ho la 太好啦 *a fabulous*
tai ho la 太好啦 *a fantastic*
tai hung yan 太空人 *n. astronaut*
tai lorng 豺狼 *n. jackal*
tai see 差事 *n errand*
tai siew 太少 *a. meagre*
tai sun chung geh 太順從嘅 *a. servile*
tai suy 踩碎 *v.t. trample*
tai tak 猜測 *n conjecture*
tai tak 猜測 *n. guess*
tai yeurng 太陽 *n. sun*
tai yeurng geh 太陽嘅 *a. solar*
tai yeurng yoot 太陽穴 *n. temple*
tak 賊 *n burglar*
tak 賊 *n. dacoit*
tak 賊 *n. robber*
tak 賊 *n. thief*
tak chuy 拆除 *v. t. demolish*
tak leurk 策略 *n. manoeuvre*
tak leurk 策略 *n. stratagem*
tak leurk 策略 *n. tactics*
tak see 策士 *n. tactician*
tak see 測試 *n test*
tam 碳 *n. carbon*
tam 氹 *v. t coax*
tam 沈 *v.i drown*
tam 沈 *v.i. sink*
tam 痰 *n. sputum*
tam 氹 *v.t. wheedle*
tam chung gam hang 沈重咁行 *v.i. plod*
tam deen mat 沈澱物 *n. sediment*
tam fan 侵犯 *v.t. infringe*
tam fan 侵犯 *n. intrusion*
tam ga 參加 *v.t. join*

tam gow 探究 n probe
tam guy 寢具 n. bedding
tam gwun 痰罐 n. spittoon
tam gwun 參觀 n. visit
tam jeem 侵佔 v. i encroach
tam jeem 侵佔 n. usurpation
tam jung geh 沈重嘅 a. massy
tam koon 侵權 v.t. usurp
tam leurk 侵略 v.t. invade
tam leurk 侵略 n. invasion
tam leurk jeh 侵略者 n. aggressor
tam ma 蕁麻 n. nettle
tam mak geh 沈默嘅 a. reticent
tam mak gwa yeen 沈默寡言 n. reticence
tam mak gwa yeen 沈默寡言 a. taciturn
tam may 沈迷 v.t. indulge
tam may 沈迷 n. obsession
tam may 沈迷 v.t. steep
tam may jow sik geh 沈迷酒色嘅 n. voluptuary
tam mwun 沈悶 a. leaden
tam pwun 談判 v.i parley
tam pwun yan 談判人 n. negotiator
tam sam 貪心 n cupidity
tam sam 貪心 a. greedy
tam see geh 沈思嘅 a. pensive
tam shoon 沈船 n. wreck
tam sik 侵蝕 v. t erode
tam sik 侵蝕 n erosion
tam sok 探索 v.t explore
tam sok 探索 n. quest
tam sok 探索 v.t. quest
tam wu 貪污 n. corruption
tam yan 氹人 v.t. amuse
tam yap 侵入 v.t. hack
tam yat 尋日 n. yesterday
tam yat 尋日 adv. yesterday
tam yee yoon 參議院 n. senate
tam yee yoon 參議員 n. senator

tam yee yoon geh 參議員嘅 a. senatorial
tam yee yoon geh 參議員嘅 a senatorial
tam yeet jam 探熱針 n. thermometer
tam yuk 貪慾 n. greed
tam yuk 貪慾 a. lustful
tan 炭 n coal
tan 塵 n dust
tan 撢 n duster
tan 襯 v.t. line
tan 塵 n. mote
tan 鏟 v.t. shovel
tan 鏟 n. spade
tan 鏟 v.t. spade
tan 襯 v.t. suit
tan bak 坦白 a. frank
tan ban 產品 n. produce
tan ban 產品 n. product
tan bo hang way 殘暴行爲 n cruelty
tan bo hang way 殘暴行爲 n. savagery
tan chuy 鏟除 v. t eradicate
tan doon 診斷 v. t diagnose
tan doon 診斷 n diagnosis
tan far mat 碳化物 n. carbide
tan fay 殘廢 a disabled
tan gan 餐巾 n. napkin
tan geh 真嘅 a. genuine
tan hai 殘骸 n debris
tan hai 殘骸 n. wreckage
tan heurng yow 檀香油 n. sandalwood
tan huk 殘酷 a. barbarous
tan jat 殘疾 n handicap
tan jee 題字 n. inscription
tan jing geh 真正嘅 a. authentic
tan jing geh 真正嘅 a. proper
tan koon 產權 n. ownership
tan kwan 襯裙 n. petticoat
tan lan geh 燦爛嘅 a. refulgent
tan leurng 產量 n yield

tan low geh 殘留嘅 a. residual
tan low man jat 殘留物質 n. residue
tan mat 親密 n. intimacy
tan ngoi 親愛 a dear
tan pai 餐牌 n. menu
tan sai 殘晒 a. worn
tan sam 襯衫 n blouse
tan sang 產生 v.t. generate
tan seurng 真相 n. truth
tan shoon gap 碳酸鉀 n. potash
tan sik 歎息 v. t bewail
tan sik 嘆息 v.i. groan
tan sor 診所 n. clinic
tan suk gwan hay 親屬關係 n. kinship
tan sun 親信 n. henchman
tan teet sing 親切性 n. amiability
tan teng 餐廳 n. restaurant
tan tik 親戚 n. kin
tan tik 親戚 n. relative
tan tik pang yow 親戚朋友 n. kith
tan ting geh 真正嘅 a. actual
tan way 攤位 n. stall
tan wun 癱瘓 n. paralysis
tan wun geh 癱瘓嘅 a. paralytic
tan yan 殘忍 n barbarity
tan yan 殘忍 a brutal
tan yan 殘忍 a cruel
tang 曾 adv ever
tang 層 n. layer
tang 橙 n. orange
tang 層 n ply
tang 撐 v.t. row
tang 層 n. stratum
tang shoon 撐船 v.i boat
tang shoon 撐船 v.i. paddle
tang sik geh 橙色嘅 a orange
tang teng sow 撐艇手 n. oarsman
tang tiew 藤條 n. cane
tang worng sik 橙黃色 a saffron
tang wu 藤壺 n barnacles
tao 炒 v.t. sack

tao lao 吵鬧 n. racket
tao lao seng 吵鬧聲 n clamour
tao seh 抄寫 n. transcription
tap 插 v.t. insert
tap 塔 n. pagoda
tap 插 v.t. plug
tap 插 v.t. spike
tap 插 n thrust
tap 塔 n. tower
tap jor 插座 n. socket
tap juy 插嘴 v.t. interrupt
tap sor 插鎖 n. latch
tap sow 插蘇 n. plug
tap tow 插圖 n. illustration
tap tow shoot ming 插圖說明 n. caption
tap yap 插入 n. insertion
tap yap 插入 v.t. penetrate
tap yap 插入 n. penetration
tap yap yu 插入語 n. parenthesis
tar yee 差異 n difference
tarm 探 v.t. visit
tarm bai 慘敗 n fiasco
tarm hao shu muk 參考書目 +n bibliography
tarm kwai 慚愧 v.t. abash
tarm kway 慚愧 a. ashamed
tarm teen 貪錢 n. avarice
tarm yu 參與 v.i. partake
tarm yu 參與 v.i. participate
tarm yu 參與 n. participation
tarm yu jeh 參與者 n. participant
tarn bo hang way 殘暴行為 n atrocity
tarn yan 殘忍 a. atrocious
tat 擦 v.t. polish
tat 七 n. seven
tat 七 a seven
tat gao hur 膝膠靴 n. wellington
tat gworng jay 擦光劑 n polish
tat hai jay 擦鞋仔 n. sycophant
tat sap 七十 n., a seventy

tat seurng 擦傷 n graze
tat yoon kam 七弦琴 n. lyre
tat yow 擦油 v.t grease
tat yow 漆油 n. paint
tay 堤 n embankment
tay 蹄 n. hoof
tay 提 v.t. inscribe
tay 梯 n. ladder
tay 睇 v.i look
tay 提 v.t. prompt
tay 提 v.t. remind
tay 睇 v.t. see
tay 剃 v.t. shave
tay 剃 n shave
tay 睇 v.t. view
tay 睇 v.t. watch
tay bar 堤壩 n. weir
tay bo jow 齊步走 n march
tay cho 體操 n. gymnastics
tay cho geh 體操嘅 a. gymnastic
tay cho yoon 體操員 n. gymnast
tay chor 睇錯 v.t. misjudge
tay chung 體重 n. weight
tay chut 提出 v.t. propound
tay chuy mat 提取物 n extract
tay dak chut geh 睇得出嘅 adj perceptible
tay dow 睇到 v. t behold
tay dow 堤道 n causeway
tay dow 剃刀 n. razor
tay dow 提到 n. reference
tay dow 睇到 v.t. saw
tay dow 剃度 n. tonsure
tay forng 提防 v.i. beware
tay gak 體格 n build
tay gao 提交 v.t file
tay go 提高 v. t elevate
tay gow 提高 v.t. raise
tay gow 提高 n uplift
tay gung 提供 v.t. offer
tay gung 提供 v.i. provide

tay gung jee gam 提供資金 v.t finance
tay gung jee sun geh 提供資訊嘅 a. informative
tay gung yam sik 提供飲食 v. i cater
tay hay 提起 v.t. refer
tay jee 提子 n. grape
tay jee gon 提子乾 n. currant
tay jee gon 提子乾 n. raisin
tay kap 提及 v.t. invoke
tay kap 提及 n. mention
tay kap 提及 v.t. mention
tay kap 梯級 n. rung
tay lay 睇來 v.i. seem
tay leen chorng 提煉廠 n. refinery
tay man 提問 a. interrogative
tay muk 題目 n. topic
tay sam 提審 v. arraign
tay see 提示 n clue
tay see 提示 n cue
tay see 提示 n. hint
tay see yan 提示人 n. prompter
tay seng 提醒 v.t. refresh
tay seng 提醒 n. reminder
tay siew 睇小 v.i trifle
tay sik 棲息 v.i. roost
tay sik chu 棲息處 n. perch
tay sik chu 棲息處 n. roost
tay sik day 棲息地 n. habitat
tay sing 提升 v. t boost
tay sing 提醒 v. t. caution
tay teep 體貼 a. chivalrous
tay teep 體貼 n. chivalry
tay teep 體貼 a. considerate
tay teep 體貼 a. thoughtful
tay yee 提議 n offer
tay yee 提議 n. proposition
tay yee 提議 n. recommendation
tay yee 提議 n. suggestion
tay yee 提議 v.t. tender
tay yeurk 體弱 a. infirm
tay yeurk 體弱 n. infirmity

tay ying 體型 n. *physique*
tay yuk cheurng 體育場 n. *stadium*
tay yuk gwun 體育館 n. *gymnasium*
tee 黐 a. *adhesive*
tee 遲 adv. *late*
tee 似 a. *like*
tee 似 prep *like*
tee 肢 n. *limb*
tee 似 n. *resemblance*
tee 似 v.t. *resemble*
tee 似 a. *similar*
tee 黐 v.t. *stick*
tee 黐 a. *sticky*
tee 刺 v.t. *sting*
tee 似 a. *such*
tee 刺 n. *thorn*
tee deen peen mow 詞典編纂 n. *lexicography*
tee deep 磁碟 n. *disc*
tee dow 刺刀 n *bayonet*
tee dun 遲鈍 n. *laggard*
tee dun geh 遲鈍嘅 a. *obtuse*
tee dun gen yan 遲鈍嘅人 n *dunce*
tee gang 匙羹 n. *spoon*
tee gik 刺激 n. *provocation*
tee gik 刺激 n. *stimulus*
tee gik 刺激 n. *thrill*
tee gik 刺激 v.t. *thrill*
tee gik mat 刺激唔 n. *irritant*
tee hak 刺客 n. *assassin*
tee hay 瓷器 n. *china*
tee hay 瓷器 n. *porcelain*
tee hung jeurk 雌孔雀 n. *peahen*
tee jang 賜贈 v. t *bestow*
tee jik 辭職 n. *conge*
tee jik 辭職 v.t. *resign*
tee jik 辭職 n. *resignation*
tee joon 瓷磚 n. *tile*
tee jor geh 遲咗嘅 adj. *belated*
tee ju 黐住 n. *adhesion*
tee ju leem yik geh 粘住黏液嘅 a. *slimy*

tee juk 持續 n. *continuation*
tee juk 持續 v.t. *perpetuate*
tee juk 持續 v.t. *ply*
tee juk 持續 v.t. *span*
tee juk geh 持續嘅 a. *perennial*
tee juk geh 持續嘅 a. *relentless*
tee juy 次序 n. *order*
tee lay gan 黐脷根 n *lisp*
tee lik 磁力 n. *magnetism*
tee luk 雌鹿 n *doe*
tee ma mi 似媽咪 a. *motherlike*
tee pai yan 持牌人 n. *licensee*
tee sat 刺殺 n *assassination*
tee seen 慈善 n. *charity*
tee seen 黐線 a *crazy*
tee seen 黐線 a. *insane*
tee seen 慈善 n. *philanthropy*
tee seen ga 慈善家 n. *philanthropist*
tee seen geh 慈善嘅 a. *charitable*
tee seen geh 黐線嘅 a. *lunatic*
tee seen geh 慈善嘅 a. *philanthropic*
tee sek 磁石 n. *loadstone*
tee sek 磁石 n. *magnet*
tee sor 廁所 n *bogle*
tee sor 廁所 n. *toilet*
tee sow 刺繡 n *embroidery*
tee suy geh 似水嘅 a. *watery*
tee tong 池塘 n. *pond*
tee worng jee gam geh 似王子咁嘅 a. *princely*
tee wu 雌狐 n. *vixen*
tee wuy 詞彙 n. *lexicon*
tee wuy biew 詞彙表 n. *glossary*
tee yam far 齒音化 v. *assibilate*
tee yee 刺耳 v. i *bray*
tee yee geh 刺耳嘅 a. *strident*
tee yee geh seng 刺耳嘅聲 v. t *blare*
tee yeurng 似樣 a *decent*
tee yiew 次要 a. *subservient*
tee yiew geh 次要嘅 a. *secondary*
tee yoon hok 詞源學 n. *etymology*
tee yuk 恥辱 v.t. *attaint*

tee yuk 恥辱 *n dishonour*
tee yuk 恥辱 *n. humiliation*
tee yuk 恥辱 *n. stigma*
teem 簽 *v.t. sign*
teem 甜 *a. sweet*
teem choy 甜菜 *n beet*
teem chu forng 簽署方 *n. signatory*
teem fuk 潛伏 *a. latent*
teem jat 潛質 *n. potential*
teem lik 潛力 *n. potentiality*
teem man hok 天文學 *n. astronomy*
teem may 甜味 *n. sweetness*
teem may geh 甜美嘅 *a. luscious*
teem meng 簽名 *n. autograph*
teem meng 簽名 *n. signature*
teem sik 甜食 *n confectionery*
teem sik seurng 甜食商 *n confectioner*
teem suy 潛水 *v. i dive*
teem suy 潛水 *n dive*
teem suy teng 潛艇 *n. submarine*
teem way 纖維 *n fibre*
teem yap suy dow 潛入水裡度 *v.i. submerge*
teen 田 *n field*
teen 前 *a. forward*
teen 前 *n. front*
teen 錢 *n. money*
teen 淺 *a pale*
teen 天 *n. sky*
teen 一千 *a thousand*
teen bay 前臂 *n forearm*
teen choy 天才 *n. genius*
teen chung 填充 *v.t. populate*
teen fan tek 千分尺 *n. micrometer*
teen far 天花 *n. smallpox*
teen far ban 天花板 *n. ceiling*
teen fu 天賦 *n. aptitude*
teen fung 前鋒 *n. striker*
teen gan ding 千斤頂 *n. jack*
teen geh 淺嘅 *a. shallow*

teen geh sap yat sing forng 千嘅十一乘方 *n. decillion*
teen geurt 前腳 *n foreleg*
teen ging wan dung 田徑運動 *n. athletics*
teen hay leen 千禧年 *n. millennium*
teen heen 天譴 *n. damnation*
teen hey 天氣 *n weather*
teen jan 天真 *a. artless*
teen jan 天真 *n. innocence*
teen jan 天真 *a. naive*
teen jan 天真 *n. naivete*
teen jan 天真 *n. naivety*
teen jeh 前者 *pron former*
teen jow kuk 前奏曲 *n. overture*
teen ju gao geh 天主教嘅 *a. catholic*
teen juy 前綴 *n. prefix*
teen king 前傾 *n. lurch*
teen man hok ga 天文學家 *n. astronomer*
teen man toy 天文台 *n. observatory*
teen meen 前面 *adv. ahead*
teen meen 前面 *a front*
teen ngan geh 錢銀嘅 *a. monetary*
teen ngor 天鵝 *n. swan*
teen sang geh 天生嘅 *a. inborn*
teen sang geh 天生嘅 *a. innate*
teen sao 前哨 *n. outpost*
teen see 天使 *n angel*
teen see jeurng 天使長 *n archangel*
teen seen 天線 *n. aerial*
teen seurng geh 天上嘅 *adj celestial*
teen sik 淺色 *n. tint*
teen tan 淺灘 *n shoal*
teen tee yan 填詞人 *n. lyricist*
teen tee yat kay 填遲日期 *v.t. post-date*
teen teng 前廳 *n. lobby*
teen tong 天堂 *n. heaven*
teen tong geh 天堂嘅 *a. heavenly*
teen torng 天堂 *n. paradise*
teen tow 鞦韆 *n swing*

teen yam 前任 n. predecessor
teen yan 前因 n. antecedent
teen yeen geh 天然嘅 a. natural
teep 妾 n concubine
teep 貼 v.t. paste
teep biew teem 貼標籤 v.t. label
teep jee 貼紙 n. sticker
teep ju 貼住 v.t. affix
teep see 貼士 n. gratuity
teep see 貼士 n. tip
teep teet 貼切 adv appositely
teet dat nay ho 鐵達尼號 a. Titanic
teet day 徹底 a utter
teet day da bai 徹底打敗 v.t. rout
teet day da bai 徹底打敗 n rout
teet day gam 徹底咁 adv downright
teet day gam 徹底咁 adv. utterly
teet day geh 徹底嘅 a outright
teet day gik bai 徹底擊敗 v.t. vanquish
teet fai 切塊 v.t. slice
teet gey 設計 v. t. design
teet gey 設計 n. design
teet ham jeng 設陷阱 v.t. snare
teet ham jing 設陷阱 v. t. entrap
teet hay 設喺 v.t. base
teet jap 鐵閘 n. shutter
teet jee 設置 v.t set
teet jeurng 鐵匠 n blacksmith
teet jeurng 鐵匠 n. smith
teet lap 切粒 v. i. dice
teet low 鐵路 n. railway
teet see 設施 n facility
teet seen 切線 n. tangent
teet siew 撤銷 v.t. countermand
teet siew 撤銷 v.t. decontrol
teet sow 鐵鏽 n. rust
teet sow tow 鐵手套 n. gauntlet
teet tam 鐵砧 n. anvil
teet tan 鐵鏟 n. shovel
teet toon 切斷 v. t disconnect
teet toon 切斷 v.t. sever

teet tuy 撤退 v.i. retreat
tek 踢 n. kick
tek 踢 v.t. kick
tek choon 尺寸 n dimension
tek dow 赤道 n equator
tek jee 赤字 n deficit
tek lor geh 赤裸嘅 a. nude
teng 請 v. t employ
teng 聽 v.t. hear
teng 聽 v.i. listen
teng choy 青菜 a. vegetable
teng dow geh 聽到嘅 a audible
teng gwa 青瓜 n cucumber
teng gwong ngan 青光眼 n. glaucoma
teng hay lay 聽起嚟 v.i. sound
teng hm dow 聽唔到 a. inaudible
teng jeh 聽者 n. listener
teng ling 青檸 n. lime
teng tung 青銅 n. & adj bronze
teng tung 聽筒 n. stethoscope
teng wah geh 聽話嘅 a. obedient
teng wah geh 聽話嘅 a. submissive
ter 嗨 interj fie
ter 斜 a. steep
ter 斜 v.i. tilt
ter 斜 n. tilt
ter bor 斜坡 n slant
ter bor 斜坡 n. slope
ter ok 邪惡 n evil
ter ok 邪惡 n. immorality
ter ok geh 邪惡嘅 a. sinful
ter ok geh 邪惡嘅 a. vile
ter ok geh 邪惡嘅 a. wicked
ter see 斜視 n squint
ter seen gung jay 扯線公仔 n. puppet
ter tay 斜體 a. italic
ter tay jee 斜體字 n. italics
ter tee 奢侈 n. luxury
ter tee ban 奢侈品 n. superfluity
ter tee geh 奢侈嘅 a. sumptuous

tey gung 提供 *v.t. supply*
tey leen 提煉 *v. t extract*
tey yee 提議 *v.t. suggest*
tiew 跳 *n. bound*
tiew 跳 *v.i. dap*
tiew 跳 *n. jump*
tiew 跳 *v.i jump*
tiew 跳 *v.i. leap*
tiew 鞘 *n. scabbard*
tiew 潮 *n. tide*
tiew 跳 *v.i. vault*
tiew chut 超出 *prep. beyond*
tiew chut seurng yan geh 超出常人嘅 *a. superhuman*
tiew dai say 調大細 *v.t. size*
tiew doy 朝代 *n dynasty*
tiew dung 跳動 *v.i. pulse*
tiew dung 跳動 *n. throb*
tiew fwun 條款 *n clause*
tiew gai 調解 *n. mediation*
tiew geen 條件 *n condition*
tiew geen 條件 *n prerequisite*
tiew geh 潮嘅 *a. tidal*
tiew gow 跳高 *n leap*
tiew gwor 超過 *v.i excel*
tiew gwor 跳過 *v.t hurdle2*
tiew gwor 超過 *v.t. surpass*
tiew gwor 超過 *v.t. top*
tiew gwor 超過 *v.i. tower*
tiew hay 挑起 *v.t foment*
tiew jay 調製 *v. t concoct*
tiew jay ban 調製品 *n. concoction*
tiew jee yeen geh 超自然嘅 *a. supernatural*
tiew jeen 挑戰 *n. challenge*
tiew jeen 挑戰 *v. t. challenge*
tiew jeet hay 調節器 *n. regulator*
tiew jeurng 肖像 *n. portrait*
tiew jing 調整 *v.t. adjust*
tiew jing 調整 *n. adjustment*
tiew jing 調整 *v.t. modulate*
tiew joy 超載 *v.t. overload*

tiew leurng gung ying 超量供應 *v.t. glut*
tiew liew 調料 *n dressing*
tiew lo 潮流 *n. trend*
tiew low 超嬲 *a. furious*
tiew man 條紋 *n. stripe*
tiew may jeurng 調味醬 *n. dip*
tiew mo 跳舞 *v. t. dance*
tiew pay 調皮 *a arch*
tiew san 朝臣 *n. courtier*
tiew san jeh 跳傘者 *n. parachutist*
tiew sap 潮濕 *n damp*
tiew sat 跳蚤 *n. lop*
tiew see 超時 *v.t overrun*
tiew seen ging 朝鮮薊 *n. artichoke*
tiew sik ban 調色板 *n. palette*
tiew sing 跳繩 *v.i. skip*
tiew sing jee luy 朝聖之旅 *n. pilgrimage*
tiew sing jeh 朝聖者 *n. pilgrim*
tiew suy 憔悴 *a. haggard*
tiew suy 憔悴 *a. wan*
tiew ta 調查 *v.t. investigate*
tiew ta 調查 *n. investigation*
tiew ta 調查 *n research*
tiew ta 調查 *n. survey*
tiew ta 調查 *v.t. survey*
tiew ting 調情 *n flirt*
tiew ting 調停 *v.i. mediate*
tiew ting 調情 *v.t. pet*
tiew ting jeh 調停者 *n. mediator*
tiew yam 調音 *v.t. tune*
tiew yam bor geh 超音波嘅 *a. supersonic*
tiew yan 超人 *n. superman*
tiew yan geh 挑釁嘅 *a. provocative*
tiew yeh 招惹 *v.t goad*
tiew yoot 超越 *v.t exceed*
tiew yoot 超越 *v.t. outrun*
tiew yoot 超越 *v.t. overhaul*
tiew yoot 超越 *v.t. transcend*
tik 剔 *n. tick*

tik 剔 *v.i. tick*
tik jak 斥責 *n. reprimand*
tik jak 斥責 *v.t. reprimand*
ting 停 *v.t. stop*
ting bok 停泊 *v.t moor*
ting chor 清楚 *a clear*
ting chor 清楚 *a. evident*
ting chor 清楚 *a. explicit*
ting chor 清楚 *a. legible*
ting chor biew dat 清楚表達 *a. articulate*
ting chun kay 青春期 *n. adolescence*
ting chun kay 青春期 *n. puberty*
ting chuy 清除 *n clearance*
ting chuy 清除 *v.t. purge*
ting chuy 清除 *v.t. remove*
ting dan 清單 *n. list*
ting fat 懲罰 *v.t. penalize*
ting fat 懲罰 *n. penalty*
ting fat 懲罰 *n. punishment*
ting fat 懲罰 *v.t. sanction*
ting fat geh 懲罰嘅 *a. punitive*
ting forng 情況 *n circumstance*
ting forng 情況 *n. situation*
ting fu 稱呼 *v.t. address*
ting fu 情婦 *n. courtesan*
ting gao tow 清教徒 *n. puritan*
ting gao tow sik geh 清教徒式 嘅 *a. puritanical*
ting geet 清潔 *v. t clean*
ting geet gung 清潔工 *n. sweeper*
ting gok geh 聽覺嘅 *adj. auditive*
ting gor 情歌 *n. ballad*
ting jan 稱讚 *n. praise*
ting jan jee 清真寺 *n. mosque*
ting jap cho 請雜草 *v.t. weed*
ting jay 停滯 *v.i. stagnate*
ting jay 停滯 *n. stagnation*
ting jay 停滯 *n. standstill*
ting jee 停止 *v. t discontinue*
ting jee 停止 *v. t. halt*
ting jee 停止 *n halt*
ting jee tung yung 停止通用 *v.t. demonetize*
ting jeen heep ding 停戰協定 *n. truce*
ting jeet kek 情節劇 *n. melodrama*
ting jik geh 挺直嘅 *a. upright*
ting juy 程序 *n. procedure*
ting juy 程序 *n. process*
ting kow 請求 *n. plea*
ting kow 請求 *n request*
ting lan 整爛 *v. t break*
ting leem 清廉 *a. incorruptible*
ting leen yan 青年人 *n young*
ting pak chu 停泊處 *n anchorage*
ting pwun 清盤 *v.t. liquidate*
ting pwun 清盤 *n. liquidation*
ting sat 證實 *n affirmation*
ting sat 證實 *v.t. verify*
ting say 清洗 *v. t cleanse*
ting shoon chu 停船處 *n. moorings*
ting siew leen 青少年 *a. adolescent*
ting siew leen 青少年 *n. teenager*
ting sik 清晰 *n clarity*
ting sik dow 清晰度 *n. lucidity*
ting sik dow 清晰度 *n. resolution*
ting sik geh 清晰嘅 *a. vivid*
ting sing 清醒 *a conscious*
ting sing geh 清醒嘅 *a. sober*
ting suy 情緒 *n. sentiment*
ting suy far 情緒化 *a. saccharine*
ting suy gik dung 情緒激動 *a. hysterical*
ting tai 情態 *n. modality*
ting tat 清漆 *n. varnish*
ting ting 澄清 *v. t clarify*
ting ting 澄清 *n clarification*
ting wa 青蛙 *n. frog*
ting wa seng 青蛙聲 *n. croak*
ting yan 情人 *n. lover*
ting yan 情人 *n. paramour*
ting yat 聽日 *n. morrow*
ting yat 聽日 *n. tomorrow*

ting yat 聽日 *adv. tomorrow*
ting yeep 停業 *n. closure*
ting yoon 庭院 *n. courtyard*
ting yoon 請願 *v.t. petition*
ting yoon jeh 請願者 *n. petitioner*
ting yoon shu 請願書 *n. petition*
tong 糖 *n. candy*
tong 糖 *n. comfit*
tong 糖 *n. sugar*
tong 糖 *n sweet*
tong jay gwan 糖仔棍 *n. lollipop*
tong jeurng 糖漿 *n. syrup*
tong jing 糖精 *n. saccharin*
tong liew beng 糖尿病 *n diabetes*
tong meng yan 同名人 *n. namesake*
tong ting 同情 *v.i. sympathize*
tong yee 躺椅 *n chaise*
toon bo 臀部 *n hip*
toon geet 團結 *n. solidarity*
toon geet 團結 *v.t. unite*
toon joot 斷絕 *n. severance*
toon tay 團體 *n. confraternity*
toon toon juk juk 斷斷續續 *a fitful*
toon toon juk juk 斷斷續續 *a. spasmodic*
toon toon juk juk 斷斷續續 *a. sporadic*
toon tow 源頭 *n. origin*
toot jee lai 脫脂奶 *n buttermilk*
toot lap 脫粒 *v.t. thresh*
toot lay 脫離 *v.i. secede*
toot lay 脫離 *n. secession*
toot lay ju yee jeh 脫離主義者 *n. secessionist*
tor 拖 *v.t. mop*
tor bwuy 駝背 *n stoop*
tor hai 拖鞋 *n. loafer*
tor hai 拖鞋 *n. slipper*
tor heep 妥協 *v. t compromise*
tor heep 妥協 *n concession*
tor ju geurt hang 拖住腳行 *v.i. shuffle*

tor lai gey 拖拉機 *n. tractor*
tor lun 舵輪 *n. helm*
tor mo bo 駝毛布 *n camlet*
tor yeen 拖延 *v.i. procrastinate*
torliew 鴕鳥 *n. ostrich*
torng 燙 *v.t. iron*
torng 堂 *n. lesson*
torng 堂 *n. session*
torng 劏 *v.t. slaughter*
torng 湯 *n. soup*
torng 糖 *n. sweetmeat*
torng dow 燙斗 *n. iron*
torng hok 湯殼 *n. ladle*
torng jeurng 糖漿 *n molasses*
torng lik suy 湯力水 *n. tonic*
torng worng geh 堂皇嘅 *a. palatial*
tow 肚 *n belly*
tow 頭 *n. head*
tow 桃 *n. peach*
tow 偷 *v.t. pilfer*
tow 偷 *v.t. rifle*
tow 偷 *v.t. rob*
tow 吐 *v.i. spit*
tow 偷 *v.i. steal*
tow 臭 *v.i. stink*
tow 肚 *n. stomach*
tow 頭 *n. tip*
tow 醜 *a. ugly*
tow bay 逃避 *n elusion*
tow bay 逃避 *n escape*
tow bay 逃避 *n evasion*
tow bay 逃避 *v.t. shirk*
tow bay jeh 逃避者 *n. shirker*
tow biew 投標 *n bid*
tow biew 圖表 *n. chart*
tow biew 圖表 *n diagram*
tow biew 圖表 *n. graph*
tow biew 投票 *n tender*
tow bo 投保 *v.t. insure*
tow chee 陶瓷 *n ceramics*
tow chuk 抽搐 *n. spasm*
tow chuk 抽搐 *v.i. throb*

tow chut 抽出 *v.t. abstract*
tow chut 抽出 *v.t. spare*
tow day 徒弟 *n. apprentice*
tow fan 逃犯 *n. outlaw*
tow far 醜化 *v.t. uglify*
tow far muk 桃花木 *n. mahogany*
tow fat 頭髮 *n hair*
tow fat 頭髮 *n lock*
tow forng 套房 *n. suite*
tow fu 屠夫 *n butcher*
tow ga 投家 *n bidder*
tow gan 頭巾 *n coif*
tow gan 頭巾 *n. wimple*
tow gow 禱告 *n. prayer*
tow gung 陶工 *n. potter*
tow gwat 頭骨 *n. skull*
tow hay 陶器 *n. crockery*
tow hay 陶器 *n. pottery*
tow hey 唞氣 *v. i. breathe*
tow ho 討好 *v. t. court*
tow ho 討好 *v.t flatter*
tow horng 投降 *v.t. surrender*
tow horng 投降 *n surrender*
tow jay 兔仔 *n. rabbit*
tow jay geh 土製嘅 *a earthen*
tow jee 投資 *v.t. invest*
tow jee 透支 *n. overdraft*
tow jee 透支 *v.t. overdraw*
tow jee 投資 *n. investment*
tow jeurng 抽象 *a abstract*
tow jeurng geh koy leem 抽象嘅概念 *n. abstraction*
tow jor lap geh 塗咗蠟嘅 *adj. cerated*
tow jow 逃走 *v.i abscond*
tow jow 逃走 *v. i decamp*
tow jow 逃走 *v.i escape*
tow juy 陶醉 *v.i. revel*
tow kow 投球 *v.i bowl*
tow kow sow 投球手 *n. pitcher*
tow kow sow geh jor ho 投球手左後 *n. mid-off*

tow kow sow geh teen yow 投球手嘅前右 *n. mid-on*
tow kway 頭盔 *n. helmet*
tow lan 偷懶 *v.i. laze*
tow liew 塗料 *n. daub*
tow lo 透露 *v. i confide*
tow low 透露 *v. t disclose*
tow low 頭腦 *n. mind*
tow low 醜陋 *n. ugliness*
tow lun 討論 *v. t. debate*
tow lun 討論 *v. t. discuss*
tow lun 討論 *n. nagotiation*
tow lun wuy 討論會 *n. symposium*
tow luy 醜女 *n. hag*
tow man 醜聞 *n scandal*
tow ming 透明 *a. transparent*
tow ming dow 透明度 *n. opacity*
tow morng 偷望 *n peep*
tow or 肚屙 *n diarrhoea*
tow or 肚餓 *a. hungry*
tow pay 頭皮 *n dandruff*
tow pay 頭皮 *n scalp*
tow peen 圖片 *n. image*
tow piew 投票 *n. poll*
tow piew 投票 *v.i. vote*
tow piew koon 投票權 *n. suffrage*
tow piew yan 投票人 *n. voter*
tow poon 頭盤 *n appetizer*
tow sat 屠殺 *v. t butcher*
tow sat 屠殺 *v.t. massacre*
tow sat 屠殺 *n. slaughter*
tow seet 盜竊 *n burglary*
tow seet 偷竊 *n. theft*
tow she 投射 *v. t. cast*
tow she mat 投射物 *n. projectile*
tow shu gwun 圖書館 *n. library*
tow shu gwun gwun jeurng 圖書館館長 *n. librarian*
tow so 投訴 *v. i complain*
tow so 投訴 *n complaint*
tow tai jor geh 淘汰咗嘅 *a. obsolete*
tow tay 偷睇 *v.i. peep*

tow tow 陶土 *n argil*
tow tow gam jow 偷偷咁走 *v.i. sneak*
tow tung 頭痛 *n. headache*
tow wah 圖畫 *n. picture*
tow wah geh 圖畫嘅 *a. pictorial*
tow yap 投入 *n. input*
tow yeem 討厭 *a abominable*
tow yeem gway 討厭鬼 *n. sod*
toy 台 *n channel*
toy 台 *n. dais*
toy 台 *n. platform*
toy 枱 *n. table*
toy fung 颱風 *n. gale*
toy fung 颱風 *n. hurricane*
toy fung 颱風 *n. typhoon*
toy seen 苔蘚 *n. moss*
toy tee 台詞 *n. speech*
toy tow ting hung hang 抬頭挺胸行 *v.i. strut*
tteen tee jee mat 天賜之物 *n. godsend*
tuk bay wu ngar 禿鼻烏鴉 *n. rook*
tuk jow 禿鷲 *n. vulture*
tun 盾 *n. shield*
tun 吞 *v.t. swallow*
tun mwut 吞沒 *v.t engulf*
tun ping 吞併 *v.t. annex*
tun ping 吞併 *n annexation*
tung 痛 *n. ache*
tung 痛 *v.i. ache*
tung 桶 *n. barrel*
tung 銅 *n copper*
tung 桶 *n. pail*
tung 痛 *v.t. pain*
tung 捅 *v.t. stab*
tung 捅 *n. stab*
tung 同 *prep. with*
tung been geh 通便嘅 *n. laxative*
tung dang 同等 *n equal*
tung dow 通到 *n. passage*
tung for gan suk 通貨緊縮 *n. deflation*

tung fu 痛苦 *n. affliction*
tung fu 痛苦 *n. agony*
tung fu 痛苦 *n. misery*
tung fu 痛苦 *n. pain*
tung fu 痛苦 *a. painful*
tung fu 痛苦 *n. tribulation*
tung fu 痛苦 *n. woe*
tung fung 通風 *n draught*
tung fung 通風 *v.t. ventilate*
tung fung 通風 *n. ventilation*
tung fung beng 通風病 *n. gout*
tung fung ho 通風口 *n. ventilator*
tung garn 通姦 *n. adultery*
tung geh 痛嘅 *a. sore*
tung gey 統計 *n. statistics*
tung gey geh 統計嘅 *a. statistical*
tung gey hok ga 統計學家 *n. statistician*
tung gowr 通過 *v.i. pass*
tung guy 同居 *v. t cohabit*
tung guy 同居 *n. concubinage*
tung gwor 通過 *v. t enact*
tung gwor 通過 *adv. through*
tung han 痛恨 *n. abhorrence*
tung hang fay 通行費 *n. toll*
tung hang jing 通行證 *n pass*
tung huk 痛哭 *v.i. wail*
tung jee 通知 *v.t. apprise*
tung jee 統治 *v.t. govern*
tung jee 通知 *v.t. impart*
tung jee 通知 *v.t. inform*
tung jee 通知 *n. notice*
tung jee 通知 *n. notification*
tung jee 通知 *v.t. notify*
tung jee 統治 *n reign*
tung jee 統治 *v.t. rule*
tung jee forng sik 統治方式 *n. governance*
tung jee forng sik 統治方式 *n. regime*
tung jee gwan 童子軍 *n scout*
tung jee kay 統治期 *v.i. reign*

tung jee koon 統治權 *n dominion*
tung ju jeh 同住者 *n. inmate*
tung juk 同族 *adj cognate*
tung jung liew fat 同種療法 *n. homeopathy*
tung jung liew fat see 同種療法師 *n. homoeopath*
tung kay ta yan yat yeurng 同其他人一樣 *n. conformity*
tung leen 童年 *n boyhood*
tung leen 童年 *n. childhood*
tung ling geh 通靈嘅 *a. psychic*
tung luy geh 同類嘅 *a. homogeneous*
tung mai 同埋 *conj. and*
tung pwuy 同輩 *n. peer*
tung see 同事 *n. associate*
tung see 同事 *n colleague*
tung see 同事 *n fellow*
tung see fat sang 同時發生 *v. i coincide*
tung see fat sang 同時發生 *v.t. parallel*
tung see fat sang 同時發生 *a. simultaneous*
tung seurng 同上 *n. ditto*
tung seurng 通常 *adv. generally*
tung seurng 通常 *adv. oft*
tung seurng 通常 *adv. often*
tung seurng 通常 *adv. usually*
tung seurng wuy 通常會 *v.i. tend*
tung sing 通勝 *n. almanac*
tung sing loon 同性戀 *a. gay*
tung sun 通訊 *n. communication*
tung sun 通信 *n. correspondence*
tung tap fan 通緝犯 *n. fugitive*
tung ting 同情 *v. t commiserate*
tung ting 同情 *n compassion*
tung ting 同情 *n. pity*
tung ting geh 同情嘅 *a. sympathetic*
tung ting sam 同情心 *n. sympathy*
tung wah kek 童話劇 *n. pantomime*
tung yat 統一 *n. standardization*

tung yat 統一 *v.t. standardize*
tung yat 統一 *n. unification*
tung yee 同意 *v.t. accede*
tung yee 同意 *v.i. agree*
tung yee 同意 *n. assent*
tung yee 同意 *v. i consent*
tung yee tee 同義詞 *n. synonym*
tung yeurng day 同樣地 *adv. likewise*
tung yung yu 通用語 *n. lingua franca*
tung...yat yeurng 同...一樣 *adv. as*
tuy 推 *v.t. push*
tuy 推 *n. push*
tuy 退 *v.t. refund*
tuy 推 *v.t. shove*
tuy 推 *n. shove*
tuy 推 *v.t. wheel*
tuy bo 退步 *v.i. backslide*
tuy chut 退出 *v.t. quit*
tuy chut 退出 *v.t. withdraw*
tuy chut 退出 *n. withdrawal*
tuy doon 推斷 *v.t. infer*
tuy dung 推動 *n. motivation*
tuy dung 推動 *v.t. propel*
tuy dung lik 推動力 *n. momentum*
tuy fan 推翻 *v.t. overthrow*
tuy fan 推翻 *n overthrow*
tuy fan 推翻 *v.t. subvert*
tuy fwun 退款 *n. rabate*
tuy fwun 退款 *n. refund*
tuy gworng 推廣 *v.t. advertise*
tuy hang 推行 *v.t. impose*
tuy hm gwan yan 退伍軍人 *n. veteran*
tuy ho 退後 *a. backward*
tuy hoy 推開 *n. jostle*
tuy hoy 推開 *v.t. jostle*
tuy jeen 推展 *v.t. nominate*
tuy jeen 推展 *n. nomination*
tuy jeen 推薦 *v.t. recommend*
tuy jeen sun 推薦信 *n. testimonial*

tuy mow 蛻毛 *v.i. moult*
tuy pay 蛻皮 *n. slough*
tuy siew 推銷 *v.t market*
tuy siew 推銷 *n. merchandise*
tuy suk 退縮 *v.i. cower*
tuy suk 退縮 *v.i. recoil*
tuy suk 退縮 *adv. recoil*
tuy tak 推測 *v. t conjecture*
tuy tak 推測 *v.i. speculate*
tuy tak 推測 *n. speculation*
tuy tak 推測 *n. supposition*
tuy tak 推測 *n. surmise*
tuy tak 推測 *v.t. surmise*
tuy tiew 退潮 *n ebb*
tuy yow 退休 *v.i. retire*
tuy yow 退休 *n. retirement*
tuy yow gam 退休金 *n. pension*
tuy yow yan see 退休人士 *n. pensioner*

uk 屋 *n house*
uk kay 屋企 *n. home*
uk kay yan 屋企人 *n family*

wah 畫 *n drawing*
wah 畫 *n. painting*
wah gar 畫家 *n. painter*
wah jeurng 畫像 *n. portraiture*
wah lay 華麗 *n. splendour*
wah lorng 畫廊 *n. gallery*
wah shu 樺樹 *n. birch*
wah tai dor 話太多 *v.t word*

wah tai dor 話太多 *a. wordy*
wai geh 壞嘅 *a faulty*
wai kuk 歪曲 *v.t. misrepresent*
wai yan 懷孕 *n. maternity*
wai yan 懷孕 *n. pregnancy*
wai yee 懷疑 *v.t query*
wai yee 懷疑 *v.t. suspect*
wai yee geh 懷疑嘅 *a. sceptical*
wai yee tai dow 懷疑態度 *n. scepticism*
wak 畫 *v.t draw*
wak 畫 *v.t. pencil*
wak gey ho 畫記號 *v.t mark*
wak jeh 或者 *adv. either*
wak jeh 或者 *adv. perhaps*
wak seen 畫線 *v.t. underline*
wan 彎 *n bend*
wan 彎 *v. t bend*
wan 雲 *n. cloud*
wan 彎 *v. t curve*
wan 玩 *v. i. dabble*
wan 暈 *v.i faint*
wan 搵 *v.t find*
wan 玩 *v.i. frolic*
wan 搵 *n hunt*
wan 玩 *v.i. play*
wan 搵 *v.i. root*
wan 搵 *v.t. search*
wan 搵 *v.t. seek*
wan 運 *v.t. ship*
wan 暈 *n. swoon*
wan 玩 *v.i. toy*
wan 彎 *n turn*
wan chut kok ding way jee 搵出確定位置 *v.t. locate*
wan day 暈低 *v. i collapse*
wan ding 穩定 *n. stabilization*
wan ding 穩定 *v.t. stabilize*
wan ding geh 穩定嘅 *a. stable*
wan ding sing 穩定性 *n. stability*
wan ding sing 穩定性 *n. steadiness*
wan dow 搵到 *v.t. found*

wan dow 溫度 n. temperature
wan dung 運動 n. exercise
wan dung 運動 n. sport
wan dung sam 運動衫 n. jersey
wan dung say bao 運動細胞 a. sportive
wan dung wuy 運動會 n. meet
wan dung ying 運動型 a. athletic
wan dung yoon 運動員 n. athlete
wan dung yoon 運動員 n. sportsman
wan fan 還返 v.t. repay
wan for ma cher 運貨馬車 n. wain
wan ga 玩家 n. player
wan ging 環境 n. environment
wan ging 環境 n. milieu
wan gor 輓歌 n. monody
wan gu 頑固 n bigot
wan gu 頑固 n bigotry
wan gu geh 穩固嘅 v.t. stable
wan hap 混合 a compound
wan hap 混合 v.t. intermingle
wan hap 混合 v.t. mingle
wan hap ban 混合品 n blend
wan hap ban 混合品 n. mixture
wan hap tay 混合體 n amalgam
wan hay 運氣 n. luck
wan hor 運河 n. canal
wan huy 允許 n. consent
wan huy 允許 v.t. consent3
wan huy 允許 v.t. permit
wan huy 允許 v.t. vouchsafe
wan jan geh 穩陣嘅 a. steady
wan jap 溫習 v.t. revise
wan jap 溫習 n. revision
wan jeurk 雲雀 n. lark
wan jiew wu 環礁湖 n. lagoon
wan jok 運作 v.i function
wan jor 彎咗 n bent
wan jorng san wu dow 環狀珊瑚島 n. atoll
wan kuk 弯曲 v.t. arch
wan kuk 彎曲 v.t. crankle

wan kuk 彎曲 n. zigzag
wan kuk geh 彎曲嘅 a. sinuous
wan look 溫暖 n. warmth
wan loon 混亂 v. t bewilder
wan loon 混亂 n. chaos
wan loon 混亂 adv. chaotic
wan loon 混亂 v. t confuse
wan loon 混亂 n confusion
wan loon 混亂 n. melee
wan loon 混亂 n. muddle
wan loon geh 混亂嘅 a. turbulent
wan low 環流 n. circumfluence
wan lut 韻律 n. prosody
wan mow 雲母 n. mica
wan ngat 還押 n remand
wan ngat ho sam 還押候審 v.t. remand
wan por 穩婆 n. midwife
wan see 輓詩 n elegy
wan sek 雲石 n. marble
wan sek 隕石 n. meteor
wan seurng 幻想 n fancy
wan seurng 幻想 a. imaginary
wan seurng 幻想 n. reverie
wan shu 運輸 n. transit
wan shu fay 運輸費 n. cartage
wan shu gung see 運輸公司 n. carrier
wan sun 溫順 a docile
wan sun 溫順 a. tame
wan sun geh 溫順嘅 a. meek
wan sung 運送 v.t. transport
wan sung for 運送貨 n. consignment
wan sung geh for 運送嘅貨 n. shipment
wan tung 頑童 n. urchin
wan wan kuk kuk 彎彎曲曲 a. serpentine
wan wan kuk kuk geh 彎彎曲曲嘅 a. tortuous
wan wo geh 溫和嘅 a.) placid
wan wor geh 溫和嘅 a. mild

wan wor geh 溫和嘅 a. temperate
wan wuy 挽回 v.t. redeem
wan yiew 環繞 v. i. circulate
wan yiew 環繞 v.i. revolve
wan yiew 環繞 adv. round
wan yiew 環繞 v.t. skirt
wan yiew 彎腰 v.i. stoop
wan yiew 環繞 v.t. wind
wan yik 瘟疫 n. pestilence
wan ying tow 混凝土 n concrete
wan yow 溫柔 a. gentle
wan yow 溫柔 a tender
wan yung 運用 v.t. wield
wang ak 橫額 n. banner
wang chung jik jorng 橫衝直撞 v.i. rampage
wang gwor 橫過 adv. across
wang gwor 橫過 prep. athwart
wang way 宏偉 n. grandeur
wang way 宏偉 a. lordly
wang way 宏偉 a. magnificent
wat 滑 v.t. glide
wat 核 n. kernel
wat ban cher 滑板車 n. scooter
wat cheurng gey 滑翔機 n. glider
wat chung 屈從 n. servility
wat dat 核突 a gross
wat dat 核突 a. hideous
wat fuk 屈服 v. t capitulate
wat fuk 屈服 n. submission
wat fuk 屈服 v.i. succumb
wat fuk 屈服 v.t. yield
wat gam heurng 鬱金香 n. curcuma
wat geh 滑嘅 a. smooth
wat gwut 挖掘 v. t. excavate
wat gwut 挖掘 n. excavation
wat hang 滑行 v.i. taxi
wat kay doon kek 滑稽短劇 n. skit
wat lun 滑輪 n. pulley
wat sam 核心 n. hub
way 餵 v.t feed
way bwuy 違背 v. t dishonour

way cheurng 圍牆 n. bawn
way choon 遺傳 n. heredity
way choon geh 遺傳嘅 n. hereditary
way dow 緯度 n. latitude
way fan 違反 n. infringement
way fan 違反 n. transgression
way fan 違反 v.t. violate
way fan 違反 n. violation
way fat 違法 n breach
way geh 胃嘅 a. gastric
way gung 圍攻 v. t besiege
way han 遺憾 n regret
way heep 威脅 v.t. intimidate
way heep 威脅 n menace
way heep 威脅 n. threat
way heep dow 威脅到 v.t menace
way hey 遺棄 v.t. abandon
way ho 胃口 n. appetite
way jee 位置 n. position
way jik 遺跡 n. relic
way jik 遺跡 n. remains
way jik 遺跡 n. vestige
way jor 爲咗 n. sake
way ju 圍住 v. t encase
way ju 圍住 v.t fence
way ju 圍住 v.t. surround
way ju 圍住 v.t. wall
way juk 遺囑 n. will
way korng 違抗 n defiance
way korng 違抗 v. t disobey
way kwun 圍裙 n. apron
way lai 餵奶 v.t. suckle
way lan 圍欄 n fence
way lan 圍欄 n. raling
way lik 威力 n. prowess
way low 遺留 v. t. bequeath
way low 遺漏 n. omission
way man 慰問 n condolence
way meet 毀滅 v.t. annihilate
way meet 毀滅 n annihilation
way meet 毀滅 v.t. decimate
way meet 毀滅 n destruction

way sang 衛生 n. hygiene
way sang geh 衛生嘅 a. hygienic
way sang geh 衛生嘅 a. sanitary
way see gey 威士忌 n. whisky
way sik geh yan 爲食嘅人 n. glutton
way sing 彗星 n comet
way sing 衞星 n. satellite
way sow 維修 n. maintenance
way suk 畏縮 v. i. cringe
way suk 畏縮 v.i. wince
way sun 威信 n cachet
way sun 威信 n. prestige
way ta ming 維他命 n. vitamin
way tan 遺產 n. heritage
way tan 遺產 n. inheritance
way tan 遺產 n. legacy
way tee 維持 v.t. maintain
way tee 維持 n. retention
way tee 維持 v.t. sustain
way tee sang wut 維持生活 v.i. subsist
way tok 委託 v. t delegate
way tok 委託 v. t entrust
way wai 毀壞 v.t. ravage
way wat 委屈 n. grievance
way wat 委屈 n hurt
way yam 委任 v.t. accredit
way yam 委任 v.t. appoint
way yat geh 唯一嘅 a sole
way yeem 威嚴 n august
way yeem 威嚴 n. stateliness
way yeurk 違約 n. default
way yiew 圍繞 v.t. begird
way yiew 圍繞 v. t. encircle
way yiew 圍繞 v.t girdle
way yiew 圍繞 v.t. wreathe
way yoon 委員 n. commissioner
way yoon wuy 委員會 n committee
way yu 謂語 n. predicate
way...yee giew oh 爲...而驕傲 v.t. pride
wik 減 v.t. moat

wing gow geh 永久嘅 a. permanent
wing gow sing 永久性 n. permanence
wing han geh 永恆嘅 a abiding
wing hang 永恒 n eternity
wing hang geh 永恆嘅 a. everlasting
wing sang 永生 n. immortality
wing yoon 永遠 a. eternal
wing yoon 永遠 adv forever
wing yoon dow hm wuy 永遠都唔會 adv. never
wing yu 榮譽 n. glory
wing yu 榮譽 n. honour
wok chuy bo lay 獲取暴利 v.i. profiteer
wok dak 獲得 v.t. attain
wok dak 獲得 v.t. procure
wok jeurng jeh 獲獎者 n. laureate
wok jun lay hoy 獲准離開 n. discharge
wok lo 鍋爐 n boiler
wong day 皇帝 n emperor
wong fan 黃昏 n dusk
wong gwun 皇冠 n crown
wong ho 皇后 n empress
wong sik 黃色 n yellow
wong sik geh 黃色嘅 a. yellow
wong suy chorng 黃水瘡 n boil
wong suy seen 黃水仙 n. daffodil
wong tung 黃銅 n. brass
wong wong day 黃黃地 a. yellowish
woo ngoy geh 戶外嘅 a. outdoor
woon jor 援助 n aid
wor chorng 窩藏 v.t harbour
wor deng 鍋釘 n. rivet
wor gai 和解 n compromise
wor gai 和解 v.t. reconcile
wor gai 和解 n. reconciliation
wor hai 和諧 n. concord
wor hai geh 和諧嘅 a. harmonious
wor hoy 禍害 v.t. peril
wor hoy 禍害 n. scourge
wor lun gey 渦輪機 n. turbine

wor muk 和睦 *n. amity*

wor muk 和睦 *n. harmony*

wor ngoy 蝸牛 *n. snail*

wor ping 和平 *n. peace*

wor ping geh 和平嘅 *a. peaceable*

wor seurng 和尚 *n. monk*

wor yam 和音 *n. consonance*

wor yoon 和弦 *n. chord*

worng bo seng 黃寶石 *n. topaz*

worng chung 蝗蟲 *n. locust*

worng dan 黃疸 *n. jaundice*

worng day geh 皇帝嘅 *a. imperial*

worng fung 黃蜂 *n. wasp*

worng gung 皇宮 *n. palace*

worng gwok 王國 *n. kingdom*

worng gwun 皇冠 *n. tiara*

worng jee 王子 *n. prince*

worng ma 黃麻 *n. jute*

worng pai 王牌 *n. trump*

worng sat geh 王室嘅 *a. royal*

worng sat sing yoon 王室成員 *n. royalty*

worng way 王位 *n. throne*

wu 弧 *n. arc*

wu 壺 *n. jug*

wu 湖 *n. lake*

wu bo 互補 *a complementary*

wu deep 蝴蝶 *n butterfly*

wu deep geet 蝴蝶結 *n bow*

wu fat fwuy fuk 無法恢復 *a. irrecoverable*

wu fuk yik 護膚液 *n. lotion*

wu gway 烏龜 *n. turtle*

wu ho 戶口 *n. account*

wu jiew 護照 *n. passport*

wu jiew fan 胡椒粉 *n. pepper*

wu jik 污漬 *n. blot*

wu jik 污漬 *n. smear*

wu jik 污漬 *n. stain*

wu jo 污糟 *a filthy*

wu jorng mat 糊狀物 *n. mush*

wu jow 污糟 *a dirty*

wu jow ghe 污糟嘅 *a. seamy*

wu lam yan 護林人 *n. ranger*

wu lay 狐狸 *n. fox*

wu lay yoon 護理員 *n. orderly*

wu low 葫蘆 *n. gourd*

wu mat 污物 *n filth*

wu muk 烏木 *n ebony*

wu ngan geng 護眼鏡 *n. goggles*

wu ngar 烏鴉 *n crow*

wu san fu 護身符 *n. amulet*

wu san fu 護身符 *n. talisman*

wu see 護士 *n. nurse*

wu seurng yee lai 互相依賴 *v.t. correlate*

wu seurng yee lai 互相依賴 *n. interdependence*

wu seurng yee lai 互相依賴 *a. interdependent*

wu seurng ying heurng 互相影響 *n. interplay*

wu sing hor 護城河 *n. moat*

wu so 鬍鬚 *n beard*

wu sow 鬍鬚 *n. moustache*

wu sow 鬍鬚 *n. mustache*

wu sung 護送 *v. t escort*

wu sung jeh 護送者 *n escort*

wu suy 污水 *n. sewage*

wu suy dow 污水道 *n sewer*

wu tow 糊涂 *adj addle*

wu way 護衛 *n. guard*

wu way wu lay 互惠互利 *a. reciprocal*

wu yeem 污染 *v.t. contaminate*

wu yeem 污染 *v.t. pollute*

wu yeem 污染 *n. pollution*

wu yeem 污染 *n. taint*

wu yeem 污染 *v.t. taint*

wu yeen lun yu 胡言亂語 *n. babble*

wu yeen lun yu 胡言亂語 *v.i. babble*

wu ying 烏蠅 *n fly*

wun 碗 *n bowl*

wun 換 *v. t convert*

wun gai kay 緩解期 *n. remission*
wun guy 玩具 *n. toy*
wun gwat 腕骨 *n. carpal*
wun hai day 換鞋底 *v.t sole*
wun jeurng 腕杖 *n. maulstick*
wun siew 玩笑 *n. banter*
wun wor 緩和 *v.t. moderate*
wun wor jorng gik 緩和撞擊 *v. t cushion*
wung wung seng 嗡嗡聲 *v. i buzz*
wung wung seng 嗡嗡聲 *n. buzz*
wung wung seng 嗡嗡聲 *n hum*
wung wung seng 嗡嗡聲 *n. whir*
wut dung 活動 *n. activity*
wut dung 活動 *n. campaign*
wut dung 活動 *n event*
wut lik 活力 *n. vitality*
wut pwut 活潑 *n. vivacity*
wut pwut geh 活潑嘅 *a. vivacious*
wut sat 活塞 *n. piston*
wut yeurk 活躍 *a. active*
wuy 會 *n club*
wuy 會 *n. meeting*
wuy 會 *v.t. will*
wuy bo 回報 *v.t. reciprocate*
wuy bo 回報 *v.t. requite*
wuy dap 回答 *v.t answer*
wuy dap yan 回答人 *n. respondent*
wuy fuk 回覆 *v.i. reply*
wuy fuk 回覆 *n reply*
wuy fuk 回復 *v.i. revert*
wuy fwun 匯款 *v.t. remit*
wuy fwun gam ak 匯款金額 *n. remittance*
wuy gey 會計 *n. accountancy*
wuy gey see 會計師 *n. accountant*
wuy gu 回顧 *v.t. review*
wuy hap 匯合 *adj. confluent*
wuy jeurng 會長 *n prior*
wuy low chu 匯流處 *n confluence*
wuy loy 回來 *n. return*
wuy say geh 會死嘅 *a. mortal*

wuy seurng 回想 *n. retrospect*
wuy sor 猥瑣 *v.t. grope*
wuy sor 猥瑣 *a. lewd*
wuy yam 回音 *n echo*
wuy yam 回音 *v. t echo*
wuy yee 會議 *n conference*
wuy yee teng 會議廳 *n. chamber*
wuy yik 回憶 *n. reminiscence*
wuy yik 回憶 *n. retrospection*
wuy yik fan 回憶返 *a. reminiscent*
wuy yik luk 回憶錄 *n. memoir*
wuy yoon 會員 *n. member*
wuy yoon san fan 會員身分 *n. membership*

Y

yam 飲 *v. t down*
yam 飲 *v. t drink*
yam 陰 *n. fringe*
yam 陰 *n. shade*
yam am 陰暗 *a cheerless*
yam am 陰暗 *a. gloomy*
yam am geh 陰暗嘅 *a. shadowy*
yam ban 飲品 *n beverage*
yam ban 飲品 *n drink*
yam ban 飲品 *n. refreshment*
yam cho day fu 陰曹地府 *n. underworld*
yam dorng 淫蕩 *a. lascivious*
yam dorng geh luy yan 淫蕩嘅女人 *n. slut*
yam dow 陰道 *n. vagina*
yam gan geh ju san 陰間嘅諸神 *a. manful*
yam ging 陰莖 *n. penis*
yam hao 音效 *n. acoustics*
yam hor 任何 *a. any*
yam hor 任何 *adv. any*

yam hor yeh 任何嘢 *n. aught*
yam jeet 音節 *n. syllable*
yam jeet geh 音節嘅 *a. syllabic*
yam kay 任期 *n. tenure*
yam leurng 音量 *n. volume*
yam mo 任務 *n. task*
yam mow 陰謀 *n. conspiracy*
yam mow 陰謀 *n intrigue*
yam mow 任務 *n. mission*
yam ok 音樂 *n. music*
yam ok ga 音樂家 *n. musician*
yam sap 陰濕 *adj. dank*
yam sik 飲食 *n. pl victuals*
yam sing 任性 *n. caprice*
yam sing 任性 *a. wayward*
yam sing geh 任性嘅 *a. perverse*
yam sing geh 任性嘅 *a. petulant*
yan 癮 *n. addiction*
yan 忍 *v.t. endure*
yan 印 *v.t. imprint*
yan 人 *n. people*
yan 人 *n. person*
yan 印 *v.t. print*
yan 印 *v.i. stamp*
yan 引 *v.t. tantalize*
yan 忍 *v.t. tolerate*
yan chor 印錯 *n. misprint*
yan chor 印錯 *v.t. misprint*
yan chorng 隱藏 *v. t bemask*
yan dow 引導 *v.t. usher*
yan dow geh 印度嘅 *a. Indian*
yan dow ju yee geh 人道主義嘅 *a humanitarian*
yan fat 引發 *v. t beget*
yan fat 引發 *v.i. spark*
yan gak far 人格化 *n. personification*
yan gan geh 人間嘅 *a earthly*
yan gung 人工 *n pay*
yan guy 隱居 *n. seclusion*
yan guy chu 隱居處 *n. hermitage*
yan gwor gwan hay 因果關係 *adj. causal*

yan gwor gwan hay 因果關係 *n causality*
yan hang wang dow 人行橫道 *n. crossing*
yan hay 引起 *v. t evoke*
yan hay 引起 *v.t. induce*
yan hey 引起 *v. t effect*
yan ho 人口 *n. population*
yan ho jung dor geh 人口眾多嘅 *a. populous*
yan ho tiew ta 人口調查 *n. census*
yan jee 人質 *n. hostage*
yan jeurng 印象 *n. impression*
yan jeurng 印章 *n. seal*
yan jeurng sam hak 印象深刻 *a. impressive*
yan jeurng sam hak 印象深刻 *v.t. lavish*
yan jo geh 人造嘅 *a. artificial*
yan jow geh 人造嘅 *a. synthetic*
yan jow lai yow 人造奶油 *n. margarine*
yan jow way sing 人造衛星 *n. sputnik*
yan jun 引進 *n. import*
yan kan 殷勤 *n. complaisance*
yan king 引擎 *n engine*
yan king goy 引擎蓋 *n bonnet*
yan lik 引力 *n. gravitation*
yan lik cher 人力車 *n. rickshaw*
yan luy 人類 *a. human*
yan luy 人類 *n. humanity*
yan luy 人類 *n. mankind*
yan mun 隱瞞 *v. t. conceal*
yan ok geh 音樂嘅 *a. musical*
yan san bo wu ling 人身保護令 *n. habeas corpus*
yan see 隱士 *n. hermit*
yan see 隱士 *n. recluse*
yan see bo 人事部 *n. personnel*
yan seurng 欣賞 *n. admiration*
yan seurng 欣賞 *v.t. admire*

yan seurng 欣賞 *v.t. appreciate*
yan so 因素 *n factor*
yan sow dow geh 忍受到嘅 *a. tolerant*
yan suy 人瑞 *n centenarian*
yan tan 姻親 *n. in-laws*
yan tat gey 印刷機 *n. printer*
yan tay far geh 人體化嘅 *a. incarnate*
yan tay mow ying 人體模型 *n. mannequin*
yan tee 仁慈 *a. gracious*
yan tee 因此 *adv. hence*
yan tee 因此 *adv. thereby*
yan way 因為 *conj. as*
yan way 因為 *conj. because*
yan way 因為 *a due*
yan way 因為 *conj. for*
yan yap 引入 *v.t. adhibit*
yan yap 引入 *v.t. innovate*
yan yee tan sang 因而產生 *v.i ensue*
yan ying 隱形 *a. invisible*
yan yow 引誘 *v. t. entice*
yan yow 引誘 *n. inducement*
yan yung 引用 *v.t. quote*
yao see suy 入市稅 *n. octroi*
yap 入 *v. t enter*
yap 入 *n entry*
yap 入 *prep. into*
yap been 入邊 *prep. inside*
yap been 入邊 *a inside*
yap been 入邊 *adv. inside*
yap been 入邊 *n. within*
yap doy 入袋 *v. i. bag*
yap hm 入伍 *v. t enlist*
yap ho 入口 *n entrance*
yap ho 入口 *n. portal*
yap hok 入學 *v. t enrol*
yap huy 入去 *n. admittance*
yap jik 入籍 *v.t. naturalize*
yap may 入迷 *a fanatic*
yarn yan ju muk geh 引人注目嘅 *a.*

remarkable
yat 一 *a. a*
yat 一 *art an*
yat 一 *a. one*
yat 一 *pron. one*
yat ba jeurng 一巴掌 *n. slap*
yat ba jeurng 一巴掌 *n smack*
yat bak 一百 *n. hundred*
yat bak jow leen 一百週年 *n. centenary*
yat bak jow leen 一百週年 *adj. centennial*
yat ban 一班 *n. gang*
yat ban yan 一班人 *n crowd*
yat bao 一包 *n. pack*
yat bao 一包 *n. packet*
yat been 一邊 *adv. aside*
yat bo 日報 *n. daily*
yat bwun 一半 *n. half*
yat chai 一切 *n all*
yat chai 一齊 *adv. along*
yat chai 一齊 *adv. altogether*
yat chay 一齊 *adv. together*
yat choon 一串 *n strand*
yat da 一打 *n dozen*
yat dai ban yan 一大班人 *n. horde*
yat dai ban yan 一大班人 *n. throng*
yat dai dam 一大啖 *n. gulp*
yat dai duy 一大堆 *n. welter*
yat dai duy yeh 一大堆嘢 *n. hotchpotch*
yat dai kwan 一大群 *n. swarm*
yat dam 一啖 *n bite*
yat dap 一沓 *n. sheaf*
yat dat 一笪 *n patch*
yat dee 一啲 *n bit*
yat dee 一啲 *n. jot*
yat dee dow mow 一啲都無 *pron. none*
yat dee dow mow 一啲都無 *adv. none*
yat dee yeh 一啲嘢 *pron. something*

yat dee yeh 一啲嘢 adv. something
yat ding 一定 v. must
yat ding 一定 n must
yat ding geh 一定嘅 adv. perforce
yat ding yiew 一定要 a compulsory
yat ding yiew geh 一定要嘅 a. obligatory
yat dow 一竇 n brood
yat doy yan 一代人 n. generation
yat duy 一對 n couple
yat duy 一堆 n. heap
yat duy 一堆 n. mound
yat duy 一對 n. pair
yat duy 一堆 n. pile
yat duy lap sap 一堆垃圾 n. tip
yat fai 一塊 n. slice
yat fan 一份 n portion
yat fan 一份 n share
yat fu dor tay 一夫多妻 n. polygamy
yat fu dor tay geh 一夫多妻嘅 a. polygamous
yat fu yat tay jay 一夫一妻制 n. monogamy
yat gey 日記 n diary
yat gey 日記 n. journal
yat gor gway juk 一個貴族 n. aristocrat
yat gow 一嚿 n block
yat gow 一嚿 n. lump
yat gow 一嚿 n. mass
yat gu 一股 n waft
yat hak 一刻 n. instant
yat hak 一刻 n. moment
yat hak 一刻 a. momentary
yat hay leet 一系列 n. sequence
yat ho kuy joot 一口拒絕 v.t. rebuff
yat hoon 一圈 n. lap
yat horng 一行 n. row
yat horng yan 一行人 n file
yat jak fa 一紮花 n bouquet
yat jan 一陣 adv. awhile
yat jan 一陣 n bout

yat jan 一陣 adv. shortly
yat jan 一陣 n. while
yat jan fung 一陣風 n. gust
yat jan kek tung 一陣劇痛 n. pang
yat jat 一紮 n. skein
yat jay 一劑 n dose
yat jee 一致 n. accord
yat jee 一致 n. oneness
yat jee geh 一致嘅 a. unanimous
yat jee tung yee 一致同意 n. unanimity
yat jik 一直 a consistent
yat jik 一直 a constant
yat jow 一組 n. group
yat kay 日期 n date
yat kay fu fwun 一期付款 n. instalment
yat kwan 一群 n. herd
yat lap 一粒 n. grain
yat leen choon 一連串 n. spate
yat leen yat dow geh 一年一度嘅 adv. yearly
yat leen yat tee geh 一年一次嘅 a. annual
yat lik 日曆 n. calendar
yat lun tow kow 一輪投球 n over
yat ngan 一眼 n. glance
yat ngan 一眼 n. glimpse
yat pai 一排 n. row
yat pay 一批 n lot
yat san gao 一神教 n. monotheism
yat san gao sun tow 一神教信徒 n. monotheist
yat san sung bai 一神崇拜 n. monolatry
yat say dam 一細啖 n nibble
yat say dam 一細啖 n. sip
yat say deem 一細點 n. speck
yat say gow 一細嚿 n. nugget
yat say jat 一細紮 n. wisp
yat say jat far 一細紮花 n. nosegay
yat seurng 日常 a. ingrained

yat seurng geh 日常嘅 *a. informal*
yat seurng geh 日常嘅 *a routine*
yat seurng see mow 日常事務 *n. routine*
yat seurng yam sik 日常飲食 *n diet*
yat sik 日蝕 *n eclipse*
yat sik sam fan 一式三份 *n triplicate*
yat tan 一餐 *n feed*
yat tan 一餐 *n. meal*
yat tan bat yeem 一塵不染 *a. spotless*
yat tay 一齊 *n. unison*
yat tay jay geh 一妻制嘅 *a. monogynous*
yat tee 一次 *adv. once*
yat tee gang 一匙羹 *n. spoonful*
yat teen 一千 *n. chiliad*
yat teen 一千 *n. thousand*
yat tiew 一條 *n. loaf*
yat tiew 一條 *n. strip*
yat tiew cheurng lung 一條長龍 *n. queue*
yat tow 日頭 *adv adays*
yat tow 日頭 *n day*
yat tow 一套 *n set*
yat wak 一劃 *n. stroke*
yat yeh jee gan 一夜之間 *adv. overnight*
yat yeh jee gan 一夜之間 *a overnight*
yat yeh see hao 日夜思考 *v.t. preoccupy*
yat yeurng geh 一樣嘅 *a. identical*
yat yeurng geh 一樣嘅 *a. same*
yat yoon 日元 *n. Yen*
yay 拽 *a. naughty*
yee 姨 *n. aunt*
yee 耳 *n ear*
yee 醫 *v.t. physic*
yee 醫 *v.t remedy*
yee 二 *n. two*
yee 而 *conj. whereas*

yee bak jow leen 二百週年 *adj bicentenary*
yee been 易變 *a fickle*
yee been gorng 耳邊講 *v.t. whisper*
yee been jat geh 易變質嘅 *a. perishable*
yee cher 而且 *adv. also*
yee cher 而且 *adv besides*
yee chuy 耳垂 *n. lobe*
yee dai lay geh 義大利嘅 *a. Italian*
yee dai lay yan 義大利人 *n. Italian*
yee duk 易讀 *adv. legibly*
yee dung 移動 *v.i. manoeuvre*
yee ga 而家 *adv. now*
yee ga 而家 *adv. presently*
yee ga geh 而家嘅 *a. present*
yee geen 意見 *n advice*
yee geen 意見 *n. opinion*
yee ging 已經 *adv. already*
yee go 耳垢 *n cerumen*
yee guy 移居 *v.i. migrate*
yee guy 移居 *n. migration*
yee gway 衣櫃 *n. wardrobe*
yee harm 易喊 *a. lachrymose*
yee hay 儀器 *n device*
yee hey 儀器 *n. apparatus*
yee ho 以後 *conj. after*
yee ho 醫好 *v. t. cure*
yee ho 醫好 *v.i. heal*
yee jay yoon 耳仔軟 *a inexorable*
yee jee 以致 *conj. that*
yee jee lik 意志力 *n. volition*
yee jee siew tam 意志消沉 *v. t. demoralize*
yee jeurng 意象 *n. imagery*
yee jeurng gwun 儀仗官 *n. beadle*
yee jik 移植 *v.t graft*
yee jik 移植 *v.t. transplant*
yee jik mat 移植物 *n. graft*
yee jorng 耳狀 *adj. auriform*
yee jun jay 二進制 *adj binary*
yee kao 依靠 *n. recourse*

yee kao 依靠 v.i. resort
yee kao geh 依靠嘅 a dependent
yee lai 依賴 n anaclisis
yee lai 依賴 v. i. depend
yee lai 依賴 n dependence
yee lai 二奶 n. mistress
yee lai 依賴 n. reliance
yee lai 依賴 v.i. rely
yee liew geh 醫療嘅 a. medical
yee ling sow forng sik 以零售方式 adv. retail
yee low 易嬲 a. touchy
yee luy 疑慮 n. misgiving
yee luy 疑慮 n. mistrust
yee man 疑問 n doubt
yee man 移民 n. immigrant
yee man 移民 v.i. immigrate
yee man 移民 n. immigration
yee man 移民 n. migrant
yee man 疑問 n. query
yee man 移民 n. settler
yee man tee 疑問詞 n interrogative
yee mat wun mat 以物換物 v.t. barter1
yee ming geh 易明嘅 a. intelligible
yee ming geh 易明嘅 a. lucid
yee mo geh 義務嘅 a. honorary
yee ngoy 意外 n accident
yee ngoy geh 意外嘅 a. untoward
yee ngoy so wok 意外收穫 n bonus
yee sang 醫生 n doctor
yee sang 醫生 n. medico
yee sap 二十 a. twenty
yee see 意思 n. meaning
yee see 醫師 n. physician
yee see 意思 n. signification
yee seurng 以上 adv above
yee seurng 異常 n anomaly
yee seurng geh 異常嘅 a anomalous
yee seurng geh 異常嘅 a. extraordinary
yee seurng geh 異常嘅 a. uncanny

yee seurng teen hoy geh 異想天開嘅 a. whimsical
yee sik 儀式 n. ceremony
yee sik 儀式 n. rite
yee sik 儀式 n. ritual
yee sik dow 意識到 v.t. realize
yee sik seurng geh 儀式上嘅 a. ritual
yee sup 二十 n twenty
yee tai 儀態 n poise
yee tan 遺產 n. patrimony
yee teen 以前 adv. before
yee teen 以前 adv formerly
yee teen geh 以前嘅 a. retrospective
yee ter 而且 conj both
yee ter 而且 adv. moreover
yee ter 而且 adv. withal
yee ting biew 議程表 n. agenda
yee tow 意圖 n. conation
yee tow gey 二頭肌 n biceps
yee way ping day 夷為平地 v.t. raze
yee yan far 擬人化 v.t. personify
yee yeen 易燃 a. inflammable
yee yoon 醫院 n. hospital
yee yoon 意願 n. inclination
yee yoon 議員 n. parliamentarian
yee yoot 二月 n February
yeem 染 v. t dye
yeem 厭 v.t fatigue
yeem 閹 v.t. geld
yeem 鹽 n. salt
yeem 厭 v.t. satiate
yeem 染 v.t. tincture
yeem cho 煙草 n. tobacco
yeem gak 嚴格 a. strict
yeem gak geh 嚴格嘅 a. rigorous
yeem geh 鹽嘅 a. saline
yeem got 閹割 n neuter
yeem jeem 奄尖 adj censorious
yeem jung 嚴重 a. acute
yeem jung 嚴重 a dire
yeem jung geh 嚴重嘅 a serious

yeem jung geh 嚴重嘅 *a. severe*

yeem jung shoon wai 嚴重損壞 *v.t. mangle*

yeem jung sing 嚴重性 *n. severity*

yeem koy 掩蓋 *v.t. overshadow*

yeem lay 嚴厲 *n. rigour*

yeem lay 嚴厲 *n. stark*

yeem lay 嚴厲 *n. stern*

yeem lay geh 嚴厲嘅 *a. stern*

yeem lay geh 嚴厲嘅 *a. stringent*

yeem lay pay ping 嚴厲批評 *v. t. castigate*

yeem liew 染料 *n dye*

yeem mwut 淹沒 *v.t. whelm*

yeem ngow 閹牛 *n bullock*

yeem say jeh 厭世者 *n. misanthrope*

yeem see 驗屍 *n. post-mortem*

yeem shu 鼴鼠 *n. mole*

yeem siew siew 染少少 *v.t. tinge*

yeem sik 染色 *v. t colour*

yeem sik 掩飾 *v.t. mask*

yeem sik 掩飾 *n. masquerade*

yeem sik 掩飾 *v.t. whitewash*

yeem sing 鹽性 *n. salinity*

yeem suk 嚴肅 *a. grave*

yeem suk 嚴肅 *n. solemnity*

yeem suk geh 嚴肅嘅 *a. solemn*

yeem suy 鹽水 *n brine*

yeem tay 掩體 *n blindage*

yeem yee 嫌疑 *n. suspicion*

yeem yee fan 嫌疑犯 *n suspect*

yeen 演 *v.i. act*

yeen 煙 *n. cigarette*

yeen 煙 *n. smoke*

yeen cheurng 延長 *v. t extend*

yeen cheurng 現場 *n. locale*

yeen cheurng 延長 *v.t. prolong*

yeen cheurng 延長 *n. prolongation*

yeen cheurng 現場 *n. site*

yeen cheurng wuy 演唱會 *n. concert*

yeen chut 演出 *n. performance*

yeen doy 現代 *a contemporary*

yeen doy far 現代化 *v.t. modernize*

yeen doy geh 現代嘅 *a. modern*

yeen doy sing 現代性 *n. modernity*

yeen fat 研發 *v. t. develop*

yeen gam 現金 *n. cash*

yeen gey 演技 *n. acting*

yeen gorng 演講 *n. lecture*

yeen gorng 演講 *n. oration*

yeen gorng 演講 *n. presentation*

yeen gorng ga 演講家 *n. orator*

yeen gorng geh 演講嘅 *a. oratorical*

yeen gorng sut 演講術 *n. oratory*

yeen han guy jee 言行舉止 *n. mannerism*

yeen ho 然後 *adv. thence*

yeen jay 延滯 *n. retardation*

yeen jee 燕子 *n. swallow*

yeen jik 筵席 *v.t. banquet*

yeen jow wuy 演奏會 *n. recital*

yeen kay 延期 *n. adjournment*

yeen kay 延期 *n. postponement*

yeen liew 燃料 *n. fuel*

yeen lun 言論 *n. remark*

yeen lun 言論 *n. utterance*

yeen mak 燕麥 *n. oat*

yeen mow 煙霧 *n. smog*

yeen sat 實現 *v.t. achieve*

yeen sat ju yee jeh 現實主義者 *n. realist*

yeen sat sang wut 現實生活 *n. reality*

yeen siew 燃燒 *v.i blaze*

yeen siew 燃燒 *v.i flame*

yeen tee 延遲 *v.t. & i. delay*

yeen tee 延遲 *v.t. postpone*

yeen tee 延遲 *n. procrastination*

yeen tow 煙頭 *n. stub*

yeen tow wuy 研討會 *n. seminar*

yeen tung 煙囪 *n. chimney*

yeen wuy 宴會 *n. banquet*

yeen wuy 宴會 *n feast*

yeen yam jeh 現任者 *n. incumbent*

yeen yoon 演員 *n. actor*
yeen yuk 煙肉 *n. bacon*
yeep 醃 *v.t. condite*
yeep 葉 *n foliage*
yeep 葉 *n. leaf*
yeep 頁 *n. page*
yeep 醃 *v.t pickle*
yeep been 頁邊 *n. margin*
yeep beng 葉柄 *n stalk*
yeep ju 業主 *n. proprietor*
yeep yu ngoy ho jeh 業餘愛好者 *n. amateur*
yeet 熱 *n. heat*
yeet 熱 *a. hot*
yeet dai 熱帶 *n. tropic*
yeet dai 熱帶 *a. tropical*
yeet dai sam lam 熱帶森林 *n. jungle*
yeet leet 熱烈 *a fervent*
yeet leet 熱烈 *a. tumultuous*
yeet leet 熱烈 *a. uproarious*
yeet leet fwun ying 熱烈歡迎 *n. ovation*
yeet ngoi 熱愛 *adj. avid*
yeet sam 熱心 *n devotion*
yeet sam 熱心 *n enthusiasm*
yeet sam 熱心 *a. keen*
yeet san 熱身 *v.t. limber*
yeet teet 熱切 *a. intent*
yeet tiew 熱潮 *n craze*
yeet ting 熱情 *a. ardent*
yeet ting 熱情 *n. ardour*
yeet ting 熱情 *adv. avidity*
yeet ting 熱情 *a enthusiastic*
yeet ting 熱情 *n fervour*
yeet ting 熱情 *n. keenness*
yeet ting 熱情 *n. passion*
yeet ting 熱情 *a. passionate*
yeet ting 熱情 *n. zeal*
yeet ting 熱情 *n. zest*
yeet ting geh 熱情嘅 *a. zealous*
yeh 惹 *v.t. incur*
yeh 惹 *v.t. provoke*

yeh 嘢 *n. stuff*
yeh 嘢 *n. thing*
yeh ang 夜鶯 *n. nightingale*
yeh choy fa 椰菜花 *n. cauliflower*
yeh gan wut dung geh 夜間活動嘅 *a. nocturnal*
yeh hok teem way 椰殼纖維 *n coir*
yeh jee 椰子 *n coconut*
yeh ju 野豬 *n boar*
yeh man 野蠻 *a. barbarian*
yeh man 野蠻 *n. barbarism*
yeh man 夜晚 *n. night*
yeh man yan 野蠻人 *n. barbarian*
yeh man yan 野蠻人 *n savage*
yeh ngow 野牛 *n bison*
yeh sang geh 野生嘅 *a. wild*
yeh so 野獸 *n beast*
yeh so 耶穌 *n. Christ*
yeh so gam geh 野獸咁嘅 *a beastly*
yeh tan 野餐 *n. picnic*
yeh tan 野餐 *v.i. picnic*
yeh tow 野兔 *n. hare*
yeh yan ngoy 惹人愛 *a. lovable*
yeng 贏 *v.t. win*
yeng 贏 *n win*
yeng ga 贏家 *n. winner*
yeurk 藥 *n cure*
yeurk 弱 *a. frail*
yeurk 藥 *n. medicament*
yeurk 藥 *n. medicine*
yeurk 藥 *n. physic*
yeurk 藥 *n. remedy*
yeurk 藥 *n. tablet*
yeurk 弱 *a. weak*
yeurk cho 藥草 *n. herb*
yeurk chuk 約束 *v.t. regulate*
yeurk chuk geh 約束嘅 *a. restrictive*
yeurk deem 弱點 *n. weakness*
yeurk doy 虐待 *v.t. abuse*
yeurk doy 虐待 *n. mal-treatment*
yeurk doy 虐待 *v.t. mistreat*
yeurk doy kwong 虐待狂 *n. sadism*

yeurk doy kwong 虐待狂 n. sadist
yeurk forng 藥房 n dispensary
yeurk forng 藥房 n. pharmacy
yeurk forng 藥方 n. prescription
yeurk geh 藥嘅 a. medicinal
yeurk gow 藥膏 n. ointment
yeurk ho geh 約好嘅 a. promissory
yeurk jat 瘧疾 n. malaria
yeurk jay see 藥劑師 n druggist
yeurk jeh 弱者 n. weakling
yeurk jow 藥酒 n. tincture
yeurk wuy 約會 n. rendezvous
yeurk yoon 藥丸 n. pill
yeurng 癢 n. itch
yeurng 癢 v.i. itch
yeurng 養 v.t. rear
yeurng 羊 n. sheep
yeurng ban 樣板 n. prototype
yeurng bwun 樣本 n. sample
yeurng fung cheurng 養蜂場 n. apiary
yeurng fung yeep 養蜂業 n. apiculture
yeurng gan jing 羊癇症 n epilepsy
yeurng giew seng 羊叫聲 n bleat
yeurng hay 氧氣 n. oxygen
yeurng jow chorng 釀酒廠 n distillery
yeurng jow leen fan 釀造年份 n. vintage
yeurng low gam 養老金 n. annuity
yeurng mo 羊毛 n fleece
yeurng pay 羊皮 n. lambkin
yeurng shu 楊樹 n. poplar
yeurng tow 陽台 n. veranda
yeurng tow cheurng 養兔場 n. warren
yeurng toy 陽台 n. balcony
yeurng wuy heurng 洋茴香 n aniseed
yeurng yuk 羊肉 n. mutton
yiew 要 v.t. acquire
yiew 窰 n. kiln

yiew 要 v.t. need
yiew 搖 v.i. rattle
yiew 搖 v.t. rock
yiew 搖 v.i. shake
yiew 搖 v.i. swing
yiew 搖 v.i. wag
yiew 腰 n. waist
yiew 搖 v.i wobble
yiew bai 搖擺 v.i. sway
yiew bai 搖擺 n sway
yiew bai 搖擺 v.i. waddle
yiew bai 搖擺 n wag
yiew bay geh 要畀嘅 a. payable
yiew bee bee 搖BB v.t. dandle
yiew dai 腰帶 n. girdle
yiew deem 要點 n. gist
yiew dung 搖動 n shake
yiew forng 搖晃 n. stagger
yiew gwai 妖怪 n. monster
yiew gwor 繞過 v.t. round
yiew ha yiew ha 擺下擺下 v.i. reel
yiew hung 遙控 n. controller
yiew kow 要求 v.t. request
yiew kow jeh 要求者 n claimant
yiew lam kuk 搖籃曲 n. lullaby
yiew larm 搖籃 n cradle
yiew seen gorn 繞線杆 n. spindle
yiew so 要素 n element
yiew ting 邀請 v. invitation
yiew ting 邀請 v.t. invite
yiew tow 腰頭 n. waistband
yiew yeen 謠言 n. rumour
yiew yiew bai bai 搖搖擺擺 v.i. stagger
yiew yuk 腰肉 n. loin
yik 液 n. sap
yik 翼 n. wing
yik at 抑壓 v.t. withhold
yik beng 疫病 a. plague
yik dow hm 亦都唔 conj. neither
yik dow hm 亦都唔 conj nor
yik far 液化 v.t. liquefy

yik jeurng 腋杖 n crutch
yik miew 疫苗 n. vaccine
yik tay 液體 n fluid
yik tay 液體 n liquid
yik tay geh 液體嘅 a. liquid
yik wat jing 抑鬱症 n depression
ying 鷹 n eagle
ying 鷹 n hawk
ying 影 v.t. photograph
ying 影 n. shadow
ying 影 n. silhouette
ying borng 英鎊 n. pound
ying borng 英鎊 n. sterling
ying dak 應得 v. t. deserve
ying dak 認得 v.t. recognize
ying dak geh yeh 應得嘅嘢 n due
ying fat geh 刑罰嘅 a. penal
ying fu 應付 v. i cope
ying fu 應付 n. tackle
ying geet 凝結 v. t clot
ying geh 營嘅 adj castral
ying gwok 英國 n albion
ying gwok geh 英國嘅 adj british
ying gworng mok 螢光幕 n. monitor
ying heurng 影響 v.t. affect
ying heurng 影響 n. influence
ying heurng 影響 v.t. influence
ying heurng 影響 v.t. jaundice
ying heurng 影響 v.i. militate
ying heurng 影響 n. thrall
ying heurng geh 影響嘅 a subject
ying heurng lik 影響力 n. impact
ying heurng lik 影響力 n. leverage
ying heurng lik 影響力 n. potency
ying heurng sam yoon geh 影響深遠
嘅 a. seminal
ying hor 認可 n. approbation
ying hor 認可 n. recognition
ying hung 英雄 n. hero
ying hung jing san 英雄精神 n.
heroism

ying jan see hao 認真思考 v.i.
ruminate
ying jorng 形狀 n. shape
ying lap suy geh 應納稅嘅 a. taxable
ying larm 型男 n gallant
ying lay 英里 n. mile
ying lay sow 英里數 n. mileage
ying loon、bong 英聯邦 n.
commonwealth
ying man 英文 n English
ying morng 凝望 n ogle
ying mow 英畝 n. acre
ying mow 鸚鵡 n. parrot
ying see 凝視 v. t daze
ying see 凝視 n gaze
ying see 凝視 n. stare
ying she 影射 n. insinuation
ying sik 形式 n medium
ying sing 形成 v.t. form
ying sing 應承 v.t promise
ying sing jik seen 形成直線 n.
alignment
ying tam 英尋 n fathom
ying tan 認真 a earnest
ying way 認為 v.i. deem
ying way 認為 v.t figure
ying way 認為 v.t. opine
ying way 認為 v.t. reckon
ying way 認為 v.t. repute
ying yan gey 影印機 n. xerox
ying yeurng 營養 n. aliment
ying yeurng 營養 n. nutrition
ying yeurng ban 營養品 n.
nourishment
ying yeurng bat leurng 營養不良 n.
malnutrition
ying yeurng geh 營養嘅 a. nutritive
ying yu 凝乳 n curd
ying yung 形容 v. t describe
ying yung geh 英勇嘅 a. heroic
ying yung hang way 英勇行為 n
exploit

ying yung tee 形容詞 n. adjective
yoom jee 原子 n. atom
yoom jee geh 原子嘅 a. atomic
yoon 遠 adv. afar
yoon 猿 n ape
yoon 縣 n. county
yoon 完 n. end
yoon 遠 adv. far
yoon 遠 a far
yoon 鉛 n. lead
yoon 軟 n. soft
yoon ai 懸崖 n. cliff
yoon bat 鉛筆 n. pencil
yoon bat pao 鉛筆刨 n. sharpener
yoon choon 完全 adv all
yoon choon 完全 a downright
yoon choon 完全 adv entirely
yoon choon 完全 adv. fully
yoon choon 完全 adv. wholly
yoon choon geh 完全嘅 a. sheer
yoon choon mo 完全無 a devoid
yoon chu 遠處 adv. afield
yoon chu ying 圓柱型 n cylinder
yoon deng uk 圓頂屋 n dome
yoon fan 緣份 n fate
yoon gam 軟禁 v.t. imprison
yoon geh 遠嘅 a distant
yoon gow 原告 n. plaintiff
yoon han 怨恨 n grudge
yoon han 怨恨 n. rancour
yoon han 怨恨 n. resentment
yoon han 怨恨 n. spite
yoon hang 遠行 v.i. voyage
yoon hok 玄學 n. metaphysics
yoon hok geh 玄學嘅 a. metaphysical
yoon hoon 圓圈 n. circle
yoon hoon 圓圈 n. loop
yoon jak 原則 n canon
yoon jak 原則 n. creed
yoon jak 原則 n. principle
yoon jak 原則 n. tenet

yoon jee lang geh 原子能嘅 a. nuclear
yoon jee wat 原子核 n. nucleus
yoon jing 完整 a complete
yoon jing 遠征 n expedition
yoon jing 完整 a. intact
yoon jing 完整 n. integrity
yoon jok geh 原作嘅 a. original
yoon joot mat 緣絕物 n. insulator
yoon jow 圓周 n. circumference
yoon ju 沿着 prep. up
yoon ju man 原住民 n. pl aborigines
yoon juk 遠足 n. excursion
yoon juy ying 圓錐形 n. cone
yoon lay 原理 n. rationale
yoon leem 懸念 n. suspense
yoon leurng 原諒 v.t excuse
yoon leurng 原諒 v.t forgive
yoon may 完美 n. perfection
yoon may geh 完美嘅 a. perfect
yoon miew geh 玄妙嘅 a. oracular
yoon mong 願望 n. wish
yoon ngay 園藝 n. horticulture
yoon ngay ga 園藝家 n. gardener
yoon on 懸案 n. subjudice
yoon say 芫荽 n. coriander
yoon seng 原聲 a acoustic
yoon sing 完成 v. t complete
yoon sing 完成 completion
yoon sing 完成 v.t finish
yoon tee geh 原始嘅 a. primeval
yoon yam 元音 n. vowel
yoon yan 原因 n. reason
yoon yee ling ting geh 願意聆聽嘅 a. receptive
yoon ying 圓形 a circular
yoon ying geh 圓形嘅 a. round
yoot 月 n. month
yoot ging 月經 n. menses
yoot ging bat tiew 月經不調 n amenorrhoea
yoot ging geh 月經嘅 a. menstrual

yoot gway 越軌 *n. pale*

yoot gway 越軌 *v.t. transgress*

yoot gway shu 月桂樹 *n laurel*

yoot hon 月刊 *n monthly*

yoot leurng 月亮 *n. moon*

yoot leurng geh 月亮嘅 *a. lunar*

yow 有 *v.t. contain*

yow 釉 *n glaze*

yow 有 *v.t. have*

yow 油 *n. oil*

yow 油 *v.t. paint*

yow 疣 *n. wart*

yow am 幽暗 *n. gloom*

yow bay dak 邱比特 *n Cupid*

yow bay mo wan 有備無患 *v.t forearm*

yow beng geh 有病嘅 *a. sick*

yow cheen 有錢 *a. affluent*

yow cho cher 油槽車 *n. tanker*

yow chorng yee 有創意 *a. inventive*

yow chorng yee 有創意 *a. visionary*

yow choy wah geh 有才華嘅 *a. gifted*

yow chuy geh 有趣嘅 *a. laughable*

yow dak jing geh 有得整嘅 *a. raparable*

yow dak king geh 有得傾嘅 *a. negotiable*

yow dan xing 有彈性 *a elastic*

yow day 郵遞 *n mail*

yow day geh 郵遞嘅 *a. postal*

yow day korng lik 有抵抗力 *a. resistant*

yow dee 有啲 *adv. some*

yow dee 有啲 *pron. some*

yow dee 有啲 *adv. somewhat*

yow deem 優點 *n excellency*

yow deem 優點 *n. merit*

yow dorng 遊蕩 *v.i. wander*

yow dow lay 有道理 *a. reasonable*

yow doy biew sing geh 有代表性嘅 *a. representative*

yow doy luy dung mat 有袋類動物 *n. marsupial*

yow duk geh 有毒嘅 *a. poisonous*

yow duk geh 有毒嘅 *a. venomous*

yow fay 郵費 *n. postage*

yow ga jik 有價值 *a. valuable*

yow gam gok geh 有感覺嘅 *a. sentient*

yow geen 郵件 *n. mail*

yow geen day 有見地 *a. judicious*

yow gey geh 有機嘅 *a. organic*

yow gey sing 有記性 *a. retentive*

yow gey sut geh 有技術嘅 *a. skilful*

yow gik duy yoon 游擊隊員 *n. partisan*

yow gik jeen 游擊戰 *n. guerilla*

yow gok geh 有角嘅 *a. angular*

yow gow yow sow 又高又瘦 *a. lank*

yow guk 郵局 *n. post-office*

yow gwan geh 有關嘅 *a. pertinent*

yow gwan geh 有關嘅 *a. relevant*

yow gwan geh 有關嘅 *a. topical*

yow gwan hay geh 有關係嘅 *a. associate*

yow gwan hay geh 有關係嘅 *a. relative*

yow gworng jak 有光澤 *a. lustrous*

yow hai 遊戲 *n. game*

yow han 休閒 *a fallow*

yow han fu 休閒褲 *n. slacks*

yow han gam 休閒咁 *a. leisurely*

yow han geh 有限嘅 *a finite*

yow han geh 休閒嘅 *a leisure*

yow han geh 有限嘅 *a. limited*

yow hang 遊行 *v.i march*

yow hang 遊行 *n. parade*

yow hang 遊行 *v.t. parade*

yow hao 有效 *a effective*

yow hao 有效 *a. fruitful*

yow hao 有效 *a. valid*

yow hao geh 有效嘅 *a. potent*

yow hao lut geh 有效率嘅 *a.* productive

yow hay morng geh 有希望嘅 *a.* promising

yow hing chuy 有興趣 *a. interested*

yow hing chuy 有興趣 *a. interesting*

yow hm tung geh 有唔同嘅 *v.t. vary*

yow ho dor 有好多 *v.i. abound*

yow hok ham geh 有學問嘅 *a.* scholarly

yow hoon 幼犬 *n. puppy*

yow hor lang 有可能 *adv. probably*

yow hor lang geh 有可能嘅 *a.* probable

yow hoy 有害 *a. injurious*

yow hoy geh 有害嘅 *a malign*

yow hoy geh 有害嘅 *a. negative*

yow hoy geh 有害嘅 *a. noxious*

yow hoy geh 有害嘅 *a. pernicious*

yow jak yam 有責任 *a accountable*

yow jak yam 有責任 *a incumbent*

yow jak yam gam 有責任感 *a.* responsible

yow jee 幼稚 *adj callow*

yow jee 幼稚 *a. childish*

yow jee 油脂 *n grease*

yow jee 幼稚 *a. immature*

yow jee gak 有資格 *a eligible*

yow jee gak 有資格 *v.i. qualify*

yow jee geh 幼稚嘅 *a. juvenile*

yow jee geh 幼稚嘅 *a. puerile*

yow jee sat king heurng 有自殺傾向 *a. suicidal*

yow jee wey 有智慧 *a. wise*

yow jee yoon 幼稚園 *n. kindergarten* ;

yow jee yoon 幼稚園 *n. nursery*

yow jeen 休戰 *n. armistice*

yow jeet jow geh 有節奏嘅 *a.* rhythmic

yow jing 郵政 *n. post*

yow jing guk jeurng 郵政局長 *n.* postmaster

yow joon yem 有尊嚴 *v.t dignify*

yow jor 有咗 *a. pregnant*

yow jun dow geh 有進度嘅 *a.* progressive

yow koon 有權 *v. t. entitle*

yow koon geh 有權嘅 *a. powerful*

yow koon way 有權威 *a.* authoritative

yow koot ham geh 有缺陷嘅 *adj.* deficient

yow kuk seen ghe 有曲線嘅 *a.* shapely

yow lai geh 有奶嘅 *a. milch*

yow lam 遊覽 *v.i. tour*

yow lam jee hay koy 有男子氣概 *a.* manlike

yow lang lik 有能力 *a. capable*

yow lang lik 有能力 *a. competent*

yow lay 有利 *v.t. advantage*

yow lay 有利 *a favourable*

yow lay geh 有利嘅 *a beneficial*

yow lay mao 有禮貌 *a. courteous*

yow lay mao 有禮貌 *a. polite*

yow lay yow geh 有理由嘅 *a.* justifiable

yow lay yu 有利於 *v. t. benefit*

yow lay yu 有利於 *n boon*

yow lay yun geh 有利潤嘅 *a.* profitable

yow leurng gor bo fan 有兩個部份 *a.* twofold

yow liew hao geh 有療效嘅 *a* curative

yow loy sing geh 有耐性嘅 *a. patient*

yow lun 郵輪 *n ferry*

yow luy 憂慮 *n agitation*

yow luy 憂慮 *a anxiety*

yow luy 憂慮 *a. anxious*

yow luy 憂慮 *n distress*

yow luy 憂慮 *v. t distress*

yow mak 幽默 *a. humorous*
yow mak 幽默 *a. jocular*
yow mak gam 幽默感 *n. humour*
yow mak jok ga 幽默作家 *n. humorist*
yow man far geh 有文化嘅 *a. literate*
yow man tay geh 有問題嘅 *a. problematic*
yow may 優美 *n. grace*
yow may geh 有味嘅 *a. odorous*
yow may geh 優美嘅 *a. picturesque*
yow may lik 有魅力 *a. winsome*
yow meen yik lik geh 有免疫力嘅 *a. immune*
yow meng geh 有名嘅 *a. renowned*
yow miew 幼苗 *n shoot*
yow ming mow sat 有名無實 *a. titular*
yow morng geh 有望嘅 *a. prospective*
yow muk 柚木 *n. teak*
yow muk dik 有目的 *v.t. purpose*
yow muk geh 遊牧嘅 *a. nomadic*
yow muk man 遊牧民 *n. nomad*
yow mun 油門 *n. throttle*
yow mwuy may geh 有霉味嘅 *a. musty*
yow ngan lik geh yan 有眼力嘅人 *n. visionary*
yow ngar 優雅 *n elegance*
yow ngar 優雅 *adj elegant*
yow ngoy sam 有愛心 *a benevolent*
yow ok yee 有惡意 *a. baleful*
yow peen geen 有偏見 *v. t bias*
yow piew 郵票 *n. stamp*
yow sam gor bo fan geh 有三個部份 *a. tripartite*
yow san lun 有神論 *n. theism*
yow san lun jeh 有神論者 *n. theist*
yow sang hey 有生氣 *a. lively*
yow say 優勢 *n. predominance*

yow say 優勢 *n. preponderance*
yow see 有時 *adv. sometime*
yow see 有時 *adv. sometimes*
yow seen geh 優先嘅 *a. preferential*
yow seen koon 優先權 *n. precedence*
yow seen koon 優先權 *n. priority*
yow seurng geh 憂傷嘅 *a mournful*
yow seurng jeurng lik 有想像力 *a. imaginative*
yow seurng jun sam geh yan 有上進心嘅人 *n. aspirant*
yow shoon jak geh 有選擇嘅 *a. selective*
yow shu 幼樹 *n. sapling*
yow sik 休息 *n break*
yow sik 休息 *n. repose*
yow sik 休息 *v.i. repose*
yow sik 休息 *v.i. rest*
yow sow 幼獸 *n cub*
yow sow 優秀 *n. excellence*
yow sow 優秀 *a. outstanding*
yow sow geh 優秀嘅 *a. excellent*
yow sow geh 優秀嘅 *a. sterling*
yow sow ho han 遊手好閒 *v.i. loaf*
yow sow ho han geh yan 遊手好閒嘅人 *n. idler*
yow sow ho han geh yan 遊手好閒嘅人 *n. sluggard*
yow sun sam 有信心 *a. confident*
yow suy 游水 *v.i. swim*
yow suy 游水 *n swim*
yow suy fuk lik 有說服力 *adj. cogent*
yow tai 郵差 *n. postman*
yow tai yan 猶太人 *n. Jew*
yow tar yee 有差異 *v. i differ*
yow tee 有刺 *a. barbed*
yow tee jee jung 由始至終 *prep. throughout*
yow tee lik geh 有磁力嘅 *a. magnetic*
yow teem lang 有潛能 *a. potential*
yow teen 有錢 *a. wealthy*

yow teen 有錢 a. well-to-do
yow teen geh 有錢嘅 a. rich
yow teng 遊艇 n. yacht
yow tiew lay geh 有條理嘅 a. methodical
yow tiew lay geh 有條理嘅 a. orderly
yow tiew lay geh 有條理嘅 a. systematic
yow wak 誘惑 v.t. allure
yow wak 誘惑 n allurement
yow wak 誘惑 v.t. lure
yow wak 誘惑 v seduce
yow wak 誘惑 v.t. tempt
yow wak 誘惑 n. temptation
yow wak jeh 誘惑者 n. tempter
yow wat 憂鬱 a blue
yow wat 憂鬱 v. t depress
yow wat geh 憂鬱嘅 a. melancholic
yow wat jing 憂鬱症 n. melancholia
yow way goon 優惠券 n. coupon
yow way goon 優惠券 n. voucher
yow way morng geh 有威望嘅 a. prestigious
yow wing jeh 游泳者 n. swimmer
yow wut lik geh 有活力嘅 a dynamic
yow wut lik geh 有活力嘅 a energetic
yow wuy 休會 v.t. prorogue
yow wuy 幽會 n. tryst
yow wuy kay 休會期 n. recess
yow yan 有人 pron. somebody
yow yan 有人 n. somebody
yow yan 有人 pron. someone
yow yan 蚯蚓 n. worm
yow yan sing geh 有人性嘅 a. humane
yow yee 猶豫 n demur
yow yee 猶疑 v. i doubt
yow yee 猶豫 v.i. hesitate
yow yee 猶豫 n. hesitation
yow yee 猶豫 v.i. shilly-shally
yow yee 猶豫 n. shilly-shally

yow yee chorng 幼兒床 n. cot
yow yee chorng 幼兒床 n. crib
yow yee geh 猶豫嘅 a. hesitant
yow yee see 有意思 a. meaningful
yow yee yee geh 有意義嘅 a. allegorical
yow yeen 油煙 n. soot
yow yik 有益 a. wholesome
yow yik geh 有翼嘅 adj. aliferous
yow yik geh 有益嘅 a. salutary
yow ying heurng lik 有影響力 a. influential
yow ying juy lik 有凝聚力 adj cohesive
yow ying yeurng 有營養 a. nutritious
yow yoon 柔軟 a flexible
yow yoon 柔軟 n limber
yow yoon 柔軟 a. supple
yow yoot 優越 a. superior
yow yoot 優越 n. superiority
yow yow gwa doon 優柔寡斷 n. indecision
yow yung 有用 v.t. avail
yow yung 有用 a. useful
yow yung geh 有用嘅 a. invaluable
yow yung geh 有用嘅 a. serviceable
yu 瘀 n bruise
yu 魚 n fish
yu 雨 n rain
yu ak 餘額 n. balance
yu bay cho see 預備措施 n preliminary
yu chun hang way 愚蠢行為 n. idiocy
yu deng 預訂 n. reservation
yu fai 愉快 n enjoyment
yu fai 愉快 a. jolly
yu fai 愉快 n. pleasure
yu fai geh 愉快嘅 a merry
yu fai geh 愉快嘅 a. pleasant
yu forng 預防 n. precaution
yu forng 預防 n. prevention

yu forng 乳房 *n. udder*

yu forng geh 乳房嘅 *a. mammary*

yu forng geh 預防嘅 *a. precautionary*

yu forng jeem jung 預防接種 *n. inoculation*

yu forng sing geh 預防性嘅 *a. preventive*

yu fu 迂腐 *n. pedantry*

yu gam 預感 *n. premonition*

yu geen 預見 *v.t foresee*

yu gey 預計 *n. anticipation*

yu gey 預計 *n bet*

yu gey 預計 *v. t expect*

yu gey 預計 *v.t. predict*

yu go 預告 *n forecast*

yu go 預告 *n. trailer*

yu gow 預告 *v.t. prophesy*

yu gway 雨季 *n. monsoon*

yu gwor 如果 *conj. if*

yu gwor hm hay 如果唔係 *conj. otherwise*

yu hao 愈合 *v.t. conglutinate*

yu hap 愈合 *n. concrescence*

yu hay 語氣 *n. tone*

yu jee 預知 *n. foreknowledge*

yu jee 預知 *n. prescience*

yu jee 魚子 *n. roe*

yu jow 宇宙 *n. universe*

yu jow geh 宇宙嘅 *adj. cosmic*

yu kay 預期 *n antedate*

yu kwan 魚群 *n. shoal*

yu lan jeh 遇難者 *n. casualty*

yu liew 預料 *v.t. anticipate*

yu liew 預料 *v.t. presuppose*

yu lok 娛樂 *n amusement*

yu lok 娛樂 *v. t entertain*

yu lok 娛樂 *n. entertainment*

yu luy 魚雷 *n. torpedo*

yu miew 魚苗 *n fry*

yu mo 羽毛 *n feather*

yu mo kow 羽毛球 *n. badminton*

yu mow 預謀 *n forethought*

yu mow 預謀 *n. premeditation*

yu mow kow 羽毛球 *n. shuttlecock*

yu say gak joot geh 與世隔絕嘅 *a. secluded*

yu see 於是 *conj. whereat*

yu see 於是 *conj. whereupon*

yu seen 預先 *n. advance*

yu seen ging go 預先警告 *v.t forewarn*

yu seen hao luy 預先考慮 *v.t. premeditate*

yu seen koot ding 預先決定 *v.t. predetermine*

yu shoon 預算 *n budget*

yu siew 預兆 *n. auspice*

yu siew 預兆 *n forerunner*

yu siew 預兆 *v.t herald*

yu siew 預兆 *n. omen*

yu siew 預兆 *v.t. portend*

yu tak 預測 *v.t forecast*

yu torng 乳糖 *n. lactose*

yu tow 乳頭 *n. nipple*

yu tow 乳頭 *n. teat*

yu wan 雨雲 *n. nimbus*

yu yam hok 語音學 *n. phonetics*

yu yan 漁人 *n fisherman*

yu yee 寓意 *n. allegory*

yu yeen 寓言 *n apologue*

yu yeen 寓言 *n. fable*

yu yeen 預言 *v.t foretell*

yu yeen 語言 *n. language*

yu yeen 語言 *n. lingo*

yu yeen 寓言 *n. parable*

yu yeen 預言 *n. prophecy*

yu yeen fung gak 語言風格 *n. locution*

yu yeen ga 預言家 *n. prophet*

yu yeen ga 預言家 *n. seer*

yu yeen geh 語言嘅 *a. lingual*

yu yeen geh 語言嘅 *a. linguistic*

yu yeen geh 預言嘅 *a. prophetic*

yu yeen hok 語言學 *n. linguistics*
yu yeen hok 語言學 *a. philological*
yu yeen hok 語言學 *n. philology*
yu yeen hok ga 語言學家 *n. linguist*
yu yeen hok ga 語言學家 *n. philologist*
yu yeurk 預約 *n. appointment*
yu yeurk 預約 *v.t. reserve*
yuk 喐 *v. i. & n budge*
yuk 肉 *n flesh*
yuk 玉 *n. jade*
yuk 肉 *n. meat*
yuk 喐 *v.t. move*
yuk dow hm yuk ha 喐都唔喐下 *a. motionless*
yuk gong 浴缸 *n bath*
yuk gway fan 肉桂粉 *n cinnamon*
yuk jeurng 肉醬 *n. paste*
yuk jut 獄卒 *n. jailer*
yuk ma 辱罵 *v.t. taunt*
yuk mong 慾望 *n. appetence*
yuk mong 慾望 *n. appetite*
yuk sow yuk geurk 喐手喐腳 *v.t. paw*
yuk tong 肉湯 *n broth*
yun wat 潤滑 *n. lubrication*
yun wat yow 潤滑油 *n. lubricant*
yung 用 *n access*
yung 溶 *v.i. melt*
yung 湧 *v.i. surge*
yung 用 *v.t. use*
yung 用 *v.t. utilize*
yung bay mor 用鼻摸 *v. nuzzle*
yung bo sek jorng sik 用寶石裝飾 *v.t. jewel*
yung chu 用處 *n. use*
yung chut geh 湧出嘅 *n spurt*
yung dai leem dow got 用大鐮刀割 *v.t. scythe*
yung fan gan say 用番梘洗 *v.t. soap*
yung far geh 熔化嘅 *a. molten*
yung far gway jeet 熔化季節 *n thaw*

yung fat 用法 *n. usage*
yung fwuy lay pow 用灰泥鋪 *v.t. plaster*
yung gai 溶解 *v.t dissolve*
yung gai dow 溶解度 *n. solubility*
yung gam 佣金 *n. commission*
yung gam 勇敢 *a. courageous*
yung gam 勇敢 *a. gallant*
yung gam 勇敢 *n. gallantry*
yung gam 勇敢 *a. interpid*
yung gam geh 勇敢嘅 *a daring*
yung gam geh 勇敢嘅 *a dauntless*
yung gam geh 勇敢嘅 *a. mettlesome*
yung gam geh 勇敢嘅 *a. valiant*
yung gan geh 用緊嘅 *a. operative*
yung guy 用具 *n. utensil*
yung gwong wun fat 容光煥發 *v. i beam*
yung gwong wun fat 容光煥發 *n. radiance*
yung gwun shu sung 用管輸送 *v.i pipe*
yung hay 勇氣 *n. mettle*
yung hay 勇氣 *n. valour*
yung hey 勇氣 *n. courage*
yung hoy meen mat 用海綿抹 *v.t. sponge*
yung huy geh 容許嘅 *a. permissible*
yung jay 溶劑 *n solvent*
yung ju seh hay say 用注射器洗 *v.t. syringe*
yung lap 容納 *v.t accommodate*
yung leurng 容量 *n. capacity*
yung lik bai 用力擺 *v.t. plank*
yung lik deng 用力掟 *v.t. pitch*
yung lik teng pow 用瀝青鋪 *v.t. tar*
yung lo 熔爐 *n. crevet*
yung mai 擁埋 *v.i flock*
yung mao 容貌 *n. physiognomy*
yung mao cho jing uk deng 用茅草整屋頂 *v.t. thatch*
yung mao gat 用矛拮 *v.t. spear*

yung mo gan mat 用毛巾抹 *v.t.*
towel

yung mow ban yan 用模板印 *v.i.*
stencil

yung ngam 熔岩 *n. lava*

yung ngar kek dung jok 用啞劇動作
v.i mime

yung seurng gwan yu 用雙關語 *v.i.*
pun

yung shoon wan sung 用船運送 *v.t*
ferry

yung shu 榕樹 *n. banyan*

yung so jee mor 用手指摸 *v.t finger*

yung sow geh 用手嘅 *a. manual*

yung sow jee gung ping 用手指公評
v.t. thumb

yung tang tiew da 用藤條打 *v. t. cane*

yung tee 用詞 *n diction*

yung tee bat dorng 用詞不當 *n.*
misnomer

yung tong ju 用糖煮 *v. t. candy*

yung wan ying tow 用混凝土 *v. t*
concrete

yung wu jeh 擁護者 *n exponent*

yung wu jeh 擁護者 *n. protagonist*

yung yan 容忍 *v.i abide*

yung yan 容忍 *n. toleration*

yung yao 湧入 *n. influx*

yung yee 容易 *a easy*

yung yee fat low 容易發嬲 *a.*
irritable

yung yee gam yeem dow 容易感染到
a. prone

yung yee seurng chu 容易相處 *adj.*
convivial

yung yow 擁有 *v.t. own*

yung yow 擁有 *v.t. possess*

yung yu luy jap gik 用魚雷襲擊 *v.t.*
torpedo